ISBN 978-0-266-26242-8
PIBN 10919714

This book is a reproduction of an important historical work. Forgotten Books uses state-of-the-art technology to digitally reconstruct the work, preserving the original format whilst repairing imperfections present in the aged copy. In rare cases, an imperfection in the original, such as a blemish or missing page, may be replicated in our edition. We do, however, repair the vast majority of imperfections successfully; any imperfections that remain are intentionally left to preserve the state of such historical works.

1 MONTH OF
FREE
READING

at

www.ForgottenBooks.com

By purchasing this book you are eligible for one month membership to ForgottenBooks.com, giving you unlimited access to our entire collection of over 1,000,000 titles via our web site and mobile apps.

To claim your free month visit:
www.forgottenbooks.com/free919714

REPORTS

OF

CASES AT LAW AND IN EQUITY

DETERMINED BY THE

SUPREME COURT

OF THE

STATE OF IOWA.

OCTOBER 7, 1897—DECEMBER 15, 1897.

BY

BENJ. I. SALINGER.

VOLUME XIV,

BEING VOLUME CIII OF THE SERIES.

DES MOINES, IOWA:
GEO. H. RAGSDALE, PUBLISHER.
1898.

JUDGES OF THE SUPREME COURT

DURING THE TIME OF THESE REPORTS.

L. G. KINNE, Des Moines, *Chief Justice.*
H. E. DEEMER, Red Oak.
GIFFORD S. ROBINSON, Sioux City.
CHAS. T. GRANGER, Waukon.
JOSIAH GIVEN, Des Moines.
SCOTT M. LADD, Sheldon.

OFFICERS OF THE COURT.

MILTON REMLEY, Iowa City, *Attorney General.*
C. T. JONES, Washington, *Clerk.*
BENJ. I. SALINGER, Carroll, *Reporter.*

JUDGES OF THE COURTS

FROM WHICH APPEALS MAY BE TAKEN TO THE SUPREME COURT.

DISTRICT COURTS.

First District—HENRY BANK, JR., Keokuk.

Second District—M. A. ROBERTS, Ottumwa; T. M. FEE, Centerville; F. W. EICHELBERGER, Bloomfield; ROBERT SLOAN, Keosauqua.

Third District—H. M. TOWNER, Corning; W. H. TEDFORD, Corydon.

Fourth District—WM. HUTCHINSON, Orange City; GEO. W. WAKEFIELD, Sioux City; F. R. GAYNOR, Le Mars; JOHN F. OLIVER, Onawa.

Fifth District—J. H. APPLEGATE, Guthrie Center; J. H. HENDERSON, Indianola; A. W. WILKINSON, Winterset; JAMES D. GAMBLE, Knoxville.

Sixth District—DAVID RYAN, Newton; BEN MCCOY, Oskaloosa; A. R. DEWEY, Washington.

Seventh District—C. M. WATERMAN, Davenport; W. F. BRANNAN, Muscatine; P. B. WOLFE, Clinton; A. J. HOUSE, Maquoketa.

Eighth District—MARTIN J. WADE, Iowa City.

Ninth District—W. F. CONRAD, CALVIN P. HOLMES, THOMAS F. STEVENSON, W. A. SPURRIER, Des Moines.

Tenth District—J. J. TOLERTON, Cedar Falls; A. S. BLAIR, Manchester.

Eleventh District—D. R. HINDMAN, Boone; S. M. WEAVER, Iowa Falls; BENJAMIN P. BIRDSALL, Clarion.

Twelfth District—JOHN C. SHERWIN, Mason City; J. F. CLYDE, Osage.

Thirteenth District—L. E. FELLOWS, Lansing; A. N. HOBSON, West Union.

Fourteenth District—LOT THOMAS, Storm Lake; WILLIAM B. QUARTON, Algona.

Fifteenth District—A. B. THORNELL, Sidney; WALTER I. SMITH, Council Bluffs; N. W. MACY, Harlan; W. R. GREEN, Audubon.

Sixteenth District—S. M. ELWOOD, Sac City; Z. A. CHURCH, Jefferson.

Seventeenth District—GEORGE W. BURNHAM, Vinton; OBED CASWELL, Marshalltown.

Eighteenth District—H. M. REMLEY, Anamosa; WILLIAM G. THOMPSON, Marion.

Nineteenth District—FRED O'DONNELL, Dubuque; JAMES L. HUSTED, Dubuque.

Twentieth District—JAMES D. SMYTH, Burlington; WINFIELD S. WITHROW, Mt. Pleasant.

SUPERIOR COURTS.

Cedar Rapids—THOMAS M. GIBERSON.

Council Bluffs—J. E. F. MCGEE.

Keokuk—JOSEPH C. BURK.

PREFACE.

The judges of the supreme court have directed that this volume and future volumes of the Reports shall not contain counsel's briefs, annotations, or Northwestern Reporter citations, which duplicate references to the Iowa Reports. This action is taken on account of changes made by the Code of 1897.

BENJ. I. SALINGER.

IN MEMORIAM.

GEORGE G. WRIGHT.

On the eleventh day of January, 1896, George G. Wright, a former chief justice of the court, an ex-senator of the United States, and for long years a leading member of the bar of the state, departed this life at his home in Des Moines.

At the January term, 1896, the court having designated February 8, 1896, for the presentation of resolutions in memory of the deceased, the following resolutions, passed by the bar of that city, were read:

The members of the bar of the city of Des Moines have learned with deep regret of the death of the Hon. George G. Wright, and they now desire to pay to his memory this last tribute of their affection and esteem:

Judge Wright's early life is the repetition of the familiar story of many of our eminent men,—he began his career with nature's gifts of youth and health and brains, and he brought to their aid tireless industry and a sturdy integrity that no one ever dreamed of questioning. His active career as a lawyer began in the territory of Iowa, and at the early age of thirty-five he was chief justice of the supreme court of the state. His first opinion was delivered in June, 1855, and is reported in the first volume of Clark's reports, page 3. The fifteen years during which he served as a member of this court were filled up with events that were of the first magnitude in the history of the nation and of the state. The Dred Scott decision, the struggle in Kansas, John Brown's raid, secession and the civil war, emancipation of the slaves and reconstruction, the amendments to the federal and state constitutions securing equal civil rights to the colored race; all these stirring events were crowded into these few years, and Judge Wright was among the foremost men in bringing the state into the front rank in the great work of making history as our children read it to-day. His six years in the senate of the United States followed his career on the bench and gave an enlarged opportunity for wise and most valuable service to the nation and his own state which he faithfully rendered. Satisfied with public honors, and with the burning questions of the civil war period settled, Judge Wright returned to his practice as a lawyer in this city to make some pecuniary provision for his family and for himself in his declining years. During these last twenty years no one in this city has been so well known, so much sought after, so readily accorded the place of honor in public or private gatherings of men or women, so looked up to by all sorts and conditions of men as Judge Wright, while in active practice, he was the first man at the bar. Among the early settlers of the state he was a friend, not merely in counsel, but in every practical way in which friendship finds expression. His great influence was freely used to aid and encourage the agricultural, the educational, the reformatory, and charitable interests of the state. The friends of his youth and early manhood were such to the end of their lives; or if they survive him, were true to the last day of his life.

By what qualities of heart and mind did Judge Wright become one of the foremost men in the history of the state?

It is quite unnecessary to answer that question to the members of this bar or this court. That such was his position as a matter of right and without effort on his part, every one took for granted

We ask the court that this brief and inadequate tribute to the memory of one of the most eminent members of this court, and the most distinguished member of this bar, be spread upon the records.

WM. CONNOR,
JAMES G. DAY,
CROM BOWEN,
Committee.

January 10, 1896.

Thereupon Hon. Jas. G. Day addressed the court as follows:

MAY IT PLEASE YOUR HONORS·

It is with the deepest sense of a personal loss that I rise to second the request which has just been made. Your honors have never been asked to turn aside, from the ordinary routine of business, to pay a last tribute of respect to one more st·ongly intrenched in the affections of the people of this state, than was he whose virtues we to-day commemorate, and whose death we to-day mourn. So closely connected and so intimately associated was Judge Wright with all that pertains to the prosperity and grandeur of the state of his adoption, that it would be impossible to write its history without according to him honorable mention and assigning to him an important place. He was closely in touch with the people in every branch of their business and in every feature of their lives. Coming to Iowa when it was still a territory, in 1840, before he had attained his majority, he settled at Keosauqua, upon the then very boundary of civilization. His commanding abilities were soon recognized and appreciated. Commencing at the very bottom round of political preferment he advanced by rapid strides until he reached almost its topmost. Soon after coming here he was elected prosecuting attorney of his county. In 1848 he was state senator. In 1855, chief justice of the state supreme court, and in 1870 he was chosen for the honorable and dignified position of United States senator. He continued to be a member of this court, with a very slight interruption, from 1855 to 1870. He came to the chief justiceship of this honorable tribunal at a time when the jurisprudence of the state was in a formation period and needed more than it has ever since needed, to be moulded and directed by wise judgment and honest purpose. As to Chief Justice Marshall, it is generally conceded that the country is indebted for properly construing and placing in efficient operation the federal constitution and laws, so it must be conceded that the people of Iowa owe a like debt of gratitude to Judge Wright for a like service as to the state constitution and laws. By his wisdom and his prudence, his courage and his justice, he laid, strong, deep, and symmetrically, the foundation of our jurisprudence, upon which his compeers and his successors have so builded, it is to be hoped, as to command confidence at home and respect abroad. Having served efficiently and faithfully a term of six years in the United States senate, he voluntarily declined a re-election, and returned to the avocations of private life. For more than fifty years he was a conspicuous and commanding figure in Iowa history. No man has been so universally esteemed nor so well beloved at half a million firesides in this state; his name has become a household word. He took a most lively interest in everything that advanced the material interests or promoted the social progress of his state. He was a man of remarkable versatility. Whether deciding grave constitutional questions in the highest state tribunal, or conducting the proceedings of a state agricultural society, or presiding over the august assemblage of the American Bar Association, or directing the proceedings of the pioneer law makers, or lecturing to a law class, or presiding at a political discussion, he was always ready and everywhere efficient. He never fell below the requirements of any occasion in which he was called upon to act. His genial good humor, his constant kindliness of manner, and his inexhaustible resource of appropriate and interesting anecdotes made him everywhere welcome, and always the center of interest and affectionate regard. This city was never so intensely stunned as when it read in the morning prints that its first citizen, the man, whom above all others, it respected and loved and honored, was dead. But two days before he was at his accustomed place at the bank, of which he was president, and but few were aware that he was not in his accustomed health. And yet those who knew him intimately and met him frequently, unwelcome as the knowledge was to them, could not hide from themselves the fact that in the past year his general health had greatly declined. Indeed he never fully rallied from the terrible blow inflicted by the death of his eldest son, around whom so many hopes were clustered, and in whom so many honorable ambitions were centered. Heroically, even cheerfully, did this grand man discharge every duty to the living, but he bore upon his heart a burden of sorrow for which earth had no antidote, and so manfully struggling, but gradually sinking, crowned with years and honors, rich in the confidence and love of a people with whom he had lived and moved without reproach for more than fifty years, he was called from the very midst of active duties, to his final reward, "like as a shock of corn cometh in his season." He needed no granite shaft or statue of bronze to perpetuate his name. He has erected for himself a monument "more enduring than brass and more everlasting than marble." As long as civilization continues, and its literature endures, so long will the memory of Judge Wright be cherished and his fame be secure. A life so pure of purpose, so grand in achievement, and so replete with success, is both an inspiration and a benediction. I second the request that the memorial read be spread upon your journals.

In Memoriam.

Remarks by Hon. C. C. Cole:

MAY IT PLEASE THE COURT:

A life well prolonged, always busy and active, largely spent in the higher planes of professional and official duties, manifesting a versatile capacity rarely equaled and never surpassed, always mindful of and obedient to all domestic and social duties, accomplishing a measure of usefulness and beneficence which command the respect and gratitude of all,—such a life, I say, cannot be even epitomized in the time properly allotted to anyone on an occasion like this. It is, therefore, alike both my purpose and my duty to him, in what I say to the one exalted avenue of Judge Wright's life work to confine myself to that wherein he accomplished most, and wherein I knew him best; indeed, I think it not egotism to affirm, that from opportunities and actualities, I knew him better therein than any other man now living. It is unnecessary for me to say in this presence that the avenue of exalted and extended usefulness to which I refer, is Judge Wright's accomplishments in jurisprudence. Judge Wright, more than any man living or dead, must be regarded and commended as the father of Iowa jurisprudence. He was the master workman therein, whoever may have been his associates for the time. There were two especially able and distinguished pioneers in the same avenue; each of them contributed much to the preparation of the way for the then future work of our departed friend and jurist, whose life and service we now commemorate. Charles Mason, the very prime pioneer in preparing for the foundation of Iowa jurisprudence, was a man of the broadest and most thorough learning, possessed of a vigorous, active and logical mind, remarkable for his accuracy and profundity in the law, as also for his ever conscientious and faithful discharge of every duty. George Greene, whose industry was untiring, and whose versatility in the knowledge of the law and its practice, seem to have been without limit; these characteristics, in connection with a sound judgment and ever abiding integrity, justly entitle him to a grateful recognition as one of the foremost in laying the sunken piers and foundations of our jurisprudence. The work of these two, together with their associates, every one of whom we delight to honor, had prepared well the way for the sys'ematic, formative, and thorough work of Judge Wright, the master workman, and his associates. Judge Wright's knowledge of the law, acquired by elementary reading and study, was broad, systematic and thorough. His superior preparation for its practice, enabled him to cope successfully from the first with the ablest lawyers in our territory and state. His career at the bar was one of marked growth and recognized success. When a change of political administration came in Iowa, Judge Wright's standing at the bar, his learning in the law, his success in its practice, and his recognized ability and integrity, pointed to him, confessedly above all others in the state, as the man and lawyer to be made chief justice of the supreme court of his state, before the close of the first decade of its history. He was made chief justice, and with two worthy associates, entered upon the work of completing the foundations and perfecting and constructing our jurisprudence thereon. The period at which he entered upon his judicial duties, and the time he continued therein, was peculiarly formative, and required not only breadth and learning as a lawyer, but sound and comprehensive discretion and judgment as a statesman. How well Judge Wright's career upon the bench has approved the wisdom of those who placed him there, as well as his own fitness, I need not discuss. It may be true, in a more philological sense, that Judge Wright was neither exrudite nor profound. However that may be, it is abundantly true and most fully approved by his work, that he possessed in a most eminent degree that sound, comprehensive, practical mind and judgment which ever kept him in wise and conservative paths. His opinions are universally models of sagacious and discreet conclusions, clothed in plain, practical and legal language, meteing out justice according to law, with satisfaction and certainty. Judge Wright was pre-eminently the lawyer and the judge. His admiration for the law, its symmetry, harmony and certainty, always kept him from being misled by outside equities and facetious presentations. To him the more or less veritable maxim "that hard cases make bad law," had no application. As a judge, he was a close and careful student first of the facts in the case before him, and then of the law applicable thereto, and he followed the law to its goal with no variation because of any supposed unjust results to which he might be led. He accepted the law as his guide, and while if he saw that it appeared to lead to unjust conclusions, he would review the facts and ascertain certainly the law, he would then apply it, and leave to the law its consequences It was my good fortune to serve as a member of this court, with Judge Wright and another of our departed members, Judge Lowe, for a few years together. Judge Lowe was distinguished for his humanity and his love of equity, and his sterling and ever abiding integrity. As judge, his love of equity, practical common sense, every day equity, as he saw it, would often incline him to that goal, rather than to the direct one to which the law in its rigidity would lead. This difference of natural and mental characteristics often brought before me in their discussions, the fact to which I allude. If the facts and law brought the accused certainly to the scaffold Judge Lowe would be nervously astute to find some equitable ground for his deliverance, while Judge Wright, in his love for the purity, excellence and certainty of the law would go unerringly to its goal, and rejoice in its wisdom and justice, while sympathizing with its erring victim. So unerringly and always was he devoted to the law, and the justice which it would measure out when properly administered, that it seemed to be a matter of indifference to him what were its consequences, regardless of whether the subject of its adverse judgment was his devoted friend or his active enemy, personal, political or otherwise. It was this characteristic of admiration for, confidence in and fidelity to the law, and his broad and accurate comprehension and application of it, that made him a pillar of strength to his associates and to the bench. As I recur in memory to his faithful and laborious work in the consultation room, and recall the times when he was well-nigh overcome with anxious, persistent and excessive labor, and yet, would faithfully stand by and perform his duty, regardless of his own discomfort and pains, I cannot hesitate to declare again that our Iowa jurisprudence, in its excellence, and in its appreciation and approval, both at home and abroad, is pre-eminently the work of its master judicial workman, Judge George G. Wright.

Remarks by Col. C. H. Gatch:

My relations with Judge Wright were such, and my esteem for him so great, that I cannot forbear expressing my full and hearty assent to the many warm and deserved tributes to his memory that have been so happily and feelingly expressed here and elsewhere, and I will not attempt more. If ever silence is golden, it is on occasions like this, when even to the most gifted, there comes a sense of the poverty and feebleness of language. All who knew Judge Wright well, have in their minds and hearts their best and fittest tribute to his great worth. To such, though he has gone from their midst, there will remain to them the pleasure, though a sad one, of continuing to live with him in memory, for "To live in hearts we leave behind, is not to die." His summons came as the shadows of evening were gathering over a long and well spent life. "Let us," in the words of unsurpassed beauty spoken by another of another, "believe that in the silence of the receding world, he heard the great waves breaking on a farther shore, and felt already on his brow the breath of the eternal morning."

Jas. H. Rothrock, Chief Justice, responded for the court, as follows:

Much has been spoken and written in the last few weeks touching the passing away of the distinguished citizen who has been prominent in the affairs of the state and nation for more than half a century. He was one of the pioneers of the territory of Iowa, and from the year 1840, down to the time of his death he was a leading factor in upbuilding the state, not only as a lawmaker and a judge of its highest court, but as a promotor of every organization for the purpose of advancing the industrial and material interest of the people. And his career as a public man was more than state wide. As a United States senator he reflected honor upon the state, as an able and dignified representative, and after his voluntary retirement from that exalted position and his return to private life, no man in this state was more generally known and more highly esteemed and beloved.

It is difficult to add anything more than has been so well and truthfully uttered on this occasion in memory of George G. Wright. It would probably be sufficient to say that every member of this court heartily and feelingly endorse these resolutions and the remarks which have been made upon his life and character. It is due to memory, however, that something should be said concerning his relation to this court as a practitioner at the bar. After the close of his services as a United States senator, he returned to the practice of his profession as the senior member of the partnership of Wright, Gatch & Wright. He represented that firm for several years in this court and argued many cases. He was in regular attendance at every term at Davenport, Dubuque and Council Bluffs, while the court was held at those places. It is not necessary to say more than that he presented his cases with consummate ability and in that persuasive and convincing manner which was characteristic of the man. He did not indulge in mere oratorical display. He was not a word painter and he gave but little attention to the rounding of periods, but at the bar and on all other occasions his speech was forcible, logical and dignified. He retired from the practice of his profession a number of years ago, but up to within a very short time before his death he manifested a noticeable interest, not only in the proceedings before this court, but the kindliest feelings for every individual member of the bench He never omitted to call upon the court at some time during each term. His last interview with the judges was about a month before his death. And now in closing these memorial services, this court joins with the bar and the public, in mourning the loss of a distinguished citizen of the state, who had much to do in laying the foundation of its present greatness and in shaping its destiny, and all classes, old and young, the high and the low, unite in remembering him as a man with a high sense of honor, sound judgment, spotless integrity, a scrupulous sense of duty and faultless manhood. faithful in every official obligation during his public life and social, genial and refined in his intercourse with all people. And above all he was a sincere christian. He has laid down his burden and is at rest. It is ordered that the resolutions presented be spread upon the records, and published in the official reports of this court.

All of which was and is accordingly done.

TABLE OF CASES REPORTED

IN THIS VOLUME.

(xv)

REPORTS

OF

CASES AT LAW AND IN EQUITY

DETERMINED BY THE

SUPREME COURT

OF

THE STATE OF IOWA

AT

DES MOINES, OCTOBER TERM, A. D. 1897,

AND IN THE FIFTY-FIRST YEAR OF THE STATE.

E. K. Brown, Appellant, v. George Taber.*

Dedication by Plat: VACATION: *Acceptance.* Where the owners of land which had been dedicated as a street in the plat of an addition to a city had disposed of none of the abutting lots, and such dedication had not been accepted by the city, they had the right
1 to vacate such street, under Code 1873, section 564, authorizing such vacation of any part of a plat, provided it does not affect the rights and privileges of other proprietors in such plats.

Title to streets adjoining: *Construction of statute.* Where a "street" as platted was vacated, under Code 1873, section 564, a proportionate part thereof did not become a part of each of the abutting lots, by virtue of section 565, authorizing the proprietors
3 of vacated *lots* to inclose a proportionate part of the adjoining street, and section 567, providing for the re-platting of such lots, as such sections relate only to the owners of "lots" which have been vacated.

103	1
105	203
103	1
106	388
103	1
120	544
103	1
125	137
103	1
130	601
103	1
134	163
134	432
103	1
135	303
103	1
142	403

*The figures on the left of the syllabi refer to corresponding figures placed on the margin of the case at the place where the point of the syllabus is decided.

SAME: *Deeds.* Under Code 1873, section 559, providing that descriptions of lots according to the number and designation thereof on the plat shall be deemed sufficient for the purposes of conveyances thereof, and section 561, declaring the acknowledgment and recording of such plat equivalent to a deed in fee simple of lands therein set apart for streets and other public uses, a deed describ-

3   ing the lands thereby conveyed as lots, by numbers as designated in the plat, included only the several parcels so specified therein; as such reference to the lots by numbers, in the deed, had the effect identical with describing them by metes and bounds as delineated on the plat, and therefore included no portion of a vacated street on which they abutted, but to which no reference was made in the deed.

Quieting Title: COMMON SOURCE. Where both plaintiff and defendant claim title to land under a common grantor, it was sufficient

2   to prove its derivation from him, without tracing his title back to the government.

Appeal from Hardin District Court.—HON. S. M. WEAVER, Judge.

THURSDAY, OCTOBER 7, 1897.

ACTION to acquire title to a vacated street between outlot 3 and block 7 in the Railroad addition to Eldora. Decree for defendant, and plaintiff appeals.—*Reversed.*

Albrook & Lundy for appellant.

Chas. L. Hays for appellee.

LADD, J.—The land platted belonged to C. C. and Abbie W. Gilman. The plat was filed in June, 1877, and that portion known as "Hammond street," was

by them vacated in December following. In
1   the meantime, none of the abutting lots had
been conveyed, and no evidence was offered
tending to show that the dedication of the street had been accepted. The title thereto did not vest in the city without acceptance. *City of Waterloo v. Union Mill Co.*, 72 Iowa, 437; *Incorporated Town of Cambridge v. Cook*, 97 Iowa, 599; *Manderschid v. City of Dubuque*, 29 Iowa,

73; *Bell v. City of Burlington*, 68 Iowa, 296; *Johnson v. City of Burlington*, 95 Iowa, 197; *Taraldson v. Town of Lime Springs*, 92 Iowa, 187; Code 1873, section 527; *Laughlin v. City of Washington*, 63 Iowa, 652. As the conveyance was not -accepted, the proprietors of the plat remained owners of the land included in the street, and, having disposed of none of the abutting lots, were free to vacate it, under the provisions of section 564 of the Code of 1873. After vacating the street, it was conveyed by Gilman and wife to Hardin, and then to John Hall, and also by Hardin to Hall. The defendant
2   urges that this evidence was offered by him, and that the plaintiff failed to trace his title back to the government. A sufficient answer to this complaint is, that both parties claim under Hall, and it was quite enough to prove derivation from him, without proving his title. 2 Greenleaf, Ev., 307; *Cooley v. Brayton,* 16 Iowa, 10; *Byers v. Rodabaugh*, 17 Iowa, 53.

II. The conveyance from Hall to plaintiff includes the vacated street, and, unless the description in the deed from Hall to King, some months previous, transferred the title to the latter, the plaintiff is owner of the land in controversy. As defendant only obtained the interest King took, his deed need not be considered. Lots 1, 2, 3, and 4 constitute block 7, which lies northwest of Hammond street, and outlot 3 to the southeast; and these are the only abutting lots. The
3   description in the deed to King simply mentions the number of these lots, without specific reference to the vacated street. It is insisted that a proportionate part of the street became a part of each lot, and passed with it to King. Sections 565 and 567 of the Code of 1873 are relied on. These relate distinctly to the owners of lots vacated. When vacated, the force and effect of the execution and recording of that part

of the plat is destroyed. Sections 563, 564. Section
567 only provides for re-platting, and what shall bo
included in such event. The lots, having been vacated,
and the proportionate part of the street, may be platted
and numbered again for convenience in conveying and
assessing the property. If the previous numbers were
retained, and the proportionate part of the street
becomes part of the lot, this would be entirely
unnecessary. Here the lots have not been vacated,
and in determining what a deed of them by number
conveys, it becomes important to consider the purpose
in platting land. Section 559 requires this to be done
with reference to some known or permanent monu-
ments, and to "accurately describe all the sub-divisions of such tract or parcel of land, numbering the
same by progressive numbers, and giving the dimensions and length and breadth thereof, and the breadth
and courses of all streets and alleys established therein.
Descriptions of lots or parcels of land in such subdivisions according to the number and designation
thereof on said plat contained, in conveyance, or for
the purposes of taxation, shall be deemed good and
valid for all intents and purposes." The reference
to lots by number thus becomes as definite and certain as though described by metes and bounds.
The width and length and the exact location is
thereby fixed to a certainty. The same is true of
the street, as the acknowledgment and recording of
the plat "is equivalent to a deed in fee simple of such
portion of the premises platted as is on such plat set
apart for streets or other public use." Section 561.
That Hammond street was vacated before its acceptance did not change the definiteness with which the
boundaries of the street were fixed in the plat, nor
obliterate any of the lines. It remained as specifically
located and described on the plat as the abutting lots.
The only effect of vacating was to withdraw it from

the public use. In the words of Lowe, C. J., in *Mil-
burn v. City of Cedar Rapids*, 12 Iowa, 246: The lots
are "designated by numbers, and it is simply by these
numbers that they are conveyed, as they are known
to represent the particular lot, with its specific boundary as represented on the map. Under such circumstances there is no room to indulge in the
presumption that the purchaser takes any more land
than is contained within the defined lines of the lot."
Referring to the lots by number in the deed, had the
effect identical with describing them by metes and
bounds as delineated on the plat. Their boundary
lines were those of the vacated street, and the deed
conveyed to King only the land included within such
lines. See *Chicago Lumber Co. v. Des Moines Driving
Park*, 97 Iowa, 25; *Burbach v. Schweinler*, 56 Wis. 386
(14 N. W. Rep. 449). As the vacated street was a distinct parcel of land, it seems hardly necessary to say
that it did not pass as incident or appurtenant to the
lots. *Jackson v. Hathaway*, 8 Am. Dec. 263; *Mendel v.
Whiting*, (Ill. Sup.) 31 N. E. Rep. 431; *Harris v.
Elliott*, 10 Pet. 25; *O'Linda v. Lothrop*, 21 Pick. 296;
Ammindown v. Bank, 8 Allen, 285.

III. The defendant claims there was an oral conveyance to King, or at least a mistake by which the
street was omitted from the deed. The evidence
offered by him, however, fails to sustain such contention. It rather tends to show that King must have
bought with knowledge that he was not obtaining the
vacated street. True, he took possession of it, but
this alone, does not establish a purchase. Nor will
the mere inference of a witness be sufficient for that
purpose. Higginbotham does not pretend to have
heard the bargain, or to testify to any of its details.—
REVERSED.

State of Iowa v. L. R. Van Tassel, Appellant.

Murder by Poison: VERDICT SUSTAINED. Defendant's wife was killed by strychnine, administered at different times. Defendant purchased and had in his possession large quantities of such drug at or about the time of her death; and, while she was suffering from its effects, he denied that he had any poison, and after her death, denied that he had purchased any before she died. Evidence given by him at a coroner's inquest on her body, and that given by him on the trial, was contradictory. He had substituted
16 some other drug for medicine left for his wife by a physician; soon after her death he removed something from some of the furniture in her room, and he objected to an inquest on the body. He showed no signs of grief at her death, he was in love with her sister, and proposed marriage to her soon after the death. There was evidence that the wife committed suicide, but, on the whole, it showed that she had no desire to take her own life. *Held*, that the evidence supported a verdict of guilty.

Evidence: COMPARISON OF WRITINGS. Where a paper that has written on it the name of a particular person, is not itself admitted in
8 evidence, it cannot properly be used as the basis of a comparison of hand writing, for the purpose of showing whether a certain signature is such person's.

IDENTIFICATION: *Sufficiency.* The evidence fully identified and accounted for certain organs from the time they were taken from deceased's body until they reached H, a toxicologist in Chicago, except for an hour or so, when they were left sealed in the office of the doctor that removed them from deceased's body, and while they were in transit by express to Chicago. Said doctor, during such hour or so, left them in a commode in his office, the door of which was locked, while he was gone, and no one was in the room.
4 The city marshal assisted the doctor in packing the jars containing the organs, and as soon as they were packed, the marshal took the box and delivered it to the express agent, who held it in his possession, and had it under his immediate supervision, until it was shipped to Chicago, where H. received the box in the apparent condition in which it was when shipped, and analyzed the contents of the jars. *Held*, that there was sufficient identification of deceased's organs to justify the admission of H's evidence of his analysis thereof, and its results, and this, though there was some conflict as to the number of jars sent and received.

EVIDENCE OF INSANITY: *Relevancy and competency.* It was not error
to exclude, as immaterial and incompetent, evidence of insanity
2 of defendant's uncle, where there was no other evidence tending
to show that defendant was insane, and the particular form of his
uncle's insanity was not shown.

ADMISSIBILITY: *Voluntary testimony at inquest.* Where defendant
6 appeared voluntarily, and gave his evidence, at an inquest held
on the body of his wife, such evidence was admissible on his trial
for her murder, for the purpose of impeaching him, and as sub-
18 stantive evidence. *State v. Clifford*, 86 Iowa, 550, *distinguished.*

SAME. Letters signed by defendant, charged with murdering his wife,
taken from a bureau not under lock and key, which the defendant
had moved to the home of his wife's parents and directed his
mother-in-law to give to his child, and a bond found in the house
of his father-in-law, and not taken from a locked drawer, are
admissible as a standard of comparison for the purpose of deter-
5 mining the genuineness of his signature to an alleged confession,
notwithstanding an objection that they were taken surreptitiously
and that he is thus compelled to give evidence against himself.
Boyd v. United States, 116 U. S. 616, *distinguished.*

EXPERTS. The court may properly instruct the jury that expert ·
11 testimony as to handwriting is far from satisfactory, and should
be received with great care and caution.

CONFESSION TO DETECTIVE. Where one of the main witnesses for the
state was a hired detective, it was not error to refuse to charge
that, if he employed falsehood, artifice and fraud in trying to
obtain an alleged confession, it very seriously affected his credibility as to whether such confession was obtained, and, instead, to
charge that the jury had a right to consider the means employed
by such detective to elicit statements from defendant, whether or
not he used deception and falsehood to induce defendant to make
10 them, as well as many other things enumerated in the instruction,
in determining the weight to be given to his evidence; and that
the jury had a right to know just what arts were employed, and
all the circumstances under which the confession was made, and
in the light of these circumstances, and in connection with·
defendant's evidence, to determine the facts in regard to the purported confession.

Confession. Where one makes a confession of murder in the belief
that he thus proves his capacity to commit crime and to become
11 an accomplice in future crimes, the confession is voluntary.

Indictment: POISONING. Under Code of 1873, section 3849, murder
by poison is murder in the first degree, hence such murder need not
1 be charged to have been committed "unlawfully, feloniously,
deliberately, and premeditatedly,"

SAME If such charge were necessary, an indictment which says that defendant by giving poison "did wilfully, feloniously, deliber-
1 ately, unlawfully and of his malice aforethought kill," is sufficient.

Instructions: HARMLESS ERROR An instruction in a trial for mur-
der by poisoning, that if the defendant administered the poison to his wife, and she partook of the same and died from the effects thereof, all the elements of murder in the first degree are proven,
7 is not cause for reversal, notwithstanding that, under it, defendant might be convicted if he gave the poison as medicine or for the good of deceased, where there is not a scintilla of evidence tending to show that he administered the poison with such intent.

INSTRUCTIONS CONSTRUED TOGETHER The court charged that "you have heard the testimony as to the autopsy held on (deceased's) body, and the removal of certain organs therefrom, and touching the chemical analysis by H, and the result of such chemical analysis as to finding strychnine in said organs, and the quantity there found;" that medical experts had been permitted to give their opinions, based in part on the result of such analysis, and their opinions were proper to be considered; that the opinions
8 were based on the assumption that the facts recited in the hypo-
thetical questions were true; that whether or not the conditions so stated were true was for the jury to determine; that they should give careful consideration to all the evidence bearing on all the facts involved in the hypothetical questions, and to the opinions of witnesses founded thereon, and that it was for them to decide whether the death was caused by poisoning Held, that the objection that the quoted part of the instructions assumed the existence of certain facts with reference to such analysis, was not valid when all the instructions were considered together.

SAME. On an issue whether defendant's wife was murdered or com-
mitted suicide, the court directed the jury to carefully consider her health, mental traits, and condition prior to her death, and that such evidence should not be permitted to obscure the "well-
proven facts," nor lead them to indulge in fanciful suppositions.
15 Held, that the instruction was not open to the objection that it clearly intimated that all the state's evidence consisted of well-
proven facts, when considered in connection with instructions relating to reasonable doubt and to what the state must prove in order to convict.

SAME: Reasonable doubt. An instruction that to authorize a conviction, the minds of the jury must be brought to an abiding conviction beyond a reasonable doubt of the defendant's guilt after a
14 full consideration of the whole case, is not erroneous because it fails to use the words "to a moral certainty," as, "abiding conviction beyond a reasonable doubt" is equivalent to that

DEGREES: *Instruction on.* Where the evidence conclusively shows
that deceased's death was caused by poison, and there is no evi-
7 dence that it was negligently administered, so that defendant is
either guilty of murder in the first degree or not guilty, it is not
error to submit to the jury the first degree, only.

Appeal: OBJECTION BELOW. Where the state in proving the genu-
iness of a signature, asserted to be defendant's, is permitted to
use a paper on which defendant's name is written, as a basis of
8 comparison of handwriting, and defendant objects merely to the
competency of the expert testifying, he cannot, on appeal, object
because the court permitted experts to use such paper, without
sufficient proof that the standard used was authentic.

Appeal from Chickasaw District Court.—HON. L. E.
FELLOWS, Judge.

THURSDAY, OCTOBER 7, 1897.

THE defendant was indicted, tried and convicted
of the crime of murder of his wife, by administering
to her a lethal dose or doses of strychnine. He was
sentenced to life imprisonment, and from the judgment of the court, appeals.—*Affirmed.*

J. R. Bane for appellant.

Milton Remley, attorney general, and *T. C. Clary,*
county attorney, for the state.

DEEMER, J.—The record is very voluminous, consisting of more than five hundred closely typewritten
pages. A large number of errors are assigned, and we
have examined the whole record with the care the
importance of the case seems to demand.

I. The indictment is questioned. It is said that it
does not allege that defendant did feloniously, wilfully,
deliberately, premeditatedly, and of his malice
1   aforethought, poison, kill, and murder his wife.
The indictment charges, "that defendant did
feloniously, wilfully, unlawfully, premeditatedly, and

of his malice aforethought, contriving and intending one Ora Van Tassel, with poison, feloniously,
wilfully, unlawfully, and with his malice aforethought, to kill and murder, * * * did privately
and secretly mix with food, water, and some other
substance * * * strychnine; * * * and the
said Ora Van Tassel did take, drink, swallow, the said
water, food, and other substance with which the
strychnine was mixed, * * * by means whereof
* * * the said Ora Van Tassel * * * died.
* * * And so the jurors * * * say that
* * * the defendant * * * in manner and
form aforesaid, * * * the said Ora Van Tas-
sel, unlawfully, feloniously, wilfully, and deliberately,
premeditatedly, and of his malice aforethought, did
poison, kill, and murder. * * *" In another count
of the indictment it is charged, "that * * * the
defendant, on account of the giving and administering of said poison * * * to the said Ora
Van Tassel, did wilfully, feloniously, premeditatedly,
deliberately, unlawfully, and of his malice
aforethought, kill and murder the said Ora Van
Tassel. * * *" Under our statute (Code 1873, section 3849), "all murder which is perpetrated by means
of poison * * * is murder in the first degree.
* * *" The unlawful administering of poison with
bad motive or intent constitutes murder under this
statute, if death ensues, and it is immaterial whether
or not there is a specific intent to kill. *State v. Wells*,
61 Iowa, 629. It is unnecessary, then, to charge that
the defendant did unlawfully, feloniously, deliberately,
and premeditately kill and murder his wife; but, if
such an allegation were necessary, we think it is sufficiently charged in the second count of the indictment,
if not in the first. *State v. Shelton*, 64 Iowa, 333;
State v. Perigo, 70 Iowa, 657.

II. The defendant's father testified to the insanity of a brother, an uncle of the defendant. At the conclusion of defendant's evidence, the state moved to strike this testimony as immaterial and incompetent, for the reason that there was no evidence that defendant himself was insane, or showed any symptoms of insanity, at the time the poison is said to have been administered. This motion was sustained. Defendant also asked an instruction relating to insanity as a defense. This instruction was refused. Of these rulings complaint is made. We do not find any evidence, aside from that above quoted, which tended to show that defendant was insane. On the contrary, the record shows him possessed of more than the ordinary grade of intelligence. The particular form of insanity with which the uncle is afflicted was not shown, and there is no evidence aside from this isolated fact, tending to show that defendant was not in his right mind. Was this single circumstance admissible in evidence, and did it call for an instruction with reference to insanity as a defense? When there is evidence of a want of motive or other evidence furnishing a basis for inquiry as to the insanity of the accused at the time of committing the criminal act, evidence of hereditary insanity may be introduced. But mere proof of insanity in a parent will not be sufficient to constitute a defense if the other evidence negatives the presence of insanity in the accused. *Lovegrove v. State*, 31 Tex. Cr. R. 491 (27 S. W. Rep. 191). Proof of hereditary insanity is admitted as cumulative evidence, and insanity of ancestors is of itself no defense. 1 Wharton & S. Medical Jurisprudence, section 377; *Laros v. Commonwealth*, 84 Pa. St. 200; *Snow v. Benton*, 28 Ill. 306; *Sawyer v. State*, 35 Ind. 80. The reason for this, undoubtedly, is that the burden is upon defendant to establish this defense by a preponderance of the evidence. *State v. Felter*, 32 Iowa, 49. And proof of an isolated case of insanity in the family, especially that of a remote relative, will not of itself overcome the presumption of sanity. The instruction asked was faulty, in that it did not apply the right test by which to determine the mental responsibility of the defendant.

III. The defendant's name appeared upon the register of the Arlington Hotel at New Hampton, and the state was permitted to use this as a basis for comparison by its witnesses in proving the genuineness of a signature attached to a confession purporting to be signed by the defendant. It is said that the signature appearing upon the hotel register was denied by defendant, and that there was no proof that defendant signed the name appearing thereon.

3

The objection now made is that it was error to permit expert witnesses to use this as a basis for comparison. No such objection was made upon the trial. The objection then made was to the competency of the expert, and not to the competency of his testimony. As defendant was then content with the identification of his signature appearing upon the register, he cannot now be heard to complain. The exhibit itself was not admitted in evidence, and could not properly have been used as a basis for comparison had timely objection been made. As it was not made, there was no error. *State v. Cater*, 100 Iowa, 501.

IV. At the conclusion of the evidence, defendant's counsel moved to strike out all the evidence of Dr. J. B. Horton, as to an autopsy held upon the body of Ora Van Tassel, the woman who it is claimed was murdered, and as to the examination and identification of certain organs of her body, because it was immaterial, irrelevant, and incompetent. The exact ground does not appear from the objection itself, and, upon turning to the argument, we find but little said in support of the objection. Evidence was introduced without objection showing that an autopsy was held; that the stomach, a part of the liver and spleen, one kidney, and part of the intestines, were removed from the body of the deceased, and placed in fruit jars or cases by Dr. Horton, preparatory to being sent to Chicago for chemical analysis. That such evidence was legitimate is plain.

Defendant also moved to strike the evidence of Dr. Haines, the toxicologist, who examined what were thought to be the organs taken from the body of Mrs. Van Tassel, on the ground that the said organs 4 were not sufficiently identified. It is claimed in argument that the identification must be complete; that the evidence must establish their identity to a moral certainty and beyond all reasonable doubt. This objection was not urged to the evidence when given, but was by motion made at the close of the introduction of the evidence; and it is questionable whether it was made in time. As said by Judge Dillon, in the case of *State v. Moore*, 25 Iowa, 138: "In a case of this kind, the party cannot sit silent and wait until the evidence is in, willing to take the benefit of it if· it shall chance to be for him, and insist as a matter of right to exclude it if it be against him." Without reference to this rule, however, we do not think the court was in error in denying the motion. The evidence fully identifies and accounts for the whereabouts of these organs from the time they were taken from the body of the deceased until they reached Dr. Haines, except for the space of an hour or so, when they were left sealed in the office of Dr. Horton, while he went to dinner, and while they were in transit by the express company from Nashua to the city of Chicago. If they were properly delivered to the express company for shipment to Dr. Haines, in Chicago, as the evidence

shows they were, this is sufficient to cover the period
of time necessary to their shipment. When Dr. Horton went to his dinner he left the jars containing the
organs he had removed from the body, in his office, but
he says that they were locked up in a commode, and
that he also locked the office door when he was away,
and that no one was in the room while he was gone.
The city marshal assisted Dr. Horton in packing the
jars containing the organs taken from the body of the
deceased, and, as soon as they were packed, the marshal took the box and delivered it to the assistant
express agent, who held it in his possession and had
it under his immediate supervision, until it was
shipped to Chicago. Dr. Haines received the box in
the apparent condition in which it was when shipped,
and analyzed the contents of the jars. Surely, this
was a sufficient identification to justify the admission
of Dr. Haines' evidence. There is some little conflict
as to the number of jars sent and received, but this is
not of itself sufficient reason for rejecting the evidence.

V. It is said that the court erred in admitting in
evidence certain letters, papers, and documents surreptitiously taken from the premises and possession
of defendant without his consent, thus compelling him
to give evidence against himself. The condition of
the record makes it difficult to say what foundation
there is for this claim. We find that, when
5   defendant was being cross-examined, he was
called upon to identify his signature to a bond,
to certain letters signed by himself, and in a memorandum book of the Capital Insurance Company. The
signature in the memorandum book was not sufficiently
identified, and it was not offered or used in evidence.
The signatures to the bond and letters were admitted
by the defendant to be genuine, but, when they were
offered, defendant's counsel objected, on the ground
that the papers were taken from him surreptitiously

and without his consent, and that their introduction
was equivalent to compelling him to give evidence
against himself. In support of the objection, the
defendant testified that he left the bond in a secretary
at his father-in-law's house, in a box, with some other
private papers, and that he gave no one permission to
take it; that the letters were locked in the small
drawer of a bureau left at his residence; and that
the bureau was his property; and that he gave no
one permission to take the letters. The evidence
adduced by the state, however, tends to show that none
of these papers were under lock and key, and, further,
that the defendant moved the bureau, with its contents, to the home of his wife's parents, about two
weeks after her death, and directed the mother-in-law
to give it to his little child. The letters were taken
from one of the unlocked drawers of this dresser.
The bond was found in the house of defendant's
father-in-law, and was not taken from a locked box.
The papers were not taken surreptitiously, nor was
the defendant compelled to give evidence against
himself. See *The Anarchists' Case*, 122 Ill. Sup. 1 (12
N. E. Rep. 977). The state produced the letters and
bond, and the defendant was properly called upon in
cross-examination to identify his signature. The case
is very different in its facts from *Boyd v. U. S.*, 116 U.
S. 616 (6 Sup. Ct. Rep. 524).

VI. Defendant was a witness at an inquest, held
upon the dead body of his wife. He appeared and
voluntarily gave his evidence. This evidence, so
given, was used against him, not only for
6   impeaching purposes, but to a certain extent
as substantive evidence. Complaint is now
made to the introduction of the evidence. Its
admissibility seems to be sustained by the authorities.
State v. Carroll, 85 Iowa, 1; Wharton, Criminal Evidence,

STATE OF IOWA v. L. R. VAN TASSEL, Appellant.

Murder by Poison: VERDICT SUSTAINED. Defendant's wife was killed by strychnine, administered at different times Defendant purchased and had in his possession large quantities of such drug at or about the time of her death; and, while she was suffering from its effects, he denied that he had any poison, and after her death, denied that he had purchased any before she died. Evidence given by him at a coroner's inquest on her body, and that given by him on the trial, was contradictory. He had substituted
16 some other drug for medicine left for his wife by a physician; soon after her death he removed something from some of the furniture in her room, and he objected to an inquest on the body. He showed no signs of grief at her death, he was in love with her sister, and proposed marriage to her soon after the death. There was evidence that the wife committed suicide, but, on the whole, it showed that she had no desire to take her own life. *Held*, that the evidence supported a verdict of guilty.

Evidence: COMPARISON OF WRITINGS. Where a paper that has written on it the name of a particular person, is not itself admitted in
8 evidence, it cannot properly be used as the basis of a comparison of hand writing, for the purpose of showing whether a certain signature is such person's.

IDENTIFICATION: *Sufficiency.* The evidence fully identified and accounted for certain organs from the time they were taken from deceased's body until they reached H, a toxicologist in Chicago, except for an hour or so, when they were left sealed in the office of the doctor that removed them from deceased's body, and while they were in transit by express to Chicago. Said doctor, during such hour or so, left them in a commode in his office, the door of which was locked, while he was gone, and no one was in the room.
4 The city marshal assisted the doctor in packing the jars containing the organs, and as soon as they were packed, the marshal took the box and delivered it to the express agent, who held it in his possession, and had it under his immediate supervision, until it was shipped to Chicago, where H. received the box in the apparent condition in which it was when shipped, and analyzed the contents of the jars. *Held*, that there was sufficient identification of deceased's organs to justify the admission of H's evidence of his analysis thereof, and its results, and this, though there was some conflict as to the number of jars sent and received,

EVIDENCE OF INSANITY: *Relevancy and competency.* It was not error
to exclude, as immaterial and incompetent, evidence of insanity
2 of defendant's uncle, where there was no other evidence tending
to show that defendant was insane, and the particular form of his
uncle's insanity was not shown.

ADMISSIBILITY: *Voluntary testimony at inquest.* Where defendant
6 appeared voluntarily, and gave his evidence, at an inquest held
on the body of his wife, such evidence was admissible on his trial
for her murder, for the purpose of impeaching him, and as sub-
18 stantive evidence. *State v. Clifford,* 86 Iowa, 550, *distinguished.*

SAME. Letters signed by defendant, charged with murdering his wife,
taken from a bureau not under lock and key, which the defendant
had moved to the home of his wife's parents and directed his
mother-in-law to give to his child, and a bond found in the house
of his father-in-law, and not taken from a locked drawer, are
admissible as a standard of comparison for the purpose of deter-
5 mining the genuineness of his signature to an alleged confession,
notwithstanding an objection that they were taken surreptitiously
and that he is thus compelled to give evidence against himself.
Boyd v. United States, 116 U. S. 616, *distinguished.*

EXPERTS. The court may properly instruct the jury that expert
11 testimony as to handwriting is far from satisfactory, and should
be received with great care and caution.

CONFESSION TO DETECTIVE. Where one of the main witnesses for the
state was a hired detective, it was not error to refuse to charge
that, if he employed falsehood, artifice and fraud in trying to
obtain an alleged confession, it very seriously affected his credibility as to whether such confession was obtained, and, instead, to
charge that the jury had a right to consider the means employed
by such detective to elicit statements from defendant, whether or
not he used deception and falsehood to induce defendant to make
10 them, as well as many other things enumerated in the instruction,
in determining the weight to be given to his evidence; and that
the jury had a right to know just what arts were employed, and
all the circumstances under which the confession was made, and
in the light of these circumstances, and in connection with
defendant's evidence, to determine the facts in regard to the purported confession.

Confession. Where one makes a confession of murder in the belief
that he thus proves his capacity to commit crime and to become
11 an accomplice in future crimes, the confession is voluntary.

Indictment: POISONING. Under Code of 1873, section 3849, murder
by poison is murder in the first degree, hence such murder need not
1 be charged to have been committed "unlawfully, feloniously,
deliberately, and premeditatedly."

demonstrates that there was no assumption of any fact
in the part of the instruction criticised.

VIII.   One of the main witnesses for the state
was a detective employed by the county authorities
to assist in ferreting out the crime.   The defendant
asked an instruction to the effect that, if he employed
falsehood, artifice, and fraud in trying to obtain the
alleged confession from defendant, it very seriously
affected his credibility as to whether such con-
10   fession was obtained or not.   In lieu thereof, the
court said to the jury that they had the right to
consider the means employed by the detective to elicit
statements from defendant, whether or not the detective used deception and falsehood on his part to induce
the defendant to make the same, as well as a great
many other circumstances which are enumerated in
the instruction, in determining the weight to be
given to the evidence of this witness.   The court also
said that the jury had the right to know just what arts
were employed, and all the circumstances under
which the confession was made; and in the light of
these circumstances, and in connection with defendant's evidence, they should determine the facts in
regard to the purported confession.   The instructions
given were clearly correct, and it was not erroneous
to refuse the one asked by defendant.   *State v. Hoxsie*,
15 R. I. 4 (22 Atl. Rep. 1059); *Commonwealth v. Mason*,
135 Mass. 555; *Commonwealth v. Trainor*, 123 Mass.
414; *State v. McKeon*, 36 Iowa, 343.

Complaint is made of the instructions 11 and 12.
Eleven relates to the alleged confession, and says
that if it was obtained with the view that defendant
should be accepted as an accomplice in the
11   commission of a proposed crime, and to dem-
onstrate to the detective that defendant was
capable of committing crime, it was voluntary.   Certainly, this a correct statement of the law.

Instruction 4 asked by defendant, relating to the weight to be given the confession, was covered by other parts of the charge.

Instruction 12 relates to the testimony of experts as to handwriting, and directs the jury that such evidence is far from satisfactory, and should be received with great care and caution. This 12 was certainly correct, and it embodied the substance of the charge asked by defendant with reference to the same subject.

The jury were instructed that they might consider the testimony given by defendant before the coroner's jury for impeaching purposes, and for that alone. In 13 argument it is said that it was inadmissible for any purpose, because obtained by duress. We have already seen that the evidence was admissible. The instruction was really favorable to defendant, and he has no cause of complaint.

The instruction as to motive or the want of it, and its effect upon the case, is complained of. We need not set it out, as it is a clear and correct statement of the law.

The instruction as to the weight of the evidence required in such cases used these words: "If, after a careful comparison of the evidence and a full consideration of the whole case, your minds are 14 brought to an abiding conviction beyond a reasonable doubt ' etc. It is said that the instruction is faulty because it fails to use the words "to a moral certainty" This criticism is captious. When the mind is brought to an abiding conviction beyond a reasonable doubt that a thing exists, it is a "moral certainty." *Commonwealth v. Costley*, 118 Mass. 23.

A question in the case was whether Mrs. Van Tassel, the wife of defendant, was murdered or committed suicide. With reference to this matter, the court

directed the jury to carefully consider the health of
the deceased, her mental traits, and condition
15   prior to her death, and further said that "such
evidence should not be permitted to obscure
the well-proven facts, nor lead you to indulge in fanciful suppositions or suspicions." It is said that this
instruction clearly intimates that all the state's evidence consists of "well-proven facts." We do not so
understand it. There is no intimation that the court
regarded any particular facts as "well proven." The
last part of the instruction is certainly correct when
construed with the other instructions relating to reasonable doubt, and as to what the state must prove in
order to secure a conviction.

A careful examination of all of the instructions
convinces us that there was no prejudicial error. On
the contrary, they clearly and accurately state the law
as applied to the facts shown in evidence, and were a
complete and authentic guide to the jury in arriving
at their verdict.

IX. Lastly, it is insisted that the verdict is without support in the evidence. That the deceased came
to her death by strychnine poisoining, administered at
different times, is clearly shown by the
16   evidence; and that defendant purchased and
had in his possession large quantities of this
deadly drug at or about the time the deceased came to
her death, conclusively appears. It also appears that
defendant, at the time his wife was suffering from the
effects of the drug, denied that he had any poison,
and that there was any poison about the premises.
There is considerable evidence to the effect that
defendant substituted some kind of a drug in place of
one left by the doctor to be given Mrs. Van Tassel, to
cure her of the effects of poison previously taken by
her. There is also evidence that defendant showed no
signs of grief when his wife died, and that shortly

after her death he went into her room, and removed
something from some of the furniture therein. There
is further evidence to the effect that he objected to
an inquest being held upon the body of his wife, and,
after the death of his wife, denied having purchased
any poison before her death. There is also some
evidence to the effect that he was in love with his
wife's sister, and that a very short time after the death
of his wife he proposed marriage to this sister. In
addition to this, the jury may well have found that
the defendant confessed his crime to the detective
of whom we have spoken in other parts of this
opinion, both orally and by a solemn written confession, made to induce the detective to believe that
defendant was low and base enough to enter into a
criminal conspiracy to wrong and defraud. The proof
of the *corpus delicti* was ample, and the confession
made to the detective, if believed, was sufficient in
itself to justify the conviction. There are, it is true,
some things which cast suspicion upon the testimony
given by this detective; but, on the other hand, there
are some physical facts which tend to support
him. The weight of his evidence was for the
jury; and as he was before them, and was subject
to a most rigid and searching cross-examination,
they were better situated than we to determine his credibility. Discarding all of his evidence,
however we think enough remains to show
that defendant is guilty of the crime with which he is
charged. In addition to some of the circumstances to
which we have referred, we find that his testimony
before the coroner's jury and his evidence given upon
the trial are contradictory and conflicting. The evidence is conflicting, but there is ample, if credited by
the jury, to justify the verdict. There is also evidence
tending to show that the deceased committed suicide,
but much of this is contradicted, and, on the whole,

we think that it shows that Ora Van Tassel was in love with life, and had no desire to take it by her own hand: She was, it is true, somewhat nervous and excitable, due no doubt to overwork in school during her girlhood days, but everything pointed to a desire on her part to live. She was interested in, and was planning for, the future, which promised a new life for her in a few months. And, while the evidence of motive is not strong, yet it frequently happens that crime is committed for which there is no apparent motive.

We have carefully examined the whole record, not only because of the importance of the case, but by reason of the fact that the crime charged was and is unnatural, and of the further fact that conviction was had largely upon the evidence of a detective whose methods are not to be commended. This examination convinces us that there was no prejudical error, and the judgment is therefore AFFIRMED.

STATE OF IOWA v. RICHARD TAYLOR, Appellant.

Evidence: HARMLESS ERROR Error, if any, in excluding, on a prosecution for rape, the question whether a matured man could
1 commit rape on a woman of about the same age and weight and in good health, is not prejudical where the jury find defendant guilty of an assault with intent to commit rape.

Exceptions: CRIMINAL LAW. A statement of the court, made in its decision overruling a motion for a new trial, may be excepted to,
4 because of Code 1873, section 4480, reserving the right to except to a decision or action of the court, whether made "before or after the trial of the indictment or on such trial."

SAME: *Bill of exceptions.* The statement of the trial court in overruling a motion for a new trial, indicating doubts as to defendant's guilt, is a matter of exception, and affects a "material or substantial right" of defendant within Code 1873, section 4480; and a bill of exceptions containing such statement may if time to settle the bill has been extended beyond the term, be settled by the signature of bystanders, where the judge refuses to sign the bill, under section 4480, providing that if the judge refuse to sign the bill it may be signed by two or more attorneys or officers of the court or disinterested bystanders. *St. John v. Wallace*, 25 Iowa, 21, *distinguished.*

Appeal from Jefferson District Court.—HON. ROBERT SLOAN, Judge.

THURSDAY, OCTOBER 7, 1897.

THE defendant was indicted and tried for the crime of rape. He was found guilty of an assault with intent to commit rape. He appeals.—*Affirmed.*

C. W. Coykendall for appellant.

Milton Remley, attorney general, and *Jesse A. Miller* for the state.

KINNE, C. J.—I. One Dr. Aylesworth, a practicing physician, was asked this question: "Suppose a man, say thirty years of age and over,—a matured man,
1
weighing about 135 pounds, in possession of all his faculties, in apparent good health,—and a female about the same age, about the same weight, in apparent good health; is it likely, or probable, that the male, under such circumstances as I have delineated, could commit a rape or have carnal intercourse against her will, provided she resisted to the extent of her ability?" This question was objected to as irrelevant, incompetent, immaterial, and because the facts stated had not been proven, and the facts proven were materially different from those set out in the question. The objection was sustained. In view of the verdict, we need not consider whether this evidence was properly rejected, nor determine whether the subject inquired about was a proper subject for expert testimony. Not having been convicted of a rape, it affirmatively appears that the rejection of the

offered evidence was not prejudicial. If answered in the negative, it could have had no possible bearing upon the question as to whether the defendant had committed the crime of an assault with intent to commit a rape,—the crime of which the defendant was found guilty.

II. In an "addendum to bill of exceptions," as it is called is found a statement of the trial court, which seems to indicate that he had doubts as to the defendant's guilt. It is said that the trial judge refused to certify to the matter therein contained. The statement set out was sworn to on the ninth day of December, 1895. At the defendant's instance, time beyond the term was given him to prepare a bill of exceptions. The bill was approved and signed on December 9, 1895. The attorney general contends that, "when a trial judge refuses to sign a bill of exceptions as drawn by a party, it is not competent to settle the same at any time other than that at which the ruling of the court was made upon the matter excepted to." It is therefore insisted that the matter embraced in the so-called "addendum" is not of record. The "addendum" having been settled as a bill of exceptions in one of the modes prescribed by law, must be treated as a part of the record unless the claim is well founded that, under the statutes, a bill settled in that manner must be settled at the very time the ruling was made upon the matter excepted to. The statute recites that the decision of the court upon certain specified matters may be excepted to. Code 1873, section 4479. It then says: "Nothing herein contained is to be construed so as to deprive either party of the right of excepting to any action or decision of the court which affects any other material or substantial right of either party, whether before or after the trial of the indictment, or on such trial." Code 1873, section 4480. Section 4483

of the Code of 1873, after providing how exceptions
may be taken, and that they shall be signed by the
judge, and filed, proceeds: "But if the judge refuse
to sign it, such refusal must be stated at the end thereof;
and it may then be signed by two or more attorneys
or officers of the court or disinterested bystanders, and
sworn to by the persons so signing the same, and filed
with the clerk, and it shall thereupon become a part
of the record of the cause." Section 4484 of the Code
of 1873 provides that the judge shall be allowed one
clear day to examine the bill of exceptions, and the
party excepting shall be allowed three clear days
thereafter to procure the signatures, and file the same.
By section 4486 of the Code of 1873 it is provided that
time shall be allowed to settle a bill of exceptions,
when necessary. Counsel for the state, in support of
their construction of the statute, refer to *St.*
3   *John v. Wallace*, 25 Iowa, 21. Judge Wright,
       in rendering the opinion of the court in that
case, held to the view that where the parties, by agreement, extended the time for settling the bill of exceptions beyond the term at which the trial was had, it ·
was not competent to settle the same by the certificate
of bystanders. The other members of the court
expressed no opinion on the question, and the motion
to strike the bill was sustained by the court on other
grounds. The case, therefore, is not authority for the
contention made by the attorney general in the case
before us. Besides, the cited case was a civil action,
and the sections of the Code touching bills of excep-
       tions in criminal cases were not involved or
4   considered. The provisions of the sections we
       have quoted are broad enough to warrant an
exception such as was taken in this case. An exception is authorized in a criminal case as to any "action
or decision" of the court which affects a material or
substantial right of a party, whether such action or

decision was made before or after the trial of the
indictment. The statement of the court was made in
its decision overruling the motion for a new trial. It
was, therefore, a decision or action of the court made
at such a time as that it might be excepted to.
5   Code 1873, section 4480.   Did it "affect" a
"material or substantial right" of the defendant?
The language used by the trial court was: "You, to
say the least, have been guilty of violating the rules
of decency and morality in going to such a place, and
in doing what you did.   The law fixes the extreme
penalty in cases of this kind at twenty years in the
penitentiary, and, while I do not feel justified in setting aside the verdict, in view of all the circumstances
in the case, and of the doubts existing as to your guilt,
I will not give you the extreme penalty of the law.
* * *" In *State v. Billings*, 81 Iowa, 116, where the
trial judge, in ruling on a like motion, expressed
doubts as to the defendant's guilt, we said: "To a
valid judgment the law requires,—*First*, that there
shall be a verdict upon evidence to satisfy the minds
of the jury beyond a reasonable doubt; *second*, that the
judge who presides at the trial shall believe that the
evidence is sufficient to justify the finding.   An affirmative showing of a want of either surely avoids a judgment." We are constrained, therefore, to hold that
the matter excepted to affected a material right of the
defendant.   Nor is there anything in the chapter
relating to bills of exceptions in criminal cases which
indicates, to our minds, an intention on the part of
the legislature to limit the right to settle such a bill
of exceptions by the signature of bystanders to the
time when the exception was taken.   Such a construction appears to be wholly unwarranted.   How can a
defendant know, until his bill is presented to the judge
for approval, whether or not he will sign it?   If, as is
manifest, he cannot know, until such presentation,

whether he will need to settle his bill by the aid of the signatures of bystanders, and, if, when so presented to the judge, he refuses to sign the same, the defendant would be remediless in case time to settle the bill had been, as it was in this case, extended beyond the term. We conclude, then, that the matter contained in the "addendum" is of record, and that a party in a criminal case may avail himself of either mode provided by the statute for settling a bill of exceptions in case time to settle the bill has been extended beyond the term.

III. It is urged that the evidence does not sustain the verdict. Considering the entire record, we cannot concur in that view. The evidence of plaintiff shows that the defendant sought to accomplish his purpose by force; that he took hold of her, and pushed her into a bedroom, that he threatened to choke her and to kill her if she did not cease making an outcry; that he dragged her on the floor and threw her on the bed, and that he inflicted bruises upon her limbs. A physician testified to an examination of these bruises two or three days after the occurrence. The defendant's conduct when he knew the officer was looking for him, was hardly that of an innocent man. The defendant admitted to the officer that he had assaulted the prosecutrix against her will. Indeed, the record shows a state of facts which would have justified the jury in finding the defendant guilty of the crime charged in the indictment. Under the evidence, there is no reasonable doubt, as it seems to us, of the defendant's guilt. We have not intended to review the evidence in detail. We are satisfied that the defendant had a fair trial, and has no just cause for complaint.— AFFIRMED.

STATE OF IOWA v. ED. BURTON, Appellant.

Instructions: DEGREE OF LARCENY: *Reasonable doubt.* An instruction giving substantially the provision of Code 1873, section 4429, that where there is a reasonable doubt of the degree of defendant's
1 offense, he shall only be convicted of the lower degree, is not required on trial for larceny of hogs, where the uncontradicted evidence shows that defendant, if guilty at all, was guilty of grand larceny.

Appeal: RECORD BY AFFIDAVIT: *Misconduct.* An affidavit alleging misconduct of counsel in making improper statements in their
2 arguments to the jury is not competent evidence of such misconduct, on appeal, but the alleged improper statements should be set out in the bill of exceptions

OBJECTIONS: *Waiver.* The right to object to the competency of affidavits as proof of statements made by a torney in argument,
3 where they are not preserved in the bill of exceptions, is not waived by the filing of counter-affidavits.

*Appeal from Jasper District Court.—*HON. D. RYAN, Judge.

THURSDAY, OCTOBER 7, 1897.

THE defendant was convicted of the crime of larceny, and appeals from the judgment which required that he he imprisoned in the state penitentiary at Ft. Madison, at hard labor, for a term of three years.—*Affirmed.*

W. R. Lewis and *John T. Scott* for appellant.

Milton Remley, attorney general, and *Jesse A. Miller* for the state.

ROBINSON, J.—The indictment charges that the defendant committed the crime of larceny in January, 1894, by stealing six hogs, each of which was of the actual value of six dollars. The verdict of the jury found the defendant guilty as charged, and fixed the value of the hogs stolen at forty-eight dollars and seventy-five cents.

I. Section 4429 of the Code of 1873, is as follows: "Where there is a reasonable doubt of the degree of the offense of which the defendant is proven to be guilty, he shall only be convicted of the lower degree." In larceny the extent of the punishment depends upon the value of the property stolen. If that be more than twenty dollars, the offense is punishable by imprisonment in the penitentiary for not more than five years; and, where the value does not exceed that sum, the offense is punishable by a fine not exceeding one hundred dollars, or by imprisonment in the county jail not exceeding thirty days. Code 1873, section 3902. The section quoted was considered in *State v. Wood*, 46 Iowa, 116, a case in which the defendant was tried for the crime of larceny. This court held that the trial court erred in not instructing the jury that, if it had a reasonable doubt, upon all of the evidence, as to the value of the property being greater than twenty dollars, it should find the value to be twenty dollars or less. But much of the evidence in that case was as to the value of the property stolen, some of the witnesses stating that it was more, and others that it was less, than twenty dollars. In *State v. McCarty*, 73 Iowa, 51 (also a case involving larceny), it was said to be the duty of the court to instruct the jury according to the rule stated in *State v. Wood, supra*, and that a failure to do so must be regarded as prejudicial error, unless there was no possible doubt, under the evidence, that the stolen property was of greater value than twenty dollars. Neither of the cases cited is authority for the rule that the instruction in question should be given in every case in which the defendant is on trial

for larceny. Where there is no room for doubt as to
the value of property taken, there is no occasion to
instruct the jury that, if there is any reasonable
doubt as to its value, it must be fixed at twenty dollars or less. This is a case of that kind. The evidence
showed, beyond question, and without conflict, that if
the defendant was guilty of the offense charged, he
had stolen six hogs, if not seven, and that their value
was not less than forty dollars. The conflict in the
evidence related to the ownership of all of the hogs
in question, not to a part of them only, nor to the
value of any of them. The court did not give the
instructions we have considered, and, in view of the
facts in the case, was not required to do so. See *State
v. Cater*, 100 Iowa, 501, and cases therein cited; also,
State v. Smith, 102 Iowa, 656.

II. The only other question presented in behalf
of the appellant, relates to alleged misconduct of
attorneys for the state in making improper statements in their arguments to the jury. The
2 alleged misconduct is shown only by affidavits,
and is not set out in the bill of exceptions. We
have frequently held, that we would not consider
charges of such misconduct which occurred, if at all,
in the presence or within the knowledge of the court,
unless it was shown by bill of exceptions. That rule
was first announced by us in *Rayburn v. Railway Co.*,
74 Iowa, 641, and has since been approved and followed in numerous cases, both civil and criminal.
State v. Bigelow, 101 Iowa, 430; *State v. Helm*, 97 Iowa,
378; *State v. La Grange*, 99 Iowa, 10. We held in
State v. Whalen, 98 Iowa, 662, that affidavits of jurors,
attached to a motion for a new trial, became a part of
the record, by being filed with the motion to which
they were attached. That conclusion was based upon
the provisions of section 4482 of the Code, which
refers to criminal cases. We did not hold, however,

that, by making an affidavit a part of the record in
that manner, it becomes competent evidence. There
is a wide difference between making a paper a part of
the record and making it competent evidence to prove
a fact. In *State v. La Grange*, 99 Iowa, 10, we held
that, although affidavits which charged that the
court had made improper remarks during the trial
were made of record by filing them, yet they were
not competent to show the alleged misconduct; that,
as what was said was necessarily known to the court,
the remarks in question should have been embodied
in a bill of exceptions. What was there said in regard
to remarks by the court, is applicable to statements
made by attorneys in the presence of the court.

3   It is said, however, that no objection was made
in the district court to showing the statements
objected to by means of affidavits, and that the state
filed counter-affidavits, thereby waiving any objection
which might otherwise have been urged to the method
of preserving the statements which was adopted, and
that the appellant does not make any objection to the
counter-affidavits, but asks that they be considered.
In the case of *Rayburn v. Railway Co.*, *supra*, counter-
affidavits had been filed; yet the effect of filing them
was not regarded as a waiver of the right to object to
the competency of the affidavits. We conclude that
we have no competent proof of statements made by
attorneys in argument, and we cannot say that there
was any misconduct of which complaint is made. If
the witnesses for the state were credible, and, in view
of the verdict returned by the jury, we must conclude
that they were, the evidence of the guilt of defendant
is ample and satisfactory. We do not find any ground
upon which to disturb the judgment of the district
court, and it is AFFIRMED.

FRANK A. HODOWAL, *et al.*, Appellants, v. A. L. YEAROUS,
et al., and A. L. YEAROUS V. FRANK A.
HODOWAL, Appellant.

Action: JOINDER OF CAUSES. An action for forcible entry and detainer
of real property cannot be consolidated with an action relating
to the same land to set aside a tax deed and permit redemption
from a sale for taxes, under Code 1873, section 2734, providing that
1 two or more actions pending in the same court which might have
been joined may be consolidated; as one is a law action, and the
other an equitable one, and therefore may not be prosecuted by
the same kind of proceedings, which, under Code 1873, section 2630,
is a condition of joining causes of action.

Affirmance of Justice's Judgment: OPENING UP. The district court
should not open a judgment affirming a judgment of a justice of
the peace entered on the motion of appellee, because of failure of
the appellant to docket the case by noon of the second day of the
2 term to which the same was returnable as required by Iowa district court rule 4, of the rules of practice in the Iowa district
courts, upon an affidavit of appellant which affirmatively shows
neglect to have the case docketed after taking the appeal, or
which merely shows that the matter was left with the appellant's
attorney, who, for some reason, did not attend to it.

*Appeal from Jones District Court.—*HON. W. P. WOLF,
Judge.

THURSDAY, OCTOBER 7, 1897.

THE first entitled action is to set aside a tax deed,
and permit redemption from a sale for taxes; the second,
for forcible entry and detention of real property. The
real estate involved in the two suits is the same. The
equity suit was commenced in September, 1895, and the
other before a justice, October 31, 1895, and the issues
tried to a jury, that returned a verdict for the defendants. The defendant appealed to the term of the district
court commencing December 10, 1895, and on the seventeenth of that month the appellant, not having the cause

docketed, as provided by rule 4 of "Rules of Practice in District Courts," the appellee procured the same to be docketed, and the judgment was affirmed. On the same day the appellant appeared, and moved the court to open the judgment, and set the case for trial, and that it be consolidated with the equity case. The motion, supported by affidavit, was sustained. Later in the proceedings, a motion to set aside the order of consolidation was denied, and a motion by defendants in the equity case to separate the causes for trial was denied, as was also a jury in the law action. The cases, as consolidated, then proceeded to trial, and a decree was entered dismissing the petition in the equity case, and awarding possession to the plaintiff in the law action. The plaintiffs in the equity suit and the defendant in the law action appealed.—*Reversed.*

W. C. Gregory and *R. W. Henry* for appellants.

No appearance for appellees.

GRANGER, J.—I. It is insisted that the causes should not have been consolidated. It seems clear to us they should not have been, if for no other reason, because the statute does not provide for the consolidation of such causes. Code 1873, section 2734, is as follows: "Whenever two or more actions are pending in the same court which might have been joined, the defendant may, on motion and notice to the adverse party, require him to show cause why the same shall not be consolidated, and if no sufficient cause be shown the same shall be consolidated." These two actions were, at the date of consolidation, pending in the same court, but they could not have been joined. One is a law action, and the other an equitable one. They are to be prosecuted by different proceedings. Code 1873, section 2630, tells what actions may be joined, as follows: "Causes of action of whatever kind, where each may be prosecuted by the same kind of proceedings, provided that they be by the same party, and against the same party in the same rights, and if suit on all may be brought and tried in that county, may be joined in the same petition." These actions are not to be prosecuted by the same kind of proceedings, are not by the same parties against the same parties, nor do they involve the same rights. The conditions do not meet the requirements of the law for the consolidation of actions.

II. It may also be said that the showing to open up the judgment is insufficient. We have examin d the transcript to know the record. The rule to govern such proceedings is as follows: "In appeals from justice's courts or other inferior tribunals in civil causes, the appellant shall cause the case to be docketed by noon of the second day of the term to which the same is returnable, and, in case of his failure so to do, the appellee may procure the case to be docketed, and will thereupon be entitled to have the judgment below affirmed. * * * But the judgment, if affirmed, may be opened at any time prior to noon of the following day of the term, by appellants making a satisfactory showing of merits and excuse for his default." The affidavit, when stripped of much that is immaterial, devoted to the question of the two actions involving the same questions as to title, etc., is no showing whatever of excuse for default. It is an affirmative showing of a neglect, after taking the appeal, to bring a transcript to the district court, and have the case docketed. Another affidavit by plaintiff in that case shows that the matter was left with his attorney, who, for some unknown reason, did not attend to the matter. We think the court erred in opening up the judgment, after being affirmed under the rule. The judgment as to both cases is REVERSED.

Mrs. J. B. RABBITT, Plaintiff, v. WILLIAM M. WILCOXEN, Receiver, Appellant, R. M. DIHEL, *et al.*, Interveners and Appellees.

Building and Loan Companies: WITHDRAWAL BY STOCKHOLDER: *Insolvency.* The by-laws of a building and savings association, whose articles of incorporation arranged for a loan fund and an expense fund, provided that any stockholder, after giving thirty days' notice, might withdraw the full amount of his payments to the loan fund, with earnings up to the last dividend period, and that the association should not be liable to pay out on account of withdrawals, during any one month, more than thirty per cent. of the cash receipts of the loan fund during such month. *Held*, that where such association was insolvent, and more than said thirty per cent had been paid out when notices of withdrawals were given, shareholders giving such notices were not creditors with claims, and entitled to be paid in full the amounts by them paid to the loan fund before other stockholders were entitled to anything, but were on a parity with other stockholders Such by-laws contemplate a going concern.

Appeal from Polk District Court.—HON. T. F. STEVENSON, Judge.

FRIDAY, OCTOBER 8, 1897.

THE following, including some provisions of the law of the association, to be noticed in the opinion, is substantially appellees' statement of the facts. "The Union Building & Savings Assoc'ation was inc.rporated under the laws of Iowa, on the twenty-sixth of June, 1890, with its principal place of business in the city of Des Moines. The object of the association, as stated in its articles of incorporation, being 'to afford profitable investment of money, and encourage and assist its shareholders in the acquisition of real estate, by loaning money to them, to be paid back in monthly installments, thereby increasing the proportion of home

owners in the country, in the manner and by the means
provided in chapter 6, title 9, of the Code of Iowa.' On
the fifteenth of December, 1894, Mrs. J. B. Rabbitt,
plaintiff in the original cause, petitioned the district
court of Polk county for the appointment of a receiver
for the association; and on the twenty-eighth day of
December, 1894, the court appointed William M. Wilcoxen, Esq., receiver, to take charge of the assets of the
association, and collect and convert the same into
money, with a view to the winding up of the association.
On the fourth day of December, 1895, R. M. Dihel, et al.,
filed their petition of intervention, and, in a few days
thereafter, others filed petitions of intervention, all of
said petitions claiming the same relief. The petitions
of intervention are substantially the same, and claim
that the petitioners filed their notices of withdrawal, as
provided by section 9 of article 13 of the by-laws, and
for that reason they are entitled to be paid, according
to said section 9 of article 13 of the by-laws, prior to
the payment or distribution of the funds among the
stockholders of said corporation who did not file their
notice of withdrawal. They claim that they are no
longer stockholders of said corporation, and have not
been since the moment of filing their notices of withdrawal, but are creditors with claims, according to the
terms of section 9 of article 13 of the by-laws. On the
seventh day of December, 1895, William M. Wilcoxen,
receiver, filed his answer, and it was agreed that this
answer should apply to all the petitions of intervention.
Said answer is found on page 11 of the abstract, and in
substance states that the association, at the time of
filing said notices of withdrawal, was insolvent; that
article 17 of the by-laws of said association provides
that said association shall not be liable to pay out, on
account of withdrawals of all classes of stock during
any month, more than thirty per cent. of the cash

receipts of the loan fund during such month; and that
there had been, since January 1, 1894, during each
month, more than thirty per cent. paid out; and, further,
it states that said interveners have not complied with
all things necessary in order to perfect their withdrawals, in accordance with the 'Articles of Incorporation and By-Laws' of the association; and, further, it is
stated that to allow the claims of these interveners to
be paid in full would impair the value of the outstanding securities, etc.; and then prays that the claims of
the interveners be adjudged to be on a parity with the
claims of the non-withdrawing shareholders of said
association, and that they be made to share their pro
rata proportion with the other shareholders in the funds
coming into the hands of the receiver." The district
court determined the issues in favor of the interveners,
and gave judgment accordingly, and the receiver
appealed.—*Reversed.*

Wm. Wilcoxen, Bishop, Bowen & Fleming, and
Sammis & Scott for appellant.

Searle & Keating for C. P. Searle, et al.

Dudley & Coffin for R. M. Dihel, et al.

E. T. Morris for W. P. Mott, et al.

C. A. Ballreich and *Read & Read* for Forston
Aker, et al.

Ayres, Woodin & Ayres for Paul Longe, administrator, et al.

J. K. Macomber for F. K. Irwin, intervener and
appellee.

GRANGER, J.—The case involves no controversy as to general creditors, nor as to any creditors except in so far as the withdrawing shareholders may be regarded as creditors, as to which fact there is some controversy in argument. There are two classes of persons who claim to be entitled to participate in the distribution of the assets of the corporation: *First,* those who gave notice of withdrawal before the appointment of the receiver, who claim to be preferred, and to be entitled to full payment before the other shareholders are entitled to anything; and, *second,* those who did not give such notice, who claim that all shareholders (that is, both classes) should share equally. The articles of incorporation provide for two funds,—a loan fund and an expense fund. The following is a provision of the by-laws under which it is claimed that the withdrawing shareholders should be preferred and first paid: "Section 9. Any shareholder in good standing, after giving thirty (30) days' notice in writing, and upon the surrender of his certificate, may withdraw, after three (3) months' dues have been paid, the full amount of his payments to the loan fund, together with the earnings up to the last dividend period. Said withdrawals shall be paid according to the priority of notice." The stock of the corporation is classed from A to F, but the classification is not important for our consideration. The following is a further provision of the by-laws: "Article XVII. This association shall not be liable to pay out on account of withdrawals of all classes of stock, during any one month, more than thirty (30) per cent. of the cash receipts of the loan fund during such month, upon all classes of stock except Class F, and except stock issued under the provisions of Sec. 2 of article VII. of the by-laws. In case of withdrawal before maturity, there shall be charged against the book value thereof a withdrawal fee of 10 cents on

each share." By a misappropriation, the loan fund has
been used for the expenses of the corporation to an
amount in excess of thirty-six thousand dollars, and
while, in argument, there is some contention otherwise,
the corporation is insolvent. In considering the rights
of withdrawing shareholders from such associations,
the cases discuss the effect of the association being, at
the time of withdrawal, "a going concern," or insolvent,
and its affairs being "wound up." It is quite evident
that the by-laws of this association were adopted with
reference to doing business, rather than with reference
to closing up its affairs. This fact is important in determining what must have been the mutual understanding
of the incorporators in their adoption of the article and
laws, and also the understanding of those who became
shareholders afterwards. Section 9 of article 13 gives
the absolute right of withdrawal on thirty days' notice,
and just as absolute a right to withdraw payments to
the loan fund, except that it must be done in a way prescribed. That method is fixed by article 17, which
exempts the association from liability for such withdrawals, so that it is not required to pay, in any one
month, more than thirty per cent. of the cash receipts
of the loan fund during such month. Speaking of such
an association as a going concern, there would seem to
be no question but that a withdrawing shareholder, on
presentation of his certificate, could demand and should
receive payment, in the order of his withdrawal, of as
much money as the treasury afforded, of the thirty per
cent. specified, and no more. If there were no provision
for such payment, none could be made from the fund,
and the shareholder must hold his stock or exchange it
in the market. The right of withdrawing the stock,—
that is, withdrawing the payments,—depends entirely
on the by-laws authorizing it. The by-law is not a
limitation on a prior right,—that is, a right existing

independent of the by-law, perforce of a person being
a shareholder,—but it is a grant of a right, and limited
by the terms of the grant.

In *Heinbokel v. Association*, 58 Minn. 340 (59 N. W.
Rep. 1050), this particular question is considered. The
by-law in that case is so like the one in this case as to
make the authority entirely applicable. It is said in
that case: "In assuming the relation of a member of
the association, plaintiff contracted with reference to,
and was to be governed by, its by-laws in so far as they
were reasonable, and not opposed to our statutory provisions regulating associations of this character. He
agreed to abide by the condition of the treasury in case
of a withdrawal, and to take his money when funds
properly applicable for the purpose were on hand. He
was not to be paid until these funds were in the treasury, and, although he could at any time cease to be a
member, and terminate his obligation to make monthly
payments, the amount to be returned to him did not
then become due or payable except in a certain contingency. If not absolutely and immediately due and
payable at withdrawal, it is difficult to see how his
cause of action was then maintainable." In that case
the questions are considered whether or not a withdrawing shareholder becomes a creditor upon complying with the law for withdrawing his payments, and
also whether he could bring an action and obtain judgment against the association when there is no money
legally applicable for the payment of his claim. It is
held that such a shareholder is not to be regarded as
having the rights of the ordinary creditor, and hence
that he could not maintain such an action. It is further
said in that case: "The right to draw and receive back
what has been paid into the treasury by a member of
the association exists solely by virtue of the by-laws or
the statute. If this right to receive the money out of

the treasury is made to depend upon its condition, the right is not perfect or absolute until that condition exists." In *Association v. Kerr* (Tex. Sup.) 13 S. W. Rep. 1020, where the right of withdrawal was given in the by-laws, and there was a provision that at no time should more than one-third of the funds in the treasury be applied to the demands of the withdrawing stockholders without the consent of the directors, it was held that there could be no recovery by such a stockholder in the absence of a showing that there were funds applicable, or that the directors had consented to the use of other funds. *Christian's Appeal*, 102 Pa. St. 184, involved a question as to the right of withdrawing stockholders to preference after the payment of the general creditors, under by-laws so similar to those in the case at bar as to make the rule of the case authority; and it is there said as to such stockholders: "If the association has been prosperous, they have the right, under certain limitations and restrictions, to demand and receive their proportionate share of the accumulated fund; but if bad investments have been made, or losses have been sustained, before actual withdrawal, they must bear their just proportion thereof. * * * When a building association has failed to fulfill the object of its creation, and has become hopelessly insolvent, it cannot be justly or equitably wound up on any other principle than that above suggested. After expenses incident to the administration of its assets are deducted, the general creditors, if any, should be first paid in full, and the residue of the fund should be distributed pro rata among those whose claims are based upon stock of the association, whether they have withdrawn and hold orders for the withdrawal value thereof or not. Both classes are equally meritorious, and, in the marshaling of the assets, neither is entitled to priority over the other. The claims of each are alike based on their relation to the association as members thereof." The case refers to *Association v. Silverman*, 85 Pa. St. 394; and, while it does not overrule or distinguish it, it announces the above rule with the former case in mind. It is not easy to reconcile the two cases in some particulars, and undoubtedly the last should be taken as the judgment of the court wherein, if at all, the cases are not in harmony. The *Silverman Case* is reviewed in *Heinbokel v. Association, supra* (the Minnesota case), and the holding is disapproved. In Endlich, Building Associations (2d ed.), section 114, it is said, speaking of the by-law provisions of such corporations, that only a proportion of the funds can be withdrawn for the purpose of paying withdrawing stockholders: "This, then, becomes a charter limitation upon the rights of withdrawing members, and operates to prevent a conflict between them and the undisturbed exercise of the association's corporate functions by narrowing them down to a certain portion of its assets as the source of their payment."

It seems to us that these authorities, as well as the language of the by-laws of the association in this case, fix a limitation on the rights of withdrawing shareholders as to the funds applicable to the payment of their claims, and that beyond such limit they cannot go. In this case there is, confessedly, no such fund available. We have seen no case in which the limitation is like the one in this case, it being limited to thirty per cent. of the monthly receipts. This limitation, throughout the authorities, in this country, seems to be of controlling importance. Insolvency but adds to the strength of such a position, and the holding in *Christian's Appeal, supra*, is in a case where the corporation was insolvent, and the rule was there applied. Both parties have quoted from, and argued the effect of, some English cases, and, conceding them to announce a different rule (and to quite an extent they do), we are still

content with the rule that is supported by the weight
of authority in this country, and best accords with reason. No one contends that such a conclusion is not the
equitable one, the contention of interveners being only
that a correct legal construction of the by-laws justified
their claim, but in that view we do not concur. As we
said at the outset, the provision of the by-laws for paying back contributions to the loan fund contemplated
monthly receipts to such fund, so that the corporation,
as a going concern, could apply a percentage thereof
to such a purpose; and there is nothing to show a purpose to make such payments after such receipts ha e
ceased, and the only business of the corporation is a
final settlement and an equitable division of the assets.
We think the judgment should be so changed as to make
a pro rata payment of all stockholders, regardless of
notices of withdrawal, and the cause is remanded for
such a decree.—REVERSED.

MARY R. BAKER, Administratrix of the Estate of
GEORGE C. BAKER, Deceased, v. A. HALLAM,
Appellant.

Deed in Blank: DECEIT. Defendant made a deed. At the request of
the grantee he erased the name of that grantee, and returned it to
him with an abstract showing title in defendant, which abstract
1   proved to be spurious. The man whose name had thus been
erased, sold to plaintiff who inserted his own name as grantee,
2   *Held,* as defendant had by his own act put a deed in blank, accompanied by such abstract, into circulation, he was liable to said
last buyer as for false representations as to ownership of the land.
though these two never came together.

RELIANCE OF VENDEE. The nature of the transaction, and the fact
5   that vendee gave valuable consideration for the land, are sufficient
to support a verdict that plaintiff relied on the representations of
ownership, by defendant.

Evidence. Where one delivers a deed which his own grantor had
3   made a deed in blank by erasure, and with it a true copy of
abstract which states the title falsely, his statements to his vendee

6 that the original abstract had been received from said grantor and
   must be returned to him. are admissible in an action for deceit
   brought by the last vendee against such original grantor.

SAME. The abstract was spurious and a forgery. One K testified
8 that the land had been offered to him, and that a deed therefor
   from defendant, accompanied by the abstract, was placed in
   escrow, while he sent a copy of the abstract to the clerk in
4 Georgia, who had certified it, and discovered it to be a forgery;
   whereupon he declined to take the land and told his reason
   plainly. He was then given other land and money as a substitute, which money was paid by defendant. Held, that there was
   evidence that defendant knew the abstract was spurious.

SAME The admission of testimony of K as to the return of the
   deeds and abstract in escrow, in connection with his other testi-
7 mony was not prejudicial error, as the purpose of the testimony
   was to show that K had notified defendant of the defective character of his title.

Appeal from Polk District Court.—HON. W. F. CONRAD,
Judge.

FRIDAY, OCTOBER, 8, 1897.

ACTION at law to recover damages for alleged fraud
and deceit in the conveyance of real estate. The issues
and facts appear in the opinion. Verdict and judgment
were rendered for the plaintiff. Defendant appeals.—
Affirmed.

Dowell & Parrish for appellant.

Cummins & Wright for appellee.

GIVEN, J.—I. There is no dispute as to the following facts: On July 8, 1889, the defendant executed
a special warranty deed to one A. Brower to two thous-
and acres of land in Camden county, Ga., described as
a part of a grant of five thousand acres made by that
         state to Robert Middleton, March 28, 1794. About
1   the first of November, 1889, Brower sold all of
         said land to one J. A. Merritt, and was about to
erase his name as grantee in said deed, when Merritt

protested that Hallam, the grantee, must consent to
the erasure. Thereupon Brower went to Hallam, who
erased the name of Brower as grantee in the said deed,
leaving it blank as to the grantee, and attaching a note
to the deed, as follows: "Nov. 1, 1889. Mr. Merritt: I
scratched the name out of A. A. Brower's deed. A. Hallam." Merritt received the deed thus made blank as to
the grantee, as a conveyance of the land. During the
transaction between Brower and Merritt, Brower presented to Merritt, as evidence of the title, what purported to be an abstract showing title in Hallam.
Brower represented to Merritt that he had promised to
return said abstract to Hallam, but that Merritt could
have a copy made of it, to retain. A copy was made by
E. Irons, who verified the same as a true copy. Merritt
continued to hold the deed in blank as to the grantee,
and said copy of the abstract, until about the first of
July, 1890, when he entered into negotiations with the
plaintiff's intestate, George C. Baker, deceased, for the
sale of said land to him. Merritt presented to Baker,
as evidence of his title, said deed from Hallam, and
said copy of the abstract. Baker gave to Merritt, in payment for said land, three hundred dollars in money and
two hundred shares of stock of the Mexican & Iron
Mountain Manufacturing Company, of the then value of
from five dollars to eight dollars per share, and received
from Merritt said deed from Hallam, in blank as to the
grantee, and said copy of the abstract. Baker filled the
blank in the deed with his own name as grantee. Plaintiff alleges that said abstract was a spurious and forged
abstract, in that certain conveyances appearing therein,
and upon which the title of defendant rested, were
never, in fact, executed or recorded, but were inserted
in said abstract over the certificate of the clerk thereto;
and that said Hallam had no title whatever to the said
lands, "and knew that he had no title thereto, and knew
that the said abstract was a forged and spurious

abstract." Plaintiff asks to recover the value of the money and capital stock paid and transferred to Merritt in consideration of said land.

II. Appellant contends, and appellee concedes, that to entitle the plaintiff to recover she must prove the following: "*First*, that the representations were made to George C. Baker by defendant, Hallam, and were made with intention to influence the action of the said George C. Baker; *second*, that the representations at the time they were made, were known by the defendand to be untrue; *third*, that the said George C. Baker believed and relied upon the said representations, and acted there n, and was damaged thereby." Upon the first proposition appellant insists that there is no evidence that he ever made any representations to Baker. It is true, so far as appears, that Baker and Hallam never came together, or exchanged words, in relation to this land. By delivering his deed in blank as to the grantee, to Merritt, appellant authorized the blank to be filled with the name of any person who might subsequently become a grantee of the land. The deed itself was a representation by him that he, at least, believed that he was the owner of the property conveyed, or had some interest in it. By putting the deed in circulation in blank as to the grantee, he must be presumed to have known that he might thereby become the grantor of a person with whom he had no personal dealings. By accompanying that deed with said abstract, he certainly intended to thereby represent to any person taking title under him that he believed the abstract to be correct. The case is not different from what it would have been if the sale had been directly from Hallam to Baker, and Hallam had presented this deed and abstract as the evidence of his title. That it was a verified copy of the abstract that came to the knowledge of Baker does not change the application of the rule, for, being a correct copy, it operated as appellant's representation as effectually as if the original abstract had been presented to Baker. This branch of the case was very clearly and concisely submitted to the jury.

III.   Appellant contends that there is no evidence that Hallam had knowledge that the representations made by the deed and abstract were untrue, or that he had no title to the land.   The abstract shows
3   upon its face title from the governor of Georgia to Robert Middleton, and from Middleton, through various persons, to Charles J. Santmeyer. Following this is a certificate of John J. Rudolph, clerk of the superior court of Camden county, Ga., who is *ex-officio* recorder of deeds, to the correctness of what precedes. Following this, the abstract shows two conveyances, the last of which is to appellant, Hallam; and after this is another certificate of said clerk, showing conveyances from Whitehead to Davis, and Davis to Hubbell, Hubbell to Austin, and Austin to Hallam. Hon. Phillip Cook, secretary of the state of Georgia, testifies in his deposition that he is custodian of the records of grants from the state; that there is a record of conveyance of fifty grants of one thousand acres each from the governor to Middleton, and of fifty-eight grants of one thousand acres each from the governor to Bryan; that only such grants are recorded in his office, and that grants between individuals are recorded in the office of the clerk of the superior court of the county where the land lays. He says this land was never surveyed or settled upon by any of the grantees; that for thirty years no taxes have been paid on the same, although due each year; that the grants have never been recognized by the state, and most of the land has been granted under the law to actual citizens and residents of the state, who lived upon them and paid taxes for the past fifty years. Mr. Rudolph testifies that seven of the

conveyances shown by said abstract between individuals are not of record in his office. He says: "I executed a certificate of abstract of title from John M. Whitehead to Christopher Davis, and from Christopher Davis and wife to Charles S. Hubbell, and from Charles S. Hubbell and wife to Charles Santmeyer, and from Hubbell to E. Austin, and from E. Austin to A. Hallam. These were the only conveyances contained in the abstract when such certificate was attached. I don't know who changed the abstract to which I attached the certificate to make it appear that all the other conveyances above were of record in Camden county. The abstract is incorrect, not only as to the place of record in the books, but as to the fact of record at all." It can scarcely be doubted, under this evidence, that the abstract is spurious and forged. As to appellant's knowledge of that

fact, there is only this evidence: One T. H.
4   Knotts testifies that at a time prior to the date
of Hallam's deed he entered into an arrangement with one Collins for the purchase of lands in Camden county, Ga., for other property; that the papers were made out, and deposited in escrow; that thereupon he corresponded with the clerk of the court of the county with respect to the title. He says: "I took the abstract, and sent it to the county clerk of Camden county, Ga., whose certificate it bore, by mail, and inquired of him if that abstract was correct. * * * He said that his certificates related only to certain transfers as being of record, and that he did not certify to the entire abstract. When I received this information, I did not make the trade. I gave my reasons direct to the party with whom I was dealing, whose name I cannot recollect at this moment." Witness testified that the letter from the clerk had been lost or destroyed, and that the papers in escrow were taken up by the respective parties. He also testifies that the deed that

was deposited in escrow was signed by Mr. Hallam, and that the copy of the abstract shown him was a copy of the one sent by him to the clerk. He also testifies that certain lands in Kentucky were substituted for the Georgia lands in the trade, the deed to which was made by Mr. Brower, and that the money difference which he received was paid by Mr. Hallam. It can scarcely be doubted, under this evidence, that Collins was representing Hallam and Brower in the deal with Knotts; that Collins learned from Knotts what the clerk said about the abstract; and we think it may be inferred that Collins imparted this information to Hallam and Brower, as showing why the trade for the Georgia land was not consummated. The question of defendant's knowledge was properly submitted to the jury, and under this evidence the jury was certainly warranted in finding that he knew that the abstract was not true and correct.

IV. Appellant insists that there is no testimony tending to show that George C. Baker relied upon the representations arising from the deed and abstract. This inquiry was also submitted to the jury, and 5 we think it was fully warranted in finding, from the nature of the transaction, that Mr. Baker did rely upon it as a representation upon the part of the grantor therein that he believed himself to be the owner of the land to the extent of the interest conveyed, and that he believed the abstract of title to be correct. It is said that there is no evidence that Baker was ignorant of the falsity of these representations as to title. Surely, if Baker had not relied upon the title, and had known that the title was not as represented by the deed and abstract, he would not have parted with the consideration that he did, for the conveyances.

V. Complaint is made of several rulings on evidence, and, first, that Merritt was permitted to testify

to what Brower said with respect to the abstract, and
        from whom he got it. Appellant having put this
6   abstract into circulation with his deed, it was
        competent for Brower to state from whom he
received it, and that Hallam required him to return it.
The reason for requiring the abstract to be returned
may have been because of the alterations that had been
made in it, or because it covered more land than the
two thousand acres involved in these transactions. We
think, under the circumstances, it was competent for
        Brower to testify as he did. It is also urged that
7   the court erred in permitting Knotts to testify
        that the papers deposited in escrow had been
returned to the parties. There was certa'nly no prejudice in admitting this testimony. The important part
of that inquiry was as to what information Knotts had
imparted to the agents of Hallam and Brower touching
the condition of the title and abstract. Complaint is
made of the instruction to the effect that the delivery
of the abstract to Merritt was in law a representation
to Baker that the defendant had title to the land. What
we have already said disposes of this contention upon
the plainest pr:ncipl s of equity and r'ght, and we w:ll
not, therefore, refer to any of the authorities cited
further than to say that, upon examination, we think
they are not applicable to the facts of this case. Our
conclusion is that the judgment of the district court
should be AFFIRMED.

STATE OF IOWA v. NICK ABEGGLAN, Appellant.

Evidence: SEDUCTION. Evidence as to the relation between the
    prosecutrix in seduction and one other than defendant, after the
    alleged seduction, which does not tend to explain their relation
    before that time is inadmissible in behalf of defendant.

Appeal from Monroe District Court.—HON. T. M. FEE,
Judge.

FRIDAY, OCTOBER 8, 1897.

THE defendant was accused and convicted of the
crime of seduction. From the judgment, which required
that he be imprisoned in the state penitentiary at Ft.
Madison for the term of eighteen months, he appeals.—
Affirmed.

T. B. Perry and *J. F. Abegglan* for appellant.

Milton Remley, attorney general, for the state.

ROBINSON, J.—The indictment charges that the
offense of which the defendant was convicted was committed on or about the fifteenth day of June, 1895.
Gertie Smith, the person alleged to have been seduced,
testifies that the offense was accomplished by reason
of a promise of marriage, in the latter part of May, 1895,
when she was fifteen years of age. She gave birth to a
child about the first of March, 1896, and states that she
never had sexual intercourse with any one excepting
the defendant.

I.   There is testimony which tends to show, and
the jury was authorized to find, that during the first
half of the year 1895 the defendant paid to the prosecutrix considerable attention, frequently being in her
company two or three times in a week, waiting upon
her to parties, and attending her from church, usually
at night, and conducting himself as her suitor. Several
witnesses testified that they had heard the defendant
say that he had had sexual intercourse with her. The
defendant offered evidence to show that, before and at
the time of the alleged seduction, the prosecutrix was

receiving the attentions of one Guy Castner, and that
he may have been the father of her child. The d fend-
ant complains of the refusal of the court to permit him
to show that Castner not only paid to the prosecutrix
the attention of a suitor prior to the alleged seduction,
but that he continued to do so after that time, and during the remainder of the year. The complaint is based
in part upon a misapprehension of the record. The
court permitted the defendant to show the relations
which existed between Castner and the prosecutrix both
before and after the time of the alleged seduction,
although it did sustain objections to some of the
evidence which was designed to show their conduct
towards each other after that time. In sustaining such
objections, the court did not, we think, err. There was
nothing in that which the defendant proposed to show
in regard to what occurred between Castner and the
prosecutrix after the seduction is alleged to have been
accomplished which could tend to explain what took
place before. If the prosecutrix accepted the attentions of another suitor after that time, that fact would
not tend to show that the defendant was n .t her su'tor
before, for it is not claimed by any one that he continued
his attentions more than a short time after the prosecutrix submitted herself to him. If she was guilty of
improper conduct after that time, that fact would not
tend to show him to be innocent of the offense charged,
for it might be one of the results of the ruin he had
wrought. The district court rightly permitted the
defendant to prove the relations which existed between
the prosecutrix and Guy Castner before and at the time
of the alleged seduction. The defendant was also permitted to show that during the year 1895 he paid much
attention to Miss Castner. The cases of *State v. Brown*,
86 Iowa, 121; *State v. Baldoser*, 88 Iowa, 62; and *State
v. Mackey*, 82 Iowa, 394, upon which the appellant relies,

do not authorize more than the district court permitted him to prove. In the case last cited, it was held that proof of acts of sexual intercourse subsequent to the one by which the seduction was alleged to have been accomplished was competent evidence on the question of the intent with which the first act was committed; but that evidence was unlike any which the district court rejected in this case.

II.   The appellant makes numerous complaints in regard to the rulings of the court on the admission of evidence, and of portions of the charge given. The rulings of the court in regard to evidence were, in most cases, so clearly right that it is not necessary to set them out. If at any time the court erred in excluding evidence offered by the defendant, the error was subsequently corrected, and proper evidence permitted. The charge, so far as it has been called to our attention, was fair to the defendant. The abstract of the defendant shows that he asked the court to make of record certain statements alleged to have been made by the attorney for the state during the trial, and in argument to the jury. The court refused to do so, on the ground that the alleged statements were not made, and bystanders thereupon made affidavit to the effect that they were made. If the district court was in error, and the bystanders were correct as to what was said, we should not be disposed to disturb the judgment of the court on that ground. It is claimed that the county attorney denounced the manner in which the defense had been conducted. If he did so, it was not without reason. Questions were persistently asked in behalf of the defendant on cross-examination of witnesses, and at other times, which were so manifestly improper that it is surprising that able and conscientious attorneys should have persisted in asking them.

III.   We do not find any ground upon which the judgment of the district court should be disturbed

There was conflict in the evidence respecting the conduct of the prosecutrix and her relations with Guy Castner, as well as in regard to other matters, which was properly submitted to the determination of the jury. That the prosecutrix was indiscreet in many things before the alleged seduction is quite probable, but the evidence to establish the guilt of the defendant is ample, and there is no apparent reason why he should not suffer punishment for his crime. The judgment of the district court is AFFIRMED.

STATE OF IOWA v. WESLEY WILTSEY, Appellant.

Constitutional Law: COMPULSORY PROCESS TO OBTAIN WITNESSES. Where the state admits that a sick witness for defendant would, if present, testify as stated in defendant's continuance affidavit, which the latter read on the trial, he has not been denied his constitutional right to compulsory process, and sections 2751 and 4556, Code, 1873, which permit the denial of a continuance under such facts, are not violative of such constitutional right.

Grand Jury: CHANGE IN STATUTE. A grand jury drawn prior to July 1, 1895, for that year, pursuant to the laws then in force, is competent to return an indictment subsequent thereto, though acts April 26, 1894, which took effect July 1, 1895, changed the law concerning the drawing of grand juries.

Adultery: EVIDENCE. The fact that a witness saw a man and woman in a cemetery, in the day time, hugging and kissing for half an hour, is not alone sufficient to justify a conviction of adultery; especially where but one witness testified to such act, both parties deny it, and intercourse at any time, and other parties who were watching them do not mention it.

Appeal from Kossuth District Court.—HON. LOT THOMAS, Judge.

FRIDAY, OCTOBER 8, 1897.

THE defendant was indicted for the crime of adultery, committed with Rose Shadle, the wife of L. K. Shadle. He was convicted, and sentenced to be confined

in the penitentiary for one year. He appeals.—
Reversed.

D. C. Chase and *Sullivan & McMahon* for appellant.

Milton Remley, attorney general, for the state.

KINNE, C. J.—I. Between the time of the drawing of the grand jury which found this indictment and the time the indictment was returned, the law touching the selection of grand jurors was changed, and said new act took effect July 1, 1895. The indictment was found in October, 1895. A challenge to the panel 1 of the grand jury was interposed on the ground that said panel was not appointed, drawn, and summoned as prescribed by law. The challenge was not allowed. The ruling was correct. *State v. Graff,* 97 Iowa, 568.

II. Defendant made a motion for a continuance on the ground of the absence of a witness named Dahl, on account of sickness. The state having admitted that the witness, if present, would testify as stated in the affidavit, the motion was overruled, and the defendant excepted. Upon the trial the defendant read 2 said affidavit to the jury. He now claims that, under the constitution, he was entitled to the personal attendance of the witness, or to a continuance. Our statute provides that "the rules of evidence prescribed in the civil part of the Code, shall apply to criminal proceedings as far as applicable and as they are not inconsistent with the provisions of this chapter." Code 1873, section 4556. Under Code 1873, section 2751, if the application be sufficient, the cause must be continued unless the adverse party will admit that the witness, if present, would testify to the facts therein stated, in which event the cause shall not be continued, but the

party may read as evidence of such witness the facts
held by the court to be properly stated. True it is that
the defendant has, by virtue of the constitution, the
right to have compulsory process for his witnesses.
That right he had in this case. On account of the sickness of the witness, such process did not avail to bring
the witness into court; but the defendant was not
thereby deprived of his constitutional right. In *State
v. Kennedy*, 20 Iowa, 372, it was held that a defendant
had no absolute right, under this provision of the constitution, to insist upon the personal attendance of a
witness who was a convict in the state penitent'ary.
In principle, that case is controlling in the case at bar.
There was no error in the court's ruling.

III. The serious question in this case is as to the
guilt of the defendant. The act of adultery upon which
conviction was had is said to have occurred in the cemetery in the city of Algona, Iowa, on April 22,
1895. One witness testifies to having seen the
defendant and Mrs. Shadle go into the cemetery
on that day; that he did not see them upon the ground.
This witness says they hugged and kissed for a half
hour. Another witness, who was with the one before
referred to, saw them in the cemetery; says they were
standing up; that they moved around some. Still
another witness saw them enter the cemetery. The
evidence shows without conflict that, after entering the
cemetery, they went towards the grave of Mrs. Shadle's
father. All this occurred in daytime. But one witness
testifies to any improper conduct at the cemetery, and
he, only, that they were hugging and kissing. No other
witness saw that, though at least one other person was
watching Mrs. Shadle and the defendant while they
were in the cemetery. The defendant and Mrs. Shadle
both deny the kissing and hugging in the cemetery.
They positively deny having, at that or any other time,

had any connection with each other. Evidence was
'introduced showing the defendant's good cnaracter.
Nothing improper is shown to have occurred at the
cemetery between these parties except the hugging and
kissing, and under the evidence it is not at all certain
that they were guilty of those acts in that place. Giving the utmost force and effect to the unsupported testimony of one witness, and these acts in the cemetery
only tended to show mutual affection, which, though
manifestly improper, was not criminal. From a close
examination of this record, we are forced to the conclusion that this verdict is not supported by the evidence.
It cannot be truthfully said that it justified the jury in
finding the defendant guilty of the crime charged,
beyond a reasonable doubt. For this reason the judgment below is REVERSED.

CARISTINA E. MORGAN v. DALLAS COUNTY, Appellant. | 108
| f125

Contributory Negligence: JURY QUESTION: *Bridges*. Plaintiff, her
1 husband and her child were driving over a bridge, and when on
the graded approach thereto, some six feet above the surrounding
land, the horse shied, forcing the buggy over the edge of the
approach, to the ground below, injuring the occupants. There
were no guard rails on the approach. There was a ford under the
bridge, the use of which would have avoided the necessity of going
on the approach. The bank on one side of the ford was steep,
and the river was about sixty-five feet wide, the water being
about up to the wheel hubs. The major portion of the travel was
by the bridge, rather than the ford, *Held*, that the question of
contributory negligence in choosing the bridge rather than the
ford, was for the jury. •

Same: *Instructions*. An instruction that assumed that a way by the
2 ford was safe, and free from all danger, was properly refused.

Instructions: APPLICABILITY. Testimony by a mother as to the
3 value of her time, and as to the amount of time given by her to
her child by reason of its injuries, supports an instruction permitting "reasonable compensation for the care of the child
occasioned by the injury."

Appeal: HARMLESS ERROR: *Evidence.* Error in allowing the driver
to testify that if there had been a guard rail along the approach
to the bridge his horse would not have backed over the side, is not
prejudicial, as it is apparent that if there had been a barrier sufficiently strong, the horse could not have gone through it.

Appeal from Guthrie District Court.—HON. A. W. WIL-
KINSON, Judge.

FRIDAY, OCTOBER 8, 1897.

WHILE J. W. Morgan, with his wife, the plaintiff
herein, and little child, were driving along the approach
to a county bridge in Dallas county, his horse shied off
the grade, and occasioned the injuries complained of.
Morgan assigned his cause of action to the plaintiff,
who brings this suit for damages sustained by both.
Trial to jury; verdict and judgment for plaintiff; and
defendant appeals.—*Affirmed.*

Edmund Nichols for appellant.

Shortley & Harpel and *S. D. Nichols* for appellee.

LADD, J.—It is insisted that the plaintiff and her
husband were guilty of contributory negligence, and,
for this reason, ought not to recover. The bridge is over
the 'Coon river, about one and one-half miles
1   southwest of Perry, and is sixty-five or seventy
feet long, with iron guard rails. Next to the
bridge is a plankway, with wooden railing, and, beyond
this, an approach, constructed by erecting a crib, and
filling it with earth, about six feet above the surface.
This approach had no barriers whatever, and from it the
horse shied, and occasioned the accident. Under the
bridge was a ford, the water being about one foot deep,
or, as said by one witness, it came up to the hub of the
wagons. In going to the south, as Morgan did, the
way was on the east side of the approach, under the

bridge, and out on the west side. In going into the river, the ground was level to the north, but there was a steep bank on the south side, making it somewhat difficult to get out. As Morgan knew the approach was without barriers, it is said he ought to have driven by way of the ford, instead of over the bridge. *Homan v. Franklin County*, 98 Iowa, 692, is relied on. In that case the defect in the bridge was such as might occasion injury without any other co-operating cause, such as to render it dangerous however used. It was shaky, and not properly braced from below. Here the approach might be used with impunity by those to whom the want of barriers was not a source of danger. The greater portion of the travelers went over the bridge, instead of through the river. Morgan had driven this very horse over it many times without harm. The approach was as constructed, and open to the public use. Under the circumstances, Morgan might well hesitate whether he would brook the dangers of the ford or those of the unguarded approach. In deciding, he was required to exercise that degree of prudence an ordinarily cautious man would under like circumstances. Whether he so did, was properly left to the jury. *Walker v. Decatur County*, 67 Iowa, 307; *Waud v. Polk County*, 88 Iowa, 617.

II. The first instruction asked by the defendant was properly refused, because it assumed that the way by the ford was safe and convenient. It cannot be said that driving across a stream sixty-five feet wide, with wife and small child, in the buggy, the water hub deep, and a difficult ascent on the further side, would have been entirely free from danger. The ninth instruction given by the court called attention to the way by the ford, and submitted the question whether Morgan was negligent in going over the bridge. It is not as specific as could have been desired, but must have been understood by the jury as indicating that

Morgan was required to choose between the two ways,
acting as an ordinarily cautious man in so doing.

III. It is said there is no evidence to support that
part of the tenth instruction permitting the jury to
allow as damages "reasonable compensation for the
care of the child occasioned by the injury." The
3   plaintiff testified to the value of her time, and
also the care given the child. This furnished a
basis from which to fix such compensation.

IV. Morgan was allowed to testify, over the objection of the defendant, that, if there had been a guard
rail along the approach, the accident would not have
occurred. This was a conclusion of the witness,
·4   and improperly received. He spoke his opinion,
only. It was without prejudice, however, as
every juror knew, as well as the witness, that, if there
had been a barrier sufficiently strong, the horse could
not have gone through it. The evidence bearing on the
character of the horse was in conflict, and rightly left
for the consideration of the jury in passing on the issues
raised by the pleadings.—Affirmed.

Charles B. Rouss, Appellant, v. M. A. Creglow.

Contracts: construction: *Understanding of parties.* Code, 1873,
   section 3652, providing that, "where the terms of an agreement
 1 have been intended in a different sense by the parties to it, that
   sense is to prevail against either party in which he had reason to
   suppose the other understood it," applies only to contracts susceptible of different constructions.

Rule applied to guaranty. A contract of guaranty provided for
   the payment of any sum "which is now, or at any time hereafter may become due and payable" upon an open account for goods
 2 sold and delivered, with the further provision. "This guaranty
 3 shall apply to all indebtedness which may accrue within one year
   from this date, and before the personal service upon us by said
   guarantor of written notice, to the effect, that he will not be

liable for any debt contracted after the service of such notice." *Held*, that the guaranty was not a continuous one, but was limited to one year.

Appeal from Clayton District Court.—Hon. L. E. Fellows, Judge.

Saturday, October 9, 1897.

Action upon a written contract of guaranty. Defendant's demurrer to the petition was sustained, and, plaintiff electing to stand on his petition, judgment was entered against him, from which he appeals.— *Affirmed.*

Blythe, Markley & Smith for appellant.

D. D. Murphy for appellee.

Given, J.—I. The written contract of guaranty sued upon is as follows: "$2,500.00.　May 7, 1892. For and in consideration of the sum of one dollar to us in hand paid by Charles Broadway Rouss, of the city of New York, receipt whereof is hereby acknowledged, I, we, or either of us, do hereby guarantee the prompt payment to him of any sum, up to twenty-five hundred dollars, which is now or at any time hereafter may become due and payable to him by Creglow Bros. upon open account for goods sold and delivered, or upon any note or evidence of debt given upon account of such sales and deliveries. This guaranty shall apply to all indebtedness which may accrue at any time within one year from this date, and before the personal service by us upon said Rouss of written notice to the effect that we will not be liable for any debt contracted after the service of such notice. Notice of the acceptance of this guaranty, and notice of any credit extended on the faith thereof, is hereby waived.

The said Rouss is at liberty to extend the time for payment of any such indebtedness, without notice to' us.
We do hereby waive the benefit of all exemption laws of
every description, including the right of homestead, as
against any liability arising under this instrument. It
is understood and agreed by the party giving this instrument as collateral security that he or they are to remit
at the rate of 10 per cent. per week of the open account
of indebtedness,whatever it is or may hereafter become
So long as this is done, they have the privilege of
extending this instrument for twelve months from its
date. In the event of a failure to do this, it is understood that this instrument immediately becomes due.
It is also understood that they have the privilege of
ordering an equal amount of goods to the remittance
sent, even should the remittance be in excess of the 10
per cent. per week. It is also understood that proceeds
for shipments made C. O. D. by freight or express shall
not be construed as a remittance to be applied on the
10 per cent. per week; in other words, remittances
must accompany the orders, or be received before orders
are filled, to be applied on the 10 per cent. agreement.
It is further understood that the sureties are fully
cognizant of these terms. Creglow Bros. M. A. Creglow." The account aga'nst Cr. g'ow Bros. set out in the
petition shows a balance of one thousand, five hundred
and five dollars and twenty-seven cents due to plaintiff
on May 7, 1892, and a continuous course of dealing from
that date to November 30, 1894, with a balance of one
thousand and two dollars and ninety-five cents then due
to plaintiff. The account also shows that the credits
largely exceed the balance due May 7, 1892, and the
amount of purchases made between that date an1 May
7, 1893. From this it is clear that the balance of one
thousand and two dollars and ninety-five cents, due
November 3, 1894, and for which judgment is asked, is
for merchandise purchased after May 7, 1893. By the

demurrer, the question is raised whether appellee is liable, under said contract of guaranty, for the indebt-edness incurred after one year from its date, namely, after May 7, 1893.

II. Appellant's contention is that this is a contin-uing guaranty, limited only by notice of its termination, or by the lapse of a reasonable time; and appellee con-tends that it is limited by its own terms to one year from its date. Appellant cites *Pratt v. Matthews*, 24 Hun. 386, and *Powers v. Clarke*, 127 N. Y. 417 (28 N. E. Rep. 402), to the effect that the words "at any time hereafter" tend strongly to show that the guaranty is a continuing one. Such language, standing alone, does so tend, but not when followed, as in this case, by a provision expressly limiting the guar-anty "to all indebtedness which may at any time accrue within one year from this date,"—the date of guaranty. We think it entirely clear that the words "or at any time hereafter" are qualified by the words "within one year from this date," and that the provision as to notice is for notice within the year. In *Shickle, Harrison & Howard Iron Co. v. Council Bluffs City Water Works Co.*, 83 Iowa, 397, it is said "that, in construing contracts of guaranty, technicalities should be avoided, and the reasonable intent of the parties, as it may be gathered from all parts of the contract, should prevail." Thus construing this contract, it is plainly a guaranty for one year from its date, and does not admit of any other interpretation.

III. Appellant filed an amendment to his petition as follows: "And now plaintiff amends his petition by stating, in addition thereto, that he intended the writ-ten instrument of guaranty to cover goods sold and credit extended after one year from the date thereof, as well as before such time, and that he accepted said instrument of guaranty, and sold and delivered goods

2 (marginal number beside paragraph II)

upon credit to said Creglow Bros. under and in pursuance of said written instrument, and in reliance thereon,
understanding and intending that it covered sales made
and credit extended after one year from its date, as well
as before; and the defendant at all times well knew
that he was so acting with such understanding and
intention, and had reason at all times so to know, yet
remained silent, and suffered the plaintiff so to act, with
full knowledge that he was so acting, and acquiesced
therein without notice or objection." Appellant cites
section 3652 of the Code of 1873, which is as follows:
"When the terms of an agreement have been intended
in a different sense by the parties to it, that sense is to
prevail against either party in which he had reason to
suppose the other understood it." Appellant
3   contends that this section "applies to any language, whether it is fairly susceptible of the
sense in which the party understood it or not." *Hop-
wood v. Corbin*, 63 Iowa, 218; *Oil Co. v. Montague*, 65
Iowa, 67; *Chicago Lumber Co. v. Tibble's Manufacturing Co.*, 80 Iowa, 369; and *Evans v. McConnell*, 99 Iowa,
326, are cited as supporting these contentions. In each
of these cases wherein section 3652 was applied, the contract was either held to be susceptible of different constructions, or the question whether it was so susceptible
was submitted to the jury. Counsel say they do not
find any case construing this statute to be limited to
cases where the writing was fairly susceptible of different meanings; but we are not referred to, nor do we
find that it has ever been applied to, any other. In
Walker v. Manning, 6 Iowa, 520, it was held not to
apply, for the reason that "there is nothing in the testimony from which it can be inferred that the terms of
the agreement have been intended by the parties in a
different sense." By this contract, appellee became a
surety, and, under familiar rules, his liability is not to

be extended by implication. "To charge him beyond its terms, or permit it to be altered without his consent, would be, not to enforce the contract made by him, but to make another for him." Brandt, Suretyship, section 80; *Gongower v. Association*, 94, Iowa, 499. To extend this plain and unambiguous contract beyond the year to which it is limited, merely because appellant so intended it, and because appellee so knew, would make a new contract. This contract being susceptible of but one construction, appellant had no reason for his alleged understanding of it, and appellee's liability cannot be extended because of that unwarranted understanding, even if he knew it. The demurrer was properly sustained, and the judgment is therefore AFFIRMED.

W. M. STEPHENS v. F. P. MITCHELL, Sheriff, Appellant, and D. A. WYNKOOP, *et al.*, Appellants, v. W. C. GREGORY, *et al.*

Redemption: FORECLOSURE. The statutes give the mortgagor twelve months in which to redeem from sale under foreclosure.
1   During the first six and the last three months, this right is exclusive in him. During the other three months his lien creditors may redeem from the sale and from each other. A sale was had under first mortgage and plaintiff bought the certificate. Within a few days later he bought a second mortgage. He foreclosed it, without objection by the mortgagor, and purchased at the sale. The mortgagor never offered to redeem from either sale, but
2   within a few days before the year of redemption from the first sale expired, he made deed to a stranger, who then paid in sufficient to redeem from the first mortgage sale, and thereupon insists that all rights under the second sale were lost. *Held:*

   a. The general rules of statutory redemption under which a
3   . mortgagor may redeem from sale under first mortgage
5   without paying the second mortgagee who has not
7   redeemed, have no application to cases where, during the period in which lien creditors may redeem, the same person holds the certificates of sale resulting from the foreclosure of both the first and second mortgages.

b. Under such circumstances, equity will consider that done
   which ought to have been done, and no rights will be
   lost because a party who owned all rights under a first
   and second mortgage and all liens, failed to pay the clerk
   enough money to redeem from the first sale, which money
   he would have been entitled to withdraw from the clerk
   as soon as it was paid in.

c. Under these circumstances, the purchase of the second
   certificate would operate as a redemption if it were
   bought within six and nine months after the first sale,
   and though the right of redemption was exclusively in
   the mortgagor for the first six months, and such purchase
   within the first six months was, therefore, technically,
   not a redemption, it will operate as one where the certificate was held during both said periods, without an attempt
   at redemption by the mortgagor.

d. Consequently, a grantee of such mortgagor could not
   make an effective redemption from the sale under the
   first mortgage without paying enough to satisfy both
   sales.

ENTRY OF CREDIT. The only effect of the failure of the assignee of
8 a certificate of sale under execution to enter on the sale book the
4 amount he is willing to credit on his claim, under the provisions
   of Code, section 8115, is to require him to credit the debtor with
   the full amount of his claims on the land.

Appeal from Jackson District Court.—HON. W. F. BRAN-
NAN, Judge.

SATURDAY, OCTOBER 9, 1897.

THE two proceedings above entitled were consolidated in the district court as involving the same subject-matter, and proper for disposition in the same trial.
The controlling issue is as to the right of the plaintiff
Stephens to a sheriff's deed to certain premises for
which he holds a sheriff's certificate of sale on execution
in a foreclosure proceeding. The district court gave
judgment for the plaintiff in the first case, and dismissed
the petition in the second case. The defendant sheriff
in the first case and the plaintiff in the second case
appealed.—*Affirmed.*

Levi Keck and *D. A. Wynkoop* for appellants.

W. C. Gregory and *L. A. Ellis* for appellee.

GRANGER, J. — The district court found, and placed of record, the facts, with its reasoning and conclusions of law, and we cannot better present the case than to set out the principal part of the opinion, as follows:

"These two cases relate to the same subject-matter, are dependent on the same facts, and by consent of parties were both tried together; the only difference between them being in the form of the actions. The first is an action of mandamus, instituted by the plaintiff Stephens, asking that the defendant Mitchell, as sheriff, be commanded to execute to the plaintiff a sheriff's deed for certain premises sold by him at judicial sales, the plaintiff being the holder of the sheriff's certificates executed pursuant to such sales. The other is a proceeding in equity, in which the plaintiffs, Wynkoop and Sloane, claim to be the absolute owners of the premises sold at such sheriff's sales. Their claim is based on a deed executed to them, before the year for redemption had expired, by one Lindenau, the execution defendant, of the said premises, and the payment by them to the clerk within the year of the amount which they allege was required for redemption. The prayer, in substance, asks that their title to said premises be confirmed and quieted; that the certificates of sale held by the said Stephens be set aside; and that Mitchell, the sheriff, whom they make a defendant, be enjoined from executing a sheriff's deed to the said Stephens on the said certificates of sale. The facts in the two cases appear to be these: On the twenty-eighth day of July, 1894, the premises in controversy were sold upon a special execution under a decree of foreclosure obtained by P. D. Griggs, as administrator of

the estate of Joshua Shanks, deceased, against Charles
A. Lindenau. The plaintiff, Griggs, administrator,
bought in the property at such sale, and the amount he
bid for it was the sum then due upon the judgment of
foreclosure, together with all interest and costs. The
judgment was consequently fully satisfied. On the
thirtieth day of July,—two days after the foreclosure
sale,—the said Griggs, as administrator aforesaid, duly
assigned to the said Stephens the certificate of sale
issued to him as purchaser of said premises by the sheriff who conducted the sale. In the said foreclosure proceeding W. C. Gregory acted as attorney for the plaintiff. Gregory himself held a mortgage on the same
premises which was junior to that of said Griggs, and
was made a party defendant in that proceeding. From
all that appears, the conclusion is that he suffered a
default to be taken against him. About or near the
time that Stephens purchased the said certificate of
sale he purchased and had assigned to him the junior
mortgage held by Gregory. Stephens, after he had thus
become the owner of the Gregory mortgage, foreclosed
the same, and under the decree obtained on this last
foreclosure proceeding the said premises were again
sold, Stephens becoming the purchaser, and receiving
the usual certificate of sale. The amount bid at this
sale, it appears, fully satisfied the amount then due
upon the judgment. Stephens thus held the certificates
of purchase executed by the sheriff for both sal s; the
first by assignment, and the other by purchase at the
sale. Wynkoop and Sloane, within a very few days
before the twelve months required for redemption from
the first sale had expired, obtained a deed from Lindenau, the mortgagor in both cases, and deposited with
the clerk the amount necessary to redeem from the first
sale. It was said in argument that it was but two days
before the time for redemption had expired, but I do

not think this makes any material difference, so long as
it was within the period for redemption. Stephens
refuses to accept the money thus tendered as redemption.

    "The principal contention on the part of the defend-
ant Mitchell in the mandamus case, and Wynkoop and
Sloane, who are the plaintiffs in the equity suit, and the
main ground on which they rely to support their
2   title under the deed to them from Lindenau, is
that Stephens, under the assignment to him of
the Gregory mortgage, did not intend to redeem the
property from the sale under the Griggs mortgage, and
took no step to that end; and that his subsequent foreclosure of the Gregory mortgage, and his purchase
under it, can be of no avail to him in this proceeding.
Section 4331 of McClain's Code gives to the defendant
in execution the right to redeem real property sold
under it. He can exercise this right at any time within
one year from the day of sale. For the first six months
and the last three-months of the year his right is exclusive. During the intervening three months, if no
redemption has been made by the defendant, lien creditors have the right to redeem from each other. It is
hardly necessary to say that such creditors, in redeeming from each other, have no unity of interest. Their
interests are generally adverse to each other. Attention has been called to the various provisions in relation
to redemption, and numerous decisions have been cited
as bearing upon the questions raised in this case. These
cases, and others not cited, have been carefully examined. * * * The contention of Wynkoop and
Sloane, the grantees of Lindenau, the judgment debtor,
as has been stated, is that their redemption from the
Griggs sale under the first mortgage completely cuts
out all rights which might have accrued to Stephens
under his subsequent foreclosure of the Gregory mortgage, and his purchase under it at sheriff's sale, since,

as they claim, there was no redemption made, and none
intended to be made, by Stephens, from the sale under the
prior mortgage. Their title to the property in dispute,
they aver, is consequently superior to any claim or
right on the part of Stephens. If the institution of the
subsequent proceeding for the foreclosure of the Gregory mortgage was irregular or unnecessary, as claimed,
the only person who could make complaint was Lindenau, the mortgagor. If he did not object to it then,
his grantees cannot object to it now.

"Every case must be determined by its own facts.
I have been unable to discover, in the multitude of
authorities cited, any case which, in all its features, is
strictly analogous to the one now in hand. We are,
therefore, in this case, required to give to the statute
authorizing redemptions by creditors such construction
as will reasonably accord with the legislative
3   object and intent. The statute, so far as it relates
to creditors, is manifestly intended to afford the
means for relief to creditors whose liens are junior and
subordinate to the lien of the elder creditor. It is true
that it authorizes a senior creditor to redeem from a
junior redeeming creditor, but that does not militate
against the proposition above stated. It therefore contemplates, and is intended to provide for, cases between
creditors of opposing interests. It does not, either in
terms or by implication, contemplate a case where all
the liens are held by the same person in his own right,
and who is, consequently, the only creditor. In this
case Stephens was the only creditor. He held, and was
the owner, by proper assignment, of the certificate of
sale under the Griggs foreclosure. He was the purchaser and owner of the certificate of sale under the
foreclosure of the Gregory mortgage. There was no
creditor, either senior or junior, from whom to make
redemption. The object of the statute requiring certain

entries to be made by creditors, is mainly, if not wholly,
intended to serve as a guide to other creditors who may
be entitled to redeem. It consequently cannot apply
to a creditor holding all the liens upon the property sold.
Especially is this true when the evidence of his liens
is a matter of public record, or at least known to the
parties undertaking to redeem. The failure to
4   make the record entries, which the grantees of
Lindenau, the execution debtor, pronounce fatal
to the rights of Stephens, would, under the circumstances of this case, have been a useless and unnecessary ceremonial. It gave no life to the deed under
which they claim. A creditor can make redemption
without the formula of a deposit with the clerk, since
he can, by mutual agreement, redeem directly from the
party holding the superior lien. *Goode v. Cummings,*
35 Iowa, 71. A junior creditor may take an assignment
of the certificate of sale, and in such case the transaction amounts to, and actually is, a redemption. *Lamb
v. Feeley,* 71 Iowa, 743. A senior creditor may, under
the statute, redeem from a junior creditor, and this can
be done by proper assignment. No possible prejudce
can result to the debtor from such transaction. In the
case at bar Stephens purchased, and had duly assigned
to him, the certificate of sale under the Griggs foreclosure. He purchased, and had duly assigned to him,
the Gregory mortgage, which appears to have been the
only remaining lien left on the property sold under the
first foreclosure. The subjecting the property to a second foreclosure under the Gregory mortgage, and purchase of it at sheriff's sale, may have been an unnecessary proceeding, still it bars Stephens of no right in the
present case. It at least accomplished this much: It
showed him to be an actual purchaser at the sheriff's
sale, and the holder of the resulting certificate.
5   He thus had united in him, through judicial procedure, the claims of all creditors of the debtor
Lindenau. Under these circumstances he was not

required to go through the form of redeeming from
himself, or from a claim he himself held. Holding, thus,
all the claims against the property, they became
merged, and constituted an entirety, and had all the
effect flowing from a formal redemption. This conclusion is plainly deducible from the decision in *Lamb v.
Feeley, supra.* In that case, as has been stated, the
plaintiff, who was the assignee of the junior mortgage,
redeemed from the prior sale by securing an assignment of the certificate of sale. He subsequently undertook to foreclose the junior mortgage, and, upon proper
defense being made, it was held that the mortgage and
the debt for which it was given, under section 3114,
Original Code (section 4343, McClain's Code), had
become extinguished. This result could only be reached
upon the theory, clearly indicated by said section, that
the redemption from the former sale operated and had
the effect of a merger of both claims. The plaintiff in
that case, like the plaintiff in this case, clearly indicated his desire to hold the property, since he took no
steps showing an unwillingness to hold it, as provided
in section 4344 of McClain's Code. It is true that in
the case of *Lamb v. Feeley* the proceeding to foreclose
the junior mortgage was commenced after the plaintiff
had obtained the sheriff's deed on the certificate of sale
assigned to him. In this case Stephens sought to obtain
a sheriff's deed on the expiration of the period for
redemption, but the sheriff refused to make it. In principle there is no essential difference between that case
and the one at bar. In each of the cases the union of
both the liens and the manner in which such union was
accomplished operated, under the statute, as a merger
of both claims; and a valid redemption can only be
made by redeeming from both liens. It is, however,
insisted by counsel that Stephens did not intend to
redeem. If by that is meant that he intended to abandon his rights as purchaser under the foreclosure of the

junior mortgage, the question naturally recurs, what
was his object in making the purchase, and thereby
satisfying the full amount of the indebtedness? He
owned, as the proof shows, business property immediately adjacent to the property in dispute, and had
therefore, a personal interest in its acquisition. If it is
meant,—as I presume it is,—that by his failure to make
the entry of redemption on the clerk's record he forfeited, as against the grantees of Lindenau, all rights
under his said purchase, counsel are equally in
6   error. But, in any event, this presents a proper
case for the application of the well-settled rule
in equity that 'equity will consider that as done that
ought to have been done,'—a rule that is repeatedly
applied to relieve purchasers from omissions that prejudice no one. If the assignment to him of the Gregory
mortgage did not take immediate statutory effect as a
redemption from the prior sale, it would, by operation
of law, have that effect at the expiration of the six
months following the first sale. The provisions of the
statute providing for and regulating redemptions by
creditors have no application to a redemption made by
the defendant. If the defendant had, in this case,
sought to make redemption at the time of his conveyance to Sloane and Wynkoop, he would have been
obliged to redeem from both sales in order to give validity to the redemption. His grantees are in no better
position, under the circumstances of this case, and have
no greater rights than he possessed. Their redemption,
to be effectual, must be from both sales. Redemption
from one will not suffice. I am clearly of opinion that
Stephens is entitled to a deed under his certificates of
sale, and judgment in his favor is accordingly ordered
in the mandamus proceeding, to which the defendant
excepts. The petition in equity filed by Sloane and
Wynkoop is ordered to be dismissed, to which they duly

except. Let judgments in both cases be in accordance
with the above. * * *

"These cases were taken under advisement, and
by consent of parties the judgment of the court was to
be entered as of the last day of the November term,
1895. W. F. Brannan, Judge."

In this court it is urged that the suit by Stephens
for a mandamus to compel the sheriff to execute a deed
is premature, because the sale under the foreclosure
of the Gregory mortgage was October 16, 1894, and the
year for redemption would not expire till October 16,
1895, before which time he was not entitled to a deed,
and his suit was commenced August 24, 1895. The
argument is based on a misapprehension of fact. It is
appellee's contention that his right to a deed is because
there has been no redemption from the sale under the
foreclosure of the Griggs mortgage; that to a proper
foreclosure from that sale it was not enough to pay in
the amount of that mortgage, with costs, but that, in
addition, there must be enough to satisfy the Gregory
mortgage or judgment, owned by Stephens. Looking to
the petition, it is plain that the action is for a deed to
which Stephens became entitled July 28, 1895, under the
foreclosure of the Griggs mortgage. The record also
shows, against appellants' contention, that there was a
demand for a deed before the commencement of the
mandamus proceedings. In expressing our con-
7   currence in the conclusions of the district court,
we wish to emphasize what is said in its opinion
as to the facts of the case being unusual, and, evidently,
not within the letter of our statutes on the subject of
redemptions. As is said, there is but a single creditor,
with the two foreclosure judgments. Both are liens,
and if both are not to be paid it is because the judgment
creditor did not observe the idle form of paying money
into court for himself. The observance of a mere form

would have protected his rights. The failure to observe
it is without prejudice to any one. The reasons for the
prescribed methods of redemption do not exist in this
case as to Stephens. Stephens bought the Gregory mortgage, and afterwards purchased the certificate under
the Griggs sale within six months of the sale. Had he
made the purchase after the six months, and within
the nine months, the transaction would have been a
redemption by Stephens from Griggs, as held in *Lamb
v. Feeley,* 71 Iowa, 742; *Lamb v. West,* 75 Iowa, 399; and
there would then be no question but that, to redeem,
Lindenau, or his assigns, must do so from both judgments. As Stephens purchased the Griggs certificate
within the six months, it was not technically a redemption, and within the six months Lindenau could have
redeemed by paying the Griggs judgment. This was
not done, and Stephens held both judgments during the
period in which he could have acquired both, and been
protected. The practical effect is the same as to the
judgment debtor.

We are cited to *Bank v. Percival,* 61 Iowa, 183,
where it is held that a creditor may redeem from himself. We do not determine in this case that it may not
be done, nor are we holding that it might not be required
in some cases. The questions in that case were between
creditors, and there was a redemption by a creditor
from himself. It is not therein held that it was necessary, but only that it could be done. There is nothing
in *Moody v. Funk,* 82 Iowa, 1, nor in *Bevans v. Dewey,*
82 Iowa, 85, not in harmony with the conclusion in this
case.

Some importance is attached to a failure of Stephens to enter on the sale book the amount he was will-

ing to credit on his claim under the provisions of Code,
section 3115. The only effect of such a failure
8   was to require him to credit the debtor with the
full amount of his liens, which we understand to
be his purpose. The judgment in both cases will stand
AFFIRMED.

76
05   STATE OF IOWA, on Relation of JAMES A. HOWE, as
06   County Attorney of Polk County, Iowa, Appellant,
l   v. THE MAYOR AND THE CITY COUNCIL OF THE CITY
         OF DES MOINES.

Constitutional Law: DELEGATION OF TAXING POWER: *Municipal corporations.* So much of Iowa Acts Twenty-sixth General Assembly,
1   Chapter 50, as attempt to confer upon the board of library trustees, appointed by the mayor with the consent of the city council,
2   the power to fix absolutely and beyond the control of the council
5   the amount of taxes to be raised for the purposes of the library,
    is unconstitutional, under the rule that the legislature cannot,
    without the consent of the people, delegate the power of taxation
    for municipal purposes to a body of persons not elected by and
    immediately responsible to the people.

SAME. The legislature may for proper and legitimate purposes
    confer the taxing power upon municipalities, but such power
1   cannot be delegated, without the consent of the people of the municipality, to any body or person not elected by, and immediately
2   responsible to the people. Citing *People v. Chicago*, 51 Ill. 17; *Howard v. Drainage Co.*, 51 Ill. 130; *Board of Commissioners v. Abbott*, 34
8   Pac. Rep .416; *McCulloch v. Maryland*, 4 Wheat. 428, and concurring opinion in *Board of Park Commissioners v. Detroit City Council*, 28 Mich. 227.

ACCEPTANCE OF LAW. The acceptance by the people of a city of the
    provisions of the Iowa statutes authorizing the establishment of
    public libraries by cities, before the adoption of Acts Twenty-
4   sixth General Assembly, which in effect, transfers the power of
    taxation for library purposes from the city council to the board
    of library trustees, appointed by the mayor with the approval of
    the council, does not operate as an assent by them to the exercise
    of the taxing power by such trustees, so as to remove the constitutional objection to such delegation of the taxing power by the
    legislature.

Appeal from Polk District Court.—HON. W. F. CONRAD,
Judge.

SATURDAY, OCTOBER 9, 1897.

ACTION for mandamus to compel the city council of
the city of Des Moines to levy a tax for the purpose of
creating a sinking fund to build a library building in
said city, and to compel said city council to levy a tax
for the maintenance of a library. Jury waived, trial
to the court, and judgment for defendants for costs.
Plaintiff appeals.—*Affirmed.*

Read & Read and *Hubbard & Dawley* for appellant.

J. K. Macomber and *Bishop, Bowen & Fleming* for
appellee.

KINNE, C. J.—I. The conceded facts in this case
are as follows: The city of Des Moines, a city of the
first class, in 1882, by a vote of its electors, accepted the
provisions of the statute of this state relating to the
establishment and maintenance of free public libraries,
and had, in the exercise of the powers conferred upon
it, established and was maintaining such a library. In
pursuance of law, a board of library trustees had been
appointed and was exercising the powers and duties
imposed upon it. On July 31, 1896, said board of
trustees did fix and determine a rate of taxation of one
mill on the dollar of the taxable valuation of the property in said city for the purpose of maintaining the
public library and at the same time did fix and determine a rate of taxation of three mills on the dollar for
the purpose of creating a sinking fund for the purchase
of a lot and the erection of a library building, and did
cause said amounts so fixed and determined to be certified to the city council of said city. Said city council

refused to levy and certify to the county auditor said amounts so certified to them by said board of library trustees, but did levy and certify one-half a mill tax for the purpose of the maintenance of the library. Thereupon this action was brought to obtain a writ of mandamus compelling the city council to levy and certify the rates of taxes fixed and determined by the board of library trustees. As is said by counsel for appellants. "The ultimate question to be determined is whether or not the city council in cities of the first class accepting the provisions of the statute relating to the establishment and maintenance of free public libraries, and maintaining such library, is bound and required to levy and certify the amount of taxes or the rate of taxation fixed and determined by the board of library trustees of said city."

II.   On the one hand it is contended that the statute vests in the board of library trustees absolute power to fix and determine the amount of the levy to be made for the purpose of maintenance of the library, and of creating a sinking fund for the purchase of a lot and the erection of a library building, subject only to the limitations in the statute; and that the duty devolves upon the city council to levy and certify the sums so certified to them by said board; that the city council is without any discretion in the matter. On the contrary, the appellees contend that the board of library trustees has no such power; that its power in the matter is advisory merely, and that the city council is invested with a discretion as to the amount or amounts which shall be levied for the purposes mentioned. As in the discussion which may follow reference may be made to various acts of the legislature touching the creation and maintenance of free public libraries, it may tend to brevity to here recite the substance of all such statutes which can have any bearing upon the

question under consideration. Chapter 45, Acts
Thirteenth General Assembly, provided that cities of
the first and second classes might levy an annual tax
not exceeding one-half mill on the dollar of the taxable
property in such city for the maintenance of a free public library and reading room, provided a suitable lot
and building be first donated for such purposes. The
city council was authorized to appoint officers for such
library and reading room. The Fourteenth General
Assembly, in chapter 47, extended the provision of the
former act so as to include incorporated towns,
increased the amount of the levy, and authorized all
the municipalities referred to in the act, out of the
money raised, to purchase land and erect buildings or
lease rooms. The act also provided that before exercising any of the powers conferred, it should be
accepted by a vote of the people. The same provisions,
in substance, were incorporated in the Code of 1873
(section 461), in which it was declared that "the establishment and maintenance of a free public library is
hereby declared to be a proper and legitimate object
of municipal expenditure." Such was the law in force
at the time the electors of the city of Des Moines voted
to accept its provisions, and to establish a free public
library. By chapter 41, Acts Twenty-Fifth General
Assembly, it was provided that in any city which had
accepted the provisions of Code, section 461, there
should be created a board of library trustees, to be
appointed by the mayor, with the approval of the
council. That act vested in said board full power
of control over the library, including the power to
appoint and remove librarians and employes; that they
should have full power over the moneys raised for the
library by taxation; and said act also contained the
following, viz.: "The board of library trustees shall,
before the first day of August in each year, determine

and fix the amount or rate to be appropriated for one
year under section 461 of the Code of Iowa for the
maintenance of such library, and cause the same so
fixed to be certified to the council, and the council shall
make such appropriation and levy the necessary tax
for such year to raise said sum and certify the percentage or rate not exceeding one mill on the dollar of
such tax to the county auditor, * * * provided
that in cities of the first class the city council may and
shall levy and certify such further sum of tax as it may
deem expedient to create a sinking fund and pay interest under the provisions of chapter 18, Acts of the
Twenty-second General Assembly, and acts amendatory thereof." By chapter 99 of the acts of the same
general assembly power was conferred upon the city
to levy and collect a tax of not exceeding three mills
on the dollar to pay interest on any indebtedness theretofore contracted or to be thereafter contracted or
incurred for the purchase of real estate and the erection of a building or buildings for a public library, and
to create a sinking fund for the payment of such indebtedness. By chapter 5, Acts Twenty-sixth General
Assembly, the tax was authorized to be collected annually. By chapter 50, Acts Twenty-sixth General
Assembly, it was provided that the board of library
trustees should determine and fix the rate, not exceeding one mill on the dollar, for the maintenance of the
library, and not exceeding three mills on the dollar
for the purpose of paying for a building and the creation of a sinking fund, and "cause each of the amounts
or rates so determined and fixed to be certified to the
council, and the council shall levy the taxes necessary
to raise said sums respectively for such year, and certify
the percentage or rates * * * of such tax to the
county auditor." In pursuance of the provisions of
chapter 41, Acts Twenty-fifth General Assembly, a

board of library trustees had been appointed. In
March, 1892, the city of Des Moines, as it then existed,
by a vote of the electors, accepted the benefit of the
law relating to public libraries. Prior to the passage
of the Acts of the Twenty-sixth General Assembly, the
city council was clearly invested with discretionary
power as to levying a tax for a library building and for
the creation of a sinking fund. The act of the Twenty-
sixth General Assembly, in terms, seems to require the
council to levy and certify the tax certified to it for
maintenance and for a building or sinking fund, so long
as the same does not exceed the amount provided by
the statute.

III.   The questions involved in this appeal are of
great interest and importance. Irrespective of our
duty to uphold the act of the legislature as constitutional, if it be possible to do so without doing violence
to well-known legal principles and accepted canons of
construction, our interest in the welfare of the people,
which is so largely promoted by the establishment and
maintenance of public libraries, would prompt us to
give the questions presented most careful con-
1   sideration. If it be conceded that a tax for
the maintenance of a public library and for the
erection of a library building is a tax for a public purpose, and hence one which, in furtherance of the general public policy of the state, may be compelled to be
levied, may the legislature authorize its levy by the
board of libary trustees? Touching the power of the legislature to delegate the taxing power, Judge Cooley
says: "It is a general rule of constitutional law that a
sovereign power conferred by the people upon any one
branch or department of the government is not to be
delegated by that branch or department to any other.
This is a principle which pervades our whole political
system, and, when properly understood, permits of no

exception, and it is applicable with peculiar force to
the case of taxation. *The power to tax is a legislative
power.* The people have created a legislative department
for the exercise of the legislative power and within
that power lies the authority to prescribe the rules of
taxation, and to regulate the manner in which those
rules shall be given effect. * * * There is, nevertheless,
one clearly defined exception to the rule that the legislature shall not delegate any portion of its authority.
The exception, however, is strictly in harmony with
the general features of our political system, and it rests
upon an implication of popular assent, which is conclusive. These exceptions relate to the case of municipal corporations. Immemorial custom, which tacitly
or expressly has been incorporated in the several state
constitutions, has made these organizations a necessary part of the general machinery of state government, and they are allowed large authority in matters
of local government, and to a considerable extent are
permitted to make the local laws. This indulgence has
been carried into matters of taxation; the state in
very many cases doing little beyond prescribing rules
of limitation within which, for local purposes, the local
authorities may levy taxes. * * * The legislature,
however, in thus making delegation of the power to
tax, must make it to the corporation itself, and provide
for its exercise by the proper legislative authority of the
corporation. * * * What is true of the state is
equally true of the municipality,—that the power
they possess to tax must be exercised by the corporation itself, and cannot be delegated to its officers or other agencies." Cooley, Taxation (2d ed.)
pp. 61, 63, 65. The doctrine laid down by the learned
author is that the delegation of the power to tax by
the legislature must be made to the municipality itself,
and that it cannot be delegated to other agencies.

The constitution of the state of Illinois contains the following provision: "The corporate authorities of counties, townships, school districts, cities, towns and villages may be vested with power to assess and collect taxes for corporate purposes." Constitution Illinois, 1848, article 9, section 5. In construing this provision, the supreme court of that state said that the phrase "corporate authorities," as used in the constitution, must be understood as "those municipal officers who are either directly elected by the people to be taxed, or appointed in some mode to which they have given their assent." *People v. Mayor, Etc., of City of Chicago*, 51 Ill. 17. The same court, in construing the same constitutional provision, said: "The power of taxation is, of all powers of government, the one most liable to abuse, even when exercised by the direct representatives of the people; and, if committed to people who may exercise it over others without reference to their consent, the certainty of its abuse would simply be a question of time. No person or class of persons can be safely intrusted with irresponsible power over the property of others, and such a power is essentially despotic in its nature, and violative of all just principles of government. It matters not that, as in the present instance, it is to be professedly exercised for public uses by expending for the public benefit the tax collected. If it be a tax, as in the present instance, to which the persons who are to pay it have never given their consent, and imposed by persons acting under no responsibility of official position, and clothed with no authority of any kind, *by those whom they propose to tax*, it is, to the extent of such tax, misgovernment of the same character which our forefathers thought just cause of revolution. We are of opinion that we do no violence to the language of the clause in the constitution we have been considering by holding that

it was designed to prevent such ill-advised legislation
as the delegation of the taxing power to any person or
persons other than the corporate authorities of the
municipality or district to be taxed. These authorities
are elected by the people to be taxed, or appointed in
some mode to which the people have given their assent,
and to them alone can this power be safely delegated."
Harward v. Drainage Co., 51 Ill. 130. In still another
case, in which the constitutionality of the metropolitan
police act of the city of East St. Louis was under consideration, and in which the police commissioners were
appointed by the act, and given power, not to levy a
tax, but to estimate what sum of money would be necessary for each fiscal year to enable them to discharge
the duties imposed upon them, and the act required the
city council to appropriate and set apart the amount
so certified out of the general fund of the city, and, in
case the council failed so to do, then it was made the
duty of the board of commissioners to issue certificates
of indebtedness in the name of the city for the amounts
so certified, the court said: "These police commissioners are not the corporate authorities of East St. Louis,
and therefore can have no power of taxation. They are
not elected by the people of that city nor appointed in
any mode to which the people have given their assent.
The act creating them has never been accepted by the
people or by the city council, but, on the other hand,
as alleged in the bill, the council has constantly denied
the authority of the commissioners." *Hinze v. People*,
92 Ill. 406. See, also, *Updike v. Wright*, 81 Ill. 49;
People v. Morgan, 90 Ill. 558.

The legislature of the state of Kansas passed an act
authorizing the creation of a board of road commissioners, and empowering them, among other things to levy
taxes. The act was held unconstitutional. *Board of
Commissioners v. Abbott*, 52 Kan. Sup 148 (34 Pac. Rep.
416). The question of the constitutionality of the same

act came before the federal court, and the court said:
"Does the constitution of the state of Kansas authorize
the legislature to delegate the power of taxation either
to the signers of these petitions or to these road commissioners? Can a tax be absolutely forced upon these
taxpayers of the county, either by the individuals or
by officials in whose appointment they have had no
voice? The power of taxation is a power inherent in
all governments. In a constitutional government, the
people, by the constitution, confer it on the legislature.
It is one of the highest attributes of sovereignty. It
includes the power to destroy. It appropriates the
property and labor of the people taxed. Unrestrained
power of taxation necessarily leads to tyranny and
despotism. Hence, in all free governments, the power
to tax must be limited to the necessities for the purposes of government, and the agencies for local taxation should be fixed, and their powers limited, by
organic law; and they should be so selected as to be
directly answerable for their official acts to their local
constituencies or districts to be taxed. If they act cor-
ruptly those directly interested may then remove them
and appoint others. If those directly interested have
no voice in their appointment, or power to remove
them, they have no means of correcting their abuses.
No other rule can secure those to be taxed from oppres-
sion and fraud on the part of the taxing officers. In
McCulloch v. Maryland, 4 Wheat. 428, Marshall, C. J.,
said: 'The only security against the abuse of this
power (the taxing power) is found in the structure of
our government itself. In imposing a tax the legislature acts upon its constituents. This is, in general, a
sufficient security against erroneous and oppressive
taxation.' This reasoning applies with equal force to
all kinds of taxation, and has been applied as well to
local assessments or improvement districts as to taxes
levied in local, political, and municipal corporations.

* * * Self-taxation, or taxation by officers chosen
by or answerable to those directly interested in the
district to be taxed, is inseparable from that protection
of the right of property that is either expressly or
impliedly guaranteed by all written constitutions
under our system of government. Of all the powers of
government the one most liable to abuse is the power of
taxation. If placed in hands irresponsible to the people
of the district to be taxed, its abuse is a mere question
of time. * * * The act is a plain violation of the
principle of self-taxation, and a clear invasion of the
right of property. The legislature is not the fountain,—
not the source,—of power. Under our system of government the legislature can exercise only such powers as
the people have delegated to that body, either expressly
or by necessary implic tion, by the constitution. All
rights not so delegated are retained by the people. The
right of life, liberty, and property is among the inherent
and inalienable rights that the people did not commit
to the legislature. Constitutions are adopted and governments administered for the protection, and not for
the destruction, of these reserved rights of the people.
Illegal or oppressive taxation is destructive of the right
of property, and is not government, under the constitution; but is misgovernment." *Parks v. Board of Commissioners*, 61 Fed. Rep. 436.

The legislature of the state of Michigan passed an
act creating a board of park commissioners to be
appointed by the governor, with authority to create an
indebtedness, and the act was held unconstitutional.
Mr. Justice Campbell, in specially concurring with
other members of the court, said: "I am not willing,
however, to leave out of view an objection which has
seemed to me quite as fundamental as the one referred
to, and more dangerous, if that be possible, in its
tendencies. I think the very essence of municipal

existence consists in a government which allows no discretionary power beyond that of mere administration
to be exercised without the *immediate or ultimate control of the freemen or their immediate representatives.*
A city is, and must be, as I conceive, a unit for purposes of government; and all bodies employed in the
service of the municipality, and not directly representing the freemen, must act as agencies subordinate to
the council. If powers in any way involving the municipal prerogative can be given to any bodies except the
common council, to the exclusion of any regulation or
control of that body, they can all be so given, and the
people may be entirely deprived of representative government. It is a misnomer to apply that term to a system where there is any legislative power over which
the people's representatives have no control. A school
district is as well organized a municipality as a city,
and may co-exist with it in territory, in whole or in
part, as a city may cover the territory of a county
wholly or partially. There is no incompatibility
between them, and both are separate, and in some sense
independent, popular representative bodies exercising
different functions. The duties of the others are no
part of the ordinary concerns of town or city corporations. But from time immemorial every municipal
government, properly so called, and acting within its
peculiar sphere, has acted through its common council,
composed either of the burgesses or their representatives, subject in some cases to checks and vetoes, but
not subject to legislation or final action in defiance of
their own decisions. Their supremacy cannot be given
up by themselves any more than it can be taken from
them. No doubt the state can limit their powers, but
it cannot transfer them. The appointment and incorporation of boards as mere agencies is competent, and
may be very convenient. But making them anything

but agencies is a direct invasion of representative government, and would bring into existence a class of
cities unknown to our constitutions, and very different
from the municipal corporations recognized by our constitution as the authorized recipients of local legislative power. Whether the law of 1871 contains any
provisions obnoxious to this principle, it is not necessary to discuss. But, if there are such provisions, I do
not conceive they could be made valid by any recognition from the city. Concurring entirely in the general
views of my Brother Cooley, I have not deemed it necessary to do more than indicate very briefly my views on
the point which he has waived, which, in my judgment,
is inseparable from the principles underlying the decisions heretofore made in *People v. Hurlbut*, 24 Mich. 44,
and *People v. Township Board of Springwells*, 25 Mich.
153. I therefore agree in the conclusion of my breth-
ren." *People v. Common Council of Detroit*, 28 Mich.
228.

Under our constitution the power of taxation has
been vested by the people in the legislature. Constitution Iowa, article 3, section 1; *City of Davenport v.
Chicago, R. I. & P. R. Co.*, 38 Iowa 643. There is no
express constitutional restriction or limitation upon
the power of the legislature in this state, and that body
may, for proper and legitimate purposes, confer the
taxing power upon municipalities. 2 Dillon, Municipal
Corporations, section 740; 25 Am. & Eng. Enc. Law, pp.
18, 71. Nevertheless, in the absence of such constitutional restriction, the power of the legislature to confer the right of taxation is limited by implication.
Prouty v. Stover, 11 Kan. 235. So it is said in *Hanson
v. Vernon*, 27 Iowa, 73: "It cannot be maintained that
the constitution confers upon the state government
absolute and unlimited legislative power, authorizing
all laws affecting the rights and property of the people,

not expressly prohibited by that instrument. * * *
There is, as it were, back of the written constitution, an unwritten constitution, if I may use
the expression, which guaranties and well protects
all absolute rights of the people. The government can exercise no power to impair or deny them.
Many of them may not be enumerated in the constitution, nor preserved by express provisions thereof, notwithstanding they exist, and are possessed by the people
free from government interference." We say,
2   then, that there is an implied limitation upon the
power of the legislature to delegate the power
of taxation. This, of necessity, must be so, otherwise
the legislature might clothe any person with the
power to levy taxes, regardless of the will of those upon
whom such burdens would be cast, and such person
might be directly responsible to no one. Whatever the
effect of the constitutional provisions in Illinois and
Kansas may be, the reasoning of the cases is in line
with the views expressed by Judge Cooley, and it is
equally applicable to cases where there are no express
constitutional limitations. It is said that it is not true
that power to determine the rate of taxes must be committed to the proper legislative authority of the corporation, and certain instances in this state are cited,
as the power given the executive council to determine
the rate of tax for state purposes. Code 1873, section
835. But counsel have cited no instance in the legislation of this state, and we have found none, where
the power to tax was conferred upon a board or officer
not elected by and immediately responsible to the
people, and we are unwilling to extend the right to delegate such power to any body or person not directly
representing the people. The danger which lies in del-
egating such power to any person or board not directly
responsible to the taxpayers is so forcibly set forth

in the citations we have made that we need not enlarge upon it. If the power to tax may be by them vested in a board of library trustees, against the will of the people, it may be reposed in any other body which is not directly accountable to the people.

Counsel for appellants rely upon the cases of *Mayor of Baltimore v. State*, 74 Am. Dec. 572, and *State v. District Court of Hennepin County*, 33 Minn. 235 (22 N. W. Rep. 625). The latter case, in its facts, is so different from the case at bar as not to support the contention of appellant; and the Maryland case sustained the constitutionality of an act authorizing the board of police commissioners to levy and collect taxes for the support of the police department of the city. If this case is sustainable at all, it is upon the theory that the state may insist upon the proper exercise of the police power by a municipality, and, if the municipality fails so to do, the state may arbitrarily provide therefor. This is on the theory that one of the objects of the government of the state is to preserve peace and good order.

We have treated this statute as, in effect, authorizing the library board to levy the tax. In fact, it in terms directs them to fix and determine the amount of the tax, which, upon being certified to the council, it must levy. The right to thus fix and determine is equivalent to the right to levy. Now, the uses to which this tax is to be put are local, and the benefits to be derived from such library must necessarily inure mostly to the people of the city of Des Moines. 3   Such being the case, we think that the legislature had no power to vest the levying of this tax in a body not directly responsible to the people of the city. The levy and collection of a tax is a taking of the property of the taxpayer against his will, and such a necessary, arbitrary and far-reaching power ought

not to be conferred upon a body of persons who are not
the direct representatives of the people, who are not
elected by them, and who, therefore, are not directly
responsible to them, unless the people assent thereto.

IV.   The remaining question is, have the people of
the city of Des Moines in any manner assented to the
exercise of the power of taxation attempted to be conferred upon and exercised by the board of library
4   trustees?   The people of the city did by vote
accept the provisions of the law as it then
existed.   The law then did not authorize any increase
of taxation, and the library was under the direct control and management of the city council, who were
elected by the people.   By subsequent acts of the legislature a board of trustees was established, and their
duties and powers fixed; the control and management
of the library was by statute vested in said board, and
the board was vested with the power of absolutely
determining the amount of tax that should be levied.
It will be seen that the people assented by their vote to
maintaining a public library, which should be under
the control of the council which they elected.   They
never consented to the creation of a board of library
trustees which should be in control of the library, and
be substantially vested with the power to levy taxes
without the consent and against the will of the people.
The placing of the extraordinary power of taxation in
a body not the direct creation of, or directly responsible to, the people, was in no way involved in the vote
of the people had before such powers were conferred or
thought of.   Here, by an act passed subsequent to the
vote of the people, the legislature empowers an irresponsible board (irresponsible in the sense that they
are not directly accountable to the people) to fix a tax
levy limited in the amount which may be raised each
year, but unlimited in duration, so that millions of dollars may be accumulated without consulting the

people, or their immediate representatives, the city
council. It may be doubted if any statute of this state
can be found wherein such extended and unlimited
power as to duration of time has been granted to a body
of persons to fix what taxes shall be levied for any such
purpose. This law authorizes a levy annually upon the
taxable property of the city for the purpose of purchasing real estate, and the erection of a building, and to
create a sinking fund; absolutely no limit as to the
number of years said tax may be levied. Under
its provisions millions may be accumulated and spent,
and if appellant's theory is correct the taxpayer
who assented to the formation and maintenance of a
public library simply was then voting upon himself a
burden of taxation for a library building and ground
which might be endless in duration as to the ultimate
amount to be raised, and which might be invested in a
building the cost of which would likewise be unlimited.
That a body or board, not elected by the people, and not
directly responsible to them, should have been clothed
by the legislature with such extraordinary powers
without proper safeguards to protect the people from
unnecessary taxation,—which is confiscation,—is mar-
velous. The people of the city of Des Moines never
assented by vote or otherwise to any such legislation.
Cornell v. People, 107 Ill. 372.

Nor can we agree to the contention that, inasmuch
as the people elect the city council and the mayor, and
the mayor appoints the library board with the consent
of the council, therefore such board is, in fact, selected
by the people, or that thereby the people assented to
the legislation creating the board and endowing it with
the power to fix and determine the taxes to be levied.
If such contention was correct, it would be difficult to
find a case of an officer or board vested with taxing
powers, no matter by whom appointed, when by the

same process of reasoning the original power could not be traced through the various offices or agencies to the people themselves. Suppose the act at bar had provided that the board of library trustees for the public library of the city could be appointed by the governor of the state, it would not be contended for a moment that the people, by voting for and electing the governor who appoints such a board, thereby gave their assent to such a mode of appointment. No more do they when they elect the mayor and council, whom they must elect in order that the proper business of the municipality may be carried on. Under such an argument any violation of the taxing power might be ultimately traced to the people, who are the original source of all political power in a government like ours. The power to determine and levy taxes is inherent in government. Its exercise for proper purposes is essential to the very existence of government. When exercised in a lawful manner, and by proper agencies of the state, the burdens imposed must be borne by those upon whom they fall; but when exercised by officers and bodies charged with no direct responsibility to the people the temptation to place upon the people unnecessary burdens under the guise of taxation, and to take from them a portion of their property not needed for legitimate purposes of government, is great. It may be admitted in the case before us that the board of library trustees is composed of high-minded, honorable men and women, and it may be that this board is better qualified to know what such tax should be than is the city council. However that may be, the principle is wrong, and the power of taxation attempted to be conferred upon the trustees is a long step in the direction of per-

mitting boards not elected by or directly responsible to
the people to determine what burden the tax-
5   payers' property shall bear. We hold that no
officer and no board not elected by and immediately responsible to the people can be made the reposi-
tory of such power. If this power was given to the city
council, and it was abused, the people could, at least,
prevent a recurrence of the wrong at the polls; but if it
be reposed in a body not elected by the people the remedy is uncertain, indirect, and likely to be long delayed.
The absolutely unlimited power of taxation, as to duration, attempted to be conferred by the act under consideration, is of itself a forcible reminder that the power
to fix, determine, and levy a tax for local purposes
should be conferred upon somebody which stands as the
direct representative of the people, to the end that an
abuse of such power may be speedily and directly corrected by those whose property must bear such burdens.
The act in question is unconstitutional in so far as it
undertakes to confer the arbitrary power upon the
board of library trustees to fix and determine the
amount of tax to be levied for the purposes therein mentioned, and the city council cannot be compelled to levy
(regardless of any discretion) the amounts fixed by the
library board, and certified to said council. The questions involved in the case were not raised or considered
in *Orvis v. Board of Commissioners*, 88 Iowa, 674. The
action of the district court in refusing a writ of mandamus and in rendering a judgment against the plaintiff for costs was correct, and the judgment is AFFIRMED.

J. A. SMITH AND MARY J. HUNTER v. M. HALL, *et al.*

Railroad Right of Way. The interest in a railroad right of way is the
2 same whether granted or condemned.

SAME. The nature and quality of the interest taken and conferred
in a railroad right of way is fixed by the legislature, and whether
8 it shall be only an easement or a full fee title is purely for its
determination. It is therefore competent for the legislature to
say to whom the land shall revert when abandoned by the company.

Reversion: RAILROAD RIGHT OF WAY. A conveyance of all the
remaining portions of a tract of land from which a railroad right
4 of way had been taken, passes to the grantee whatever right to
the reversion the grantor then had.

SAME. Under section 2660 Code of 1873, providing for the reversion of
a railroad right of way to the owner of the tract from which it was
1 taken, an abandoned right of way reverts to him who owns such
tract at the time of the reversion, and not to him who owned it
when the right of way was taken.

Appeal from Chickasaw District Court.—HON. L. E.
FELLOWS, Judge.

SATURDAY, OCTOBER 9, 1897.

ACTION to quiet title to an abandoned right of way.
The answer alleged that Margaret Smith was the owner
of the southeast quarter of the northwest quarter of
section 17 in township 94 north, of range 14 west, of fifth
P. M., in 1871, and conveyed the right of way, one hundred feet wide, diagonally through said land, to the Milwaukee & Nashua Railroad Company. Afterwards she
sold that east of the east line of the right of way, and
the Nashua Driving Park Association became the
owner thereof. She conveyed that west of the west line
of right of way to J. W. Smith, who divided it into acre
lots, and deeded them to the other defendants. The

railroad company graded and partially completed its
road, but work finally ceased and was never in good
faith resumed. The above conveyances were made
before the right of way reverted, under the statute, by
reason of non-user; and, after such reversion, Margaret
Smith conveyed any interest she had in the right of
way, to the plaintiffs. On this deed they base their claim
to the land. The demurrer to this answer was overruled, and, plaintiffs having elected to stand on the ruling, decree was entered quieting title in the defendants.
Plaintiffs appeal.—*Affirmed*.

A. G. Lawrence for appellants.

B. A. Billings for appellees.

LADD, J.—When the right of way of a railroad
company is lost by non-user, to whom does it revert,—
to the original owner thereof, or to the then owner of
the remaining portion of the tract of land from
1　　　which it was taken? The determination of this
question involves the construction of section 1260
of the Code of 1873, as follows: "Provided, however,
that if said roadbed or right of way, or any part thereof,
shall not be used or operated for a period of eight years,
or in any case where the construction of a railway has
been commenced by any corporation or person, and
work on same has ceased and has not been in good faith
resumed by any corporation or person for a period of
eight years, the land and the title thereto shall revert
to the owner of the section, subdivision, tract or lot
from which it was taken." The interest in the
2　　　right of way is the same whether granted or condemned. *Brown v. Young*, 69 Iowa, 625. The
easement is not that spoken of in the old law books, but
is peculiar to the use of a railroad, which is usually a
permanent improvement, a perpetual highway of travel

and commerce, and will rarely be abandoned by non-user. The exclusive use of the surface is acquired, and damages are assessed, on the theory that the easement will be perpetual; so that, ordinarily, the fee is of little or no value, unless the land is underlaid by quarry or mine. *Hollingsworth v. Railway Co.*, 63 Iowa, 443; *Cummins v. Railway Co.*, 63 Iowa, 397; *Clayton v. Railway Co.*, 67 Iowa, 238. The nature and quality of the interest taken and conferred is necessarily limited and fixed by the legislature, and whether only an easement or a full fee title, is purely for its determination. See *Aldrige v. Railway Co.*, 23 Am. Dec. 307; *Leggett v. Dubois*, 28 Am. Dec. 413; *De Varaigne v. Fox*, 2 Blatchf. 95 (Fed. Cas. No. 3836). It was competent for
3   the legislature to say to whom the land occupied
          and used by a railroad company should revert when abandoned. This necessarily follows from its right to fix the extent of the interest in the property appropriated. See *Noll v. Railway Co.*, 32 Iowa, 66; *Central Iowa R. Co. v. Moulton & A. R. Co.*, 57 Iowa, 249.

The fee to the right of way was not conveyed by Margaret Smith to the grantors of the defendants, in express terms, but, in conveying all the remaining portion of the tract from which it was taken, she
4   parted with whatever right to the reversion she
          then had, and her grantees became vested, under the statute, with such right. The legislature could not have intended that the title revert to the original owner, and it be traced down to his descendants or those of his grantees. Such a holding would result in much litigation, and the land, owing to its condition and situation, would be of little value to the person obtaining it; while the construction casting the reversion on the owners of the remaining portion of the tract from which taken renders those entitled to it certain and easily ascertained, and vests the land in those to whom it will be

of some advantage. The words of the statute, when fairly construed, can only refer to the owner of the tract at the time of the reversion. That the "section, subdivision, tract or lot" is mentioned and emphasized, confirms this view. Had the intention been to return the land to 'him from whom taken, the statute would have so stated. In referring to the owner in the present tense, and especially to the tract from which taken, instead of the owner from whom taken, or the fee, the present owner is very evidently intended.—AFFIRMED.

MARSHALL ALLBRIGHT, Appellee, v. A. HANNAH, Executor, Appellant.

Land Sale by Contract: STATUTE OF FRAUDS. A married daughter's parents, anxious that she should be near them, promised their
1 son-in-law that if he would erect a house on land belonging to them, clear the land, and put it in cultivation, he should have it when they were done with it. The son-in-law performed the
2 conditions and lived on the premises until after his wife's death. *Held*, that the contract was valid, being either the present transfer of the fee subject to a life estate, or an agreement for a devise.

ABANDONMENT. The mere fact that the son-in-law removed from the
3 land was not conclusive evidence of an abandonment of his contract rights where he continued to claim an interest, and where his grantors have a life estate.

Homesteads. The owner of an uncleared forty acres of land on one side of which, close to the line bounding another forty acres of
4 cleared land owned by him, his residence was situated, abandons his right to claim the former forty acres as a homestead, at least as
6 to all except the part on which the dwelling house is situated, by agreeing with his son-in-law to give the land to him at his death
7 if he clears it off, fences and improves it, in reliance upon which the latter performs his part of the contract.

Evidence: TRANSACTION WITH DECEDENT. Under Code, section 3639, excluding a party's testimony regarding any personal communi-
8 cation between him and a deceased person, such a witness may testify to a conversation which he heard between a person since deceased and another, and in which witness took no part.

SELF SERVING DECLARATIONS. In a proceeding to establish a claim
against a decedent's estate, based on the assumption that
11 deceased had sold and agreed to convey certain land to claimant, self serving declarations made by decedent during his life
time, as to how and under what right claimant claimed the land
are not admissible.

ASSESSOR'S BOOKS. Assessor's books are inadmissible to show that
land situated within the township was assessed to defendants
9 intestate, in a proceeding to establish a claim against the estate,
under an agreement by the deceased to give such land to the
claimant if he would clear it off, fence, and improve it.

TAX BOOKS. Tax books are inadmissible in evidence to show that a
specified person paid the taxes, where the testimony of the witness
10 who produced the books shows that they furnished no guide as to
who, in fact, paid the taxes.

Instructions. An instruction which announces the correct doctrine
5 on any theory applicable to facts involved, must be upheld.

New Trial. A new trial for newly discovered evidence which is
12 merely cumulative is properly refused.

Appeal from Davis District Court.—HON. F. W. EICHEL-
BERGER, Judge.

SATURDAY, OCTOBER 9, 1897.

THIS is a proceeding to establish a claim against
the estate of Louis Remey, deceased, based upon the
assumption that Remey sold and agreed to convey to
the claimant forty acres of land in Davis county, and
that, instead of making the conveyance as agreed, the
land was sold by Remey before his death, to claimant's
damage in the sum of one thousand, two hundred dollars. Defendant denies the sale or conveyance of the
land to plaintiff; pleads the statute of limitations and
the statute of frauds; avers that the land was the homestead of Remey, and that his wife did not concur in the
conveyance. A reply denied the affirmative allegations
of the answer, and also pleaded certain other facts not
necessary to be here recited. The case was tried to a

jury, resulting in a verdict and judgment for plaintiff,
and defendant appeals.—*Affirmed.*

John F. Scarborough and *Steck & Smith* for appellant.

Traverse & Taylor for appellee.

DEEMER, J.—The exact claim made by plaintiff in
his petition is that he married the daughter of Remey
about twenty-three years ago, and at or about the time
of the marriage, Remey and his wife promised
1   that if plaintiff would move a house, which he
had then commenced to build upon his father's
land, to the land in question, clear it off, fence and
improve it, he (deceased) would give it to plaintiff, or
that it should be plaintiff's at the time of his (Remey's)
death or when he (Remey) was done with it; that plaintiff moved onto the place, made improvements thereon,
cleared it off, and fenced it, relying upon said contract
of purchase; that, in March, 1895, Remey sold the land,
without the knowledge or consent of plaintiff, receiving
one thousand two hundred dollars therefor. The
defenses relied upon in argument are (1) a denial of the
contract; (2) an abandonment by plaintiff of his rights
under the contract, if he ever had any; (3) that the property was the homestead of Remey, and, as his wife did
not join in the contract, it is void; and (4) certain errors
in the rulings of the court made during the progress of
the trial.

I. The first complaint is that there is not sufficient
evidence of the contract to sustain the verdict of the
jury. The court instructed that it must be clearly, definitely, and unequivocally established that there was
such a contract as claimed by plaintiff. If the case were
triable *de novo*, we would have no hesitation in saying
that plaintiff had not made out his case. It is not so

triable, however, and the question is not whether the
alleged contract has been established to our satisfaction, but rather whether there is evidence from which
a jury, free from passion or prejudice, might find for
the plaintiff. Without attempting to set out the evidence, it is enough to say that the jury may have found
the following to be the facts: That in the year
2   1870 appellee married the only daughter of
deceased; that at the time of the marriage plaintiff had commenced to build a house on land belonging
to his (plaintiff's) father; that deceased and his wife, who
were anxious that their daughter should be near them,
promised the appellee that if he would move the house
onto the land in question, clear the land out, and put
it in cultivation, he should have it when Remey was
done with it; that, on the strength of this agreement,
plaintiff moved his house onto the land, cleared it up,
put it in cultivation, and otherwise improved it; that
he lived on the premises for about six years, and unt'l
after the death of his wife, when he removed to another
tract, which he had purchased in the meantime; that,
without the knowledge and consent of plaintiff, Remey
sold the land which he promised to give to his son-in-
law, and afterwards made a will, in which plaintiff was
not remembered. The evidence as to the contract made
between the parties is not in exact harmony, but the
jury was justified in finding therefrom the above state
of facts. It is conceded that such a contract, if made,
was good. Indeed, it could not well be questioned, for
it has frequently been held that a promise, based upon
a good consideration, to will certain property to another,
is valid, and may be specifically enforced against all
persons having notice or knowledge thereof. Beach,
Modern Equity, section 602; *Carmichael v. Carmichael,*
72 Mich. 76 (40 N. W. Rep. 173); *Parsell v. Stryker,* 41
N. Y. 480; *Johnson v. Hubbell,* 10 N. J. Eq. 332. If

such a contract can be specifically enforced, it follows that damages may be assessed for its breach. The contract in this case was that plaintiff should have the land upon the death of Remey, or when he and his wife were done with it; and it was either the present transfer of the fee, subject to a life estate, or an agreement to will the property to the plaintiff. Whichever it may have been, it was good if plaintiff accepted it and acted thereon, and took possession of the land thereunder. *Franklin v. Tuckerman*, 68 Iowa, 572.

II. Appellant contends that there was an abandonment by plaintiff of his rights to the land, if he ever had any therein. This is an affirmative defense, the burden being on defendant to establish it. We do not think there is such evidence of abandonment as to justify us in interfering with the verdict. The mere fact that the appellee moved off of the land in the year 1876 is not conclusive of this question. Under his theory of the case, the Remeys were entitled to a life estate in the land. They were to hold the legal title until they were through with it. The jury may well have found that Remey recognized the validity and force of the contract down to within a year of his death; and there is also evidence that plaintiff, after he had moved off the land, was claiming an interest in it.

III. Another defense is that the land was the homestead of Remey and his wife at the time it is claimed the contract was made. That Remey and his wife were living upon the forty acres in dispute, and but a few feet from the line between that and another lying south, which they owned at the time the agreement is said to have been made, is conceded; and that they were entitled to a homestead out of this eighty acres is also conceded. Bearing upon this issue, the court gave the following instruction, of which complaint is made: "As to the claim of the

executor that the land was a homestead, you are
instructed that if you find beyond doubt that Louis
Remey and wife urged plaintiff to move onto the north
forty, and promised and agreed with plaintiff that if he
would do so, and would clear off and put in cultivation
such forty, *he should own said forty at their death, or
when they were done with it;* and if you further find
that plaintiff accepted such proposition, and in good
faith complied with his part of such contract, if one
was so made, relying on said promise; and if you also
find that Remey and wife are both dead, and left no
child or children surviving them,—then the executor
could not now be permitted to defend against the claim
of plaintiff on the ground that the contract was not
valid because the land was the homestead of Louis
Remey and wife." This instruction does not say that,
under the facts assumed, there would be an abandonment of the homestead; nor does it in terms hold that
the agreement would not constitute a sale or disposition
of the homestead. Neither does it indicate upon what
theory the court held that, under the facts stated, the
executor could not defend against the claim on the
ground that the property covered by the contract was
a homestead. When we find that it announces
5   the correct doctrine upon any theory applicable
to the facts stated, it must be upheld. This much
the instruction does fairly assume, viz.: that the land
was a homestead before the making of the alleged contract. Now, it has been held by the supreme court of
Wisconsin, in construing a statute quite like our
6   own, that a sale by the husband alone of the fee
title to the homestead, in which he reserved
the right to use and occupy the property during the life
of himself and wife, was valid and binding. *Ferguson
v. Mason*, 60 Wis. 377 (19 N. W. Rep. 420); *Whitemore
v. Hay*, 85 Wis. 240 (55 N. W. Rep. 708). See, also, *Smith*

v. Provin, 4 Allen, 516; *Doyle v. Coburn,* 6 Allen, 71.
We have, to a certain extent, at least, recognized this
doctrine. *Harkness v. Burton,* 39 Iowa, 101; *Railroad
Co. v. Swinney,* 38 Iowa, 182; *Railway Co. v. McWil-
liams,* 71 Iowa, 164. But, without committing ourselves
to it at this time, it is sufficient to say that the instruction was correct on the theory that there was an abandonment by Remey and his wife of any homestead right
they may have had in the premises. In the case of
Drake v. Painter, 77 Iowa, 731, we held that an oral contract for the sale of homestead, followed by possession
taken thereunder, amounted to an abandonment of the
homestead by the grantors. And in the case of *Winkleman v. Winkleman,* 79 Iowa, 319, we held that an oral
contract by parents to sell their homestead to a son,
followed by the son's taking possession thereunder,
amounted to an abandonment of the homestead. These
cases seem to be based upon the proposition that there
cannot be two separate homesteads in the same tract of
land, and that, when the grantee acquires one by the
consent and acquiescence of the grantors, they (the
grantors) lose their homestead rights by abandonment.
See, also, *Jones v. Currier,* 65 Iowa, 533; *Bradshaw v.
Remick,* 90 Iowa, 409. Aside from this, however, there
is little, if any, evidence that Remey or his wife intended
to claim any part of the north forty acres as their homestead. The south forty was in cultivation when they
made the agreement with their son-in-law, and the evidence tends to show that they claimed this as their
homestead. The house they occupied was upon the
north forty, but was very close to the line; so close,
indeed, that it is difficult to say from the evidence
whether or not they knew it was not on the south forty
acres. This much is true, however: that neither of
them intended to claim any part of the land in controversy as their homestead. If they did intend to so

claim it, they, as we have seen, abandoned this intent when they made the agreement with their son-in-law.

Another proposition is conclusive of this question. Remey had the right to select the land upon which his improvements were located (about one-half acre in extent), and all of the south forty, except an amount equal to that occupied by the dwelling. The right granted by the statute is not confined to congressional subdivisions. Now, from the record before us, it 7 is quite clear that both husband and wife abandoned all claim to any part of the north forty, save the small tract upon which their buildings were located, and that plaintiff, if he made the contract as claimed, is entitled to the value of that land. Defendant does not defend on the ground that the land occupied by the house is homestead. He says that the whole north forty acres are of that character, and that the contract is therefore void.

IV. Claimant was permitted to testify, over defendant's objections, to a conversation he heard between Remey, his wife, and his (plaintiff's) father, in which he (plaintiff) took no part. This evidence 8 was proper, and was not subject to the objection lodged against it. *Smith v. James*, 72 Iowa, 515. The case of *Muir v. Miller*, 82 Iowa, 700, is not in point. Defendant offered in evidence the assessor's books for the township in which the land was situated, to show that the land was assessed to Remey. They 9 were properly rejected. *Adams v. Hickox*, 55 Iowa, 632. He also introduced the tax books, for the purpose of showing that Remey paid the taxes. These were also properly rejected, for the testimony of the witness who produced them 10 showed that they furnished no guide as to who, in fact, paid the taxes. Appellant also complains because the court would not permit him to

prove certain declarations made by Remey during his
        lifetime, as to how and under what right appellee
'11   claimed the land. This evidence was also prop-
        erly rejected. Plaintiff was allowed to show
over defendant's objections that Remey claimed the
south forty acres of land as his homestead. This evi-
        dence was certainly proper under the issues pre-
12   sented. Appellant filed a motion for a new trial,
        based upon newly-discovered evidence. The
motion was properly overruled, because the evidence
was clearly cumulative. Some other unimportant questions are presented, which we do not consider. We
have examined the record, and discover no prejudicial
error, and the judgment is AFFIRMED.

STATE OF IOWA v. B. F. BOOMER, Appellant.

Fraudulent Banking. A bank which is still receiving deposits,
1   although most of its business has been transferred to another
     bank, is within Acts Eighteenth General Assembly, chapter 153,
     making it a felony for any officer of a bank to knowingly receive
8   any deposits when the bank is to his knowledge insolvent.

EVIDENCE. Papers used in another action tending to show by defend-
     ant's admission that he was sole owner of a bank are admissible
7   in evidence in a prosecution for knowingly receiving money on
     deposit in such bank, while it was insolvent.

SECONDARY EVIDENCE. On a trial for fraudulent banking, where the
     books of defendant's bank are in his possession, and he cannot be
5   required to produce them, witnesses that have been employed by
     defendant and have become familiar with the books in the course
     of their employment, may testify as to their contents.

OPINION EVIDENCE. Such witnesses, being familiar with the banking
     business, the bank books, and the value of the property then
6   owned by defendant could state their opinions as to defendant's
     solvency when the depo-it in question was received.

PUNISHMENT. Under Acts Eighteenth General Assembly, chapter 153,
     section 2, making it a felony for an insolvent bank to receive a
     deposit, a judgment of conviction requiring defendant to be
     impr.soned in the penitentiary, at hard labor, for the term of five
     years, as is not reversible for being excessive punishment.

Indictment: VARIANCE IN PROOF. Acts Eighteenth General Assembly, chapter 153, section 1, provides that no insolvent bank shall receive on deposit moneys or currency "or other notes, bills, or drafts circulating as money or currency." Code 1873, section 4306, provides that no indictment shall be held insufficient for surplusage where there is sufficient matter alleged to indicate clearly the offense and the person charged, or for any matter
2 which does not tend to the prejudice of the substantial rights of defendant, on the merits   An indictment for receiving a deposit after known insolvency charged that the deposit was "in lawful money of the United States, a particular description of which to the jurors is unknown"   The evidence given by the clerk who received the deposit was that it was currency, but that he did not notice whether it was national currency, greenbacks, silver certificates, or gold certificates.   Held, that the words "of the United States" could be rejected as surplusage, and hence there was no material variance.

TIME DEPOSIT.   A deposit payable after a stated time, with interest,
4 is within the statute against fraudulent banking.

DOCUMENTARY EVIDENCE.   Documentary evidence which was before
8 the grand jury need not be returned with the indictment or be noted thereon.

NOTICE OF WITNESSES.   A notice served on defendant in a prosecution for knowingly receiving a deposit while a bank owned by him was insolvent, stating that the clerk of the district court would be examined as a witness, and that it was expected to prove by him
7 that he was such clerk, and that as such he had the custody of the records of the court and would introduce and identify its records, showing a specified list of judgments, is sufficient to authorize the examination of such clerk and identification by him of papers in a case to which defendant has been a party, tending to show that he was the owner of the bank.

Appeal from Allamakee District Court.—HON. A. N. HOBSON, Judge.

SATURDAY, OCTOBER 9, 1897.

THE defendant was accused and convicted of the crime of fraudulent banking, and from the judgment, which required that he be imprisoned in the penitentiary at Anamosa at hard labor for the term of five years, he appeals.—*Affirmed.*

Dayton & Dayton, Stilwell & Stewart, and *H. T. Reed* for appellant.

Milton Remley, attorney general, *E. M. Woodward,* county attorney, and *J. H. Trewin* for the state.

ROBINSON, J. — The indictment charges "that said B. F. Boomer, at the county of Allamakee, state of Iowa, on or about the fifteenth day of August, 1893, was engaged in the banking business at Waukon, in said county and state, under the name and style 'Bank of Waukon, Boomer Bros.,' and he, the said B. F. Boomer, the Bank of Waukon, and Boomer Bros., were then and there insolvent; and while and when he, the said B. F. Boomer, the Bank of Waukon, and Boomer Bros., were so insolvent, and while and when he, the said B. F. Boomer, was so engaged in the banking business at the time and place aforesaid, he, the said B. F. Boomer, then and there being president and manager of said Bank of Waukon, did, knowing of such insolvency as aforesaid, knowingly and unlawfully receive on deposit in said Bank of Waukon, from one Michael Regan, the sum of two hundred dollars, in lawful money of the United States, a particular description of which is to the grand jurors unknown, contrary to and in violation of the laws of the state of Iowa." The evidence authorized the jury to find that the following were established facts: In the year 1878 the defendant and his brother, J. H. Boomer, commenced the banking business at Waukon, under the name of the "Bank of Waukon, Boomer Bros." The capital of the bank belonged to the defendant, but his brother, who acted as cashier, was to have one-half of the profits of the business after paying the defendant interest on one-half of the capital. In the year 1891, J. H. Boomer moved to South Dakota, and does not appear to have had any interest in the

bank after that time, although his name continued to
appear as cashier. The bank was carried on thereafter
by the defendant, but without any change in the name.
He did not personally keep the books of the bank, but
was advised as to its condition. In addition to the banking business, he was engaged in buying and selling live
stock. In the spring of the year 1893, the First National
Bank of Waukon was organized, and in June commenced doing business; and the defendant became the
owner of a part of its capital stock, and arranged to
transfer to it the banking part of his business. The
business of both banks was thereafter carried on in the
same room, the defendant using the back part of it for
the Bank of Waukon and for his stock business.

1   Nearly all of the banking business was, in fact,
transferred to the First National Bank; and the
defendant insists that he had ceased to do a banking
business at the time the transaction for which he was
indicted took place. But it is shown that the Bank of
Waukon continued to receive occasional deposits. On
the fifteenth day of August, 1893, that bank received
from Michael Regan two hundred dollars in money, and
gave to him a certificate, of which the following is a
copy:

> "Bank of Waukon,
> "Boomer Brothers,
> "Waukon, Iowa, Aug. 15, 1893.
> "Michael Regan has deposited in this bank two hundred
> dollars, payable to the order of himself in current funds on the
> return of this certificate properly indorsed, 12 months after
> date, with interest at 5 per cent. per annum for the time speci-
> fied only.
> "Matures 8, 15, '94·
> "J. H. Boomer, Cashier."

Certificate of deposit not subject to check.

Within a week after that time, the defendant gave
mortgages and transferred property to a large amount
for the purpose of securing debts, and the Bank of
Waukon was closed.

The state claims that the money was received from Regan in violation of chapter 153 of the Acts of the Eighteenth General Assembly, which contains the following:

"Section 1. No bank, banking house, exchange broker, deposit office, or firm, company, corporation, or party engaged in the banking, broker, exchange, or deposit business, shall accept or receive on deposit, with or without interest, any moneys, bank bills or notes, or United States treasury notes, or currency or other notes, bills or drafts circulating as money or currency, when such bank, banking house, exchange broker, or deposit office, firm or party is insolvent.

"Sec. 2. If any such bank, banking house, exchange broker, or deposit office, firm, company, corporation, or party, shall receive or accept on deposit any such deposits aforesaid, when insolvent, any officer, director, cashier, manager, member, party, or managing party thereof, knowing of such insolvency, who shall knowingly receive or accept, be accessory, or permit or connive at the receiving or accepting on deposit therein, or thereby, any such deposits as aforesaid, shall be guilty of a felony. * * *"

I. At the close of the evidence, the defendant asked the court to direct a verdict of not guilty on several grounds, one of which was that there was a material variance between the indictment and the proofs.

2   The alleged variance was as follows: The indictment charges that the deposit in question was "in lawful money of the United States, a particular description of which is to the grand jurors unknown", while the proof failed to show that it was in coin of the United States or notes or certificates which it was required to redeem. The testimony of the employe who received the deposit was that it was two hundred dollars; that it was currency, but that he did not notice "whether it was national currency or greenbacks or

silver certificates"; that there "might have been a gold
certificate." It is not claimed that, to constitute the
offense of fraudulent banking by receiving a deposit
when the bank or person receiving it is insolvent, it is
essential that the deposit consist of money issued by
the United States. The language of the statute cited
leaves no room for such a claim, but includes "all currency or other notes, bills or drafts circulating as money
or currency." The claim is that the proof must conform
strictly to the charge, even though that be made with
unnecessary particularity. There are undoubtedly
many decisions which tend to sustain that claim. 1
Greenleaf, Evidence, section 65. In *State v. Newland*,
7 Iowa, 242, the indictment charged that the defendant
passed counterfeit bills which purported to have been
issued by "a corporation duly authorized for that purpose, by the state of Massachusetts"; and it was held
incumbent on the state to prove that averment. So, in
State v. Crogan, 8 Iowa, 523, where the indictment
charged that the defendant kept a place resorted to
for the purpose of gambling, in a building on a lot specified, it was held that, although it was unnecessary to
have described the location of the place further than to
show the proper venue, yet, as it was more specifically
described, the proof must show that the place was on
the lot specified. Those cases did not arise under the
statutes which govern this case. Section 4305 of the
Code of 1873 provides that an indictment "is sufficient
if it can be understood therefrom: * * * (5) That
the act or omission charged as the offense, is stated
with such a degree of certainty, in ordinary and concise
language, and in such a manner as to enable a person of
common understanding to know what is intended, and
the court to pronounce judgment upon a conviction
according to the law of the case." Section 4306 provides
that "no indictment is insufficient, nor can the trial,

judgment, or other proceedings thereon be affected by
reason of any of the following matters:　*　*　*　(4)
For any surplusage or repugnant allegation, or for any
repetition, when there is sufficient matter alleged to
indicate clearly the offense and the person charged;
nor (5) for any other matter which was formerly deemed
a defect or imperfection, but which does not tend to the
prejudice of the substantial rights of the defendant
upon the merits." The case of *State v. Hesner,* 55
Iowa, 494, arose under those statutes, and is especially relied upon by the appellant. In that case
the indictment charged the defendant with the crime
of selling intoxicating liquor known as "whisky," in
violation of law; and it was held that an instruction
which authorized a conviction on proof of the sale of
intoxicating liquors other than whisky was erroneous.
But the charge that the defendant was guilty of selling
whisky illegally was so specific and definite as to be
well calculated to exclude, by implication, illegal sales
of other liquors, and thus mislead the defendant, to his
injury, in the preparation of his defense. That case is
so unlike this in important particulars as not to be in
point. The deposits which the statute which creates
the offense of fraudulent banking is designed to prevent
are of any kind of money, bank bills, or notes, treasury
notes issued by the United States, currency, or other
notes, and bills or drafts circulating as money or currency; and it is wholly immaterial whether the deposit
be of money issued by the general government or not.
The statute does not specify "lawful money of the
United States." In a general sense, such money is any
lawful money which is circulated in the United States.
In a comprehensive sense, money is "any currency usually and lawfully employed in buying and selling."
Webster Inter. Dictionary. It includes "whatever is
lawfully and actually current in buying and selling, of

the value and as the equivalent of coin." 15 Am. & Eng.
Enc. Law, 701. See, also, *Klauber v. Biggerstaff*, 47
Wis. 557 (3 N. W. Rep. 357). In view of the purposes of
the statute, and the popular understanding of the term
"lawful money," and the absence of any more definite
designation than "lawful money of the United States,"
we conclude that the indictment was designed to
include any money which was lawfully circulated in
the United States; and hence that the words "of the
United States" may be rejected as surplusage. Had the
indictment charged that the deposit was of money particularly described, as of gold coin, or of treasury notes
of a particular denomination and number, it may be
that no part of the description could have been rejected
as surplusage, and that the case would have been within
the rule of *State v. Hesner, supra.* For the reasons
shown, we are of the opinion that there was no variance
in proof which was prejudicial to the defendant. See
State v. Ean, 90 Iowa, 536; *Tracy v. State*, 46 Neb. 361
(64 N. W. Rep. 1071).

II. The defendant claims that the evidence did
not show that he was engaged in the banking business
when the transaction in question occurred. It shows
that nearly all the banking business, such as
3   making loans, discounting notes, selling
exchange, and making collections, had been
transferred to the First National Bank of Waukon
before that time; but the bank of Waukon had
continued to receive deposits, and had not therefore fully closed its banking business and was doing
that business, within the meaning of the statute,
when it received the deposit in question. Nor can we
say that transaction was not a deposit, within the

meaning of the statute, but a mere loan of money. *State v. Cadwell*, 79 Iowa, 434. The statute

4   contemplates time deposits, for it includes deposits on which interest is paid. The certificate given to Regan shows that the transaction was a time deposit, and the evidence justified the jury in so finding, and in finding that the deposit was received by authority of the defendant, expressly given.

III. The defendant complains because the district court permitted witnesses Hager and Mitchell, who had examined the books of the Bank of Waukon, to

testify as to their contents. The witnesses had

5   been employed by that bank, and had become familiar with the books in the course of their employment. The books were in the possession of the defendant, and he did not produce them. It is not claimed that he could be compelled to do so. Constitution Iowa, article 1, section 8; Code 1873, section 3636; *Boyd v. U. S.*, 116 U. S. 616 (6 Sup. Ct. Rep. 524); *Counselman v. Hitchcock*, 142 U. S. 547 (12 Sup. Ct. Rep. 195). But it is said the state cannot be permitted to do indirectly what it can not do directly, and substitute secondary evidence for that to which it is not entitled. We do not think that objection, as applied to the facts in this case, is well founded. The witnesses became familiar with the contents of the books in question, with the knowledge and consent of the defendant; and proof of the information they thus obtained is as competent for the state, in the absence of the books, as would be proof of declarations the defendant had made. It was the best evidence which could be obtained without the consent of the defendant, and the state should not be debarred from its use merely because the defendant might be regarded as admitting it to be true if he did not introduce the books to disprove it. The same

result would follow his failure to contradict as a witness declarations which the evidence tended to show he
had made.

IV. The defendant also complains because
Hager and Mitchell were permitted to state their
opinions, based on their knowledge of the books they
had examined, as to the solvency of the defendant when
the deposit in question was received. The wit-
6   nesses were familiar with the banking business,
understood bank books, and had a knowledge of
the value of the property then owned by the defendant.
Their testimony to which the defendant objects was
fully authorized by what we said of similar testimony
in *State v. Cadwell, supra.*

V. The state was permitted to introduce as a witness the clerk of the district court, who testified to his
official position, and identified certain papers in a case
to which the defendant had been a party, which
7   were then introduced in evidence. The papers
which were thus received tended to show by the
admission of the defendant that he was the sole owner
of the Bank of Waukon, and were competent for that
purpose. But the defendant objects to them, on the
ground that the clerk was not examined before the
grand jury, his name was not indorsed on the indictment, and notice was not given to the defendant of
an intention to examine the witness with reference
to the papers introduced. A notice was in fact duly
served upon the defendant, which informed him that
the clerk of the district court would be examined as a
witness, by whom "it was expected to prove that said
witness is such clerk; that, as such, he has the custody
of the records of said court, and will introduce and
identify the records of said court showing the following judgments against the defendant,"—giving a list
of judgments. This notice was sufficient, under section
4421 of the Code, to authorize all the evidence which

the witness gave. That section provides that the notice
which must be given of the testimony of a witness who
was not examined before the grand jury shall state the
substance of what is expected to be proven by him on
the trial. Notice of what is expected to be proven by
documentary evidence is not required. *State v. Far-
rington*, 90 Iowa, 681. This rule is in harmony with
that applicable to the return of evidence taken
before the grand jury. It is not necessary to
return with the indictment documentary evidence which was before the grand jury, nor is it
required that such evidence be noted. *State v. Mullen-
hoff*, 74 Iowa, 274. The purpose of returning with the
indictment minutes of the evidence taken before the
grand jury is the same as that of giving notice of the
examination of a witness who did not testify before the
grand jury. *State v. Yetzer*, 97 Iowa, 423. It has
been held frequently that the examination of witnesses
who testified before the grand jury need not be confined strictly to the matter set out in the minutes of
the testimony. *State v. Harlan*, 98 Iowa, 458, and cases
therein cited. And the same rule is applicable to the
examination of witnesses who were not before the
grand jury, but testify on notice. *State v. Yetzer,
supra*. The examination of the clerk was confined to a
statement of his official position, and an identification
of the documentary evidence introduced, and the notice
under the authorities cited, was sufficient to authorize
that examination. Notice of the pleadings and judgment entries was not required.

VI. The defendant complains of the refusal of
the court to give instructions asked by him, and of portions of the charge given. The first four instructions
asked by the defendant and refused, were in conflict
with the law as we have stated it, and with the facts as
the jury was authorized to find them, and therefore

were properly refused. So far as the instructions asked were material and correct, they were virtually included in the charge as given. That, in the particulars of which the defendant complains relating to the meaning of the word "insolvent," as used in the statute, was substantially the same as the portion of the charge approved in the case of *State v. Cadwell, supra.* It is true this case differs from that in that the defendant had ceased to transact a full banking business when he received the deposit in question, and that the charge of the court did not recognize that difference, but the omission to do so could not have prejudiced the defendant. The charge as given was applicable to the facts in this case.

VII. It is claimed that attorneys for the state were guilty of misconduct during the trial in asking questions relating to the books of the defendant, in bringing them to the attention of the jury after the court had ruled that such references were improper, and in other matters. We cannot say that there was error in anything of which complaint is thus made. Some of the things said by attorneys, and now objected to, were authorized by the record. It appears from a statement made by the court that an attorney for the defendant had at some time during the trial suggested that the defendant had not refused to produce his books; and we cannot say that the court abused its discretion in permitting what was done, nor that the attorneys for the state were guilty of misconduct.

VIII. We have examined all questions presented in argument without finding any error in the record prejudicial to the defendant. The case has been presented with much care and ability, but we are satisfied that the conviction of the defendant should be sustained. The evidence of his guilt is ample. He was insolvent, and must have known that fact; yet he

expressly authorized his agent to receive the deposit in
question. We cannot say that the punishment for
which the judgment provides is excessive. What we
have said disposes of all the material questions in the
case, and the judgment of the district court is AFFIRMED.

THE NATIONAL IMPROVEMENT AND CONSTRUCTION COM-
PANY, Appellant, v. A. D. MAIKEN, et al.

Principal and Agent: RATIFICATION. Where an agent, with written
1 power, merely, to receipt for money due his principal, settles a
2 claim with one who knows the terms of such power, but, relying
4 on the agent's representations that he has the authority to make
5 the settlement, pays money thereon in good faith, the principal,
   by accepting and retaining the money, with full knowledge of
   what has been done, ratifies the settlement.

RESCISSION: *Tender.* A creditor whose agent, authorized simply to
   receive money and receipt therefor, accepts part of the claim in
   full settlement of the same, cannot repudiate the settlement
8 without returning the money to the debtor at the place where it
   was obtained; and it is insufficient to deposit it in another city to
   the credit of the debtor, at which place no one authorized to
   receive such money is present. None of the exceptions arising in
   cases of gratuities or fraud have application.

Appeal from Appanoose District Court.—HON. T. M.
FEE, Judge.

MONDAY, OCTOBER 11, 1897.

SUIT in equity to recover the contract price for
erecting a canning factory for the defendants at
Moravia, Iowa, and to establish and foreclose a
mechanic's lien against the property upon which the
factory was erected. The defendants deny that the
factory was constructed according to contract. They
also plead a settlement with one Silvers, an agent of
the plaintiff. Plaintiff, in reply, denies the settlement,
and denies the authority of Silvers to do more than
receive and receipt for such money as the defendants

might see fit to pay on the contract. From a decree
dismissing the plaintiff's petition, it appeals.—
Affirmed.

D. P. *Stubbs* and C. T. *Howell* for appellant.

T. B. *Perry* for appellees.

DEEMER, J. — The individual defendants, who
are the promoters and stockholders of a corporation
known as the Moravia Canning Factory Company,
entered into a written contract with the plaintiff, a
co-partnership, by which it undertook to build and
equip a canning factory in the town of Moravia, in
Appanoose county, Iowa. By the terms of this contract, the plaintiff undertook to build and erect the
factory according to certain plans and specifications,
and to equip it with certain machinery, which was
described in the contract, for the consideration of six
thousand, nine hundred and fifty dollars, to be paid
when the factory was completed and in operation.
The contract also contained these provisions: "Payment shall be due from date of completion of and operation of said factory. If time is requested by the party
of the second part, the National Improvement and Construction Company hereby agrees to accept one-half
when factory is completed, balance one-half in three
months from date of completion if approved bankable
note is furnished, drawing interest at the rate of six
per cent. only. Said factory is to be completed in ninety
days or thereabouts after above amount ($6,950.00) is
subscribed. * * * As soon as the above amount
($6,950.00) is subscribed, or in a reasonable time there-
after, the said subscribers may among themselves
incorporate under the state laws as therein provided,
fixing the aggregate amount of stock at not less than
the amount subscribed, to be divided into shares of

$100.00 each. Said share or shares, as above stated, to be issued to the subscribers in proportion to their paid-up interest; and it is agreed that each stockholder shall be liable only for the amount subscribed by him. Extra stock may be subscribed in excess of contract price; and it is hereby agreed that all money collected after paying the first party net contract price shall belong to the party of the second part, and may be used by them as surplus or working capital." There was also attached to this contract a slip containing the following words: "Said factory shall be furnished with all necessary machinery for canning all kinds of fruits and vegetables at the rate of from ten thousand (10,000) to twenty thousand (20,000) cans per day of ten hours." Whether this was a part of the original contract, or was added thereto without authority after the contract was fully executed, is one of the disputed questions of fact in the case. The suit is upon the contract to recover the agreed price, less a credit of three thousand, nine hundred and thirty-five dollars, indorsed by the plaintiff upon the account, on September 11, 1894. The petition recites the making of the contract and the performance by plaintiff on its part of all its conditions, and asks judgment for the balance due. There is a dispute as to the contents of defendant's answer, but a brief statement of the undisputed recitals of that pleading is sufficient. The defendants say that plaintiff did not furnish the factory with the necessary machinery for canning all kinds of fruit and vegetables at the rate of ten thousand to twenty thousand cans per day of ten hours; allege that it did not have half of this capacity; and further deny that plaintiff ever tested the same, or offered to do so. They further plead that a dispute arose between the parties to the contract as to whether it had been fully complied with by the plaintiff, and that negotiations leading to a settlement of the matters in dispute were had between

the defendants and an agent of the plaintiff, which
finally resulted in a compromise by which plaintiff
agreed to accept four thousand dollars in full of its
claims under the contract; that defendants accepted
the proposition, paid the four thousand dollars, and
received back the contract, together with a conveyance
of the property and receipts in full to each of the
defendants for their liability under the contract. The
plaintiff admits the settlement made by Silvers, but
says he had no authority except to receive payments
under the contract, which the defendants well knew;
that, after receiving the money from the agent, it
repudiated and rescinded his action, because of lack of
authority and of fraud practiced upon him by the
defendants, and offered to return the money received,
and demanded the return of the property; that the
defendants refused to return the property, and plaintiff
thereupon credited the amount (less a small sum which
was allowed some of defendants for soliciting stock)
to defendants' account, which is the credit it refers to
in its petition.

These were, in substance, the issues upon which
the case was tried, resulting in the order and judgment
appealed from. Several questions are argued which
we do not regard as controlling, and they will not be
referred to except incidentally. For instance, the conflict as to what was in the contract when it was originally agreed to is only important, as we view it, to
show that there was an actual dispute between the
parties at the time the agreement of settlement is said
to have been made. It is not important to determine
which was right in this dispute. Sufficient is it
1   to say that such a dispute existed, and that one
representing the plaintiff attempted to settle it.
That an agent for the plaintiff went to Moravia, met the
defendants, and did, in fact, settle this claim, is conceded. But plaintiff insists that he had no authority to

do so, and that it rescinded and repudiated the settlement as soon as it learned of it, and, after such repudiation, demanded of defendants the return of the contract, and a re-coveyance of the property. The actual authority conferred upon this agent is evidenced by a power of attorney, the material parts of which are as follows: "Know all men by these presents, that National Improvement and Construction.Company, of the city of Chicago, county of Cook, in the state of Illinois, has made, constituted, and appointed, and, by these presents, does make, constitute, and appoint, J. B. Silvers, of the city of Chicago, county of Cook, and state of Illinois, true and lawful attorney for it, and in its name, place, and stead to receive and receipt for any and all sums of money due it at Moravia, Iowa, and to give its own receipt therefor." Of this the defendants had knowledge. Silvers claimed, however, that he had full authority to settle and adjust the claim. Relying upon this claim, and believing in his authority, defendants made the settlement pleaded by them in their answer, and received the documents as therein stated. Silvers returned to Chicago, and reported his settlement to the plaintiff, giving full information as to what he had done. Thereupon plaintiff sent defendants a written notice, in which it recited its claim under the contract, and, further, gave notice that it refused to ratify or justify his (Silvers') acts, and that it had deposited in the Lake Street Manufacturing Block, in the city of Chicago, to the order of A. D. Maiken, of Moravia, Iowa, the sum of three thousand, nine hundred and thirty-five dollars; that it demanded a surrender of the factory, and the possession of the original contract and the power of attorney executed to Silvers. The notice concluded as follows: "And, in pursuance of this demand, states that if, within ten days from the date of this document, said property and said papers are not so delivered to

said first party by the said second party, then the first
party will credit or indorse on the said contract the
said $3,935.00, and will proceed by action at law or
equity to recover from said second party $6,950.00, with
interest, and the present possession of the aforesaid canning factory at Moravia, Iowa, and present possession
of the original contract, with all the subscriptions
thereon and equities therein, and present possession of
the power of attorney aforesaid, and will hold the second parties jointly and severally responsible to it for
any and all damages that the first party may have sustained by reason of these premises. [Signed.]"

2   Now, it must be conceded that Silvers did not
have authority to settle the dispute between
these parties. He assumed to possess this power, however, and defendants paid him, relying upon the truth
of his claim. He received the money, delivered up the
contract, conveyed the property to the defendants, delivered them his power of attorney, and took the money
received in settlement with him to Chicago. When he .
arrived there, he reported his doings to his principal.
As soon as they were advised as to what he had done,
they attempted to repudiate and rescind his action, and
the controlling question in the case is whether or not
they did rescind.

The well-settled rule of law is that, when an agent
transcends his power, his principal, upon being
informed of the transaction, must repudiate or rescind
the same within a reasonable time, or he will be held
to have ratified the act. It is also elementary that a
principal cannot ratify a part of the agent's unauthorized acts, and reject the remainder. The rule has thus
been stated in the case of *Bryant v. Moore*, 26 Me. 84:
"There is no doubt that if one person knows that another
has acted as his agent without authority, or has
exceeded his authority as agent, and with such knowledge accepts money, property, or security, or avails

himself of advantages derived from the act, he will be
regarded as having ratified it. * * * If, for
instance, a merchant should authorize a broker, by a
written memorandum, to purchase certain goods at a
price named, and the broker should exhibit it to the
seller, and yet should exceed the price, and this should
be made known to the merchant when he received the
goods, if he should retain or sell them he would ratify
the bargain made by the broker, and be obliged to pay
the agreed price." And in the case of *Benedict v. Smith*,
10 Paige, 126, the court, in discussing a question ruled
by the same principle as the one at bar, said: "* * *
But where one person assumes to act as the agent of
another, without authority, the person for whom he
assumes to act cannot claim the benefit of his agency
in part only, and reject it as to the residue of the transaction. And where the attorney of record goes beyond
his general power in compromising or taking security
for a debt intrusted to him for collection, if the client,
upon being informed of the transaction, does not dissent without any unreasonable delay, the court may
presume the attorney had a special power thus to act;
especially where the client receives the benefit of the
securities taken for him by the attorney." Appellant
recognized this rule of law, and, in giving the notice
to which we have referred, attempted to repudiate the
transaction; and the real question is whether or not it
did so. It gave notice of the repudiation, and demanded
the return of the property and of the papers delivered
to the defendants, but the only return it made of the
money was to deposit it to the order of the president
of the canning company, in a building in Chicago, with
notice that, if the property and papers were not returned
and the money accepted, it would credit it upon
3   defendants' account. Having received the money
from the defendants at Moravia, it was the duty
of plaintiff, in case it desired to rescind, to offer the

same back to them at that place. Defendants were not required to go to Chicago or to any other place to get it. It had come into the possession of plaintiff through the acts of its agent,—unauthorized though they may have been,—and it was its duty to tender the same back to the defendants at the place where received. *Eadie v. Ashbaugh*, 44 Iowa, 519; Parsons, Contracts (6th ed.), p. 679; Story, Agents, section '259; *Miles v. Ogden*, 54 Wis. 573 (12 N. W. Rep. 81); *Strasser v. Conklin*, 54 Wis. 102 (11 N. W. Rep. 254); *Elwell v. Chamberlin*, 31 N. Y. 611; *Hatch v. Taylor*, 10 N. H. 538; *Bank v. Oberne* 121 Ill. 25 (7 N. E. Rep. 85).

As the plaintiff did not restore the money collected by Silvers on the faith of the settlement, but, on the contrary, accepted it, and undertook to apply it on the defendants' account, it cannot be heard to say that the acts of its agent were not authorized. Defendants were not compelled to act under the notice given them by the plaintiff until their money was returned, or offered to be returned, at Moravia, Iowa. An offer to deliver it to them at Chicago was not sufficient, unless, possibly, they or some of them authorized to receive it were present in Chicago when the tender was made. The case relied upon by appellant, *Harper v. Insurance Co.*, 5 C. C. A. 505 (56 Fed. Rep. 281), clearly announces this doctrine. There are a few exceptions to these general and well-recognized rules. For instance, it is held that, when a party has fraudulently procured the execution of a contract, he is not entitled to an offer to restore what he has received as a condition precedent to rescission. *Hendrickson v. Hendrickson*, 51 Iowa, 68. Again, it has been held that if one, by fraudulent representations, procures a settlement and discharge of a cause of action, it is merely a receipt for a gratuity, and plaintiff may maintain his action without returning the money paid. *O'Brien v. Railway Co.*, 89 Iowa, 644.

These cases are based upon the doctrine that one who attempts to rescind a transaction on the ground of fraud is not required to restore that which he would be entitled to retain either by virtue of the contract sought to be set aside or of the original liability. See, also, *Allerton v. Allerton*, 50 N. Y. 670; *Bebout v. Bodle*, 38 Ohio St. 500. Another exception recognized by some of the authorities is to this effect: that "ratification does not arise when the principal accepts the results of an unauthorized act, not as a matter of choice, but merely for his own protection, to prevent further loss or liability therefrom." This exception is recognized in the following, among other cases: *Triggs v. Jones*, 46 Minn. 277 (38 N. W. Rep. 1113); *Mills v. Berla* (Tex. Civ. App.), 23 S. W. Rep. 910; *Nye v. Swan*, 49 Minn. 439 (52 N. W. Rep. 39); *Crocker v. Appleton*, 25 Me. 131. Without committing ourselves to this last-named exception, it is sufficient to say that there is no claim, either in the pleadings or in argument, that plaintiff was justified in withholding the money under any such rule. Its claim in this respect is that defendants knew of the agent's authority, and that they were guilty of fraud in making the settlement, and that the case comes under the first exception named, which we have recognized as being the law. True it is that defendants knew
4   of the terms of the agent's power of attorney, but it is also true that they believed, from his representations, and from the construction they placed upon the instrument, that he had full power to settle the dispute and compromise the claim. There is no evidence that, in effecting the settlement, they intended to defraud the plaintiff. On the contrary, they acted in the utmost good faith. They did not intend to pay plaintiff any money except in settlement of the claim; nor can their payment be said to be a mere gratuity, as in the *O'Brien Case*. The case of *Stainer v. Tysen*, 3 Hill, 280,

relied upon by appellant, is not in point. But, aside from all this, the question here is not one of repudiation of contract or settlement because of fraud, but rather as to an agent's power to make a settlement, and the exception has no application. If, with the authority of the agent conceded, there was a question as to the character of the settlement, there might be room for application of the doctrine announced in the *Hendrickson Case.*

The ultimate question here is the authority of the agent. He was not, as we have seen, expressly authorized to make the settlement. He, however, assumed to do so, and his principal accepted the benefits 5   thereof with full knowledge of what had been done. Having ratified the acts of its agent, the transaction was the same in law as if expressly authorized. If authorized, there was no fraud, and consequently the plaintiff was not justified in retaining the money while at the same time asserting that its agent was guilty of fraud. It cannot take the benefits of its agent's contract, and at the same time repudiate its burdens. The case of *Hakes v. Myrick,* 69 Iowa, 189, recognizes this distinction, although it is not made as prominent as it might have been. As the account was fully settled by plaintiff's agent, it is not entitled to recover.—AFFIRMED.

|1

W. P. L. MUIR, Administrator, Appellant, v. M. J. MILLER, *et al.*

Fraudulent Conveyance. The defendant, being indebted to his wife for various loans made to him, evidenced by his two notes, trans-
1 ferred to her the note of a third party for a similar amount, in consideration of the cancellation of his notes. *Held,* to be a valuable consideration, and not in fraud of creditors.

HUSBAND AND WIFE. A wife has a right to secure the payment of her
2 just claim against her husband, however much it may hinder or
5 delay the collection of other claims.

SAME. Where the testimony in regard to loans by a wife to her husband is direct, reasonable and positive, and free from contradic-
4 tion, all presumptions of fraud that may arise from their relation
of husband and wife will be overcome.

DISCONNECTED TRANSFERS. A note given by a husband to his wife
for a good and sufficient consideration, is not void as to the hus-
3 band's creditors because another note was given by him to her
without consideration, in an entirely distinct transaction.

Appeal from Van Buren District Court.—HON. M. A.
ROBERTS, Judge.

MONDAY, OCTOBER 11, 1897.

GARNISHMENT proceedings, commenced as at law,
and subsequently transferred to the equity docket.
There was a hearing on the merits, and a decree, from
which the plaintiff appeals.—*Affirmed.*

Wherry & Walker for appellant.

Mitchell & Sloan for appellees.

ROBINSON, J. — In October, 1888, the plaintiff,
as administrator of the estate of S. J. Miller, deceased,
recovered in the Van Buren district court judgment
against the defendant M. J. Miller for the sum of two
thousand, two hundred and twenty-seven dollars and
twelve cents, with interest and costs. In July, 1891, a
general execution was issued on the judgment, and the
defendant Ellen L. Miller was garnished as a supposed
debtor of the defendant M. J. Miller, and her answers
were taken by a commissioner appointed by the court.
The answers thus taken showed that M. J. Miller was
the husband of the garnishee, and that she held and
claimed to own a note made to her by one Thomas
McAllister on the seventeenth day of January, 1888, for
the sum of two thousand dollars, with interest thereon
at the rate of eight per cent. per annum, on which

interest for three years had been paid. That note was
given in lieu of one which had been made by McAllister,
to S. J. Miller, the plaintiff's intestate, and which the
garnishee claims was transferred by him to her husband. The answers of the garnishee further state that
her husband surrendered that note, and caused the
note she holds to be made for it, in part payment of a
note which he was owing to her. To the answers of
the garnishee the plaintiff filed a pleading in which he
alleged that the surrender of the original McAllister
note, and the taking of a new one in lieu thereof, payable to the garnishee, was fraudulent, and for the purpose of aiding M. J. Miller to cheat and defraud his
creditors, and that he is insolvent. To that pleading
the garnishee filed a reply, in which she asserted that
she was the absolute owner of the McAllister note, and
denied the plaintiff's allegations of fraud. The reply
further pleaded an adjudication of the ownership of the
note in her favor by the circuit court of Scotland
county, in the state of Missouri. When the pleadings
had been filed, the cause was transferred to the equity
docket, as already stated. The district court found
and adjudged that the plea of former adjudication was
not sustained, that the transfer to the garnishee by her
husband of a note made by one Fatherson was not for
a valuable consideration, and in good faith, but that
the transfer of the McAllister note was valid and
invested the garnishee with the ownership thereof.
Judgment for the amount of the Fatherson note and
one-half the costs was rendered against the garnishee
in favor of the plaintiff. Since the garnishee does not
appeal, it is not necessary to review the action of the
district court so far as it related to the Fatherson
note.

I. In the year 1885, S. J. Miller, the father of the
defendant M. J. Miller, died intestate, and the plaintiff
was appointed and qualified as administrator of his

estate. Soon after the appointment of the plaintiff as stated, he commenced this action against M. J. Miller, claiming that in October, 1884, the decedent was feeble in body and mind, and incapable of transacting business of any importance, especially that of dividing or giving away his property; that in the month specified, and while the decedent was in the condition stated, M. J. Miller, by taking advantage of that condition, wrongfully obtained from the decedent, through persuasion and undue influence, money, promissory notes, mortgages, accounts, and securities of the aggregate value of six thousand, four hundred and thirty-nine dollars and fifty cents. Judgment for the possession of the property, or, if it could not be found, for its value, was demanded. The cause was tried to a jury in the year 1886, and a verdict for seven thousand, two hundred and twenty-two dollars and twenty-five cents was returned in favor of the plaintiff. All in excess of one thousand, eight hundred and forty-six dollars and forty-seven cents was remitted, and judgment for that amount, but not for the return of the property, was rendered in favor of the plaintiff. That judgment was reversed by this court on appeal (see 72 Iowa, 585), and in the year 1888 the case was again tried in the district court, and the result was a verdict and judgment in favor of the plaintiff for the sum of two thousand, two hundred and twenty-seven dollars and twelve cents, with interest and costs. It was an ordinary judgment for the recovery of money only, not authorizing the recovery of the property in dispute, and was affirmed by this court in the year 1891. See 82 Iowa, 700. Execution was issued on that judgment, and Ellen L. Miller was garnished thereunder, and that garnishment is the basis of the proceedings which we are asked to review.

It will be observed that the form of the judgment rendered in favor of the plaintiff precludes him from

claiming title to the McAllister note as the property
of the estate of which he is administrator. He relies
upon the claim that the note in controversy was the
property of M. J. Miller, but was transferred to his
wife fraudulently, for the purpose of placing it
1   beyond the reach of his creditors. The garnishee
testifies, in support of her claim, that the note
was given to her in payment of an indebtedness due
to her from her husband; that in the latter part of the
year 1878 she loaned to him four hundred dollars,
which she had earned by teaching and other work, for
which he gave her his note about October 15, 1878, and
that about the fifth day of April, 1882, he gave her his
note for nine hundred dollars, for that amount of
money which she loaned him at that time, and which
she had obtained from her father's estate; that each
note bore interest at the rate of ten per cent. per
annum; that no interest had been paid on the notes
until November, 1886, when her husband conveyed to
her certain property for the sum of four hundred and
fifty dollars, which was credited on the notes; that the
amount due her on these notes when the McAllister
note in controversy was given was two thousand and
sixteen dollars, and that she accepted that note for
two thousand dollars, and sixteen dollars, and some
cents in money, for the two notes of her husband, which
she surrendered to him. She is corroborated in regard to
the amount of money which she obtained from her father's estate by evidence which shows that she received
a tract of land from that estate valued at a little more
than eight hundred dollars, and which she sold, after
holding it for something more than one year, for eight
hundred and fifty dollars. That sum, and fifty dollars
which had been paid to her for one year's use of the
land, she states made up the amount she loaned to her
husband in the year 1882. Her testimony in regard to

the two loans she made to him, and in regard to the
sources from which she' obtained the money for that
purpose, is not in any manner contradicted, and shows
a good and sufficient consideration for the note
2   in controversy. The appellant contends that
because of the relationship existing between the
garnishee and M. J. Miller, the transaction in question
should be closely scrutinized, and attention is called
to the fact that some circumstances disclosed by the
evidence tend to show that the garnishee has not at
all times acted in good faith towards the creditors of
her husband, but manifested a disposition to aid him in
placing some of his property beyond their reach. Her
connection with the Fatherson note is cited as an
example of that kind. The evidence in regard to that
note was given by her husband, and it is said that her
testimony respecting the money she loaned to him
shows that she did not give any consideration for the
note. She did not testify directly in regard to it,
3   but, conceding that she did not take that note
in good faith, it does not follow that she was
guilty of any wrong in obtaining the note in suit. There
was no connection between the two transactions, and,
while it is true that this cause was pending against
the husband, and undetermined, and that she
4   probably knew that fact, yet she had a right to
secure the payment of her claim, even though
she knew that by making payment to her the husband
would be, to the amount of the payment, unable to pay
other creditors. If her object in getting the note in
suit was not to hinder or delay other creditors of her
husband, but only to obtain the amount justly due to
herself, the transaction was valid, however much it
may have hindered the collection of other claims. See
Fowler Co. v. McDonnell, 100 Iowa, 536; *Sprague
5   v. Benson*, 101 Iowa, 678. The testimony of the
garnishee in regard to the loans she made to her
husband, in payment of which the McAllister note was

taken, is so direct, reasonable and positive, and so free
from contradiction, that all the presumptions, if any,
which arise from the circumstances alleged to show
fraud, upon which the appellant relies, have been overcome, and the right of the garnishee to the note in controversy and the proceeds thereof must be regarded as
fully established. This conclusion makes it unnecessary to determine other questions discussed, and the
decree of the district court is AFFIRMED.

B. G. TIFFANY v. H. L. TIFFANY AND W. S. WORTHING-
TON, Guardian, Appellant.

Fraud: ESTOPPEL: *Equity.* One who takes title to land purchased
by him, in the name of his sister, for the purpose of defrauding
his wife, cannot in equity, and after the death of the sister, set up
the fraud to defeat his sister's title.

*Appeal from Hamilton District Court.—*HON. S. M.
WEAVER, Judge.

MONDAY, OCTOBER 11, 1897.

PLAINTIFF avers, as grounds for the relief asked, in
substance as follows: That he is the son and sole heir
of H. S. T. Jay, who died intestate December 23, 1891;
that the defendant H. L. Tiffany is a brother of said
deceased; that said H. L. Tiffany has been adjudged
insane, and the defendant Worthington is his duly-
appointed guardian; that prior to the death of H. S. T.
Jay, and the proceedings adjudging said Tiffany insane,
said Jay had given into hands of said Tiffany a large
sum of money to be loaned and to be invested in her
name; that said Tiffany so loaned and invested said
money for her benefit, and that no part thereof has been
repaid to said Jay, or to her estate; that part of said
money was invested in real estate described, and in

other real estate, title to some of which was taken in
the name of said H. S. T. Jay; that part of said money
was invested in notes, mortgages, and tax receipts in the
name of said Jay, about eight hundred dollars of which
have been paid to said Tiffany or his guardian. Plaintiff prays for an accounting, and for judgment, and that
his title be quieted and confirmed, with possession, to
such of the property as he may be entitled to. D. C.
Chase was appointed guardian *ad litem* for H. L. Tiffany, and appeared for said Tiffany, and answered,
"Denying each and every allegation in plaintiff's bill."
Decree was entered quieting title in plaintiff to the
premises as prayed for, with judgment against Worthington for costs, and the bill as to personal property
was dismissed without prejudice. Defendant appeals.—
Affirmed.

D. C. Chase for appellant.

J. L. Kamrar for appellee.

GIVEN, J.—I.   There is no dispute but that, in
1862, H. S. T. Jay did place in the hands of H. L. Tiffany
a certain sum of money, claimed by the plaintiff to have
been four hundred dollars, and by the defendant to
have been but two hundred and fifty dollars. Plaintiff
claims that this money was invested, and, with its
accumulations, re-invested from time to time, by Tiffany, for the benefit of his sister, and that the property
purchased and standing in her name was purchased
therefor, and that, in addition thereto, Tiffany is liable
for other sums realized from the investment of that
money and its accumulations. It is contended on behalf
of the defendant that Tiffany repaid all the money that
he received, many years ago, in sums of money paid to his
sister at different times, and two sewing machines furnished to her, and in support given to her and her son,

this plaintiff, in his family. It is further claimed by the defendant that about ten years ago,—long after his sister had been fully paid,—anticipating trouble with his wife, he, to prevent her from getting his property, commenced using the name of his sister in his business transactions for the purpose of covering his property from any claim that his wife might make thereon. Much of the evidence relied upon by the defendant to sustain his claim is clearly inadmissible, but, taking it all into consideration, it falls far short of being convincing, or satisfactory. Indeed, the claim of neither party can be said to be conclusively established. We are led to the conclusion that the matters relied upon as constituting payment of the sum received by Tiffany from his sister was not so intended, and that Tiffany did retain her money, and invested it to some extent, as claimed, taking title to her in some instances. If it be true, as claimed by the defendant, that he took title to property purchased in the name of his sister to defraud his wife, he will not now be heard to assert that fact to defeat her title. It is true, he was adjudged insane, but it is neither alleged nor contended that his insanity is ground for applying any different rule. It is not alleged nor shown that he was insane at the time he took these titles in the name of his sister. While, as we have said, the evidence is not entirely satisfactory, we think the preponderance is in favor of the plaintiff as to the real estate, the title to which is in his deceased mother, and therefore the decree of the district court is AFFIRMED.

L. H. DUNHAM, J. L. SLOAN, and MARY B. DUNHAM, Appellants, v. ALBERT BENTLEY, Defendant, and J. L. STAMAN, Administrator, Garnishee, PHILOMA BENTLEY AND MURRAY & FARR, Interveners.

Husband and Wife: CONVERSION: *Creditors.* While money given by a wife to her husband, without promise of repayment, will not
4 enable her to base a claim against his creditors, this rule has no application to cases where her rights against the husband might be enforced by suit under section 2204, Code, 1878, and hence a
5 settlement in which the wife takes an assignment of a note on account of her property which her husband has *converted*, is valid against his creditors.

Attorney's Fees: ORDER OF COURT. A son contracted that his attorneys should have twenty per cent. of his share of his father's estate, for services rendered in proceedings brought to appoint a guardian for his father, on account of insanity. At the end of
7 the controversy the court ordered payment to said attorneys of a certain sum out of the father's estate, with proviso that it should be in full compensation for all services rendered, and the attorneys accepted said sum under protest. *Held,* they could claim nothing under the son's contract, as it would be presumed that they had received full compensation.

CHAMPERTY: *Fraud.* An agreement by one to whom her husband has assigned his interest in his father's estate, to pay attorneys a
6 specified per cent. of the claim for protecting her interest as against the creditors of her husband, is valid if the assignment was valid.

Contingent Interest Sale: RATIFICATION. Though an assignment of
8 a son's prospective interest in a father's estate is invalid, yet it may become operative by a ratification after the father's death.

Executions: REVIVOR. An execution issued in the name of a deceased plaintiff is absolutely void where there is no indorse-
1 ment thereon of the name of his representatives, as required by Code 1878, section 3130.

ABANDONMENT. The issuance of a void execution does not operate as
2 an abandonment of a prior execution.

RETURN. The return of an execution does not, under Code 1878, sec-
3 tion 3052, affect garnishment proceedings commenced after the issuance of the execution.

Appeal from Jackson District Court.—HON. WILLIAM
F. BRANNAN, Judge.

MONDAY, OCTOBER 11, 1897.

IN 1886, L. B. Dunham obtained a judgment against
Albert Bentley for nine hundred and sixty-seven dollars
and forty-two cents. The judgment plaintiff died in
1892, and, on August 19, 1893, execution was issued on
this judgment in the name of L. H. Dunham, as administrator of L. B. Dunham, deceased, on which appeared,
in the handwriting of the clerk, the indorsement: "L.
H. Dunham appointed administrator of the estate of
L. B. Dunham, and his commission as such is still in
force." J. L. Staman, as administrator of David Bentley, deceased, and others, were duly garnished, and the
execution returned by the sheriff October 4, 1893. A
new execution in the name of L. B. Dunham, without
any indorsement, was issued April 23, 1894, and Staman
again garnished. December 8 following, Staman
answered that, as administrator of the estate of David
Bentley, he then held the sum of eight hundred and
twenty-five dollars as Albert Bentley's share of his
father's estate, and that this was claimed by Philoma
Bentley and Murray & Farr. Thereafter such claimants
filed a petition of intervention, setting up an assignment of Albert Bentley's share in his father's estate,
made January 28, 1893, and ratified shortly after the
death of David B. Bentley. L. H. Dunham, J. L. Sloan,
and Mary B. Dunham, as heirs and persons entitled to
the estate of L. B. Dunham, deceased, attack the assignment as being fraudulent and without consideration.
Trial to court, judgment for interveners, and L. H. Dunham, J. L. Sloan, and Mary B. Dunham appeal.—
Reversed.

Levi Keck and *D. A. Wynkoop* for appellants.

Hayes & Schuyler, Wm. Graham, and *Murray &. Farr* for appellees.

LADD, J.—The judgment plaintiff died before the second execution was issued. No indorsement what-ever was made by the clerk, as required by section 3130 of the Code of 1873, and the defendant has entered no complaint of this omission, though, under section 3134, he might have enjoined or moved to quash the execution. The record, then, raises the question whether an execution without indorse-ment, issued after the death of the judgment plaintiff, is void, or only voidable. A judgment, at common law, became dormant in a year and a day, but it might be revived by resort to the *scire facias.* An execution issued after the lapse of this time, and without so doing, was only voidable. If the defendant chose to interpose no objection to its regularity, others could not do so for him, and he was not permitted to do so collaterally. Freeman, Executions, section 29. Where the time within which execution may be issued has been extended by statute, the same rule is adopted. *Mariner v. Coon*, 16 Wis. 468; *Bank v. Spencer*, 18 N. Y. 154. So, too, where the time within which an execution may issue after a previous one, is limited, an execution issued therefor, without revivor has been adjudged voidable only. *Gard-ner v. Railway Co.*, 102 Ala. 635 (48 Am. St. 84, 15 South. Rep. 271); *Eddy v. Coldwell*, 23 Or. 163 (37 Am. St. 672, 31 Pac. Rep. 475.) In analogy with the principle involved in these cases some courts have held an execution issued after the judgment creditor's death, and without revivor, not void. *Day v. Sharp*, 34 Am. Dec. 509; *Hughes v. Wilkinson*, 37 Miss. 482; *Darlington v. Speakman*, 9 Watts & S. 182; *Jenness v. Lapeer*, 42 Mich. 469 (4 N. W. Rep. 220). With

1

better reason such an execution has been adjudged void
on two grounds: (1) By the death of plaintiff, the party
to whom authority was given to enforce the judgment
is withdrawn; (2) a new party, benefited and concerned
in the judgment, is introduced in the record. *Brown v.
Parker*, 15 Ill. 307; *Meyer v. Mintonye*, 106 Ill. 414; *Bel-
linger v. Ford*, 21 Barb. 311; *Morgan v. Taylor*, 38 N. J.
Law, 317; *Stewart v. Nuckols*, 50 Am. Dec. 127. This
last case overrules *Day v. Sharp, supra*. The grounds
for holding such an execution void seem unassailable.
If the sole plaintiff is dead, the right of another to stand
in his stead ought to be first determined, and the record
show in whose behalf the benefits accruing under the
judgment are taken. This insures the proper application of the amount collected to the satisfaction of the
debt. It avoids an unexplained variance in the record.
That letters of administration have issued is not presumed, and the authority given plaintiff to resort to the
legal processes of compulsory payment ought not to be
exercised by another until his rights to do so be fully
ascertained. Such a rule serves a double purpose; it
guards the rights of the judgment defendant, and protects the property of the deceased plaintiff. The provisions of the statute recognize, rather than obviate, the
necessity of some kind of a revivor. Upon the filing of an
affidavit with the clerk of court, setting forth the death
of the plaintiff, the names of his heirs or representatives,
and, if the latter, accompanied by a certificate of qualification, he is required to indorse on the execution the fact
of such death, and the names of those entitled to the
judgment; and when this is done the sheriff proceeds as
though the parties whose names are so indorsed were
the only plaintiffs. Sections 3131-3133, Code 1873. If
the personal representatives or heirs are not properly
stated in the indorsement, the execution may be
quashed; and, if not entitled to the judgment, its
enforcement may be enjoined. Section 3134. A remedy

is thus provided where there is a defective indorsement;
none, in event of no indorsement. Nor, in such a case,
was any necessary, as the execution, being void, would
be no protection in the hands of the officer, and a levy
thereunder amount to no more than a trespass. This
view is in harmony with the conclusion arrived at in
Meek v. Bunker, 33 Iowa, 169, where it is said of such
an execution that it "could not have vitality to sustain
a levy," and that, "being invalid, the property levied
upon under it could not be held." See *White v. Secor,*
58 Iowa, 533. It follows that the execution was void,
and the garnishee not held thereunder.

II. The issuance of the second execution, as it was
void, did not amount to an abandonment of the first
one. *West v. St. John,* 63 Iowa, 287; *Friyer v. Mc-
Naughton,* 67 N. W. Rep. 978 (Mich.). Nor
2   did the return of the first execution in any way
affect the garnishment proceedings. Section
3052, Code 1873. The proceeds thereof may be readily
appropriated, under the order of the court, to the satisfaction of the judgment, without the use of the original
execution. No question is made as to the sufficiency of
the indorsement on the first execution, and any property
held by Staman, as administrator of David Bentley,
deceased, belonging to the defendant Albert Bentley,
must be accounted for thereunder.

III. The assignment by the defendant of his
prospective share in his father's estate to Philoma Bentley and Murray & Farr prior to his father's death was
fully ratified after that event, so that the policy
3   of permitting transfers of contingent interests of
this character need not be considered. But the
plaintiffs contend that there was no consideration for
the assignment to Philoma Bentley. The evidence,

when fairly considered, quite satisfactorily shows that
she received one thousand dollars from her
4   father's estate, and afterwards loaned it to Morris & Griffin, taking their note therefor; and that
she received a note of five hundred dollars from the
estate of her mother. These notes were collected by her
husband, the defendant, in 1883, and the proceeds
appropriated by him to his own use. With six per cent.
interest, the sums so appropriated, together with forty-
five dollars loaned to him, amounted to something over
two thousand dollars in 1886, and for this amount he
then executed his promissory note, which is the consideration of the assignment. It will thus be seen that
the facts in this case do not bring it within the rule
that a gift of money or property by the wife to the husband without any promise to return or repay as a consideration will not sustain a subsequent transfer of
property by the husband to her when attacked by creditors. *Hanson v. Manley,* 72 Iowa, 51; *Porter v. Globe,*
88 Iowa, 565. Here the wife did not give or loan money
to her husband. He simply took the notes, collected
them, and appropriated the proceeds to his own use.
He was under the same obligation to account to his
wife for this misappropriated money as he would have
been in case of a stranger. Section 2204 of the Code of
1873 provides that when either husband or wife obtains
possession or control of property belonging to the other,
the owner of such property may maintain an
5   action therefor. If Mrs. Bentley could maintain
an action for this money, as she surely had the
right to do under this section, then certainly she could
settle the claim by taking the note. But it is insisted
that she was never the owner of the note. It was
executed at a late hour of the night, and at the time of
several other transactions, and was handed to her the
next day. She then indorsed it to Hosea Goodenow, to

whom her husband had transferred substantially all his
property. The purpose seems to have been that any
surplus remaining after satisfying the indebtedness due
Goodenow be applied on her note. Goodenow sent the
note back to Mrs. Bentley through his son. We think
the evidence warrants the conclusion that the note
remained the property of Mrs. Bentley, and was only
indorsed to Goodenow for the purpose above stated.

IV. A contract was entered into between Mrs.
Bentley and Murray & Farr, by the terms of which the
firm was to receive thirty per centum of the money in
the hands of the administrator, for their services in protecting Mrs. Bentley's interest in such property against
the suit of Dunham and other creditors of defendant,
and for collecting the same. This contract, it is
6   said, is void, because its purpose was to aid the
assignee in defeating the defendant's creditors.
Such an agreement, when carried out, and made effective, may have that result, because inevitable in protecting the *bona fide* rights of the purchaser. If there was
a fraudulent purpose in the original transfer of the
property, neither the purchaser nor the contingent
interest of the attorney will be protected. But, if this
property belonged to Mrs. Bentley, then she had the
right, under the decisions of this court, to contract payment of a portion of the property recovered for the services of her attorneys in protecting it. *Winslow v. Railway Co.*, 71 Iowa, 197; *Jewel v. Neidy*, 61 Iowa, 299;
McDonald v. Railway Co., 29 Iowa, 170.

V. Under the assignment of the defendant, Murray & Farr were to receive twenty per centum of the
net share of the defendant in his father's estate, for
services by them rendered as attorneys in first resisting
the appointment of a guardian for his father, and after-

wards procuring the appointment thereof because of
insanity.   At the end of that controversy the
7   attorneys engaged therein filed a stipulation that
each firm receive out of the estate, for services,
the sum of one hundred and fifty dollars.   The court
ordered the payment of this amount, but provided that
it should be in full compensation for all services rendered. This condition in the record entry was known
to Murray & Farr, and, though they protested, they
received the money. On what ground the protest was
based we can only surmise, as it does not appear in the
record. We conclude that it must have been owing to
the fact that this condition was not contained in the
stipulation. That the court was authorized to fix the
fees for the services rendered is not questioned, nor
could it be after receiving the payment provided. The
firm had the option of taking or refusing this money,
but, having taken it, they are not in a situation to object
to the condition on which it was paid. If the order was
erroneous, it might have been modified or corrected.
The value of the services rendered does not appear, and,
in the absence of evidence, it will be presumed the compensation allowed by the court was entirely adequate.
Having received payment in full from the guardian of
David Bentley, whose estate was primarily liable for
such services, compensation cannot be exacted a second
time from Albert Bentley, or his property. Nor will
the assignee be permitted to accomplish indirectly that
which could not have been done in direct action. The
consideration for the assignment having been fully discharged, it cannot be insisted on as against Albert Bentley nor his creditors, who are permitted to avail themselves of every defense he might urge. The twenty per
centum of his inheritance remained his property, and
should be applied in satisfaction of the judgment.—
REVERSED.

MICHAEL ZIMMERMAN V. C. B. BRANNON AND C. HOLLI-
DAY, Appellants.

Fraud in Sale: EVIDENCE ON INTENT. Where plaintiff alleged fraud
in the sale of hogs that he purchased out of a drove, from defend-
1 ants, their statements, as to the soundness of the hogs in the
drove, made to other prospective purchasers, are admissible in
evidence to show their intent in making representations of soundness to plaintiff.

SAME: Where defendants sold hogs that were affected with cholera
2 and that had come from certain stock yards, where there had been
hog cholera for years, it is proper to show that defendants falsely
stated that the hogs came from some other place, on the question
of fraud in selling the hogs, as tending to show defendant's
knowledge as to the condition of the hogs.

CONSTRUCTION OF WARRANTY. Defendant, sued on a warranty, that
4 hogs sold by him were all right and healthy, cannot testify that he
did not intend to guarantee the hogs, where his language would
fairly import a warranty.

Instructions. Though an instruction is erroneous when considered
3 alone, yet it is not reversible error, where such instruction, taken
together with other instructions, gives the proper rule, so that the
jury could not have misapprehended the law of the case.

Appeal from Wayne District Court.—HON. H. M.
TOWNER, Judge.

MONDAY, OCTOBER 11, 1897.

THE defendants bought, at the stock yards at
Omaha, Neb., a lot of hogs, and shipped them to Corydon, Iowa, and sold four of them to the plaintiff. Three
of them afterwards died of hog cholera, or swine
plague, and plaintiff brings this action to recover damages, alleging fraud in the sale, and a warranty that the
hogs were sound and free from disease. The answer

was a general denial. Upon the trial there was a verdict for the plaintiff, and from a judgment thereon the
defendants appealed.—*Affirmed.*

Miles & Steele for appellant.

Freeland & Evans for appellee.

GRANGER, J. — I.   Of the hogs shipped to Corydon, some were sold to James Keho and to others, and
parties talked with defendants with a view of buying,
but did not. It appears that some of the hogs
1   were diseased when sold, and died soon after,
Keho, and some others, who purchased, and
others who talked with defendants about the hogs, but
did not purchase, were witnesses for the plaintiff, and
were permitted to state, against objections, that
defendant Brannon, who did the selling, represented
the hogs as all right, and healthy. The court, in admitting the evidence, regarded it proper on the question of
fraud. The evidence was as to the same lot of hogs
from which plaintiff purchased, and the statements by
Brannon were made about the time of plaintiff's purchase, but not in his presence. It appears from the evidence that hog cholera had been in the stock yards at
Omaha for years, and that the hogs came from those
yards; but it does not appear that any of these hogs
were diseased while there. It is in evidence that there
was no appearance of disease among those hogs while
at the yards in Omaha. It clearly appears that the
hogs did not appear well in the yards at Corydon, and
that Brannon accounted for their appearance because
of being jammed on the train, and worried. There is
considerable in the evidence from which it might be
found that Brannon had reason to believe the hogs
were not healthy; and as he was, at the time of the
different conversations, engaged in the sale of the

same lot of hogs, we think his statements to the different persons were proper to be considered in determining his motives or intent in making the representation of soundness to the plaintiff. The rule has clear support in *Porter v. Stone,* 62 Iowa, 442, and also in *Starr v. Stevenson,* 91 Iowa, 684. See, also, *Baldwin v. Short,* 125 N. Y. App. 553 (26 N. E. Rep. 928). In *Mather v. Robinson,* 47 Iowa, 403, it is said: "It cannot be proven that fraudulent representations are made to one person because the same or other false representations were made to another." The statement is not incorrect, taken literally. It should not, however, be construed as meaning that other fraudulent acts may not be shown in corroboration of other proof to show a fraudulent intent, in a proper case. In *Gardner v. Trenary,* 65 Iowa, 646, there is no more than a statement that the rule might be as claimed by appellants in this case, but not an announcement of such a rule. The later cases have clearly put the rule at rest, so that any seeming conflict should be regarded as settled. In *Land Co. v. Heilman,* 80 Iowa, 477, it appears that the representations held to be improperly in evidence were such as could not have influenced the making of the contract, and held improper for that reason. The question involved in this case was not considered in that.

II.   Thomas Beal was a witness for plaintiff, and he was permitted to testify that Brannon told him he bought the hogs at Lincoln, Neb. The ruling is thought to be error, because the issues present no such question.

2   There was no error. The testimony was proper on the question of fraud. It appeared that cholera had been in the yards at Omaha, and such a false statement might well be considered on the question of Brannon's knowledge or belief as to the condition of the hogs. The purpose of the statement must have been to avoid the suspicions as to the disease, if the hogs came from the yards at Omaha. It

was a fraudulent statement, made about the time of the sale to plaintiff, and under the rule of *Starr v. Stevenson, supra,* it was proper to be shown.

III. It is contended by appellants that, in order to constitute a warranty because of an affirmation of quality, on which the buyer relies, it must appear that the parties, including the seller, intended a warranty; and this seems to be the rule as stated in *Figge v. Hill,* 61 Iowa, 430, and other cases. The difficulty is, that appellants have selected one instruction, which, considered alone, would be erroneous, but, when considered with other instructions, gives, we think, the rule contended for. The instructions from 1 to 4 are on the subject of warranty, and the following is No. 2: "The words 'warrant' or 'warranty' need not be used to constitute a warranty. Neither is it necessary that it be shown the seller intended to cheat or deceive the purchaser in the sale. Nor is it necessary, as to this issue, that it appear the seller at the time knew the representations made to be false. The purchaser has a right to believe and rely on said statements made, if such statements constitute a warranty. But mere praise or commendation of property offered for sale does not constitute a warranty. Neither is a bare affirmation of the soundness of an animal exposed for sale, of itself, a warranty. It must appear that the seller intended, by statements made to the purchaser as to the quality or condition of the thing sold, that such statements should be believed and relied on, and thus be effective and operative in effecting the sale; and this intention is to be determined by the jury from the language used, and the acts of the parties at the time, and the circumstances surrounding the transaction, as disclosed by the testimony." With other instructions on the subject, it is a full compliance with the rule given in *Figge v. Hill, supra.* The instruction does no less than make the warranty depend on the intention of the parties.

IV. Brannon was a witness for the defense, and on direct examination he was asked this question: "Now, I will ask you to state if, in any of those conversations or statements you had with Mr. Zimmerman at the time he purchased these hogs, or during the negotiations of this trade, if there was any intent on your part to guarantee those hogs." The answer was excluded on objection by plaintiff, and the ruling is said to be error. A rule in substantially the following language has many times been stated: "It is a general rule that, where the intention or motive of a witness is a material question in the case, the witness may state what his intention or motive was." The language quoted was used in *Frost v. Rosecrans*, 66 Iowa, 405. Quite similar language is used in *Watson v. Chesire*, 18 Iowa, 202, and in *Browne v. Hickie*, 68 Iowa, 330. The first two cited cases involve issues of fraud, and in such issues, as well as those involving malice or criminal intent, as material facts in the case, the rule, as stated, is apparently universal. Nearly all the cases to which we are referred involve such issues. See *Heap v. Parrish*, 104 Ind. 36 (3 N. E. Rep. 549); *Kerrains v. People*, 60 N. Y. 221; *Spalding v. Lowe*, 56 Mich. 366 (23 N. W. Rep. 46). In *Delano v. Goodwin*, 48 N. H. 203, an action on contract, the following language is used: "Before the statute making parties competent witnesses, the ordinary way to prove their intent or understanding was by circumstantial evidence. But, now that the party himself is admittted to testify, there is no reason for confining his testimony to a variety of circumstances tending to show his purpose or understanding, when he knows and can testify directly what that purpose or understanding was. Accordingly it has been held, that

where the intention or good faith of a party to a
suit becomes material, it may be shown directly as
well as from circumstances; and the party himself, if
a competent witness, may testify to his intention or
understanding, unless prevented by some other principle of law applicable to the case." We have seen no
broader statement of the rule than this, and this statement recognizes that there are cases to which the rule
is not applicable. We have cited *Browne v. Hickie* as
stating the rule of appellant's contention, but it is
there stated only to show that the case is an exception,
and not governed by it. After citing *Watson v.
Cheshire* and *Frost v. Rosecrans, supra,* it is said: "But
the present case is not governed by that rule. The questions to be determined were whether the parties
entered into a contract for the termination of the lease,
and, if so, what were the terms and conditions of their
agreement. These questions must be determined from
the conduct and language of the parties during the
negotiations. If an agreement was entered into by the
parties, the undertaking of plaintiff therein must be
determined alone from what was said and done by him
at the time. His secret motives or intentions are
entirely immaterial." The question of intent was as
clearly involved in that case as in this. It hardly needs
argument to show the danger of such a rule in this class
of cases, where, after language is used on which a
party relies as a warranty, and on which he has a right
to rely, the other party may go behind the fair understanding from his language, and say, "I did not so
intend," and thus do injustice to another by taking
advantage of his own wrong. The rule that permits the
intention to be found from the acts and words of the
parties places them on an equality, which is desirable
in the administration of justice. The case differs from
those in which a specific unlawful intent is pleaded in

avoidance of a contract, as in *Counselman v. Reichart,* 103 Iowa, *post.* See, also, *Selz v. Belden,* 48 Iowa, 451.

V. It is thought that there is a conflict between the second and fourth instructions that constitutes reversible error. We have said that the fourth instruction, taken alone, is erroneous; but, when the instructions are taken together, we think the jury could not have misapprehended the law of the case. Conceding a technical error in the fourth instruction, we should not reverse the case because of it. The judgment will stand AFFIRMED.

O. R. SHULTZ v. A. P. GRIFFITH, Appellant.

Dogs: LIABILITY OF OWNER FOR INJURY BY. Under Code, section 1485, making the owner of a dog liable to a person injured, for all damages done by it, except when such person is doing an unlawful act, negligence of the person injured does not exempt the owner from liability, unless the negligence amounts to an unlawful act.

RULE APPLIED. Plaintiff left his horse and buggy in defendant's livery stable, and at about 8 P. M. went into the barn yard to see that his buggy was put under shelter; and to get some articles therefrom While at the buggy, he was bitten by defendant's dog. *Held,* that, though the property was in care of defendant, plaintiff was not a trespasser in going to it when and for the purpose he did, without permission, and it is immaterial whether defendant's employes knew of his presence.

EVIDENCE OF OWNERSHIP. A person having a dog in his possession, and harboring it on his premises, as owners of dogs usually do, will be deemed the owner of the dog, in an action unner Code, section 1485, for injuries done by it.

Pleading: DAMAGES: *Future suffering.* Future pain and anguish cannot be considered in assessing damages under a pleading which alleges pain and injury in the past tense only, where the petition does not allege that there has been a failure to make recovery and where the evidence is confined to showing disablement up to time of trial.

Negligence Defined. An instruction that "negligence is the failure or
8 omission to do that which an ordinary prudent and cautious man
   would do under similar circumstances" is incomplete as lacking
   the element of commission.

Appeal from Bremer District Court.—HON. P. W. BURR,
Judge.

TUESDAY. OCTOBER 12, 1897.

ACTION to recover damages alleged to have been
caused by plaintiff's being bitten by a dog owned by
defendant. Defendant answered, denying generally,
and a verdict and judgment were rendered for plaintiff
for four hundred dollars. Defendant appeals.—
Reversed.

G. W. Ruddick for appellant.

Gibson & Dawson for appellee.

GIVEN, J.—I. The following facts are undisputed: Defendant was the keeper of a feed and livery
barn open to patronage by the public. The plaintiff
was traveling by team, and on the evening of October
2, 1894, he left his team and buggy in care of the defendant, to be kept in said barn over night, for which he
        paid seventy-five cents. When the team was put
1   in the barn, the buggy was left standing near by
        in the barn yard. Between 8 and half past 8
o'clock that evening plaintiff went into the barn yard
for the purpose of seeing that his buggy was put under
shelter, and of getting some articles belonging to him,
therefrom. While at the buggy he was attacked and bitten on the leg by a dog, which caused a painful wound.
The only disputes as to facts are whether defendant's employes at work at the barn knew of plaintiff's
presence before he was bitten, and the identity and ownership of the dog, and the extent of the injury. In the

view we take of the case, it is not material to plaintiff's right to recover whether his presence was known to defendant's employes or not. We think the jury was warranted in finding, under the instructions, that defendant owned the dog that did the biting, and that plaintiff was injured to the extent returned.

II. We have said the jury was warranted in finding as it did under the instructions, but the question remains whether the court erred in giving or refusing instructions in any of the particulars complained of. The court instructed that "under the laws of the state of Iowa the owner of any dog attacking or attempting to bite any person without fault or negligence upon the part of the person injured shall be liable to the person so injured for all damages done by his dog, except when the party injured is doing an unlawful act." Appellant does not complain of this instruction, and, as will be seen hereafter, could not reasonably do so. Following this, the court instructed to the effect that, if the jury found the facts to be as we have stated them above, then "that his going on said premises for said purpose at the time he states he did go there was not unlawful, and you should not so find it to be." Appellant asked an instruction, which was refused, as follows: "The defendant would be bound to keep the property until the next morning, and, if the plaintiff wished to take possession before that time, he should ask permission of defendant, and if he went upon the defendant's premises to intermeddle with the property so left, without permission of defendant, he would be doing an unlawful act, and your verdict must be for the defendant." The instruction given is correct, and there was no error in refusing that asked. The barn and yard were places to which the patrons of the business were invited to come at seasonable hours. Plaintiff went there before half past 8 o'clock in the evening, and while defendant's son and a hired hand, with a lighted lantern, were at work at the barn. He went there to see that his buggy was put under shelter, and to get some article belonging to him, from the buggy. Surely the time was seasonable, the purpose proper, and, therefore, the act was not unlawful. Though the property was in the care of defendant, plaintiff was not a trespasser in going to it when and for the purpose that he did, without permission, and it is, therefore, immaterial whether defendant's employes knew of his presence or not.

III.   The court instructed that "negligence is the failure or omission to do that which an ordinary prudent and cautious man would do under similar or like circumstances." Appellant contends, and cor-

3   rectly so, that this is an incomplete definition, and that the words, "or doing something that a reasonable person would not do," should be added. The question of negligence involved in this case, under the instruction first referred to, was of commission, and not omission. These two instructions, taken together, were more favorable to appellant than he was entitled to, and therefore not prejudicial to him. Section 1485 of the Code makes the owner of the dog "liable to the party injured for all damages done by his dog, except when the party is doing an unlawful act." Negligence by the injured party, whether of omission or commission, does not exempt the owner of the dog from liability, unless that negligence amounts to an unlawful act. We think the court erred in giving any instruction on the subject of negligence, as mere negligence, not amounting to an unlawful act, is no defense. These instructions were more favorable to appellant than he was entitled to, and therefore not prejudicial to him.

IV.   On the question of the ownership of the dog the court gave this instruction: "If you find from the

weight of the evidence introduced on the trial that the
dog was in the possession of the defendant, and
4   that the defendant was harboring him on his
premises, as owners usually do with their dogs,
then he will be deemed to be the owner of the dog,
within the meaning of the law." It is true that, under
said section 1485, it is only owners of dogs that are made
liable, but possession and harboring, as owners usually
do, have been held to be sufficient evidence of ownership.
See *O'Harra v. Miller* 64 Iowa, 462. There is no error in
this instruction.

. V.   On the question of damage the court gave this
instruction: "(2) If you find for the plaintiff, then in
assessing his damages you may allow him such sum as,
under the evidence, you find will compensate him for
the wound he received as shown by the evidence, if any;
the pain and anguish, mental and physical, if any,
which he has suffered, or which the evidence
5   shows it is reasonably certain he will hereafter
suffer, if shown by the evidence, and caused by
the injuries received." Appellant contends that no
claim is made in the petition for future pain and
anguish, and that, therefore, the court erred in submitting that as an element of damage. It is alleged in the
petition that by reason of the wound "plaintiff became
sick, sore, and lame, and suffered great bodily and
mental pain and anguish, and continued to suffer for
a long time thereafter; that plaintiff has suffered great
pain and loss of time, and was put to great expense."
These allegations are all in the past tense, and do not
even inferentially allege or claim damages for future
pain or anguish. Appellee cites *Meier v. Shrunk*, 79
Iowa, 22. In that case the plaintiff alleged that he was
not yet recovered from injuries, and we held that was
a sufficient allegation to warrant the court in submit-.
ting the question as to future damages. Appellee contends that the fair import of this ruling is that, when

the petition does not show a recovery, future damages
may be submitted to the jury. Its import plainly is
that the claim is only to be submitted when the petition
alleges that there has not been a recovery. Appellee contends that evidence of future disability was admitted
without objection, and therefore the instruction was
proper. Whether that would justify the instruction we
need not determine, as we do not find that such evidence
was introduced. True, p'a'ntiff testified to his condition up to and at the time of the trial, but there is no
evidence whatever to show that that condition would
continue. Even his attending physician was not asked
whether the injuries were such as to cause future pa'n
or anguish. Our conclusion is that the court erred in
instructing the jury to consider future pain and anguish
in assessing damages, and that appellant was prejudiced thereby. For this reason the judgment of the
district court is REVERSED.

EDWARD H. GILLETTE, Appellant, v. THOMAS MEREDITH.

Estoppel. A director in a corporation, who acquiesces in the acts of
other directors in urging and inducing a third person to purchase
a mortgage executed by the corporation, to prevent its foreclosure,
is estopped as against such purchaser to deny the validity of the
mortgage.

Appeal from Polk District Court.—HON. T. F. STEVEN-
SON, Judge.

TUESDAY, OCTOBER 12, 1897

ACTION to enjoin the foreclosure of defendant's
mortgage executed by the Farmers' Tribune Company.
From a decree dismissing the plaintiff's petition, he
appeals.— *Affirmed.*

C. C. Cole for appellant.

Mackenzie & Dewey and *Read & Read* for appellee.

LADD, J.—A newspaper known as the *Iowa Trib-une* was established by J. B. Weaver and E. H. Gillette, and then transferred to the Iowa Tribune Publishing Company. Afterwards, the property of this company was sold to the Farmers' Tribune Company, a part of the consideration being the assumption of all the indebtedness of the former company, including certain notes of Weaver and Gillette to S. S. Gillette, which the Iowa Tribune Publishing Company had agreed to pay. Under a decree in an action for divorce, Gillette became owner of the indebtedness on these notes, and, as such creditor of the Farmers' Tribune Company, instituted this action to enjoin the foreclosure of the defendant's mortgage. This mortgage appears to have been executed by said company to F. H. Hunter, October 25, 1892, securing three notes, amounting to two thousand, four hundred and seventy-eight dollars and forty-four cents. Gue had a claim against the company of one thousand, two hundred and sixty-three dollars and thirty-three cents, and to him Wooster assigned his claim of seven hundred and three dollars and eleven cents, Roe his of four hundred dollars, and Scott his of one hundred and four dollars and eighty cents. All these were transferred to Hunter, who thereupon demanded payment, and received the notes and mortgage in settlement. The plaintiff insists that only four of the nine directors were present at the meeting authorizing the execution of the mortgage, which covered all the property of the company, and that it had its inception in fraud, and was without consideration. In the view we take of the case, it is not necessary to inquire into the validity of the indebtedness, or whether all requirements were observed in giving the mortgage. It is enough to say that the records of the company show that five of the nine directors were present ordering the making of the notes and mortgage, and the defendant purchased them without any notice whatever of the fraud alleged or want of consideration, if such there was, or of the fact that Hunter was not the unqualified owner. The defendant pleads that plaintiff is estopped from questioning the validity of his mortgage, and the evidence fully sustains the plea.

When the first note became due, Hunter began foreclosure proceedings, and the defendant, as one of the directors, was importuned by at least four other directors to purchase the mortgage, and avoid foreclosure. The defendant lived at Atlantic, and Wooster, to induce him to part with his money, labored with him two days and a night without avail. Scott and Roe made the same attempt, only to fail. Weaver, with one of these, interviewed him, with no better results. Finally, he was telegraphed to come to Des Moines, and, by the representations of the four parties named, all of whom were directors of the company, was induced to buy and take an assignment of the mortgage. Gillette, who was also a director, knew of the efforts being put forth and the purpose had in doing so, and, as he says, acquiesced in what the rest did. He had an interest other than director and creditor, for, under an agreement with the company, he and Weaver had recently sold a large amount of stock on their representation that it was a good investment, and a foreclosure "would cut out all these parties" purchasing. He testifies that "the situation was extremely distressing to us, and therefore the effort to get Col. Meredith to purchase that mortgage to prevent its foreclosure." He afterwards admitted to Meredith "having told them to go and get five thousand dollars of you to pay those mortgages off, and put that paper on its feet." At a meeting

of the stockholders, in November, 1892, after the execution of the mortgage, and before its purchase by Meredith, Gillette being present, a resolution was adopted
unanimously ordering the directors, by mortgage or
otherwise, to liquidate the indebtedness of the concern
in whole or in part. But the plaintiff says he did not
know of the defects inhering in the mortgage until
shortly before this action was begun, sixteen months
afterwards. He heard of the giving of the mortgage,
however, a few days after its execution, and says he was
astonished by the information. By the exercise of
ordinary diligence, he might have known all the circumstances connected with the mortgage, and as, in
the capacity of director, he was charged with the protection and care of the company's property, he ought
to have learned these before encouraging the purchase
of the security. The plaintiff insists that he sent no one
to Meredith, but the evidence shows that he was fully
informed of what the others were doing, and fully
acquiesced therein, and encouraged every effort to
induce Meredith to make the purchase, and was very
anxious for him to do so. He was willing to stand by,
as he testifies, and see Meredith put his money into an
enterprise that he knew was ruined a year before, for
he "wanted to see that paper rise like an eagle out of
its ashes." The defendant having acted in such complete harmony with the wishes and aspirations of the
plaintiff, and having been induced to purchase the mortgage by the efforts and representations of the four
directors, in all of which the plaintiff fully acquiesced
and agreed, he will not now be permitted to question
the transaction or the title to the property purchased.—
AFFIRMED.

THE FARMERS' TRUST COMPANY, Appellant, v. ANNA
LINN, Intervener.

Fraudulent Conveyance: EVIDENCE. Where money is obtained by a
loan on the homestead, standing in the name of the wife, a purchase of personalty in the name of the wife, paid for by a portion
of the money so obtained, is not fraudulent as to the creditors of
the husband.

Appeal from Woodbury District Court.—HON. G. W.
WAKEFIELD, Judge.

TUESDAY, OCTOBER 12, 1897.

THIS action was commenced at law against the
defendant, Charles Linn, to recover the amount of a
promissory note, and was aided by attachment. The
writ of attachment was levied upon a grading machine
of which the intervener claims to be the owner. Her
claim of ownership was presented by a petition of intervention, to which the plaintiff filed an answer. There
was a trial by jury on the issues thus presented, which
resulted in special findings and a judgment in favor of
the intervener. The plaintiff appeals.—*Affirmed.*

Lohr, Gardiner & Lohr for appellant.

Carter & Brown for appellee.

ROBINSON, J. — I.   On the twenty-fourth day of
July, 1890, Charles Linn entered into an agreement
in writing with the Austin Manufacturing Company
for the purchase of the grader in question. It was
delivered to him, and on the twelfth day of August,
1890, he paid therefor the contract price, one thousand,
two hundred dollars. The money thus paid, and fifty

dollars for freight, was obtained of a local bank on two
promissory notes which were signed by Linn, J. P.
Blood, and F. B. Robinson, one of which was for four
hundred and fifty dollars, and the other for eight hundred dollars. Blood and Robinson signed as sureties,
and to secure them, Linn gave to them a mortgage on
the grader. Robinson testifies that the four hundred
and fifty dollar note was paid in the fall of the year
1890, or in the spring of the next year; that a part of the
other note was paid in the year 1890, and the remainder
in the year 1892 or 1893; and that these payments
were made with money which belonged to Charles Linn
and to Charles and A. B. Linn. In the year 1892,
Charles Linn sold the machine to his brother, A. B.
Linn, and took from him a mortgage on it, which, as we
understand the record, was security for the unpaid part
of the purchase price. In the latter part of the year 1890,
John Brown and Anna Brown, through their agent,
Robinson, made a loan of one thousand, two hundred
dollars to Charles Linn, or to him and his wife, the intervener, and took as a security therefor a mortgage on
the homestead of Charles Linn and his wife and upon
an adjoining lot, and afterwards took an assignment
of the mortgage on the grader given by A. B. Linn.
That mortgage was renewed by A. B. Linn to the
Browns, and the new mortgage was foreclosed by them,
and the grader was sold thereunder in January, 1894.
The sale was made to the mortgagees, although Robinson states that it was made for Charles Linn, who did
not wish to be known as the purchaser; and that he
afterwards directed that a bill of sale for the grader
be made by the Browns to his wife, which was done.
Charles Linn denies that he told Robinson that he did
not wish to be known as the purchaser, and claims
to have told him that the grader belonged to his
wife from the first. The intervener claims that it was

in fact purchased of the Austin Manufacturing Company for her, and was paid for from the proceeds of the loan on the homestead. It is shown that the title to the homestead which the intervener and her husband mortgaged to the Browns was vested in the intervener, and that she had paid the larger part of the purchase price therefor with money which belonged to her. Both the intervener and her husband testify that the grader was purchased with the money which was obtained from the Brown loan, and that it belonged to her when the attachment was levied. The bill of sale given by the Browns was then on record, and the grader stood on a vacant lot near the premises of the intervener. Robinson testifies that the proceeds of the Brown loan were used, under the direction of Charles Linn, chiefly in paying his debts, and that only about two hundred dollars were paid to him, and that the notes for the grader were paid with money obtained from other sources. It is quite probable that this testimony is true, and that the intervener and her husband did not know just what application had been made of the money obtained from different sources, as Robinson appears to have paid out the money for the benefit of Linn, and probably under his direction, and retained possession of nearly all of his notes which were paid. But, however that may have been, the intervener could have obtained title to the grader when it was originally purchased substantially as she claimed, even though her husband used the proceeds of the homestead loan for his own purposes, and replaced them by money obtained from other sources. The purchase by the Browns at foreclosure sale, so far as is shown, was valid, although the consideration recited in the bill of sale is only one dollar, and the intervener did not pay anything for it at that time. The real character of the transaction between the Browns, Charles Linn, and the intervener, which included the foreclosure sale and the giving of the bill of sale, is not fully shown. It does not appear that the foreclosure sale was invalid, and there is no ground for presuming that it was. The jury was authorized to find that it vested the title to the grader in the Browns, and they had the right to transfer it to the intervener, even for a nominal consideration. It appears that Charles Linn regarded the transfer as rightly vesting in the intervener the title to the grader, because of the money which had been obtained on her property, and used as stated. That the money so procured and used furnished a sufficient consideration for the transfer by the bill of sale, if procured by Charles Linn, is clear. We conclude that the evidence is sufficient to support the special findings of the jury, and that they authorized the judgment rendered in favor of the intervener.

II. The appellant complains of the ninth paragraph of the charge, which is as follows: "Par. 9. Plaintiff alleges the machine attached was at the time the property of Charles Linn, and that the transfer by bill of sale to intervener was without consideration, and made to defraud creditors of Chas. Linn, and therefore void. As a matter of law, the burden of so proving is upon plaintiff. If the bill of sale was without consideration, and made for the purpose of hindering or delaying creditors, the same would not be a defense against the attachment. So, if you find from the evidence that Charles Linn originally bought said machine, sold it to A. B. Linn, taking a mortgage; that said Chas. Linn thereafter foreclosed the mortgage, and caused a bill of sale to be made to intervener without any consideration paid or given by her, and with intent and purpose on his part to hinder, delay, or defraud his creditors,—then find for plaintiff against intervener." The appellant contends that the court erred in giving the last half of the paragraph, for the

alleged reason that the evidence showed without contradiction that Charles Linn did originally buy the
machine, and cause it to be transferred to his wife without consideration.   That, as we have seen, is not the
case.   There was evidence from which the jury may
have found a purchase by the wife for a full and valid
consideration.   The paragraph is criticised in other
respects, but what we have said disposes of most of
the questions thus presented, and the others are unimportant.   Although there is some evidence which tends
strongly to sustain the claims of the appellant, we do
not find any sufficient ground for interfering with the
judgment of the district court, and it is therefore
AFFIRMED.

GAMET & OGDEN AND Z. T. NOYES v. W. R. SIMMONS
   AND GEORGE A. WALLACE, Appellants, and GAMET
   & OGDEN AND Z. T. NOYES v. MAHULDA WALLACE
   AND W. R. SIMMONS, Appellants.

Fraudulent Conveyance: EVIDENCE.   A conveyance by a man heavily
2   indebted, to his son-in-law and his stepdaughter, neither of whom
    had any money or property with which to meet the payments,
    which it is claimed were to be made for it, and which were evi-
    denced by their notes, given while they lived in the family of the
    grantor, and while they knew of his indebtedness, is fraudulent
    as to grantor's creditors.

SAME: *Notice.*   Where a purchaser of land has knowledge of such
8   circumstances as would put a prudent person on inquiry as to the
    intent of the grantor to hinder or delay his creditors, the convey-
    ance is fraudulent.

CONSIDERATION.   A transfer of land to one's stepdaughter, based
4   on a promise which is not binding on the promisor, is voluntary
    and fraudulent as to creditors, where he has no other property
    left with which to pay debts.

Rule Applied.   The promise by a stepfather, to deed land to his
4   stepdaughter, as soon as she was married, if before that time she
    will travel with and take care of him, is not binding upon him
    where she is a minor, and he is standing in *loco parentis.*

ACTION TO SET ASIDE: *Joinder.* Several judgment creditors may
1 join in an action to set aside a fraudulent conveyance.

LADD, J., took no part.

Appeal from Harrison District Court.—HON. SCOTT M.
LADD, Judge.

TUESDAY, OCTOBER 12, 1897.

CREDITORS' bill to subject certain real estate, the
legal title to which is in George A. Wallace and
Mahulda Wallace, to the payment of certain judgments against W. R. Simmons. From a decree granting the relief prayed, defendants appeal.—*Affirmed.*

J. S. Dewell for appellants.

S. H. Cochran for appellees.

DEEMER, J. — The plaintiffs in the two suits
entitled as above are the same, and they were brought
against a common defendant, W. R. Simmons, to set
aside two certain conveyances made by Simmons,—one
to George A. Wallace, his son-in-law, and the other to
Mahulda Wallace, his stepdaughter. The two suits
were tried at the same time, and upon practi-
1   cally the same evidence. To the petitions, which
are in the usual form, defendants filed a motion
to require plaintiffs to elect as to which of them they
would prosecute, and to dismiss as to the other, for the
reason that there was a misjoinder of parties plaintiff
and causes of action. From the petitions it appears
that each of the plaintiffs obtained judgment against
W. R. Simmons on the same day, and that the conveyances in question were made with intent to defraud
the creditors of the judgment debtor. In the case of
Gorrell v. Gates, 79 Iowa, 632, we held that several
judgment creditors may join in an action to set aside

a fraudulent conveyance. The defendants' motion was properly overruled.

II. Appellees obtained their judgments against Simmons in April of the year 1894. The conveyances which they seek to set aside were made on the thirteenth day of December, 1893. Simmons is a blind man, who puts in most of his time begging. Prior to the making of the deeds he married a widow with one daughter, Mahulda. This girl was then six years of age. After the marriage the child traveled with and helped to care for Simmons during his pilgrimages, until she was about twelve years of age. About a month prior to the time the conveyances were made, Mahulda married George Wallace, and the two have lived with Simmons ever since. At the time the deeds were executed, Simmons was heavily in debt, of which fact both George and Mahulda Wallace had knowledge. He owned or had title to about two hundred and fifty acres of land of the value of about two thousand dollars. One hundred and seventy acres of this land he conveyed to George Wallace in consideration, as he says, of an assumption by Wallace of the indebtedness then standing against it, and the execution of notes to the amount of nine hundred dollars. Wallace had no property at this time, and no means whereby he might reasonably expect to pay his obligations. Forty acres, incumbered to the extent of 'four hundred dollars, he transferred to Mahulda Wallace, in consideration, he says, of a promise made her that, if she would travel with and take care of him, he would deed her some land as soon as she was married. He also conveyed to her ten acres of the land, for which she gave him her note for one hundred dollars. He also transferred forty acres to one Sconlar at or about the same time, and retained forty acres as his homestead. Almost immediately upon receipt of the notes

Simmons delivered them to a relative in Appanoose county, to whom he claims to have sold them. The one hundred dollar note given by Mahulda Wallace she paid from proceeds of timber cut from the ten-acre tract. Without setting forth even the substance of the evidence relied upon by appellees to sustain their plea of fraud, it is sufficient to say that we are constrained to believe that their claim is established. Neither of the grantees in these deeds had any money or property with which to meet their notes. They lived in the family of the grantor, and knew that he was heavily involved, and we are satisfied that Mahulda Wallace did not know of the conveyances to her until some time after they were made. We doubt very much the story with reference to the execution, delivery, and transfer of the nine hundred dollar notes by George Wallace. The evidence tends to show that these notes were handed to Mrs. Simmons, the wife of the grantor, and were placed in a trunk by her. George Wallace was, according to his claim, a purchaser of the land; and

3   the rule is well settled that, if a purchaser has knowledge of such facts and circumstances tending to show that the debtor intends by the sale to hinder, delay, or defraud his creditors as would put a prudent person upon inquiry, the sale is fraudulent. *Redhead v. Pratt,* 72 Iowa, 99. That he had knowledge of such facts is apparent, and the conveyance is, therefore, fraudulent. The same rule obtains as to the ten acre tract conveyed to the stepdaughter. The

4   conveyance of the forty acres calls for the application of another principle. The alleged promise on which the conveyance was based was made by Simmons to his stepdaughter, while she was a minor, and he was standing in *loco parentis,* and it was not binding upon him. *Dick v. Grissom,* 1 Freeman Ch. (Miss.) 434; *Gerdes v. Weiser,* 54 Iowa, 591; *Irish v.*

Bradford, 64 Iowa, 304; *Swartz v. Hazlett*, 8 Cal. 118.
A transfer based upon such a promise was voluntary,
and under the showing made in this case, was for
that reason, fraudulent. Bump, Fraudulent Conveyances, p. 230; *Elwell v. Walker*, 52 Iowa, 256; *Peterson
v. Rone*, 76 Iowa, 447. The decree of the district court is
right and it is AFFIRMED.

LADD, J., took no part.

JOSEPH MERRYFIELD v. P. F. SWIFT AND WILLIAM
KRANER, Appellant.

Intoxicating Liquors: ABATEMENT OF NUISANCE. A decree ordering
that a building be closed, and that the owner shall pay the costs
and attorney fees incurred in proceedings to enjoin the continuance of a liquor nuisance in such building, is unauthorized where
the sale of intoxicating liquors was made by a trespasser without
the owner's knowledge or consent, and the sale of the liquor and
the occupancy of the trespasser had ceased before the petition
was filed.

*Appeal from Keokuk District Court.—*HON. D. RYAN,
Judge.

TUESDAY, OCTOBER 12, 1897.

THIS is an action in equity to enjoin the continuance of a liquor nuisance. Swift made default. A
decree was entered against the defendants, abating the
nuisance, enjoining the carrying on of the business,
and ordering the building closed for one year; also,
that the furniture, fixtures, and movable property in
said building be sold, and the proceeds of such sale
applied in payment of the costs. The costs, including
attorney's fees and costs of abatement and sale, were
decreed to be a lien upon said real estate. The defendant Kraner excepted and appeals.—*Reversed*

.   *Steck & Smith* for appellant.

Hamilton & Donohoe for appellee.

KINNE, C. J.—The defendant Kraner owned a building in the town of Hedrick, in Keokuk county, Iowa. He resided in the city of Ottumwa. The defendant Swift, in September, 1895, without any lease from Kraner, and without his knowledge or consent, entered said building, and for two or three days illegally sold liquor therein. These sales and Swift's occupancy of the building had ceased prior to the time the petition in this case was filed. Under these facts there was no occasion to commence this action against the owner of the building. Swift was a trespasser upon the premises. He had no right there whatever, and Kraner did not know that he had ever been an occupant of his building, or selling liquors therein, until the notice in this case was served on him.

The decree below, in so far as it ordered the building closed, and made the costs and attorney's fees and costs of abatement and sale a lien upon the property of Kraner, was unwarranted. *Drake v. Kingsbaker*, 72 Iowa, 441; *Eckert v. David*, 75 Iowa, 302; *Morgan v. Koestner*, 83 Iowa, 134; *State v. Lawler*, 85 Iowa, 564; *State v. Severson*, 88 Iowa, 714; *State v. Price*, 92 Iowa, 181. The decree below, in the respects above mentioned, being erroneous, it is REVERSED.

STATE OF IOWA v. FRANK DORLAND, Appellant.

Intent in Manslaughter: INTOXICATION: *Jury question.* Where it is
1 the law of the case that conviction of manslaughter must depend
  upon whether defendant aided another in a deadly assault, the
4 intent of defendant is so involved as that his being intoxicated
  bears upon the formation of such intent; and it is erroneous to

charge the jury that his intoxication does not affect his guilt or innocence of manslaughter.

Province of Jury: WEIGHT OF EVIDENCE. In an instruction as to
3 the effect of intoxication on the guilt of a defendant charged
2 with murder, it is error to state that there is some evidence tending to show that defendant was under the influence of intoxicating liquors, as the word "some" would be expressive of the opinion
of the court as to the quantity and weight of the evidence of
intoxication.

Appeal from Fayette District Court.—HON. L. E. FEL-
LOWS, Judge.

TUESDAY, OCTOBER 12, 1897.

INDICTMENT for murder. Verdict of manslaughter. Judgment thereon, and the defendant appealed.— *Reversed.*

Ainsworth & Ainsworth and *W. E. Fuller* for appellant.

Milton Remley, attorney general, and *Jesse A. Miller* for the state

GRANGER, J.—I.   The indictment is for murder in the first degree against Frank Darland and Willie Smith. Separate trials were granted. On the eleventh of December, 1894, Dorland, Smith, one Bowser, and Andrew and Jacob Nelson started from West Union, in Fayette county, Iowa, in a wagon. It seems that Bowser owned and drove the team. Dorland, Bowser, and Andrew Nelson occupied a seat, with Dorland between the other two. Jacob Nelson and Smith stood up behind the others. They had some alcohol, and had been drinking. Some three miles from West Union, the men became involved in a quarrel, resulting in the death of Andrew Nelson. The circumstances

under which the party was found may be best understood by part of the testimony of John Blunt, as follows: "I reside three miles and a half from town, east
of the Clermont road. I am a farmer. Reside over half
a mile from the scene of the trouble, south, and a little
east. Know defendant Dorland and Willie Smith. On
the eleventh of December last, I heard something
unusual on the Clermont road. It was a still evening,
and I heard loud talk over there. Could hear nothing
in particular, more than some curse words,—swearing.
Don't think anybody could tell what they were saying.
Told the boy to go and get the horse, and saddle him up.
Didn't hear this loud talk and swearing but a short
time. Would not think it was more than a minute or
two. Then I went into the house, got my coat, and told
the boy to get my horse. Then I went back into the
house, and then went on to the barn, got the horse, and
started over where the noise was. There is a road
across from my place to the Clermont road,—a track
where the milkmen drive. There is a gate at the
Clermont road. Went through that. It was east of
the scene of the alleged crime about twenty-five rods.
While at the fence, I hard some one say, 'For God's
sake, don't pound them any more!' I was then at the
gate on the south side of the road, twenty-five or thirty
rods from them, east of where the trouble occurred.
Came up within three or four rods of the boys. Heard
somebody say, 'Keep still, there is somebody coming;'
and then I think it was Smith or Frank said, 'That is
John Blunt,' or 'It is John Blunt's horse,' and they said
'Hallo!' and I answered them; and then they came out
where I was, and took hold of me. Both of them got
hold of me, and went on to tell me that they had had a
hell of a fight. They said they had had a hell of a
damned fight, and one of them had struck Willie, and
shot at him or 'shot at us.' They said they didn't know

whether the damned fools shot at them or shot in the
air, and I asked them where the fellows were that they
had the fight with, and they said, 'There the son of
bitches are,—out there, on the ground.' We got along
up to where Dave stood by the wagon, and they said
they had taken the revolver away from them, and Dave
had it in his pocket. From that I went out to where
Andrew lay on the south side of the track, and asked
him if he was hurt. He lay there with his head to the
east and south, and his feet to the north,—in that
direction (indicates); and the wagon was off in this
direction, and I went to the one nearest the wagon, the
same one I went to first, raised him up, and asked him
if he was hurt. He didn't make any answer. Felt of
his pulse, and thought from the way his pulse beat he
was pretty near dead. He lay stretched out full length
on his stomach and side. I went over to the other body.
It lay on the north side, in almost the same direction
and position, just about, on his left side; that is, on his
stomach or side. Asked him the same question, and
he didn't reply. Then went back to the boys, and told
Dave we would have to do something with those boys;
that they would chill out there on the ground. And
Dave said he couldn't do anything; he couldn't leave
his team. Told him he would have to unhitch them; we
would have to get them up. Frank heard what I said,
and said he would help put the boys in, and he did help
put them in. Andrew was put in first. The boys were
lying a rod or more apart; yes, more than a rod. One
was further east than the other. There would be more
than a rod's difference between the two from the
wagon. We put Andrew in first. Put him in feet first.
Frank and Mr. Shmuhl helped put him in, and I got in
the wagon, to straighten him around, and to lay him
down in the wagon. When I got him about half down,
he made a struggle, raised up, made a struggle, and

kicked both feet right out over the wheel. The horses
were started and backing. I helped him set up against
the end gate like, and took his feet, and put them back
into the wagon; then straightened him down in the
wagon, and laid him out, and put something under his
head, and laid him down there. As I was doing this,
the other one laid over west a ways. The horses had
started maybe four or five feet. Frank went and got
hold of the other one, and lifted him up pretty near to
the wagon. Then I got out, and we put him in head
first. Frank helped put him in. I put a coat under
the one's head we put in last; pulled him up and put a
coat under his head. I told the boys to get ready and
go. Frank said he wanted his overcoat; wanted to
know where his overcoat was. Told him I didn't know;
I put a coat under those Norwegians' heads. He went
up and said 'that no lousy son of a bitch of a Norwegian
could bleed on his coat,' and pulled it out. During this
time Bowser was standing by the wagon, holding his
team. Father drove up. The boys were talking with him,
and I told them that they would have to go; that the
boys were lying there in the wagon. When I came up,
both of the boys came up. Smith and Dorland were
bloody. Both were in their shirt sleeves. After father
came up, Dorland wanted his hat. We went back, and
found it about a rod or so west of the cottonwood tree.
Think the cottonwood tree was about eight rods west
of where the difficulty occurred, and on the north side of
the road. After we got the bodies in the wagon, the boys
got in, but, before they got in, Willie Smith called my
attention to his coat. He wanted to show me how it
was torn, and said that they tore his coat clear around,
and he turned around and showed it to me. It was
kind of a nappy coat. I didn't ride in the wagon when
they started off. Willie got into the seat and Frank
stood behind. Dave Bowser was in the seat. I followed behind them on horseback. They went on and ;

stopped at my father's, whose place was about eghty
rods east from the alleged crime, and on the same road.
Didn't stop at my father's very long. Hitched up a
team (one of my horses and one of his) onto a lumber
wagon, and went on to Mr. Howe's, where we got up
with the boys. Mr. Howe's is about a half a mile from
my father's and about three-quarters from the scene of
the crime. Went on to Mr. Howe's, and, when I got
there, they were standing around the wagon, and Mike
Fritz asked me to get out and see what I thought about
them. Got out and examined them. Went to Andrew
first. He was lying in the hind end of the wagon. I
told him he was dead. Then he looked at him, and felt
of him, and told them he was dead, and Frank says,
'You don't say so.' And I said, 'Yes, he is dead.' And I
turned around to the other one, with his head the
other way. Looked at him, and Frank came around,
and asked me how he was. I says, 'He is pretty near
dead, too; and you will have to do something for them
to keep them warm.' Frank said, 'They can have anything I have got;' they could have his coat. Took off
his coat, and covered it over the dead body. Told him
he didn't need to cover him up. 'Cover the other up,
and keep him warm.' Don't know whether he made
the change or not. Told Dave Bowser he better take
them to his house, and take them in where it was warm,
and I saw that somebody ought to go for the doctor.
When Bowser spoke of taking them home, it was down
to their shanty, and I told him it was better to take
them to his own house, and then I left, and they went
on. Think, when they went on, Smith and Dorland got
into the wagon. Don't think any one else got in with
them. I then came to town for the doctor, and got Dr.
Ainsworth, and went down to the jail, and got Mr. Phillips." The testimony of the physicians who examined
the body of Andrew Nelson shows that his body was
considerably mutilated by cutting, and that one of the

wounds, under the arm, was fatal necessarily, and that
death would result from such a wound in from three
to five minutes. The testimony further shows that
both Andrew and Jacob Nelson were severely
1   bruised by beating. It is likely true that the
cutting was done by a knife in the hands of
Smith, and we gather from the record and arguments
that whatever was done by Dorland was with his fists.
The precise facts leading to and during the quarrel or
fight, resulting in the death, cannot be known, because
of the different versions of it by those present, and
there were none other than those riding in the wagon
that we have named. There is no dispute but that a
fight was brought on in some way, and that both Nel-
sons, Smith and Dorland were engaged in it, with
the results stated. The court gave instructions as to
murder in both degrees and manslaughter.

Complaint is made of the nineteenth instruction,
which is as follows: "(19) There is some evidence tending to show that the defendant, at the time of the commission of the alleged crime, was to some extent
2   under the influence of intoxicating liquors. If,
from the evidence, you find that the defendant
was to any extent under the influence of intoxicating
liquor, you are instructed that unless the intoxication of the defendant was, at the time of the commission of the act, so great as to deprive him of the
power to deliberate and form a guilty intent, it
is no excuse or palliation for the act. This question
of intoxication can only be considered by you in
determining whether or not the defendant is guilty
of murder. It cannot affect the question of his being
guilty of the crime of manslaughter, and it is
entirely immaterial whether or not the deceased furnished the liquor drank by defendant.". Com-
3   plaint is first made as to the words, "There is
some evidence tending to show that the defendant, at the time of the commission of the alleged crime,

was to some extent under the influence of intoxicating liquors." The criticism is on the use of the word "some," and reliance is placed on our holding in *State v. Donovan*, 61 Iowa, 369. That was an indictment for an assault with intent to commit rape, and the court, in an instruction, said: "There is some evidence tending to show that the defendant was drunk." The instruction was held erroneous because of the word "some," in that "it would be understood as expressing the opinion of the court as to the quantity and weight of the evidence on the question of the defendant's drunkenness, which was unfavorable to him." In that case the drunkenness became material on the question of the defendant, at the time of the act, being in a condition of mind to be capable of forming the intent to do the unlawful act. The crime charged in the indictment in this case being murder, the intent in making the assault became material; and the instruction complained of was given to properly guide the jury on that branch of the case; and the court said to the jury that the intoxication of the defendant was proper to be considered in determining whether he had the mental capacity to deliberate and form a guilty intent. We cannot see why, in this case, the use of the word "some" is not equally fatal to the instruction on the question of murder that the use of the same word was in the *Donovan Case*, and for the same reason. But it is said that the cases differ; that in the *Donovan Case* the defense offered evidence to show intoxication, while in this case it did not, but only claimed that the entire party had been drinking to excess, and that the natural result would cause them to be intoxicated; and it is said that the defendants had been drinking, but were not drunk. The argument does not reach the difficulty. The court submitted the case to the jury on the theory of a state of evidence that the jury must

or might find it necessary to determine therefrom if
Dorland was so intoxicated as to be incapable of forming a guilty intent. The court regarded, as we think it
should, the question of intoxication as important on
the question of murder. As this case and the *Donovan
Case* involve precisely the same reasons for holding
the use of the word "some" in the instructions erroneous, of course the same holding must follow.

II. If, however, it may be said that on the question of murder there could be no prejudice to the defendant, because of the practical acquittal of the crime of
murder by a verdict of manslaughter, we are brought
to consider some complaints as to the instruction as
bearing on the latter crime. Instruction No. 15 specifies the facts and conditions under which Dorland
could be convicted of manslaughter. It is as follows:
"(15) If you find from the evidence, beyond a reasonable
doubt, that the defendant Dorland, in sudden passion or
heat of blood, without premeditation and without malice towards Andrew Nelson, and without any specific
intent to injure him, unlawfully assaulted and struck
said Nelson violent blows, while said Nelson was being
assaulted by his co-defendant, Smith, and for the purpose of assisting said Smith in his assault upon Nelson,
and that neither Dorland nor Smith were acting in self-
defense, and that the death of Nelson resulted from
such assaults made by either or both defendants, then
the defendant Dorland was guilty of the crime of manslaughter and you should find him guilty of that
offense. If, however, the defendant Dorland took part
in the affray for no other purpose than that of stopping
the same, and did no more than was reasonable and
proper under the circumstances to accomplish that
purpose, then he was acting lawfully, and you should
acquit him." It will be seen that the instruction only
permits a verdict for manslaughter if Dorland, in doing

what he did towards causing the death of Nelson, did so
for the purpose of assisting Smith in his assault upon
Nelson; and, in view of the quite conclusive showing
that the death was caused by the knife cuts by Smith,
the theory of the instruction in this respect seems correct. While the instruction as to intoxication, applied
to independent acts of persons charged with manslaughter, is correct, it is thought not to be so when the
acts constituting the offense involve an intent or purpose, so that without that intent or purpose, the
crime cannot exist. Because of this, it is urged
that the instruction, in the use of the word "some,"
is erroneous, and, besides, that it is erroneous
in holding that the fact of intoxication has no bearing
on the crime of manslaughter. It seems to have
4   been the theory of the prosecution that, inasmuch as Smith's acts in using the knife took the
life of Nelson, Dorland's guilt must depend on his
having unlawfully aided in so doing, through a concert
of action; and the court adopted it to the extent of holding that there must have been an intent by Dorland to
aid Smith in his unlawful acts. Now, if the state of the
record was such that the jury might consider the intoxication of Dorland in determining if he were capable of
forming an intent to kill, we do not see why it should
not be permitted to consider it in determining the fact,
submitted to it, of his having formed an intent or purpose to help Smith in his unlawful acts. Instruction
No. 16 seems to have reference to the guilt of the
defendant for any crime included in the indictment,
and it is as follows: "(16) The defendant in this case
is jointly indicted with another, one Willie Smith. Evidence has been introduced for the purpose of showing
the acts and conduct of both parties indicted, so as
to enable you to determine whether or not both these
parties were acting in concert and with a common intent

or otherwise. If, from the evidence, you find, beyond a reasonable doubt, that both the defendant Dorland and Smith were acting together, with a common purpose, aiding and assisting each other, and that, while so acting in concert, the life of the deceased was taken, it matters not which of the indicted persons inflicted the fatal injuries. The defendant would be guilty although he may not have inflicted the fatal wound himself, but the degree of his guilt would depend upon his own condition of mind as to the malice afore-thought, premeditation, deliberation, or the absence of any or all of these conditions of his mind." This instruction shows the theory on which a conviction must rest, and that the fact of Dorland and Smith aiding and assisting each other, with a common purpose, was important. In fact, there is no theory of the instructions on which a conviction could rest in the absence of an element of intent. It seems to us the court erred in saying that the fact of intoxication could not be considered in determining whether the defendant was guilty of manslaughter. There are no other questions that we regard it necessary to consider, in view of a new trial.—REVERSED.

HARRY HOLIDAY v. THE AMERICAN MUTUAL ACCIDENT ASSOCIATION OF OSHKOSH, WISCONSIN, Appellant.

Accident Insurance: CLASSIFICATION. One insured as a bookkeper, against accident, by a policy classifying as more hazardous the
1 occupation of "hunter or hunting," and providing that if injury occurs "while performing any act pertaining to an occupation classed as more hazardous" than the one under which the policy is issued, "or while engaged in a more hazardous occupation,"
8 insured shall be entitled only to such indemnity as the premiums paid would purchase in the class in which such occupation is classed, is not prevented from recovering the indemnity provided for a bookkeeper, though shot by discharge of a gun he was carrying while hunting for recreation.

WAIVER OF DEFENSE. Defense, under provision in an accident
2 policy against recovery for injuries resulting from exposure to
unnecessary danger, is waived by offer to confess judgment for
an amount less than claimed, on the ground that insured's occu-
4 pation was more hazardous than that under which he was insured,
and, by motion, after the evidence was in, for verdict in accordance with such offer.

Appeal from Des Moines District Court.—HON. JAMES
D. SMYTH, Judge.

WEDNESDAY, OCTOBER 13, 1897.

THE plaintiff became a member of the defendant
association on the first day of December, 1894. The
association classifies its risks from "AA" to "G." Those
classed as AA are preferred, and the loss of a
1   foot above the ankle entitles the holder of such
a certificate to two thousand dollars. Persons
admitted to this class are bookkeepers, lawyers, clergy-
men, artists, etc. Class ½ AA is for the same persons,
but the indemnity is but one-half of that of class AA.
Class E includes "hunter or hunting," and indemnity
for the loss of a foot above the ankle is five hundred
and eighty-five dollars. On the sixth of August, 1895,
the plaintiff was out hunting with a party; and on his
return, in getting through a wire fence, by an accidental
discharge of his gun, he was injured so as to necessitate
the amputation of his left foot above the ankle joint.
The indemnity provided in such a case, where payable,
was in eighteen equal monthly installments. The association declined payment in this case, and after five
months, this action was commenced, claiming two hundred and seventy-seven dollars and eighty-eight cents,
as the five installments due; and later, by an amendment to the petition, the amount was raised to five hundred dollars, because of two more installments becoming due. Plaintiff's claim is based on the classification

¼ AA, being that specified in the certificate of membership. Defendant, in its answer, admits a liability, and
offers to confess judgment for two hundred and ninety-
two dollars and fifty cents, being one-half the indemnity
provided for such a loss in Class E, in which class is
specified "hunter or hunting," but denies a liability, as
claimed under a classification ¼ AA. At the close of
the evidence, the defendant moved the court to direct a
verdict for it, based on three separate grounds, which
the court denied, and sustained a motion by the plaintiff for a verdict in his favor for five hundred dollars,
and from a judgment thereon the defendant appealed.—
Affirmed.

Dodge & Dodge and *Phillip & Hicks* for appellant.

Kelley & Cooper for appellee.

GRANGER, J.—I.   It is first urged that the court
erred in directing a verdict for plaintiff, because there
was a question of fact whether the plaintiff, at the time
of the injury, was not engaged in a more hazardous occupation than the one in which he was insured, being that
        of a bookkeeper.   It appears in the statement
2   that there was an offer to confess judgment for
        two hundred and ninety-two dollars and fifty
cents; and in defendant's motion to direct a verdict, in
one division thereof, it asks the court to direct a verdict
for plaintiff for that amount "up to the time of the tender, as set forth in defendant's answer." This condition
of the record fixes a right of recovery, leaving only the
question of amount, which is made to depend on the
classification under which a recovery can be had.   The
following is a provision of the certificate: *"Fourth.*
That the association shall have the power at any time
to cancel this certificate upon refunding any balance
of the premium standing to the credit of such member

on its books; and if injury occurs while performing an act pertaining to an occupation classed by it as more hazardous than the one under which this certificate is issued, or while engaged in a more hazardous occupation, such member or beneficiary shall be entitled to such an amount of indemnity as the premiums paid would purchase in the class in which such occupation is classified." It will be seen that a main contention arises over whether the plaintiff, when injured, was engaged in the occupation of a hunter or hunting, within the meaning of the contract, so as to change the classification under which he is entitled to indemnity from $\frac{1}{2}$ AA to E. The facts are not in dispute, and are substantially as follows: The plaintiff and others had been hunting, and plaintiff was carrying a hammerless gun, which cocked only by breaking it down to insert the shells containing the charge of powder and shot. There were no hammers to catch, as is many times the case, and discharge the gun. There was a safety catch, which, when "set at safety," prevented a discharge until pushed "to shoot." Plaintiff was coming to the wagon, which was in the highway, from a field; and, as there was no gate, he had to cross a wire fence. With his gun, as claimed by him, at "safety," he placed it across a wire of the fence, with one hand on the stock, and the other on the barrels, so as to press down a wire of the fence, and make an opening through which to pass. He passed his left foot through to the other side, and bent his body, and passed through; and as he was straightening up, after being through, he stumbled, because of a hole in the ground; and in some way the safety catch was changed, and the gun discharged, causing the injury. It should perhaps appear that there is doubt as to the condition of the safety catch on the gun. Every essential fact from which to reach a conclusion is in this statement. That, for the time being, the plaintiff was engaged in a more hazardous work than that of a bookkeeper, admits of no quest on, and the jury must have so found had the question been submitted. In fact, the court could have so stated to the jury. There is no other question of fact. Whether that fact has the effect of changing the clas ification is one of law, and we do not think there was a disputed question of fact in the case for the jury to d termine.

II. A more difficult que tion is how the fact affects the classification. We may fairly present the question in this way: Does the association intend, and should one accepting its propo sition for member-

3   ship understand, that, if accepted under the classification AA, wherein the indemnity is larger because of the decreased risk, such indemnity is to be paid only if accident occurs while he is doing those things because of which he is admitted to such classification? As, if a minister, must the accident occur while doing the distinguishing duties of a minister; or, if a lawyer, while doing his professional work; or, if an artist, while doing the work of an artist,—with, perhaps, in each case, the essential duties of home, of society, and of citizenship? Or does the association intend, and should such a person understand, that the classification is based on the decreased risk because of the effect of such callings lessening the hazard, in view of the usual experiences of such men, not professionally, but as a whole? It seems to us that reason and authority sustain the latter rule.

An authority relied on by appellant is *Insurance Co. v. Martin*, 133 Ind. Sup. 376 (33 N. E. Rep. 105). In that case, the classification in which the assured was accepted was that of a passenger brakeman, and twenty dollars would purchase two thousand dollars in that class. The occupation of brakeman on a construction train was ten times more hazardous, and the assured,

after the insurance, changed his occupation to that of
a brakeman on a construction train. The case holds
that the recovery should be in the latter classification,
and, we think, correctly so. In *Knapp v. Accident Association*, 53 Hun, 84 (6 N. Y. Supp. 57), where a policy
issued to a person classed as a "retired gentleman,"
with a proviso against liability for injuries resulting
from exposure not incident to the occupation under
which he received membership, and he was injured
while operating a buzz saw for amusement, it was held
there could be no recovery. It was hardly to be contemplated, when the policy issued, that working with
a buzz saw would be an amusement of a retired gentleman; but, on the contrary, it would be one of the
resorts for amusement that would not be contemplated.
The known danger of such a resort would suggest its
exclusion. The case of *Aldrich v. Accident Association*,
149 Mass. 457 (21 N. E. Rep. 873), is where the certificate
issued to a "spare conductor, through freight." The
assured was killed while acting as brakeman on a
through freight, under another as conductor. The risk
of brakeman was classed as more hazardous than that
of conductor. A recovery was only allowed under the
more hazardous risk. It will be seen that in these cases,
except the *Knapp Case* there was a change of occupation or employment, at least temporarily. The case of
Accident Association v. Frohard, 134 Ill. 228 (25 N. E.
Rep. 642), is quite similar to this. The assured was a
teacher, and was killed while overlooking the construction of a building he was having erected. It was said
in the case: "The word 'occupation' * * * must
be held to have reference to the vocation, profession,
trade, or calling which the assured is engaged in, for
hire or profit, and not as precluding him from the performance of acts and duties which are simply incidents
connected with the daily life of men in all occupations,

or from engaging in mere acts of exercise, diversion, or recreation." In *Insurance Co. v. Burroughs*, 69 Pa. St. 43, the business of the assured was that of an earthenware manufacturer, and he was killed while on a visit to his grandfather, and assisting in hauling in and unloading hay. Speaking of a change of occupation, it is said: "But this was not a change of his occupation or business, within the meaning of the policy. To give the word such a construction would prevent the assured from performing any act or service outside of his usual avocation or business without rendering the policy null and void." We do not overlook the particular language of the certificate that limits the liability where the accident "occurs while performing any act pertaining to an occupation classed by it as more hazardous than the one under which the certificate is issued." This language is more doubtful than that as to a change of occupation. With considerable study, we are not able to give the words quoted a meaning in connection with the facts of the case. As applied to this case, "occupation" must mean hunting. We think, within the meaning of the certificate, the plaintiff was not engaged in the occupation of hunting when the injury occurred, so that the liability of the defendant can be lessened for that cause. That he was hunting, there is no question; and, by all authority, there may be hunting without its being an occupation. The classification by which the hazard of hunting is fixed is that of hunting as an occupation. Now, the plaintiff was carrying a loaded gun, and getting through the fence. What was the act pertaining to the occupation of hunting? There could be nothing more than the fact that he was hunting; and if the mere fact of hunting for recreation is not such an occupation, within the meaning of the policy, how does it *pertain* to it,—that is, pertain to the occupation (which the authorities hold to mean, not hunting for amusement, but as a business or calling for profit or hire)? Such a

carrying of the gun no more pertained to the occupation
of hunting than would the carrying of a gun from one
place to another with no intention to hunt. The carrying of the gun would be an act to be done in hunting,
and it might pertain to hunting, but not to it as an
occupation. The entire classification of the defendant
association is before us, and it seems to be entirely
based on occupations; that is, occupations, and not
acts, are the basis of classification. In *Accident Association v. Frohard, supra,* the policy contained the term
"any act or occupation," and the case is quite in point
on this question. After some consideration of this question, it is said: "There is not in the by-laws or in the
record any classification of hazards in respect to acts;
in other words, there is no act which is classified as
more or less hazardous than another, and no act is
classed as more hazardous than the occupation designated in the certificate of insurance issued to the
deceased. The case, then, does not stand otherwise than
it would if the word 'act' were not found in the contract." We do not see why this language is not applicable to this case.

III.   A provision of the policy prevents a recovery
for injuries resulting from exposure to unnecessary
danger. Such a defense goes to the entire right of recovery. In view of the offer to confess judgment for
4   two hundred and ninety-two dollars and fifty
cents, and of the motion made after the evidence
was in, we do not see how this question is longer
involved. The offer to confess and the motion are an
acknowledgment of a right of recovery, so that the only
question was as to the classification that should fix the
amount. The fact of unnecessary exposure has no bearing on that question. The judgment is AFFIRMED.

G. W. PICKERING, Appellant, v. W. W. CAMERON.

Indorsement of Draft: TITLE TO PROCEEDS. Defendant indorsed a sight draft to a bank, with which he had an account, and the same was placed to his credit. Said bank forwarded it to the drawee bank, where it was protested, and on its return, it was given back to defendant, and charged to him. Defendant then sent it the second time to the drawee, to whom the drawer then paid it. *Held*, that defendant was the owner of the funds in the hands of the drawee, in such sense, that he might recover damages of the drawer because he attached said fund without sufficient reason to believe that the drawee was indebted to him.

Appeal from Page District Court. —HON. W. R. GREEN, Judge.

WEDNESDAY, OCTOBER, 13, 1897.

THIS action was commenced by attachment against the defendant, a non-resident of the state, to recover an alleged indebtedness of sixty-seven dollars and sixty-eight cents. The attachment was served by garnishing the First National Bank of Shenandoah, Iowa, which held the proceeds of a check drawn by the plaintiff in favor of the defendant. Defendant appeared, and answered, denying plaintiff's cause of action, and setting up a counter-claim on the attachment bond for damages, alleging that the attachment was wrongfully and maliciously sued out, for that plaintiff had no reasonable grounds for believing that defendant was indebted to him in any sum whatever. Plaintiff replied, denying the counter-claim, and denying that the money attached was, at the time of the garnishment the property of the defendant. The jury found against the plaintiff on his cause of action, and in favor of the defendant on his counter-claim in the sum of two hundred and fifty dollars. Judgment was rendered on the verdict, and for costs, including fifty dollars attorney's fee, against the plaintiff, from which he appeals.— *Affirmed.*

W. P. Ferguson for appellant.

Parslow & Scott for appellee.

GIVEN, J.—This appeal is from the judgment rendered on the counter-claim, and the only question presented is whether the money in the hands of the garnishee was the money of the defendant at the time of the levy. For the purpose of abbreviating the record, counsel have stipulated that the following ultimate facts are established by the evidence: "(1) That at the time of the commencement of this suit and suing out of attachment therein defendant was a non-resident of the state, but not indebted to plaintiff in any sum whatever. (2) That in suing out such attachment the plaintiff acted without sufficient reason for believing that any such indebtedness in fact existed; hence without justifiable grounds in suing out such attachment. (3) That if defendant is entitled to any affirmative judgment for actual or exemplary damages, then it is conceded that he would be entitled, under the evidence, to the full amount of judgment rendered in the district court. (4) That a partial transcript of the official report of the evidence in said cause filed in the office of the clerk of the district court April 29, 1896, together with this stipulation, to which it is attached, shall, for the purposes of this appeal, constitute a complete record of all the evidence offered or introduced on the trial of said cause. It being the intention and purpose of the parties on this appeal to limit the issues to be presented to the supreme court on appeal to the one question, namely, whether the defendant, W. W. Cameron, had any such interest in the draft in question, or proceeds thereof, as to entitle him to damages because of the levy of the attachment writ, which was by service of garnishment summons." The partial transcript of the evidence shows that the defendant alone was examined on the issue joined on the counter-claim. His evidence shows, in substance, as follows: That in the spring of 1895 he had settlement with the plaintiff at Chester, Neb., and that plaintiff gave him his fifteen days' sight draft on the First National Bank of Shenandoah, Iowa, guarantied by one Hindman, for one hundred dollars, the balance due to defendant. Defendant indorsed the draft to the Blue Valley Bank, of Hebron, Neb., with which he had an account, and the same was placed to his credit. The draft was forwarded by the Blue Valley Bank to the Bank of Shenandoah for payment, and protested. While defendant's evidence is somewhat confused as to what followed, the jury was fully warranted in finding that on the return of the draft protested it was returned to the defendant, and charged to him by Blue Valley Bank. Defendant says that, when the draft was returned protested, "I notified Mr. Hindman, surety, and at his instance sent it to Shenandoah a second time." It appears that after the draft was sent the second time to the Bank at Shenandoah the plaintiff paid it to that bank, and then commenced this action for an alleged indebtedness that he had no sufficient reason for believing did exist, and garnished the money in the hands of the bank. That the attachment was wrongfully sued out is conceded, and the only defense offered to defendant's right to damages is that he did not own the money held by the garnishee. Whether, if the draft had still been held by the Blue Valley Bank, defendant might, because of his liability as indorser, recover damages, we need not determine, as it is entirely clear that the draft was exclusively his at the time of the garnishment. Appellant's argument is based upon isolated statements as to the ownership of the draft. A careful examination of defendant's testimony shows that when he speaks of it as owned by the bank he has reference to the time after he indorsed it, and before its return to him protested. The jury were not warranted in finding otherwise than that the money in the hands of the garnishee was the property of the defendant at the time the notice of garnishment was served, and therefore there was no error in either of the respects assigned.—AFFIRMED.

S. M. WINCHELL v. THE IOWA STATE INSURANCE COMPANY, Appellant.

Insurance: ESTOPPEL. An insurer is not estopped to deny its
2 approval of an application, by its retention of a non-negotiable
8 premium note accompanying the same, and the failure of the
9 soliciting agent to return the application or notify the insured of
10 its rejection, although the insured, in the belief that the applica-
3 tion had been accepted, failed to take out other insurance, in the
absence of any notice to the insurer that he entertained such
belief. Citing *More v. Insurance Co.*, 130 N. Y. 537; *Insurance
Co. v. Johnson*, 23 Pa. St. 72; *Insurance Co. v. Beatty*, 119 Pa. 6;
Haskin v. Insurance Co., 78 Va. 700; *Insurance Co. v. Helzgrafe*,
53 Ill. 516; *Harp v. Insurance Co.*, 49 Md. 307; *Heiman v. Insurance Co.*, 17 Minn. 153.

Same: *Agents.* The failure of a soliciting agent of an insurer to pay
the applicant for livery hire which he accepted as the cash pay-
4 ment, does not estop the insurer to assert that it did not approve
6 of the application, in the absence of any evidence that the agent
had any actual or apparent right to contract for livery service at
the expense of the insurer.

AGENTS. A mere soliciting agent of an insurance company, without
1 power to make contracts, has no power to construe an application
5 for insurance and a premium note, nor to declare their legal
effect.

Contract of Insurance: APPLICATION. Receiving an application for
7 insurance accompanied by a premium note, does not of itself constitute a contract for insurance.

Appeal from Poweshiek District Court.—HON. BEN
McCOY, Judge.

WEDNESDAY, OCTOBER 13, 1897.

ACTION at law to recover the amount of an alleged
contract of insurance. There was a trial by jury, and a
verdict and judgment for the plaintiff. The defendant
appeals.—*Reversed.*

McVey & Cheshire for appellant.

No appearance for appellee.

ROBINSON, J. — On the twenty-fifth day of May,
1894, the plaintiff, who was the keeper of a livery stable,
signed and delivered to D. F. White, a soliciting agent
of the defendant, a mutual fire insurance company, an
application to it for insurance against loss or damage
by fire, for the term of six years from that date. The
insurance asked was for two hundred and fifty dollars
on work horses and mules, and one hundred and fifty
dollars on buggies, carriages, and harness. Attached
to the application was a promissory note for the sum of
forty-eight dollars, payable on assessment; but not
exceeding fifteen per centum thereof was collectible in
any one year. The application was made subject to the
conditions of the policy to be issued and the by-laws
and charter of the defendant, and provided that the
policy should be sent to the applicant. The application
described two barns as the premises in which the property to be insured was kept. On the first day of June,
1894, the application, having been received by the
defendant, was rejected "for specific amount on each
barn, and also for rate of four per cent. on the contents
of barn No. 1 and two per cent. on barn No. 2," and was

returned, with the note, to the agent, White. He testifies that he received the two papers on the fourth day
of June, and that on the next day he saw the plaintiff,
informed him that his application had been rejected,
stating the reason for that action, and proposed to
increase the note, and meet the requirements of the
company; and that the plaintiff said he was about to sell
the property to be insured, and would have the purchaser insure it. White further testifies that he then
delivered the note to the plaintiff, who destroyed it, but
retained the application, on account of the description
of property, which it contained, for use in preparing
another application. On the twenty-second day of
August, 1894, property covered by the application, of an
aggregate value exceeding four hundred dollars, was
destroyed by fire. The plaintiff admits that he was
with White several hours on the fifth day of June, and
that he saw White again in August, before the fire; but
states that he did not inquire for the policy, that the
matter of insurance was not referred to on either occasion, and that his note was not returned to him. He
also admits that he told White that two young men
were to buy the property. Proof of loss was mailed to
the defendant on the twentieth day of October, 1894.
The claim made in the original petition of the plaintiff
was that a contract of insurance was effected by the
signing and delivery of the application and note.

1   In an amendment to the petition the plaintiff
states that the application was made at the solic-
itation of White, and signed without reading, because
the plaintiff was unable to read it without great labor;
that White represented that the making of the application and note constituted and was the defendant's contract of insurance from that date; that the plain-

2   tiff, not knowing the rules, provisions of policies,
or by-laws of the defendants, believed White's
statements to be true, and from that time relied thereon

as the contract of insurance of the defendant, and
because thereof did not procure other insurance; that
the defendant, through its agent, knew that the plaintiff
believed and relied upon the statement of the agent, and
for that reason did not procure other insurance;
3   that the defendant retained the application and
note, and did not notify the plaintiff that his
application had been rejected until after the destruction
of the property, and is now estopped to deny its liability
as the insurer of the property. The answer of the
defendant denies liability, and pleads various matters,
which we need not refer to in detail. At the close of the
evidence the defendant moved the court to direct a verdict in its favor, but the motion was overruled. The
district court instructed the jury in regard to the elements of an estoppel, and directed it to return a verdict
for the defendant if the evidence failed to show that it
was estopped from asserting that it did not approve the
application. Therefore the controlling question for us
to determine is, did the evidence authorize the jury to
find that the defendant was estopped to assert that it
did not approve the application?

White was a soliciting agent, without power to
make contracts for the defendant, and the plaintiff had
no sufficient reason for believing that he had such
power. The plaintiff had seen White a few times
4   when the application was made, but was not
acquainted with him. It does not appear that
White made any representations in regard to the contents of the application, nor that the plaintiff asked to
have it read, or expressed any desire to know its contents. The plaintiff states that White told him
5   the contract of insurance would take effect at
noon of the day the application was signed, but
it was not the duty, nor within the power, of White to
construe the application and note, nor to declare their

legal effect. *Dryer v. Insurance Co.*, 94 Iowa, 471. The plaintiff states that he understod that White was to write a policy for him when the application was taken, and did not understand that he was to submit the application to the defendant for its approval; but in that he contradicts other testimony which he gave, to the effect that he supposed the application would be sent to the defendant, to be approved by it before the policy would be issued, and that White did not say anything to him about the policy. A by-law of the defendant provides that "any person wishing to become a member of the company shall, previous to being insured, deposit his application and premium note with the secretary or agent, upon which note he shall pay five per cent., and, if said application be approved by the directors, the policy of insurance shall bear date of that day, and take effect at noon, unless otherwise directed by the appli-

6   cant." When the application of the plaintiff was taken, he did not pay any money, but White agreed to take the five per cent. cash payment required by the by-law referred to in livery service, and that was furnished him. White says he offered to pay the plaintiff the livery hire when the application was returned, but that the plaintiff declined to receive the money, stating that it could be applied on the insurance when taken. The plaintiff denies this, and states that the money has never been paid nor tendered to him, and for the purposes of this appeal we must assume that his statement is true. But, if true, it would not affect his rights, for the reason that, so far as appears, White did not have either the actual or apparent right to contract for livery services at the expense of the defend-

7   ant. It is well settled that the receiving of an application for insurance, accompanied by a premium note, does not constitute a contract of insurance. The delivery of the note and application is in the nature

of a proposition for insurance which requires the assent
of the insurer to constitute a contract. *Walker v.
Insurance Co.*, 51 Iowa, 680; *Armstrong v. Insurance
Co.*, 61 Iowa, 215. But, if an application and
8   premium note be sent to the insurance company,
and it rejects the application, but does not notify
the applicant of the fact, does its silence estop it to deny
an approval of the application? In *Atkinson v. Insurance Co.*, 71 Iowa, 340, it appeared that an application
and premium were received by a soliciting agent of the
insurance company, and mailed to, but never received
by, it. This court held that there was no contract of
insurance, although it said, "If the defendant had
received the application and premium, and retained the
same, and remained silent, it may be that it should
be held to have approved the application." But the
question thus suggested was not involved in the case,
and was not determined. Ordinarily, mere silence in
regard to a proposal to enter into a contract will not
authorize the presumption that the proposal has been
accepted. This case differs from such a case in that the
proposal or application for insurance was accompanied
by a premium note, which, if the plaintiff is to be
believed, was retained by the defendant. But it
9   was not negotiable, and could have been made of
value only by accepting the application. As that
was rejected, the note was valueless, and the defendant
was not in any manner benefited, nor the plaintiff
harmed, by the failure to return it before the fire. The
plaintiff has failed to show that the defendant
10   knew, or had any reason to know, that he relied
upon the belief that his application had been
accepted. The defendant had promptly returned the
application and note, when rejected, to White, with the
evident intention that he should inform the plaintiff of
what had been done. It may be conceded that it was a

duty which White owed to the defendant to give that information; but the defendant and the plaintiff were alike interested in making the contract, and it was as much the duty of the latter to inquire whether it had been entered into as it was the duty of the former to give that information. The plaintiff admits that he was with White eleven days, and again more than two months, after the application was delivered, and yet claims that he did not make any inquiries with respect to the policy. He does not claim to have been misled by anything which was done or said by the defendant or White, excepting the statements of the latter in regard to the effect of the application and note, to which we have already referred; but the plaintiff relies upon the silence of the defendant as creating an estoppel. However, under the circumstances we have related, there was no obligation to speak. The views we have expressed find support in the following authorities: *More v. Insurance Co.*, 130 N. Y. 537 (29 N. E. Rep. 757); *Insurance Co. v. Johnson*, 23 Pa. St. 72; *Insurance Co. v. Beatty*, 119 Pa. St. 6 (12 Atl. Rep. 607); *Haskin v. Insurance Co.*, 78 Va. 700; *Insurance Co. v. Holzgrafe*, 53 Ill. 516; *Harp v. Insurance Co.*, 49 Md. 307; *Heiman v. Insurance Co.*, 17 Minn. 153; 1 Beach, Insurance, section 499; 2 May, Insurance, section 508. We conclude that the evidence was not sufficient to sustain a verdict for the plaintiff, and that the district court erred in not directing a verdict for the defendant. Its judgment is therefore REVERSED.

HERSHEY, BROWN & COMPANY v. CATHERINE NYENHUIS, Appellant.

Appeal: BILL OF EXCEPTIONS. The trial judge has no power, in the absence of an agreement of consent, to sign a bill of exceptions
1   after the final adjournment of the term; and if consent is given,

the bill must be filed within the time agreed upon, or it will not be considered, under Code 1873, section 2831.

ESTOPPEL. Appellee is not estopped to deny that the bill of exceptions was filed in due time, by correcting in its amended abstract alleged errors and inaccuracies in the appellant's abstract, where
2 the appellee denies the statement that the evidence was immediately after the trial certified by the trial judge and made a part of the record, and states the facts showing that the bill was not allowed by the judge during the term of court, or within the time after adjournment allowed therefor.

Appeal from Muscatine District Court.—HON. C. M. WATERMAN, Judge.

THURSDAY, OCTOBER, 14, 1897.

ACTION at law upon a promissory note. Defense, payment and a counter-claim for money deposited with plaintiff as bankers. Trial to the court without a jury. Judgment for plaintiff, and defendant appeals.—*Affirmed.*

D. M. Lambert, E. M. Warner, and *Earle & Prouty* for appellant.

Jayne & Hoffman for appellee.

DEEMER, J. — The judgment from which the appeal is taken was rendered on the twenty-fourth day of July, 1895. On January 21, 1896, the trial court made a certificate to the shorthand notes, the material parts of which are as follows: "I hereby certify t' at I believe the foregoing is the official report of the ab)ve-entitled cause; that it contains, together with the documentary evidence therein referred to, all of the evidence that was offered or introduced on the trial of said case, and all of the objections and rulings made and exceptions taken; and the said official report in shorthand is here' y made a part of the above-entitled cause." This certificate was attached to the shorthand notes, and filed in the clerk's office, January 23, 1896. The transcript of the shorthand notes was certified by the judge on January 9, 1896, and filed with the clerk January 20 of the same year. The action is at law, and it was the duty of appellant to file his bill of exceptions during the term, or within such time thereafter as might be fixed by the court. Code 1873, section 2831. In the absence of express agreement or consent, the judge has no power to sign a bill of exceptions after the final adjournment of the term; and, if consent is given, the bill must be filed within the time agreed upon, or it will not be considered. *Bunyan v. Loftus*, 90 Iowa, 122; *Wadsworth v. Bank*, 73 Iowa, 425.

In addition to reciting the facts above stated, appellee, in its amended abstract, proceeds to correct certain alleged errors and inaccuracies in the appellant's abstract. It is contended that, by so doing, it has estopped itself from saying that there was no proper and timely bill of exceptions. *Wells v. Railroad Co.*, 56 Iowa, 520; *Balm v. Nunn*, 63 Iowa, 641; and *Wilson v. Palo Alto County*, 65 Iowa, 20, are relied upon in support of this contention. None of these cases are in point, for the reason that in none of them did the appellee, as in this case, deny the statement made in the abstract that the evidence was properly made of record, by bill of exceptions or otherwise. On the contrary, it appears in each of these cases that the appellee set out certain evidence which he claimed was found in the record, and omitted from the appellant's abstract. Upon such a state of facts, we held that appellee was estopped from thereafter claiming that there was no proper bill of exceptions. The case which comes nearest to sustaining appellant's contention is *Conners v. Railroad*, 74 Iowa, 383, in which we said that, notwithstanding appellee alleged in his amended abstract that the evidence was not preserved by bill of exceptions, yet, as he set out portions of the evidence which he claimed were omitted, he would not be permitted to deny that the evidence was properly preserved; citing numerous cases. This case differs from that, in this: In this case, appellant, in his abstract, alleged that the evidence was, immediately after the trial, certified by the trial judge, and made a part of the record. Appellee denies this statement, and proceeds with a statement of the facts which are recited at the beginning of this opinion, and finally says that the evidence was never preserved by bill of exceptions, nor was there any bill of exceptions ever prepared, signed, or filed. It thereupon proceeds to state that certain entries of record are omitted from appellant's abstract, and further says that certain evidence is incorrectly abstracted, and makes corrections therein. These facts afford no good ground for saying that appellant is estopped from claiming that the bill of exceptions was not filed in time. The evidence was certified as stated, but the bill of exceptions was not filed in time. Appellant is not taking inconsistent positions in saying that the evidence was not properly made of record, while at the same time affirming that the evidence which was filed is not correctly abstracted. Examination of the cases cited as sustaining the rule announced in the *Conners Case* will disclose that they do not go to the extent claimed, and if there be a conflict between this case and that, it is overruled. All questions in the case depend upon a consideration and examination of the evidence, and, as it was not properly preserved, the judgment is AFFIRMED.

CLOSZ & MICKELSON, Appellants, v. JAMES MIRACLE.

Negotiable Instruments: DEMAND AND NOTICE. Presentment and
1 demand on one of two makers of a note is not sufficient to hold
2 the indorser.

WAIVER. To prove a waiver of demand and notice by an indorser, it
4   must be shown that he made a waiver with knowledge of the facts
that discharged him from liability.

DEMAND. There can be no such demand of payment as to charge an
1-2 indorser of a note, by mailing a letter to the maker.

SAME. The necessity of a demand of payment upon a maker of a
1   note after maturity, as a condition of holding an indorser. is not
obviated by making a demand upon him before maturity, and the
2   statement of another maker that he could not make the payment.

Plea and Proof: WAIVER. A waiver of demand and notice of non-
8   payment cannot be proved in an action against the indorser of a
promissory note, under a petition alleging demand and notice.

Appeal from Hamilton District Court.—HON. D. R.
HINDMAN, Judge.

THURSDAY, OCTOBER 14, 1897.

CY AND KATIE ASHPOLE executed to James Miracle
their note of one hundred and twenty-five dollars,
dated March 31, 1893, payable September 15 of the
same year. About June 27, 1893, Miracle sold this
note to the plaintiff, indorsing it in blank. The petition alleges that Miracle orally guarantied payment of
the note when he sold it, and also seeks to hold him as
indorser. The answer denies these allegations, and
avers that it was agreed the indorsement was to be
without recourse. Trial to jury. Verdict and judgment for defendant, and the plaintiff appeals.—
Affirmed.

Geo. Wambach for appellant.

A. N. Boeye for appellee.

LADD, J.—The indorsee and the makers of the
note lived in the same neighborhood, and no excuse
appears in the record for the failure to present the

note and demand payment personally or at the resi-
· dence or place of business of the makers. The
1   statute permits notice by mail to the indorsers,
but the law merchant controls with respect to
presentment and demand. Code 1873, section 2095. In
this case the indorsee, Closz & Mickelson, mailed letters to the makers, Cy Ashpole, and Katie Ashpole,
some time before the day the note matured,
2   demanding payment. Cy Ashpole called upon
the indorsee, and stated he could not make payment, and it is said that this obviated the necessity of
a demand. See *Gilbert v. Dennis*, 3 Metcalf (Mass.) 495.
But presentment and demand on all the makers are
required before the indorser may be held liable. *Blake
v. McMillen*, 22 Iowa, 358 (33 Iowa, 150); *Bank v.
Orvis*, 40 Iowa, 332. The note was never presented to
or payment demanded of Katie Ashpole, and the mailing of the letters referred to is the only evidence thereof.
That under such circumstances the indorser will not be
held has been expressly determined by this court.
Graul v. Strutzel, 53 Iowa, 712. See, also, *Bank v.
Green*, 11 Iowa, 476.

II.   Whether the demand and notice were waived
was not in issue. The petition alleged demand and
notice, not waiver thereof. To be of any avail a waiver
must be pleaded. *Lumbert v. Palmer*, 29 Iowa,
3   104; *Peck v. Schick*, 50 Iowa, 281. Nor was such
an issue supported by the evidence. The
indorser, before he may be said to have waived demand
on the makers, must be shown to have had knowledge
of the facts which in law discharged him from
4   liability. *Ballin v. Betcke*, 11 Iowa, 204; *Hughes
v. Bowen*, 15 Iowa, 446; *Freeman v. O'Brien*,
38 Iowa, 406.

III.   The issue as to whether the indorsement was
to be without recourse became immaterial upon the
failure to establish liability of defendant as indorser.

There was evidence, however, tending to show that
the note was taken at the risk of the plaintiff; and, if
so, under the evidence, there could have been no oral
guaranty. Telling the jury, then, to find for the
defendant if the indorsement was to be without
recourse, amounted to no more than an instruction to
return a verdict for him in event he did not guaranty
the payment of the note. No errors prejudicial to the
plaintiff appear in the record, and the judgment must
be AFFIRMED.

R. R. SAATOFF v. T. B. SCOTT, Appellant.   103
138

Plea and Proof: FAILURE OF PROOF   Where plaintiff sued for a
breach of a written contract for the sale of land, and the evidence
showed merely a contract made by defendant's agent, and signed
by plaintiff alone, there was a total failure of proof, within Code
1878, section 2688, providing that when the allegation to which the
proof is directed "is unproved in its general meaning" it shall not
be deemed a variance, but a failure of proof.

Variance. Damages for breach of an oral contract to convey land
cannot be recovered under a petition on a written contract, in the
absence of an amendment thereof to conform to the evidence.

Evidence: HARMLESS EXCLUSION.   Error in striking out the statement
of a witness, who thereafter testifies to substantially the same
facts, without any objection being made, is harmless.

Appeal from Franklin District Court.—HON. D. R.
HINDMAN, Judge.

THURSDAY, OCTOBER 14, 1897.

ACTION to recover damages for a failure to convey
land in accordance with a certain contract. Verdict
and judgment for plaintiff. Defendant appeals.—
Reversed,

E. P. Andrews for appellant.

Taylor & Evans for appellee.

KINNE, C. J.—I. There was no prejudicial error in the rulings of the court in striking out answers by the defendant, Scott, as to the authority of his agent, Musser, as the same witness afterwards testified to substantially the same facts without objection.

II. At the close of the plaintiff's evidence the defendant moved the court to direct a verdict for him, because plaintiff had failed by a preponderance of the evidence to support the allegations of his petition. We think the motion should have been sustained. The plaintiff sued on a written contract providing for the sale and conveyance of certain real estate to the defendant The evidence on part of the plaintiff not only wholly fails to show any written contract, but from it, as well as from all of the evidence, it conclusively appears that no written contract was ever entered into between the parties. The most that plaintiff's evidence shows is that one Musser, defendant's agent, made a contract with the plaintiff for the sale of the land, and plaintiff claims that he (plaintiff) signed said contract, and executed a mortgage and some notes. It nowhere appears that either the defendant or his agent ever signed the contract relating to the sale of said land. There was, therefore, a total failure of proof as to the claim made in the petition. Code 1873, section 2688. Under the evidence there could be no recovery on a written contract, as no such contract was shown to have been entered into by the parties. While it may be that plaintiff might have so amended his petition as to conform to the evidence, no attempt was made to do so. Recovery, therefore, if had at all, must be upon a written contract; and, as no such contract was proven, the motion

for a verdict should have been sustained.   2 Thompson,
Trials, p. 1606.

Other questions are argued, which, in view of the
conclusion we have reached, need not be considered.—
REVERSED.

PETER MEARS v. THE CHICAGO & NORTHWESTERN RAIL-
WAY COMPANY, Appellant.

Railroads: TRESPASSING STOCK. An engineer has the right to pre-
2 sume that the track is clear of stock at a point where the company
has inclosed the right of way, and he owes no duty to the owner
4 in relation to trespassing horses until their presence is discovered,
and then only the duty of using ordinary care to avoid injuring
them. Citing *Harrison v. Railway Co* , 6 S. D. 100 (60 N. W. Rep.
405); *Railway Co. v. Noble,* 14 Ill. 578; *Railway Co. v. Barlow,* 71 Ill.
410.

CONDUCT OF ENGINEER. Where the engineer of a train by which
horses were killed first saw such horses as they were getting on
the track, and on seeing them whistled for brakes, and reversed
3 the engine, which was running down grade at twelve to fifteen
miles an hour, toward an open bridge, there was no showing of
negligence in the management of such train; and it was proper to
omit the usual stock alarm whistle.

NEGLIGENCE: *Gates.* Where the gate in a right of way fence at a
farm crossing, which was an ordinary gate, sliding between two
posts at each end, and to open which it was necessary to shove it
back on a line with the fence, and then carry it around, appeared
1 to have been opened by pushing it back and towards the railroad
track, permitting the escape of horses to the right of way, no
want of ordinary care in the construction or maintenance of such
gate was shown, in the absence of evidence that it was defectively
constructed, or out of repair, or required some other mode of fastening.

Appeal from Clinton District Court.—HON P. B. WOLFE,
Judge.

THURSDAY, OCTOBER 14, 1897.

ACTION to recover the value of three horses killed
by one of defendant's trains.   Defendant answered,

denying generally, and verdict and judgment were rendered for plaintiff. Defendant appeals.—*Reversed.*

Hubbard & Dawley for appellant.

Walter I. Hayes and *F. P. McGinn* for appellee.

GIVEN, J.—I.   It is not disputed but that plaintiff's horses got upon defendant's right of way through a gate in the right of way fence at a farm crossing, and were struck and killed by one of defendant's trains. Plaintiff alleges as grounds for recovery that said gate was defective, and that defendant's agents negligently and carelessly ran said train over and upon said horses. Defendant contends that there is no evidence to sustain either of these allegations, and that, therefore, the court erred in overruling its motion for a verdict and its motion for a new trial.   The gate is described, by all the witnesses who speak concerning it, as an ordinary sliding gate, such as is in common use. "The gate was slid in between two posts, with a piece of board between the two posts.   At the other end the posts stood apart, and the gate shoved in between the posts.   It was a common sliding gate.   There was no fastening on the gate."   There is no evidence that the gate was defectively constructed, was out of repair, or that any other fastening than placing the ends of the boards between the posts was required or used on such gates.   To open this gate, it was necessary to shove it back on a line with the fence, and then carry it round.   On the morning preceding that on which the horses were killed, the gate was standing closed, and after the horses were killed it was found to be pushed back about four feet, and towards the track about four feet.   We think it highly improbable that the horses did, or could have, opened this gate as it was opened, but more probable that it

was opened by some person. If it be conceded that
the horses did, in some way, work the gate open, still
there is no evidence of want of ordinary care on the
part of the defendant in the construction or maintenance of the gate. It was just such a gate as is in common use, and was in good order.

II. The train that killed the horses was a freight
of twelve or fifteen cars, going west. In approaching
the place of the accident the train came up a steep
grade to a point thirty-six rods east of the bridge where
the horses were killed, from which point it is down
grade, west to the bridge. The up grade from the east
is such that horses on the right of way between the summit and the bridge cannot be seen from the cab of the
engine until the engine is near the summit. The
2   track being inclosed for a long distance east
        and west, the trainmen had no reason to expect
that horses would be on the right of way at the place
of the accident; but when known to be there it was
their duty to exercise ordinary care to avoid injuring
them. The engineer testifies: "I first saw the animals on the track. They came up on the left-hand side
and I didn't see them until after they got onto the track.
I saw them getting onto the track. They came over
from the left-hand side onto the track. When I saw
them, I whistled for brakes and reversed my engine. I
applied brakes, and did everything in my power to stop
the train." The train was running down grade at
twelve to fifteen miles an hour towards an open bridge.
Therefore, it is entirely reasonable that the engineer
would have done just what he says he did do, and his
testimony stands uncontradicted. True, a witness who
was some distance away, says he "just heard one little
whistle. Just about the time they whistled the train
stopped." This rather confirms than contradicts the
engineer's testimony that he whistled for brakes, as

evidently but a brief time elapsed between the call
for brakes and the stopping of the train. With
3   the frightened horses fleeing before the train as
they were, towards the open bridge, there was
no occasion for any other whistling that the call for
brakes; indeed, it may be questioned whether it would
not have been negligence to have sounded the usual
stock alarm. We do not find any evidence that the
trainmen were negligent or careless in the management of the train, nor that the defendant was negligent
in the construction or maintenance of said gate. We
think the court erred in not sustaining defendant's
motion for a verdict, and its motion for a new trial on
the ground that the evidence did not justify a verdict
for the plaintiff.

III. The defendant asked instruction to this
effect: That, having inclosed its right of way at the
place where these horses were, it was not bound to
anticipate that horses or cattle would be there
4   on the track, but had a right to presume that the
track was clear; and that defendant owed no
duty to the plaintiff in relation to his trespassing horses
until their presence was discovered, and then only owed
the use of ordinary care to avoid injury to the horses.
That such is the law, see *Baker v. Railway Co.*, 95 Iowa,
163; *Connyers v. Railway Co.*, 78 Iowa, 410; *Thomas v.
Railway Co.*, 93 Iowa, 248; *Railway Co. v. Barlow*,
71 Ill. 640; *Harrison v. Railway Co.*, 6 S. D. 100; (60 N.
W. Rep. 405), and *Railway Co. v. Noble*, 142 Ill. 578 (32
N. E. Rep. 684). The instructions given were not explicit
on this subject, and those asked should have been given.
Other errors assigned and argued are sufficiently con-
sidered and disposed of in what we have already said.
It follows that for the errors named above, the judg-
ment of the district court must be REVERSED.

W. S. BENNETT, Appellant, v. THE NATIONAL STARCH
MANUFACTURING COMPANY.

Accretions Defined. In a suit commenced in 1893 and tried in 1895,
between the respective owners of adjoining lots, numbered ten to
fifteen, bounded on the south by the Des Moines river at a point
where it flows east, the question was whether certain ground
south of the original river bank, forming the boundary of lot ten,
was accretion. When the section of which such lots are a part
was surveyed by the United States, the river near such lots was
separated by an island, into two parts, and the place in controversy was covered by the north one of the two channels Subse-
5   quently a large part of the island was cut away, and the north
channel partially filled, discharges from sewers above contributing to such result; and for several years prior to 1895 water had
not covered the tract in question, except in times of high water.
In October, 1895, a rise of nine feet would have been required to
cause water coming down the river to flow over it, though a considerable portion would have been covered by back water, from a
smaller rise. The deposits in the old north channel are of sand and
refuse from sewers. The soil thus formed does not produce
grass, and is not suitable for agricultural purposes; cottonwood
trees, willows, weeds, and sand burrs growing on it. The two
banks are distinct, and in most places several feet higher than the
place in question: and the river would overflow all of that before
it could overflow either bank. For several years before the trial
such tract had not been overflowed, and it had on it cottonwood
trees and willows of three or four years' growth; but the river
had been unusually low for several years. *Held,* that the ground
in question was not an accretion.

Boundaries: WATERS. The title to land derived under conveyances
made while the Des Moines river was regarded as navigable,
2   describing the premises conveyed as bounded by the bank of such
river, only extends to the edge of the bank, notwithstanding that
the river is not now regarded as navigable.

SAME. The owners of land bordered by a navigable stream own only
1   to ordinary high water mark,—that is, to the edge of the bank,—and
the whole bed of the river belongs to the public.

SAME. The line which separates the bed of a navigable stream from
the land owned by the riparian proprietor is not the line reached
4   by unusual floods, but that which is shown by the character and
condition of the soil and vegetation to be the limit which high

water ordinarily reaches. Citing *Carpenter v. Board*, 56 Minn., 513 (58 N. W. Rep. 295).

ACCRETIONS. Accretions between the meander line and a navigable
3 river belong to the riparian proprietor.

Injunction: WATER. The discharge of sewage from a manufactory
into a running stream will not be enjoined on the complaint of a
lower riparian owner that it emits disagreeable odors, where the
6 causes of offense for which the defendant was responsible were
almost wholly removed before the action was commenced, and
the use which it is making of the river is a proper one, in view of
the business which it carries on and the conditions which exist in
the locality.

Appeal from Polk District Court.--HON. T. F. STEVEN-
son, Judge.

THURSDAY, OCTOBER, 14, 1897.

ACTION in equity to enjoin the maintenance of a
sewer on land claimed by the plaintiff, to abate an
alleged nuisance, and for other relief. There was a
hearing on the merits, and a judgment for the defendant. The plaintiff appeals.—*Affirmed*.

Day & Corry for appellant.

C. C. & C. L. Nourse for appellee.

ROBINSON, J. — The plaintiff is, and has been for
many years, the owner of a tract of land now known as
"lot numbered 10, of official plat of section 12, in township 78 north, of range 24 west of the 5th P. M." In the
year 1870 he sunk on the lot an artesian well, from
which he obtained and sold mineral water, and in the
year 1874 or 1875 he built a sanitarium for use in connection with the well, to which for a time many people
resorted. A family residence was also erected a few
rods from the site of the sanitarium. For some time
prior to the year 1890 the Gilbert Starch Company
owned and operated a starch factory, which was located

on lot numbered 15 of the official plat of section 12, west of and adjoining the lot owned by the plaintiff. Both lots were bounded on the south by the Des Moines river, which there flows along an irregular course, the general direction of which is from west to east. For the purpose of discharging the sewage from its factory into the Des Moines river, the Gilbert Starch Company had maintained an open board sewer which extended from the factory to the river bank. That was well defined and constituted the southern boundary of the two lots we have described, when section 12 was surveyed by the general government; but about the year 1889 the channel of the river in that vicinity seems to have been changed to the southward, and thereafter, and until the time of the trial in the district court, the water in the river, when at an ordinary stage or lower, did not reach the original bank. In the year 1890 the Gilbert Starch Works were transferred to the defendant. A few days later the factory was burned, but was rebuilt in the latter part of the year 1892, and the new factory was put in operation in April, 1893. In December, 1892, the defendant constructed a new sewer by laying a fifteen-inch tile pipe on the bottom of the old one until the end of the latter was reached at the old river bank, and from that point, which was but a few feet west of the west boundary line of the lot of the plaintiff, constructed an extension in a southeasterly direction to the bank of the river as it then existed. That extension of the sewer is now a little more than seven hundred feet in length, and its outlet is four hundred and twenty feet south of the original north bank of the river, and six hundred feet southwest of the sanitarium of the plaintiff. The defendant has used that sewer since April, 1893, and during that time has discharged through it the sewage from its factory. This action was commenced in September of the year 1893, and

the trial of the cause was commenced in the district
court two years later, and finally concluded the last of
October, 1895. The plaintiff claims as follows: (1)
That the change in the river channel is permanent, and
that by accretion the south boundary of lot 10 has been
extended south to the bank of the river as it now flows;
that all of the extension of the defendant's sewer which
is east of the west boundary line of lot 10 produced to
the new bank is on the land of the plaintiff without
his consent, and that its maintenance and use on his
land constitute a trespass. (2) That the sewage which
flows through the sewer is deposited in such manner
and in such quantities as to contaminate the water of
the river, and impregnate the atmosphere with a stench
so great and offensive as to prevent the comfortable
enjoyment of the premises of the plaintiff by himself
or others, and endanger their health and lives, thereby
constituting a nuisance. The district court found that
neither of these claims was sustained by the evidence,
and rendered judgment in favor of the defendant for
costs.

I. We are first required to determine whether the
premises in controversy are a part of the river bed, or
whether they have become a part of lot 10 by the process
of accretion. It is the settled rule in this state
1   that the owners of land bordered by a navigable
stream own "only to ordinary high-water mark,
—that is, to the edge of the bank,"—and that the whole
bed of the river belongs to the public. *Musser v.
Hershey*, 42 Iowa, 361. The conveyances through
which the plaintiff derived title to his lot described the
premises conveyed as bounded on the south by the
north bank of the Des Moines river, and,
2   although the river is not now regarded as navigable, the rule which limits the ownership of the
plaintiff to land bounded by the ordinary high-water
mark applies. *Serrin v. Grefe*, 67 Iowa, 198; *Railway*

Co. v. Porter, 72 Iowa, 429. The appellant does not dispute these propositions, but contends that the premises in question are now above high-water mark, and therefore constitute an accretion to his original lot.

3   It is true that accretions between the meander line and the river belong to the riparian proprietor. *Coulthard v. Stevens*, 84 Iowa, 242; *Cook v. City of Burlington*, 30 Iowa, 99; *Kraut v. Crawford*, 18 Iowa, 549. The line which separates what belongs to the river bed from that which is owned by the
4   riparian proprietor is not the line reached by unusual floods, but that which is shown by the character and condition of the soil and vegetation to be the limit which high water ordinarily reaches. Soil which is submerged so long or so frequently, in ordinary seasons, that vegetation will not grow upon it, may be regarded as part of the bed of the river which overflows it. *Houghton v. Railroad Co.*, 47 Iowa, 370. In *Carpenter v. Board*, 56 Iowa, 513 (58 N. W. Rep. 295), it is said: "High-water mark means what its language imports,—a water mark. It is co-ordinate with the limit of the bed of the water; and that only is to be considered the bed which the water occupies sufficiently long and continuously to wrest it from vegetation, and destroy its value for agricultural purposes." See, also, *Plumb v. McGannon*, 32 U. C. Q. B. 14; Gould,
5   Waters, section 76. When section 12 was surveyed by the general government, the river near what are now known as lots 10 and 15 was separated by an island into two parts, and the place in controversy was covered by the north one of the two channels thus formed. Since that time a large part of the island has been cut away by the river, and the north channel has been partially filled; discharges from the sewers of numerous factories located near the river and above the land of the plaintiff doubtless having contributed to that result. The main channel of the river is now

further south than it was fifteen years ago, and for
several years water has not covered the tract in
question excepting in times of high water. In October,
1895, a rise of nine feet would have been required before
water coming down the river would have flowed over
it, although a considerable portion would have been
covered by back water from a smaller rise. The deposits
which have been made in the old north channel are of
sand and the refuse from sewers. The soil thus constituted is not suitable for agricultural purposes, nor
does it produce grass. Cottonwood trees, willows,
weeds, and sand burs comprise what grows upon it.
The two banks are distinct, and in most places rise
several feet higher than does the tract in question. The
river would overflow all of that before it could overflow
either bank. For several years the tract has not been
overflowed, and cottonwood trees and willows of three
or four years' growth were found upon it at the time of
the trial, but it appears that the river had been unusually low for several years. A witness who had lived
near the river for forty years stated that it was lower
during the preceding three years than it had been
during the remainder of the time he had known it.
We are satisfied that a preponderance of the evidence
shows that the tract in question has the characteristics
of a river bed uncovered for a few years by reason of
unusually low water, and a change in the channel of
the stream, which may be only temporary; that it is
subject to overflow in ordinary times of high water,
and is worthless for agricultural purposes. We conclude, therefore, that it is not a part of the lot owned
by the plaintiff, and that the defendant is not a trespasser in placing and using its sewer on it.

II. The evidence in regard to the kind, quantity,
and effect of the discharges from the sewer is some-

what conflicting. There is no doubt that at times it has emitted disagreeable odors. In the spring of the year 1893 high water formed a sand bar near to and above the mouth of the defendant's sewer, which formed a bay into which the sewer discharged, and for a time the sewage was troublesome; but in July the sewer was extended through the bay and the sand bar to the current of the river, and that difficulty was remedied. At another time a break in the sewer occurred where it crossed the bay, and there was a leakage of sewage, which was offensive; but that also was remedied. Since February, 1894, very little of an offensive nature passed through the sewer, and the defendant has used due care to keep the sewer in good order, and to prevent any considerable discharge from it of offensive matter. The causes of offense for which the defendant was responsible were almost wholly removed before this action was commenced; and the use which the defendant is now making of the river appears to be a proper one in view of the business it carries on and the conditions which exist in that locality. Some witnesses state that the discharge from the defendant's sewer caused disagreeable odors, while other witnesses, whose opportunities for knowing the fact have been equally as good, state that the odors emitted were not of a serious character. Some of the testimony relates to the discharges from the old Gilbert Starch Company sewer, for which the defendant is not responsible. The sanitarium of the plaintiff is vacant, but he is not certain that he had rented it more than once, and then for a single winter, during the ten years preceding the trial. The evidence is not sufficient to sustain the claim that the sewer as it is operated by the defendant is a nuisance, nor to show that the plaintiff has sustained injury from any unauthorized use of it. The judgment of the district court is therefore AFFIRMED.

JAMES HOLLENBECK, Appellant, v. P. E. HALL.

Libel. To publish of one that he has for several years owed for medical services; that his attention has been repeadly called thereto to no purpose; that finally, being sued therefor, he, having no other defense, has cowardly slunk behind that of the statute of limitations; and that such a course is not in accordance with the writer's idea of strict integrity,—is not actionable, within Code 1873, section 4097, defining libel as malicious defamation of a person by writing tending to expose him to public hatred, contempt or ridicule, or to deprive him of the benefits of public confidence and social intercourse.

Appeal from Cedar Rapids Superior Court.—HON. T. M. GIBERSON, Judge,

FRIDAY, OCTOBER 15, 1897.

THE plaintiff alleged in his petition that "on or about the first day of June, 1893, the defendant, P. E. Hall, for the purpose of injuring the good name and reputation of the plaintiff herein, and to expose him to the public hatred, contempt, and ridicule, and to deprive him of the benefit of public confidence and social intercourse, did publish of and concerning the plaintiff the following false, libelous, and defamatory matter to-wit: 'Cedar Rapids, Iowa, Dec. 7, 1892. P. E. Hall, Pres. C. R. & M. C. R'y Co., Cedar Rapids, Iowa—Dear Sir: For some years past, one of your old and trusty conductors, Mr. James Hollenbeck, has owed us a bill for professional services rendered his family in the way of consultations with his family physician at his home in Marion. His attention has been repeatedly called to the subject, but to no purpose. We finally sued him, to which he responds by employing an attorney, and contesting the claim. Having no other defense, he cowardly slinks behind that of statutory limitation.

Such a course is not exactly in accordance with our idea of strict integrity. So far as we are concerned, we would prefer not to be connected in an official capacity with a corporation giving employment to men of this character; especially when permitted to occupy positions of trust. Yours, courteously, H. & J. M. Ristine.'" Then follows a denial in detail of the statements contained in the letter, the allegations that it was published by mailing copies to persons named, and that plaintiff has been damaged in the sum of five thousand dollars, for which amount judgment is prayed. No special damages are alleged. To this petition the defendant demurred in these words: "(1) No sufficient publication of the alleged libel is shown to render the defendant liable. (2) The alleged letter or publication set out in the petition is not libelous or actionable, even if published. It is not libelous to charge plaintiff with having availed himself of the statute of limitations, and no language is contained in the alleged letter or publication from which injury or damage to the plaintiff can be inferred." The demurrer was sustained, and, the plaintiff electing to stand on the ruling, judgment was entered against him for costs, and he appeals. —*Affirmed.*

J. H. Crosby, *H. Rickel*, and *John T. Christie* for appellant.

Chas. A. Clark for appellee.

LADD, J.—Conceding the letter to have been published, was it libelous? Our statute defines "libel" to be "the malicious defamation of a person made public by any printing, writing, sign, picture, representation or effigy, tending to provoke him to wrath or expose him to public hatred, contempt or ridicule, or to deprive

him of the benefits of public confidence and social intercourse." Code 1873, section 4097. "Defamation" is
defined by Webster as "the taking from another's reputation." Odgers, in his work on Libel and Slander,
says: "Words which produce any perceptible injury
to the reputation of another are called defamatory."
It is "a false publication calculated to bring one in
disrepute." Cooley, Torts, 193. The derivation of
the word leaves no doubt as to its meaning. Was
there anything in the letter injurious to the good
name of the plaintiff, or tending to bring him into
disrepute? It is not dishonorable to be indebted to
another, nor is it libelous to publish of another that he
owes money. *Regina v. Coghlan,* 4 Fost. & F. 316.
To be in debt is very common, and to be unable to
make payment does not necessarily involve moral ter-
pitude. Nor is the debtor's reputation brought in question by making a defense which the law sanctions, and
which rests .on sound reason and long experience
Formerly, pleading the statute of limitations was
looked upon with disfavor. Lord Mansfield remarked
in *Quantock v. England,* 5 Burrows, 2630, "that, in
honesty, a defendant ought not to defend himself by
such a plea." The statute is now generally conceded to
be beneficial, and the defense as legitimate as any
other. As said by Justice Story in *Spring v. Gray,* 5
Mason, 523: "The defense, therefore, which it puts
forth, is an honorable defense, which does not seek to
avoid the payment of just claims or demands, admitted
now to be due, but which encounters, in the only practical manner, such as are ancient and unacknowledged,
and, whatever may have been their original validity,
such as are now beyond the power of the party to meet,
with all the proper vouchers to repel them. The natural
presumption certainly is that claims that have been
long neglected are unfounded, or, at least, are no longer
subsisting demands. And this presumption the statute

has erected into a positive bar. There is wisdom and policy in it, as it quickens the diligence of creditors, and guards innocent persons from being betrayed by their ignorance, or their overconfidence in regard to transactions which have become dimmed by age." See 3 Parsons, Contracts, 61; *Penley v. Waterhouse*, 8 Iowa, 418. It cannot be libelous to accuse one of doing what the law approves. In *Homer v. Englehardt*, 117 Mass. 539, it was held that to accuse one of availing himself of the prohibitory liquor law, in order to defeat an indebtedness for liquor sold, is not libelous, the court remarking that, "the plaintiff having the right to make this defense, it is not libelous to publish the statement that he had done so." *Bennett v. Williamson*, 4 Sandford, 60, is precisely in point. Since the law recognizes this defense as legitimate and honorable, to accuse one of making it would not amount to defamation. Bishop, Noncontr. Law, section 283.

II. The entire letter must be considered, and therefrom the plain import and natural meaning as intended, and the sense in which it was understood. determined. The alleged facts are clearly stated. There is no mistaking them from the opinions expressed by the writers of the letter. The characterization of the acts is based entirely on the assumption that the conduct of the plaintiff in availing himself of the defense was not honest and in accord with their standard of integrity. The spirit and purpose of the letter may well be said to indicate an element of character quite as inconsistent with the golden rule as that which permits omissions in the matter of pecuniary obligations. Such a letter may be the subject of just criticism, but its publication does not expose to public hatred or contempt in the sense or to the degree required by the law of libel. See *Urban v. Helmick*, 15 Wash. 155 (45 Pac. Rep. 747); *Donaghue v. Gaffy*, 54 Conn. 257 (7 Atl. Rep. 552).—AFFIRMED.

FRANK E. SMITH, Appellant, v. JAMES CALLANAN
et al.

18   **Taxation:** REDEMPTION NOTICE. Code 1873, section 894, provides
that, after the expiration of two years and nine months from the
date of sale of land for taxes, notice may be served on the person
in possession of the land, and also on the person in whose name
the same is taxed, stating that the right of redemption will expire,
1   and a deed for said land be made, unless redemption is made
within ninety days from service of said notice   *Held,* that the
notice should be given to the person in whose name the property
is taxed, at the time the notice is in fact given, and not necessarily
to the person to whom it is taxed at the end of the two years and
nine months from the date of sale.

TAX BOOK: *Sale.* Code 1873, section 845, provides for the placing
upon the tax books, opposite each parcel of land, the year or
years for which taxes remain due and unpaid, and that sales for
taxes not so entered are invalid.   The treasurer's tax book, in the
8   column "1878," showed the figures "75," written with lead pencil,
and crossed over, as if to mark them out.   In column "1879,"
appeared "74" in the same condition.   In the column "1880"
appeared the letters "ad," unexplained.   *Held,* not a compliance
with the statute.

Limitation of Action: COMMENCEMENT OF SUIT: *Action to redeem.*
Code 1873, section 2532, which is found in the general chapter on
the limitation of actions, and provides that delivery of the original notice to the sheriff of the proper county, to be served imme-
3   diately, "is a commencement of the action," is applicable to an
action to redeem from a tax sale and to quiet title, though there is
a special limitation for such action not found in the general
chapter on limitations. *Hintrager v. Nightingale,* 86 Fed. Rep.
847, *disapproved.*

Appeal from Kossuth District Court.—HON. GEORGE H.
CARR, Judge.

FRIDAY, OCTOBER 15, 1897.

ACTION to redeem from certain tax sales, and to
quiet title. Decree for defendants. Plaintiff appeals.—
Reversed.

George E. Clarke for appellant.

Davis & Davis for appellee.

KINNE, C. J.—I.   The facts in this case are that this action was commenced in the district court of Kossuth county to set aside and redeem from a certain tax deed made to the defendants by the treasurer of said county on October 28, 1887, and which was recorded October 29, 1887. The real estate involved is the south half of the southeast quarter, and the undivided one-fifteenth of the southeast quarter of the southwest quarter, all in section 13, township 99 north, of range 29 west, of the fifth P. M. The petition in this case was filed November 3, 1892. The original notice was delivered to the sheriff of Kossuth county for service on all of the defendants on October 10, 1892, and was served on J. C. Stahl on November 23, 1892. An original notice was delivered to the sheriff of Polk county, Iowa, for service on the defendants James Callanan and J. C. Savery, on October 28, 1892, and was served on them October 31, 1892. Plaintiff is the owner of the patent title to the land in controversy, and defendants Callanan and Savery are the owners and holders of the tax title to the south half of the southeast quarter, and an undivided one-fifteenth of the southeast quarter of the southwest quarter of the land heretofore described under a tax deed. Said deed was made to one Atkins, and he quitclaimed to Callanan and Savery. For the years 1884 and 1885 said land was assessed and taxed to the American Emigrant Company, and for the years 1886 and 1887 to Callanan and Savery. The tax deed was taken upon notice served by publication against James Callanan and J. C. Savery, which publication was completed July 15, 1887, and filed with the treasurer July 22, 1887. Said land was sold

on October 2, 1882, for the taxes of 1874 and 1875.
Defendants claim title to said land under the tax deed.
In a counter-claim they plead said tax deed as an affirmative ground for relief, and ask for a decree quieting
the title in them. They further plead that this action
was not commenced within five years after the completion and recording of said tax deed, and that plaintiff's
action is barred.

II. Was the notice for a tax deed served upon
the proper party? It is to be observed that, at the
expiration of the period of two years and nine months

1
from the date of sale, the land in question was
assessed and taxed to the American Emigrant
Company. When the notice was in fact given,
the land was assessed and taxed to James Callanan and
J. C. Savery, and the notice was given to them. The
controversy is as to whether the notice should be given
to the person in whose name the land is assessed, and
taxed at the end of the two years and nine months from
the date of sale, or to the person in whose name it is
assessed and taxed at the time the notice is in fact
given. The statute provides: "After the expiration of
two years and nine months after the date of sale of the
land for taxes, the lawful holder of the certificate of
purchase may cause to be served upon the person in
possession of such land, * * * and also upon the
person in whose name the same is taxed in the manner
provided by law for the service of original notices, a
notice; * * * and until ninety days after the
service of said notice, the right of redemption from
such sale shall not expire." Code 1873, section 894.
We think the notice was properly given to James Callanan and J. C. Savery. They are the persons in whose
name the land was assessed, and to whom it was taxed
when the notice was given. The provision of the statute requiring notice to be served on the person in possession and the person in whose name the land is taxed is

for the benefit of the owner of the land. To construe the statute as contended for by appellant would require the service of notice in cases like this upon persons having no interest in the land, whatever. The purpose of the law is to advise the owner that a deed will be taken unless redemption is made within the time provided by statute. It was said in *Heaton v. Knight*, 63 Iowa, 686: "The statute declares that notices served must be served on the person in whose name the land is taxed. This undoubtedly means at the time the notice was served, as the statute was clearly enacted for the benefit of the owner." And see *Cahalan v. Van Sant*, 87 Iowa, 597; *Hall v. Guthridge*, 52 Iowa, 410. We have carefully examined all of the cases cited by appellant, and in none of them has the question here presented been determined. In some of the cases language might be found which, standing alone, might give some support to appellant's contention; but, when considered in connection with the facts of the case wherein such language is used, it in no way aids appellant herein. We have no doubt that our construction of this statute is correct, and the only one which in any way tends towards accomplishing the purpose which the legislature had in mind in its enactment; that is, of giving notice to the owner, so that he might redeem.

III.   The statute provides that "no action for the recovery of real property sold for the non-payment of taxes shall lie unless the same be brought within five years after the treasurer's deed is executed and recorded." Code 1873, section 902. A material question in this case is as to when this action was "brought." Was the action brought when the original notice was placed in the sheriff's hands for service, or was it brought when service of the notice was actually made on the defendants? If service was essential in order to constitute the commencement or bringing of the action, then this action is barred; otherwise it is not. An action is brought when it is commenced. We are therefore to determine when this action was commenced. Code 1873, section 2532, provides that "the delivery of the original notice to the sheriff of the proper county with intent that it be served immediately, which intent shall be presumed unless the contrary appears, * * * is a commencement of the action." Section 2599 provides: "Actions in a court of record shall be commenced by serving the defendant with a notice. * * *" Section 2605 provides: "If the notice is placed in the hands of a sheriff, he must note thereon the date when received, and proceed to serve the same without delay. * * *" It is clear that section 2599 throws no light upon the subject of our inquiry. That section simply points out or provides the manner in which an action shall be commenced. Section 2605 is only material as indicating the duty of the officer as to service, but, like 2532, is not, in terms, limited in its application to chapter 2 of title 17 of the Code of 1873. We, then, have but one section of the Code of 1873 which undertakes to provide what shall be deemed to be the commencement of an action so far as the statute of limitations is concerned, and that is section 2532. That section is found in chapter 2 of title 17 of said Code. That chapter treats of the limitation of actions generally. In determining whether section 2532 furnishes the rule for ascertaining when the action referred to in section 902 is brought, it is well to consider briefly some decisions of this court. So far as it is material to the question to be determined in this case, it may be said that the statutes referred to are in substance the same as they appeared in the Code of 1851 and in the Revision of 1860.

The decisions of this court which tend to throw light upon the question before us may be grouped under the following heads: (a) Cases of attachment and injunction, wherein it has been held that the filing of the petition and the service of the writ operates to commence the action. *Sweatt v. Faville*, 23 Iowa, 321; *Hargan v. Burch*, 8 Iowa, 310. In the last cited case, the court, in speaking of the corresponding section of the Code of 1851, says: "The intention here is that, when the precise time of the commencement of an action becomes material, the fact referred to in section 1663 is made to define that time." (b) Cases wherein the provisions of the general statute of limitations have been held not to apply to or to control the contract stipulations limiting the time within which the action must be brought. *Parkyn v. Travis*, 50 Iowa, 438; *Proska v. McCormick*, 56 Iowa, 318. *Harrison v. Insurance Co.*, 102 Iowa, 112. In *Parkyn's Case* and *Proska's Case* it was held that section 2532 fixed the time for the purpose of determining the rights of the parties under the statute of limitations, and that section 2599 contains the general provision as to what is the commencement of an action. (c) Cases arising under special limitation statutes, not found in chapter 2 of title 17, and in which this court has either held directly or assumed that section 2532 was controlling in determining what constituted the commencement of the action. *Snyder v. Ives*, 42 Iowa, 157; *Wilson v. McElroy*, 83 Iowa, 595. (d) Cases arising under other sections in chapter 2 of title 17 of the Code of 1873, and in which section 2532 has been held to be of general application. *Heaton v. Fryberger*, 38 Iowa, 185, in which the court considered the sections of the Code of 1851 and of the Revision of 1860, which are the same as section 2532 of the Code of 1873. (e) Other cases which bear on the question. *Ware v. Howley*, 68 Iowa, 633; *Lesure Lumber Co. v. Ins. Co.*, 101 Iowa, 514.

We have referred to the foregoing cases, not

but rather to show the tendency of judicial construction, and as indicating to some extent the view the
court has taken as to whether section 2532 is controlling in determining what is the commencement of
the action when the limitation is a special one, not
found in the general chapter on limitation of actions.
It is apparent that in one or two cases the court, without expressly holding that section 2532 was applicable
in all cases where special limitations were provided,
has applied it in such cases. We do not think that the
mere fact that section 2532 is found in the general
chapter on the limitation of actions is of itself con
trolling in determining whether it shall be applied to
cases of other limitations found in the Code, and especially as it is in its terms general and unrestricted.
Our attention is called by appellee's counsel to the case
of *Hintrager v. Nightingale,* 36 Fed. Rep. 847, a case
like that at bar, wherein Judge Shiras held that section
2532 did not control, and that the commencement of the
action in such a case was the service of the notice. He
construes the case of *Proska v. McCormick, supra,* as in
effect deciding that section 2532 applies only to the
limitations provided for in the chapter in which it is
found. Such a conclusion does not necessarily follow
that holding. That was a question as to whether section 2532 applied to a contract limitation, and had no
relation whatever to the question as to whether special
statutory limitations, not found in the general chapter
on the limitation of actions, should be governed by
section 2532 in so far as determining when the action
was commenced was concerned. We discover no good
reason for following the cited case. Certain it is, the
same rule should obtain as to what shall constitute the
commencement of an action, as to the statute of limitations, whether the limitation be found in the general
chapter or elsewhere in the Code, unless there is something in the statute itself indicating to the contrary, or

unless some recognized rule of construction will be violated in so holding. We think, therefore, that, except in the classes of cases wherein section 2532 of the Code of 1873 has been held not to be controlling, or in other like cases, as a general rule, said section must be held applicable to cases of special limitations of actions, in determining what shall constitute the commencement of an action. It follows that, the notice having been placed in the sheriff's hands in time, the action in this case is not barred.

IV. Only one other question need be considered. Section 845 of the Code of 1873 provides that "the treasurer, on receiving the tax books for each year, shall enter upon the same in separate columns, opposite each parcel of real property or person's name, on which, or against whom any tax remains unpaid for either of the preceding years, the year or years for which such delinquent tax so remains due and unpaid. And any sale for the whole or any part of such delinquent tax, not so entered, shall be invalid." An inspection of the treasurer's books for 1881 and of the abstract shows that the above statute was not complied with. In the treasurer's books in the column "1878," the figures "75" have been written in with a lead pencil, and said figures have been crossed over as if it was intended to mark them out. In the column "1879," in like manner, have been marked the figures "74," and they are also crossed out; and in the column "1880" appear the letters "ad." The letters "ad." appearing opposite the tracts of land in controversy, unexplained, mean nothing. The other marks referred to, especially in view of their condition,—being crossed out,—cannot be held to constitute a compliance with the statute. There is therefore nothing to show that the tax of 1874 and 1875 was brought forward as the law requires. Under such circumstances, the sale was invalid, and the

deed should be set aside, and the plaintiff be permitted
to redeem. *Gardner v. Early*, 69 Iowa, 44; *Barke v.
Early*, 72 Iowa, 273; *Hooper v. Bank*, 72 Iowa, 280.—
Reversed.

J. W. EWING, Appellant, v. THE CITY OF WEBSTER
CITY, *et al.*

Injunctions: PENAL ORDINANCES. Proceedings to enforce a penal
ordinance enacted by authority of the legislature are criminal, within the rule that the validity of a criminal statute will
2 not be tested, nor its enforcement enjoined by a court of equity,
unless the party seeking such relief will otherwise sustain irreparable injury for which he has no plain, speedy, and adequate remedy
at law. *Sylvester v. City*, 130 Mo. 323, *disapproved.*

EQUITY JURISDICTION. Plaintiff, who had been twice convicted and
fined for violating an ordinance requiring grain to be weighed on
the city scales, and had appealed, brought suit, during pendency
1 of the appeals, to restrain the city from enforcing the ordinance,
and from further prosecuting plaintiff or any of his customers
thereunder, on the ground that the ordinance was void; alleging
that plaintiff's corncribs were one-half mile from the city scales,
that all the eligible locations near the scales were occupied by
other dealers, that sellers of corn refused to sell to plaintiff unless
3 the corn could be weighed near his cribs, and that the granting
of the relief demanded would avoid a multiplicity of suits.
Held, that plaintiff could avoid a multiplicity of suits by obeying
the ordinance, and that, though he must suffer some loss of business pending his appeals, or pay enough to secure the corn he
desires, the loss would not be so great as to warrant the interference of equity. Citing *Poyer v. Des Plaines*, 123 Ill. 111; *West
v. New York*, 10 Paige, 539; *Manchester v. Smyth*, 64 N. H. 380 (10
Atl. Rep 700); *State v. Patterson* (Tex. Civ. App.) 37 S. W. Rep. 478.

Appeal from Hamilton District Court.—HON. B. P.
BIRDSALL, Judge.

FRIDAY, OCTOBER 15, 1897.

ACTION in equity to restrain the defendants from
enforcing an ordinance of the city of Webster City. A
temporary injunction was issued, but on subsequent

hearing on the pleadings and affidavits was dissolved, and from that order the plaintiff appeals.—*Affirmed.*

Geo. Wambach, J. L. Kamrar, and *Wambach & Richard* for appellant.

C. A. Weaver and *D. C. Chase* for appellees.

ROBINSON, J.—In the latter part of the year 1895 the plaintiff commenced buying and cribbing corn in the city of Webster City. In August, 1889, an ordinance had been enacted which provided for establishing at the city market place city scales suitable for weighing commodities of various kinds. The ordinance also provided for a city weigher, and fixed the fees to be paid for weighing. Sections 6 and 7 of the ordinance are as follows:

"Sec. 6. It shall be unlawful for any person, persons, firm, or corporation to buy or sell by weight, within the city of Webster City, Iowa, any stock or any grain, hay, straw, stone, coal or other commodity, commonly sold by weight, and weighed on wagon or stock scales, where the quantity exceeds 600 pounds, without procuring a draft of such stock or commodity to be made on the city scales. This section shall not be construed so as to prohibit the buying or selling of stock by the head, or commodity by the bulk, or otherwise than by weight. Nor shall it apply to persons living on farms, within the corporation, so as to prevent their buying produce for feeding purposes thereon, outside of the platted portion of the city. The buying or selling of any commodity embraced in the foregoing provisions, and weighed on other scales than the city scales, shall be presumptive evidence that the same is bought and sold by weight.

"Sec. 7. Any person found guilty of a violation of this ordinance shall be fined a sum of not less than five dollars, or more than twenty-five dollars, and stand committed until such fine is paid."

On the twelfth day of December, 1895, the plaintiff was arrested, and fined five dollars, and required to pay the costs of the prosecution, for buying corn not weighed on the city scales; and on the next day he was again arrested, and required to pay a like fine and costs for a similar offense. From each judgment the plaintiff in this case appealed to the district court, and the appeals are now pending in that court, and undetermined. The distance from the city scales to the cribs of the plaintiff is about one-half mile, and on account of that distance sellers of corn refuse to sell to the plaintiff unless the corn can be weighed near the cribs. The location of the cribs is the nearest one to the scales which the plaintiff can procure, for the reason that all eligible locations which are nearer are already occupied by other dealers. The defendants are the city and its mayor and marshal. They threaten to prosecute the plaintiff and his customers if they do not weigh the corn sold on the city scales, and in consequence of the threats and prosecutions the business of the plaintiff has been greatly diminished. He states that the facilities for weighing furnished by the city are inadequate, and that the ordinance to which we have referred is unreasonable and void. He asks that the defendants be restrained from enforcing the ordinance, and from further prosecuting the plaintiff, or any of his customers, under the ordinance; and as one ground for the relief asked states that it will avoid a multiplicity of suits. A temporary injunction was issued to restrain the defendants from enforcing the ordinance as prayed. The answer of the defendants contains a general denial and pleads various matters in justification of the ordinance. A motion to dissolve the temporary injunction was filed by the defendants. The district court dissolved it on the ground "that the remedy

by injunction will not lie; that the court has no power
to determine the validity of the ordinance in question
in a suit in equity, but that the plaintiff must be rele-
gated to the suits brought for the enforcement of the
ordinance, wherein, if the ordinance is void, it will be
a complete defense to such prosecutions." Webster
City contains more than five thousand inhabitants, and
is incorporated as a city of the second class. The defendants claim that the ordinance in question was authorized by section 456 of the Code of 1873, which provides,
among other things, that incorporated cities and towns·
have power to establish and regulate markets, to
provide for the measuring or weighing of hay, coal,
or any other article of sale; and by section 482,
which authorizes such corporations to enforce obedi-
ence to ordinances by fine or imprisonment. These
sections authorized the city to adopt an ordinance
of the general scope and purpose of that in question; but an ordinance so adopted, to be valid,
must be reasonable. In *Davis v. Town of Anita*,
73 Iowa, 325, an ordinance similar to that in question
was considered, and held to be authorized, and this
court held further, in effect, that for the town of Anita
it appeared to be reasonable, and that an injunction to
restrain its enforcement should not have been granted.
But the power of a court of equity to grant an injunction to restrain prosecutions under such ordinances
does not appear to have been considered. A
2   court of equity will not interfere by injunction
where the party desiring it has a plain, speedy,
and adequate remedy in the ordinary course of the law.
Thomas v. Manufacturing Co., 76 Iowa, 738; *City of
Council Bluffs v. Stewart*, 51 Iowa, 391. To prevent a
multiplicity of suits is a well-recognized and favorite
ground for the granting of relief by injunction. 1 High,
Injunctions, section 12. But it is the general rule that

the validity of criminal statutes will not be tested, nor
their enforcement restrained, by a court of equity.
1 High, Injunctions, section 20. Whether that rule is
applicable to municipal ordinances which provide for
penalties has been questioned by some authorities. In
the state of Missouri the doctrine prevails that such
ordinances are not criminal, and therefore that the rule
last stated does not apply to them. See *Sylvester Coal
Co. v. St. Louis*, 130 Mo. 323 (32 S. W. Rep. 649, 51 Am.
St. Rep. 566), and cases therein cited. Whether offenses
against municipal ordinances are to be regarded as
criminal within the constitutional meaning of the term,
for all purposes, we have no occasion to decide. See
City of Davenport v. Bird, 34 Iowa, 524. But it is the
established rule of this state that, for most purposes, at
least, the violation of a municipal ordinance enacted by
authority of the state is a crime, and that proceedings
for its punishment are criminal. *City of Creston v. Nye*,
74 Iowa, 369; *State v. Vail*, 57 Iowa, 103; *Jaquith v.
Royce*, 42 Iowa, 408. Therefore the rule in regard to
testing the validity of criminal enactments applies
in this state alike to statutes of the general assembly
and to municipal ordinances enacted pursuant to legislative authority. There are cases where a court of
equity will enjoin an act, even though it be punishable
as a crime, as an act which would cause irreparable
injury. Thus an injunction would issue to prevent the
unlawful destruction of trees, on the ground that they
could not be replaced, and that the benefit their owner
would derive from them cannot be accurately meas-
ured from a pecuniary standard. *Musch v. Burkhart*,
83 Iowa, 301, and cases therein cited. See, also, *Bolton
v. McShane*, 67 Iowa, 207; *Deems v. Mayor of Baltimore*, 80 Md. 164 (30 Atl. Rep. 648, 45 Am. St. Rep.
339). In *Vegelahn v. Guntner* (Mass.) 44 N. E. Rep.
1077, it was said that "a continuing injury to property or business may be enjoined, although it may

be punishable as a nuisance or other crime." In *City of Austin v. Austin City Cemetery Association*, 87 Tex. 330 (28 S. W. Rep. 528, 47 Am. St. Rep. 114), it was said that the general rule that the aid of a court of equity cannot be invoked to enjoin criminal proceedings is "subordinate to the general principle that equity will grant relief where there is not a plain, adequate, and complete remedy at law, and when it is necessary to prevent an irreparable injury." It was accordingly held that the execution of a void ordinance in regard to the interment of the dead, which greatly prejudiced the property rights of the appellee, might be enjoined. In *Gas Co. v. Tyner* (Ind. Sup.) 31 N. E. Rep. 59, it was said to have been long settled "that a private citizen may maintain an action for a public wrong if he suffers an injury peculiar to himself, and not sustained by the public in general." We are of the opinion that if the ordinance in question be void, its enforcement may be enjoined, provided the plaintiff has shown that, if it is enforced, he will sustain irreparable injury, for which he has no plain, speedy, and adequate remedy in the ordinary course of the law. Has he shown that such would be the case? We think not. It is true, there are some averments in the petition and affidavits to the effect that the business of the plaintiff will be ruined if all the corn he buys must be weighed on the city scales; but in view of the facts shown, those averments are not reasonable. Provisions for weighing on the city scales appear to be ample. The defendant can avoid all danger of the prosecution of himself and the persons of whom he buys by having the corn weighed as required by the ordinances. His cribs are half a mile from the scales, but those of other buyers must be removed from them some distance, and he must suffer the loss of business which is inevitable from the attempt to do business in a location less desirable

than that occupied by others, or pay enough for what
he buys to secure the corn he wishes to purchase. This
he may do while he is prosecuting his appeals and
obtaining a decision as to the validity of the ordinance
in question from a court of competent jurisdiction, in
the manner provided by law. While he may suffer
some inconvenience, and even some pecuniary loss,
pending the determination of his cases, yet they will
not be so great as to warrant the interference of a court
of equity. There is no occasion for a multiplicity of
suits. Our conclusion finds support in the following
authorities: *Poyer v. Village of Des Plaines*, 123 Ill.
111 (13 N. E. Rep. 819), and cases therein cited; *West v.
New York*, 10 Paige, 539; *City of Manchester v. Smyth*
64 N. H. 380 (10 Atl. Rep. 700; *State v. Patterson* (Tex.
Civ. App.) 37 S. W. Rep. 478; 2 High, Injunctions, section 1244. The order of the district court dissolving
the temporary injunction appears to have been correct,
and it is AFFIRMED.

IN THE MATTER OF THE ESTATE OF JONAS PROCTOR,
Deceased. FLORA A. MACK, *et al.*, v. CHARLES
PROCTOR AND N. H. DuFOE, Administrator, Etc.,
Appellants.

Dower: ELECTION. A widow is not necessarily put to her election
between dower which in Iowa is an estate in fee simple, and a
devise in her husband's will, of a life estate in all his real property, as such a devise is not inconsistent with the right of dower.

SAME. A widow will not be held to have elected to take under her
husband's will in lieu of dower, by her asking for the probate of
the will which nominates her as executor, and accepting her
appointment as such and selling real property which under the
will she had power to dispose of if necessary for her support, and
keeping possession of the personal estate which the will bequeathed
to her for life, where all her acts are referable to her position as
an executor, and there is nothing to indicate that they were done
in any other capacity.

SAME. A widow is not required to take under the will, in lieu of her
1 distributive share under the statute, where such will does not
2 expressly, or by clear implication, show that the devise to her was
8 so intended, nor where such devise is not inconsistent with the
statutory right, nor where an election has not been made to take
under the will.

DESCENT AND DISTRIBUTION: *Husband and wife.* The heirs of a
5 widow may have her distributive share of the estate of her
deceased husband set off to them in personalty where she made
no such election to take under her husband's will as to divest her
of such share, as, upon her husband's death, it vested in her immediately, subject to her right of election to take under the will.

Practice: *Probate.* The heirs of a widow may maintain a petition
6 against representatives of the deceased husband to have the
7 widow's dower assigned to them, and her distributive share
admeasured and set apart to them, although they were not legatees or devisees under the husband's will.

DOWER. The heirs of a widow whose dower was not assigned during
5 her lifetime may have it set off to them, in the absence of an
election on her part to take under her husband's will in lieu of
dower.

Costs: ESTATES. The personal representatives of a decedent cannot
avoid liability for costs under Code 1873, section 2933, providing
8 that costs shall be recovered by the successful party, upon the
ground that the defense to the petition of the successful party was
made in good faith and on reasonable grounds.

Appeal from Black Hawk District Court.—HON. A. S.
BLAIR, Judge.   ◦

FRIDAY, OCTOBER 15, 1897.

DEFENDANTS' demurrer to plaintiffs' petition was
overruled, and defendants electing to stand on their
demurrer, and refusing to plead over, judgment was
rendered against them, from which they appeal—
Affirmed.

M. F. Edwards and *J. C. Scott* for appellants.

Courtright & Arbuckle for appellees.

Given, J. — I.   Upon the submission of the demurrer, it was stipulated as follows: "It is admitted for the purpose of a hearing on the demurrer of Charles Proctor and N. H. Du Foe, administrator, to the application for admeasurement that the will of Jonas Proctor and all papers filed in the estate be considered a part of the application, the intention being to determine the case as fully on the demurrer as could be done by a trial on the merits of the case." We understand by this stipulation that all facts appearing in the record in the estate, material to the questions raised by the demurrer are to be considered as if set out in the petition. Thus considered, we have the following matters alleged by the plaintiffs as ground for the relief asked: Jonas Proctor died, testate, October 28, 1891, seized of certain real and personal property described, leaving Susan Proctor, his widow, surviving

1   him. By his will, after providing for the payment of debts and funeral expenses, he devised and bequeathed to his wife, Susan, "all the rest, residue, and remainder of my estate, both real, personal, and mixed, to have and to hold unto my said wife during her life, with full power to sell, transfer, and dispose of same as much as may, from time to time, be needed for her support and the cancellation of any indebtedness now and hereafter existing." It is further provided that, after the death of his wife, all the then remaining property of his estate, real and personal and mixed, "shall revert to, and is hereby given, devised, and bequeathed to, my son, Charles Proctor, to have and to hold unto himself, heirs, and assigns, forever." It is further provided that after the decease of his wife, and after Charles has received all of the property as aforesaid, he shall pay to the testator's grandchildren, Susie May and Freddie Perrin, the sum of one thousand dollars, to be divided equally among them as

they respectively arrived at the age of twenty-one years. Susan Proctor was nominated in the will to be the executrix thereof, without bonds. Upon her application, the will was admitted to probate, and Mrs. Proctor was appointed and qualified as executrix thereof, and took possession of, and proceeded to settle, the estate. While thus acting as executrix, "she sold and conveyed lots 5 and 7 in block 23, Root's addition to the town of New Hartford." No debts were proven against the estate within the required time. There was no notice to Susan Proctor to elect whether she would take under the will or otherwise, nor is there any record entry expressly showing an election by her. Pending the settlement of said estate, to-wit, April 25, 1893, Susan Proctor died, intestate, leaving surviving her, as her heirs at law, the plaintiffs Flora A. Mack, J. N. Gould, Melissa Gould, Hattie Whipple, and Nellie Thomas, the other plaintiffs being the grandchildren named in the will, of whom A. T. Perrin is guardian. Upon her death, the defendant N. H. Du Foe was appointed administrator *de bonis non* of the estate of Jonas Proctor, and administrator of the estate of Susan Proctor. On September 11, 1893, these plaintiffs filed their petition to have the distributive share of Susan Proctor admeasured and set apart to them. A question arising as to the fee granted by the will, plaintiffs, with the leave of court, withdrew said petition, and applied for a construction of the will. The will being construed, 95 Iowa, 172, the plaintiffs renewed said application for admeasurement and setting apart of said share to them, and this is the application under consideration.

To the petition as thus construed, the defendants demurred on six grounds, in substance as follows: (1) That the petition shows that Susan Proctor "did take and receive all the personal and real estate devised to her by the terms of said will, thereby consenting to take

under said will." (2) That the terms of said will are
inconsistent with the right of the widow to take both
under the will and her distributive share under the
statute, and are inconsistent with the dower right,·
which shows an intention that the devised share be in
lieu of dower. (3) That the provisions of the will being·
inconsistent with the distributive share, and such share
not being assigned to her, or claimed by her, during her
lifetime, her heirs cannot now be given that right, it
being a personal one to be exercised by the widow. (4)
That the rule of law which permits a widow, in certain
cases, to take under the will and law both, applies
only to real estate, and that, the widow having taken
under the will, her heirs cannot have her share set off
to them in personalty. (5) That the relief asked has been
adjudicated in this court. (6) That the applicants are
not entitled to the relief demanded, for the reason that
they are not parties in interest, not being legatees or
devisees under the will.

II.   Our first inquiry is whether the petition shows
an election by Mrs. Proctor to take under the will.
Appellant cites *Craig v. Conover*, 80 Iowa, 358, and
  other cases holding that, if the record discloses
2 an act or declaration of the widow plainly indicating a purpose to take under the will, she will
be held to have so elected.   Upon these authorities, it
is contended that, because of what the record shows
the widow to have done in connection with the will and
the settlement of the estate, she should be held to
have had notice of the provisions of the will, and to
have elected to take under it.   While the matters shown
leave no doubt but that she knew the provisions of the
will, they do not, as we view them, even tend to show
an election on her part.   She asked that the will be
probated, as it was her duty to do, and, being nominated
therein, asked to be appointed to execute it.   Being

appointed and qualified, she took possession of the estate as executrix, and, as such, proceeded to settle it. Even the lots alleged to have been sold by her are alleged to have been sold "while she was acting as executrix of the estate of said decedent." Not an act relied upon as showing an election is pointed out but is plainly referable to her nomination and appointment as executrix and to her duties as such, or which, in the least, indicates an election on her part. The rule is well established and undisputed that the election must appear in the record. *In re Frank's Estate*, 97 Iowa, 704 In *Craig v. Conover*, *supra*, it is said: "If the record discloses an act or declaration of the widow plainly indicating a purpose to take under the will, she will be held to have so elected." In that case, the widow, as one of the executors, filed a report in effect accepting under the will, and accompanying the report with her receipt as an individual to the executors for all the property bequeathed to her. There is no such record in this case, and each of the many cases cited is equally foreign in its facts to this case so far as relates to an election. It is said in argument that Mrs. Proctor used all of this estate during her lifetime, and authorities are cited that such use is inconsistent with a dower right. So far as we discover, there is nothing to show that Mrs. Proctor made use of any part of this estate for any individual purpose, and yet she would not come within the rule of the cases cited by using it for her maintenance. We say again that her entire contact with this estate, as shown by this petition, is plainly referable to her position as executrix, and does not indicate an election upon her part to take under the will.

III. In support of the second ground of their demurrer, appellants say: ."In this we affirm that it is clearly deducible from the terms of said will that it was the intention of the testator that the devise to the

widow should be in lieu of dower, and, having elected
to take under the will, cannot now take under the statute in addition thereto." We have seen that the widow
did not make an election, and therefore, had she sur-
vived, she would be privileged to do so. *In re Proctor's
Estate*, 95 Iowa, 172, this will was construed as devising
a life estate to the widow, and not a fee simple.
4   According to a long line of decisions by this
court, such a devise is not inconsistent with the
right of dower. See *Daugherty v. Daugherty*, 69 Iowa,
677; *Watrous v. Winn*, 37 Iowa, 72; *Parker v. Hayden*,
84 Iowa, 493. In *Metteer v. Wiley*, 34 Iowa, 214, it is
held that, where there is no expressed declaration in the
will that the devise shall be in lieu of dower, the intention that it should be must be deduced by clear and
manifest implication from the will. In this will there
is no such expressed declaration, nor do we think that
such an intention is deducible therefrom by clear and
manifest implication. Three sufficient reasons appear
why this second ground of the demurrer was properly
overruled, namely, that the will does not expressly nor
by implication show that the devise was intended to be
in lieu of dower. That the devise named is not inconsistent with the dower right, and that no election had
been made by the widow to take under the will.

IV. The third ground of the demurrer, namely,
that the heirs of Mrs. Proctor cannot now be given the
right to elect, it being a personal right to be exercised
by the widow, is grounded upon the claim that the provisions of the will are inconsistent with the dower
right. It is said in argument: "It seems to be the
holding in *Potter v. Worley*, 57 Iowa, 66, that where
the provisions of the will are not inconsistent with
dower, and the widow's dower is not assigned during
her lifetime, her heirs may have it set off to them. Our

contention is that in this case the provisions of the will are inconsistent with the dower right."

5   Holding, as we do, that the provisions of the will are not inconsistent with the dower right, the *Case of Potter* would seem to be controlling. There are, however, very potent reasons why the heirs of Mrs. Proctor may now ask the relief demanded. It is true that the right of election ceased with the widow's death, and equally true that her heirs take whatever she died seized of. The distributive share of the widow vested in her immediately upon the death of her husband, qualified by her right of election to take under the will, and to the rights of creditors of the estate to the extent that the personal property might be applied to the payment of debts. We have seen that there were no debts and no election by the widow to divest her in whole or in part of the distributive share that vested in her immediately upon the death of her husband. Being seized of the right to her distributive share in her husband's estate at her death, that right passed to her heirs immediately upon her decease. See *Potter v. Worley, supra*, and *Blair v. Wilson*, 57 Iowa, 177.

V. The fourth cause of demurrer is grounded on the assumption that Mrs. Proctor had elected to take under the will, and therefore it is insisted that her heirs cannot have her share set off to them in

6   the personal property. Mrs. Proctor, not having made an election, died seized of the right to take under the statute in both real and personal property, and this right descended to her heirs upon her death. The proceeding for the construction of this will was not an adjudication of any of the questions presented in this application, nor, indeed, could they have well been adjudicated in that proceeding. While it is true

7   that the plaintiffs, heirs of Mrs. Proctor, are not legatees or devisees under the will, they are parties in interest, and entitled to maintain this proceeding. Our conclusion is that the demurrer was

properly overruled as to each and all of the grounds thereof.

VI. The court below found that the will gave to Mrs. Proctor a life estate only; that the same was not inconsistent with a right of dower in addition thereto; and that the heirs of Mrs. Proctor have the right to have her distributive share set apart to them; and that said share consisted of one-third of the estate of Jonas Proctor. It was ordered that the demurrer be overruled, and that one-third of the estate of Jonas Proctor be admeasured and set apart as part of the estate of Susan Proctor, and that N. H. Du Foe, administrator of Susan Proctor's estate, credit himself with one-third of the personal property in the Jonas Proctor estate, and charge himself therewith in the Susan Proctor estate. Referees were appointed to admeasure said share in the real estate, and the costs were taxed against the defendants. While it is left somewhat obscure, we understand that Mr. Du Foe was appointed administrator *de bonis non* of the estate of Jonas Proctor, and administrator of the estate of Susan Proctor. This being true, the order of the court as to the personal property effectuates just what the heirs of Susan Proctor are entitled to; and the order for the admeasurement of their share out of the real estate is authorized by the conclusions we have reached. We think the complaints against the decree in these respects are not well founded

Appellants also complain that the costs are taxed to them, and insist that as their defense is made in good faith, upon reasonable grounds, the costs should be paid out of the estate of Susan Proctor. The 8   general rule is that "costs shall be recovered by the successful party." Code 1873, section 2933. That a defense has been made in good faith, and upon reasonable grounds for making it, forms no exception to this rule. The decree of the district court is AFFIRMED.

J. E. RICHARDSON v. M. L. PROBST, et al., Appellants.

Attachment: JOINT OBLIGORS. That the surety on a note is financially responsible, does not affect the right of the holder to an attachment in a suit against the maker, if any of the grounds of
1 attachment specified by the Code exist as against him; and it is prejudicial error to admit testimony showing the existence of such a surety.

Appeal. Where an appellee presents no brief or argument, the
2 supreme court will consider only such questions as are essential to determine the appeal.

Appeal from Jackson District Court.—Hon. W. F. BRANNAN, Judge.

FRIDAY, OCTOBER 15, 1897.

ACTION on an attachment bond. Verdict and judgment for plaintiff, and the defendants appealed.— *Reversed.*

B. F. Thomas and *Hayes & Schuyler* for appellants.

No appearance for appellee.

GRANGER, J. — Defendant Probst brought an action against the plaintiff herein on a note, and sued out an attachment, and defendant Stickley was surety on the attachment bond. This is an action on the bond, on the ground that it was wrongfully sued out. The answer was, for the purposes of our consideration, a denial. One Jane Preston was surety on the note sued on in the attachment proceeding, but was not a party to that suit, and is not to this. At the trial of this suit, the plaintiff, Richardson, was a witness in his own behalf; and, after stating that Jane Preston was surety on the note in the attachment suit, he was permitted, against objections, to state her financial condition, and complaint is made of the ruling. In the absence of an argument for appellee, we are left to assume the purpose of the testimony, and we think of no other purpose than as bearing on the question of the wrongful suing out of the attchment. The answer showed her

1   to be possessed of property. We discover nothing in the law authorizing attachments, where a ground therefor exists, as to one of the makers of the note, and such a suit is brought, to make the pecuniary responsibility of another maker material, on the question of an attachment being properly sued out. The alleged ground for the attachment was that the defendant was about to remove from the state, and had started to leave the state, and refused to make any arrangements for the securing of the payment of the debt when it became due. Such facts are statutory grounds for an attachment. The law does not make the fact that there are others, who are responsible, liable for the payment of the debt, a limitation on the right; but the right to the writ is made to depend on facts as to any obligor against whom payment could be enforced. Our law gives a right of action against any or all the joint makers of a note. Code, section 2550.

We think it was error to admit the evidence to show the responsibility of the surety on the note, and such testimony could hardly have been otherwise than prejudicial. As we are without an argument by

2   appellee, we limit our consideration to such questions as are essential to determine the appeal. *Dodd v. Scott*, 81 Iowa, 319. The judgment is REVERSED.

MRS. C. D. CROCKER V. MRS. ANNIE HOGIN, Appellant.

Assignment of Insurance Certificate: DEFENSES BY INSURER. McClain's
Code, section 3262, providing that when, by the terms in an instru-
1 ment its assignment is prohibited, "the assignment of it shall
nevertheless be valid," but the maker may avail himself of any
8 defense or counter-claim against the assignee which he may have
had against the assignor, applies to life insurance policies and certificates of mutual benefit associations.

SAME. The assignee of a mutual benefit certificate cannot, where the
2 assignment is void and no recovery can be had against the society,
recover the amount of the certificate from a trustee to whom the
society voluntarily paid it, to be held by him until the rights of the
7 original beneficiary and the assignee should be determined.

SAME. Acts Twenty-first General Assembly, chapter 65, section 7,
provides that no association, "organized or operating" under it
1 shall issue certificates unless the beneficiary is the wife, relative,
legal representative, heir, or legatee of the insured member, and
4 that an assignment of such certificate shall be void. A certain
association issued a certificate upon the life of a husband. At
the time, its articles of incorporation prohibited the assignment of
5 any certificate in payment of or security for debt. Husband
and wife assigned the certificate as security for debt. Held, the
6 assignment is absolutely void as against the wife, in a suit
between her and the assignee, over the proceeds of the policy, if
said association was operating under said act, though it had not
fully complied with its provisions.

Appeal from Polk District Court.—HON. W. F. CONRAD,
Judge.

FRIDAY, OCTOBER 15, 1897.

THIS is a controversy over the rights of the
respective parties to a fund now in the hands of a
trustee, the avails of a policy of insurance or certificate
of membership in the Ancient Order of United Workmen of the State of Iowa, issued to one George B. Hogin
during his lifetime, and in which Annie B. Hogin was
the beneficiary. The trial court found the plaintiff was

entitled to the larger part of the money by virtue of
an assignment of the policy to her, and defendant
appeals.—*Reversed.*

Ayres, Woodin & Ayres for appellant.

Bishop, Bowen & Fleming and *Nourse & Nourse*
for appellee.

DEEMER, J.—In the year 1882 the Grand Lodge
of the Ancient Order of United Workmen, a mutual
benefit association, doing business on the assessment
plan, issued to George B. Hogin a certificate of membership, in which it agreed to pay to his wife, Annie B.
      Hogin, in case of his death, the amount named
1   in the certificate. In 1890 a new certificate for
    the sum of two thousand dollars was issued in
lieu thereof, in which Mrs. Hogin was the beneficiary.
In 1889 George B. Hogin borrowed of the plaintiff one
thousand dollars, and executed his note therefor; and
on the same day he, with his wife, executed to plaintiff
the following assignment: "We, George B. Hogin and
Annie B. Hogin, husband and wife, of Pasadena, California, in consideration of C. D. Crocker, of Los Ange-
les, California, having loaned said George B. Hogin one
thousand dollars, and said George B. Hogin and Annie
B. Hogin hereby assign our right, title, and interest
to the life insurance policy hereto attached, being
numbered 12,705, for two thousand dollars, to the said
C. D. Crocker. The purpose of said assignment is to
secure payment of the one thousand dollars, heretofore
referred to, to the said C. D. Crocker, Pasadena, Cal."
This assignment was attached to the first certificate,
and the certificate, with the assignment, was delivered
to plaintiff. In 1890 the note was renewed, and some
small payments have since been made upon it. George

B. Hogin died on the sixth day of February, 1895,
      leaving his wife and two children surviving. The
2   society made no question as to its liability, but
      refused to pay the amount of the insurance to
Mrs. Hogin because she could not surrender the certificate assigned to plaintiff. Thereupon a stipulation was
made between the parties, by which one Martin was
to receive the money as trustee, and hold it until the
rights of the contending parties were determined. The
validity of the assignment of the certificate is questioned upon two grounds, to-wit: (1) It is said that,
by the terms of the constitution and by-laws of the
grand lodge, the assignment was prohibited; (2) that
the laws of the state in force at the time the assignment
was made prohibited such contracts. The articles of
incorporation and by-laws of the Ancient Order of
United Workmen provided that, when the certificate
issued, no certificate should in any manner be assigned
in payment or as security for any debt, and also provided that the beneficiary might be changed to some
legal member of the family of the assured by the assent
of the association, but not otherwise. The association
is making no defense. It has recognized its liability,
and has paid the money to the trustee, in order that the
controversy between these litigants may be settled.

Plaintiff, as assignee, is seeking to recover upon a
contract which, by its terms, is non-assignable. That
she may do so seems to be settled by statute,—McClain's
      Code, section 3262,—which provides "that when
3   by the terms of an instrument, its assignment is
      prohibited, the assignment of it shall neverthe-
less be valid, but the maker may avail himself of any
defense or counter-claim against the assignee which
he may have had against the assignor." This statute
applies to policies of insurance. *Mershon v. Insurance
Co.*, 34 Iowa, 87. And the Code expressly recognizes the

validity of such assignments or arrangements. See
McClain's Code, section 3576, which provides, in effect,
that any sum of money made payable by any benevolent
society upon the death of the member is not subject to
the debts of the deceased except by special contract or
arrangement. The assignment was and is valid, unless
it contravenes some statute, or is contrary to public
policy. It has frequently been held that certificates,
such as the one in question, are *choses* in action, and
are assignable, and that action thereon may be brought
in the name of the assignee. *De Ronge v. Insurance Co.*,
23 N. J. Eq. 486; *Collins v. Dawley*, 4 Colo. 138; *Merrill
v. Insurance Co.*, 103 Mass. 252; *Souder v. Friendly Soc.*,
72 Md. 511 (20 Atl. Rep. 137); *Bussinger v. Bank*, 30
Wis. 75 (30 N. W. Rep. 290); *Brown v. Mansus*, 64
N. H. 39 (5 Atl. Rep. 768); *Martin v. Stubbings*, 126 Ill.
Sup. 387 (18 N. E. Rep. 657).

Chapter 65 of the Acts of the Twenty-first General
Assembly relates to the organization and operation of
mutual benefit associations, and requires of all corporations or associations organized under the laws
4   of the state upon the mutual assessment,
co-operative, or natural premium plan, for
purpose of insuring the lives of individuals, or of
furnishing benefits to widows, heirs, orphans, or
legatees of deceased members, compliance with the
provisions of the chapter before commencing business. The act further provides, in section 7 thereof,
that "no corporation or association organized or
operating under the act shall issue certificates *
* * unless the beneficiary * * * shall be
the husband, wife, relative, legal representative, heir
or legatee of such insured member; nor shall any such
certificate be assigned, * * * and any certificate
issued or assignment made in violation of this section
shall be void. Any member of any corporation, association or society operating under this act, shall have the

right at any time, with the consent of such corporation,
association or society, to make a change in his beneficiary without requiring the consent of such beneficiary." The act also relieved companies already duly
incorporated and operating under the laws of the state
from reincorporating, and further provided that it
should not relieve any corporation or assessment association then doing business in the state from the fulfillment of any contract theretofore entered into with
its members, and further relieved such companies from
the operation of the general insurance laws of the state
regulating life insurance. The Grand Lodge of the
Ancient Order of United Workmen was doing business
in the state under certain amended articles of incorporation adopted in the year 1884, as a charitable or
benevolent institution, under chapter 40 of the Acts of
the Fifteenth General Assembly, and continued to do
business under these articles until July 1, 1893, when it
filed its report with the auditor of state, and for the
first time received authority to do business under the
Acts of the Twenty-first General Assembly. Its articles
provided that it was organized for the purpose of creating a fund to be paid upon the death of a member, and
that no certificate should be made payable to any person not a member of the family or heir of the member,
and that no certificate should be in any manner assigned
in payment of or as security for any debt. It is clear
that section 7 of chapter 65 of the acts before quoted
expressly avoids the assignment of the certificate if the
association is of the class included in the act. That it
is, is demonstrated by a consideration of section 20 of
that act, which is as follows: "Any corporation or
association doing business in this state which provides
in the main for the payment of death losses or accident
indemnity by any assessment upon its members or upon
the natural premium plan, shall, for the purpose of this

act, be deemed a mutual benefit association, and shall
not be subject to the general insurance laws of this
state, regulating life insurance." It is said,
5   however, that the Ancient Order of United
Workmen organization did not comply with the
provisions of the act, and was not operating thereunder
at the time the certificate was assigned, and that for
this reason section 7 does not apply. If the controversy
were between plaintiff and the association, there might
possibly be some force in the position. But this is not
the true status. The association is neutral as between
the parties to this suit, and neither plaintiff nor defendant should be prejudiced because of failure of the association to comply with the law. If the insurance or
indemnity is of the kind and character contemplated by
the act, the statute should apply to a controversy
between the claimants of the avails thereof. The fact
that the lodge was not complying with the insurance
laws of the state should not prejudice the defendant's
rights to the benefits provided. We regard it as entirely
immaterial that the society was not complying with
the law. Again section 7 is made to apply to all
6   associations operating under the act. That the
grand lodge was operating under it, although
not fully complying with all its provisions, is clear; and
we are of opinion that the act applies, and that the
assignment was and is void. As supporting our conclusions, see *Briggs v. Earl*, 139 Mass, 473 (1 N. E.
Rep. 847); *Basye v. Adams*, 81 Ky. 368; Bacon, Benevolent Societies, sections 311, 312. The case of *Grimes v.
Legion of Honor*, 97 Iowa, 315, is not in conflict with
these views. This statute is not for the benefit of the
society, and does not in any manner affect its ultimate
liability. Violation of section 7 would be no defense
to an action brought by the designated beneficiary.
The only effect of that part of it relating to assignment

is to render such assignment void. An unauthorized
and void assignment does not affect the policy. In
the case of *Wendt v. Legion of Honor*, 72 Iowa, 682, we
said, in discussing an attempted change of beneficiary
made by the assured, that the provisions of the certificate relating to change of beneficiary were binding
upon all claimants under the certificate. See, also
Stephenson v. Stephenson, 64 Iowa, 534.

That the money was voluntarily paid to a trustee
by the Ancient Order of United Workmen can make no
difference in the rights of the parties. If appellee could
not have recovered the benefits promised, by
7   direct action against the association, she ought
not to recover them in this action. *Ballou v.
Gile*, 50 Wis. 614 (7 N. W. Rep. 561). The general
assembly enacted the prohibition we are considering
for the purpose of preserving to the designated beneficiaries the benefits to be derived from insurance in such
associations, and not only limited the persons who
might profit by membership therein, but expressly prohibited assignments of the certificates. It is not
important to consider the reasons which led to, nor the
policy of, such legislation. That it exists, and renders
void all such assignments as are relied upon by
appellee is plain, and our duty to enforce it is equally
clear. The judgment of the district court is REVERSED.

THE S. HAMMILL COMPANY, Appellant, v. GIDEON VAN
LOON AND WILLIAM VAN LOON.

Mortgage: FRAUDULENT PAYMENT, WHAT IS NOT. The failure to file
a chattel mortgage does not render a mortgagee liable for the proceeds realized on a sale of the mortgaged property by the mortgagor with his permission, and received by him under arrangement with the latter, to creditors whose claims accrued after the
mortgage and before the sale, but who acquired no lien on the
mortgaged property.

*Appeal from Lucas District Court.—*HON. ROBERT
SLOAN, Judge.

SATURDAY, OCTOBER 16, 1897.

Will B. Barger and *Hughes & Roberts* for appellants.

Stuart & Barthelomew for appellees.

KINNE, C. J.—Plaintiff firm, being creditors of
the defendant Gideon Van Loon, bring this action in
equity, wherein they ask to have a mortgage held by
the defendant William Van Loon upon the stock of
goods of the defendant Gideon Van Loon set aside as
fraudulent and void as to them, and for personal judgment against said William Van Loon. Their claim is
that the said William Van Loon, by withholding his
said mortgage from record, induced them to extend
credit to said Gideon, which would not have been
extended had they had notice of the existence of said
mortgage. The facts disclosed by the pleadings and
evidence are substantially as follows: Gideon Van
Loon was in 1894 engaged in the grocery business at
Chariton, Iowa. In December of that year, Gideon gave
to William a note for two hundred and fifty dollars,
payable April 1, 1895, and a mortgage on his stock
securing the same. March 20, 1895, William, upon the
promise of Gideon to pay the note, canceled the mortgage of record. Afterwards, and on the same day,
Gideon concluded not to pay the note at that time.
William informed him that he (William) had already
canceled the mortgage supposing he was going to pay
the debt. Finally Gideon gave William a new note
and mortgage for the same debt. William neglected to
file this mortgage for record until September 20, 1895.
On that day he filed for record the mortgage above

mentioned, and also another mortgage, the consideration of which was a debt paid by William for Gideon, and the securing the repayment of one hundred dollars which William had loaned to Gideon. Afterwards Gideon mortgaged his stock of goods to another creditor, which mortgage was purchased by William. About September 20, 1895, William Van Loon had an arrangement with Gideon whereby the latter agreed to place the proceeds from the sale of the goods in a bank to the credit of said William, and William was to apply such proceeds on the mortgage debts he had, which he did. In this way the two first mortgages were paid, and a small amount was paid on the last mortgage. Gideon retained possession of the goods, and sold all of them. Plaintiff firm extended credit to Gideon Van Loon, after the cancellation of the mortgage, for certain goods, which have not been paid for, and for which they now have a judgment against Gideon Van Loon. The district court dismissed plaintiff's petition at their costs, and they except and appeal.

Much is said in argument touching the effect of the failure of William Van Loon to record his mortgage, and it is contended by appellants that thereby a legal fraud was perpetrated upon them, and that, therefore, the defendant should be prevented from asserting any right under his mortgage. They also insist that the acts of William Van Loon constitute an estoppel as to him, and in favor of the appellants. We do not find it necessary to decide these questions. The evidence before us does not show that William Van Loon ever took possession of the goods covered by the mortgage; hence he cannot be liable in this action. True it is that he has received, by reason of the arrangement with Gideon Van Loon, sufficient of the proceeds of the sale of the goods to satisfy the mortgage which it is claimed he negligently failed to record; but by such an arrangement William did not take possession of the goods or

exercise any dominion over them. Gideon had a perfect right to pay his debt in the way he did,—by depositing the proceeds of the sales of the goods in the bank to
the credit of William Van Loon. Plaintiff, having no
lien on the goods, cannot complain that their proceeds
were actually applied on other debts owing by the
mortgagor. As we have said, the debtor had a right to
pay him in preference to plaintiff who had no lien upon
the goods. The decree below is AFFIRMED.

W. R. GREEN v. THE SCHOENHOFEN BREWING COM-
PANY, Appellant.

Contracts: PUBLIC POLICY: *Sureties.* At a time when selling liquor
in original packages was legal, a non-resident appointed an agent
to so sell. He sold by the glass in violation of his contract of
appointment, and, the liquors of his principal being thereupon
seized, he became the surety of the principal on a replevin bond
in an action to reclaim the liquors. He was ultimately compelled
to make payment on account of said bond. *Held,* he is not
estopped to recover such payment.

Appeal from Crawford District Court.—HON. Z. A.
CHURCH, Judge.

SATURDAY, OCTOBER 16, 1897.

THIS appeal is by the defendant from a ruling sustaining plaintiff's demurrer to its answer, and judgment
in favor of plaintiff upon defendant's refusing to further
answer.—*Affirmed.*

Hayes & Schuyler and *P. E. C. Lally* for appellant.

W. R. Green and *E. H. Swasey* for appellee.

GIVEN, J.—I.   Plaintiff states as his cause of
action that the defendant, a corporation organized and
doing business under the laws of Illinois, commenced

an action in replevin against William S. Armstrong,
sheriff, to recover possession of certain property; that
defendant executed a replevin bond in the sum of eight
hundred dollars, with John Mullen as surety; that
judgment was rendered in said action in favor of the
defendant therein on said bond for four hundred dollars and costs, which judgment was affirmed on appeal
to this court (89 Iowa, 673); that this defendant failed to
pay said judgment; that execution was issued thereon,
and that said John Mullen was compelled to pay the
same, with interest and costs, amounting to over five
hundred dollars; that defendant refused to pay said
Mullen on demand; and that thereafter Mullen, for a
valuable consideration, assigned said claim to the plaintiff,—wherefore plaintiff asks to recover six hundred
dollars and costs. The defendant's answer, in effect,
admits the allegations of the petition, and alleges that
it is under no obligation to reimburse said Mullen,
because of the following facts: That its business is
the manufacture and sale of lager and other beers, and
its place of business is in the city of Chicago, Ill. That
it entered into a contract in writing with said Mullen,
as follows: "This agreement, made this 1st day of
May, A. D. 1890, between the P. Schoenhofen Brewing
Company, a corporation of the city of Chicago, county
of Cook, and state of Illinois, party of the first part,
and John Mullen, of the town of Audubon, county of
Audubon, and state of Iowa, party of the second part,
witnesseth: That, for and in consideration of the sum
or sums of money hereinafter mentioned, paid to the
said party of the second part, the said party of the first
part has and does employ the said party of the second
part to sell the beer made and manufactured by the
said party of the first part, and to give all his time and
attention to their said business in the town last aforesaid, and adjacent territory. The said party of the second part agrees to remit to said party of the first part

all the moneys which he may collect for said party of
the first part in their said business immediately and
without delay, and to sell only for cash, at the follow-
ings prices: Keg beer: 'Select' or 'Standard,' per barrel, $10.00; 'Edelweiss,' per barrel, $12.00. Bottled beer:
'Export,' per case, 2 doz. qts., net, $2.75; per barrel, 9
doz. qts., net, $———. 'Edelweiss,' per case, 2 doz. qts.,
net, $3.00; per barrel, 6 doz. qts., net, $3.00. Party of the
second part further agrees, that, when payments are
delinquent, to push the collection of the same to the
best of his ability. For and in consideration of the
afore-mentioned covenants and agreements, the said
party of the first part agrees to pay said party
of the second part the sum of fifty ($50) dollars
per month during the term of the existence of this contract. The said party of the first part reserves to itself
the right to abrogate or cancel this agreement at any
time. In witness whereof, the said parties have here-
unto set their hands and seals, the day and year first
above mentioned." That on the same day a written
contract, identical in terms, was entered into between
defendant and one William Burns, of Audubon county,
Iowa. That on May 6, 1890, each of said contracts was
modified by writings signed by said Mullen and Burns,
respectively, as follows: "In consideration of the P.
Schoenhofen Brewing Company, of Chicago, Illinois,
allowing me a rebate of four dollars per barrel of keg
beer, and ——— per barrel of bottled beer, and eighty-
five cents per case of bottled beer, from the retail prices
in my town on all beer manufactured by them, and sold
by me, I covenant and agree to relinquish any and all
claims I now have, or may hereafter have, against the
said P. Schoenhofen Brewing Company .for work in
placing their goods, wares, and merchandise on the
market, and also for allowances, if any, agreed to be
paid me by the said P. Schoenhofen Brewing Company

in a former agreement, bearing date May 1, 1890. The
above reduction may be hereafter modified by mutual
agreement, if found necessary by any change in the
market or in the price of the raw material. I also bind
myself to pay to said P. Schoenhofen Brewing Company
for all beer sent me by said company, or to other parties
in the state of Iowa on my order." That said contracts,
so modified, were in force from their date until after
said judgment was rendered. Defendant further states
in said answer as follows: That after the making of
said contracts, and prior to the seventh day of July,
1890, the said defendant shipped to itself at said Audubon, and there turned over to said John Mullen and
William Burns, certain intoxicating liquors,—beer,—
so manufactured by it, which was so shipped under
and by virtue of said contracts, and which was so
received and held by said John Mullen and said William
Burns, being divided between them as they saw fit,
each with full knowledge of all facts in connection
therewith, as herein alleged, and with intent to sell
the same in Iowa, according to and under the terms
of said contracts, and from which they did so sell at
wholesale, retail, and by the glass at said place; and,
while the same was so being held by them, part of each
separately, search warrants were issued by a justice of
the peace in and for said Audubon county against each
of them, under the provisions of section 1544 and subsequent sections of the Code of Iowa, for the purpose
of seizing and destroying said liquor, as being kept in
violation of the laws of the state, and under and by
virtue of which warrant the sheriff of said county,
being the William S. Armstrong mentioned in the petition, seized the same, and, while the said liquors were
so held by said sheriff, and on or about the seventh day
of July, 1890, the said John Mullen, for said defendant,
and in the name of the defendant herein, brought an

action in replevin therefor in the district court of the
state of Iowa in and for Audubon county, and thereunder took possession of said liquors, the said John
Mullen signing the bond in said action as surety, which
is the same suit and proceeding mentioned in the petition, and which proceeded to judgment as therein set
out. The defendant admits the issuing of execution and
the payment of said judgment by said Mullen, as
alleged, but says that, by reason of the facts hereinbefore set out, no obligation exists upon its part to either
reimburse said Mullen, or contribute towards the payment by him of said judgment.

The plaintiff demurred to said answer upon the
following grounds: (1) That the agreements set forth
therein, and alleged to have been made by and between
the defendant and John Burns and William Mullen on
the first day of May, 1890, and on the sixth day of May,
1890, are not in any way contrary to, nor do they provide for any act contrary to, public policy. (2) It is
nowhere alleged in said answer that the proceedings
referred to in the petition as a basis for plaintiff's action
were provided for, contemplated by, or done under and
in pursuance of, said contracts, or either of them. (3)
That it is not alleged therein that there was any understanding, at the time when said agreements were made,
that any illegal acts should be carried on through or by
means of said contracts, or the liquors referred to
therein, nor is it alleged that any illegal act was done
under and in pursuance of said contracts, or any understanding had between the parties making the same, at
the time they were made.

II. Appellant's first contention is that said contracts were made with a view to the sale of beer in
this state, in violation of the laws thereof, that the
seizure and replevin of the beer grew out of this unlawful purpose, and that, Mullen being a party to the

wrong, his assignee cannot enforce contribution. Plaintiff stands in the place of Mullen, and cannot recover unless Mullen could. The contracts were entered into May 1, modified May 6, and the beer turned over to Mullen and to Burns was seized before, and replevied and the bond given on, July 7, 1890. It is not questioned that, under the decision of the supreme court of the United States in *Leisy v. Hardin*, 135 U. S. 100 (10 Sup. Ct. Rep. 681), it was lawful for the defendant corporation to bring its beer into this state in the original packages, and to sell it in such packages, during all the time between May 1 and July 7, 1890. The contracts, as first made, provide expressly for sales "per barrel" and "per case," and do not authorize any other kind of sales than in these original packages, and the modification does not change the contract in this respect. These contracts were neither illegal nor contrary to public policy, and there is nothing therein that contemplates or authorizes a violation of law. Appellant cites *Harley v. Stapleton*, 24 Mo. 248; *Muscatine County v. Carpenter*, 33 Iowa, 41; *Marienthal v. Shafer*, 6 Iowa, 223; and *Reynolds v. Nichols*, 12 Iowa, 399. In each of these cases the action was upon a contract held or claimed to be illegal, while in this it is upon a legal contract.

III. It is said in the answer that Mullen and Burns did separately sell said beer "at wholesale, retail, and by the glass at said place." It is insisted that, by selling at retail and by the glass, Mullen violated the law, and caused the seizure that necessitated the replevin of the beer, and therefore plaintiff is estopped from recovering. The contracts set up have no reference whatever to the giving of a replevin bond. When Mullen executed that bond as surety for the appellant, the law implied a contract on the part of appellant to reimburse him for whatever he might have to pay on the bond. It is conceded that the ownership of the beer remained in the appellant; that appellant authorized the bringing of the replevin action and the execution of the replevin bond. If Mullen sold beer at retail, in violation of his powers as agent and of the laws of the state, that presents no reason why appellant should be exempted from liability upon a legal contract between them.—AFFIRMED.

G. B. LIBBEY, Appellant, v. JOHN YOUNG, *et al.*

Adverse Possession. Adverse possession of a part of the land will be considered, for the purpose of title by adverse possession, under
1 the Iowa statute, to extend to the whole sub-division to which the occupant holds color of title or makes claim of right.

PRESUMPTIONS. The presumption that possession of land extends to the entire congressional sub-division called for by the occupant's conveyance or claim of right, does not obtain where, with his
2 knowledge, and that of his grantors, another person has been in possession of part of the sub-division, under color of title or claim of right, for more than ten years.

Appeal from Webster District Court.—HON. B. P. BIRD
SALL, Judge.

SATURDAY, OCTOBER 16, 1897.

SUIT in equity to enjoin and restrain defendants from trespassing upon certain lands lying east of the Boone river in Webster county. The defendants claim title to the land by prescription. The trial court dismissed the plaintiff's petition, and he appeals.— *Affirmed.*

Hyatt & Hyatt for appellant.

J. A. O. Yeoman and *W. S. Kenyon* for appellees.

DEEMER, J.—Each party claims title to the land by adverse possession. It is true that appellant pleads a patent title, but he has failed to prove it, and his right to the land, if he has any, is based upon prescription. His claim of right and color of title is based upon certain conveyances from one Bell (who went into possession of some of the land situated in the same congressional subdivision as the land in dispute, in the year 1858) to Nathan Baker, in the year 1865, from Nathan Baker to James Baker in the year 1874, and from James Baker to appellant in the year 1891; and the possession of these various grantees is relied upon by appellant as

1   establishing his title. Appellees claim title through a parol conveyance of the land in dispute from a Mrs. Gleason, the widow of one Solomon Gleason, who, it is claimed, bought the land from one Lamphere, who took possession in the year 1869. Lamphere claims to have purchased the land from one McGrath, who claimed to have purchased from Nathan Baker. Appellant's evidence makes a *prima facie* case of ownership of the land, and he is entitled to it unless the appellees have established their claim of adverse possession. To this we now turn our attention. Boone river runs through the southeast quarter of section 25—87—27, and the land which lies east of that river is the property in dispute. When Nathan Baker purchased the land, he made his improvements upon the west side of the river, but he also took such possession of that lying upon the east side, that appellant is entitled to the land unless appellees have shown title by adverse possession. The evidence establishes the following facts with reference to this possession: Lamphere settled upon the land east of the river in 1869, and held possession of about three hundred acres in the southeast quarter of section 25 until he sold to Gleason. When Lamphere sold to Gleason

he gave him possession, and Gleason continued to use and occupy the land until his death, which occurred in the year 1880. The widow and heirs of Gleason cultivated it the summer after the father died, and in the spring of 1882 Mrs. Gleason sold to appellee Young, who immediately took possession, and proceeded to cultivate the land, and has ever since held possession. In the year 1885, James H. Baker, who then claimed to own the land on the west side of the river, endeavored to purchase the land in dispute from appellee Young. He offered him a horse or one hundred dollars in money for the land. Appellant claims that Gleason went into possession of the land as a tenant of Baker, and introduces some evidence to establish the fact. But Baker denies that he leased to Gleason, and we are of opinion that the claim is not established. Appellant also claims that there was an hiatus in appellees' possession, but this is not true, as we understand the evidence. Upon this state of facts it is clear that plaintiff cannot recover. Defendant and his grantors have been in possession of the land under color of title or claim of right for more than ten years. Their possession has been actual and continuous, notorious and hostile, for the period prescribed by statute. But for the fact that appellee Young and his grantees have had possession of the land for more than ten years, the presumption would be that appellant had been in possession of all the congressional subdivisions called for by his conveyance, or claimed as of right. But appellee and his grantors have, as has been seen, been in possession, with the knowledge of the appellant's grantors, for such length of time that their title has become perfect. *Railway Co. v. Allfree,* 64 Iowa, 506. That appellee Young has held possession under claim of right or color of title is fully established by the cases of *Hamilton v. Wright,* 30 Iowa, 489; *Teabout v. Daniels,* 38 Iowa, 161; and *Brown v. Bridges,* 31 Iowa, 138. The attempt by James H. Baker to purchase the land of Gleason is a strong circumstance in appellee's favor. *Davenport v. Sebring,* 52 Iowa, 364; *Litchfield v. Sewell,* 97 Iowa, 247.

Appellant further contends that in no event should appellees be decreed to own or hold more of the land than was actually occupied by them. We have already referred to the presumption which obtains in

2   such cases, to the effect that possession of a part will be considered to extend to the whole subdivision to which the occupant holds color of title or makes claim of right. *Watters v. Connelly,* 59 Iowa, 217. In this case appellee and his grantors made claim to all of the southeast quarter of section 25 lying east of the river, and their possession must be as broad as their claim. The decree of the district court is right and it is AFFIRMED.

JOHN SWAN v. T. L. MATHRE, Appellant.

103
129

Fraudulent Representation: BONA FIDE PURCHASER. A statement by the promoter of a corporation, that stockholders would receive
1 from ten to twenty-five per cent. on their money paid for stock, is an expression of an opinion, and the fact that the corporation became
2 insolvent and ceased to do business six months later, does not invalidate a note given in payment for stock.

SAME: *Evidence.* In an action on a note given in payment for stock, brought by a purchaser before maturity, the defense was that the note was void for want of consideration, and for fraud in its inception, and that plaintiff had knowledge of its invalidity
8 when he purchased it. *Held,* evidence as to the insolvency of the corporation, as to plaintiff's knowledge of the insolvency, as to the sum plaintiff had paid for his own stock in the corporation, and as to why he did not sue the indorser of the note, is irrelevant, and inadmissible

Appeal from Hamilton District Court.—HON. B. P. BIRD-
SALL, Judge.

SATURDAY, OCTOBER 16, 1897.

ACTION at law to recover the amount of a promissory note. After the evidence had been submitted, the
district court sustained a motion of the plaintiff for
judgment upon the note, and rendered judgment in his
favor for costs. The defendant appeals.—*Affirmed.*

D. C. Chase for appellant.

Wesley Martin for appellee.

ROBINSON, J. — The note in suit was made by the
defendant on the twenty-fifth day of June, 1891, for the
sum of one hundred and twenty-five dollars, payable on
or before two years after its date to Tjernagel Bros.,
with interest at the rate of six per cent. per annum after
one year. It was given for capital stock of an incorporation known as the Scandia Publishing and Printing
Company, and was transferred to the plaintiff by an
indorsement in blank. The defendant alleges that the
note was procured by means of false and fraudulent
representations, without consideration, and that the
plaintiff knew of the fraudulent character of the note
before he obtained it, and is not an innocent purchaser
for value. The Scandia Publishing and Printing Company was located at Story City, and appears to have
been organized by Tjernagel Bros. in March or April,
1891. L. J. Tjernagel, who, we infer, was a member of
that firm, solicited and finally prevailed upon the
defendant to take some of the capital stock of the com-

pany, and to give the note in suit, and another for a like
amount, in payment for it. To make the sale,
1   Tjernagel represented to the defendant that the
capital stock of the company was fifty thousand
dollars, one-half of which was to be retained by Tjernagel Bros. and the remainder was to be sold; that the
stock was worth fifty thousand dollars; that the company was running nights; that it was to buy a Norwegian paper called *Amerika*, and would make one
of the largest printing companies. The affairs of the
company did not prosper; the business was not profitable; the company became insolvent, and it ceased to do
business in November or December, 1891. The plaintiff
and L. J. Tjernagel became partners in the banking busi
ness in the year 1889. In January, 1891, Tjernagel withdrew from the bank all his investments, and had no
interest in it, nor control of the business, after that time,
although his name continued to be used therein until
the year 1892. In March, 1891, the plaintiff became a
stockholder of the Scandia Company. At different
times in the spring of that year he purchased notes
which had been given for capital stock, and on the
eighth day of August, 1891, he purchased of L. J. Tjernagel the note in suit, with other notes to the amount
of about one thousand five hundred dollars, paying
therefor the face of the notes, less the regular bank discount. The claim of the defendant is that the note was
void by reason of want of consideration and fraud in
its inception, and that the plaintiff, by reason of his
connection with the company and with Tjernagel, and
the information he obtained through them, was chargeable with knowledge of the invalidity of the note at the
time he purchased it. The burden of proving the claim
thus made was upon the defendant.

I. The defendant stated that, to induce him to
purchase stock, and give his notes, Tjernagel stated

that "I would have so big a per cent. on my money; I
would have from 10 to 25 per cent. on my money."

2   A motion to strike that part of the testimony was
sustained, and of that ruling the defendant
complains. We think it was correct. The company had
been but recently organized, and the statement of Tjernagel was clearly but an expression of opinion in regard
to what would be done in the future. It was not a representation as to what had been done, nor respecting an
existing condition. The false statements which were
held to be material in *Parks v. Burbank*, 58 Iowa, 707,
and *McKown v. Furgason*, 47 Iowa, 636, were in regard
to alleged existing facts, or what was alleged to have
been done, and were not mere expressions of opinion.

II. The appellant complains of numerous rulings
of the court in excluding answers to questions which
he had asked. Among such questions were some asked
the plaintiff, as follows: "Was this insolvent,
3   this Scandia Co? Is it a fact that as stockholder you knew the Scandia Co. was insolvent
at the time you took them? State whether or not the
stock of the Scandia Co. was paid up. How much did
you pay for your stock? Why did you not sue Tjernagel
Bros. if they were indorsers of the note?" Numerous
other questions of a somewhat similar character were
also asked, and objections thereto were sustained. We
are of the opinion that these rulings, so far as they have
been commented upon by the appellant, were correct.
The answers sought, so far as they were indicated by
the questions, would not have tended to establish any
issue in the case. Whether the Scandia Company was
insolvent, whether the plaintiff knew that it was
insolvent when he purchased the notes of its stockholders, whether its stock was paid up, what the plaintiff paid for his stock, and why he did not sue the indorsers of the note in controversy, were all matters which

did not relate to the alleged fraud in the inception of
the note, nor to t' e knowledge of that fraud possessed
by the plaintiff when he purchased it. The defendant
testified, it is true, that Tjernagel stated to him that
"there was fifty thousand dollars capital in there, and
it was worth that much." But the defendant also testified in regard to the same conversation, in substance,
that he did not recollect whether Tjernagel said how
much the shares were then paying annually, and that
he "could not just say whether he said whether the stock
was paid up, or what it was really." It is clear that the
statements of Tjernagel upon which the defendant
relied were in the nature of mere expressions of opinion
as to present values and future earnings, and statements in regard to the plans of the company, which do
not afford the defendant any ground for relief in this
case, however much he may have been misled by them.

III.   We have read the evidence submitted to us
with care, and reach the conclusion that it would not .
have sustained a verdict for the defendant, and that
the case was properly taken from the jury. It is not
shown that the note in suit was without consideration.
The actual financial condition of the company when the
note was given does not appear. The value of the
material, machinery, and type owned by the company is
shown not to have exceeded fifteen thousand dollars in
value; but there is not competent evidence as to the
value of all of the assets of the company, although one
witness, not shown to know the condition of the company, stated, in answer to a question as to the value of
all the property of the company at the time of its organization, "Well, I do not really just remember, but I guess
that is about all,—from twelve thousand dollars to
fifteen thousand dollars." So far as we are advised,
there was a sufficient consideration for the note when it

was given. The plaintiff is not shown to have been concerned in the management nor responsible for the failure of the company, nor to have had any actual or constructive knowledge, when he purchased the note in
suit, of the fraud, if any, alleged to have been perpetrated upon the defendant to obtain it. We conclude
that the judgment of the district court must be, and it is,
AFFIRMED.

OLIVIA ANDERSON, Appellant, v. M. J. COSMAN AND S. J.
PATTERSON.

Homesteads: ABANDONMENT. A wife will be deemed to have abandoned her homestead in land held by her husband, under a con-
1 tract of purchase reserving the title to the vendor, where her
husband with her knowledge and apparent acquiescence surrendered the contract to the vendor, who in pursuance of the husband's request conveyed the land to a purchaser from him, and
8 she afterwards remained on the land with him under a lease from
the grantee, apparently recognizing a title unincumbered by the
homestead, in the latter. *Bradshaw v. Remmick*, 90 Iowa, 409,
followed.

LEASED LANDS. A homestead right under the Iowa statute may exist
2 in lands leased, or held under a contract of purchase, the legal
title remaining in the vendor.

Appeal from Crawford District Court.—HON. Z. A.
CHURCH, Judge.

SATURDAY, OCTOBER 16, 1897.

S. J. PATTERSON owned the one hundred and sixty
acres of land in question, and on the third day of January, 1890, he contracted in writing to sell the same to
Henry Anderson, the husband of the plaintiff. The consideration expressed in the agreement was two thousand, one hundred and twenty dollars, the first payment of which was to be made December 30, 1890, and

the last payment December 30, 1897, with annual intervening payments. A warranty deed was to be executed
by Patterson on full payment. The following is a stipulation of the contract: "In case the second
1   party shall fail to make the payments aforesaid,
or any of them, punctually, and upon the strict
terms and times above limited, and likewise to perform
and complete all and each of his agreements and stipulations aforesaid strictly and literally, without any failure or default, the times of the payments being of the
essence of the contract, then the first party shall have
the right to declare this contract null and void, and all
rights and interests hereby created or then existing in
favor of said second party, or derived under this contract, shall utterly cease and determine, and the
premises hereby contracted shall revert to and revest
in the said first party (without any declaration or forfeiture or act or re-entry, or without any other act by
said first party to be performed, and without any right
of said second party for reclamation or compensation
for moneys paid or improvements made) as absolutely,
fully, and perfectly as if this contract had never been
made. If, however, the said first party shall elect not
to declare this contract null and void, in case the second
party shall fail to make the payments, or any of them,
as above stipulated, the second party agrees to pay
interest at the rate of 8 per cent. per annum on all payments of both principal and interest from the date of
their maturity." Anderson, with his wife and family,
took possession of the land, made improvements
thereon, and occupied the same as a home till May, 1894.
Payments aggregating about five hundred dollars were
made by Anderson, but not at the maturity thereof. In
May, 1894, Anderson made arrangements with defendant Cosman to sell the land to him. Prior to this time
there had never been any election by Patterson to forfeit

the contract for default in payment. A conference with
Patterson by Anderson led to an agreement by which
the written contract held by Anderson was surrendered
to Patterson, marked on the back "Surrendered and
canceled," and Patterson conveyed the land by deed to
Cosman, and Cosman leased it to Anderson for one
year, for one-third of the crop. This action was commenced in February, 1895, by the plaintiff, who is the
wife of Anderson, reciting in her petition the facts as to
the contract of purchase of the land; the occupancy of
it as a homestead, and improvements made; that payments have been made; the transactions leading to the
sale to Cosman; and that she has never joined with her
husband in a conveyance of the land, or relinquished
her homestead rights therein,—and she asks that the
contract of conveyance by her husband to Cosman be
set aside, and for other relief. The answer makes some
admissions and denials, and pleads, with other facts,
that Anderson made defaults in his payments, the provisions of the contract in regard thereto, the cancellation and surrender of the contract by agreement, and
the conveyance of the land to Cosman in pursuance
thereof. The district court dismissed plaintiff's petition, and she appealed.—*Affirmed.*

R. Shaw Van and *Shaw & Kuehnle* for appellant.

J. P. Connor and *McKenzie, Brockett & Dewey* for
appellees.

GRANGER, 'J.—It is provided by section 1990 of
the Code of 1873, as to homesteads, that "a conveyance
or incumbrance by the owner is of no validity unless the
husband and wife, if the owner is married, concur in
and sign the same joint instrument." Plaintiff bases

her right to relief on the fact of a homestead right in
the premises, and the provision of the Code
2   above quoted. There can be no question but that
a homestead right may exist in land leased, or
sold under contract, where the legal title remains in
the vendor. *Pelan v. De Bevard*, 13 Iowa, 53; *Stinson v.
Richardson*, 44 Iowa, 373; *Belden v. Younger*, 76 Iowa,
567. And it may be conceded that the plaintiff and her
husband had a homestead right in the land in controversy, modified by the terms of the lease, which gave
all the right plaintiff or her husband possessed. It may
also be conceded that, had the husband desired to convey the land, in a legal sense, it could not have been
done except by the concurrence of the wife in the way
provided by law. There was never any election on the
part of Patterson to forfeit the contract, but, on the
contrary, he seemed disposed to extend to Anderson
further time to meet his payments and save the land.
It was only when Anderson came to Patterson, and
desired him to convey the land to Cosman, that there
was a talk of canceling the contract. At that time,
however, the agreement was made to surrender and
cancel the contract, because Patterson refused to make
any conveyance to Cosman while the contract was outstanding. At the time of the sale of the land by
3   Patterson to Cosman, and of the surrender of the
contract of sale by Anderson, he (Anderson), in
writing, leased the land of Cosman from May 15, 1894,
to March 1, 1895, at a rental of one-third of the crop
grown on the land; and he occupied the land in pursuance of the lease, and paid the rental agreed upon. As to
Anderson, it is not to be doubted that he intended to
and did abandon all interest he had in the land, including homestead occupancy. It is said there was also an
abandonment by the plaintiff, and the conclusion is
sustained by the record. She knew that her husband

was not paying for the place as the contract required;
that he was trying to dispose of the land; that his title
was only by contract requiring payment to secure a
title. She had the contract in her possession, or at least
it was in a drawer to which she, most of the time, held
the key; and, when Anderson called for the contract to
be taken to Patterson, she got it for him, knowing what
was to be done; and when her husband returned, the
same day, he told her what had been done, so that she
had knowledge of the surrender of the contract, the conveyance by Patterson to Cosman, and the lease from
Cosman to Anderson. She nowhere pretends that she
made any objection, and the only reasonable inference
is that she acquiesced in what was then thought to be
best, because of her husband's inability to pay for the
land. After the transaction they occupied the land
under the lease (that is, Anderson did), paying the rent,
with her actual knowledge of such payments, and under
circumstances entirely inconsistent with any claim of
right in the land except that of lessee. The rents had
been assigned by Cosman to one Way, who collected
them; and it is to be said that, if she was not in accord
with what had been done, and living on the land only
as the wife of a lessee, she was practicing a deceit, for
she well knew that the land was held adversely to any
other claim, and in good faith. She must have known
that her husband had abandoned any homestead right
and she knew equally well that it was supposed she
claimed no such right. Deceit is not fairly to be
imputed to her. Her acquiescence and participation in
the abandonment of all interests in the land except
under the lease was in a way not unusual for a wife. It
is true that Anderson says she said to him, when he
came home with the lease, that she did not want to pay
rent, but his testimony is discredited to an extent that
it should not be given force in this particular. Again,

it is not made to appear what was meant by the expression. It does not appear that she did not want to pay
rent because she had or claimed any right in the land.
It appears almost conclusively that Anderson could not
pay for the land, and any homestead right in it must
be lost. This fact, known to her, may well be considered as largely accounting for what appears to have
been a mutual understanding between Anderson and
his wife that their occupancy after the sale to Cosman
was only by virtue of the lease. The case is quite like
that of *Bradshaw v. Remick*, 90 Iowa, 409, in which we
held there was an abandonment of the homestead by the
wife by virtue of an occupancy under a lease. We think
the decree of the district court is right, and it is
AFFIRMED.

THE NATIONAL CASH REGISTER COMPANY, Appellant, v.
J. C. BROEKSMIT AND J. W. HAYES.

Attachment Levy: PROPERTY HELD ON CONDITIONAL SALE: *Notice to
Officer.* A levy of an attachment on all the goods, wares, merchandise, furniture, and fixtures "belonging to" defendant, and
1   contained in a certain building, covers an article sold to defendant on condition that the title is not to pass from the seller until
2   the purchase price is paid in full, where the contract of sale is not
recorded, and neither the officer making the levy nor the attach-
4   ment creditor had notice of the existence of the condition, when
the levy was made.

Levy: ABANDONMENT. The abandonment of personal property by
the receiver of a corporation by failing to inventory and appraise
3   it, and to include it in a sale of the property of the corporation,
does not constitute an abandonment of a levy legally made by
him as marshal prior to his appointment as receiver, in an attach-
5   ment issued at the instance of a creditor who subsequently became
a purchaser at the receiver's sale.

Appeal from Linn District Court.—HON. WILLIAM P.
WOLF, Judge.

MONDAY, OCTOBER 18, 1897.

ACTION to recover possession of a certain cash register and damages for the retention thereof. The issues and facts appear in the opinion. The case was tried to the court, and judgment rendered in favor of the defendant. Plaintiff appeals.—*Affirmed.*

U. C. Blake and *Jno. M. Redmond* for appellant.

C. J. Deacon for appellee.

GIVEN, J.—I.   The case was submitted upon an agreed statement of facts and the testimony of A. R. West, called by the defendant. The facts necessary to be noticed are as follows: On August 4, 1893, the plaintiff corporation sold the cash register in controversy to a corporation known as the "Cone Company," then engaged in the jewelry business in a room known as "No. 17 South Third Street," Cedar Rapids, Iowa. The contract of sale is in writing, and shows the price to be two hundred and twenty-five dollars, with a deduction of forty-five dollars "allowed for a Peck register," the balance to be paid in monthly payments of fifteen dollars. The contract contains the following: "It
1   is agreed that the title of the said cash register
shall not pass until the same is paid for in full, and shall remain your property until that time." It also provides that, "in default of any payment, you or your agent may take possession and remove said cash register without legal processes." It also provides: "Should there be any default in the payment of any note, it is agreed that all the remaining notes shall at once become due and payable, anything in the notes to the contrary notwithstanding." Said cash register was delivered to the Cone Company prior to November 15, 1893, and upon delivery was placed and thereafter used in said store as a part of the furniture and fixtures

thereof. The Cone Company made default in the payment due February 15, 1894, and there is one hundred and seventy-five dollars, with interest from July 4, 1895, due to the plaintiff from the Cone Company, under said contract. Said contract was not filed for record. On December 29, 1893, defendant Broeksmit commenced an action, aided by attachment, to recover three thousand, five hundred dollars and interest from said Cone Company. An attach-
2   ment was issued and delivered to A. R. West, marshal of the city of Cedar Rapids, whose return shows that on December 29, 1893, at 11:30 o'clock A. M., he attached, assessed, levied upon, and took possession of, the following described personal property, as the property of the defendant, Cone Company, to-wit: "All of the goods, wares, and merchandise of every description, furniture and fixtures, contained in the building known as 'No. 17 South Third Street,' Cedar Rapids, Iowa, consisting of jewelry, clocks, watches, furniture, fixtures, safes, silverware, opera glasses, pens, chinaware, tools, and all other property contained in said No. 17, in the basement and all parts of said No. 17, occupied by the defendant Cone Company, and belonging to the said company." It appears that neither Broeksmit nor West had at that time any notice of said contract of purchase. The cash register in controversy was in said room at that time. February 6, 1894, judgment was rendered in favor of Broeksmit, against the Cone Company, for the amount claimed. On December 30, 1893, the Kimball Building Company commenced an action, aided by landlord's attachments, against the Cone Company, for rent then due for the use of said room No. 17, asking that a receiver be appointed. Said A. R. West was appointed receiver. Broeksmit and other defendants answered in said action of the Kimball Company. The receiver filed an

inventory and appraisement of the goods, furniture, and fixtures, enumerating the various items, but not mentioning said cash register. Mr. West gives as 8   a reason that after the levy, and before the making of said inventory, he had been informed that the plaintiff made some claim to said cash register. Such proceedings were had that thereafter said receiver was ordered to sell said property belonging to said Cone Company, and he sold the same to defendant Broeksmit for three thousand dollars, and for which property the receiver executed to the purchaser a bill of sale, which was thereafter approved by the court. The cash register still remained in said storeroom; and, all the goods sold being therein, the receiver made delivery by turning over the keys to the room to the purchaser. It does not appear why J. W. Hayes was made a defendant, and the case is submitted as between the plaintiff and defendant Broeksmit.

II. Plaintiff submits, as the first question, "whether or not there was, in fact and in law, a valid levy or attachment on the register." According to the return, a levy was upon "all goods, wares, merchandise, furniture, and fixtures contained in said building, belonging to the Cone Company." We do not 4   understand plaintiff to question the sufficiency of this levy as to property belonging to the Cone Company, but contend that as, under the contract, title to the cash register was not to pass to the Cone Company until paid for in full, and not being paid for in full, it did not belong to the Cone Company, and was therefore not covered by the levy. Under the conditions of the contract and the fact that the register was not paid for in full, title did not pass to the Cone Company as between the parties to the contract, but not so as to third persons who did not have notice of this condition in the contract. The officer executing the attachment found the cash register in the store of the Cone

Company, and in use by that company as a part of its furniture and fixtures, and having no notice of plaintiff's rights under said contract, included it in his levy. In the absence of the recording of said contract and of notice of its existence, the officer and the defendant Broeksmit had a right to treat the cash register as the property of the Cone Company. We think that, under the facts, the levy was sufficient to include the cash register.

III.   Mr. West held the property levied upon until he was appointed receiver, and, as receiver, he had a detailed inventory and appraisement thereof made, which did not include the cash register. Mr. West says it was not inventoried and appraised, "for the reason that after I took possession as receiver, and before I had an opportunity to make an inventory under my levy, Mr. Blake notified me of the claim for the cash register, and informed me of the conditions of the contract; and, there being a question about it, I didn't put it in the inventory here as receiver for that reason, leaving the matter to be adjusted in the future by the parties." Plaintiff contends that the order of sale, the sale, and bill of sale made by the receiver to the defendant Broeksmit were only of the goods inventoried and appraised, and did not include the cash register. Whether this be true or not we need not determine; for, if it be conceded, still, we think, the plaintiff is not entitled to possession of the register as against the defendant. By the levy of his attachment, the defendant Broeksmit became entitled to have said cash register, as well as the other property levied upon, applied to the payment of his judgment against the Cone Company, subject only to the claim for rent, and that the proceeds arising from the sale made were insufficient to satisfy defendant's judgment. It is contended that as West, as receiver, did not include the register in his inventory, he must be held to have abandoned his levy thereon. While it may be that

West, as marshal, might abandon the levy under certain
circumstances, yet, as receiver, he could not abandon
the levy legally made by him as marshal, so as to defeat
the right of the attaching creditor under the valid levy.
There was a valid levy upon the cash register. There
has been no abandonment of that levy; and though it
be true as claimed, that it was not included in the
receiver's sale, the valid levy still continuing, the plaintiff is not entitled to possession of the register as
against the levy. It follows from these conclusions that
the judgment of the district court must be AFFIRMED.

GEORGE H. FITCHNER & COMPANY v. THE FIDELITY MUTUAL FIRE ASSOCIATION, Appellant.

Insurance Policy: REFORMATION. A mutual mistake in an applica-
1 tion for insurance on a stock of merchandise is clearly established,
where both the insured and the agent soliciting the application
testify that it was agreed that there should be twelve thousand dollars of concurrent insurance on the stock, and such agent
erroneously fixed this amount as the limit of concurrent insurance
on both the stock and the building containing it.

PRINCIPAL AND AGENT: *Notice.* The insurance company is charged
8 with the knowledge of its soliciting agent that the insured desired
and was placing twelve thousand dollars of concurrent insurance
on the merchandise.

Estoppel. Insured, if without negligence, is entitled to have his
policy reformed so as to increase the amount of concurrent insur-
4 ance allowed, where the company's agent knew, when the application was made that the insured was actually arranging for
other insurance and had definitely fixed its amount, which by the
agent's mistake was understated in the application, and such right
is not dependent upon the authority of the agent to contract
with reference to insurance, as the company is estopped to avail
itself of the agent's mistake.

NEGLIGENCE. The mere failure of the insured to read the applica-
2 tion or the copy of it on the policy, or to read the policy, does not
constitute such negligence as deprives him of the right to a
reformation of the policy to correct a mistake of the agent
respecting the amount of concurrent insurance to be allowed.

INCUMBRANCES. The condition of a policy of insurance against
6 incumbrances is not broken by the execution and recording of a
mortgage on the insured property to a fictitious person for the
purpose of protecting the mortgagor against possible misconduct
of his partner, the mortgage never having been delivered.

Pleading: PRAYER—INSURANCE. A prayer in a petition in an action
in equity on a policy of insurance, that the policy be so reformed
5 as to permit concurrent insurance of a specified amount and for
such other and further relief as plaintiff may be or show himself
entitled to, is broad enough to include relief from a provision of
the policy rendering it void if the insured "now" has or shall
"hereafter" procure any other insurance, unless consent in writing
is indorsed hereon.

Appeal from Polk District Court.—HON. C. P. HOLMES,
Judge.

MONDAY, OCTOBER, 18, 1897.

ACTION in equity on a policy of insurance against
loss by fire in the sum of one thousand dollars on the
building, and the same amount on stock of goods contained therein. At the time of the loss there was
twelve thousand dollars insurance on the stock and
eight thousand dollars on the building. The application and also the policy contained this clause: "$12,000
total concurrent insurance allowed;" and the plaintiffs
ask that this be so reformed as to be twenty thousand
dollars, instead, and that the twelve thousand dollars be
limited to insurance on the merchandise. There was
also an issue with reference to incumbrances. Decree
was entered for plaintiffs, and defendant appeals. On
re-hearing.—*Affirmed.*

Dudley & Coffin for appellant.

McVey & McVey and *J. P. Conner* for appellees.

LADD, J.—I. The three questions presented are:
Was there a mistake? If so, can it be corrected? And

was there any incumbrance on the property? The firm
of George H. Fitchner & Co., composed of Fitchner,
who lived at Correctionville, and H. C. Laub, whose
home is at Denison, was engaged in trade at Correctionville, owning a building valued at from nine thousand
dollars to twelve thousand dollars, and a stock of merchandise estimated to be worth from fourteen thousand
dollars to twenty thousand dollars, at the date of the
policy. P. A. Doughty, as soliciting agent of the defendant and other companies, procured from Laub, at Denison, applications for six thousand dollars insurance on
the stock and five thousand dollars on the building. The
applications were written by Doughty, and, being

1   unable to complete them before leaving, were fin-
ished after Laub had signed them. The latter
testifies that he told Doughty that he wanted to
place twelve thousand dollars insurance on the merchandise and eight thousand dollars on the building,
and that Doughty advised him to take more, and
wanted to write applications for all of it. This
Laub refused, stating he had promised insurance
in a company in Sioux City, and some to parties
at Council Bluffs. Doughty concurs in all this,
except as to the amount on the building, and says
Laub requested permission for other insurance, and
he told him he might exercise his discretion in that,
provided he did not exceed three-fourths of the value of
the stock; that in writing the application, through a
clerical error, the total concurrent insurance was fixed
at twelve thousand dollars on all the property, instead
of being limited to the merchandise. While there was
talk that the stock would be increased later in the fall,
this had no reference to the arrangement concerning
the amount of insurance at that time. These were the
only witnesses to the transaction, and, without doubt,

both understood there was to be twelve thousand dollars insurance on the stock, and that it was not so limited through the error of Doughty in writing the application. Seldom is a mistake more conclusively established.

II. It is said Laub ought to have discovered the mistake. The applications were very hastily prepared by Doughty, as he wished to make a train. He worked on them till near midnight. Laub testifies that he was tired out and did not read the applications. They were signed, and afterwards completed by the agent. The amount of insurance he wished to carry had been fully discussed and agreed to. Doughty was the agent of the company, and acted in that capacity in preparing the applications. The insured ordinarily rely upon the agent to properly set out the facts in the applications, and Laub did as men usually do, in assuming that the defendant's agent had done his duty. *Stone v. Insurance Co.,* 68 Iowa, 737; *McComb v. Insurance Co.,* 83 Iowa, 247. The mere failure of the assured to read his application, or the copy of it on the policy, does not establish negligence. *Bennett v. Insurance Co.,* 70 Iowa, 600; *Hagan v. Insurance Co.,* 81 Iowa, 321; *Donnelly v. Insurance Co.,* 70 Iowa, 693; *Boetcher v. Insurance Co.,* 47 Iowa, 353. Nor is the mere omission to read the policy negligence. *Barnes v. Insurance Co.,* 75 Iowa, 11; *Jamison v. Insurance Co.,* 85 Iowa, 229; *Boetcher v. Insurance Co., supra.* Laub had no reason to suppose the policy and application were drawn differently than understood. As to matters affecting the rights of the firm at the time the policy was delivered, or in the future, it must be charged with notice, but the law did not require him to search through the policy to ascertain past mistakes or misstatements of the agent or company. Under the circumstances disclosed, it cannot be said that the plain-

tiff was negligent in failing to discover the error of the
defendant and its agent.

III.   Doughty had the information that the firm
then desired and was placing twelve thousand dollars of
concurrent insurance on the merchandise, and the company was charged with the same knowledge.
3   This was a condition of things then existing, and
incident to the very business of insurance.
Applications to all of the companies could not be made
at precisely the same time, nor could the policies be so
issued. If the plaintiff was actually arranging for other
insurance to cover the same property at that time, and
had definitely fixed its amount, this was a fact, and not
in the nature of an expression of a desire to procure
other insurance at some future date. This rule is recognized in *Insurance Co. v. Wood* (Neb.) 69 N. W. Rep.
941, relied on by the defendant, and sustained in *Hagan
v. Insurance Co., supra.*

IV.   Whether a soliciting agent may enter into a
contract with reference to insurance is not involved in
this case. Doughty was bound to set out the material
facts as stated by Laub in the application, and,
4   through a mistake on his part, failed to do so.
Under such circumstances, the company is
estopped from availing itself of the error in the application in order to defeat recovery. *Stone v. Insurance
Co., supra; Eggleston v. Insurance Co.,* 65 Iowa, 308;
Reynolds v. Insurance Co., 80 Iowa, 563; *Key v. Insurance Co.,* 77 Iowa, 174; *McComb v. Insurance Co., supra.*
Here the mistake has been carried into the policy. This
the company issued on the basis of facts disclosed to
the agent, and the conditions as they existed, and of
which it is presumed to have knowledge. Having
accepted and retained the premium and issued its
policy, it is presumed to have intended to do so with
reference to existing conditions known to it; and its

failure to do so, while it may have resulted from the mistake of its agent, amounted to a fraud on the plaintiff. That equity will grant relief in such cases is not an open question, see *Boetcher v. Insurance Co., supra; Esch v. Insurance Co.,* 78 Iowa, 334; *Barnes v. Insurance Co., supra; Jamison v. Insurance Co.,* 85 Iowa, 229.

V. This clause is contained in the policy: "This contract shall be void and of no effect unless consent in writing is indorsed hereon by the secretary in each of the following instances, viz.: If the insured shall now have, or hereafter make or procure, any other contract of insurance, whether valid or not, on property covered in whole or in part by this contract." Applications for other insurance on the building were prepared by the same agent at the same time, and policies issued thereon. If, then, the policy is not reformed, as no estoppel is pleaded, the taking of additional insurance on the building, without permission, rendered it void from the day it was delivered. But the prayer of the petition, in asking that the policy be reformed so as to permit twenty thousand dollars concurrent insurance, "and for such other and further relief as plaintiff may be or show himself entitled to," includes this relief. It was not necessary to state the very phrase the plaintiff would have included in the policy, but making the allegations and prayer broad enough to include the relief to which the plaintiff is entitled, was quite sufficient. The evidence shows that Laub represented that the firm was then arranging for and placing eight thousand dollars insurance on this building, and that this was omitted in the application. The policy should have been so drawn as to permit this amount of concurrent insurance thereon. An amendment to the petition alleges a contract between the plaintiff and defendant's agent. No contract was made by such agent, nor did he have authority so to do. Apparently the

pleader intended to allege that Laub and the agent
agreed there might be an unlimited amount of insurance on the building, and twelve thousand dollars on
the stock.   What contracts these parties may have
made is quite immaterial.   The important question is,
what material facts connected with this policy of insurance did Laub make known to Doughty, which the
latter failed to include in the application, and which
the company omitted from the policy?   And as to
those, the plaintiff is entitled to relief.

VI.   In 1888 the plaintiff executed a mortgage to
Eliza Ann Hughes on the building and lots, and, after
being recorded, it remained in the possession of Laub.
The mortgagee was a fictitious person, and the
6   mortgage was never delivered.   It seems to have
been prepared by Laub with the purpose of protecting himself against any possible misconduct of his
partner.   But as there was no debt, no mortgagee, and
no delivery, there could have been no incumbrance
such as is prohibited by the policy.—AFFIRMED.

JOHN KEATLEY, Administrator of the Estate of ROBERT
    KEATLEY, Deceased, v. THE ILLINOIS CENTRAL
        RAILROAD COMPANY, Appellant.

Negligence: FELLOW SERVANTS: *Railroads.* The foreman of a gang
    of bridge repairers, who was furnished with a flag, and charged
    with the duty of signaling approaching trains to slow up if the
    condition of the bridge required it, is engaged in the operation of
    the railroad, within the meaning of Code 1873, section 1307, which
    renders railroad companies liable for injuries to employes caused
    by the negligence of co-employes "engaged in the operation of
    any railway;" and the railway company is liable for the death of
    an employe who was killed by the derailment of a train while
    crossing the bridge, owing to the foreman's neglect to signal the
    train to slow up.

Appeal from Dubuque District Court.—HON. J. L. HUS-
TED, Judge.

MONDAY, OCTOBER 18, 1897.

PLAINTIFF, as the administrator of Robert Keatley,
deceased, brings this action to recover damages of the
defendant for causing his death. There was a trial to
a jury, and a verdict for plaintiff, upon which a judgment was entered. Defendant appeals.—*Affirmed.*

W. J. Knight and *Hubert O'Donnell* (*James Fen-
tress,* of counsel) for appellant.

James H. Shields for appellee.

KINNE, C. J.—I. Robert Keatley, the decedent,
was killed on October 24, 1890, near bridge 26 on the
defendant company's railroad, by reason of a freight
car on said road leaving the track and falling on
him. At the time of the accident, the defendant company was engaged in building an iron bridge over a
creek, in place of a wooden one, which had been
removed. This bridge was seventy-one feet long, and its
ends rested on stone abutments. On the day mentioned,
there were two gangs of men at work, one working
erecting the bridge, and known as the "iron gang," of
which one Mantz was foreman, and the other known as
the "stone gang," with one Egan as foreman. The latter
gang were not working on the bridge or its abutments,
but were engaged in building a retaining wall from the
north end of the east abutment of the bridge, east-
wardly, along the north line of the right of way. The
iron gang were at work finishing the superstructure of
the bridge, and expected to complete it the following
day. The bridge was on the main line of the defendant's railway, and, while it was being erected, the traffic

of the road was carried on, the trains passing over this
bridge before it was fully completed. The stone gang
had a derrick for use in raising stone for use in the
retaining wall. The platform on which this derrick
stood was built on the north side of the track, and
about seven feet from it, and some ten or fifteen feet
east from the new east abutments. It was about two
feet lower than the rails of the track. The work of
each gang of men was independent of that of the other.
Decedent was about fifteen years of age, and was
employed by Egan, the foreman of the stone gang, to
carry water to the members of that gang, and to do
such other work as the foreman might direct. Shortly
after 5 o'clock on the day of the accident, decedent was
on the derrick platform. He and other members of his
gang were engaged in securing the boom of the derrick, preparatory to ceasing work for the day. The iron
gang was on the bridge. A freight train, containing
twenty loaded cars, came from the west. The engine
and ten cars passed over the bridge on the rails. The
next two cars were derailed, but passed over the bridge
on the ties, and, as they came opposite the derrick platform, one of them rolled off the trestle, fell on the derrick platform, and killed the deceased. The bridge went
down with the remainder of the train, and was pushed
eastward, off the west abutment.

The negligence charged is "that, at the time, the
bridge was but partially completed; that its ends were
resting on abutments about seventy feet apart; that it
was not supported or held in place by guys, rods, or other
supports; that the rails of the track crossing the same
were not securely spiked to the ties, but were, negligently and carelessly allowed to lie in a loose, unspiked,
and insecure condition for the passage of trains
thereon; that said bridge, in its unfinished and insecure
condition, with the loose and unfastened rails thereon,

was negligently and carelessly allowed to lie and
remain in such dangerous and insecure condition; that
while decedent was employed on and about the
same, where his duty called him to be, and while said
bridge and the ties and rails thereon were in said insecure and dangerous condition, a heavy freight train
was, negligently and at a high and dangerous rate of
speed, run by appellant, from the west, down a steep
grade, around a curve, and onto said bridge; that the
track, rails, and ties thereon, were thereby spread and
thrown apart; that said train was derailed, and was
thrown with great force against and upon the said
bridge; that the same was thrown down; that decedent
was thereby thrown under said bridge and train, from
the effects of which he died; * * * that said accident, injury, and death of decedent were caused by the
grossly negligent, careless, and improper condition of
said bridge, and the ties and rails thereof, so allowed
to be by appellant, and the negligent and dangerous
act of so running said train at a dangerous rate of
speed over the same, and without fault or negligence on
the part of decedent." In an amendment to the petition
it is charged "that the employes and servants of defendant engaged in the construction of the superstructure of
said bridge, at the time of said accident, negligently
and carelessly omitted, in violation of the rules of
defendant, to give notice and warning to those in charge
of said freight train, so run at a dangerous rate of speed,
as aforesaid, of the incomplete, unsafe, and dangerous
condition of said bridge, by setting out a red flag or
other warning, and omitted and neglected to give any
warning or notice whatsoever to those in charge of said
approaching freight train of the unsafe and incomplete
condition of said bridge at the time of said accident, and
as was done at other times previous to the day of said
accident." In a further amendment it was charged that

at the time of the accident the ties of said bridge were
loose and unspiked, and that the same were spread
apart, and were sawed and cut on the ends thereof, and
were allowed to be in that negligent condition when
said train ran on the bridge, and caused the accident.
The answer was a general denial. It was also averred
that the accident was caused by the decedent's negligence. It was also claimed that the decedent was not
in the defendant's employ, in the operation of defendant's railroad, and not engaged in any duty which
brought him within the protection of section 1307 of the
Code of 1873.

II. This is the second appeal in this case. The opinion in the former hearing will be found in 94 Iowa, 685.
On the last trial the court instructed the jury that the
foreman of the stone gang was not guilty of negligence,
and that the engineer and other employes in charge
of the freight train were not guilty of any negligence.
In the sixth instruction given to the jury, the court
charged as follows: "The decedent, Robert Keatley,
was, at the time of the accident and injury complained
of, upon the derrick platform, in the line and discharge
of his duty, under the direction of the foreman of the
gang with which he was employed; and if you find from
the evidence and under these instructions that the foreman of the iron gang negligently permitted a train to
run at a dangerous rate of speed, upon an unfinished,
insecure, or unsafe bridge, by reason of which the cars
left the track, and caused the death of deceased, then,
under the statute of this state, the defendant is liable
herein." In the eleventh instruction given to the jury,
the court charged: "If the bridge in question, including
the rails and ties, was in such a condition or stage of
completion that ordinary care and prudence demanded
that trains should be operated in approaching and
crossing said bridge at a slow rate of speed, then it was

the duty of the foreman of the steel gang to, by placing
out a slow flag, give warning to the approaching trains,
so that the employes operating such trains might know
that it was necessary to approach and cross such bridge
slowly; and if the accident or injury complained of was
caused by the unsafe condition of the ties and rails upon
the bridge, and the speed of the train, which was not
reduced, by reason of the failure of the foreman of the
iron gang to properly warn the approaching train, then
the defendant is liable." No other grounds of negligence were submitted to the jury. Much is said in argument by the appellant to the effect that this boy Robert
Keatley and his stone gang and the iron gang were fellow servants, and that, in the absence of the statute
(section 1307 of the Code of 1873), there could be no liability under the established facts. It is then insisted
that the facts do not bring the case within the provisions of the statute. Appellant's contention is that the
negligence of the foreman of the iron gang was not the
negligence of one engaged in the operation of the road,
within the meaning of the statute, and that decedent
was not injured by reason of the negligent operation of
the road. On the former appeal this language was used
in the opinion: "Applying the facts attending the
employment of the deceased to the statute, we think
that if he was not out of the line of his duty in standing
on the derrick platform, and the employes of the defendant negligently ran the train at a dangerous rate of
speed, upon an unfinished and unsecure and unsafe
bridge, by reason of which the cars left the track, and
caused the death of the deceased, he was within the
statute, and a right of action accrued." Counsel now
insists that plaintiff cannot recover unless it appears
that the injury complained of was caused by or through
the negligence of the employes who were running or
operating the train, and, as the trial court instructed

the jury that said employes were not negligent, there
can be no recovery under the statute. The language of
the former opinion is to be construed with reference to
what was said before the court, and the issues as then
made. It was then said that no charge of negligence
on the part of employes for failing to put out a flag or
other sign to stop the train was made in the petition.
The case is now before us on allegations of negligence
not made before; and, in view of this situation, there is
nothing in the former opinion justifying the claim counsel now make for it, as applicable to the facts now
before us. The statute of 1873 (Code, section 1307) is
as follows: "Every corporation operating a railway
shall be liable for all damages sustained by any person,
including employes of such corporation, in consequence
of the neglect of agents, or by any mismanagement of
the engineers or other employes of the corporation, and
in consequence of the wilful wrongs whether of commission or omission of such agents, engineers, or other
employes, when such wrongs are in any manner connected with the use and operation of any railway, on or
about which they shall be employed, and no contract
which restricts such liability shall be legal or binding."
We do not intend to review all of the cases construing
this statute. Many of them are discussed and reviewed
in the following cases: *Butler v. Railway Co.*, 87 Iowa,
213; *Keatley v. Railroad Co.*, 94 Iowa, 685; *Canon v. Railway Co.*, 101 Iowa, 613; *Smith v. Railway Co.*, 78 Iowa,
584; *Haden v. Railway Co.*, 92 Iowa, 229. On the
former appeal we held that the employment of decedent
placed him within the protection of this statute. *Keatley v. Railroad Co., supra.* Upon the record now before
us, the facts touching his employment are the same as
they appeared upon the former trial. We discover no
reason for not adhering to our former holding in that
respect.

In determining whether the accident resulted from the negligent operation of the train, it is not necessary, as counsel argue, that such negligence must be the act or failure to act of employes who are actually on the train. A train may be controlled by those upon it, or it may be controlled by one not on it, by signals given to those operating the train. It can make no difference, as to the right of recovery, whether the negligence, if any, which resulted in causing the accident, was the act or failure to act of one of the trainmen, or of some other · man in the defendant's employ, and who was charged with the duty of controlling the movements of the train by flag signal or otherwise. The foreman of the iron gang had control over the speed of trains across this bridge, and if he failed to signal the engineer of the train, and, as a result, it moved across the bridge at a dangerous rate of speed, thereby killing the decedent, the negligence was that of one charged with responsibility with respect to the movement of the train. Suppose this foreman of the iron gang had signaled the engineer to go slow across the bridge, and the engineer disobeyed the signal, would any one question the liability of the company if such disobedience resulted in Keatley's death? Surely not. There can be no doubt, then, of liability when another employe (foreman of the iron gang), who is charged with a duty with reference to the moving train, fails to perform it, and as a result a man is killed. *Pierce v. Railway Co.*, 73 Iowa, 140; *Doyle v. Railway Co.*, 77 Iowa, 608. Counsel is in error when he says: "In the case at bar there was no negligence in the operation of the railroad by any one engaged in its operation." The foreman of the iron gang, while not an operative upon the train, engaged in the physical labor of controlling its movements, was at the bridge, furnished with a slow flag, charged with the control of the operation of the train over that uncompleted structure, and to that extent it was his duty to control the operation of the train, by giving the proper signal to slow up the train in case the condition of the bridge required it. If he neglected that duty, he neglected a duty touching the operation of the road, because, so far as the duty enjoined upon him to signal the train was concerned, he was as much engaged in operating the road, within the meaning of the statute, as the engineer on the train.

Now, the evidence was conflicting as to the condition of the bridge at the time of the accident, and especially so as to the distance between the ties; some of the evidence showing that in some places they were several feet apart, and other evidence showing that the distance was proper. There was evidence as to what was necessary to complete the bridge; and the evidence of defendant in this case showed that some of the ties had been taken out before this accident; that, of the remaining ties, every other one was spiked; and that such spikes were loose enough to permit the ties to be moved back and forth. Whether the bridge was in such a condition as to be safe for trains to cross at the rate of speed attained by this train, which killed Keatley, was a question for the jury, under all of the evidence. Failure to flag the train is now pleaded as negligence, and the evidence is ample to show that the foreman of the iron gang was furnished with a slow flag, and that it was his duty to use it in case the bridge was not safe. Whether he was negligent in that respect was a matter properly submitted to the jury. They must have found that the condition of the bridge was such as to have required the train to be flagged, and that the foreman of the iron gang was negligent in failing so to do; and the verdict has such support in the evidence that we should not disturb it. In view of what we have said, the court did not err in refusing to instruct the jury that plaintiff could not recover.

III.   Claim is made that the cars were derailed by a cause other than the condition of the bridge; that a brake shoe or brake beam was the real cause of the accident. There was evidence that, as the train came on the bridge, fire was seen to fly from the rails or wheels, but what caused it does not appear. This evidence was all before the jury, and considered by it; but, as we have said, the evidence sustains the verdict, and the judgment must be AFFIRMED.

HOAG & GRIFFITH V. A. J. HAY AND RUTH HAY, Appellants.

Mechanic's Lien: CONTRACT FOR OWNER. A son who is farming his father's land, and with his father using the proceeds as he sees fit,
1 had no interest in the land; and no lien attaches to the land for lumber furnished for improvements thereon under a contract
2 with the son in his own name, and for the purchase price of which he executed his individual notes.

JUDGMENT AGAINST MAKER OF CONTRACT. One who contracted for material used in the construction of a building on another's property is not liable to a personal judgment in a suit in which it is
4 sought unsuccessfully to charge the property with a mechanic's lien, where the plaintiff's have not surrendered, and do not offer to surrender, the notes made by him, which cover the claim.

Limitations of Actions: OPEN ACCOUNT. Settling the amount due upon an open running account and giving a note for such amount
8 interrupts the continuity of the account for the purposes of the rule that the statute of limitations does not commence to run against an open running account until the last item is furnished.

SAME. The doctrine that the statute of limitation does not commence to run against an open running account until the last item
8 is furnished does not apply to a cause of action for lumber, furnished under separate contracts.

Appeal from Franklin District Court.—HON. S. M. WEAVER, Judge.

MONDAY, OCTOBER 18, 1897.

SUIT in equity to establish and foreclose a mechanic's lien. The defenses are that the action is barred by
the statute of limitations, waiver of the right to a lien
by acceptance of the notes of A. J. Hay, and that defendants were not the owners of the real estate, and could
not charge it with a lien for material furnished. The
trial court established the lien, and the defendants
appeal.—*Reversed.*

Taylor & Evans for appellants.

F. M. Williams for appellees.

DEEMER, J. — During the years 1891, 1892, and
1893, the defendant A. J. Hay was living upon his
father's farm, in Franklin county, using the machinery
and personal property upon the place. His father
1   was living with him, and using such of the proceeds of the farm as he saw fit. This defendant
also owned a farm in the same county. In the year
1891 A. J. Hay made a contract with the appellees, who
are lumbermen, for the purchase of certain building
material to be used in the erection of an addition to a
house upon the father's land, and to build a hog lot,
either upon his own land, or upon the land of his
father. Pursuant to this contract, appellees delivered
to A. J. Hay during the year 1891 lumber and material
to the amount of one hundred and forty-seven dollars
and sixty-four cents. Part of this lumber was used on
the farm belonging to Hay, and part on the land belonging to his father. In February of the year 1892, Hay
executed his notes to appellees for the sums of twenty-
seven dollars and thirty-six cents and thirteen dollars
and forty-six cents, respectively. These notes represent
the amount of lumber and material purchased during
the year 1891, together with some other charges for
coal. The notes were dated January 1, 1892. The

smaller one, which included articles from March 19 to and including August 14, was for lumber used in building the addition to the house, and this note was afterwards paid in full. The remainder of the account was for lumber used in building corn cribs and erecting fences on the land of both A. J. Hay and his father. In 1892 A. J. Hay purchased more lumber from appellees for the purpose of building some "shanties" upon his father's land, and erecting some additional fences upon his own land. The lumber purchased during the year 1892, the last item of which was furnished October 19, amounted to forty-six dollars and one cent. May 26, 1893, A. J. Hay executed to appellees a note for eighty-one dollars and fifty-three cents, representing the amount of the lumber bill purchased during the year 1892, as well as some other items for coal. July 6, 1893, Hay purchased some more lumber, amounting to the sum of three dollars and twenty-nine cents for the purpose of making a hay rake and building a watering trough. This last item Hay paid January 16, 1894. G. N. Hay, the father, died testate on the sixth day of May, 1894. He devised his real estate to his daughter Hay, one of the appellants herein. This suit is to establish and foreclose a mechanic's lien upon the property formerly owned by G. N. Hay. The trial court established the lien, and gave personal judgment against A. J. Hay for the sum of one hundred and fifty-eight dollars and thirty-nine cents, and it is from this judgment and decree that the appeal is made.

The statute provides that every person who furnishes any material for any building or improvement upon the land by virtue of any contract with the owner, his agent or trustee, shall have a lien for such material upon the land of such owner, to secure the payment of the materials furnished, upon complying with certain requirements of the law as to the filing of a statement with the clerk of the district court. This statement must be filed within ninety days from the date on which the last of the material shall have been fur-

2 nished. The statutes also provide that every person for whose immediate use or benefit the building or improvements are made shall be included in the word "owner." In the cases of *Getty v. Tramel*, 67 Iowa, 288, and *Wilkins v. Litchfield*, 69 Iowa, 465, we held, in substance, that the statute gives no lien upon any interest, except by virtue of a contract between the material man and the owner of that interest. A. J. Hay had no interest in the land. He was but a bare licensee, and had no authority, either express or implied, to bind his father for the purchase price of any of the material. He made the contract for the lumber in his own name, executed his individual notes therefor, and there is no evidence that the plaintiffs relied upon the land owned by the father as security for their claim. In this respect, the case is much like *Getty v. Tramel, supra,* wherein we held that the remedy in such cases must be confined to personal judgment against the purchaser. That case also answers appellee's claim that they are entitled to a lien against the improvements. The moment the improvement was made, it became an integral part of the entire structure, the title to which was in the elder Hay. If the evidence established the fact that A. J. Hay had such an interest in his father's land as that the improvements were made for his (appellant's) immediate use or benefit, it may be that a lien should be established against the improvements, and a decree rendered by which such lien might be enforced. But there is no such showing, and in no event would appellees, under the facts disclosed by this record, be entitled to a lien upon the land. The improvements were not made for the immediate use or benefit of A. J. Hay. The evidence is that he was farming the

land, and his "father was getting his living, and using the proceeds of the farm as he saw fit."

There is another insuperable objection to the greater part of plaintiff's claim for a lien. The material was furnished under separate and distinct contracts. The lumber which was contracted for in the year 1891 was all furnished prior to October 12, 1892. This action was commenced January 16, 1895. All items furnished under the original contract are barred by the statute of limitations. Phillips, Mechanics' Liens, section 324. It is said, however, that the lumber was furnished under a general contract to supply whatever might be needed, and that the statute begins to run from the date of the last item. We do not think it was so furnished. The contracts were separate and distinct and were so treated by the parties when the notes to which we have referred were given. It is also contended that the items charged against defendants form a continuous, open, running account, and should be treated as furnished under an entire contract. We are of opinion that the account cannot be so considered, for the plain reason that the parties themselves did not so treat it. The amounts due were computed and settled from time to time, and notes representing these amounts were given by Hay. This has been held to break the continuity of the account. *Porter v. Railway Co.*, 99 Iowa, 351. And for this reason plaintiffs' position is not tenable. But we have already seen that the lumber was furnished under separate contracts, and the doctrine contended for has no application. Appellees claim that they furnished certain material during the month of October, 1892, amounting to something like nineteen dollars. In the former part of this opinion we, in effect, conceded that their claim is correct, although there is a dispute about these items. In view of the conclusions reached on the first branch of the case, we need not consider this dispute. Appellees 4 are not entitled to a personal judgment against A. J. Hay for the reason that they have not surrendered, nor do they offer to surrender, the notes made by him which cover the account upon which this suit is brought. For the reasons pointed out, the judgment of the district court is REVERSED.

RICHARD HACKETT, Appellant, v. FREEMAN & GRAVES, *et al.*

Evidence: DECLARATIONS OF ACCOMPLICE: *Conspiracy.* Declarations of a thief, made before the theft, that he had made arrange-
1 ments to sell property of plaintiff to defendant, and declarations after the theft that he had sold the property to defendant, are not a part of the *res gestæ* and are not admissible against defendant, if made in his absence, unless a conspiracy between him and the thief is shown.

Witness: IMPEACHMENT. The pendency of an appeal from a judg-
3 ment of conviction does not render the conviction incompetent for the purposes of Code 1873, section 3648, providing that a witness may be interrogated as to his previous conviction for a
4 felony, but no other proof of such conviction is competent except the record thereof.

SAME. A "conviction" as used in said statute requires both a verdict
8 of guilty and judgment thereon.

Appeal from Pottawattamie District Court, at Avoca.— HON. W. R. GREEN, Judge.

MONDAY, OCTOBER 18, 1897.

ACTION at law to recover the value of eight hogs alleged to have been taken from the plaintiff wrongfully, and converted by the defendants to their own use. There was a trial by jury, and a verdict and judgment for the defendants. The plaintiff appeals,— *Reversed.*

Benjamin & Preston for appellant.

Turner & Cullison for appellees.

ROBINSON, J. — The defendants are the co-partnership of Freeman & Graves, and W. H. Freeman and
Henry Graves, the partners who compose the firm. The
plaintiff claims that in the latter part of March in the
year 1894 eight hogs which he had were stolen from
him and sold to the defendants, and that the defendants
received the hogs, and converted them to their own use.
This action is brought to recover the value of the hogs.

I. Edwin Bird testified that he and G. A. Brown
stole the hogs in question from the plaintiff about 11
o'clock at night, and drove them to Brown's place, where
they were at once loaded into wagons, and that Brown
started with them for Oakland early the next morning.
The defendant Graves admits that he purchased of
Brown, in Oakland, eight hogs, a little after sunrise the
next morning. Bird also testified that, before the
hogs were taken Brown told him that he had arranged
with Graves to take all the hogs he could get from
the plaintiff. The district court admitted that
4   testimony to show the arrangement between Bird
and Brown, but not as binding on Graves, and of
that the plaintiff complains. Bird further testified that
he did not go with the hogs to Oakland, but that he met
Brown at that place about 11 o'clock of the morning the
hogs were taken there, and that Brown said that he had
sold them to Graves. The court sustained an objection
to that testimony, and of that ruling the plaintiff also
complains. We think that both rulings were correct.
The statements of Brown made in the absence and
without the knowledge of Graves were not evidence
against him. Those testified to were not made at the
time of the taking and selling. The first one was made

before the enterprise is said to have been commenced,
and the last one was made after it had closed. Therefore, neither was a part of the *res gestae*. It is claimed
that there was evidence of a conspiracy, to which Bird,
Brown, and Graves were parties, and that the statements were admissible as the declarations of a co-con-
spirator. We doubt there having been any evidence of
a conspiracy, competent as against the defendants, and
there was certainly none at the time the rulings in
question were made. Moreover, the statements shown
were not made during the existence of the alleged conspiracy, and in aid of the common design. The court
might well have said that the statements in question
were not binding on any of the defendants, but its failure to do so, and its limiting their effect to Graves alone,
could not have prejudiced the plaintiff.

II. Brown testified for the defendants that the
hogs he sold were his own. On cross-examination he
testified that he did not think that he had ever been
convicted for a felony, and, when asked if he knew,
answered in the negative. The plaintiff offered in evidence records of the district court of Pottawattamie
county, which showed that Brown had been tried for
the crime of larceny, found guilty by the jury, and
adjudged to be imprisoned in the state penitentiary at
Fort Madison, at hard labor, for the term of two years,
and to pay the costs of the prosecution. It also
2   appeared that Brown had taken an appeal from
the judgment, and filed an appeal bond. The
offered records were excluded by the court, and we are
asked to review that ruling. Formerly persons rendered
infamous by reason of the commission of heinous
offenses were incompetent to testify as witnesses.
Under the statutes of this state, they are competent if
of sufficient capacity to understand the obligation of
an oath, but "facts which have heretofore caused the

exclusion of testimony may still be shown for the purpose of lessening its credibility." Section 3648 of the
Code of 1873 was enacted in aid of the change in the law
thus made, and is as follows: "A witness may be interrogated as to his previous conviction for a felony. But
no other proof of such conviction is competent except
the record thereof." It is the theory of the defendant
that the trial, verdict, and judgment of the district
court cannot be regarded as a conviction, within the
meaning of the statute, while the appeal is pending.
The word "conviction," as applied to criminal offenses,
has different meanings. A man may be self-convicted
by confession, or he may be convicted by the verdict of
a jury before judgment. Thus, in *Commonwealth v.
Lockwood*, 109 Mass., 325, it is said: "The ordinary
legal meaning of 'conviction,' when used to designate a
particular stage of a criminal prosecution triable by a
jury, is the confession of the accused in open court, or
the verdict returned against him by the jury, which
ascertains and publishes the fact of his guilt, while
'judgment' or 'sentence' is the appropriate word to
denote the action of the court before which the trial
is had, declaring the consequences to the convict of the
fact thus ascertained." See, also, *Schiffer v. Pruden*, 64
N. Y. 52; *Blair v. Commonwealth*, 25 Grat. 850, and
notes; 1 McClain, Criminal Law, section 110; 1 Bishop,
Criminal Law, section 361. But, as often used,
3   the word includes both the ascertaining of the
guilt of the accused and judgment thereon by
the court. *Blaufus v. People*, 69 N. Y. 107; *Schiffer
v. Pruden, supra; Commonwealth v. Gorham*, 9
Mass. 452; *Smith v. Commonwealth*, 14 Serg. &
R. 69; *Smith v. State*, 6 Lea, 637; *State v. Mooney*,
74 N. C. 98; 1 Greenleaf, Evidence, section 375. We

think as used in the statute quoted, the word has
the meaning last given, and we next inquire,
4 does the taking of an appeal operate to so far
suspend the judgment that it cannot be shown
in evidence as affecting the credibility as a witness of
the person convicted? Section 2223 of the Code authorizes the granting of a divorce to the wife of a man "when
he is convicted of felony after his marriage." It was
held in *Vinsant v. Vinsant*, 49 Iowa, 639, that the conviction there meant was not one from which an appeal
was pending, and which might be reversed; and that
holding was followed in *Rivers v. Rivers*, 60 Iowa, 380.
See, also, *Rivers v. Rivers*, 65 Iowa, 569. Does the rule
of those cases apply to the question under consideration? No appeal can be taken in a criminal case until
after judgment has been rendered. Code 1873, section
4522. The appeal, when taken, does not affect the judgment, unless bail be put in, and, when that is done,
the effect of the bail is to stay the execution of the judgment. Code 1873, section 4528. This court does not try
the case anew, but it may affirm, reverse, or modify the
judgment, and render such judgment as the district
court should have rendered, and may, if necessary or
proper, order a new trial. Code 1873, section 4538. If
this court render a judgment of affirmance, the original
judgment is to be executed as this court shall direct.
Code 1873, section 4541. Hence, until the judgment of
the district court is modified or reversed, it continues in
force, although the right to execute it may be suspended. It is true in some cases, and may be true generally, not only that the right to execute the judgment
is suspended, but that no action to enforce a right based
upon it can be maintained pending an appeal, where
bail is put in. To sustain such an action it must appear
that the judgment is final. The judgment is not otherwise affected, however, before it is reversed or modified
by this court. Until that time the conviction stands,

and may be shown as bearing on the credibility of the
person convicted, when he testifies as a witness. It
has been held in some cases, under peculiar statutes,
that the conviction of a witness cannot be shown to
discredit him as a witness, if he has taken an appeal
therefrom which is undetermined. See *Jones v. State*,
32 Tex. Civ. App. 135 (22 S. W. Rep. 404; *Arcia v. State*,
26 Tex. App. 193 (9 S. W. Rep. 685). It has also been
held that if an appeal has been taken from a judgment
of conviction, and the case is dismissed by the state,
pending the appeal, the conviction ceases to have any
effect. *Card v. Foot*, 57 Conn. 431 (18 Atl. Rep. 713). But
these cases have no application to the question we are
considering. It follows from what we have said that the
district court erred in excluding the record of Brown's
conviction. For this error, the judgment of the district
court is REVERSED.

ELIZABETH A. GAMMEL, Appellant, v. L. W. GOODE, *et al.*

Covenants: RELEASE OF MORTGAGE   A covenant in a mortgage for
 1 the partial release of one or more acres from its operation, on
    the payment at any one time of eight hundred dollars for each acre
    so released, runs with the land, and inures to the benefit of the
 2 grantee of the mortgagor, though the words "heirs and assigns" are
    not used in the covenant.

SAME. The right to a partial release, by the payment of a stipulated
 8 sum "at any one time," is available after default in payment, and
    the commencement of a foreclosure suit.

PARTIAL RELEASE. A mortgage on platted land stipulated for a
    partial release of one or more acres on the payment of a speci-
 1 fied sum per acre, or of lots "on the same basis " *Held*, that, in
    determining the proportionate amount to be paid on the release of
 4 one of the lots, the streets and alleys in the acre should be taken
    into consideration, and payment need not be made for the land
    included in such streets and alley.

Appeal from Polk District Court.—HON. W. A. SPUR-
RIER, Judge.

MONDAY, OCTOBER 18, 1897.

LOWRY W. GOODE and Eldridge T. Likes purchased
of plaintiff ten acres of land for the agreed price of
seven thousand, five hundred dollars, the land being
platted into lots, and known as "Oakland," and a part
of the city of Des Moines. Goode and Likes executed a
mortgage on the land to secure the payment of notes
given for the purchase price. These notes were so given
that one matured January 1, 1885, and one each year
thereafter to January 1, 1891. The last two notes are
for one thousand dollars each, and this suit is based
thereon. Lot No. 32 is one of a series into which the land
was divided, and this action is to foreclose the mortgage
as to that lot, the other lots having been released from
the operation of the mortgage by virtue of a stipulation
in the mortgage to that effect upon partial payments of
the mortgage debt. The lot in question, as well as
others, was conveyed to E. J. Goode subject to the
mortgage in suit. E. J. Goode is a defendant and
answers, reciting his purchase of the lots, and the stipulation in the mortgage by which the lots should be
released from the operation of the mortgage by the payment of a stipulated amount for each acre or lot; that
under such stipulation the amount necessary to release
the mortgage on lot No. 32, is one hundred and thirty-
eight dollars, but in no event will it exceed two hundred
dollars, and he offers to pay the amount found due by
the court; but insists that the lot is not liable for the
unpaid balance of the purchase price of the land. Plaintiff asks a foreclosure judgment for the full amount.
The district court found the lot liable for only one hundred and thirty-eight dollars, with the interest thereon,

and gave judgment accordingly. The plaintiff appealed,
—*Affirmed.*

N. B. Raymond for appellant.

Bishop, Bowen & Fleming and *Earle & Prouty* for
appellees.

GRANGER, J. — I.   The stipulation in the mortgage is as follows: "And it is hereby particularly
agreed between the above-named parties of the first and
second part that the parties of the first part
1   shall have the privilege of receiving a release
of one or more acres from the operation of this
mortgage by the payment at any one time of eight
hundred ($800.00) dollars for each acre to be so
released, or they may receive releases of lots on the
same basis, provided that, in case lots are to be released,
the aggregate contents of same shall not exceed one
acre for each payment of eight hundred ($800.00) dol-
lars made under this agreement."   Under this stipulation lots have been released from time to time, so
that but lot 32 now remains; and, if it is only liable for
a proportionate share of the purchase price of the land,
there will remain a part of such price unsecured.
The question is thought to turn largely upon whether
the covenant as to releases is one personal between the
parties to it or runs with the land.   On this question it
may be said that the authorities are somewhat in conflict.   Mr. Jones, in his work on Mortgages (volume 1,
section 79), speaking of such releases, says: "Whether
such a covenant running only to the mortgagor without
mention of his assigns is personal in character and cannot be enforced by a purchaser from him, is a question

upon which the authorities are not agreed; but the
better view is that such a covenant runs with
2   the land." Some cases attach importance to the
absence of the word "assigns," or some equivalent expression, and hold such a covenant to be personal
only. See *Pierce v. Kneeland,* 16 Wis. 672; *Squier v.
Shepard,* 38 N. J. Eq. 331. These cases are determined
upon somewhat different stipulations and facts from
the case at bar. *Vawter v. Crafts* 41 Minn. 14 (42 N. W.
Rep. 483), is a quite similar case to the one at bar, and
such a covenant is held to be one running with the
land. In that case it is said: "Much abstruse and technical learning has been wasted in discussing the question what are and what are not covenants running with
the land. But we think it will be found, by considering
the principles underlying the subject, that, according
to the best considered modern authorities, the law cor-
responds with common sense, and annexes a covenant
to the land, when the subject of it is something to be
done or refrained from, about or touching, concerning
or affecting, the covenantee's land (though not upon it),
which would benefit the same, or increase its value in
the hands of the holder." Such covenants are usually,
if not always, induced by a purpose to sell parts of the
land mortgaged, and to free it from the incumbrance.
It was true in this case. In the Minnesota case cited
it is said: "The rule, we think, is universal that the
benefit passes with the land to which it is incident. In
the case at bar the agreement or covenant is one relating to the rights of the parties in the land. It affects
the title, and hence affects the value of the estate to the
holder. The release is for the benefit of the owner; in
fact, no one but the owner could be benefited by it."
In *Frederick v. Callahan,* 40 Iowa, 311, in considering
the question of a covenant running with the land, and
the effect of the absence of the word "heirs" or
"assigns," it is said: "Under our statute a covenant of

real property, even in fee, need not contain the word
'heirs' or 'assigns' in order to pass the title." It is also
said in that case: "The performance of the covenant,
on the part of the plaintiff, to build the house upon the
land, became beneficial to the reversioner, and to no
other person." That fact is especially true in this case.
It seems true that the parties to the mortgage had in
view the sale of lots, and provided a way for the purchasers to take the lots freed from the incumbrance.
See, generally, on the question of such releases, *Nims v.
Vaughn,* 40 Mich. 356. We think it the better rule,
supported by the weight of authority, that the covenant
runs with the land.

It is urged that the effect of such a construction is
to defeat the intent of the parties to the mortgage
wherein the land was pledged as security for the entire
debt, and to become void on the payment thereof. It is
doubtless true that the purpose of the mortgage was as
security for all the debt, but there is no doubt about the
purpose to release each acre upon the payment of eight
hundred dollars. Had the lots not been platted, we do
not think it doubtful that every acre must have been
released upon the payment of the stipulated amount;
and one can readily see that, with accumulated interest, the security for a part of the debt would have been
lost. However that may be, it was the bargain, and
the courts cannot import into it a provision to relieve
from such consequences.

It is urged that the rights of E. J. Goode are not
superior to those of the mortgagors. We are not, in this
case, holding that they are. We do not determine that
question. The covenant in the mortgage gives the right
to the release to the mortgagor, and, as it runs with the
land, it inures to the grantee of the mortgagor.

It is thought that the right is not available after
default in payment, and the commencement of suit to

foreclose. There is no such limitation in the covenant.
The right seems co-extensive with the existence
3   of the mortgage. We do not see how the doctrine
of laches can affect this right of release, under
the terms of the stipulation. The only laches claimed
is the default in payment. When E. J. Goode purchased
the lot in question, he had the right to understand that,
upon the payment of so much, he would be entitled to
a release. The stipulation in the mortgage does not
say upon payment of so much in a particular time,
or without default, but on payment of so much "at any
one time."

II. The district court fixed the amount necessary
to release the lot from the mortgage at one hundred and
thirty-eight dollars. In the answer of E. J. Goode it is
said: "Defendants aver that in the platting of
4   said ten acres there were laid off and and numbered on the plat four lots to the acre; and under
the terms of said mortgage, as set out by plaintiff in her
petition, the proportionate amount of incumbrance
upon said lot 32, taking into consideration the streets
and alleys, would amount to about one hundred and
thirty-eight dollars, and, excluding the streets and
alleys, to two hundred dollars, and they aver that the
said proportionate amount to each lot would have paid
off all the indebtedness secured by said mortgagee." It
is thought that the answer is an admission that two
hundred dollars is necessary to release the lot. We
do not so construe the answer. In another paragraph
it is said that when he purchased the lot it was estimated that the amount necessary to release would be
one hundred and thirty-eight dollars, and the averment as to the two hundred dollars is to show the
amount if it should be held that the streets and alleys
are not to be excluded. The district court, as we understand, fixed the area by including the streets and alleys,
and we think that is the correct solution of the question.

When the mortgage was made, the land was platted; and the mortgage, in terms, conveys all right, title, and interest of the grantors in and to the streets and alleys. The stipulation provides for a release of one or more acres, at any one time, or of lots on the same basis; and we think, in case of lots, the estimate should include all the land as in case of a release by the acre. The difference is, in case of lots, that the release is of smaller parcels of land; but, in the aggregate, the amount and area must be the same. The judgment seems to us to be right, and it is AFFIRMED.

READ & TRAVERSY AND J. A. CAMPBELL, Trustee, v. THE STATE INSURANCE COMPANY, Appellant.

Insurance: INCUMBRANCES: *Lease.* The lease of the building in which the insured stock of goods is situated, if an incumbrance, is not within condition of the policy rendering it void, if, without
1 written consent indorsed thereon, the property is incumbered by mortgage or lien,—where the policy expressly requires *existing* incumbrances at the time of making the application, to be set forth in the application,—and that consent shall be required as to future incumbrances, only.

ARBITRATION: *Condition precedent.* Arbitration is not made a con-
8 dition precedent to an action on a policy of insurance by the mere provision thereof that a difference of opinion as to loss or
4 damage shall be submitted to arbitration, and that the award shall be binding as to the amount of loss or damage.

ESTOPPEL Either party to an agreement to arbitrate differences who intentionally prevents or unreasonably delays the stipulated method of adjudicating their rights, will not be permitted to
5 plead failure to arbitrate as a defense to an action subsequently brought on the original cause of action. Citing *Powers Dry Goods Co. v. The Imperial Fire Insurance Co* , 48 Minn. 380 (51 N. W. Rep.) 123); *Uhrig v. The Insurance Co.*, 101 N. Y. 362 (4 N. E. Rep. 745).

Same. A party charged with the duty of choosing an appraiser to determine differences of opinion as to loss or damage under a policy of insurance is bound to choose an appraiser who will act with reasonable promptness in naming an umpire, if one becomes
1 necessary, and in the submission of the dispute, or, on his failure to do so, to replace him with another; and the other party, if

without fault of his own, will not be made to suffer from his dereliction in that respect.

EVIDENCE. It is competent, for the purpose of ascertaining the amount of insured goods in a store at the time of the fire, to show the last previous invoice, the goods bought and the amount 8 received on sales in the mean time, and the average profit on such sales.

Same. Plaintiff in an action on a policy of insurance on a stock of goods may testify that, after the fire, he tried to sell the damaged goods, and as to what per cent. of the cost price he could get 9 therefor, as the defendant may develop by cross-examination the facts in relation to the depreciation, or other matters affecting the value of the testimony.

Same. An insurance company which, for the purpose of showing the amount of goods in stock at the time of the fire, has, on cross-examination of plaintiff's witness, entered into the subject of the 9 proceeds from retail sales during a certain period, cannot complain of the testimony of the witness on re-direct examination, as to the cost incurred in making such sales.

HARMLESS ERROR. Where the court instructs that arbitration is a condition precedent to suit on an insurance policy, and, by the 6 terms of the policy, arbitration is not a condition precedent, defendant is not prejudiced by thus requiring plaintiff to prove more than the law requires.

LIMITATION OF ACTIONS. A policy of insurance provided that no action thereon should be maintained unless commenced within 2 six months after the fire. *Held,* that the limitation did not begin to run until sixty days after notice of proof of loss were furnished the company, which was the time of payment fixed by the policy.

Special Interrogatory. To require the submission of an interrogatory to the jury under Code 1873, section 2807, the fact to be found 10 must be one inhering in, and necessary to determine in arriving at, the general verdict, and the method or elements considered in reaching the ultimate facts cannot be called for by special interrogatories.

RULE APPLIED. Under Code 1873, section 2807, providing that a special verdict shall find only the ultimate facts as established by the evidence, special interrogatories, in an action on an insurance 10 policy, calling for the damages to goods in different parts of the store, and the value of those totally destroyed, are properly refused, as calling for the method or elements considered in reaching the facts.

Appeal from Polk District Court.—HON. C. P. HOLMES, Judge.

TUESDAY, OCTOBER 19, 1897.

ACTION on insurance policy for damages to stock of goods, occasioned by fire. Trial to jury, verdict and judgment for plaintiffs, and defendant appeals.— *Affirmed.*

O. B. Ayres, Earle & Prouty, and *McVey & Cheshire* for appellant.

Carroll Wright and *Cummins, Hewitt & Wright* for appellees.

LADD, J.—The policy contains a clause concerning the property insured, in these words: "Or if, without written consent hereon, the title of the property is

1   transferred or changed, in whole or in part
         (except by death of the insured); or if same, or
         any part thereof, is incumbered by mortgage, lien, contract or sale, or otherwise, or is assigned for the benefit of creditors; or any existing incumbrance at the time of making application is not set forth in the application; or if there is any other insurance, valid or invalid; or if there is any change in the occupant or occupancy of the premises insured, * * * then, and in every such case, this policy shall be void." The goods insured were in a building leased February 15, 1893, for a term of three years, five and one-half months, at the rental of two hundred and eight dollars and thirty-three cents per month, payable in advance. The policy was issued March 14, 1893, for one year. The fire occurred August 18 following, and this suit was begun March 22, 1895. If, then, the lease constituted an incumbrance on the property, it existed at the time

the policy issued, and does not come within the prohibition of this clause.   There is no room for construction,
as the policy, in unambiguous terms, provides that existing incumbrances must be disclosed in the application,
and future incumbrances permitted by the company,
else it will be void.   Nor can any other intention be
imputed to the defendant.   The greater part of the merchandise of the country is kept in buildings leased for
terms, and a lease is not commonly understood to be an
incumbrance.   In preparing its form of contract the
defendant could not have had in view the invalidity of
a large portion of its insurance for which adequate compensation had been received.   Nor do the cases relied on
sustain the contention now made.   The instruments
considered in *Peet v. Insurance Co.*, 7 S. D. 410 (64 N.
W. Rep. 206, and *Insurance Co. v. Vanlue*, 126 Ind.
410 (26 N. E. Rep. 119), are construed to be mortgages,
and the rulings rest on that ground alone.   It is well
settled that such contracts must be strictly construed
against the insurer, and a forfeiture avoided, if possible.
If the lien for rent to accrue or for unpaid taxes,—created by statute,—is to invalidate a policy of insurance,
it should so provide in unmistakable terms.

II.   Was the action barred by the contract of limitation contained in the policy?   It will be noticed the
suit was begun within six months after the proofs of
loss were furnished, but more than that time
2   after the fire.   The policy stipulates that "no
suit or action against the company for the recovery of any claim under or by virtue of this policy shall
be sustained in any court of law or equity unless commenced within the term of six months next after the
fire shall have occurred."   In *Ellis v. Insurance Co.*, 64
Iowa, 507, the policy provided that "action shall be commenced within six months next after the loss shall
occur."   The court held the period began to run when
the cause of action had accrued; i. e. sixty days after

the notice and proof of loss had been furnished. This ruling is expressly approved in *Miller v. Insurance Co.*, 70 Iowa, 704, and finds support in *Steen v. Insurance Co.*, 89 N. Y. 321; *Insurance Co. v. Fairbank*, 32 Neb. 750 (49 N. W. Rep. 711); *Barber v. Insurance Co.*, 16 W. Va. 658; *Chandler v. Insurance Co.*, 21 Minn. 85. Authorities to the contrary may be mentioned. *Travelers' Ins. Co. v. California Ins. Co.*, 1 N. D. 151 (45 N. W. Rep. 703); *Johnson v. Insurance Co.*, 91 Ill. 92; *Chambers v. Insurance Co.*, 51 Conn. 17; *Insurance Co. v. Wells*, 83 Va. 736 (3 S. E. Rep. 349); *Riddlesbarger v. Insurance Co.*, 7 Wall. 386; *Law v. Association*, 94 Mich. 266 (53 N. W. Rep. 1104). The policy considered in *McConnell v. Association*, 79 Iowa, 757, stipulated that no action should be maintained unless "commenced within six months after the happening of the death on account of which the action is brought." The court, through Beck, J., said: "It is a familiar and just rule, recognized by the courts, that a bar created by a statute or by the contract to an action for a breach of its conditions by reason of the lapse of time will not commence to run until the right of action accrues; that is, the plaintiff must have the full time given by the statute or contract after his right of action accrues, in which to commence his suit." The action was begun more than six months after death, but within that time after the right of action accrued, and held to be in time. This ruling is approved in *Matt v. Association*, 81 Iowa, 135. These cases are decisive. The period must be held to have commenced to run sixty days after the notice and proof of loss were furnished the defendant,—the time of payment fixed by the policy. Parties may waive the limitation fixed by statute, and adopt one for themselves, if reasonable; but, in cases like this, the time agreed upon will be construed to begin to run when the right of action accrues. That the rule is a wholesome one is illustrated by an examination of many of the cases cited. In some

of them a strict construction of the language employed
would cut off all recovery, and in others leave the time
limited with which an action might be brought, unreasonably short. In this state the insured has sixty days
within which to furnish the company notice and proof
of loss, and may not maintain an action within ninety
days thereafter. *Quinn v. Insurance Co.,* 71 Iowa, 615.
This would leave one month only within which suit
might be brought. The property involved in this controversy was covered by policies issued by twenty-four
different companies, and the length of time required
to begin so many actions need only be suggested. Were
the question before this court for the first time, we
might deem it more appropriate for the legislature to
establish such a rule; but as it is not inimical to justice,
and may well be presumed to have been followed in
making contracts throughout the state for many years,
we are content to adhere to it. It finds support in
Hong Sling v. Insurance Co., 8 Utah, 135 (30 Pac. Rep.
307); *Insurance Co. v. Davis,* 40 Neb. 700 (59 N. W. Rep.
698); *Friezen v. Insurance Co.,* 30 Fed. Rep. 352. To the
contrary, see *Meesman v. Insurance Co.,* (Wash.) 27
Pac. Rep. 77 *McElroy v. Insurance Co.,* 48 Kan.
Sup. 200 (29 Pac. Rep. 478); *Hart v. Insurance Co.,* 86
Wis. 77 (56 N. W. Rep. 332).

   III.   Was arbitration a condition precedent to the
bringing of this action? The policy contains this provision: "If differences of opinion shall arise between
      the parties hereto as to the amount of loss or
3   damage, the subject shall be referred to two dis-
      interested and competent men, each party to
select one (and, in case of disagreement, they to select a
third), who shall, under oath, ascertain, estimate, and
appraise such loss or damage separately; and their
award in writing shall be binding on the parties hereto
as to the amount of loss or damage, but shall not decide
the liability of the company under this policy." There

is nothing in the policy making submission to arbitration a condition precedent to the payment of the loss or to the maintenance of an action, nor can such a condition be inferred from its terms. The authorities recognize the rule as stated by Sir George Jessel, M. R., in *Dawson v. Fitzgerald*, 1 Exch. Div. 257: "There are two cases where such a plea as the present is successful: *First*, where the action can only be brought for the sum named by the arbitrator; *secondly*, where it is agreed that no action shall be brought until there has been an arbitration, or that the arbitration shall be a condition precedent to the right of action. In all other cases where there is, first, a covenant to pay, and, secondly, a covenant to refer, the covenants are distinct and collateral, and the plaintiff may sue on the first, leaving the defendant to bring an action for not referring," etc. This court has recognized the right of parties to bind themselves to make payment of a sum to be fixed or estimated by an arbitrator or third person. *Flynn v. Railway Co.*, 63 Iowa, 490; *Ross v. McArthur*, 85 Iowa, 203; *McNamara v. Harrison*, 81 Iowa, 486. Also the right to make arbitration a condition precedent to the maintenance of an action. *Zalesky v. Insurance Co.*, 102 Iowa, 613. A mere provision in the policy, however, that, in event of a disagreement, the amount of damage shall be ascertained by arbitrators, will not prevent the assured from maintaining an action, unless arbitration is made, by the terms of the policy or necessary inference therefrom, a condition precedent. In such a case the agreement to arbitrate is collateral to the main purposes of the policy,—an independent agreement,—a breach of which, while it will support a separate action, cannot be pleaded in bar to a suit on the principal contract. *Hamilton v. Insurance Co.*, 137 U. S. 370 (11 Sup. Ct. Rep. 133); *Insurance Co. v. Pulver*, 126 Ill. 329 (18 N. E. Rep. 804); *Reed v. Insurance Co.*, 138 Mass. 572; *Canfield v. Insurance*

Co., 55 Wis. 419 (13 N. W. Rep. 252); *Seward v. City of Rochester,* 109 N. Y. 164 (16 N. E. Rep. 348); *Insurance Co. v. Alvord,* 9 C. C. A. 623 (61 Fed. Rep. 752); *Lumber Co. v. Insurance Co.,* 101 Iowa, 514. See *Gere v. Insurance Co.,* 67 Iowa, 272. The condition considered in each of the above cases was, in substance, like that set out, and in each adjudged not to require arbitration before bringing suit. In the authorities cited and relied on by appellant, arbitration is either made a condition precedent by the express terms of the contract or by necessary inference therefrom. Here there is no such provision in the policy, and the agreement to arbitrate must be regarded as independent, and repudiated by the beginning of this action. The remedy open to the defendant was not a plea in bar, but in an action for breach of contract to refer to appraisers. The court erroneously ruled that arbitration was a condition precedent.

IV. Each party selected an appraiser on August 26, 1893, and these were unable to agree upon an umpire. September 11 following, defendant replaced the party selected by it with another, but the attempt of these to fix upon a satisfactory person also failed. The plaintiff declared, on the sixteenth of the same month, it would proceed with the arbitration no further, but afterwards said, if there was no delay, the appraisers might proceed with one Redstone as umpire. When it was learned Redstone was about to leave for Chicago, plaintiff refused to submit the matter at all. A great part of the evidence and a very voluminous correspondence between the attorneys was introduced bearing on the question as to whether the plaintiff was justified in refusing to proceed further with the arbitration. The law seems to be well settled 5 that, if either party to an agreement to arbitrate intentionally prevents or unreasonably delays the stipulated method of adjusting the rights of the parties, he will not be permitted to plead failure to arbitrate as defense to an action subsequently brought. *Dry Goods Co. v. Insurance Co.*, 48 Minn. 380 (51 N. W. Rep. 123); *Uhrig v. Insurance Co.*, 101 N. Y. 362 (4 N. E. Rep. 745). The arbitrator, by whomsoever selected, represents neither party in the work of determining the issues submitted, but is bound to act impartially, and with no other purpose than that of arriving at a just conclusion. In selecting an umpire, he owes no other duty to the party appointing than that of promptly securing an impartial and capable person to act in that capacity. Either party may well be permitted to state valid objections to any person under consideration for such position, but may not control therein, or unduly influence, either arbitrator. If an umpire is not chosen, owing to the interference of either party, with the purpose of preventing or delaying the submission unreasonably, this ought to estop him from pleading no arbitration, because he has rendered it impossible by his own acts. Nor will an arbitrator be permitted, on his own motion, by wilfully or negligently postponing the selection of an umpire, to unreasonably delay the adjustment of the controversy; else the very purpose of arbitration, which is the speedy and inexpensive settlement of disputes, would be defeated. A person cannot be tied up forever, without his fault, by an ineffectual arbitration. It is better to hold the party appointing to the duty of choosing an appraiser who will act with reasonable promptness in naming an umpire, and in the submission of the dispute, or, on his failure so to do, replace him with another, than that the other party to the controversy shall suffer without any fault of his own. This is not in conflict with the rule that, when the award is set aside because of misconduct of arbitrators, a new appraisement, if not impossible, will still be necessary. See *Levine v. Insurance Co.*, 66 Minn. 138 (68 N. W. Rep.

855); *Hiscock v. Harris*, 80 N. Y. 402; *Carroll v. Insurance Co.*, 72 Cal. 297 (13 Pac. Rep. 853). Here, there is a failure to act at all, and a party may well be required to name an appraiser who will proceed to the performance of his duties as such without unnecessary delay. The instructions of the district court were in harmony with these views, and are approved as correctly stating the law. See *McCullough v. Insurance Co.*, 113 Mo. 606 (21 S. W. Rep. 207); *Chapman v. Insurance Co.*, 89 Wis. 572 (62 N. W. Rep. 422).

V. The defendant urges that the finding of the jury that Kenyon, the appraiser selected by it, unreasonably delayed the choice of an umpire, is not sustained by the evidence. We shall not take the trouble to determine this, for the reason that, had the finding been different, the plaintiff would have been entitled to recover. The only question proper for the consideration of the jury was the amount of damages to be allowed. In requiring the plaintiff to establish an excuse for failure to arbitrate, the court imposed an additional affirmative issue on it to establish; but this was insisted on by the defendant, and many instructions asked by it submitting that issue, so that it is not in a situation to complain of any prejudice occasioned by the holding of the court that arbitration was a condition precedent. Nor did any result. The court correctly instructed on that issue, and, by submitting it to the consideration of the jury, announced the law as more favorable to the company than it was entitled to have it. The defendant was not prejudiced by the ruling that plaintiff must prove more than the law required. See *Phoenix v. Lamb*, 29 Iowa, 352; *Hahn v. Miller*, 60 Iowa, 96; *Miller v. Root*, 77 Iowa, 545.

VI. It is also insisted that the finding of the jury that the damage to the stock of goods occasioned by the fire was thirty-four thousand dollars has not sufficient support in the evidence. The testimony of Read and

Traversy warranted this finding. Other reputable witnesses placed the damages at only a fraction of such
amount. The value of the evidence offered depended
very largely on the familiarity of the witnesses with the
goods, and the attention given to them before and after
the fire. While we might not have placed the damages
as high as the jury did, the evidence is such as to preclude any interference with the verdict.

VII.   For the purpose of ascertaining the amount
of goods in the store at the time of the fire, the plaintiff
was permitted to show the last previous invoice, the
goods bought in the meantime, the amount
7   received on sales in the meantime, and the average profit on such sales. Of this the defendant
seriously complains, but suggests no other way of fixing
the value of the merchandise before the injury. It is
the usual way of determining such value, and often the
only method of fixing the damage in event of the partial
or total loss of a large and miscellaneous stock of merchandise. If the statements and computations are correct, a comparison with the amount and value of the
goods immediately after the fire will fix the loss suffered thereby. See *Levine v. Insurance Co., supra;
Insurance Co. v. Weide,* 9 Wall. 677; *Insurance Co. v.
Weides,* 14 Wall. 375. The possibility of a great many
other dispositions of the property is suggested by counsel, but the evidence tended to show none other had
been made. So with reference to other causes of depreciation. These were undoubtedly the subject of inquiry,
and the defendant had the opportunity of calling them
to the attention of the jury either in cross-examination
or by such evidence as it might deem proper to offer.

VIII.   Read testified that after the fire he tried to
sell the damaged goods, and was asked what per cent.

of the cost price he could get. It is said that this was
improper, because the cost price might not repre-
8   sent the true value, as the goods may have depre-
icated by being shelf-worn, or out of style, and
for other reasons. It is sufficient to say that the examination followed the well-known custom of merchants
generally in making all computations from the cost
price; and, had there been any depreciation owing to
the numerous causes suggested, the defendant had
ample opportunity for developing them on cross-examination.

IX. In cross-examination Read testified that of
the stock twenty-four thousand, four hundred and
ninety-six dollars and eighty-two cents was received for
goods sold between September 25, 1893, and March
following, and merchandise invoicing seventeen thousand dollars then remained. The evident purpose was
to show that the goods actually sold for more than the
value fixed by him. The plaintiff, in re-direct
9   examination, was then permitted to show the
cost incurred in making these sales. Certainly,
if the selling price at retail may be considered in fixing
the value, the expense of making such sales ought to be
taken into consideration. The defendant, having elected
to enter such an investigation, cannot be heard to complain because followed into the same field of inquiry.

X. Special interrogatories, calling for the damage
to goods in different parts of the store, and the value of
those totally destroyed, were asked by the defendant,
and refused. The ruling was not erroneous, as
10   the inquiries were not for ultimate facts material
to the issue. It was simply an attempt to require
the jury to state the different items of damage resulting
from the same cause, making up the amount of their
verdict. A special verdict must present the ultimate
facts as established by the evidence. Section 2807, Code
1873. "Ultimate," as defined by Webster, means: "Last

in the train of progression or consequences; tended
toward by all that precedes; arrived at as the last
result; final." The fact to be found must be one inhering in and necessary to determine in arriving at the
general verdict. The method or elements considered in
reaching the ultimate facts cannot be called for by
special interrogatories. See *Lawson v. Railway Co.*, 57
Iowa, 672; *Bonham v. Insurance Co.*, 25 Iowa, 334;
Savings Bank v. National Bank, 101 Iowa, 530; *Pheonix
v. Lamb, surpa; Hawley v. Railway Co.*, 71 Iowa, 717;
Scagel v. Railway Co., 83 Iowa, 380; *Dreher v. Railway
Co.*, 59 Iowa, 599.

XI. The seventh instruction is not open to the
criticisms urged, but contains a clear and full statement of the correct measure of damages. The jury are
there told, in substance, to determine the reasonable
market value of the goods totally destroyed or rendered
worthless, and then the amount of the damage or depreciation, if any, to the market value of the goods not
destroyed or rendered worthless, and, in doing so, to
consider the purposes for which plaintiff owned and
kept the merchandise; and, after cautioning the jury
only actual damages could be allowed, proceeded: "You
are instructed that, if the goods insured could not, in
ordinary course of trade or business, be sold at as high
prices after as before the fire, such difference was an
actual damage, for which the plaintiffs are entitled to
recover; and the aggregate of these sums will be the
amount of plaintiff's loss or damage." It is said the
measure of damages is the difference between the market value of the goods immediately before and after the
fire. That is what the court told the jury. The fair
market value is what property will bring in the ordinary course of trade or business. It is claimed depreciation from other causes might be considered under
this instruction. But, in stating the issues, the jury
were told that damages occasioned by fire were claimed,

and such damages only were under consideration. If
the goods decreased in value from cost from other
causes, this would be taken into account in determining
what they were worth at that time. All the evidence
was directed to fixing the value before and after the
fire. The jury could not have failed to understand this
instruction to mean all defendant claims it should.

XII. Many other matters are discussed, but do
not require consideration. The arguments of appellant
are prolix, and many of the objections urged are captious. Without reviewing them in detail, we may say
they are without merit. The judgment is AFFIRMED.

SARAH L. PRIESTMAN, Appellant, v. WILLIAM PRIEST-
MAN.

Judgments: VACATION: *Motion and petition.* Under Code 1873, section 3154, authorizing the vacation or modification of a judgment
1 for irregularity or for fraud practiced by the successful party in
obtaining it, a claim of irregularity in obtaining the judgment
cannot be considered, unless made by motion on the second day
of the next succeeding term, as provided by the Code, though a
petition to vacate for want of jurisdiction or for fraud of the successful party may be considered if filed within one year after such
judgment was rendered.

JURISDICTION: *Notice by publication.* Under Code 1873, section
26 8, providing that "service may be made by publication when an
2 affidavit is filed that personal service cannot be made on the defendant within the state, * * * where the action is for a divorce,
if the defendant is a non-resident of the state, or his residence is
unknown" and section 2630, that, "when the foregoing provisions
has been complied with, the defendant, so notified, shall be
required to appear as though personally served within the county
in which the petition is filed on the day of the last publication,"—
there was no service where such affidavit was not filed until after
there publications of the notice; as the filing of such affidavit is
a condition precedent to such publication.

Collateral attack. An adjudication that such prerequisite had been
8 complied with is subject to attack in a proceeding to vacate such
judgment.

*Appeal from Page District Court.—*HON. WALTER I. SMITH, Judge.

TUESDAY; OCTOBER 19, 1896.

AUGUST 30, 1894, defendant obtained a decree of divorce from the plaintiff, in an action wherein he charged her with desertion and adultery. Original notice in that case was served by publication. This is a suit to set aside that decree, and for a new trial, based upon the grounds that the allegations in the petition in the original action that plaintiff had deserted defendant were untrue; that the alleged adultery had been condoned; that the affidavit of non-residence was not filed until after the notice had been published for three consecutive weeks; that the publication was made in an obscure paper, published many miles from the place of defendant's residence, with intent that plaintiff should not learn it; that the decree was obtained through fraud and perjury practiced by defendant; and that plaintiff has at all times been a resident of Page county, Iowa, and was at the time the notice was served, of which fact defendant was aware when he caused the notice to be published. The trial court dismissed the plaintiff's petition, and she appeals. —*Reversed.*

G. I. Miller and *C. S. Keenan* for appellant.

W. P. Ferguson for appellee.

DEEMER, J.—Two claims are made in the petition. One is that the court was without jurisdiction to render the original decree, and the other is that the decree was obtained through perjury and fraud; and a new trial is asked under the provisions of Code 1873, section 3154, which authorizes the vacation or modification of a judgment for irregularity or for fraud practiced by the successful party in obtaining it.

1   This action was brought on the fifteenth day of August, 1895. The Code of 1873 provides that proceedings to vacate a judgment because of irregularity in obtaining it must be by motion made on the second day of the next succeeding term. There was a term of the district court held in Page county in January, 1895, and another in April. As no motion was filed as required by the statute, we cannot consider plaintiff's claim of irregularity in the obtaining of the judgment. The Code of 1873 also provides that proceedings to obtain a new trial for fraud practiced by the successful party in obtaining the judgment shall be by petition setting forth the facts, and commenced within one year after the judgment or order was made. The application to vacate on the ground of irregularity cannot be considered, because not made in time. In

2   so far as it is a petition to set aside the judgment because of want of jurisdiction, and to vacate it because of fraud of the successful party, it is timely, and may be considered. The evidence establishes without dispute that the affidavit of non-residence was not filed until there had been three issues of the paper in which the notice was published. The first publication was July 20, and the last August 10. The affidavit was filed August 4 of the same year. The statutes with reference to such matters are as follows: Code 1873, section 2618: "Service may be made by publication when an affidavit is filed that personal service cannot be made on the defendant within this state * * * where the action is for a divorce, if the defendant is a non-resident of the state, or his residence is unknown." Section 2620 provides that, "when the foregoing provisions have been complied with, the defendant, so notified, shall be required to appear as if per-

sonally served within the county in which the petition
is filed on the day of the last publication." It has frequently been held that the requirements of the statute
as to the constructive service must be strictly followed
and literally complied with. *Abell v. Cross*, 17 Iowa,
174; *Tunis v. Withrow*, 10 Iowa, 305; *Broghill v. Lash*,
3 G. Greene, 357; *Smith v. Smith*, 4 G. Greene, 266;
Pinkney v. Pinkney, 4 G. Greene, 324. Applying this
rule, we have held that the filing of an affidavit is a
condition precedent to the service of notice by publication, and that a judgment rendered without an appearance by the defendant, served only by publication,
when the affidavit has not been filed, is void. *Carnes
v. Mitchell*, 82 Iowa, 605; *Chase v. Kaynor*, 78 Iowa,
450; *Bradley v. Jamison*, 46 Iowa, 69. The filing of the
affidavit is a condition precedent to the service of
notice, and, if not filed before the notice is published,
the court is without jurisdiction to try or consider the
case. *Snell v. Meservy*, 91 Iowa, 323. It is not a case
of defective service, as was *Woodbury v. Maguire*, 42
Iowa, 341, and *Griffith v. Harvester Co.*, 92 Iowa, 634.
If the necessary preliminary steps had been taken, and
the notice was defective, simply, in form or substance,
then the rule contended for by appellee, and established
by these cases, would apply. But here a vital prerequisite to the validity of the notice is wanting. True, the
affidavit was filed before the last day of publication, but
there was nothing on file which justified the first publications. The statutes say that such service may be
made when an affidavit reciting the proper facts is filed.
Until this is done, there is no authority to publish the
notice. It is not a case of defective service, but of no
service; and the fact that the court which rendered the
decree found and recited in the decree that service had
been made is of no consequence. *Bradley v. Jamison,
supra*. The distinction between those cases which hold
that a judgment may be collaterally attacked because

of the absence of certain jurisdictional facts, and those which hold that it must be directly assailed when there is a notice supported by proper preliminary proceedings the sufficiency of which is subject to construction, and

3   upon which the court must judge of its own jurisdiction, is apparent. In the one case the judgment or decree may be collaterally attacked, while in the other the adjudication is good until set aside in some direct proceeding. In this case there is an absence of a certain condition precedent to the publication of any notice, and the adjudication of the court that this preliminary step had been complied with is not binding, but is subject to attack in this proceeding.

II. The evidence does not establish any fraud or irregularity in publishing the notice in an obscure paper, as claimed. Nor do we think the plaintiff is entitled to a new trial because of perjury committed in the original case. We are also of the opinion that the plaintiff was a non-resident at the time the notice was published. The real merits of the case are not open to consideration. The condonation claimed by plaintiff was purely defensive, and, if the notice had been properly served, the decree of the court below in granting the divorce would have been conclusive. As the court was without jurisdiction, the decree is of no validity, and should have been set aside. This conclusion relieves us of the necessity of considering the question as to whether plaintiff has a good defense to the defendant's claim for divorce. The decree of the district court is reversed, and the cause is remanded for further proceedings in harmony with this opinion.— REVERSED.

/1
/el

W. H. HAMILTON, Appellant, v. THE CHICAGO, MIL-
WAUKEE & ST. PAUL RAILWAY COMPANY.

Carriers: CONVERSION: *Tender.* A shipper who, after a wrongful
1 delivery of the goods by the carrier to a third person, agrees to
wait for a delivery of the goods until the return of the station
2 agent, may treat the goods as converted and maintain an action
for their value, where the carrier fails for seven days after the
return of the agent to recover and deliver the goods, and a tender
made thereafter, and after notice to the carrier of the shipper's
election to treat the goods as converted, is too late.   •

Attachment: WHAT MAY BE SEIZED: *Converted property.* Where a
1 common carrier fails and refuses to deliver to the consignee prop-
3 erty shipped over its line, the consignee has a right to elect to
claim damages for the value of the property, and to waive all title
to it; and, after the carrier has been notified of such election, the
property belongs to it, and is not subject to attachment in its
hands as being the property of the consignee

Evidence. Evidence that the cashier of a station agent is liable for
losses resulting from a wrong delivery of shipments by him, and
is under bond to secure that delivery, is inadmissible in an action
4 against the carrier for the conversion of the shipment, for the
purpose of affecting defendant's liability, but may be admissible
to show the interest of the cashier as a witness, and if introduced
should be limited to that purpose by an instruction to the jury.

Appeal from Cedar Rapids Superior Court.—HON. T.
M. GIBERSON, Judge.

TUESDAY, OCTOBER 19, 1897.

PLAINTIFF states, in his petition filed September 24,
1895, his cause of action, in substance, as follows: That
on August 31, 1895, the defendant, a common carrier,
received from C. H. Stone, for carriage from Strawberry
Point to Cedar Rapids, Iowa, "one box containing one
Bohemian wheel of fortune, one box containing fixtures
for said wheel, one roll of canvas," of which said Stone
was the owner, and it was consigned to him; that said

goods were on that day transported to Cedar Rapids, and on that day defendant, without authority or consent of said Stone, delivered said articles to one B. B. Hewitt; that Stone thereafter demanded said goods; that defendant refused to deliver the same; and that they were of the value of three hundred dollars. Plaintiff alleges that for valuable consideration said Stone did, on the twenty-fifth of September, 1895, assign said claim in writing to the plaintiff, which writing is set out, and that the claim is due and owing to plaintiff; wherefore he asks judgment for three hundred dollars and costs. The defendant answered, admitting that it is a common carrier; that the goods were shipped, consigned, transported, and delivered to Hewitt as alleged, except the roll of canvas, which it alleges was delivered to one Hawkins, on a written order of Stone. This allegation is not disputed, and therefore the canvas will not be considered in what is hereafter said. The defendant denies that the goods were of the value of three hundred dollars, and avers that they were of no value, and denies that it is indebted to the plaintiff in any sum whatever, and for want of information and belief denies the assignment of the claim to plaintiff. As further defense, the defendant avers, in substance, as follows: That Hewitt was entitled to the delivery of said articles, for the reason that he was the owner thereof, and that he represented to defendant that he was authorized by Stone, as consignee, to receive and take charge of said property. That on October 8, 1895, defendant, being in possession of said property, tendered the same to the plaintiff by tender in writing, as set out, together with all costs of suit; and that plaintiff made no complaint as to the condition of the property, or the amount of costs, or form of tender, but refused to receive said property and costs. That it is now unable to produce said boxes of freight in court, for the reason that the

same were taken from its possession upon writs of
attachment against the property of C. H. Stone, of
which fact defendant notified plaintiff in writing on
October 28, 1895, which notice is set out. "Defendant
avers that the said property were and are implements
of gaming, and contraband articles, and of no value
whatever; and alleges the same to have been used by
C. H. Stone and others in Iowa, in violation of the laws
of said state, for gambling and gaming purposes, and
that said property was shipped to Cedar Rapids for such
use." Plaintiff filed his motion in fourteen paragraphs
to divide the answer into counts, to require more specific statement in certain particulars, and to strike out
parts of the answer. The motion was sustained so far
as to require the defendant to separate its answer into
counts, and to strike the division of the answer quoted
above. It was overruled as to the other grounds of the
motion. Thereupon plaintiff demurred to the second
division of the answer, on the ground that the facts
stated therein, if true, do not constitute a defense. This
division is the one wherein defendant alleges the delivery to Hewitt. The demurrer was overruled, and thereafter the defendant amended its answer by alleging, in
substance, as follows: (1) That the property was delivered to Hewitt by mistake, innocently made, and with
no intention to deprive the consignee of his property.
(2) That, upon being informed by the consignee that
the property belonged to him, defendant promptly
informed him that they would procure the property
immediately, and deliver same to him; and that they at
no time disputed his right to the possession thereof. (3)
That it was then agreed between defendant and Stone
that Stone would accept the property when the defendant would procure the return thereof from Hewitt, and
deliver it to him. That thereupon defendant diligently
set about to procure the return of the property, and did

procure the same in good condition, and tendered the
same to the plaintiff, and he refused to receive the same
as such, in the answer now on file. Plaintiff moved to
strike from this amendment paragraphs 2 and 3 as
incompetent, irrelevant, and immaterial, which motion
was overruled. On March 20, 1896, the case was tried
to a jury, and verdict and judgment rendered in favor
of the defendant. Plaintiff appeals.—*Reversed.*

Rickel & Crocker and *John A. Reed* for appellant.

Rothrock & Grimm and *J. C. Cook* for appellee.

GIVEN, J.—I. The material questions raised by
plaintiff's motions and demurrer that were overruled
were again raised and preserved on the trial. The
motions are long and complicated, and we will not
attempt to state them or the demurrer more in detail,
but proceed to consider these questions argued, after
first noticing the material facts in the case.

1   There is no dispute but that Stone did ship the
goods of which he was owner, and that they were
transported to Cedar Rapids, were wrongly delivered
to Hawkins without authority, and that, upon Stone's
thereafter applying for the goods, the defendant was
then unable to and did not deliver them to him. There
is a dispute as to what understanding or agreement
was then entered into between Stone and the defendant's agent, Jacobs, with respect to the delivery of the
goods at a future time. Stone admits that he then consented to wait for the goods for two or three days, while
Jacobs says that he agreed to wait until the defendant's
station agent, Mr. Bates, who was then absent, would
return. Soon after this first interview, and before the
return of Bates, Stone and his attorney again demanded
the delivery of the property, and they say that Jacobs
refused to deliver it then or thereafter, and told them to

hunt it themselves, or go ahead and sue. Jacobs denies
that he refused to thereafter deliver the wheel, or that
he told them to hunt it themselves, or to go ahead and
sue. He says he never disputed Stone's right to the
property, nor refused to get it, and deliver it to him.
"I always promised to get his wheel, and, furthermore,
he always promised to wait on me." Mr. Bates returned
September 14, and this action was commenced on the
twenty-fourth, Stone having assigned the claim for
damages to the plaintiff by written assignment dated
September 21, 1895. The validity of this assignment is
put in issue, but there is no evidence upon which to
question its validity. The defendant having regained
possession of the wheel and fixtures, caused to be served
on the plaintiff, on October 8, 1895, a tender in writing
as follows: "You are hereby notified that the defendant in the above entitled cause hereby tenders you in
court two boxes of freight, one of which contains a
Bohemian fortune wheel, and the other the fixtures for
the said wheel; together with all costs of suit. These
boxes of freight are the ones in suit, and claimed by you
in the above entitled cause, as set out in your petition
herein." On October 12, 1895, one Menear commenced
an action before a justice of the peace, aided by attachment against Stone, in which an attachment was issued,
and under which the wheel and fixtures in question were
on that day taken from the possession of the defendant,
and afterwards sold on execution in that case. On
October 28, 1895, the defendant caused written notice
of said seizure to be served on the plaintiff.

II. It cannot be disputed that, if the defendant
failed to deliver the property to Stone within the time
in which it was entitled to deliver it, and within which
Stone was bound to receive it, the defendant is
2   liable for its value as for a conversion. Mr. Bates
returned on September 14, 1895. Let it be conceded that Stone did extend the time for delivery until

Mr. Bates' return, we have seen that nothing was done
by the defendant towards delivering the property until
the tender made October 8 following. Surely, this was
not an offer to deliver upon Mr. Bates' return, nor
within a reasonable time thereafter. It appears by the
assignment from Stone to the plaintiff that on September 21, 1895, they had elected to make the claim for
damages instead of the property, of which the defendant had notice by this petition filed September 24.
Surely, the time that elapsed between Mr. Bates' return
on the fourteenth and the making of this assignment on
the twenty-first was a sufficient time in which to have
returned the property; and, the defendant having failed
to return it within that reasonable time, Stone and the
plaintiff had a right to thereafter treat it as converted,
and to claim its value in damages. A tender of the
property, to be effectual, must have been made within
the time in which the defendant was entitled to deliver
it and the plaintiff bound to receive it. The tender
made was not until long after the lapse of this period,
and, not being accepted, is no bar to plaintiff's right
to recover. The defense pleaded, that the property was
a gaming implement, and used for gambling, was
stricken out on plaintiff's motion; and, defendant not
having appealed, we are not called upon to consider
the correctness of the ruling on that motion.

III. The remaining question is whether the
defendant should be exempt from liability because of
the seizure of the property under a writ of attachment.
The attachment was not levied until October 12,
3   1895, long after the time within which the
defendant was entitled to deliver the property,
and long after it had been notified that Stone and the
plaintiff elected to claim damages, and were claiming
damages in this action. Under this condition of things
it cannot be doubted that the defendant was entitled

to hold this property as against the attachment. By the
election of Stone and the plaintiff to claim damages,
as they had a right to do, they waived all claim to the
property, and it thereafter became the property of the
defendant, and therefore not subject to attachment as
the property of Stone. This being true, it is no defense
to this action that the property was taken under an
attachment when it was.

IV.   Mr. Jacobs was permitted to testify, over
plaintiff's objection to this effect: That he was employed
by Mr. Bates, the station agent at Cedar Rapids,
as his cashier; that he was paid by and acted
4   as agent of the defendant; that under his employment he was liable to Mr. Bates for losses result
ing from a wrong delivery of shipments; and that he had
given to Mr. Bates a bond to secure him on that liability.   This evidence was clearly inadmissible for the
purpose of affecting defendant's liability, as the fact
that the loss might ultimately fall upon Mr. Jacobs is
no defense.   While this evidence was clearly immaterial and inadmissible as affecting defendant's liability, we think it was admissible as showing the interest
of the witness Mr. Jacobs, but the jury should have
been plainly instructed to that effect.   For the reasons
already stated, we think the court erred in overruling
plaintiff's motion to strike, and in the giving and refusing of instructions with reference to the questions
which we have considered.   The judgment of the district court is therefore REVERSED.

MINNIE Boos, Appellant, v. ALFRED DULIN.

Pleading: VERIFICATION. An amendment of the answer in an action
1   to recover the possession of real property from a tenant, alleging
a reduction of the rent because of a mistake as to the acreage,
2   upon which no affirmative relief is asked, does not introduce a
new and distinct cause of action or counter-claim, within Code

1873, section 2680, authorizing courts to permit unverified amendments to pleadings unless a new and distinct cause of action or counter-claim is thereby introduced.

Same: *Appeal from justice.* An answer in an action commenced in a justice's court to recover the possession of leased property from
1 a tenant, may be amended in the district court after an appeal
2 from the justice's court, by setting up facts showing a payment of
3 the rent, under Code 1873, section 3591, permitting amendments in the district court in cases appealed from the justice's court, where they do not set up any new demand or counter-claim; and such an amendment may be filed at any time before trial in district court begins.

Statute of Frauds: PAROL VARIANCE. The rule that a written contract cannot be varied by parol relates to oral agreements made
1 prior to or contemporaneous with the writing, and is not violated
2 by proof that, subsequent to the execution of a written lease, the lessor orally agreed to accept a smaller rent than that stipulated for therein.

Appeal: FORCIBLE ENTRY: *Abandonment by tenant.* The supreme court will not undertake to set out and discuss alleged errors
4 which, at most, are merely technical, and do not affect any substantial right of the parties, where the only practical effect its decision can have is to determine who is liable for the costs.

Appeal from Pottawattamie District Court, at Avoca.—
Hon. Walter I. Smith, Judge.

Tuesday, October 19, 1897.

Action to obtain the possession of real property which had been leased to the defendant, and of which he is alleged to hold wrongful possession after the termination of his lease. There was a trial by jury, a verdict of not guilty, and a judgment in favor of the defendant for costs. The plaintiff appeals.—*Affirmed.*

C. H. Converse for appellant.

Barton & Van Slyke and *Benjamin & Preston* for appellee.

Robinson, J.—In November, 1889, the parties to this action entered into a written agreement by which the plaintiff leased to the defendant, for a term of three years from the first day of March, 1890, a farm containing one hundred and thirty acres of land. The stipulation of the lease in regard to the payment of rent is as follows: "At the annual rent of three dollars per acre for fifty acres, to be paid as follows, to-wit: First payment of fifty dollars payable March 1, 1890, the same annually for the term of three years; one hundred dollars payable January 1, 1891, each year, according to this lease; fifty acres to give fifteen bushels of corn per acre each year, being seven hundred and fifty bushels, to be delivered in Hancock, shelled, and to be delivered at option of first party: the balance, thirty acres, to be sowed, eight acres to wheat, eight to oats, and fourteen to barley, each year. Said second party is to give for rent one-third of same each year, to be delivered to granaries of first party. Also, first party reserves one-half of the straw delivered at her stable and sheds." The lease also contained a provision as follows: "And it is further agreed that if any rent shall be due and unpaid, or if default shall be made in any of the covenants herein contained, it shall then be lawful for the said party of the first part (Minnie Boos) to re-enter the said premises, or to distrain for such rent; or she may recover possession thereof by action of forcible entry and detainer, notwithstanding the provisions of section 3612 of the Code." The defendant took possession of the leased premises. On the eighth day of March, 1892, the plaintiff filed in justice's court a petition, in which she alleged that the defendant had violated the terms of the lease, in that he had failed to deliver the grain and straw, and pay the rent, as required by the lease. She asked judgment for the immediate possession of the leased premises, and for

costs. The defendant filed an answer, which contained
a general denial, and alleged that the action was barred
because he had been in peaceable possession of the
premises, with the knowledge of the plaintiff, more
than thirty days after the alleged violation of the terms
of the lease. The answer further alleged a tender of
fifty dollars in payment of the rent due March 1, 1892,
and a payment thereof into court. The plaintiff filed a
reply, which denied the sufficiency of the alleged tender,
and averred that no tender had been made. There was
a trial in justice's court, and judgment in favor of the
plaintiff. The defendant perfected an appeal to the
district court, and there filed an amendment to his
answer, in which he alleged that the plaintiff agreed
with the defendant to accept seven hundred and five
bushels of corn each year in lieu of the quantity specified in the lease, for the reason that a mistake had been
made in the lease in regard to the corn land, which contained three acres less than the number specified in
the lease. The plaintiff filed a motion to strike
the amendment, which was overruled. The plaintiff
thereupon filed a reply. Thereafter the defendant filed
an additional amendment to his answer, in which he
alleged that, while he was in possession under the lease,
the plaintiff informed him that all crops grown on the
leased premises should be hauled to the elevators in
Hancock, at least enough thereof to pay rent, and that
the managers of the elevators should withhold a sufficient amount of the corn crop or of the proceeds thereof
to pay the rent; that, by virtue of that arrangement, C.
C. Smith, manager of one of the elevators at Hancock,
and W. J. Martin, manager of the other, became the
agents of the plaintiff to receive the rent that might
become due; that, by virtue of that arrangement, the
defendant hauled to the elevator managed by Smith
sufficient grain for the payment of the fifty dollars
which became due March 1, 1892, and that sum was

deposited with Smith, as the agent of the plaintiff, before that date, and remained in his possession, subject to her order, until the day of the trial in justice's court, when it was paid by Smith to the justice. A motion to strike that amendment was overruled, and the plaintiff then filed a reply in the nature of a general denial, and a trial was had, with the result already stated. This cause has been submitted twice for our consideration. On the first submission we inadvertently treated as a part of the record an additional abstract which had been stricken from the files. When that fact was called to our attention, after an opinion had been filed, a re-hearing was granted, and the case is again submitted for our determination.

I. The motion to strike the first amendment to the answer filed in the district court was based upon two grounds, the first of which was that the amendment was not verified; and in the present condition of the record that appears to be true, and it also appears to be true that the petition was verified. But section 2680 of the Code of 1873 authorizes courts to permit unverified amendments to pleadings "unless a new and distinct cause of action or counter-claim is thereby introduced." The amendment in question did not introduce a new and distinct cause of action, nor a counter-claim, and was therefore permissible. It is also urged that the motion should have been sustained because the amendment introduced a defense not set up in justice's court, and because the matter pleaded was within the statute of frauds. Neither of these grounds was referred to in the motion, nor otherwise presented in the district court. It is further urged in support of the motion that the amendment sought "to change by parol evidence the terms of a written contract." The language of the amendment justifies the inference that the alleged agreement to accept seven hundred and five bushels of corn in lieu of the seven

hundred and fifty bushels provided for by the lease was
entered into some time after the lease was made; and
therefore it is not within the rule in regard to varying
a written contract by proving a parol contemporaneous
agreement which the plaintiff seeks to invoke. We conclude that the motion to strike the first amendment was
properly overruled.

II. It is insisted that the district court erred in
overruling the motion to strike the second amendment
to the answer. The ground of that motion was that the
amendment was filed too late, and that the mat-
3   ters therein alleged were immaterial and incompetent. The cases of *Dicks v. Hatch,* 10 Iowa,
380, and *Hollen v. Davis,* 59 Iowa, 444, are relied upon
to sustain the claim that the matters set out in the second amendment could not be rightfully pleaded for the
first time in the district court. Neither case is in point.
Amendments which do not set up any new demand or
counter-claim are allowable in the district court in
cases appealed from justice's court. Code 1873, section
3591; *Type Foundry v. Medes,* 60 Iowa, 525. The amendment in question did not set up any demand or counter-
claim, and was authorized by the section cited. The
trial of the cause had not been commenced when the
amendment was filed; hence it was not too late, and
was properly permitted to remain on file.

III. The appellant complains of rulings of the
district court in regard to the admission of evidence,
and of portions of the charge given. We have examined
the matters of which complaint is made, but do
4   not find any error which could have prejudiced
the plaintiff. It is evident that there is no substantial merit in this appeal. If the defendant failed
in any respect to comply with the terms of his lease,
the failure was little more than nominal; and on or
about the middle of March, 1892, a few days only after

the time fixed by the plaintiff for him to surrender the premises, he left them, and the plaintiff, by herself or tenant, has occupied them since that time. Hence the only practical effect our decision can have in this case is to determine who is liable for the costs. Under these circumstances, we cannot undertake to set out and discuss alleged errors which, at most, are merely technical, and do not affect any substantial right of the parties. It is sufficient to say that we do not find any reason for disturbing the judgment of the district court, and it is AFFIRMED.

LEWIS R. ROGERS v. THE EQUITABLE MUTUAL LIFE AND ENDOWMENT ASSOCIATION, Appellant.

Accident Insurance: WHEN CERTIFICATE TAKES EFFECT. Where an application for accident insurance is made to an agent of a mutual association, who has no authority to accept a person to membership, and who has to send the application to the association by mail for acceptance, on such acceptance and issuance of the certificate of membership, the latter does not relate back to the time the application was made, in the absence of anything in the application that binds the association in the interim of time; and in case of accident to the applicant after the application is made, and before its acceptance, the association is not liable, although the application is made a part of the certificate.

*Appeal from Boone District Court.—*HON. D. R. HIND-MAN, Judge.

TUESDAY, OCTOBER 19, 1897.

'ABOUT 2 o'clock P. M., December 17, 1895, the plaintiff made application, at Boone, Iowa, to one Aylesworth for membership in the accident department of the defendant association located at Waterloo Iowa. Aylesworth was the defendant's soliciting agent at Boone. The application was in writing. The application was mailed at Boone on the afternoon of the day it

was made, and reached Waterloo on the forenoon of
the next day, and was accepted, and a certificate issued,
dated December 18, 1895, which was mailed to Aylesworth at Boone, and by him delivered to the plaintiff
within a day or two thereafter. On the evening of the
seventeenth of December, and before the application
had reached Waterloo, the plaintiff was injured, and
this action is to recover on the certificate. The answer
puts in issue a liability, for the reason that when the
accident occurred the certificate was not in force,
because the application had not then been received,
nor the plaintiff accepted to membership. The cause
was tried without a jury, and a judgment entered for
plaintiff, from which the defendant appealed.—
Reversed.

Boies & Boies for appellant.

R. F. Jordan for appellee.

GRANGER, J.— The following are provisions of
the certificate: "That the Equitable Mutual Life and
Endowment Association, Accident Department, in consideration of the warranties and agreements made in
the application for membership, and of the sum of
three dollars, and of the quarterly payment of three
dollars and seventy-five cents,—the first quarterly payment falling due January 18, 1895, and the second May
1, 1895, and quarterly thereafter.—hereby accepts
Lewis R. Rogers, by occupation, profession, or employment a freight brakeman, postoffice address, Boone,
county of Boone, state of Iowa, as a member of the
accident department of said association, and entitled to
the benefits hereinafter described, provided all the conditions contained herein, and the by-laws of said association, as now or hereafter amended, are complied
with. In the event the member herein named shall

sustain wholly disabling accidental injury, effected
through external, violent, or accidental means alone,
without the intent and meaning of this contract and
the conditions now or hereafter made, there shall be
due and payable ($6) dollars per week for a period
immediately following said injury, and during such
total disability, not exceeding fifty-two consecutive
weeks; provided, always, that this certificate is issued
and accepted subject to the provisions, conditions,
limitations, and exceptions herein contained or referred
to, and upon the express agreement that all the statements and declarations made by the member in his
application for membership are warranted to be true
in all respects, and that said application, together
with classification of risks indorsed thereon, are
referred to, and made a part of this certificate. The
member is accepted under classification special hazardous." The parties are in contention as to when the
certificate took effect so as to become a contract of
insurance; it being that of appellant that it was at the
date of the certificate, while appellee contends that,
when the certificate issued, it related back, so as to be
of force from the date of the application. The application is simply one for membership in the association,
and the fact of membership is the basis of a right to
indemnity. It is nowhere contended that the agent at
Boone had authority to accept a person to membership.
The application contained the date on which the association was to determine the question of membership.
It is not claimed that there would be a liability had the
certificate not issued, but that, when issued, it had a
retroactive operation. Appellee's reliance for such a
legal proposition is some language in Wood on Fire
Insurance (volume 1), from sections 18 and 20, as follows: "When application is made for insurance by
mail, and the agent taking the application has no
authority to bind the company during the pendency of

the application, or there is nothing in the application itself that binds the company in the interim of time, the risk does not attach until it is actually accepted by the company. But as soon as the risk is accepted, and acceptance is signified by the posting of a notice thereof, the contract is complete, and has relation back to the time when the application was made. or the time designated in the application, if any. when the risk should commence, and covers a loss occurring before the acceptance. When a risk is accepted upon the terms designated in the application, whether the same is made by writing or parol, the contract is complete, and neither can recede therefrom, and, whether a policy has been executed or not, the risk attaches at the date of the application, or the time designated therein; and the insurer is liable for any loss that occurs after the time when the risk, by the contract, commenced, even though it occurred before its acceptance thereof." In view of the authorities cited in support of the text, there is reason to doubt a meaning as broad as that claimed by appellee. The text takes for its support *Lightbody v. Insurance Co.*, 23 Wend. 18; *Kohn v. Insurance Co.*, 1 Wash. C. C. 93. In both of these cases the policies were executed, but not delivered, and there was held to be a completed contract of insurance. Neither case allows the contract or the liability of the company to antedate the policy. The author also cites *Insurance Co. v. Ruggles*, 12 Wheat. (erroneously cited 1 Wheat.) 408. The case makes no holding whatever on a question like the one at bar. It is a fact in the case that the loss occurred before the policy was effected, but no question is made of that fact affecting the insurance because the policy was not in force. The case turned on the misconduct of the master of the sloop that was insured. Appellee also refers to *Keim v. Insurance Co.*, 42 Mo. 38. In that case the application was filed in the office of the secretary of the company February 9. The policy was made

out and was to take effect at noon of that day, and the
application and policy were permitted to remain in the
office of the secretary. A loss occurred February 14,
and the policy was held in force. *Baldwin v. Insurance
Co.*, 56 Mo. 151, is also cited. In that case the application was accepted and the policy made out, but held
for the payment of the premium, which was not paid
till after the loss; and it was held that, after the payment of the premium and the delivery of the policy, the
contract related back to the date of the policy, even
though the company had no knowledge of the loss. In
short, there is no case coming to our notice that holds
to the rule of appellee's contention. In fact, we do not
find a case where the question is considered as to a company being liable on a policy where an acceptance of
the application was necessary to complete the contract,
and the application had not been received when the loss
or accident occurred, that an acceptance afterwards is
held to relate back to the date of the application. Such
a rule would be violative of all general rules governing
the taking effect of contracts. There are cases in which
recovery has been sustained for losses occurring before
the policies issued, but they all turn on a different state
of facts from this case. In such cases the contract of
insurance was complete without the policy, and the
policy was to issue in pursuance of such a contract. In
2 May, Insurance, section 400, it is said that the policy,
if delivered, takes effect from its date, unless it be otherwise stated. That seems to be the uniform rule where
not otherwise provided. It is thought that the fact
that the policy provides that the application is made a
part of the certificate favors appellee's construction,
but we think not. Nothing in the application or certificate indicates such an intent. The object in making the
application a part of the certificate is to know the intent
of the parties, by construing the two together, as they

are largely dependent instruments. We think, under
the undisputed facts of the case, there can be no recovery, and the judgment must stand REVERSED.

FRED. E. BRIGGS v. J. C. YETZER, *et al.*, Appellees, and
CLAUS H. CLAUSEN, Appellant.

Judgment by Confession: STATEMENT   A statement of the facts
under the statutes for confession of judgment upon a certificate
of deposit against a bank and guarantors is sufficiently specific
where it sets forth a copy of the certificate which purports to be
issued to the payee for a deposit made by him of a specified
amount on a specified date and to be payable to him in current
1   funds on return of the certificate four months after date, and a
guaranty and waiver of protest signed by two of the defendants
and a transfer from the payee to the plaintiff, and states that
there is "now" justly due the plaintiff on the certificate a specified
sum. Citing *Clifton v. Dodson*, 111 Mo 195 (19 S W. Rep. 711); *Dunham v. Waterman*, 17 N. Y. 9; *Dow v. Platner*, 16 N. Y. 562; *Sharp v.
Railway Co* , 106 N. C. 308 (11 S. E. Rep. 530). *Distinguishing
Kern v. Chalfant*, 7 Minn. 487; *Reading v. Reading*, 24 N. J. L.
858; *Davidson v. Alexander*, 84 N. C. 621.

VERIFICATION.   A statement for confession of judgment signed by
defendants, followed by the jurat of a notary public. in the usual
form, stating that it was subscribed and sworn to, without stating
2   by whom, is verified by defendants as required by Code 1873, section 2896. *Averill v. Boyles*, 52 Iowa, 672, *distinguished.*

DUTY OF AGENT.   An agent to collect a certificate of deposit is bound
to exercise the degree of diligence and foresight an ordinarily
prudent man would under like circumstances, and has implied
4   authority to procure a confession of judgment thereon   Citing
Davis v. Waterman, 10 Vt. 526; *Ryan v. Tudor*, 81 Kan. 866; *Dolun
v. VanDemark*, 85 Kan. 304 (10 Pac. Rep. 849); *Merrick v. Wagner,*
44 Ill. 266; *Moore v. Hill*, 48 Mich. 145.

Principal and Agent: TERMINATION OF AUTHORITY. The authority
of an agent intrusted with a certificate of deposit for collection
8   to procure a confession of judgment thereon, was not terminated
by the fact that in anticipation of the payment of the certificate
5   he remitted to his principal the amount thereof in stock of a
loan association of which he (the agent) was secretary, where he
had no authority as secretary to issue the stock without payment
in cash, although the association ratified the issuance of the stock

after a certificate of sale under the judgment by confession had
been assigned to it; since the certificate of deposit never belonged
to the association.

Appeal from Cass District Court.—HON. N. W. MACY,
Judge.

WEDNESDAY, OCTOBER 20, 1897.

JUDGMENT by confession was duly entered in favor
of the plaintiff and against the Cass County Bank, J. C.
Yetzer, and Isaac Dickerson, December 23, 1893, for
the sum of three thousand and eighty-six dollars and
sixty-seven cents, and execution issued thereon, and
certain land belonging to Yetzer sold. Claus H. Clausen
obtained judgment against Yetzer and Dickerson February 14, 1894, and, on November 26 of the same year,
filed his motion asking that the plaintiff's judgment and
sale thereunder be set aside. The motion was overruled, and Clausen appeals.—*Affirmed.*

Willard & Willard and *De Lano & Meredith* for
appellant.

, *J. B. Rockafellow* for appellees.

LADD, J.—The statement of facts out of which the
indebtedness arose is in these words: "On the eighteenth day of August, 1893, the Cass County Bank issued
to Geo. E. Pennell a certificate of deposit in the
1   sum of three thousand dollars, in words and figures to-wit: 'Cass County Bank. $3,000. Atlan-
tic, Iowa, August 18, 1893. Geo. E. Pennell has deposited
in this bank three thousand dollars, payable to himself,
in current funds, on the return of this certificate,
four months after date, with interest at the rate of eight
per cent. per annum until due only. A. W. Dickerson,
Cashier.' And on the back of said certificate is the following: 'We hereby guarantee and waive protest and

notice of protest, payment of the within certificate of
deposit. J. C. Yetzer. Isaac Dickerson.' And the following transfer: 'Pay to the order of Fred E. Briggs.
[Signed.] Geo. E. Pennell.' 'There is now justly due
said plaintiff on said certificate of deposit the said sum
of three thousand, eighty-six and 67-100 dollars. J. C.
Yetzer. Isaac Dickerson.' " The certificate indicates
that it was issued for three thousand dollars deposited
by Pennell. On the authority of *Brown v. Barngrover*,
82 Iowa, 204, no further detail of facts was required.
But it is insisted that more ought to have been stated
as to the liability of Yetzer. The guaranty is set out,
and fully apprises all of the nature of the obligation.
The law requires the facts to be concisely stated, so as
to direct the attention of third parties to the nature and
character of the consideration. It must be brief, not
specific or particular. *Bernard v. Douglas*, 10 Iowa,
370; *Vanfleet v. Phillips*, 11 Iowa, 558. And it has been
held sufficient if the transaction is identified, and a clue
furnished the creditor which will enable him to start
to investigate. *Claflin v. Dodson*, 111 Mo. 195 (19 S. W.
Rep. 711): *Dunham v. Waterman*, 17 N. Y. 9. If the
statement is full enough to enable third parties to investigate and judge of the good faith of the transaction,
and sufficiently definite to fix this, then the object of
the statute in requiring the statement has been met.
The consideration of the security was not stated in
Dullard v. Phelan, 83 Iowa, 471, but the court held the
facts sufficiently set out. Our statute is like that of
New York, and in *Dow v. Platner*, 16 N. Y. 562, a statement of facts in these words, "My drafts on Peck, Myers
and Brownson, of the city of New York, dated January
14, 1851, payable at sixty days from date, for eight
hundred dollars, and indorsed by said Daniel Dow, Jr.,
as my surety and for my benefit," was sufficient to warrant judgment in favor of Dow. See, also, *Sharp v.
Railroad Co.*, 106 N. C. 308 (11 S. E. Rep. 530). The facts

out of which the indebtedness arose were the loaning
of the money to the bank, and the guaranty of its payment by Yetzer and Dickerson, and a statement to this
effect was all that was required in order to comply with
the statute. From these facts creditors could readily
investigate and learn the character of the transaction.
The cases relied on by appellant are not opposed to this
conclusion. In *Kern v. Chalfant*, 7 Minn. 487 (Gil. 393),
the consideration of the bond on which defendant was
surety was not stated. The other cases construed
statutes essentially different from ours. *Reading v.
Reading*, 24 N. J. Law, 358; *Davidson v. Alexander*, 84
N. C. 621.

II. Was the statement properly verified? It was
signed by Yetzer and Dickerson, but they did not sign
the annexed affidavit, and their names were not written
in the jurat. The law does not require the state-
2   ment to be accompanied with an affidavit. It
must be signed and verified by the defendant.
Code 1873, section 2896. The jurat of the notary is in
the usual form, with the names of the affiants omitted.
Subscribed and sworn to by whom? The very persons,
and the only ones, who had subscribed to the statement.
No other inference can be drawn. And such a jurat is
held sufficient in *Stone v. Miller*, 60 Iowa, 243; *Stoddard
v. Sloan*, 65 Iowa, 680; and *Kirby v. Gates*, 71 Iowa, 100.
Averill v. Boyles, 52 Iowa, 672, is not in point, as, under
the statute, interrogatories attached to a pleading must
be verified by affidavit.

III. It is urged that Pennell, the party procuring
the confession of judgment, did so without the request
or knowledge of Briggs. The latter handed the certificate of deposit to Pennell in October, 1893, with
3   instructions to collect it when due, and invest
the amount received, in stock of a building and
loan association. The officers of the bank promised on
December 27, 1893, that the certificate would be paid

the following morning; and Pennell, relying on this promise, issued and mailed to Briggs three thousand, four hundred and eighty dollars in stock the same evening,—he being the secretary of the association. The same day, but after the stock had been mailed, the bank went into the hands of a receiver, and never paid the certificate. Pennell had no authority, as secretary of the building and loan association, to issue any stock until it was actually paid for, and the association refused to ratify what he had done until it received an assignment of the certificate of sale under the plaintiff's judgment. At the time of the judgment, the certificate of deposit had not been transferred by Briggs, nor had he received payment. He had not undertaken to sell or assign it to any one, nor had the association in any way arranged to receive it. He, then, continued the owner thereof. Pennell took it with instructions to collect. The manner of doing this was left to his discretion, as no other instructions were given. He 4   was required to exercise that degree of diligence and foresight an ordinarily prudent man would under like circumstances. If so, he had the right to resort to the means, if necessary, which are usually adopted to compel payment, and might bring suit. *Davis v. Waterman*, 10 Vt. 526; *Ryan v. Tudor*, 31 Kan. 366 (2 Pac. Rep. 797); *Dolan v. Van Demark*, 35 Kan. 304 (10 Pac. Rep. 848); *Merrick v. Wagner*, 44 Ill. 266; Mechem, Agents, sections 348, 386; *Moore v. Hall*, 48 Mich. 145 (11 N. W. Rep. 844). Had Pennell, with the opportunity of doing so, failed to procure the confession of judgment, he would, under the circumstances disclosed, have been lacking in fidelity to his trust. With it, collection of the certificate was certain, without it, extremely doubtful. That Pennell may not have made known all the facts to Briggs, or the latter have fully

understood the situation, will not change the legal
status of the parties at the time.   But it is said
5   the ratification of the issuance of the stock by
the association related back to the time Pennell
mailed it to Briggs.   Suppose it did.   The certificate
had never belonged to the association, but had been
collected through the judgment and the sale of the
land; and the ratification was on the express consideration of the assignment of the certificate of sale owned
by Briggs, though in Pennell's name.   The association
never had anything to do with the certificate of deposit
or the judgment until it received this certificate of sale.
—AFFIRMED.

C. JENNEY v. THE CITY OF DES MOINES, *et al.*, Appellants.

106
f11
111
103
127

Public Improvements: MUNICIPAL CORPORATIONS: *Specifications.*
Plans and specifications of a public improvement furnished by
the city engineer to the board of public works of a city as required
1   by Code, Twenty-second General Assembly, chapter 1, section 8,
are not insufficient because not as full and complete as it was possible to make them, if they are sufficiently comprehensive, definite, and elaborate for the purpose intended.

SAME.   The requirements of Code, Twenty-second General Assembly,
chapter 1, section 5, that the proposals for bids for a public improvement shall state the amount and different kinds of material to be
furnished, are sufficiently complied with, where the plans and specifications which are made a part of the proposal, and are on file in
2   the office of the board of public works, and open to the inspection
of all persons, furnish all the data from which to determine the
exact amount and kind of all the material required for the completion of the structure, although the amount for the several
kinds of material are not computed and written out.

SAME.   The requirement in the specifications for a public improvement that each bidder shall submit with his bid "strain sheet and
fully detailed plans," does not affect the validity of the award of
the contract where the bids were made upon the plans and specifi-
8   cations furnished by the city, and the detailed plans furnished by

the bidders were merely to advise the authorities of the bidder's interpretation of the plans and specifications and their method of execution.

Appeal from Polk District Court.—HON. C. P. HOLMES, Judge.

WEDNESDAY, OCTOBER 20, 1897.

ACTION in equity to cancel a contract for the erection of a bridge, and to enjoin the city council and the board of public works from proceeding thereunder. Decree for plaintiff, and defendants appeal.—*Reversed.*

J. K. Macomber, city attorney, for appellants City of Des Moines, John Sherman, and George C. Sims.

Read & Read and *J. I. Myerly* for appellant John H. Killmar.

Barcroft & McCaughan for appellee.

KINNE, C. J.—I. A careful consideration of this case leads us to the conclusion that the following statement of the facts in the argument of counsel for appellant Killmar is substantially correct: "The bridge in question was ordered constructed by an ordinance of the city council duly passed; that plans and specifications for said bridge were prepared by the city engineer, and submitted to and approved by the board of public works, before the board advertised for proposals; that the board did duly advertise for proposals for the construction of said bridge, as required by law; that the defendant John H. Killmar and others submitted bids, in response to said advertisement, for the construction of the bridge according to the plans and specifications of the city on file, as stated in the advertisement for bids; that all of the bids were regularly filed with the board of public works on or before the last day fixed for

receiving bids; that Killmar's bid was the lowest of all
the bids submitted; that Killmar's bid was accepted by
the board of public works and the city council, and a
contract entered into with the said Killmar by the board
of public works, on behalf of the city of Des Moines, on
the sixth day of August, 1896; that said contract so
entered into was regularly approved by the city council;
that there has been no bad faith or fraud, or any unfair
advantage or intentional wrong, on the part of the city
council or city engineer or board of public works or
Killmar, with respect to any of the transactions relating
to the letting and construction of this bridge; that all of
the steps required to be taken by the board of public
works, the city engineer, and city council, by the ordinances of the city or statutes of the state, have been duly
complied with, unless it be, as it is claimed, that the
plans and specifications which were prepared by the
city engineer and adopted by the board, and upon which
proposals were invited and submitted, were not such as
the law required. It is claimed in the petition,
among other things, that the plans and specifications of the city were such that competitive bids
could not be, and in fact were not, made thereon; that
Killmar's bid was not the lowest bid." Plaintiff's contention as to the illegality of the contract is based upon
the following provisions of the statutes of the state and
of the ordinances of the city: In chapter 1 of the Acts of
the Twenty-second General Assembly (section 3), it is
provided: "The city engineer shall furnish said board
(board of public works) from time to time estimates of
the cost of material for any improvement to be ordered
or advertised for by said board, together with the plans
and specifications therefor." Section 5 of the same
act provides: "Said board of public works shall advertise for bids and make all contracts on behalf of the
city * * * whenever the same shall be ordered by
the city council, * * * and proposals for bids shall

be published at least two weeks in two of the daily
newspapers in such cities. * * * The proposals for
bids shall state the amount and different kinds of material to be furnished, and kinds of improvement, and the
time and conditions upon which bids shall be received.
The board shall have power to reject any and all bids.
All such contracts shall be made with the lowest bidder,
but it shall not be necessary before proposals are published or bids received to determine specifically the kind
of material to be used." The provisions of the ordinance
being substantially the same as the requirements of
section 3 of the statute, they need not be stated. It
appears that the city engineer did furnish the board
with plans and specifications for the bridge in question,
which we think were in compliance with the statute.
Now, a plan is a design, a delineation, or projection on
a plane surface of the ground lines of a structure, which
are reduced in size, the relative positions of which, and
their proportions, are preserved. A specification is said
by the same author to denote a particular or detailed
statement of the various elements involved. Black,
Law Dictionary, tits. "Plan," "Specification." It is
not practicable to set out in this opinion the plans and
specifications in fact furnished. The evidence shows
without dispute that, while the plans and specifications
were not as full and complete as it was possible to make
them, still they were quite comprehensive, and sufficiently definite and elaborate for the purpose intended,
and conformed to the statutory requirements.

II.   It is said that the advertisement of the board
of public works for proposals was defective in not stating the amount and different kinds of material to be
furnished. The statute and ordinance required
2   that "proposals for bids shall state the amount
and different kinds of material to be furnished."
Now, by the very terms of the printed advertisement
inviting bids, the plans and specifications heretofore

mentioned were made a part of said proposals. A fair
construction of the statute and ordinance would not
require the advertisement to contain in detail the number of pounds of iron or other material to be used in the
structure. If, from the advertisement, and the plans
and specifications which were a part of the proposal,
and which were on file in the office of the board, and
open to the inspection of all persons, the amount and
different kinds of material appeared, or if from what
did appear in said plans and specifications the amount
and different kinds of material might be determined
beyond question by mere computation, then the spirit
and intent of the law and ordinance were complied
with, even though said amount of the different kinds
of material was not computed and stated. In other
words, here we have an advertisement for proposals
wherein the plans and specifications are so full that
they furnish all the data from which to determine the
exact amount and kind of all the materials which were
necessary for the completion of the structure. Nothing
remained to be done save to make the computations
from the data given, and to state the result. Every
bidder was, by the facts and data given, enabled to
know by computation what material would be needed,
and the amount of it. It would be technical construction, indeed, which would hold that, though the proposals had furnished data from which all holders could
compute and with certainty arrive at the exact amount
of the several kinds of material to be used, still, because
the city engineer had not made the computation, the
proposals should be held insufficient. It is a question,
simply, whether, under the statute, we should hold this
proposal insufficient because the amounts of the several kinds of material were not computed and written
out, when every fact was given from which any bridge
man could compute with accuracy the amounts of said
several kinds of material. The evidence shows that,

from the data furnished, any man competent to build a
bridge could, by simple computation, arrive at the exact
amount of the several kinds of material required. To
illustrate, the dimensions of the floor of the bridge, and
the kind and thickness of the lumber it shall be built of,
are stated, but the number of feet of lumber to be contained in it is not computed and stated. Are we therefore to hold that the statute has not been complied
with? Such a construction, it occurs to us, would be
unwarranted.

III. In the specifications it is provided that each
bidder must submit, with his bid, "strain sheet and
fully detailed plan." Counsel argue that the proposals
called for bids based upon said plans furnished
3   by the bidder, and hence each man bid on his own
plans and specifications, and therefore there
could be no lowest bidder. This claim we do not think is
sustained by the record. The bids were made upon plans
and specifications furnished by the city, and the
detailed plans furnished by bidders were to advise the
city authorities of the interpretation of its plans and
specifications by the bidder, and their method of execution. The bids were competitive, were made from the
city's plans and specifications, and no fraud or bad faith
is claimed to have existed or been exercised. No one
is here claiming that the work was let for too large a
sum, and, in fact, the whole case impresses us as one
wherein pure technicalities are relied upon by appellant which go to the form rather than to the substance
of the provisions of the statute and ordinances. The
decree of the district court is REVERSED.

ALBERT NOBLE v. SILAS WHITE, Appellant.

Malicious Prosecution: MALICE. Bringing a criminal prosecution for
wilful trespass on land, knowing that the only remedy is a civil
action for the possession of the land, shows malice, even if the

19 person instituting the prosecution is entitled to the possession of
    the land.

ADVICE OF COUNSEL.   An attorney who has testified as to the advice
 8 he gave defendant as to the bringing of prosecution cannot be
14 asked, on cross-examination, what his advice would have been on
    a state of facts which was not disclosed to him by defendant.

INSTRUCTIONS: *Pleadings.* In an action for maliciously instituting
    criminal prosecutions for wilful trespass on land, where the undis-
 4 puted evidence shows the existence of a lease of the land by
    defendant to plaintiff, it is not error for the court to recognize
16 that fact in its instructions to the jury, though the lease is not
    specifically pleaded.

INSTRUCTIONS.   An instruction in an action for malicious prosecu-
    tion, that the fact that the grand jury ignored the information,
    and that the defendant was acquitted before a justice of the
    peace, is no evidence of want of probable cause, but the testi-
    mony on that point is only admitted to show that the prosecution
15 has ended, is as favorable to defendant as a requested instruc-
    tion, that the ignoring of the indictment by the grand jury can-
    not be considered in evidence to show absence of probable cause
    or as showing malice on his part.

EVIDENCE: *Cross-examination.*   A witness cannot be cross-examined
    as to whether he has been fined for contempt of court for inter-
 8 ference in the suit, where the evidence does not tend to show any
    feeling on his part against the party cross-examining him.

Same.   Plaintiff in an action for malicious prosecution who has tes
    tified that the claim belongs to him, cannot be asked on cross-
 7 examination whether there is any one to get a share of the
    damages. with a view to showing that his attorney was to have
    a contingent fee.

Evidence of Prosecution.   Evidence showing that the prosecution on
 4 which an action for malicious prosecution is based has been
    ended is admissible, where the answer denies that it has been
    ended

Harmless error.   It is not prejudicial error to permit the amount of
    notes to be shown by the testimony of a witness instead of by
 5 producing the notes, where there is not dispute as to the amount
    thereof.

Leasing.   The retention of rent notes by a principal and his consent
 2 to the occupancy of the farm by the tenant is evidence of a ratifi-
17 cation of an unauthorized lease by his agent.

Same.   The lease is the best evidence of land conveyed thereby, and
 6 it is not competent to ask a witness on cross-examination if the
    lease does not describe a certain tract of land.

Rebuttal. Defendant is not prejudiced by the admission of a declaration against him, in rebuttal, which was competent evidence for
18 the plaintiff, in chief, where he was afforded an opportunity to deny or explain the same

Relevancy. Evidence that it was a damage to a place to have the sod plowed up is inadmissible in an action by a tenant against his
9 landlord for malicious prosecution based on charges made by the latter against the former for wilful trespass in plowing land, where the plaintiff's guilt or innocence of the criminal charges
11 depended upon whether or not he had authority under the lease to plow the grass land.

Same. The testimony of defendant in an action for malicious prosecution based on charges of wilful trespasses upon his land, that some of the best men said that the plaintiff was damaging his
9 property to the amount of five hundred dollars, is inadmissible even if defendant has a right to show what rumors as to the destruction of his property had come to his knowledge, before filing the information.

Reputation of plaintiff. Evidence as to the reputation of plaintiff in an action for malicious prosecution for being quarrelsome and a
12 bully is inadmissible. where the plaintiff's guilt or innocence of the criminal charges made against him depends upon whether or not he had authority under a lease from the latter to plow the latter's grass land.

Self-serving declarations. A party cannot testify to declarations made by him in his own favor to a witness, in the absence of the
10 other party, where they are not in rebuttal of anything said by the witness.

Verdict: IMPEACHMENT OF Statements made by jurors to others of the panel, after retiring to consider of their verdict, which are calculated to arouse sympathy for defendant, and to reduce the
20 verdict against him, cannot be assigned as error by him, *first,* because they inhere in the verdict and *secondly,* because they were not prejudicial to *defendant.*

Appeal. An additional abstract of the evidence filed by the appellee
1 which is necessary to the full presentation of the cause to the supreme court, will not be stricken from the files.

Appeal from Page District Court.—HON. W. R. GREEN
Judge.

WEDNESDAY, OCTOBER 20, 1897.

ACTION in two counts to recover damages for two criminal prosecutions commenced by the defendant against the plaintiff for wilful trespass on the land of another, which prosecutions are alleged to have ended, and to have been prosecuted through malice, and without probable cause. One information was filed May 4, 1895, before a justice of the peace, and the other July 9, 1895, before the same justice. Defendant answered, admitting that he filed said informations, and denying every other allegation in the petition. Verdict and judgment were rendered in favor of the plaintiff, and defendant appeals.—*Affirmed.*

C. S. Keenan and *G. B. Jennings* for appellant.

D. H. Chiles and *Parslow & Scott* for appellee.

GIVEN, J.—I. Appellant moves to strike an additional abstract filed by appellee, on the grounds that it is only a correction of clerical and typographical errors, and that it gives questions and answers. The
1   additional abstract is no more open to these objections than is the abstract of appellant. It appears that said additional abstract is necessary to a full presentation of the case, and the motion is therefore overruled.

II. Appellant argues twenty-two assignments of error based upon rulings on evidence, and other assignments based upon the instructions. To an understanding of these questions, it is necessary to state in a general way the facts and circumstance out of which the
2   criminal prosecutions grew. Defendant authorized one Thompson to lease a farm owned by defendant, and Thompson leased the same from September, 1894, to March 1, 1896, to the plaintiff, they executing, in duplicate, a written lease, and the plaintiff

executing his two promissory notes, with Peter Lavine as surety, for the rent. Plaintiff went into possession, and Thompson delivered the notes and one copy of the lease to the defendant, who thereafter continued to hold the same. There is a dispute whether defendant had authorized Thompson to lease the land on the terms that he did. The jury was warradted in finding that he did so authorize, and that he acquiesced in the terms of the lease and of the plaintiff's possession under it, for a time. It appears that defendant became dissatisfied with the terms of the lease, especially because it permitted the plaintiff to plow and plant the grass land, and and claims that he and plaintiff agreed upon a cancella-that thereafter he sought to have the lease canceled, tion, and that he tendered back said notes to the plain-tiff. The jury was warranted in finding that defendant did authorize Thompson to lease on the terms that he did; that plaintiff did not agree to a cancellation of the lease; and that the notes were never tendered to the plaintiff. Defendant was absent during the winter of 1894, and on his return found that the plaintiff was plowing the grass land, and it was for this that the prosecutions were instituted. The jury was war-

3   ranted in finding that the defendant was not justified by the advice of counsel in bringing the prosecutions, for that he did not lay all the facts known to him before counsel, and for that one or more of those whom he consulted advised him that his remedy was by civil action. They were also warranted in finding that the defendant resorted to these criminal prosecutions to secure possession of the farm, instead of a civil action, for the purpose of avoiding responsibility for costs. We have stated sufficient to show that a material question in the case is whether the defendant had probable cause for commencing said prosecutions, and that the jury had sufficient warrant for finding that he did not have probable cause.

III.   We now proceed to consider the assignments of error argued.

Appellant's first complaint is that the court allowed evidence to be introduced showing that the prosecutions had been ended, and in assuming in the instructions that they were ended. The answer denies that
4   they were ended. Therefore the evidence was properly admitted, and, as it showed without conflict that they were ended, the court had a right to accept that fact in instructing.

There was no error in permitting the plaintiff to state the amount of the notes, and that they were given for the rent. There was no dispute
5   as to either of these facts, and the ruling, if erroneous, was without prejudice.

The plaintiff was asked if any part of the damages claimed had been paid to him. It is contended that this was leading, but not objectionably so, we think. Appellant asked a witness on cross-examination if the
6   lease did not describe three quarter sections of land, and showed him the paper. The paper was the best evidence, and the objection was properly sustained.

Plaintiff, having testified that this claim belonged to him, was asked by appellant if there was any one to get a share of the damages, with a view, no
7   doubt, of showing that counsel had a contract for a contingent fee. Whether or not this was true was immaterial to the defendant.

Appellant asked the witness Thompson with reference to the lease: "That does not express your contract." There was no question but that the lease expressed the contract as made between Thompson and plaintiff, and no error in the ruling disallowing it to be answered.

Witness Ming was asked by appellant on cross-examination if he had been fined for contempt of court for interference in this suit. Appellee's
8   objection was properly sustained, as the evidence did not tend to show any feeling upon the part of the witness against the defendant.

G. I. Miller, an attorney at law, was called by the defendant to establish his defense that he acted under the advice of counsel. Appellant asked him: "Now, he had explained to you the nature of this, what he termed an 'irregular lease,' that did not describe his ground, had he?" This was objected to, and properly sustained, as leading.

Appellant, being examined in his own behalf, said: "Some of the best men said they were damaging my property to the amount of three hundred dollars." This
9   the court excluded, it being conceded that the plaintiff was plowing the grass land,—a fact which was undoubtedly known to defendant at the time he filed the informations. Let it be conceded that defendant had a right to show what rumors as to the destruction had come to his knowledge before filing the informations; yet, with this concession, there was no error in withdrawing the statements from the jury.

Appellant was asked on re-direct examination what he said to John Good in which the subject of a shotgun was mentioned, if it was mentioned. The
10   objection was properly sustained, because the matter called for was not in rebuttal of anything said by Good, and called for the statements of the appellant himself; and there was no error in the statement of the court that appellant could not introduce his own declarations here in his own support.

Appellant complains that one Olson was not permitted to answer whether it was a damage to appellant's place to have the sod plowed up at that time.

11   Plaintiff's guilt or innocence of the criminal charges depended upon whether he had authority under the lease to plow the grass land, and under the issues there was no error in excluding the opinion of the witness.

The same witness was asked if he knew the general reputation of plaintiff for being quarrelsome and a bully. The objection was properly sus
12   tained, as these traits of character were not involved in the issue.

One Cromwell, having testified to a conversation with appellant in the summer of 1894, about renting his farm, stated as follows: "I had another conversation with him in a few days, near the same place. He (Mr. White) told me then: 'If you want to rent the farm now, you must speak to Mr. Frank Thompson, because I have left it with him. Whatever you do with him is
13   all right with me.' That was near a week after the other conversation." The court excluded the first conversation and admitted that quoted above. This was competent evidence for the plaintiff in chief, and, while it is true that it was introduced in rebuttal, appellant was not prejudiced by that fact, as an opportunity remained to him to deny or explain the statement.

Mr. Good, with whom appellant had counseled, was asked on cross-examination: "If a man was irresponsible financially, and was destroying a man's property, would he advise a criminal proceeding if the party was wilfully doing it?" The objection was
14   properly sustained, as it is immaterial what the witness might have advised under such circumstances. It was only the circumstances as disclosed to him, and advice that he gave thereon, that were material in this case.

Other objections to rulings on the evidence are sufficiently answered in what we have said. We do not discover any errors prejudicial to the appellant in any of the rulings on evidence complained of.

IV. We now consider the exceptions to instructions refused and given.

Appellant asked an instruction to the effect that the ignoring of the indictment by the grand jury cannot be considered in evidence, as tending to show absence of probable cause, or as showing malice on the part of the defendant. This instruction was marked "Modified and given," and the court instructed that "the fact that the grand jury ignored the information, and that defendant was acquitted before the justice of the peace, is no evidence of want of probable cause, but the testimony on this point is only admitted to show that the prosecutions in question have ended." The instruction given was quite as favorable to the defendant as that asked.

In further instructing on the subject of probable cause, the court used this language: "Even if the lease was not authorized or ratified, if the plaintiff, in going upon the premises, acted under an honest belief of right so to do, then a prosecution therefor would not be well founded; and, if defendant knew that plaintiff so acted, then the prosecution would be without probable cause, the same as it would if the lease had been authorized or ratified. If, on the other hand, the lease was not authorized or ratified, and the defendant had reason to believe, from a talk had with plaintiff with reference to a settlement of damages claimed by defendant, or from other matters, that the plaintiff knew that his claim to the premises was unfounded, but persisted, against the objections of defendant, in going upon the prem-

ises in question, then the defendant would have probable cause for instituting the prosecutions."

16   Appellant contends that, as no lease was pleaded
or put in evidence, it was error for the court to
recognize the existence of a lease. The undisputed
evidence showed the existence of a lease, and it was
not error for the court to recognize that fact in the
instructions.

It is further contended that the retention of the
notes by the defendant, or his consent to the
17   occupancy of the farm, was not evidence of ratl-
fication; but we think it was directly so.

Appellant insists that it was error to instruct that,
if plaintiff acted upon an honest belief of right to
occupy the premises, then the prosecutions were not
well founded, for the reason that plaintiff's belief could
not influence the action of the defendant in bringing
the prosecutions. This claim ignores the fact that in
the same connection the court said: "If the defendant
knew he so acted, then the prosecution would be without probable cause;" thus making defendant's knowledge an element of the inquiry.

The court defined malice as "such a state of mind
as leads to the intentional doing of some wrongful act
knowing it to be without just cause or legal
18   excuse." Appellant complains of this definition,
and contends that "malice in law is in the
doing of a wrongful act." The definition given is
correct as applied to this case.

The court instructed that "if the defendant knew
that his only remedy was in a civil action, and wilfully
or recklessly commenced the criminal prosecutions,
this would show malice, although the defendant
19   was in fact entitled to the possession of the
premises; and malice would especially be shown
if the defendant had in fact authorized Thompson to

lease the premises upon the terms upon which it was leased by the latter, but, by reason of having got a better offer on the land, instituted the criminal prosecutions for the purpose of forcing the plaintiff to abandon the land in question." He may be said to have been actuated by malice. Appellant contends that there is no evidence that there was a better offer on the land, but we think otherwise. Appellant also complains of that part of the instruction to the effect that, if defendant knew that his remedy was in a civil action, this would show malice in commencing the criminal prosecutions. It is insisted that his remedy was not in civil action; but, be that as it may, one or more of the counsel whom he consulted so advised him, and the inquiry is as to the knowledge under which he acted. It is claimed that the court erred in saying that there could be malice in bringing the prosecutions, "although the defendant was in fact entitled to the possession of the premises." Taken alone this might be error, but taken in its connection it is not. It was bringing the prosecutions knowing that his only remedy was in a civil action that shows malice, even if he was entitled to possession.

We discover no error in refusing or giving instructions.

V. Appellant complains of the overruling of his motion for a new trial, on the grounds that the verdict is contrary to the evidence, and is the result of passion and prejudice, as shown by certain alleged misconduct of the jury, as shown by the affidavits of some of the jurors. For reasons already stated, we are of the opinion that the verdict is fully sustained by the evidence. It appears by these affidavits that after it had been decided to find for the plaintiff, and before the amount had been determined, remarks were made by some of the jurors to others of the panel as to

20

the mental condition, conduct, and disposition of the defendant, and were made with respect to the amount of the verdict to be returned. In so far as the statements relate to matters inhering in the verdict, they were incompetent, and cannot be considered. *Darrance v. Preston*, 18 Iowa, 396; *Bryson v. Railway Co.*, 89 Iowa, 677; *Dunlavey v. Watson*, 38 Iowa, 398; *Fulliam v. City of Muscatine*, 70 Iowa, 436. It does not appear that appellant was prejudiced in any of the statements made, but, on the contrary, if they had any effect, it was to arouse sympathy for him, and to reduce the amount of the verdict.

We find no error in either of the particulars assigned and argued, and the judgment is therefore AFFIRMED.

I. WHITNEY, Appellant, v. WARREN GAMMON, *et al.* |108|114

Levy and Sale: NOTICE TO SHERIFF. After exempt property had |106|119 been seized on execution, the judgment debtor sold it to plaintiff. To induce the sheriff to sell the property, the judgment creditor
1 executed bond to indemnify the sheriff and any claimant. Code, 1873, section 3055, provides that if, on levy of execution, the officer receives notice that the property is claimed by a third person, he may release the levy, unless bond is given, but that he shall be
2 protected from liability until he receives such notice *Held*, that plaintiff's right to sue on the bond was unaffected by failure to give the sheriff notice of his claim; the object of the notice being merely to enable the officer to protect himself by demanding indemnity which, here, he had taken without such notice

EXEMPT PROPERTY. As the judgment debtor need not give such notice when he claims such property as exempt, no notice need be
3 given by one who purchases from him after the levy, since he takes it with all the rights of the seller.

PUBLIC POLICY. A bond given to indemnify a sheriff against damages from the seizure and sale of personal property under an execution, and to secure to any claimant of the property any damages
4 he may sustain by reason of such seizure and sale, is not void, although it turns out that the property was exempt and not subject to levy, where there was a controversy between the parties at the time the bond was given, as to the character of the property.

Citing *Miller v. Rhodes,* 20 Ohio St. 494; *Marsh v. Gold,* 2 Pick. 285; *Mays v. Joseph,* 84 Ohio St. 22.

Limitation of Actions: INDEMNITY BOND. While an action against the sheriff for wrongful levy must be brought within three years, 2 an action seeking to recover damages on account of such levy 5 may be brought against those who made a bond to indemnify the sheriff for making it, within ten years after the execution of such bond.

Appeal from Shelby District Court.—HON. W. S. LEWIS, Judge.

WEDNESDAY, OCTOBER 20, 1897.

ACTION at law upon an indemnifying bond. Defendants demurred to the petition, and their demurrer was sustained. Plaintiff appeals.—*Reversed.*

B. I. Salinger and *Whitney Bros.* for appellant.

Byers & Lockwood for appellees.

DEEMER, J.—I. Lacey & Wells held a judgment against Daniel Whitney. Execution issued upon this judgment, and the sheriff seized two horses thereunder, which were exempt from execution, in the hands of Whitney. Thereafter, and on the same day, D. Whitney sold the horses to the appellant, I. Whitney. To induce the sheriff to sell the horses, Lacey & Wells, with Gammon and Wheeler as sureties, executed an indemnifying bond to the sheriff, and the horses were sold on the twenty-third day of February, 1889. The bond was executed on the ninth day of the same month. This action is upon the bond to recover the value of the horses. The defendant demurred to the petition reciting these facts, upon the grounds: (1) That plaintiff failed to give the sheriff any notice of her claim to the property; (2) that the bond was void, because given to the sheriff to indemnify for the sale of exempt property;

(3) that the action is barred by the statute of limitations. This demurrer was sustained.

II. The statutes (Code 1873) relating to the giving of notice and the taking of bonds are as follows:

"3055. An officer is bound to levy an execution on any personal property in the possession of, or that he has reason to believe belongs to the defendant, or on

1   which the plaintiff directs him to levy, unless he has received notice in writing from some other person, his agent, or attorney that such property

belongs to him; or if after levy he receives such notice, such officer may release the property unless a bond is given as provided in the next section; but the officer shall be protected from all liability by reason of such levy until he receives such written notice.

"3056. When the officer receives such notice he may forthwith give the plaintiff, his agent or attorney, notice that an indemnifying bond is required. Bond may thereupon be given by or for the plaintiff, with one or more sufficient sureties, to be approved by the officer, to the effect that the obligors will indemnify him against the damages which he may sustain in consequence of the seizure or sale of the property and will pay to any claimant thereof the damages he may sustain in consequence of the seizure or sale, and will warrant to any purchaser of the property such estate or interest therein as is sold; and thereupon the officer shall proceed to subject the property to the execution, and shall return the indemnifying bond to the district court of the county in which the levy is made."

The bond contained these conditions: "Now, if the said obligors shall and will indemnify the said G. S. Rainbow against all damages which he may sustain in consequence of the seizure or sale under said writ of the following described personal property, to-wit, one light bay horse, with star in forehead, and white hind feet, four years old; one dark bay horse, two white collar marks on right shoulder,—*and shall and will pay to any claimant of said property the damages he may sustain in consequence of the seizure and sale thereof,* * * * then this obligation to be void; otherwise to remain in full force and effect." It was given, not only to indemnify the sheriff, but to secure to any claimant of the property any damages he might sustain by reason of the seizure and sale of the property.

2   This action is not against the sheriff for his trespass, but is to recover from the principal and sureties on the bond, under the last condition therein named, the damages sustained by a claimant of the property. That part of section 3055 relating to notice before bringing suit has no application to this action. *Bradley v. Miller,* 100 Iowa, 169. The notice is for the protection of the sheriff, who is required to levy upon any property which the execution plaintiff directs him to seize, and has no reference to the liability of the execution plaintiff. Moreover, the object of the notice is to enable the officer to demand indemnity. If he has in fact taken the indemnity without notice, neither he nor the principal can be heard to complain; certainly the principal cannot. *Ayres v. Dorsey Produce Co.,* 101 Iowa, 141; *Sanxey v. Glass Co.,* 68 Iowa, 546; *Waterhouse v. Black,* 87 Iowa, 321. Aside from

3   this, we have held that, when the execution defendant claims the property as exempt, he is not required to give the notice provided by statute in an action against the officer. *Parsons v. Thomas,* 62 Iowa, 319; *McCoy v. Cornell,* 40 Iowa, 457. Plaintiff was not the owner of the property at the time the execution was levied. She purchased after the seizure, and is relying upon the fact that the property was exempt to D. Whitney when the levy was made. She is entitled to all the rights held by D. Whitney at the time the property was seized, may plead and prove the exemption, and need not do more to establish her claim than would

have been required of the execution defendant. *Red-field v. Stocker*, 91 Iowa, 383. At the time of plaintiff's purchase, the levy had been made, and she bought subject to it. She has, therefore, just such rights as her grantor had, and is entitled to assert them as he could have done. He was not required to give notice, and there is no reason why she should be.

III. It is alleged in the petition that the property levied upon was in fact exempt, but that Lacey & Wells claimed that it was not, and that to induce the officer to sell they executed the bond in suit. It thus 4 appears that there was a controversy between the parties as to the character of the property. In such case the bond is not void, although it turns out that the property was not subject to levy. Bishop, Contracts, sections 484, 493; *Miller v. Rhoades*, 20 Ohio St. 494; Mechem, Public Officers, section 890; *Marsh v. Gold*, 2 Pick. 285; *Mays v. Joseph*, 34 Ohio St. 22. The case of *Cole v. Parker*, 7 Iowa, 167, is not in conflict with this rule.

IV. The third ground of the demurrer is that the action is barred by the statute. The suit was commenced on the seventeenth day of August, 1893. If it 5 were against the sheriff, it would be barred by subdivision 3 of section 2529 of the Code of 1873.

As the action is upon the promise contained in the bond, it is not barred until ten years after the cause thereof accrued. Code, section 2529. Lacey & Wells could be sued for their trespass independent of the sheriff. They gave bond to secure any claimant of the property who might suffer through their act. It is in no sense an obligation to answer for the wrong of the sheriff, except as he might demand indemnity from them for any damages adjudged against him. The fact that plaintiff might have sued the sheriff instead of declaring upon the bond is of no consequence, for the sheriff is not the principal in the bond. He is one of the obligees, and the fact that no action can now be brought against him is entirely immaterial. The petition states a good cause of action, and the demurrer should have been overruled.—REVERSED.

AMANDA M. HUBNER v. WILLIAM F. REICKHOFF, Executor, Appellant.

Jurisdiction: NOTICE OF PUBLICATION: *Idem sonans.* Where service, in an action for divorce against a non-resident, is by publication, and defendant makes default, and does not appear, the court cannot assume that the name "Keesel" in the published summons should be understood as "Keisel," defendant's real name, on the principle of *idem sonans;* and a decree based on such a service is void, and is subject to collateral attack

KINNE, C. J., took no part.

Appeal from Plymouth District Court.—HON. F. R. GAY-
NOR, Judge.

WEDNESDAY, OCTOBER, 20, 1897.

WILLIAM REICKHOFF died, testate, on the eighth day of September, 1894, and the defendant is the executor of his will. The plaintiff presented a claim against the estate for damages based on a breach of promise of marriage. There is a denial by operation of law. The cause was submitted to a jury, that returned a finding for plaintiff, and the defendant appealed.—*Reversed.*

Haines & Lyman, I. S. Struble, and *G. W. Pitts* for appellant.

Argo & McDuffie for appellee.

GRANGER, J. — I.   It became necessary for the plaintiff, in order to show a valid marriage contract with William Reickhoff, to establish a divorce from Heindrick Keisel, to whom she had been married. She

had left him in Germany, and she presented to the
court a certified copy of a decree from the district court
of Nebraska in and for Douglas county, showing a
divorce of Amanda M. Keisel from Heindrick Keisel, on
the second day of September, 1888. The decree shows
that jurisdiction was obtained by a service of notice by
publication. In support of objections to the decree, as
evidence, the defendant presented the record, from
which proof of service must be found. The notice was
addressed to Heindrick Keesel signed by "Amanda M.
Keesel, by J. E. Smith, Attorney." The notice, as
shown of record, required the defendant to appear and
answer on or before December 26, 1888. It is argued
by appellant as if it was 1887; and, as appellee makes
no question as to the fact, we will consider 1887 as the
proper date. It appears that the decree was entered,
on default of the defendant, on the second day of
November, 1888. The affidavit *for* publication was filed
November 4, 1887, and that *of* publication October 13,
1888, showing the publication to have been from November 12 to December 3, 1887. The cause seems to have
been continued from the return day, December 26, 1887,
to November, 1888, before default or judgment was
entered.

The court instructed the jury that the decree as
offered was *prima facie* evidence of a divorce, and the
decree was admitted in evidence against numerous
objections as to its competency. The question of fact,
as to the residence of plaintiff in Nebraska for such
time as to give jurisdiction, the court submitted to the
jury, with the instruction as to the *prima facie* effect of
the decree. Among the objections urged then and now
to the decree is the variance in name between that of
plaintiff's husband, "Keisel," and that in the notice,
"Keesel." It is urged that the variance is fatal to the
decree. The following rule is invoked by appellee, found

in 16 Am. & Eng. Enc. Law, 122: "The absence of a
definite set of rules for the spelling and pronunciation
of the names of persons, and more especially of sur-
names, has led the court to the adoption of a principle
known as the rule of *idem sonans.* This rule may be
stated to be that absolute accuracy in spelling names
is not required in legal documents or proceedings, either
civil or criminal; that if the name as spelled in the document, though different from the correct spelling
thereof, conveys to the ear, when pronounced according
to the commonly accepted methods, a sound practically
identical with the correct name as commonly pronounced, the name as thus given is a sufficient designation of the individual referred to, and no advantage can
be taken of the clerical error." The author has collected a very extended list of names to which the rule
has been applied, and another to which it is held not
applicable. In some cases it has been held that the
question of whether the rule is applicable is one of fact
for the jury, and in others that the issue presents a
question for the court. We have examined many, but
not all, of the cases cited by the author, and from them
no very definite rule can be gathered. Many of the
cases are criminal, and the question is one of identity
of the person charged with the person on trial, and
many others present the question of the identity of the
person in court, sought to be charged with an obligation
or duty, with the one named in an instrument or document. It is, in such cases, a question whether the person against whom the adjudication is sought is the one
represented by the name in the instrument. The rea-
sonableness of the rule in such cases is apparent. An
examination of the cases will show that the variance in
orthography in names has been held fatal or otherwise,
as the facts of the case would warrant, having in view
safety in the application of the rule, and just results.

This case is unlike any that we have seen. It is conceded that the name "Keisel" is pronounced by giving to the diphthong the long sound of "i." If that pronunciation is to obtain for the purpose of the case, the rule of *idem sonans* could not be made to apply; and, so far as can be known, it is a fact that it was so pronounced. But, if the sound of long "e" should be permitted, ought the rule to obtain in this case? The test suggests this query: Where a service is by publication, which is made conclusive because of a presumption that it comes to the notice of the person, can the court assume as a matter of law that the name "Keesel" would or should be understood as "Keisel?" Can it be said to be a rule of law that one of the latter name, on seeing the former name in a notice, must or should understand it to mean him? Let it be conceded that, if he were in court, the identity of the person as the one intended might be shown; but can it be assumed as a legal conclusion that "Keesel" should be understood as "Keisel?" It is hardly to be doubted that, while "Reed" could be held to apply to "Read" or "Reade," with the person in court, and an issue of identity made, a court would not assume, in a publication service, that it meant, or should be understood to mean, either of the others. The danger of such a holding is apparent, because of the fact that all three words are names of persons pronounced alike, but of different orthography. Under some conditions either name might be held to apply to either of the persons, but not in a case where a name, not his own, is published in a notice, to which he has not responded, and the failure to respond is to be taken as a confession of the truth of charges, as the record recites in the divorce proceeding. The corrupt practices in divorce proceedings could hardly be aided by the courts better than to open the door for a variance between the actual name of the defendant in the record and that in the notice constituting the service, and giving the court

jurisdiction. It would seem as if the dissolution of the
marriage relation should depend on greater accuracy of
procedure than a variance involving such doubt and
uncertainty. The divorce case, on the face of the record,
is strange in the respect of the defendant's name, if not
somewhat suspicious. The plaintiff was a person of the
same name, and, of course, knew it well. In the proceedings the name appears as "Keisel" and "Kiesel,"
which is a mere reversal of the letters of the diphthong;
but nowhere, except in the notice, does the name appear
as "Keesel," which is enough of a departure to indicate
another name. As we understand the record, the published name is neither spelled nor pronounced like that
of the defendant in the divorce proceeding. But if pronounced the same, and if under some circumstances,
such as we have suggested, the variance in spelling
might be held immaterial, we do not think the rule
can be made to apply in this case, where the defendant
was not in court, and there could have been no issue
or facts from which he should be held to answer to a
name not his own, or be adjudged in default. The
decree in evidence and the instructions of the court
were conclusive on the question, and the effect was to
hold, as a matter of law, that the person named in the
notice was the husband of the plaintiff, and we do not
think the conclusion was warranted. We think, with
this affirmative showing, the decree should have been
denied as evidence, on the ground that the person served
did not appear to be the person named in the proceeding.

This question being jurisdictional, it cannot well
be claimed that the decree in the divorce proceeding is
conclusive against collateral attack. If the substituted
service was not, as a legal conclusion, on Heindrick
Keisel, there was an entire want of jurisdiction, and
the decree is absolutely void, and may be attacked in

any proceeding in which it is sought to be made effective. 1 Black, Judgments, section 170; *Jordan r. Brown;* 71 Iowa, 421. It is not a case of a defective service of notice, but one of no notice on Heindrick Keisel. In such a case a foreign judgment is void, notwithstanding the recitals of a service. *Stone v. Skerry*, 31 Iowa 582. An entire want of notice is not a defective notice. *Haws v. Clark*, 37 Iowa, 355.

We are better satisfied with our conclusion because of the fact that the record is not an affirmative showing of good faith in the divorce proceeding in Nebraska. The court submitted to the jury the question of a timely residence of plaintiff in Nebraska, so as to give jurisdiction to that court; and the jury found there was such residence, but upon evidence of very doubtful sufficiency. Conceding it to be of such a nature as to sustain the finding, its doubtful character. in connection with the mode of service, which we hold to be insufficient, makes it a case with no equitable features to make the application of the rule as to service appear harsh or in any way unjust. Because of the conclusiveness of the question we have considered, it is not important that we consider others. The judgment is REVERSED.

KINNE, C. J., took no part.

M. J. CONWAY v. THE CHICAGO GREAT WESTERN RAILWAY COMPANY, Appellant.

Master and Servant: RAILROADS. It is the duty of a foreman in charge of a coal house of a railroad company to keep the appliances, if properly constructed, in suitable condition for use; and he cannot recover for personal injuries caused by the failure to keep them in such condition.

Appeal from Chickasaw District Court.—HON. A. N. HOBSON, Judge.

THURSDAY, OCTOBER 21, 1897.

ACTION for personal injuries. Judgment for plaintiff, and the defendant appealed.—*Reversed.*

D. W. Lawler, Lyon & Lenehan, and *H. T. Reed* for appellant.

H. L. Spaulding and *Springer & Clary* for appellee.

GRANGER, J. —· I.   For some time prior to December 14, 1894, plaintiff was an employe of the defendant, as foreman of its coal house at Elma, Iowa. The coal house consists of a house proper and sheds for the storing of coal and loading it into engines by the use of a derrick and chutes. A way to and from a floor of the coal house, to and from which plaintiff was required to go, was a ladder on upright posts or timbers, made by placing thereon strips of 2x4 lumber. At the top of the ladder was a projection of the floor in a way to effect getting to and from the ladder safely. At the head of the ladder, and on the floor or platform, was placed a handhold for the use of the persons using the ladder. On the fourteenth day of December, 1894, the plaintiff, in descending the ladder, fell to the ground, and was injured, and, for the damage sustained, this action is brought. The petition charges negligence in various ways, and we copy the averments as follows: "That, in the construction of said coal house and the machinery and appliances used therein, the defendant, its agents, servants, and employes, put in for use two stationary ladders leading from the ground to the coal chutes; that said ladders were negligently constructed

and built, in this: that at or near the top thereof they
were not provided with any or sufficient rounds or appliances to grasp in passing to or from the said ladders and
the adjacent coal chutes; that said ladder and chutes
adjoining thereto were built close to the end of said
building; said ladder was perpendicular, and under-
neath the projecting end of the chute and timber supporting the same, the handhold on the platform above
said ladder, and which is used in descending the same,
was constructed of a solid piece of wood nailed upon a
flat board, the same being so placed as to afford an insecure grasp or handhold, the same being placed so near
to the side of the building as to prevent the free use and
exercise of a person's limbs while using said ladder, and
that the framework, timbers, and boards comprising
said building and chute were so placed over and beyond
said ladder as to compel a person in descending the
same, to climb over said obstructions, thereby causing
said ladder to be dangerous when used; that no appli-
ance or round of said ladder was so placed as to give a
person descending the same a handhold to protect himself from falling, within a space of four feet from the
top of said chutes and ladder, and no provision made
whereby a person descending said ladder could safely
take hold of anything to assist him in the descent
thereof; that the rounds of said ladder were too large to
be safely grasped; that the ends of the board and timber
used in the construction of said chute were placed too
near the top of the ladder, projected over the same, and
thereby formed an obstruction." It is conceded that
the main contention on the trial as to negligence was in
the way the handhold on the top of the platform, which
it was necessary to use in starting down the ladder, was
placed; plaintiff contending that it was nailed flat on
the floor or platform, so that a grasp of it was insecure,
and defendant contending that the 2x4 strip, serving as

a handhold, was nailed on two other strips of 2x4, so as
to leave a space of two inches between the handhold and
the floor, and a foot in width. Considerable testimony
was directed by both parties to this particular question. During the examination of a witness for plaintiff
on the direct, the following stipulation was offered
by plaintiff, and agreed to: "It is stipulated that the
ladder in question, the same being the north ladder in
said coal house, is in the same condition now that it was
when originally constructed, and was in such condition
at the time of the injury, and there has been no change
in it since made, and that the ladder was constructed
originally by defendant."

The particular question whether the handhold was
nailed flat to the floor, or with the two-inch space, was
made the turning point as to negligence so far as the
handhold was concerned; and it appears that each party
was so confident of being right that the stipulation was
made. Later in the trial, some photographs, taken
before the stipulation was made, were put in evidence,
amounting to a practical demonstration that the handhold was not flat on the floor. At the conclusion of
defendant's evidence, plaintiff moved the court for leave
to withdraw so much of the stipulation as admitted that
the ladder was as it was originally constructed, and, as
a reason, stated that the admission was inadvertently
made; that, within two or three days before making the
stipulation, the handhold had been changed without
his knowledge, and with intent to deceive him, and procure the stipulation. The court denied the motion, and
the admission remained for the purpose of the case.
Plaintiff, in his testimony, says that he knows of no
other reason for his fall except that he could not grasp
the handhold; and, although the petition contains
other averments as to negligence, there is no proof of
any other negligence causing the injury. Plaintiff alone
knows how he came to fall, and he attributes his fall to

no other cause; and hence this particular charge of
negligence became the controlling one. There are but
two ways of accounting for a verdict for plaintiff in
view of the record,—*First*, that the jury disregarded
the stipulation of fact as to the handhold, or that it
found that, after the stipulation, the handhold was
changed. Appellee, in argument, practically concedes
the latter. It is there said: "Was this handhold
changed after the stipulation was entered into? The
jury evidently thought so, for they certainly found that
to be the case." There is not a particle of evidence on
which such a finding could be based. The only evidence
bearing on the question was that showing its condition before the stipulation was made; no evidence whatever of a change afterwards. The photographs and
other evidence so fixed the fact that, when the stipulation was made, the handhold was not flat on the floor,
that the motion to withdraw part of the stipulation
concedes, in effect, that fact, and seeks to avoid it by a
withdrawal. This the court refused, so that, as we view
the record, the fact of defendant's negligence in the construction of the ladder and shed was disproven. It is
this situation that necessitates the extreme resort of
sustaining the verdict by assuming the jury to have
found a fact of which there was no proof. Assuming,
then, that the handhold was properly constructed, the
only reason why it did not properly serve the purpose
intended, at the time of the accident, seems to be that
coal dust had accumulated under it, so as to prevent
properly taking hold of it. Plaintiff was foreman of
the coal house, and it was his duty to keep the appliances, if properly made, in suitable condition for use.
Stroble v. Railway Co., 70 Iowa, 555. The legal proposition is not questioned. If, then, the accident was
caused by such accumulations, it was plaintiff's negligence that caused it. There seems to be nothing further

to elaborate. The point is made by appellant that the verdict is not supported by the evidence, and it seems to be well taken.

II. The court, in its first instruction, presents as an issue the negligence of the company in permitting the ladder to get out of repair, and remain so for an unreasonable length of time; and complaint is made because no such negligence is charged. It is true the negligence charged is only as to the construction originally, and there is reason to think the language was inserted through inadvertence, caused by some changes in the pleadings. We notice the point to avoid a repetition on another trial. The judgment is REVERSED.

F. J. Brown, Assignee, Appellant, v. F. C. Bradford, Receiver of the Buena Vista State Bank, The Buena Vista State Bank, John R. Lemon, J. Royal Lemon, John K. Lemon, E. B. Walker, John Aldinger, S. W. Hobbs, and Guilford, Martin & Co.

Banks: CONVEYANCES TO. Plaintiff's assignor made a transfer of land to a bank in which he was the principal stockholder. The
1 resolution of the directors accepting the grant recited that the
2 transfer was made to cover a shortage in the capital stock, that the grantor should receive pay for the land from the future
8 undivided profits of the bank, and that he might retain posses-sion, and receive the rents; and provided for a re-conveyance at
5 his request at any time before payment. Held, that as to the bank and its depositors the conveyance was absolute, but as to the stockholders, it was a loan which they agreed to pay from the undivided profits of the bank.

Same. The acceptance by a state bank of a conveyance of real prop-
2 erty to make good an impairment of its capital stock, is not ultra vires, although the bank under ordinary circumstances has no
8 authority to purchase real estate except such as may be convenient or needed for use in its business.

Powers. Directors of a bank have no authority to pledge the future
8 earnings, in the absence of express authority from the stock-holders.

FRAUDULENT CONVEYANCE. A conveyance absolute on its face is not
4 fraudulent in law because of a secret trust rendering it a mort-
5 gage, where no fraud was intended, and none of the grantor's
creditors were in fact misled.

SAME. An assignee for creditors is not entitled to judgment against
a receiver of a bank for the purchase price of property conveyed
1 by the assignor to the bank for the purpose of making good an
impairment of its capital stock, under an agreement that he
should be paid out of the undivided profits of the land, where
there are no special profits, notwithstanding that a release by the
7 assignor of the agreement for payment is set aside at the instance
of the assignee, as fraudulent.

Recording. A conveyance absolute on its face is not fraudulent in
law because of a secret trust, where such trust does not enter into
6 the consideration for the deed. The mere non-recording of deeds
does not render them fraudulent in law as to creditors, where no
fraud was intended, and no one was misled.

Badges. That a transaction which was in fact a mortgage was put in
the form of a conveyance absolute on its face, while a badge of
6 fraud as to creditors of the mortgagor, is not conclusive as to
fraud.

Sales: VENDOR'S LIENS. A deed absolute on its face was made to a
bank by an officer thereof to cover an impairment of the capital
stock, with a collateral agreement for payment of the price out
1 of future profits of the bank   This agreement was released upon
8 the promise of the bank examiner that the management of the
5 bank would not be interfered with. Through the bank examiner,
a receiver was subsequently appointed for the bank   *Held*, that,
as the payment was to be made from a particular fund the
grantor could not have a lien established on the land for the price.

Appeal from Buena Vista District Court.—HON. LOT
THOMAS, Judge.

THURSDAY, OCTOBER 21, 1897.

SUIT in equity to set aside a conveyance of certain
land made by one John R. Lemon, plaintiff's assignor, to
the Buena Vista State Bank, and to annul the transfer
between the same parties of certain property known as
"Auxiliary Savings Banks." It is claimed that the
conveyance and transfer were void because the bank
had no authority to receive deeds of real estate, because

the deed was never delivered, and because made with intent to hinder, delay, and defraud the creditors of John R. Lemon. The defendant Bradford, receiver, pleaded that the conveyance and transfer were made to meet an impairment of the capital of the Buena Vista Bank, and denies fraud in the transaction. The trial court dismissed plaintiff's petition, and he appeals.— *Affirmed.*

F. J. Brown, James De Land, and *J. E. Buland* for appellant.

F. H. Helsell for appellees.

DEEMER, J. — Prior to March 1, 1893, John R. Lemon, one of the defendants in this case, was engaged in business as a private banker in the town of Storm Lake. On that date he, with others, who were relatives or close friends, organized and incorporated an institution known as the Buena Vista State Bank. The capital stock of this bank was fixed at five hundred shares, of the par value of one hundred dollars each. John R. Lemon took three hundred and twenty of these shares in exchange for the building and fixtures, in which he had theretofore been doing business, at an agreed valuation of twenty-five thousand dollars. The auditor of state, through his officers, made an examination of the bank in June, 1894, and, after looking over its assets and liabilities, claimed there was, or had been, an impairment of the capital stock, which must be made good. John R. Lemon thereupon, and on the twenty-sixth day of June, 1894, executed and delivered to the bank deeds for eight hundred acres of land situated in Dakota, Iowa, Nebraska, and also transferred to said bank what is known as "200 Burns & Barclay Auxiliary Savings Banks" for five hundred dollars. For reasons to be hereafter explained, these deeds were not recorded

until August and September of the year 1895. On the
twenty-fifth day of June, 1894, the board of directors of
the bank, without the knowledge or consent of the state
authorities, adopted a resolution, of which the follow·
ing are material parts: "Whereas, the Iowa
1   bank examiner at the last examination of this
    bank appraised the real estate at fifteen thou-
sand dollars, and the personal property, including
furniture and fixtures, at two thousand dollars, thus
making a deficit of seventy-four hundred and six dollars
and fifty-nine cents in the former and five hundred and
ninety-three dollars and forty-one cents in the latter, a
total deficit of eight thousand dollars in the capital of
the Buena Vista State Bank; and whereas, John R.
Lemon proposes to make good this deficit by contribution of real estate and other property, and agrees to
take his pay for the same from and out of the undivided
profits of the bank in amount not to exceed four thou
sand dollars in any one year until all is paid, and for
this purpose proposes to sell to this bank the following
described real estate at the price below named, to-wit,
* * *   also two hundred Burns & Barclay Auxiliary
Savings Banks for five hundred dollars; it being agreed
and understood that at any time before the said Lemon
receives pay for the above property the bank will
re-convey it to him, or any part of it, at the aforesaid
prices, upon his request in writing, the amount to be
indorsed on the amount then due him for the same; and
upon the request of the cashier in writing the said
Lemon will re-purchase any part of the aforesaid land
at the prices above named, and to indorse the amount of
the same upon the amount due said Lemon. It is also
stipulated that the said Lemon shall have the use of said
land as compensation for the amount contributed by
him as above until the same shall be paid out of the
undivided profits as above stated. Resolved, that the

Buena Vista State Bank accepts the above proposition of the said John R. Lemon, and upon the delivery of the proper deeds of conveyance the cashier is authorized and directed to execute a contract with John R. Lemon in compliance with the above." Pursuant to this resolution, the following contract was entered into between the parties whose names are attached: "This agreement, made and entered into this 26th day of June, 1894, between the Buena Vista State Bank, party of the first part, and John R. Lemon, party of the second part, both of Buena Vista county, Iowa, witnesseth: That in consideration of $8,000, contributed by said John R. Lemon to the capital of said bank, in compliance with the action of the directors at a meeting held on the 25th day of June, 1894, the Buena Vista State Bank agrees to pay to said John R. Lemon, his heirs or assigns, the aforesaid sum of $8,000, the same to be paid out of the undivided profits of the bank, but in amount not exceeding $4,000 in any one year; this agreement to bind the heirs and assigns of the parties herein represented. Witness our hands the day and year first above written. Buena Vista State Bank, by J. K. Lemon, Cashier. John R. Lemon." The bank examiner, when he discovered the resolution passed by the board of directors, and the contract based thereon, insisted upon the surrender of this contract, to which Lemon finally consented; and on the twenty-ninth day of August, 1895, Lemon wrote across the face of it, "Surrendered and canceled, Aug. 29, 1895." The following release also appears in the book of minutes of the bank and upon the contract: "August 29th, 1895. For the purpose of making good a part of the impairment of the capital stock of the Buena Vista State Bank in accordance with the original intention, I hereby surrender this contract, and all my interest, including the right of occupancy and rents in and to the property deeded

by me to said bank on or about the date of the above
contract, acknowledging that such transfer was an
absolute conveyance. [Signed] John R. Lemon." Notwithstanding this release, the state authorities were
convinced that the bank was not able to longer continue
business, and an action was brought on the thirtieth
day of August, 1895, by the attorney general, to close
up its affairs. In this action F. C. Bradford was
appointed receiver, and as such took possession of the
real estate in controversy. Thereafter, and on the second day of September following, John R. Lemon made
a deed of general assignment of all his property for the
benefit of creditors, in which he named F. J. Brown
assignee. Brown qualified as such assignee, and thereafter brought this suit to set aside the conveyances and
transfers heretofore referred to, upon the grounds: (1)
That the transactions were *ultra vires*, and beyond the
power of the bank; (2) that the conveyances were void,
because made with intent to hinder, delay, and defraud
creditors, void because of a secret trust reserved to
John R. Lemon, and void because the deeds were withheld from the records by agreement between the parties.
The assignee also asked as alternative relief that, if the
conveyances be not set aside, that the contract of
release made by Lemon be set aside and the original
agreement made between him and the bank be restored.

I. Appellant's first point is that a state bank has
no authority to purchase real estate except such as may
be convenient or needed for use in its business, and
that the transfer in question amounted to a purchase
with an agreement to re-sell. We are not called
2   upon to determine this question, for we do not
regard these transactions as a sale to the bank,
as that term is ordinarily used. The resolution adopted
by the bank under date of June 25, 1894, discloses
that the bank examiner found a deficit of eight
thousand dollars in the capital of the bank, and

that John R. Lemon proposed to make this good
by the transfer of the land and the auxiliary savings
banks stock, upon condition, however, that he should
receive pay for the same out of the undivided
profits of the bank, as shown in said resolution.
Whether this impairment was due to an overvaluation
of the real estate given by Lemon in exchange for his
stock does not clearly appear, although this is a fair
inference from the transaction. But, whether this be
true or not, Lemon, as one of the stockholders, made
the conveyance and transfer for the purpose of securing
this impairment; and it does not lie in his mouth, nor in
that of his representative, to say that this was not the
proper way to secure it. The transaction was an executed one, voluntarily entered into and accepted and
relied upon by the bank; and it is not material that the
statutes (chapter 29, Acts Twenty-fifth General
Assembly) provide another manner by which this
impairment shall be met. It was met in another manner, and presumably because John R. Lemon felt himself under obligations to so meet it. The agreement
entered into on June 26, a copy of which we have heretofore set out, is a release of the future unearned profits
of the bank pledged to Lemon to reimburse him for the
transfers. In other words, the bank undertook to direct
its earnings to the extent of not exceeding four thousand dollars a year to the reimbursement of Lemon for
his transfers. Whether it had authority to do this is a
mooted question. Conceding, for the purposes of the
case, however, that it had such authority, yet it appears
that this contract was surrendered, canceled, and
released by Lemon on August 29, 1895, by the release of
that date, heretofore set out. In this release Lemon
says that it was the original intention to make good the
impairment of the capital stock by the conveyances
before referred to, and he acknowledged that such

transfers were absolute conveyances. Viewed from our present standpoint it is the same as if the conveyances had been made by him on August 29, 1895, for the purpose of making good the deficiency in the capital stock. What reason is there for saying that such conveyances were void? It is not a case where the bank goes into an open market and deals in real estate. Such a transaction might be *ultra vires*. On the contrary, the convey; ances were made for the purpose of securing the depositors and creditors of the bank against loss growing out of a diminution of the capital stock; a loss for which Lemon acknowledged his responsibility by making the conveyances. That a bank may take real estate

3   security for any debt due, is conceded. See Boone, Banking, section 23, and cases cited. Such a transaction is not *ultra vires;* and if it were, strictly speaking, without authority of the bank, we doubt whether Lemon or his representatives could take advantage of it. The conveyance, as between Lemon and the bank, or as between Lemon's assignee and the receiver of the bank, was good, unless it was made with intent to defraud. There is no evidence whatever that either the conveyances or the release of date August 29, 1895, were made with intent to defraud creditors of John R. Lemon. While he may have been, and doubtless was, insolvent on the last named date, yet neither the state officials nor the other officers of the bank knew anything of his insolvency. The conveyances and release were made at the suggestion of the state auditor and bank examiner for the laudable purpose of securing the creditors and depositors of the bank, and without any purpose or intent of wronging or delaying other creditors.

It is said the conveyances were void, because of a secret trust reserved in Lemon by the contract of date

June 26, 1894, and because Lemon was permitted to
receive the rents and profits of the land after the
4   conveyances were made. The agreement was to
return to Lemon, from the undivided and
unearned profits of the bank, the sum of eight thousand
dollars. This, in effect, was a loan made by Lemon to
the stockholders of the bank, which they agreed to
repay from future profits of the institution. As to the
bank and its depositors the conveyance was absolute,
and for their benefit; but as to the stockholders and
directors it was a loan which they agreed to repay from
their undivided future earnings. The agreement as to
possession was made of record upon the bank minutes,
and possession was in fact retained by Lemon. The
deeds were not recorded, as we have said, until the latter part of August or the first of September, 1895. No
creditor of Lemon's was, in fact, misled by these transactions. Again, the whole transaction is between
5   Lemon and the bank, as it originally stood, was,
in effect, a mortgage of the property to the bank
to secure the sum of eight thousand dollars. True, conveyances absolute on their face were made; but such
fact, while a badge of fraud, is not conclusive. *Fuller v.
Griffith*, 91 Iowa, 632. We find affirmatively that no
fraud was, in fact, intended, and, as none of Lemon's
individual creditors were misled thereby, the conveyances were not fraudulent. Moreover, it does not appear
that the right to the rents or the privilege of re-purchase was a part of the consideration for the conveyances, as in the case of *Macomber v. Peck*, 39 Iowa, 351,
and other authorities cited by appellant. There was a
consideration for the transfer of the property, and the
use of the same by Lemon was of benefit, rather than
of disadvantage, to his creditors. The transaction, on
the face of it, as it appears from the deeds and records
of the corporation, was in sooth a mortgage until the
agreement of release of August 29, 1895; and under the

statutes of this state a mortgagor of real estate is
entitled to the possession and to the rents and profits.
Code 1873, section 1938. See, also, *Suiter v. Turner*, 10
Iowa, 517. Now, as the conveyance was not made absolute in form for the purpose of defrauding creditors, it
will be given force and validity, and treated as a mortgage until the execution of the agreement of release of
date August 29, 1895. At that time the conveyance
became absolute, and Lemon relinquished all rights to
the possession of the land, without fraud or purpose on
his part of hinder or delay his creditors. There is, as
we have said, no evidence that anyone was, in fact,
misled on account of the form of the transaction; and
no reason is offered why the assignee should be allowed
to set aside the various transfers and agreements made
by his assignor. While the deeds were not
6   recorded until August and September of the year
1895, yet this did not result from any agreement
between the parties. Delivery was made of them to the
bank, and mere inadvertence is responsible for their not
being recorded. This does not render them fraudulent.
In re Bloomfield Woolen Mills, 101 Iowa, 181.

Appellant further contends that the consideration
for the release of date August 29 was an agreement
on the part of the bank examiner that the management
of the bank should not be interfered with; that this
officer disregarded his agreement, and proceeded to
have a receiver appointed for the bank; and that by
reason thereof the consideration for the release has
failed, and that he is entitled to have the conveyances
set aside, or a lien established upon the premises for
the purchase price, to-wit, eight thousand dollars.
There are two answers to this proposition. *First,* we do
not think he has established the agreement said to have
been made by the examiner. We are of opinion that
the examiner made no such promise, and that the
release was executed because of a statement from that

officer that the impairment in capital stock must be
made good, and that the only feasible way to do it was
to execute the release. But if we should assume
7   that such promise was made, and that for this reason it should be set aside, plaintiff is not entitled
to judgment for the purchase price, for this was payable
out of a particular fund, to-wit, the earnings of the
bank. Neither the bank nor any other person or corporation promised to pay eight thousand for the land and
auxiliary savings banks stock. The transaction before
the release was, as we have said, a loan or mortgage to
the bank or to the stockholders to meet a deficit in the
capital, and was to be paid from the future earnings of
the bank. If there was or is any liability to Lemon, it
is from the individual stockholders. But, as the
8   officers and directors had no authority as such to
pledge the future dividends, for such purposes,
without the consent of the stockholders, it is likely
there is no liability on their part. It must be borne in
mind that these conveyances were dictated by the state
officials who were vested with authority to examine,
and, to a certain extent, direct, the management of state
banks; and that officers and directors of the bank, in
accepting these conveyances, were acting as trustees
for the depositors as well as other creditors; and it may
well be doubted whether their resolution of date June
25, 1894, and the agreement were of any validity. They
certainly had no authority to pledge the future earnings of the bank in the absence of express authority
from the stockholders. And without deciding the question we may say that we much doubt whether fraud
committed by them upon the creditors of John R.
Lemon in accepting the conveyances, even if it had been
shown, would have been chargeable upon the depositors, or upon the receiver, who represented them.

Some other questions are presented, which are not regarded of controlling importance, and need not be considered. The decree of the district court is equitable and just, and it is AFFIRMED.

ED. WELCH v. WILLIAM SPIES, Appellant.

Sale: DELIVERY. Plaintiff sold to defendant not less than sixteen hundred nor more than twenty-three hundred bushels of corn at
1　so much a bushel, and received fifty dollars of the purchase money. The corn was in two cribs, one containing sixteen hun-
3　dred bushels intact, and the other, which had been opened, about seven hundred bushels. Plaintiff reserved the right to retain two hundred or three hundred bushels, if he needed them, and a third party was entitled to fifty bushels. Before any corn had been separated from the mass the entire lot was burned. *Held*, that, as to sixteen hundred bushels, at least, the title had passed to defendant.

SAME. The fact that part of the corn was to be shelled and delivered
3　by plaintiff at a place designated by the defendant, did not prevent the title from passing.

SAME. The intent of the parties is of controlling importance in determining whether or not the title to personal property, the
2　subject of the contract of sale, has passed to the purchaser, and the fact that it remains to weigh or measure the property sold is not conclusive as to such intent.

EVIDENCE. Evidence that the seller of personal property notified the wife of the person having the possession thereof that he had sold
5　the same is admissible on the question as to whether the title had passed before the destruction of the property, as tending to show what he did to complete delivery.

Cross-Examination. Plaintiff in an action to recover the purchase price of personal property, in which defendant has pleaded that the property was raised on the land of a third person cannot be
4　cross-examined with reference to a lien thereon for unpaid rent at the time of the sale, where he did not touch on that subject in his direct examination.

Appeal from Cass District Court.—HON. A. B. THORNELL, Judge.

THURSDAY, OCTOBER 21, 1897.

ACTION at law to recover the unpaid portion of the price of corn alleged to have been sold and delivered by the plaintiff to defendant. There was a trial by jury, and a verdict and judgment for the plaintiff. The defendant appeals.—*Affirmed*.

Willard & Willard and *Jas. B. Bruff* for appellant.

Curtis & Follett for appellee.

ROBINSON, J.—The plaintiff claims that in the latter part of July, in the year 1894, he sold and delivered to the defendant two thousand three hundred bushels of corn contained in two cribs, at the agreed price of fifty cents per bushel. The defendant admits that he entered into a verbal agreement with the plaintiff for the purchase of not less than one thousand, six hundred nor more than two thousand bushels of corn at the price stated, and that fifty dollars were paid to the plaintiff by virtue of the agreement; but denies that the corn was delivered, and alleges that the plaintiff has failed and refused to perform his part of the agreement. Soon after the sale is alleged to have been made, and while the corn remained in the crib, it was destroyed by fire. The verdict was for eight hundred and twenty dollars and ninety-three cents, and the judgment rendered was for that sum, with interest and costs.

I. The chief controversy between the parties to this action relates to the delivery of the corn. When the agreement in question was made, one crib, which had not been opened, contained one thousand, six hundred bushels. Corn had been taken from the other crib, but it then contained about seven hundred bushels. The grounds upon which the defendant insists that the corn was not delivered are stated to be that he purchased but a part of the corn in the two cribs, and there was never any separation of the part he

purchased from the remainder; that the plaintiff
reserved the right to retain two or three hundred
bushels for his own use, and that he had not set it apart;
that a man named Hunter was entitled to fifty bushels
of corn, which had not been separated from the mass;
and that five or six hundred bushels were to be shelled
by the plaintiff, and delivered to a brother of the
defendant, and that had not been done. There is some
evidence to sustain the claims thus made. But the evidence on the part of the plaintiff tends strongly to show
that by the agreement and the payment of the fifty dollars, the parties intended to transfer to the defendants
the title to all the corn, subject to the right of the plaintiff to retain for his own use two or three hundred
bushels from the broken crib, and that when the money
was paid the defendant said to the plaintiff: "The
money is yours, and the corn is mine," to which the
plaintiff assented. Some claim is made that the plaintiff was to haul the corn to the place where the defendant wished to have it delivered, but the jury was authorized to find that, although the plaintiff was to render
some assistance in hauling, that was not to constitute
any part of the delivery. The rule in regard to the sale
and delivery of personal property was stated in *Cook v.
Logan*, 7 Iowa, 142, to be "that, where some act remains
to be done in relation to the articles which are the subject of the sale,—as that of weighing or measuring, or,
as in this case, that of separating and setting them
apart from the bulk, so that they may be distinguished
and identified,—the performance of such act is a prerequisite, and until it is performed the property does
not pass to the vendee." That rule was, in effect, applied
or approved in *Courtright v. Leonard*, 11 Iowa, 32;
Rosenthal v. Risley, 11 Iowa, 541; *McClung v. Kelley*,
21 Iowa, 509; *Snyder v. Tibbals*, 32 Iowa, 448; *Harwick*

v. Weddington, 73 Iowa, 303; *Mellinger v. Hunt*, 94
Iowa, 351. But the title to property which is the
2   subject of a contract of sale may pass at once,
even though something remain to be done to
ascertain and fix the rights of the parties,—as, to weigh
or measure the property sold. The intent of the parties
is of controlling importance. In *Bank v. Reno*, 73 Iowa,
146, it was said: "The question whether the title to
personal property which is the subject of a contract has
passed to the vendee under the agreement is one of
intent. If there has been an actual delivery, and nothing remains to be done to ascertain the price or quality
of the article, the strong presumption is that the intention was to pass the title." In *Riddle v. Varnum*, 20
Pick. 283, it was said: "But in the case of sales where
the property to be sold is in a state ready for delivery,
and the payment of money, or giving security therefor,
is not a condition precedent to the transfer, it may well
be the understanding of the parties that the sale is perfected, and the interest passes immediately to the vendee, although the weight or measure of the article sold
yet remains to be ascertained. Such a case presents a
question of the intention of the parties to the contract."
See, also, *Brown v. Wade*, 42 Iowa, 649; *Hurd v. Cook*,
75 N. Y. 454; *Kimberly v. Patchin*, 19 N. Y. 330; *Mac-
kellar v. Pillsbury*, 48 Minn. 396 (51 N. W. Rep. 222);
Leonard v. Davis (66 U. S.), 1 Black, 476; *Cushman v.
Holyoke*, 34 Me. 292; *Waldron v. Chase*, 37 Me. 414; 21 Am.
& Eng. Enc. Law, 476, *et seq.* We are of the opinion
3   that the jury was authorized to find that the
parties to the contract in question fully intended
that the title should pass to the vendee at the time
the contract was made, excepting as to the corn which
the plaintiff reserved for himself and Hunter. That,
however, was to be taken from the broken crib. If a
part of the corn was to be shelled and taken by a brother
of the defendant, that fact did not prevent the transfer

of title which the parties intended. The plaintiff had not decided what quantity of corn 'he would retain; and, if it be conceded that for that reason the title to the corn in the broken crib did not pass, there was nothing to prevent the absolute transfer of title to the corn in the other crib, for the reason that no part of it was reserved, and nothing remained to do but to ascertain the number of bushels contained in the crib. The jury evidently found that the agreement was effectual to transfer the title to that corn only, for the reason that its verdict, taken with the charge of the court, shows that no allowance was made for any corn in the broken crib. The evidence to sustain that finding is ample.

II. The defendant alleged in his answer that the corn in controversy had been raised on land owned by one Erickson, who had a landlord's lien on the corn for unpaid rent; and for that reason the plaintiff had no right to sell the corn. The plaintiff testified as a witness. He was asked on cross-examination in

4	regard to the rent. An objection to a question which inquired as to the amount of rent due was sustained, and of that ruling the defendant complains. It was based on the ground that the question was not proper cross-examination, and, we think, was correct.

III. It appears that a man named Hunter had possession of the farm where the cribs containing the corn in question were at the time it was sold, and that he had charge of the corn. The plaintiff testified that when the sale was made he went to that farm, but that Hunter was gone, and he spoke to Hunter's wife. He

5	was then asked if he notified Mrs. Hunter that he had sold the corn to the defendant, and to let him have it when he came for it, and was permitted to answer, notwithstanding an objection of the defendant, "Yes, I notified her that I had sold the corn to Mr. Spies." Mrs. Hunter was also permitted to testify that the plaintiff, at the time and place stated, told her that he had sold the corn to the defendant. The defendant complains of these rulings on the ground that the statement testified to was not made in his presence, and that it tended to corroborate the plaintiff's claims in regard to the sale, and was prejudicial. We do not understand that it was proven to establish a sale, but to show what the plaintiff did to complete the delivery of the corn. What was said to Mrs. Hunter was designed for her husband, and, under the circumstances of the case, was properly given in evidence.

IV. It appears that in February, 1893, the plaintiff executed to his mother a mortgage upon all of his crops to be grown on the Erickson farm during that year. The mortgage purported to secure a promissory note for the sum of one thousand and seventy dollars, was recorded, and does not appear to be satisfied of record. It was pleaded by the defendant to show that the plaintiff did not have a right to sell the corn in question. The plaintiff testified that he had executed the mortgage, and caused it to be recorded, before he told his mother of it; and that, when informed in regard to it, she had refused to accept it. The defendant makes some objection to his testimony upon that point, but, as he does not argue the objection, we need not notice it further. This is true of other objections referred to by the defendant.

Paragraphs of the charge to the jury are criticised, but, so far as the objections thus made are material, they are disposed of by what we have already said. There does not appear to be any sufficient ground for disturbing the judgment of the district court, and it is AFFIRMED.

EMMA INGHRAM, *et al.*, v. THE NATIONAL UNION, Appellant.

Appeal: REVIEW OF VERDICT. Under Code, section 2837, subdivision 6, providing that when a verdict is not sustained by
sufficient evidence, or is contrary to law, a new trial can be
1 granted, a verdict will not be disturbed on the ground that it is
not sustained by the evidence, unless it is so manifestly against
the weight of evidence as to show that it was the result of passion or prejudice.

RULE APPLIED. In an action on a life policy the defense was suicide.
Deceased was county clerk   A witness testified that on Sunday
morning about nine o'clock he went into the clerk's office, and
heard two shots, and on opening the vault door found the gas
4 burning, and deceased's body at the foot of the stairs in the vault,
and a revolver, with two empty chambers, lying near. There
were two wounds on the body of deceased, one of which was sufficient to cause death   *Held*, that a verdict that deceased did not
commit suicide was not supported by the evidence.

New Trial. Where a motion for new trial urges that a motion for
verdict should have been sustained in spite of a conflict in the
2 evidence, that conflict must be resolved against the moving party.
If, then, there is not sufficient evidence to sustain a verdict the
motion for new trial should be sustained and, otherwise, overruled.

Burden of Proof: SUICIDE. Where the defense to an action on a
8 life policy is suicide, the burden of proof to establish the same is
on the defendant.

Special Interrogatories. In an action on a life policy, a refusal to
submit a special finding, "Do you find that the deceased committed suicide?" was proper, where the defense was suicide, as
5 such finding was directly involved in the general verdict.

SAME: *Accidental death.* A refusal to submit a special finding, "Do
you find the deceased was killed by any other person?" was properly refused, as not presenting a controlling issue, for defendant
5 would be liable if the death was by accident, no matter who
caused it.

Appeal from Des Moines District.—Hon. James D. Smyth, Judge.

Thursday, October 21, 1897.

This action is to recover upon a certificate of life insurance issued by the defendant on the life of W. D. Inghram in the sum of three thousand dollars, wherein the plaintiffs are named as the beneficiaries. The application of W. D. Inghram, which is made a part of the certificate and contract, contains this provision: "I further agree that no benefit whatever shall be paid upon my death should I suicide within two years after becoming a beneficial member, whether at the time of committing suicide I shall be either sane or insane." Question is made in the pleadings as to whether the death of Mr. Inghram occurred within the two years after he became a beneficial member. The court instructed as claimed by the defendant, namely, that the death did occur within two years after deceased became a beneficial member. This was favorable to the defendant (appellant), and it makes no complaint of the instruction; and, the plaintiffs not having appealed, this instruction must be accepted as the law of the case. The only defense pleaded is "that the said decedent died on or about the 14th day of October, 1894, and within two years of becoming a beneficial member of said defendant committed suicide, by reason whereof any and all rights of the said W. D. Inghram and of his family and beneficiaries became and were forfeited." The plaintiffs, in reply, denied these allegations, and herein we have the only issue in the case. Verdict and judgment were rendered in favor of the plaintiffs for the amount claimed, from which judgment the defendant appeals.—*Reversed.*

Chas. J. Kavanagh, Geo. S. Tracy, and *Sam'l K. Tracy* for appellant.

Seerley & Clark for appellees.

GIVEN, J. — I. Subdivision 6 of section 2837 of the Code provides that a new trial shall be granted when "the verdict, report, or decision is not sustained by sufficient evidence, or is contrary to law."

1   Appellant moved for a new trial on these grounds, and now complains that said motion was overruled, contending that the verdict is not sustained by sufficient evidence. The only question submitted to the jury was whether or not the deceased committed suicide, and the court instructed that, if the jury found that he did, its verdict should be for the defendant; and, if it failed to so find, it should be for the plaintiffs. The correctness of this instruction is not questioned, and it therefore stands as the law of the case. The verdict being for the plaintiffs, the jury must have failed to find that the deceased committed suicide, and the question now to be considered is whether there is sufficient evidence on this issue of suicide to sustain the verdict. It is a well established rule that the verdict of a jury will not be disturbed by the appellate court on the ground that it is not sustained by the testimony, unless it is so manifestly against the weight of evidence as to show it to have been the result of passion or prejudice. See note to subdivision 6, section 2837, Miller's Code. It is also an established rule that, where the evidence is conflicting, it is the province of the jury to pass upon the conflict, and the courts will not interfere in such cases. See same note. *Meyer v. Houck,* 85 Iowa, 319, does not modify nor change these rules. Under the rule of that case it is the duty of the

judge to direct a verdict "when, considering all the evidence, it clearly appears to him that it would be his duty to set aside his verdict if found in favor of the party upon whom the burden of proof rests." In

2   ruling upon the motion for a verdict or a motion for a new trial on the ground that the verdict is not sustained by sufficient evidence, where the evidence is conflicting, the conflict must be resolved in favor of the party against whom the motion is made, and, if then there is not sufficient evidence to sustain a verdict for that party, the motion, should be sustained, but, if otherwise, it should be overruled. We may say here, however, that in our view of this case, there is no substantial conflict in the evidence bearing upon the issue of suicide, and that the only room for contention is as to the conclusion that should be drawn from this uncontroverted evidence. The instruction referred to above is grounded upon the presumption that where death is shown it will be presumed to have resulted from natural or accidental causes, and not from murder or suicide.

The court also instructed,—and correctly so,—

3   that the burden was upon the defendant to establish its defense of suicide. Guided by these rules, we now inquire whether this verdict is sustained by sufficient evidence.

II.   On October 14, 1894, W. D. Inghram was clerk of the court for Des Moines county, which office he had held for several successive terms, and was then the nominee of his political party for election to another term. Defendant sought to prove that charges of defalcation had been made against Mr. Inghram in a daily paper published on the thirteenth and fourteenth days of October, but this was excluded, because no evidence was offered tending to show that Mr. Inghram had knowledge of such accusations. Evidence of an investigation of his accounts after his death was taken with a view of showing whether or not he was a defaulter. This evidence is quite unsatisfactory, and leaves it doubtful whether he was a defaulter in any considerable sum; and we think it is not very material to the inquiry to determine whether or not he was a defaulter. On Saturday, October 13, 1894, for some cause, Mr. Inghram was not at his office, but left it to the care of his deputy, Mr. Irwin. On the night of the thirteenth, Mr. Irwin closed the shutters to the window in the vault in the office, locked up the vault, turned the combination of the vault, and locked the office. C. C. Fowler, guardian of these plaintiffs, and who was called by them, testifies, in substance, as follows: That on Sunday morning, October 14, 1894, about 10 o'clock, he went into the clerk's office; that while there he heard two shots, ten seconds apart, but was not able to locate them; that he thought they were in the basement, and that on leaving the office he noticed the handle of the safe; that he went into the hall, and from there into the auditor's office, where Mr. Guelich, Mr. Garret, and Mr. Southerland were; that after two or three minutes he spoke to these persons about hearing the shots, whereupon they all went into the clerk's office. These four gentlemen and Dr. Fleming, who was immediately called, substantially agree as to what followed. The found the vault doors closed, with the handle turned, but not locked. Upon opening the door, they found powder smoke in the vault, the window shutters closed, and a gas jet in the vault burning, and turned low. After opening the vault, they heard several groans, but, owing to the darkness, could not see anything in the vault. After procuring a light, they found the dead body of Mr. Inghram at the foot of the spiral stairs in the vault, and a self-cocking revolver, with two empty chamber, lying near the body. The only conflict in the evidence of these witnesses is as to the distance the revolver lay from the body, some saying that it was two or three feet, and one that it was six or eight feet; but this discrepancy is explained by the fact that the revolver had been taken up and laid down again. They all agreed that the revolver was not in the hand of the deceased. Mr. Irwin identified the revolver found in the vault as being similar to one that had been used on a criminal trial, and that had been put away in the vault, with the loads in it, for preservation, by direction of the deceased. Mr. Irwin was not able to say whether or not this was the identical revolver. Upon removing the body from the vault, Dr. Fleming discovered a gunshot wound, which he says was sufficient to cause death. He says: "I didn't examine carefully enough to find the second wound until the next day. That was right back of the ear." Mr. Unterkircher, the coroner and undertaker, who was also present, observed that there were two wounds on the body at the time it was taken from the vault; "one right back of the ear, and the other in the temple on the right side, right in the hair." It is evident that the wound observed by Dr. Fleming on Sunday was the one in the temple in front of the ear. Mr. Unterkircher says: "When I washed the body, there were no discolorations or powder burns on the hair or body. The hole in the temple showed kind of jagged edges about the size of a lead pencil. There was no singeing of the hair, and no powder burns on either of the wounds. There was no *post mortem* examination had." The defendant also introduced in evidence the verdict of the coroner's jury, which was identified by the coroner, wherein the jury found "that the deceased came to his death by a pistol shot, self-inflicted while in a state of temporary insanity, caused by financial trouble." It is upon this evidence that the defendant relies as establishing the defense of suicide. In rebuttel, the plaintiffs

introduced evidence of which the following is the substance: Dr. J. W. Holliday, having shown himself qualified as an expert, testified as follows: "A wound
inflicted with a 38-caliber revolver through the head,
right in front of the hair, is considered a mortal wound;
as also a wound made by a revolver back of the ear, and
in the hair. * * * Two fatal wounds inflicted on the
same individual are generally considered to be done
by some one else, and not self-inflicted. It is not very
satisfactory to tell the cause of death from an external
examination of the body after death, without making
a *post mortem* examination. Where a wound having
been inflicted in the head as was stated, the shot of the
first mortal wound would practically make it impossible for him to make the second one, on account of the
shock. He couldn't make the second shot. The usual
effect upon the muscles of the hand holding the weapon
in a self-inflicted wound is that the weapon is held tight
in the grasp in case of sudden death." The doctor
further testified to the effect that, where the person
shoots himself with a pistol held in his hand, there
would be powder burns and singeing, unless the weapon
was held directly against the body, in which case the
powder and ball would go directly into the wound, and
there would be no flash outside. He further said: "I
don't pretend to tell the jury that the man shot himself,
and did not fire two shots; only give the general rules.
Yes, sir; the general rules have exceptions." Dr.
Fleming identified certain works as standard, parts of
which were offered in evidence, and it was agreed that
Doctors Stone and McKitterick would testify the same
as Dr. Holliday. The extracts from the standard works
offered in evidence sustain the general rule as testified
to by Dr. Holliday, and show but little, if anything, in
addition, material to this inquiry. The plaintiff also
introduced evidence in rebuttal showing that deceased

"shot left-handed," and that "he couldn't see out of his
right eye to amount to anything." This, with the testimony of Mr. Fowler, already noticed, was all the evidence offered in rebuttal.

III.   W. D. Inghram's death was not from natural
causes, but from a pistol shot wound or wounds in the
head inflicted by himself, accidentally or intentionally,
or by another. The present inquiry being whether it
was by himself intentionally, we only consider the
probabilities or improbabilities of accident or homicide, as they may tend to prove or disprove death by
suicide. In our view of the evidence introduced by the
defendant, and that of Mr. Fowler, introduced by the
plaintiffs, we think that but one conclusion can be
fairly and properly arrived at therefrom, and that is
that Mr. Inghram's death resulted from pistol shot
wounds intentionally inflicted by himself. It is true
that the evidence does not clearly disclose a reason for
such an act, and that mere conjecture may not be
resorted to to find the reason. It is often true that the
motive of the suicide is undiscovered; but that is no
reason for ignoring established facts in an investigation
like this. The time, place, and circumstances of the
death, as shown in the evidence before us, seem to be
inconsistent with any other conclusion than that of suicide. It was on the Sabbath, and in the seclusion of the
vault, where the act was least likely to be interfered
with. The four men were at the vault within five minutes after the shots were fired, and found the doors
closed, the vault full of smoke, and no person was seen
or heard to go from the place. There were no powder
marks or singeing, as there would have been had the
shots been fired within seven feet of the head, unless
the weapon had been against the head. If the shots had
been fired by another, it would most likely have been at
some distance from the head, yet, because of the size of
the vault, within seven feet; and in that case, according

to the testimony, there would have been powder marks
and singeing of the hair. The absence of these is quite
convincing that the death was not by the hands of
another. The fact that there were two wounds renders
the theory of accident highly improbable, for it is difficult to conceive how the deceased could have accidentally inflicted these two wounds upon himself. It
may be that it would have been impossible for deceased
to have inflicted these wounds "shooting left-handed,"
but Mr. Anderson, who says he shot left-handed, seems
to have observed this when shooting by sight. That,
when shooting by sight he shot left-handed, was probably because of the blindness of his right eye; but it
does not follow that in the darkness of that vault he did
not shoot right-handed. It seems highly probable that
the wounds were inflicted with the pistol, with the two
empty chambers, found in the vault, and that this is
the pistol that was placed in the vault as stated by Mr.
Irwin. If this is true, it is improbable that it was fired
by another than deceased. The general rules given by
Dr. Holliday and by the authors of the works in evidence are undisputed, but it remains to see their application to the facts of this case. The doctor says a
wound inflicted with a 38-caliber revolver through the
head, in front of the hair, or back of the ear, is considered a mortal wound. He also says that two fatal
wounds inflicted on the same individual are generally
considered to have been done by another, and not self-
inflicted. To apply these rules, let us inquire whether
there was a wound through the head in front of the hair,
or back of the ear, and whether there were two fatal
wounds. Dr. Fleming was the only physician who
examined the body, and he tells us that at the time it
was taken from the vault he found a hole in the front
of his head at the commencement of the hair, which
was sufficient to cause death; and that he did not discover the wound back of the ear until the next day.

The doctor gives no further description of the wounds. Mr. Unterkircher, the only other witness who gives any description of the wounds, describes the one in the temple as already quoted, but gives no description whatever of the other wound, further than to say that it was back of the ear. No witness says that the wound back of the ear was through the head, that it penetrated the head, or that it was a fatal or mortal wound; therefore that wound does not come within either of the general rules first stated by Dr. Holliday. We may well infer from the fact that this wound was not discovered by Dr. Fleming on his first examination, and is not described other than as we have stated, that it was not a mortal or fatal wound, and that the cause of death was the wound in the temple. This being true, it was entirely possible for the deceased to have inflicted the wound back of the ear, and in ten seconds thereafter to have inflicted the mortal wound in front of the ear; for, under the rule as stated, it is only when two fatal wounds are inflicted that the presumption is against suicide. The reason of the rule is that, having received one fatal wound, the suicide is incapable of inflicting another. It is further stated as a general rule, that "the usual effect upon the muscles of the hand holding the weapon, in a self-inflicted wound, is that the weapon is held tight in the grasp in the case of sudden death." From this it is argued that, as the pistol was not in the grasp of the deceased, the death was not suicidal. If by sudden death is meant instant death, this was not such, for the deceased was heard to groan several times after the witnesses had come to the vault. Whether the weapon would be retained in the grasp would depend upon circumstances,—such as the position of the body at the time the shots were fired, and the manner in which it fell. Deceased was lying at the foot of the spiral stairs, but whether upon the stairs or elsewhere, when he fell, we do not know. In the face of other facts tending so strongly to show suicide, we think it should not be said, merely because of this one circumstance, that the other facts should be ignored. Another rule relied upon as rebutting the claim of suicide is the absence of powder marks or singeing. Dr. Holliday's testimony shows that where a shot is fired from a 38-caliber revolver at from two to seven feet from the body powder marks will show, but when the revolver is held directly against the head the powder and ball would go directly into the wound, and there would be no flash outside. We have seen that there were no powder marks or singeing about those wounds, and this, we think, is quite convincing, not only that death was not caused by another, but intentionally by the deceased himself, in placing the weapon directly against his head. It may be said that, if this is true, then surely the wound back of the ear penetrated the head; but not necessarily so. Dr. Holliday says: "It is not very satisfactory to tell the cause of death from an external examination of the body after death without making a *post mortem* examination." No such examination was made, and the probability seems to be that the shot back of the ear was fired at such an angle as not to penetrate the head, and that thereupon the mortal wound upon the temple was inflicted. Our examination of the facts leads us to the conclusion that the verdict is not supported by the evidence before us.

IV. Appellant complains of the refusal to give certain instructions asked. We have examined these instructions, and find that the legal principles presented therein were quite fully covered by the instruc-
5　tions given. Appellant also complains of the refusal of the court to submit two special findings to the jury, namely: "Do you find that deceased committed suicide? Do you find that deceased was

killed by any other person?" The first was properly
refused, because it was directly involved in the general
verdict. The second was properly refused, because it
did not present an ultimate and controlling question, as
it does not follow that, because the deceased was not
killed by another, the appellant would not be liable, it
being liable if the death was by accident. For the
reasons already stated, the judgment of the district
court is REVERSED.

R. B. BEESON v. L. C. AND M. D. GREEN, Appellants.

Deed: ASSUMPTION. A grantee by accepting a deed containing a cov-
1 enant by the grantees to pay a mortgage on land is as effectually
bound as though he had signed an agreement to that effect.
Citing *Crawford v. Edwards*, 35 Mich 854; *Huyler v. Atwood*, 26 N.
J. Eq. 504; *Spaulding v. Hallenbeck*, 35 N. Y. 206; *Deck Co. v.
Leavitt*, 54 N. Y. 33.

ACTION AT LAW UPON. An action at law may be maintained against
3 a grantee in a deed on a covenant assuming the payment of a
mortgage debt, without first foreclosing the mortgage. Citing
Burr v. Beers, 24 N. Y. 178; *Follansbe v. Johnson*, 28 Minn. 311
(9 N. W. Rep. 882); *Campbell v. Smith*, 71 N. Y. 26.

PAROL VARIANCE. In the absence of fraud, a covenant in a deed for
2 payment of a mortgage by the grantee is binding upon the latter
who accepted the deed, until reformed, although its incorporation
in the deed was contrary to the previous contract   Citing *Follansbe v. Johnson*, 28 Minn. 311 (9 N. W. Rep. 882); *Coolridge v.
Smith*, 129 Mass. 554.

Appeal from Dickinson District Court.—HON. W. B.
QUARTON, Judge.

THURSDAY, OCTOBER 21, 1897.

ACTION at law on a covenant in a deed assuming
and agreeing to pay a mortgage on certain land. Trial
to jury. Judgment on verdict directed for plaintiff, and
defendants appeal.—*Affirmed.*

J. W. Cory for appellants.

C. M. Brooks and *L. E. Francis* for appellee.

LADD, J.—This action is based on a covenant in a conveyance of a tract of land in Murray county, Minn., by William Deyoe to L. C. and M. D. Green, by the terms of which the grantees assume and agree to pay certain mortgages, including the one sued on, executed by Deyoe to Adeline Dwinell, and assigned by her to the plaintiff. This deed was made and delivered to the defendants in November, 1893, and by them immediately placed on record, and subsequently they sold and conveyed the land. There was no objection to the deed until the beginning of this action, more than two years afterwards. That the deed was accepted is not questioned, nor could it be, under such circumstances. The defendants had made all the use of the instrument for which it was designed. It had served the purpose of transferring title to them, and had enabled them to convey the estate to another. They insist, however, that the deed was made in their absence, and that they never agreed to pay the mortgage. But the agreement to pay is in writing. By accepting the deed they obligated themselves as effectually as though they had signed it. *Crawford v. Edwards*, 33 Mich. 354; *Huyler's Executors v. Atwood*, 26 N. J. Eq. 504; *Spaulding v. Hallenbeck*, 35 N. Y. 206; *Dock Co. v. Leavitt*, 54 N. Y. 35. The terms of the covenant are clear and unambiguous, and oral evidence is not admissible to vary them. Authorities need not be cited in support of this elementary rule, but see *Muhlig v. Fiske*, 131 Mass. 110, where it is said: "The defendant, having, by the delivery, which the jury had found, accepted the deed of conveyance, and thereby obtained the estate which he afterwards conveyed to a third person, and so

made himself liable to the burden which by the terms
of the deed he had assumed, could not (no fraud in the
execution or delivery of the deed being suggested)
impair the legal effect of his own act by oral evidence
that he had never agreed to assume and pay the mortgage, nor authorized nor knew of the insertion of such
an agreement in the deed. Such evidence, except so far
as it tends to show that there had been no delivery of
the deed, was therefore rightly excluded, independently
of a question of pleading." The appellants rely on
Rogers v. Castle, 51 Minn. 428 (53 N. W. Rep. 651), and
Gold v. Ogden, 61 Minn. 88 (63 N. W. Rep. 266). These
are not in point, as in each case it is simply held that
the grantee named took the land as trustee, and did not
accept the deed with the burden imposed. There
2   is no evidence tending to show that any fraud
was practiced on the defendants to induce them
to take the deed, and no excuse is presented for doing
so without reading it. Even though contrary to the
previous contract, they accepted it as prepared, and,
until reformed, are bound by it as fully as though drawn
precisely as agreed. This is the rule ordinarily applied
to written contracts, and finds support directly in point
in *Follansbe v. Johnson,* 28 Minn. 311 (9 N. W. Rep.
882), and *Coolidge v. Smith,* 129 Mass. 554. Whether
the facts presented a case for reformation of the deed
need not be determined, as such relief is not sought, and
could not be granted in an action at law.

II. It is insisted the defendants are not personally
liable for the payment of the debt until the mortgaged
property is exhausted. A stranger to a contract made
for his benefit may maintain an action thereon. *Mills
v. Brown,* 11 Iowa, 314; *Johnson v. Collins,* 14 Iowa, 63;
Johnson v. Knapp, 36 Iowa, 616; *McHose v. Dutton,* 55
Iowa, 728; note to *Linneman v. Moross,* 38 Am. St. Rep.
531 (57 N. W. Rep. 103). A mortgagee may maintain an
action at law on the covenant to pay in the mortgage or

on the note, *Banta v. Wood*, 32 Iowa, 469; *Brown v. Cascaden*, 43 Iowa, 103, and may thereafter foreclose his mortgage, *Morrison v. Morrison*, 38 Iowa, 73. It is not perceived on what tenable ground the same rules do not apply to a grantee in a deed assuming to pay a mortgage for which the grantor is personally liable. Such grantee becomes obligated for the payment of the debt. *Moses v. Clerk of Court*, 12 Iowa, 139; *Wood v. Smith*, 51 Iowa, 156. And on foreclosure personal judgment will be rendered against him. *Corbett v. Waterman*, 11 Iowa, 86; *Thompson v. Bertram*, 14 Iowa, 476; *Bowen v. Kurtz*, 37 Iowa, 239; *Ross v. Kennison*, 38 Iowa, 396; *Bank v. Mesarvey*, 101 Iowa, 285. Applying the

3   rule permitting a stranger to a contract for whose benefit it was made to enforce it, under the cited authorities, there is no escape from the conclusion that an action at law may be maintained against a grantee in a deed on the covenant assuming the payment of the mortgage debt, without first foreclosing the mortgage. *Burr v. Beers*, 24 N. Y. 178; *Follansbe v. Johnson, supra; Campbell v. Smith*, 71 N. Y. 26.—AFFIRMED.

J. E. HILL v. THE CITY OF CLARINDA, Appellant.

Municipal Corporations: OFFICE ROOM FOR MAYOR. Where a city fails to provide an office for the mayor at some convenient place, as required by Code, section 518, he may furnish one himself, and collect from the city the actual, reasonable expense thereof.

SAME. A city which fails to provide the mayor with an office as required by Code, section 518, is only chargeable with its fair share of the rent, fuel, and lights of an office used by the mayor as such, in common with a law firm of which he is a member, although he released his partner from all liability for the rent in consideration of the latter's submitting to the inconvenience incident to having the mayor's office therein.

TRIAL TO COURT: *Evidence.* The action being tried to the court, it was not error to apportion the expense of the office between said firm and the city without proof of the relative value of the use by each.

FINDINGS IN. In a law action tried to the court, the findings and judgment have the force and effect of a verdict by a jury.

Appeal from Page District Court.—HON. WALTER I. SMITH, Judge.

THURSDAY, OCTOBER 21, 1897.

ACTION by J. E. Hill against the city of Clarinda to recover for rent, etc., of an office used by plaintiff as mayor. From a judgment for plaintiff, defendant appeals.—*Affirmed.*

Parslow & Scott for appellant.

F. E. Clark for appellee.

KINNE, C. J. — This was a law action. A jury was waived, and a trial had to the court. The court below filed a written opinion, a portion of which we here set out: "It appears that the plaintiff was mayor of the defendant city from the spring of 1891 to the spring of 1895. He brings this action to recover for office rent, fuel, and lights during said period, which he alleges cost him, and were reasonably worth, five hundred and thirty dollars. The defendant claims to have furnished a proper office for plaintiff as mayor, and that the office rent which he seeks to recover is rent for his own law office, which he used instead of the one furnished him by the city, simply as a matter of choice, and that it was not the intention of either plaintiff or defendant that he should be paid rent for said office. It also sets up that plaintiff never made any demand on the defendant that it furnish him an office. It is provided by section 518 of the Code of 1873: "He (the mayor) shall keep an office at some convenient place in the city, to be provided by the council.' It appears from the evidence that a number of years ago the defendant constructed a two-story building a short distance from the public square, the lower story of which is used as a fire-engine house, and the upper story of which has been used as a council chamber, and for a dance hall and the like. This room or hall is the office which the defendant claims to have furnished plaintiff. The evidence shows it was sometimes used by the mayor as a place in which to try cases which collected a large crowd of spectators. The evidence fails to show that it was ever assigned for use by the mayor as his office by the council of the defendant, and the evidence does not show that it was ever known as a mayor's office. It is a large hall, wholly unsuited for office purposes. I have made a personal examination of the room in question, under an agreement made by the parties in the trial; and, while its situation is not particularly inconvenient, I find it is not reasonably adapted for use as a mayor's office, and has never been known or designated as such. I therefore find that defendant's council wholly failed to provide plaintiff an office at a convenient place in the city, as required by law. It appears from the evidence that when the plaintiff became mayor he was engaged in the practice of law at Clarinda, in partnership with Mr. T. E. Clark, and that, wishing to use the same room for a mayor's office and for the firm law business, he informed Mr. Clark, in substance, that, if he would submit to the inconvenience incident to having the mayor's office in their office, he would release Mr. Clark from all liability for his share of the rent; and he now wishes to collect of defendant the entire rent of the room, with cost of heating and lighting it. I am of the opinion that, the defendant having failed to furnish a proper office for plaintiff, he had the right to furnish one, and collect the actual, reasonable expense of the city. 19 Am. & Eng. Enc. Law, pp. 540-543. I am also of the opinion, however,

that plaintiff could not use the office in question both
as mayor's office and as a law office for the firm of Clark
& Hill, and charge the city with more than its fair share
of the rent, fuel and lights." The court found that the
plaintiff was entitled to a judgment for two hundred
and fifty dollars, with interest and costs, which was
entered in his favor. Appellants complain of certain
rulings upon the rejection of evidence. In every case
the ruling was proper.

Complaint is made because the court allowed a
part of the claim, in the absence of evidence showing
the relative value of the use by the city and of that by
Clark & Hill. There was no error in the action of the
court. He had the evidence before him, showing the
total rent, and amount for fuel and lights paid. It also
showed what use was made of the office by the firm,
and by the plaintiff as mayor; and, in view of all of the
evidence, the allowance of the court was fair and reasonable. In a law action tried to the court, the findings
and judgment have the force and effect of a verdict of a
jury. The evidence is ample to support the judgment,
and it is AFFIRMED.

GARFIELD GOODRICH, Appellant, v. THE BURLINGTON,
CEDAR RAPIDS & NORTHERN RAILWAY COMPANY.

Railroads: NEGLIGENCE: *Jury question.* The fact that a railway
company lays its tracks in a public street, with the space between
the main rail and guard rail wider than is usual or necessary, and
1 without properly filling below the balls of the rails, will warrant
a jury in finding negligence in an action by one whose foot was
crushed by approaching cars before he could extricate it from
between the main rail and the guard rail, where it was caught
while he was walking along the street.

SAME. The question as to the negligence of a railroad company in
failing to stop detached cars before reaching a boy whose foot
was caught between the main and guard rail of a switch track
running laterally through a much used public street, is for the

3 jury upon evidence that the boy's foot was caught just as the cars
·   were started toward him from a point ninety feet distant, that
they moved only at the rate of two or three miles an hour, that sev
4 eral employes were in close proximity to the cars and heard the
emergency signal which another employe gave just as they were
started, and other evidence tending to show that the cars might
have been stopped before they reached the boy.

CONTRIBUTORY NEGLIGENCE: *Jury question.* A boy fourteen years
old is not, as matter of law, guilty of contributory negligence in
permitting his attention to be diverted to a moving train as he
was crossing a railroad track running laterally through a city
5 street, precluding recovery for injuries from being struck by moving cars while his foot was held between the main and the guard
rail of the track, although he could have easily avoided catching
his foot if he had noticed the condition of the track, where he
was unaware of such condition.

Same. Contributory negligence of a boy in catching his foot between
the main and guard rail of a switch track does not preclude his
recovery for injuries from being run over by moving cars if the
4 cars could have been stopped before reaching him by the use of
due diligence on the part of the employes, after seeing his dangerous condition.

HIGHWAYS. A railroad company is bound so to construct, maintain,
and use its tracks laid in a city street as not unnecessarily to
2 endanger persons who use the street properly, and is liable to a
person, in the exercise of due care, who is injured by reason of its
failure to observe such duty.

SAME. A railroad company does not, in the absence of an express
provision to that effect, have the right to the exclusive use of the
portion of the street in which its tracks are laid, and the people
2 are not confined to the sidewalk, but are entitled to use all parts
of the street in a proper manner and for proper purposes, subject
to the rights of the company.

Evidence. Evidence that the narrow walk on one side of a street was
made dangerous by a guard rail of a railroad track which was
near, if not in, the walk is admissible in behalf of the plaintiff in
7 an action against a railroad company for personal injuries, where
the defendant claims that he should have used that walk instead
of walking in the middle of the street.

Ordinances. Municipal ordinances are competent to show that the
6 right of a railroad company to the use of the street in which its
tracks are laid laterally, is not exclusive.

Appeal from Linn District Court.—HON. W. P. WOLF,
Judge.

FRIDAY, OCTOBER 22, 1897.

ACTION at law to recover for personal injuries
alleged to have been caused by negligence on the part
of the defendant. A jury was impaneled for the trial
of the cause, and evidence was submitted. At the close
of the evidence for the plaintiff, the district court sustained a motion of the defendant to direct a verdict in
its favor. A judgment was rendered against the plaintiff for costs, and he appeals.—*Reversed.*

Rickel & Crocker for appellant.

Preston, Wheeler & Moffit and *S. K. Tracy* for
appellee.

ROBINSON, J. — The plaintiff is a minor, and
appears by his next friend. In June, 1894, when he was
about fourteen years of age, while he was walking
across Fourth street, in Cedar Rapids, his left foot was
caught between a main rail and a guard rail of one of
the defendant's railway tracks, which were laid in the
street, and was run over by a car, and so injured that
the limb was necessarily amputated. The evidence
tends to show the following facts: Fourth street
extends from north to south, and is crossed at right
angles by several streets, among which are C and D
avenues, the latter being farthest north. From a point
south of C avenue, to a point a considerable distance
north of D avenue, several railway tracks, including
switches, are laid and maintained in Fourth street. In
the morning of the day of the accident, the plaintiff,
with a companion named Oudkirk, went north along
Fourth street, to bathe in the river north of it. They

returned a short time afterwards, and walked for some
distance on the platform of a freight house which is on
the west side of Fourth street, and north of D avenue,
and then started across the street in a southeasterly
direction, in search of a keg of drinking water, which
was usually kept in that locality. They crossed several
tracks without finding the water, and then continued
southward on the street, between railway tracks crossing D avenue. As they approached C avenue, they saw
that it was obstructed by cars which were standing on a
track which was west of them; and wishing to reach C
avenue at a point west of the standing cars, to avoid
them, and when about one hundred feet north of C
avenue, they turned in a southwesterly direction. They
crossed one of the two tracks which were then west of
them, and, in attempting to cross the last rail of the
west track at a switch, the plaintiff's foot slipped
between the rails and below the balls, and was caught
and held so firmly that the plaintiff and Oudkirk could
not loosen it. An instant before that occurred, the cars
which were in charge of a switching crew were started,
the two at the north end were cut off, and propelled
northward on the track in which the plaintiff was
caught, and were not stopped until they had passed
over the plaintiff's foot. The petition alleges that the
accident was due to negligence on the part of the
defendant in the following particulars: In maintaining and operating its track at a place where it did not
have the right to do so; in permitting the guard and
main rail to be in a worn and dilapidated and unsafe
condition, with the opening between them unnecessarily large, without proper safeguards; and in not
using due care in switching the car which caused the
injury, including the keeping of a proper lookout for
danger to persons in the street; in not heeding warnings
of the plaintiff's danger, and obeying signals to stop, in
time to avoid the accident.

I. The evidence tended to show that the space
between the guard and main rails where the plaintiff's
foot was caught was wider than was usual or necessary;
that it had not been properly filled below the
1   balls of the rails; and that had the space between
the rails been of the ordinary width, and filled in
part, as it might have been, the plaintiff's foot could not
have been caught, and the accident would not have
happened. Fourth street, from O avenue northward,
is a public thoroughfare, much used by pedestrians.
There is a walk on the west side, which was used, however, by but a small part of the people who walked
along the street. It was narrow, and so near the railway tracks that passing cars would endanger those who
used it. The rights of the people were not con-
2   fined to the sidewalk, but they were entitled to
use all parts of the street in a proper manner, and
for proper purposes, subject to the rights of the railway
companies having tracks in it. That is well settled.
Bryson v. Railway Co., 89 Iowa, 677; *Railway Co. v.
Bennett*, 9 Ind. App. 92 (35 N. E. Rep. 1033); *Railway
Co. v. Phillips*, 112 Ind. 59 (13 N. E. Rep. 132); *Railway
Co. v. Head*, 80 Ind. 117; *Railway Co. v. Pointer*, 9 Kan.
620; *Railway Co. v. Walker*, 70 Tex. 126 (7 S. W. Rep.
831); Elliot, Roads & S. 478; Patterson, Railway Accident Law, section 154; 24 Am. & Eng. Enc. Law, 33. It
was the duty of the defendant to maintain and use its
tracks and appurtenances with reference to the rights of
the public and the use made of the street. To so construct and maintain its tracks, or to so use them, as to
unnecessarily endanger persons who use the street properly, would be negligence; and, in the absence of contributory negligence, the defendant would be liable for
resulting damages. *Clampit v. Railway Co.*, 84 Iowa,
72; *Smedis v. Railroad Co.*, 88 N. Y. 20; *Frick v. Railroad Co.*, 75 Mo. 599. The evidence would have authorized the jury to find that the defendant was negligent in

not having the guard rail properly placed with respect
to the main rail, and in not having the space between
them properly blocked.

II.   At the time of the accident, cars were being
switched in Fourth street by an engine and crew of the
defendant. The engine was at the south end of a train
of eight or ten cars, the north end of the train being in
O avenue. When the plaintiff stepped between
3   the rails of the track on which he was hurt, the
engine was moved so as to start the north two
cars which had been cut off from the others northward,
towards the plaintiff, on the track he was crossing, at a
speed of two or three miles an hour. An instant after
the cars were started, the plaintiff's foot was caught.
He was then about ninety feet from the cars. One of
the switching crew, named Binko, was opposite the
middle or south end of the north car, a few feet east
of it. Wiley, the foreman of the crew, had cut the cars
off, and was standing near the southeast corner of the
south car. Zeedick, another member of the crew, was
on top of the third car from the north end of the train,
or the first one remaining after the cars were cut off.
Augustine, another member of the crew, was more than
one hundred feet north of the plaintiff. As soon as the
plaintiff was caught, he made an outcry. Oudkirk
turned, and, discovering his condition, joined in the
outcry, and tried to free him. Augustine heard the
cries, and, seeing the plaintiff's danger, he gave Binko
the signal to stop, halloed, gave a second signal to stop,
and ran for the approaching cars. He reached them
when they were yet several feet south of the plaintiff,
but, before he could climb upon and stop them, they
had passed over the plaintiff's foot, although they were
stopped within two or three feet of him. A boy who
heard the outcry, after waiting a few moments to satisfy
himself as to the cause, ran a distance of more than
three hundred feet, and reached the plaintiff before the

north car touched him. It is not shown that any of the
men with the train saw the plaintiff before the accident, but the evidence tends to show that Binko saw
Augustine's signal to stop, and repeated it to the men
in charge of the engine, and that the hallooing of the
plaintiff, Oudkirk, and Augustine was so loud as to be
heard the distance of a block or more south of where
Binko and Wiley were. See *Ford v. Railway Co.*, 69
Iowa, 627. The signal given by Augustine was an
emergency signal, and was designed as a direction, not
only to stop the train, but also the detached cars. Had
there been a brakeman on one of the moving cars, on
the lookout for danger to persons on the track, it is
clear that the cars would have been stopped in time to
avert the accident. Some of the evidence tended to
show that Binko and perhaps others of the crew could
have stopped the car after he received Augustine's signal. We do not say that it was the duty of the defendant to be on the lookout for persons caught in its guard
rails, but it was required to use reasonable care and
diligence, in view of the condition of its yard and tracks,
and the use which pedestrians rightly made of the
street, to prevent accidents. Considering the use made
of the street, the positions occupied by employes of the
defendant, the distance of the moving cars from the
plaintiff, the signals given and outcry made, we are of
the opinion that whether the defendant was negligent
in not sooner stopping the cars was a question of fact
4   for the jury; and this, we think, is true, even
though it be found that the plaintiff was negligent in permitting his foot to be caught by the
guard rail. If, after his danger was known to the
defendant, it failed to use due diligence to stop the cars
and avoid the accident, it would be liable. *Sutzin v.
Railway Co.*, 95 Iowa, 304; *Orr v. Railway Co.*, 94 Iowa,
423; and cases therein cited.

III.   It is said that negligence on the part of the
plaintiff contributed to the accident, and for that reason
he should not recover.   Whether he was negligent
     depends upon all the circumstances of the case.
5   He was not a trespasser upon the street, but was
     there by right.   Until he discovered that the
crossing at C avenue, in the direction in which he
wished to go, was blocked by cars, he was in a place of
safety.   When he found the crossing blocked, he
attempted to cross the street at a safe distance from a
train which was not in motion.   He did not know anything of the condition of the guard rail which he
attempted to cross, nor did he know anything of the
danger of being caught by it.   His attention appears to
have been drawn to the train which was moved while
he was in the act of crossing the track.   It is evident
that, had he observed the opening formed by the guard
rail, he could easily have stepped over it; but in view
of the facts stated, and his youth and lack of knowledge,
it cannot be said, as a matter of law, that in permitting
his attention to be diverted from the place where he
was walking, to the train, he was negligent.   The
defendant, in support of the claim that the plaintiff was
negligent, relies upon the rule that a person having
two ways of travel is negligent if, without good reason,
he leaves the safe for the unsafe way, and cites numerous cases as applicable in this case.   Among them are
Hansen v. Building Co., 100 Iowa, 672, *Ferguson v.
Railway Co.*, 100 Iowa, 733, *Ely v. Des Moines*, 86 Iowa,
55, which clearly are not in point.   The case of *O'Laughlin v. City of Dubuque*, 42 Iowa, 539, involved the liability of the city for injuries sustained by one who, without
reason, left the walks provided for pedestrians, and
attempted to cross an icy street, the condition of which
he knew; and is readily distinguishable from this.   In
Cosner v. City of Centerville, 90 Iowa, 33, it appeared

that the plaintiff knowingly and without sufficient reason attempted to pass over a portion of a sidewalk
which he claimed was unsafe, but the condition of
which he knew. The case of *Thomas v. Railway Co.*, 93
Iowa, 249, involved an alleged trespass upon the
defendant's right of way. The cases of *Merryman v.
Railway Co.*, 85 Iowa, 634, and *Masser v. Railway Co.*,
68 Iowa, 602, also involved trespasses. The plaintiff in
Richards v. Railway Co., 81 Iowa, 426, followed, without
sufficient reason, a route which he must have known to
be dangerous, without making reasonable effort to
anticipate and avoid danger. We do not think any of
these cases sustain the claim that the acts of the plaintiff constituted negligence in law.

IV. The appellant complains of the refusal of the
district court to permit the introduction in evidence of
certain ordinances of the city. As we understand the
claim of the appellant, they were intended to
6   show that the defendant's right to the use of
Fourth street was not exclusive. The ordinances
did not refer to the defendant, but if it can be shown
that it succeeded to the rights granted by the ordinance,
and is subject to the restrictions therein contained, the
ordinances would be competent for the purpose stated,
as tending to show the rights of the defendant. Whether
the ordinances were competent for any other purpose
we do not determine.

V. Complaint is made of the refusal of the court
to permit the plaintiff to show that the narrow walk on
the west side of Fourth street was made dangerous by
a guard rail which was near, if not in, the walk.
7   In view of the conclusion we reach, it is only
necessary to say as to this that if the defendant
claims that the plaintiff should have used that way,
instead of walking in the middle of the street, he should

be permitted to show that it was dangerous. We conclude that the district court erred in taking the case
from the jury, and its judgment is REVERSED.

108   4
105   1

The First National Bank of Sigourney and The
Keokuk County Bank v. Redhead, Norton,
Lathrop & Company, Appellants, Elizabeth K.
Woodman, Executrix, *et al.*

Appeal: ORDER NUNC PRO TUNC: *Transcript.* The courts may order
a correction of their records of a prior date to conform to the
facts as they existed at that date, but they cannot change the
records so as to show that a fact existed on a prior date that did
not then in truth exist; and an order that a transcript of evidence
for the purposes of an appeal be filed *nunc pro tunc* as of a date on
which it was not actually on file is not authorized and does not
cure the failure to file the transcript within the time allowed by
the statute.

Appeal from Keokuk District Court.—Hon. Ben McCoy,
Judge.

Friday, October 22, 1897.

This appeal is by the defendants Redhead, Norton,
Lathrop & Co. from a decree rendered under the opinion
of this court on a former appeal. 93 Iowa, 668. The
defendant, Elizabeth K. Woodman, executrix, alone
appears to this appeal. She also appeals from an order
of the district court correcting the record. Redhead,
Norton, Lathrop & Co., having first appealed, will be
designated as "appellants." ·

Nathaniel B. Raymond for appellants Redhead
Norton, Lathrop & Co.

Hubbard & Dawley for appellee Elizabeth K.
Woodman.

G. D. Woodin and *J. P. Talley* for plaintiff appellees.

Hamilton & Donohue for appellee W. O. Childs.

Given, J.—We are first confronted with a series of motions and resistances based upon affidavits and amendments to and denials of abstracts, and the appeal from the order correcting the record. These motions and proceedings are quite complicated and lengthy, and to treat them in detail would require more space than should be given to them in this opinion. The following will be sufficient to say concerning them: The decree appealed from was rendered January 6, 1896, and notice of appeal served February 6, 1896. On September 23, 1896, appellee filed her motion to dismiss the appeal and affirm the judgment because no abstract was on file. Appellants served their abstract September 22, and filed it October 7, 1896, and show sufficient reasons for the brief delay. Therefore this motion is overruled. On January 23, 1897, appellee moved to strike from the abstract all that part purporting to set out the evidence, and to affirm the judgment, on the ground that the judge's certificate to the transcript of the evidence does not certify that it contains all the evidence offered, but simply that it contains the evidence introduced, and that the transcript, with the certificate of the judge (afterwards signed) that it does contain the evidence offered, was not filed until July 7, 1896, which was after the time allowed for filing such transcript. Prior to this motion appellants sent the transcript that had been filed March 30, 1896, to the judge, for further certification; and on July 6, 1896 the judge signed a second certificate to said transcript, certifying that it contained all the evidence offered or introduced. This transcript, thus certified, the judge on that day placed

in the express office at Oskaloosa for transmission to
the clerk at Sigourney, with a written order "to re-file
the transcript of the shorthand notes of the evidence
taken in said cause and heretofore filed in said cause
March 30, 1896. You are further directed to enter the
foregoing as of date July 6, 1896, *nunc pro tunc.*" In
the ordinary course of transit, the transcript would not
reach Sigourney until between 5 and 6 o'clock P. M. of
July 6, and did not reach the clerk's office until July 7,
on which day the clerk entered the same as then filed,
but did not make any record of the order of the judge.
On February, 1897, appellants filed their motion in
the district court, asking, among other things, that the
entry and filing mark of said transcript be changed to
read, "Re-filed July 6, 1896." Appellee appeared and
resisted this motion, and on the hearing the motion was
so far sustained as to order the clerk to enter upon the
record, *nunc pro tunc,* said written order of the judge
made July 6, and from this order defendant Woodman
appeals. Appellees' motion to strike and her appeal
rest upon the fact that the transcript, duly certified,
was not filed within the time required, and the claim
that the court had no power to order it filed as of July
6. In the recent case of *Calef v. Cole,* 93 Iowa, 681, it
is said of section 2742 of the Code of 1873: "Under this
section, it has always been held that unless the translation of the reporter's shorthand notes is filed in the
lower court within six months from the time of entering
the decree, or, as has sometimes been said, within the
time allowed for an appeal, the case cannot be tried
de novo in this court;" citing prior cases. This
transcript, duly certified, was not in fact filed in the
lower court within the time required, unless said order
of the judge, made July 6, and the subsequent order
of the court that said order of the judge be entered of
record *nunc pro tunc,* constitutes a filing as of July 6.

That courts may order a correction of their records of a prior date to conform to the facts as they existed at that date is not disputed, but we do not find it to have ever been held that they may change the records so as to show that a fact existed on a prior date that did not then in truth exist. It is an undisputed fact that this transcript, duly certified, was not on file July 6, and therefore we conclude that the order for filing it as of that date was unauthorized. Such being our conclusion, it follows that the order that said transcript be filed as of July 6 must be reversed, on the appeal of Mrs. Woodman, and her motion to strike sustained. In this condition of the record, there is nothing further for this court to consider, and the decree of the district court is therefore affirmed on the appeal of Redhead, Norton, Lathrop & Co. We may add that we are content with this result, as, upon an examination of the case on the record as presented by appellants, we think the decree now appealed from is in entire harmony with our former opinion. *Reversed* on the appeal of W. K. Woodman, and *affirmed* on the appeal of Redhead, Norton, Lathrop & Co.

SUSAN E. MOORE v. THE UNION FRATERNAL ACCIDENT ASSOCIATION, F. R. CROCKER, and J. E. LOCKWOOD, Appellants.

Insurance: POLICY, BY-LAWS AND STATUTE: *Notice.* A member of a mutual life insurance association is advised that the indemnity is limited to a percentage of the assessment upon the membership as provided by the articles of incorporation and by-laws of the association, notwithstanding that the policy on its face is an absolute promise of indemnity, where it contains an indorsement on its back to the effect that it is issued pursuant to Iowa Laws 1886, chapter 65, under which "the benefits herein provided are derived from payments by policy holders, as ordered by the board of directors."

INCORPORATIONS: *Recovery against.* An officer or incorporator of a mutual insurance association cannot, in the absence of fraud or deception, be held liable to a beneficiary because the policy on its
8 face was an absolute promise of indemnity, whereas the indemnity is limited by statute and the articles of incorporation to the amount of an assessment, where the member, in securing the insurance, knows that the company was mutual and constructed on the assessment plan.

SAME: *Evidence.* That an insurance association is precluded from proving the application in an action on the policy because a copy thereof was not attached to or indorsed on the policy as required by Acts Eighteenth General Assembly, chapter 211, section 2, does
8 not preclude an officer or incorporator sought to be held liable because of the misleading form of the policy, from using the application to show that the insured was not misled to his detriment by the form of the policy.

Misappropriation: EVIDENCE. No misappropriation of funds by the officers of a mutual benefit society is shown by evidence merely
4 indicating the receipts and amounts expended for different purposes, without any showing as to whether these were improper.

Incorporation of Mutual Benefit Society: CONSTRUCTION OF STATUTE: *Notice.* Acts Twenty-first General Assembly, chapter 65, enacted to regulate the organization and operation of mutual benefit societies is complete in itself; and persons organizing under it
1 need comply only with its requirements, and need not publish notice of intention to incorporate, nor include the word "mutual" in the title of the society, as required by Code 1873, sections 1122 and 1140.

Appeal from Council Bluffs Superior Court.—HON. J. E. F. McGEE, Judge.

FRIDAY, OCTOBER 22, 1897.

ACTION at law by plaintiff, as beneficiary of a certificate of life insurance issued April 27, 1892, to John D. Moore, who died December 7, 1893. Trial to court; judgment against defendants for the full amount of the policy; and they appeal.—*Reversed.*

T. M. Stuart for appellants.

Mayne & Hazelton for appellee.

LADD, J.—The first question arising on the record
is whether the Union Fraternal Accident Association
was organized as required by the statutes of this state.
All the provisions of chapter 65 of the Acts of
1   the Twenty-first General Assembly were complied with. But it is insisted this was simply
amendatory of the law as it existed, and that by failing
to follow the provisions of sections 1122 and 1140 of the
Code of 1873, by publishing notice of intention to incorporate, and by including the word "Mutual" in the title,
the incorporation was not perfected, and the incorporators are chargeable as partners. An examination of
chapter 65, referred to, demonstrates that, excepting
statutes applicable to all insurance alike, it is complete
in itself, and was so intended by the legislature. It was
enacted for the purpose of regulating the organization
and operation of mutual benefit associations, as plainly
stated in the title; and such associations as are not
already in existence are prohibited from engaging in
business before complying with all the provisions of the
act. On the other hand, upon compliance with the act,
the auditor of state is required to issue a certificate
authorizing the association to transact business for one
year from April 1 of the year of its issue. Section 18.
The association is therefore organized to do business
without doing more than comply with the conditions of
this act. Throughout the chapter associations are
referred to as "organized under this act," and penalties
are imposed for violations thereof. The publication of
notice, as required in section 2, after approval of the
articles of incorporation, obviates the necessity of some
other kind of notice, and the whole plan is essentially
different than that provided in section 1122 and 1123
of the Code. By fixing a rule for the adoption of a name
in section 3, the other method seems to be excluded; and

the necessity of including the word "Mutual" is obviated by requiring each application to have printed in
red ink, in a conspicuous manner along the margin of
the application, these words: "It is understood and
agreed that the amount to be paid, when the certificate
or policy issued on this application becomes a claim,
shall be dependent upon the amount collected from an
assessment to meet such claim." Section 4. The term
"Mutual" shall be included only in the titles of companies organized as provided in chapter 4 of the Code,
and there was no attempt to organize this association
under that chapter. The laws of the Twenty-first General Assembly take the whole subject of insurance
under mutual benefit companies out of chapter 4 of the
Code, prohibit such insurance "upon any other event
than that of death or disability resulting from accident
to the member," and make complete and ample provisions for their organization, management, and
control.

II. It is said the policy on its face is an absolute
promise of indemnity. That part preceding the naming
of benefits is in these words: "In consideration of the
warranties in the application of this certificate,
2   which application is made a part of the contract,
and the sum of five dollars as a membership fee,
and of such future payments as may be required under
its articles of incorporation and by-laws, does hereby
accept John D. Moore, of Brimfield, state of Illinois,--
occupation, proprietor and salesman agriculture store,
—a member of this association, subject to all the conditions hereinafter contained, and entitled to the following benefits." No conditions other than above set
out appear in the body of the policy, but under the
heading "Agreement and Conditions under Which This
Certificate is Issued and Accepted," on the back of the
policy, is this among other provisions: "This policy is

issued pursuant to chapter 65 of the Laws of 1886 of the
State of Iowa, under which the benefits herein provided
are derived from payments by policy holders, as ordered
by the board of directors." So that the insured was
fully advised that payments should be made as required
by the articles of incorporation and by-laws. These
were expressly referred to as controlling the future payments, and became a part of the policy. *Simeral v.
Insurance Co.*, 18 Iowa, 319; *Davidson v. Benefit
Society*, 39 Minn, 303 (39 N. W. Rep. 803); *Walsh v.
Insurance Co.*, 30 Iowa, 133; *Hobbs v. Association*, 82
Iowa, 107. The articles limit the amount to be paid in
event of loss to one assessment less ten per cent. That
the company was managed on the assessment plan was
in fact fully understood by the assured. On the application signed by him was printed, in red ink, the clause
heretofore referred to, clearly stating how the
indemnity, in event of loss was to be provided.

3   A copy of the application was not attached to or
indorsed on the policy, as required by section 2 of
chapter 211 of the Acts of the Eighteenth General
Assembly, and for this reason the company could not
plead or prove the application in an action on the policy. *Cook v. Association*, 74 Iowa, 746; *McConnell v.
Association*, 79 Iowa, 757. But this does not preclude an
officer or incorporator sought to be held liable for loss,
from using such evidence in showing that the insured
was not misled to his detriment. Annual dues and a
number of assessments had been paid by Moore. Surely,
if he, in securing the insurance, knew the company was
mutual, and conducted on the assessment plan, his beneficiary is not in a position to complain against members or officers with reference to the mere form of the
policy. Under such circumstances there was no fraud
or deception upon which to base a cause of action. To
permit one member to recover from another in such a

case would violate the plainest principles of justice. See *Foster v. Pray*, 35 Minn. 458 (29 N. W. Rep. 155).

III.   Were the funds of the company misappropriated by its officers?   The original articles provided that ten per cent. of each assessment shall be reserved and invested in a fund, and "be used to guarantee 4   members of this association against excessive assessments in any one year." This was amended at the members' annual meeting, October 13, 1891, and before the certificate of Moore was issued, so as to permit the use of such fund in defraying the reasonable expenses of collecting the assessments and adjusting losses, and any excess over this was to be transferred to the benefit fund.   Also, any surplus derived from membership fees or dues over the requirements to properly conduct the business were to be transferred to the reserve fund.   Now, the evidence fails to show that of the ten per cent. anything remained after payment of the cost of collecting assessments and adjusting losses; nor does it appear that there was any surplus of dues and membership fees after payment of the amount required to manage the business.   A membership large enough to pay losses in full was very desirable to every member, and much of the expense was incurred to this end.   The officers did not profit by it.   Whether the efforts were legitimate we are not advised.   It was not a profitable enterprise to them or the insured.   The evidence utterly fails to show any misappropriation of funds.   It simply indicates the receipts and amounts expended for different purposes, and as to whether these were proper the record is silent.   The judgment must be REVERSED.

KINNE, C. J., took no part.

CHAS. COUNSELMAN & COMPANY, Appellant, v. EMANUEL
REICHART.

Gambling Contract: EVIDENCE. Defendant telegraphed plaintiff:
"Buy five thousand Sept. oats below thirty-one. Draw on me for
margins," and by a subsequent telegram directed plaintiff to "sell
September, and buy May." Defendant failed to put up margins
and the May oats were sold at a loss. Plaintiff paid the loss, and
8 sued to recover the same, but failed to disclose from whom he
purchased, or to produce any memorandum of the transactions;
while defendant denied that the purchases were actually made,
and testified that in ordering such purchases he did not intend
any delivery of the grain to him. *Held,* that a verdict for
defendant was warranted.

SAME. To render a contract in grain futures void as a mere speculation on the chances of rise and fall of the market, with no intention to deliver the grain, both parties thereto must have contem-
1 plated that no delivery would be made; and the contract between
commission merchants and a customer is not void on that
ground, although the customer intended, only, to speculate on
margins without a delivery of the grain, if the commission merchants intended an actual delivery.

SAME: *Intent.* A party to a contract in grain futures may attack
it on the ground that it is a mere gambling contract and may
testify as to his intention with reference to the delivery of the
2 grain when he made the purchase. Citing *Pope v. Hanke,* 155
Ill Sup. 617 (40 N. E Rep 839); *Crandell v. White,* 164 Mass. 54
(41 N. E. Rep 204).

PRESUMPTIONS The jury are warranted in drawing an inference
unfavorable to the existence of the intention on the part of a
commission merchant in purchasing "futures" grain for a cus-
4 tomer, that there should be an actual delivery, from his failure to
produce the paper and documents showing a purchase by him
on the market, in response to the demand of the other party.

Appeal from Cass District Court.—HON. A. B. THOR-
NELL, Judge.

FRIDAY, OCTOBER 22, 1897,

THE plaintiff firm is engaged in the commission business in Chicago, Ill. The defendant, in 1894, was engaged in the grain business at Neola, Iowa, and shipped grain to the plaintiff in Chicago. This action is brought to recover a balance of five hundred and five dollars and forty-three cents on account. June 14, 1894, the defendant, by telegram, directed plaintiff to buy for him five thousand bushels of September oats. On the thirty-first of August, 1894, defendant directed plaintiff to sell the oats, and to buy for him five thousand bushels of May oats. Plaintiff reported to defendant a loss on the September oats of six dollars and twenty-five cents, and charged a commission of six dollars and twenty-five cents, making an aggregate charge against defendant on that transaction of twelve dollars and fifty cents. The purchase of the May oats was reported as made, and, after a neglect or refusal to put up margins by defendant, the grain was closed out January 25, 1895, with a loss, including commission, of three hundred dollars. The losses on the two oats transactions, including commissions, and a balance on account of grain shipped to Chicago, make up the aggregate of plaintiff's claim. As to the balance of one hundred and ninety-two dollars and ninety-three cents, on account of grain shipped, there is no question, and defendant offered to confess judgment for the sum of two hundred and twenty dollars, being for that amount with interest. The contention is as to the claims based on the two transactions in the purchase of oats. The defendant denies the purchase, and avers that the transactions were illegal, as being gambling contracts, in that they were mere speculations in margins, with no intention to make actual purchases or sales of grain. The issues were tried to a jury that returned a verdict for plaintiff for two hundred and seventeen dollars and six cents, being less than the offer of judgment. There was a

judgment on the verdict, and the plaintiff appealed.—
Affirmed.

De Lano & Meredith for appellants.

Swan & Bruce for appellee.

GRANGER, J. — The court instructed the jury that,
inasmuch as it appeared from the evidence that plaintiff, as agent for defendant, made the purchase of the
May oats, and because of defendant's failure to put up
the margins the oats were sold at a loss by plaintiff,
and as it is not claimed that plaintiff, in so doing,
exceeded its authority, and as plaintiff paid the loss, it
is entitled to recover the amount of the loss, with interest, "unless it further appears from the evidence that
the purchase of said oats by plaintiff was, in contemplation of law, a gambling contract." There are some
questions argued quite extensively, about which there
is no dispute, and they may be set at rest without
extended notice. Contracts for grain, where the
1   intention is to merely speculate on the chances
of a rise or fall of the market, and no delivery is
intended, are gambling contracts, and void. It is not
enough, to render a contract void, that the buyer
intends it as a gambling contract, unless the seller par-
ticipates in that intention; that is, if, in the case at bar,
the defendant, in ordering the purchase of the oats, only
intended a speculation upon margins, without a
delivery of grain, and the plaintiff purchased the grain
for actual delivery, it would not be a gambling contract.
To make the contract void as between these parties, the
intention to make a gambling contract must have been
mutual. McClain's Code, section 5349; Acts Twentieth
General Assembly, chapter 93, section 1. The court so
instructed the jury. It also said in its instructions: "In

deciding what the intention of said parties was in making said contracts, you have the right to consider, not
only the direct evidence of the parties as to their intentions, but also, as far as shown by the evidence, how
the contract or contracts were made, and their terms,
who was the purchaser and seller, how the losses on
said contracts were in fact settled, whether any grain
was in fact handled or delivered in the settlement
thereof, and every other fact and circumstance shown
by the evidence, and throwing light thereon."

2   The court permitted the defendant to testify as
to his intentions in ordering the purchase of the
oats, whether there was to be a delivery; and it is
thought the court erred in so doing. We think not. It
was a fact directly involved, and the question we are
considering was ruled in *National Bank v. Packing Co.,*
66 Iowa, 41. In that case, speaking of the intention of
the purchaser in such a transaction, it is said: "This
essential element in the case the defendant was bound
to establish, and there was no better evidence by which
to show it than by proving the intention of the very
party who made the contract in behalf of the defendant." In *Pope v. Hanke,* 155 Ill. Sup. 617 (40 N. E. Rep.
839), speaking of how the mutual intention may be
established, it is said: "This intention may be established, not merely by the assertion of the parties, but
by all the attending circumstances of the transactions."
See, also, *Crandell v. White,* 164 Mass. 54 (41 N. E. Rep.
204). It is said that the uncommunicated motive or
intention of the defendant should not have been
admitted in evidence, because it did not enter into, nor
become a part of, the contract between the plaintiff and
the defendant. If both had that intention, it made a
meeting of minds upon that fact, and that is what made
the contract. It is not to be fairly said that such transactions are carried on without an understanding about
so important a factor of the transaction as whether the

grain is to be delivered or not. Defendant's intention would not control, but it was essential to be known in connection with the intentions of the plaintiff. When both are known, they fix the fact of whether or not there was a mutual intention that the grain was not to be delivered. There was no purpose to make defendant's uncommunicated intentions a part of the contract, except in so far as they were understood, and, together with plaintiff's intentions, completed an understanding.

Much importance is attached to the fact by appellant that the only communications by the parties were by letter and telegrams, which are in evidence, and they make no disclosure of a purpose not to deliver the

3   oats. The directions to buy were: "Buy five thousand Sept. oats below thirty-one. Draw on me for margins." "Sell September, and buy May." It was upon these telegrams that the purchases and sale were to be made. They are evidence on their face that the parties understood what was not expressed. Neither telegram purports to express all that is intended to be understood. In several particulars they are incomplete as to details essential to a complete contract. In view of the generally known fact that business on the board of trade is conducted on a plan of non-delivery of produce, but as a speculation in margins or differences, it may well be said that the fact of whether there was to be a delivery of the grain in question was one of understanding between the parties, independent of the orders for purchases. This understanding, under the issues, was a matter to be established by proof. Each party testified to the intention as to delivery. Other evidence was submitted, and the jury may have found that no purchase was made by plaintiffs, or, if made, that it was with no intention of a delivery.

4   Plaintiffs, if they made the purchases in good faith, knew of whom they made them, and the particulars; so that they could have disclosed the facts.

They were asked to make exhibits of papers and documents showing the transactions, and they said the written memoranda of the purchases would be furnished by the bookkeepers. None was so furnished. A fair inference is that none could be furnished favorable to plaintiffs. In the face of a denial that such purchases were made, and a charge that the transactions were illegal, and with exclusive knowledge of the particular facts, and how they could be disclosed, the plaintiffs failed to give light as to the facts, where it especially devolved on them to do so because of such exclusive knowledge. We think the verdict has support in the evidence, and the judgment will stand AFFIRMED.

FRANK ODELL, Appellant, v. W. H. COQUOLETTE, *et al.*

Appealable Order. An order setting aside a default is not appealable because it is not one which affects a substantial right and, in effect, prevents a judgment from which an appeal might be taken; and such appeal will be dismissed on the court's own motion.

Appeal from Linn District Court.—HON. WILLIAM THOMPSON, Judge.

SATURDAY, OCTOBER 23, 1897.

ACTION for the recovery of specific personal property. There was a default entered for plaintiff, because of a failure of defendants to appear. This default was entered April 9, 1896. April 28, 1896, the court, on motion of defendants, set aside the default, and plaintiff appealed from such ruling.—*Dismissed.*

Arthur A. House for appellant.

A. J. Vinton and *Giffen & Voris* for appellees.

GRANGER, J.—The appeal, as we have said, is
from an order setting aside the default. The effect of
the order was to permit a trial on the merits, and a
judgment from which an appeal could be taken. Code,
section 3164, specifies what orders are appealable. The
only provision of the section that could be claimed to
authorize an appeal in this case is subdivision 1, as follows: "An order made affecting a substantial right in
an action, when such order, in effect, determines the
action and prevents a judgment from which an appeal
might be taken." In *Walker v. Pumphrey*, 82 Iowa,
487, in considering what orders are appealable, it is said
that the question of whether one is rightly held to be in
default does not pertain to the rights of the parties to a
remedy, but simply to the course to be pursued to
obtain a remedy; that such an order does not affect a
substantial right, which "determines the action and prevents a judgment from which an appeal might be
taken." In *Quinn v. Insurance Co.*, 82 Iowa, 550, speaking of certain rulings, it is said: "These were all matters pertaining to the practice, the course of proceedings in the case, and did not pertain to or affect the
rights of the parties to remedies or defenses, if pursued
as required by law. The same remarks are applicable
to the order overruling the motion to strike, and for a
default made by plaintiff." In this case the default
had been entered, but, notwithstanding, the order did
not prevent a judgment from which an appeal might be
taken. From that judgment plaintiff might not desire
to appeal. If he did, he could, with a proper record,
have reviewed the ruling on the motion to set aside the
default. The question we consider is jurisdictional, and
we are required to take notice of it, whether presented
by the parties or not. *Quinn v. Insurance Co., supra.*
As we are without jurisdiction, the appeal is DISMISSED.

THE OTTUMWA SCREEN COMPANY, *et al.*, Appellants, v. THOMAS STODGHILL, Sheriff, *et al.*

Corporations: TRANSFER OF STOCK: *Notice.* The knowledge by an attaching creditor and the officer levying the attachment on corporate stock, of a previous transfer thereof by the debtor, which has not been entered upon the books of the company, does not
1 protect the transfer from the effect of Code 1873, section 1078, providing that the transfer of shares of stock is not valid, except as between the parties thereto, until it is regularly entered upon the books of the company. Citing *Bank v. Hasting,* 7 Colo. App. 129 (43 Pac. Rep. 691); *In re Murphy,* 51 Wis. 519; *Bank v. Cutler,* 49 Me. 315; *Weston v. Mining Co.,* 5 Cal. 186; *Bank v. Folsom,* 7 N. M. 611 (37 Pac. Rep. 253).

Costs: REVIEW OF APPEAL. The supreme court will not disturb the
2 taxation of costs where the record does not show what the costs were, and no abuse of the court's discretion is shown.

Appeal from   Wapello District   Court.—HON. F. W. EICHELBERGER, Judge.

SATURDAY, OCTOBER 23, 1897.

THIS is an action in equity to restrain the defendant sheriff from selling certain shares of stock. The lower court found for the plaintiffs as to ten shares of the stock, and perpetually enjoined their sale. As to the other shares in controversy, the finding was for the defendants, and as to them the temporary injunction was dissolved, and a special execution ordered to issue for their sale. It was further decreed that plaintiffs pay two-thirds of the costs, and the defendants pay one-third. The plaintiffs except and appeal.— *Affirmed.*

W. S. Coen for appellants.

Morris & Lowenberg for appellees.

KINNE, C. J.—I.   It appears from the record that
one Antrobus owned certificates of stock in the plaintiff company embracing eleven shares, and that the
same were assigned in writing to one Thayer, and were
by him deposited with the secretary of the company;
that the Ottumwa Screen & Construction Company held
a certificate for five shares of stock in plaintiff company, which, when issued, was, by the.holder, deposited
with plaintiff company, under an oral assignment, as
collateral security for two notes which had been signed
by the Ottumwa Screen & Construction Company, E.
B. Jones, and J. H. Antrobus.   Other certificates are
referred to in the record.   As, however, the court found
in plaintiff's favor as to them, they need no further consideration.   Fair, Williams & Co., having a judgment
in their favor as plaintiffs, and against the Ottumwa
Screen & Construction Company as defendants, caused
an execution to issue thereon, and a levy thereunder
to be made by the sheriff upon the shares of stock
before mentioned.   Plaintiffs claim that before
1   the sheriff made the levy he had actual notice
that the stock had been transferred as before
stated.   As to this the evidence is conflicting, though
we think it preponderates in favor of plaintiffs' contention.   No entry had been made of the transfer of said
shares on the books of the company prior to the completion of said levy.   It appears that when the shares
were transferred they were deposited with the secretary
of plaintiff company, where they had remained until
levied upon; that, where the assignment was in writing,
it was attached to the certificate, and in case of oral
transfer the company were also notified of it.   Each of
the certificates of stock contained this provision:
"Transferrable only on the books of said company, in
person or by attorney, on surrender of this certificate."

Plaintiffs claim that the transfers were made in substantial conformity to the statute, and that they were as effectual as if entered upon the books of the company. It is also said that, as the officer making the levy had actual notice of the transfer before said levy, the object of the statute was accomplished, and the creditor acquired no lien thereon superior to plaintiffs' lien. On the other hand, it is insisted that the statute provides that, except as between the parties, a transfer of shares not entered on the books of the company is invalid. The statute reads: "The transfer of shares is not valid, except as between the parties thereto, until it is regularly entered on the books of the company, so as to show the name of the person by and to whom transferred, the numbers or other designation of the shares and the date of the transfer. * * * The books of the company must be so kept as to show intelligibly the original stockholders, their respective interests, the amount paid on their shares, and all transfers thereof. * * *" Code 1873, section 1078. The question before us is: Will a transfer made in any other way than that provided in the statute be effectual to transfer the shares as against a creditor of the transferror who has actual notice of such transfer? While this court has held that a transfer of shares not entered on the books of the company will not be valid as against an attaching creditor who has no actual notice of such transfer, the effect of actual notice in case it exists, has not been determined. *Lumber Co. v. Batavian Bank*, 71 Iowa, 270. In that case, in discussing the meaning of the statute, it was incidentally said: "If attaching creditors of the transferror had knowledge of the transfer, it may be that a court of equity would protect the transferree's rights. It has frequently been so held, but that question is not before us." We think the statute should be construed to mean just what it says. We are

not authorized to insert another exception in the statute, which, in effect, we must do if we hold that the
attachment lien is not superior to the claims of plaintiffs. Plaintiffs construe the statute as if it read: "The
transfer of shares is not valid except as between the
parties thereto, and except as between the transferee
and an attaching creditor of the transferror who has
actual notice of the transfer." That would be ingrafting upon the statute an exception it does not contain.
The holding in the case just cited is followed in *Moore
v. Opera House Co.*, 81 Iowa, 45. The case of *Bank v.
Haney*, 87 Iowa, 106, relied upon by appellants, does
not involve a transfer of stock, and has no application
to the question here presented. The precise question
before us was determined in the case of *Bank v. Hast-
ings*, 7 Colo. App. 129 (42 Pac. Rep. 691). The statute of
that state provides that "no transfer of stock shall be
valid for any purpose, except to render the person to
whom it shall be transferred liable for the debts of the
company, unless it shall have been entered in the proper
book of the company within sixty days from the date of
the transfer, by an entry showing to and from whom it
was transferred." General Statute, section 269. It
was held that the requirement of the statute was absolute, and that the actual notice or knowledge of a creditor that a transfer had been made before his levy
amounted only to knowledge that the transferees had,
by their neglect to have the transfer entered upon the
proper books, lost their right to the stock, and that it
belonged to their transferror, and was subject to attachment at the suit of his creditors. Now, the right of
an attachment or execution creditor to take shares
appearing in his debtor's name upon the company's
books is derived from the act of the legislature, and we
do not discover upon what principle courts can deprive
a creditor of such right simply because he or the sheriff

had actual notice of a transfer of the stock before the
levy was made, when no such exception is to be found in
the statute. 1 Morawetz, Corporations, section 199.
Under statutes in effect like ours it has often been held
that all transfers not entered on the books of the corporation are absolutely void, not because they were
without notice, but because made so by statute. *In re
Murphy*, 51 Wis. 519 (8 N. W. Rep. 419); *Bank v. Cutler*,
49 Me. 315; *Weston v. Mining Co.*, 5 Cal. 186; *Bank v.
Folsom*, 7 N. M. 611 (38 Pac. Rep. 253). The statute
provides that a transfer of stock shall not be valid, as
to third parties, until it is regularly entered on the
books of the company. Its language is explicit.   It
points out just what must be done to protect the purchaser of stock in his holding as against the claim of
creditors of the seller. Its meaning is obvious, and no
argument is needed to show the wisdom of its provisions.   What might be the rule in case a transferee
had exhausted all reasonable means in attempting to
procure the officers of a corporation to make the proper
entries of a transfer on their books, and they had failed
and refused so to do, we need not determine, as no such
case is before us.   The provisions of the statute requiring an entry in the books of the company is imperative,
and in no wise affected by the fact that the creditor
seeking to obtain a lien upon the stock, or the officer
holding the process, may have actual notice of the
transfer before the levy is made.

II. Complaint is made of the order of the
court in apportioning the costs.   No abuse of the
court's discretion is shown.   It does not appear
2   from this record what the costs amounted to.
Upon the whole record, the decree below must be
AFFIRMED.

442|
450

ANNA FAULK v. IOWA COUNTY, Appellant.

Bridges: LIABILITY OF COUNTY. A county chargeable with knowledge of defects in the railing on an approach to a county bridge,
1 is liable for injuries of which the defective railing was the proximate cause

REASONABLE CARE: *Jury question.* Where a team of small horses, hitched to a light road wagon, backed the wagon about eight feet
1 and against a defective railing on a bridge approach, which gave way, it was a question for the jury whether the wagon was backed with force enough to have broken the railing had it been in good condition.

SAME The frightening of a horse, and its consequent backing of a vehicle off a bridge approach, are not such unusual occurrences as
2 to excuse reasonable precautions by the bridge authorities to provide against the accident.

CONTRIBUTORY NEGLIGENCE. A driver whose horse took fright and backed off a bridge approach was not chargeable with contrib-
8 utory negligence because he was driving without a whip, where it appeared that none was ordinarily used or required, and that he
· had no reason to anticipate the act of the horses

EVIDENCE. In an action for personal injuries resulting from the breaking a bridge railing against which a team backed a vehicle, it was not error to admit evidence that a part of the railing near
4 the place of the accident was missing some time before the accident occurred, to show the condition of the remaining rail and notice to defendant.

Reserving Ruling: PREJUDICE. The taking under advisement a motion to strike out testimony is without error where the ruling
5 finally sustaining the motion is accompanied by an instruction to the jury not to regard the testimony.

Appeal: BILL OF EXCEPTIONS: *Misconduct of counsel.* It does not follow from the fact that affidavits showing remarks by attorneys
6 in their arguments to the jury were made a part of the record on appeal by bill of exceptions, that they are competent to prove a disputed fact.

Appeal from Johnson District Court.—HON. M. J. WADE, Judge.

SATURDAY, OCTOBER 23, 1897.

ACTION at law to recover for personal injuries alleged to have been caused by a defective bridge. There was a trial by jury, and a verdict and judgment for the plaintiff. The defendant appeals.—*Affirmed.*

C. E. Vance, county attorney, and *Remley, Ney & Remley* for appellant.

D. H. Wilson and *Slater & Hunt* for appellee.

ROBINSON, J.—On the twentieth day of October, 1894, the plaintiff, two other women, and a man named Sullivan, left the town of Marengo, in a northerly direction, for the town of Watkins. They were riding in a two-seated road wagon drawn by two horses, and Sullivan was driving. When but a short distance from Marengo, they were overtaken and passed by several men who were in a wagon drawn by two horses. The men seemed to be somewhat intoxicated. A few minutes later they drove onto a bridge which crosses the Iowa river, and there stopped for a short time. They then drove over the main part of the bridge, and onto an approach of trestlework one thousand feet in length. When they had proceeded on the approach a distance of three or four rods, they met a team going southward, and stopped, and began to talk with its driver, who also stopped his team. The two teams then so occupied the bridge that Sullivan could not pass them. When the team going northward passed Sullivan, he slackened the speed of his team, but drove over the main part of the bridge, and went within a short distance of the two teams which were obstructing the bridge. The north team was restless, and trying to back, and, to avoid trouble from it, and thinking to avoid the obstruction and delay, and perhaps also because his horses were restless, Sullivan commenced to turn his team towards the northeast, for the purpose of driving down

an inclined way which led from a platform on the east
side of the approach at that point northward to the
bottom land below. The way appears to have
been intended for stock, but seems to have been practicable for horses and wagons. The witnesses do not
agree in regard to the distance Sullivan's horses had
proceeded in the direction of the inclined way, some
stating that they were merely turned in that direction,
while others say that they were on the incline. The
plaintiff objected to going down the incline, stating that
it was closed. At that moment the team commenced to
back, the wagon was forced against the west rail of the
trestle, which was broken down, and the wagon, its occupants, and the horses were precipitated over the side of
the approach to the ground below, a distance of about
nine feet. When the plaintiff was found, she was under
one of the horses, and had received serious injuries, for
which she seeks to recover. She claims that the accident was caused by a defective and insufficient railing,
and that the defendant was negligent in not making it
safe. The defendant denies all negligence on its part,
and avers that, if the plaintiff sustained any injuries
as alleged, she contributed to them by her own negligence. The verdict was for three thousand dollars, and
judgment was rendered in favor of the plaintiff for that
sum, with accrued interest and costs.

I. The railing in question had been in existence,
at the time of the accident, about thirteen years. It
was about three and one-half feet high, and consisted
of posts four by four inches in size, bolted to the outside
of the outside joists or stringers of the approach; a top
cap or railing of the same size, cut half way through
over the tops of the posts to which it was spiked; a hub
board two by four inches in size; and a snow board,
twelve inches wide, nailed to the inside of the posts.
There is some conflict in the evidence in regard to the

condition of the railing, but the jury was fully warranted in finding that its timbers and the stringers to
which the posts were attached were much decayed, that
nails and bolts would not hold in the wood, that one of
the posts which was forced off was held to the stringers
by a single half-inch bolt, which was without a burr or
nut, and that the railing at the place of the accident
was in bad condition, of little strength, and insufficient.

 The approach was a part of a county bridge, and
1 the evidence shows that the defendant was
 chargeable with knowledge of and is liable for
the defects, if any, which existed in the railing. See
Miller v. Boone County, 95 Iowa, 5. The appellant contends that the weakness of the railing was not the proximate cause of the accident; that the wagon in which
the plaintiff was riding was backed against the railing,
with such force that it would have been broken, and the
accident would have happened, even though the railing
had been sufficiently strong to resist all pressure which
reasonable care should have anticipated; and that the
accident was due to the viciousness and bad conduct of
the horses which Sullivan was driving. We think the
jury was justified in finding that this claim was not well
founded. The horses were small, each weighing but
about six hundred pounds. They had been used in the
butcher business about four years, and had been accustomed to back into the slaughter house used in the
business, and would do so quickly, and would sometimes
back in other places; but it is not shown that they
backed with much force, nor that the practice was a
dangerous one. They were active and spirited, but are
not shown to have been vicious nor unmanageable,
under ordinary circumstances. When they commenced
to back on the bridge, Sullivan tried to stop them by
speaking to them, and by slapping them with the reins,
but without effect. The wagon was light, and was
spoken of by most witnesses as a buggy. The pole had

been splintered, but was considered sufficiently strong
to use in driving about the country. The approach was
but sixteen feet in width, and the distance the wagon
was backed does not appear to have been more than
eight feet, and may have been less. · It is not shown ·
that it was backed against the railing with much force,
and we think the jury may well have found that the
force applied was not great, and that it was not sufficient to break down the railing, had it been in good condition. It was said in *McClain v. Incorporated Town
of Garden Grove,* 83 Iowa, 235, to be the duty of the
defendant in that case to provide for the use of the
bridge there in controversy in the usual manner, to
guard against ordinary contingencies or those which
might reasonably be apprehended, and to provide rail-
ings of sufficient height and strength to resist any
. weight or pressure which would be applied under
            ordinary circumstances. It is not so uncommon
2   for horses to become frightened on a bridge, and
            back the vehicle to which they are attached, that
it can be said to be a contingency for which the corporation responsible for the bridge should not be required
to provide; and, while the corporation should not be
held responsible for the failure to provide a railing
which would successfully withstand all pressure which
could be applied by such means, yet it may well be held
liable for the failure to provide against the pressure
which the jury may rightly have found was applied in
this case. In other words, the occurrence in question
was not of such an unusual character that it was not
the duty of the defendant to provide against it. See
Manderschid v. City of Dubuque, 25 Iowa, 109; *Byerly
v. City of Anamosa,* 79 Iowa, 205; *Miller v. Boone
County,* 95 Iowa, 5. Much is said in regard to contrib-

utory negligence of the plaintiff or on the part of Sullivan which is alleged to be imputable to her. It

3   is true that Sullivan did not have a whip, but it
is shown that none was ordinarily used or
required with the horses he was driving, and it does not
appear that he had any reason to anticipate their act in
backing against the railing. We think the jury was
authorized to find that he acted with reasonable care
and prudence, and that neither he nor the plaintiff contributed to the accident by any negligence on their
part. We have examined the authorities upon which
the appellant relies, but we think they are not in point,
or, in view of the settled law of this state, that they
should not lead us to a different conclusion.

II. A witness stated that a part of the cap or top
rail eight feet in length at or near the place of the accident was missing some time before the accident
occurred. The defendant asked to have that por-

4   tion of the testimony stricken out, but the court
denied the request. We think the testimony was
proper, especially when taken with other evidence, as
tending to show the condition of the railing at the place
of the accident, and upon the question of notice to the
defendant, of its condition. *McConnell v. City of Osage,*
80 Iowa, 297; *Munger v. City of Waterloo,* 83 Iowa, 560.

III. A witness testified that one post and a part of
the railing were out at or near the place of the accident
for a considerable length of time before the accident
occurred, and he was then permitted to state that he
had on two different occasions informed the county
auditor of the defendant of the condition of the railing.
The defendant objected to the testimony respecting
notice to the auditor. The ruling on the objec-

5   tion was reserved for some time, but the objection was finally sustained, and the testimony
was stricken out. The appellant complains because the
ruling was not made when the objection was first stated.

It is not uncommon for courts to take questions presented to them under advisement, and we do not think
any abuse of discretion in deferring the ruling in question is shown.   Moreover, the court charged the jury
not to consider the evidence in regard to the notice to
the auditor, and prejudice could not have resulted to
the defendant from the alleged error.

IV.   Other rulings on evidence are objected to and
paragraphs of the charge to the jury are criticised.   We
have examined the objections thus made, but do not
think any of them are well founded.   The trial was fair,
and the charge was quite favorable to the defendant.

V.   The appellant complains of remarks made by
attorneys for the plaintiff in their argument to the jury.
The alleged remarks are not shown by the certificate of
the trial judge, but by affidavits.   It appears that
6   the affidavits were made a part of the record by
bill of exception.   It does not follow that, because
they are of record, they are competent to prove a disputed fact.   *State v. La Grange,* 99 Iowa, 10; *State v.
Burton,* 103 Iowa, 28.   But it is said that the remarks
in question were made in the absence of the trial judge,
and hence were not within his knowledge, and could
only be shown by affidavit.   Conceding, for the purposes
of this case, that under the circumstances stated it was
competent to show the remarks of attorneys, by affidavit,
counter-affidavits could also be used for the same purpose, and they were filed in this case.   When the affidavits and counter-affidavits are considered together,
they do not show that the attorneys for the plaintiff
made any remarks which could have been prejudicial
which were not authorized by the evidence in the case,
or the statements of adverse attorneys.   It appears that
at least a part of the matters in dispute was investigated
at the time by the trial judge, and that his conclusion
was against the claim made by the appellant.   We are

of the opinion that cause for disturbing the judgment
of the district court has not been shown, and it is
AFFIRMED.

STATE OF IOWA V. J. A. PRESSMAN, *et al.*, Appellants,
and thirty-one like cases.

Mulct Law: CONSENT OF VOTERS. Section 17, chapter 62, Acts of
the Twenty-fifth General Assembly, provides, among other
things, that the payment of a specified tax, and filing with the
county auditor of a written consent to the sale of liquor, signed
by a majority of the voters of a city, shall, upon the "following
conditions," be a bar to proceedings under the statute prohibiting
1   such sale. One of the succeeding conditions is the filing with the
auditor of a copy of a resolution of consent of the city council.
Held, that the action of the city council in passing such a resolution is not a determination of the sufficiency of the statement of
consent signed by the voters, which will protect it from collateral
attack in a suit to enjoin a liquor nuisance.

EVIDENCE. In an action involving the sufficiency of such statement
of consent, the best evidence of who were legal voters of the city
2   at the last election is the poll books and registration lists of that
election, although they are not records in such sense, as that they
may not be attacked for fraud.

GRANGER, J., dissenting.

Appeal from Polk District Court.—HON. W. A. SPUR-
RIER, Judge.

SATURDAY, OCTOBER 23, 1897.

ACTION to enjoin the maintenance of a nuisance
in keeping and selling intoxicating liquors. The petition is in the usual form. The answer, in addition to a
general denial, alleges compliance with all the conditions of chapter 62 of the Acts of the Twenty-fifth General Assembly; and that, before engaging in the business of keeping or selling intoxicating liquors, the city
council of Des Moines, acting as a license board, passed
upon the statement of consent, and determined it to be
sufficient, and adopted a resolution consenting that said
business be conducted within the city; and that, owing

to the action of the city council, the court is not authorized to investigate the facts concerning said statement. Decree being entered as prayed, defendants appeal.— *Affirmed.*

C. H. Sweeney and *E. T. Morris* for appellants.

J. J. Davis and *Harvison & Mershon* for the state.

LADD, J.—It is conceded that this case cannot be tried *de novo* in this court, for the reason that all the evidence is not contained in the abstract. Several errors are assigned, only two of which are argued. The first is thus stated by the appellant: Did the city council determine the validity or sufficiency of the petition or statement of consent when it granted the resolution of consent to the defendants? The determination of this question involves the construction of portions of section 17 of chapter 62 of the Acts of the Twenty-fifth General Assembly, which are here set out: "Sec. 17. In any city of five thousand or more inhabitants, the tax hereinbefore specified may be paid quarterly in advance on the first days of January, April, July, and October, of each year, and after a written statement of consent, signed by a majority of the voters residing in said city, who voted at the last general election, shall have been filed with the county auditor, such payments shall, upon the following conditions, be a bar to proceedings under the statute prohibiting such business: (1) The person appearing to pay the tax shall file with the county auditor, a certified copy of a resolution regularly adopted by the city council, consenting to such sales, and a written statement of consent from all the resident freeholders within fifty feet of the premises where said business is carried on. But in no case shall said business be conducted within three hundred feet of any church or

school house." The second condition requires the filing
of a bond, approved by the clerk of the district court,
with the county auditor. Then follow eight other subdivisions relating to the place and manner of conducting the business, and another relating to the payment
of the tax. The filing of the statement of consent and
the payment of the tax are independent of the conditions operating as a bar,—the basis, as it were, without
which these would be of no avail. Only after such statement has been filed and the tax paid will compliance
with the conditions be considered. If this has been
done, then, by observing every condition mentioned in
the eleventh subdivision of the section, including the
filing of "a certified copy of the resolution regularly
adopted by the city council, consenting to such sales,"
such payment becomes a bar, and not otherwise. The
statement must be filed with the county auditor, and
his action filing it is ministerial only. *State v.*
1   *Ashert*, 95 Iowa, 210. The members of the city
council have only such right to inspect it when
so filed as is accorded to citizens generally. Section 21.

If it had been intended that the council pass upon
the sufficiency of the statement of consent, why file it
with the county auditor, instead of the city clerk? No
more importance is attached to the filing of a copy of a
resolution of consent as a condition than the written
consent from resident freeholders owning property
within fifty feet of the premises where the business is
to be carried on, or the filing of the bond approved by
the clerk, except that the council may withdraw its consent. Section 19 provides that "whenever any of the
conditions of this act shall be violated, or whenever the
city council or trustees of the incorporated town shall,
by a majority vote, direct it, or whenever there shall be
filed with the county auditor a verified petition signed

by a majority of the voters of said city, town, or county
as the case may be, as shown by the last general election, requesting it," then the bar shall cease. This
would occur without any action on the part of the
council if the verified petition referred to were filed
with the county auditor. If the council is required to
pass upon the sufficiency of the statement of consent,
why not upon that of the petition withdrawing consent?
Certainly, that of withdrawing consent is quite as
important to the welfare of the city.

It is urged that somebody should determine
whether the statement has a sufficient number of signatures, and has been properly prepared. There is no
greater necessity for this than that compliance with
other conditions named be adjudicated in advance. The
party engaging in this business is required to know
that all the conditions have been complied with, and
must plead and prove compliance therewith in order to
avail himself of the bar. *State v. VanVliet*, 97 Iowa,
387; *Ritchie v. Zalesky*, 98 Iowa, 589. Section 18 of
the act fixes the condition on which any city or town of
less than five thousand inhabitants may come within
the provisions of section 17, heretofore referred to.
Under the rule contended for, each council of such city
or town, in adopting a resolution of consent, must pass
upon the sufficiency of the statement filed with the
county auditor. Municipal councils are not free from
the infirmities which beset the rest of mankind, and
might well be expected to reach different conclusions
upon a question so closely touching the preference,
sentiment, or prejudice of every citizen. An adjudication of an issue by one tribunal of original jurisdiction,
not appealed from, has heretofore been deemed quite
enough to end a controversy. Here it is insisted there
shall be as many adjudications, all conclusive, upon
the one identical issue,—that of the sufficiency of the

statement of consent,—as there are cities and towns
with less than five thousand inhabitants in the county.
Such an anomaly was never intended. Nor could it be
expected that councilmen would make the needed
investigation necessary for the ascertainment of the
truth when the law does not expressly require it. The
decision in *State v. Forkner*, 94 Iowa, 733, rests on the
ground that the liquor traffic is placed under the control
of the municipalities of the state, in the exercise of the
police power. The council may prevent such traffic
by withholding its consent thereto, or discontinue it by
withdrawing such consent after given. It may levy
and collect additional taxes, and adopt rules and ordinances for the regulation of the traffic not inconsistent
with the act. The statement of consent is only a condition precedent to the exercise of such control. Cases
are cited in which statutes are considered requiring an
election to be ordered by the board of supervisors or
township trustees when a petition is filed by a certain
proportion of the electors. The ground on which it is
held that such petition may not be investigated in a
collateral attack in subsequent proceedings is well
stated in *Ryan v. Varga*, 37 Iowa, 78: "The petition for
the vote stands in substantially the same relation to the
subsequent proceedings as an original notice or summons does to the proceedings which it inaugurates. If
it is defective in fact, but is adjudged sufficient by the
tribunal having jurisdiction to decide upon it, such
adjudication becomes conclusive until reversed or set
aside upon an appeal, writ of error, *certiorari*, or the
like." The petitions in such cases are presented to the
body which, in ordering an election, necessarily passes
upon their sufficiency. The action of the city council
is not in terms made dependent on the filing of the
statement, while the order for an election can only be
made upon the filing of a proper petition. The statement is filed with an officer not officially connected with

the duties devolving upon the council, nor is it subject
to its inspection except in the office of another municipality, often located at a considerable distance. Had
the legislature intended to so place the burden of
investigation, it certainly would have provided ready
access to, and the use of, necessary papers, and a method
of procedure. Clearly, such was not the intention, but,
rather, that the person engaging in the liquor traffic
know at his peril that all the prerequisites and conditions required by the law have been fully complied with.
By section 2450 of the Code, adopted since the submission of this case, the board of supervisors of the
county is authorized to pass upon the statement of consent, thus confirming by legislative construction the
conclusion we have reached.

II. The court held that the poll books and registration lists were the best evidence of who were at the
election. The registration laws of this state are strict
and explicit. No ballot can be received
2   at a general election in a city of over
two thousand, five hundred inhabitant unless
the name of the person offering it be on the reg-
istry; and, if any is so received, it is void, and
must be rejected when the result of the election is
involved. Acts Twenty-first General Assembly, chapter
161, section 8. But, for certain reasons, an elector who
has not previously registered may procure a certificate
of registration on the day of election, and cannot vote
without so doing. The lists and certificates are carefully preserved for eighteen months. The name of each
person, when his ballot is received, is entered on two
poll books, one of which is filed with the county auditor,
and becomes a part of the records of his office. The registration lists and the poll books, prepared with such
care, when duly authenticated, and coming from the
proper custodian, are the best evidence of who cast the

ballots at the election. 6 Am. & Eng. Enc. Law, 427, and cases cited; *Dixon v. Orr*, 49 Ark. 238 (4 S. W. Rep. 774); Paine, Elections, 756. This, of course, does not mean that they are records in such a sense that they may not be attacked on the ground of fraud. We discover no error in the rulings of the district court, and its decree must be AFFIRMED.

GRANGER, J., dissents.

THE WESTERN IMPROVEMENT COMPANY v. THE DES MOINES NATIONAL BANK, Appellant.

Corporations: PAID UP STOCK. By plaintiff's articles of incorporation, and by indorsements on its certificates of stock, provision was made that the stock should be subject to assessment for the
1   payment of a mortgage on real estate conveyed to the company by its shareholders, in exchange for shares, and constituting the capital stock of the corporation, which was expressed as paid in
2   full, though the mortgage was outstanding. *Held*, though expressed as paid in full, the stock was not paid for, except in so far as liability to assessment was payment, and the shareholders were bound by the condition making the shares subject to assessment.

SAME: *Personal liability of shareholder.* The assessment being for an unpaid balance due on the stock, the shareholders are personally liable under Code, section 1082, providing that the stockholders
3   shall not be exempt from personal liability for unpaid installments, although the articles of incorporation simply confer power "to assess the capital stock"

Same. A stockholder is individually liable, under Code, section 1082,
3   for an assessment for an unpaid balance due on the stock, even if
7   the articles of incorporation restrict the remedy for failure to pay an assessment, to a sale of the stock.

Same. The exemption of stockholders from corporate debts and the provision of the Code, section 1082, making them individually
3   liable to the amount of the unpaid installments on their stock, to creditors of the corporation, do not apply in an action by the cor-
7   poration for an assessment for an unpaid installment of stock.

ASSESSMENT. There is no merit in defendant's contention that the assessment is void because shares purchased by plaintiff at a sale

4   under a previous assessment were not assessed. The assessment
5   would have to be met by the outstanding shares, as they represent the whole property of the corporation, including the purchased shares.

Notice. Directors of a corporation are required to take notice of an
adjourned session of the annual meeting of the directors ι t which
6   an assessment is made upon the stock, and a notice thereof is not
necessary.

Same. The call for an assessment of the stock of a corporation is
not invalid because it does not name the time, place, or person to
whom the payment is to be made, where the corporation has a
6   place of business and an officer authorized to receive money due
it, as the time under such circumstances is on demand and the
place of business of the corporation is the place the person to
whom payment is to be made, such officer.

Same. The articles of incorporation authorizing assessment to pay
principal and interest on the mortgage debt, and for improving
the real estate, and for other necessary expenses, an assessment
6   made, "to meet outstanding maturing obligations for taxes, bonds,
interest," etc., states with sufficient definiteness, in connection
with the articles of incorporation, the object of the assessment.

STOCK REDUCTION. The purchase of shares of its own stock by a cor-
1   poration having authority to do so, does not operate as a reduction
of the capital stock, where it does not reserve to itself the power
4   to reduce its capital stock.

Banks: CORPORATIONS: *Real estate holding.* The assumption by a
national bank of stock of a corporation which is subject to
8   assessments, for the improvement of real estate other than that
used by the bank, is not *ultra vires* because of the prohibition
against national banks engaging in the improvement of real
estate.

Appeal from Polk District Court.—HON. W. F. CONRAD,
Judge.

SATURDAY, OCTOBER 23, 1897.

THIS action by the plaintiff corporation is to recover
from the defendant corporation, as a stockholder, the
amount of an assessment alleged to have been duly
made upon the stock of the plaintiff corporation. The
issues and facts sufficiently appear in the opinion. The

case was tried to the court, and judgment rendered in favor of the plaintiff.   Defendant appeals.—*Affirmed.*

Dudley & Coffin for appellant.

Barcroft & McCaughn and *Bishop, Bowen & Fleming* for appellee.

GIVEN, J.—It is necessary to an understanding of the question discussed to notice at considerable length the character of the plaintiff corporation. Appellant's counsel makes the following statement, which is 1' sufficiently full, and is supported by the record: "In February, 1891, the plaintiff corporation was organized 'to own, buy, sell, exchange, and lease real estate, * * * to improve the same by erecting buildings thereon and otherwise, and to deal in real and personal property and choses in action,' with a capital stock of 'fifty thousand dollars, divided into shares of one hundred dollars each, to be paid in full at the time of the commencement of this corporation by conveyance to the corporation of the following described real estate, valued at sixty-eight thousand dollars (thereafter amended to read seventy-eight thousand dollars), to-wit: Lots one (1) and two (2), in block ten (10), original town of Fort Des Moines, now included in the city of Des Moines, Polk county, Iowa; and such shares of stock so to be issued to the several stockholders to be according to their interest in said real estate so to be conveyed.'   Provision is made to increase the capital stock by a vote of two-thirds of the outstanding stock to an amount not exceeding one hundred thousand dollars, but no provision is made for reducing it. Sections 3 and 4 of the articles of incorporation are: 'Sec. 3. The board of directors shall have power to assess the capital stock of this corporation at such times and in such amount as may be necessary to meet the several payments of principal and interest upon the mortgage incumbrance which may hereafter be placed upon the real estate above named, or made by this corporation, for refunding of the same as such payments become due. It may be further assessed only for the purpose of improving said real estate, or for other necessary expenses of the corporation; all such assessments for purposes other than the payment of the mortgage incumbrance and interest thereon not to exceed in the aggregate ten per cent. of the capital stock, nor to exceed two per cent. of the capital stock at any one time, nor to be called oftener than once in thirty days. Sec. 4. On the failure of any stockholder to pay any assessment when due, his stock may be sold at a meeting of the stockholders called for that purpose, of which meeting, and the object thereof, the stockholders shall have thirty days' notice by mail by registered letter or by personal service; and the proceeds of the sale of the stock shall be applied to the payment of such assessment, the balance remaining, if any, to be paid on demand of the owner of said stock, whereupon his obligation to the corporation shall cease.' The article also provides: 'The private property of the stockholders of this corporation shall not be liable for any of its debts or obligations,' and 'the annual meeting of the stockholders shall be held on the last Saturday in January of each year,' and 'special meetings of the directors may be called at any time by the president or vice-president.' On the organization of the corporation, the entire capital stock of fifty thousand dollars was issued to the different shareholders, the certificate being in words as follows: 'This certifies that ———— is the holder of ———— shares of the capital stock of the Western Improvement Company, of Des Moines, Iowa, subject to the articles of incorporation of the company, and to the terms and conditions printed on the back

hereof, which are hereby made a part of this certificate.
Transferrable only on the books of the company, in person or by attorney, on the surrender of this certificate.
Witness the seal of the company and the signature of
the president and secretary, this —— day ——, 189 —.'
On the back of each certificate is the following: 'This
stock is fully paid up, but may be assessed at such times
and in such amounts as may be necessary to meet the
payments of principal and interest on the mortgage
incumbrance placed on the property by the Western
Improvement Company, which does not exceed the
amount of twenty-eight thousand dollars, and can never
be increased.   Said incumbrance is payable as follows:
Seven thousand dollars on or before January 27, 1894,
and seven thousand dollars on or before the 27th day of
January of each year thereafter until all is paid.   Said
incumbrance bears interest at the rate of seven per
cent., payable semi-annually on the 27th day of July
and January of each year.   It may be further assessed
only for the purpose of improving said property, or
for other necessary expenses of the company.   All
such assessments for purposes other than payment of
said mortgage incumbrance and interest thereon not to
exceed in the aggregate ten per cent. of the capital
stock, nor to exceed at any time two per cent. of capital stock, nor to be called oftener than once in thirty
days.'   On November 26, 1893, appellant acquired fifty
shares of the capital stock of the plaintiff corporation.
The annual meeting of the plaintiff's stockholders held
January 27, 1894, was adjourned until February 5, and
on that day was adjourned until February 15, 1894, on
which day a directors' meeting was held, and a resolution, as follows, adopted: "On motion of Mr. Wellslager, it was unanimously resolved that an assessment
of twenty-two dollars per share, to use so much thereof
as may be necessary, by levying [be levied] upon the

capital stock of the company outstanding to meet outstanding matured obligations of the company, taxes,
bonds, interest, etc.   *   *   *   All members of the
board being present except W. F. Dummer, and representing all the outstanding stock of the company,
except that held by Mr. Dummer, those present severally waived notice of the assessment on the capital stock
as this day made." Mr. Dummer was a resident of Chicago, and had never attended any of the meetings.
Appellant refused to pay this assessment, and thereupon this action was brought to recover the same, to
which appellant makes several defenses that will be
considered in the order in which they are presented in
argument.

II.   Appellant's first contention is stated as follows: "Corporate stock has been issued as fully paid, by
which act the corporation is bound.   Consequently,
there is no right to assess for unpaid install-
2   ments on the stock, and, if there is a right to
assess, the power exists by virtue of an express
contract." The articles of incorporation provide that:
"The capital stock of this corporation shall be fifty
thousand dollars, divided into shares of one hundred
dollars each, to be paid in full at the time of the commencement of this corporation by conveyance to the
corporation of the following described real estate,
valued at sixty-eight thousand dollars (thereafter
amended to read seventy-eight thousand dollars),
to-wit: Lots one and two, in block ten, of the original
town of Fort Des Moines, now included in the city of
Des Moines." The certificates of stock were subject to
the articles and to the conditions presented thereon.
While the indorsement recites that "this stock is fully
paid," it expressly declares, in immediate connection
therewith, and as a condition thereof, that the stock
represented by the certificate is subject to assessment

for the purposes named. The fifty thousand dollars of
stock was issued in consideration of the property, and
to each shareholder according to his interest in the
property to be conveyed. The plaintiff corporation
accepted the property subject to the payment of twenty-
eight thousand dollars, and protected itself by providing for assessing the stock to pay the same. If the liability to assessment was payment, then the stock was
fully paid, but the liability remained; but, if it was not
payment, the liability is for the unpaid portion of the
stock. We have seen that the consideration for the
stock was the conveyance to the corporation of the real
estate described, clear of incumbrance. This the stockholders did not do, but the corporation accepted the
conveyance subject to the debt of twenty-eight thousand dollars, and made provisions in its articles for
assessing the stock to meet the liability. The certificates are "subject to the articles," and the indorsements
thereon make reference to this incumbrance, and the
right to assess the stock. In receiving the stock the
holder must be held to have consented to these conditions, and to hold it subject thereto. It is plain that
of the consideration to be paid for the fifty thousand
dollars of stock twenty-eight thousand dollars thereof
remains unpaid, and that the stock is assessable for the
payment of this balance. The stock has not been paid
in full, except as the conveyance of the real estate and
the liability to assessment for the twenty-eight thousand dollars constitute payment. This case is similar
in its facts to *Wishard v. Hansen,* 99 Iowa, 307, wherein
it is held that the stock was not fully paid up. This
stock not being paid for in full, the holders thereof are
liable to assessments for the unpaid balance, as provided in the articles of incorporation, and also under
section 1082 of the Code of 1873, which is as follows:
"Neither anything in this chapter contained, nor any

provision in the articles of incorporation, shall exempt
the stockholders from individual liability to the amount
of the unpaid installments on the stock owned by them,
or transferred by them for the purpose of defrauding
creditors, and execution against the company may to
that extent be levied upon the private property of any
such individual."

III.   The articles of incorporation confer power
"to assess the capital stock," and provide that on a failure of any stockholder to pay any assessment, his stock
may be sold.   Appellant contends that it is the
3   stock only, and not the stockholder, that may be
assessed; that the only remedy is the sale of the
stock; and that the stockholder is not personally liable
for such assessments. This assessment being for an
unpaid balance due on the stock, the holder thereof is
individually liable therefor under said section 1082,
even if the articles provide otherwise.   The articles
recognize the obligation as that of the stockholder, in
providing that when his stock has sold for enough to
pay the assessment which he has failed to pay "his obligation to the corporation shall cease."

IV.   It appears that a number of the five hundred
shares of stock were sold for non-payment of previous
assessments, and bid in by the plaintiff, and are now
held by it.   The plaintiff had authority to pur-
4   chase this stock, *Lumber Co. v. Foster*, 49 Iowa,
25; but, not having reserved to itself the power
to reduce its capital stock, the purchase did not operate
as a reduction, Cook, Stocks and Stockholders, section
282. Counsel agree that it is unnecessary to determine
the legal status of these shares. It is manifest, however,
that they were not canceled by the purchase, and that

they were owned and held by the plaintiff at the time
this assessment was made, and were not included
5   in it. Appellant contends that, as the assessment
was not made upon the entire five hundred
shares, it is illegal and void. It is argued that, if plaintiff may omit one share from the assessment, it may
omit all but one, and thereby cause the one to bear the
entire burden. Appellant cites the rule that no stockholder is responsible beyond the proportion which the
shares held by him bear to the whole number into which
the capital stock was divided by the charter; that to
fix the extent of his liability the whole amount of the
par value of the stock held by all stockholders, and the
amount to be paid by the assessment, must be ascertained, and the stockholder be held to contribute to
the payment of the debt for which the assessment is
made, in the proportion that his stock bears to the whole
amount of the capital stock. By the purchase of said
shares they became the property of the corporation.
The outstanding shares represent the entire property
of the corporation, including these purchased shares.
To include the purchased shares in the assessment
would increase the amount to be paid to that extent, as
their assessment must be paid by the outstanding
shares. It is said these purchased shares should have
been assessed precisely as if they were held by an outside party. If so held, the outside party would be liable
for the assessment; but, being held as they were, and
represented by the other shares of stock, there was no
prejudice to the holders of these other shares in
omitting the purchased shares from the assessment.

V. Appellant contends that this assessment is
illegal, for that it was made at a special meeting of the
board of directors of which one of the members, not
present, had no notice; that the call did not give notice
of time, place, or person to whom payment was to be

made, and did not express distinctly the object for
which the assessment was made. The assess-
6   ment was ordered at an adjourned session of the
annual meeting, of which directors were required
to take notice; not at a called meeting. The call does
not name the time, place, or person to whom payment
was to be made. The time was, therefore, on demand;
and, the plaintiff corporation having a place of business,
and an officer authorized to receive money due to it,
that place and that officer were the place and person at
and to whom payment was required to be made. *In re
Cawle & Co.*, 31 Am. & Eng. Corp. Cas. 425, cited by appellant, holds that a resolution for a call, to be valid, must
state the time at which it is to be paid. In that case the
time was not stated in the call, but was fixed by a subsequent resolution, and it was held that there was no
proper call until the second resolution. This decision
is based upon provisions in the company's articles as to
fixing time and place of payment that do not appear in
the articles of this plaintiff. In *Railroad Co. v. Spullock*, .
88 Ga. 283 (14 S. E. Rep. 478), also cited, the action was
brought without any assessment being made. We do
not think these cases are in conflict with what we have
said as to the time and place at which, and the person
to whom, payment was required to be made. The
articles authorized assessments to pay principal and
interest upon the mortgage debt, for improving the real
estate, and for other necessary expenses of the corporation. The assessment was made "to meet outstanding
maturing obligations for taxes, bonds, interest," etc.
Taken in connection with the articles, the resolution
is plain and distinct as to the objects for which the
assessment was made.

VI. Appellant calls attention to the fact that the
private property of these stockholders is exempt from
corporate debts, and cites section 1082 of the Code,

making them individually liable to the amount of the unpaid installments on their stock to creditors of the corporation. From this it is claimed that this action

7   cannot be maintained until the assets of the corporation are exhausted. This is not an action by a creditor, but by the corporation for a debt due to it, and neither the exemption from personal liability for corporate debts nor section 1082 apply to the case.

VII. Appellant further contends that in acquiring the stock upon which this assessment is made its act was *ultra vires*. It is conceded that as a national

8   bank it might acquire stock in another corporation, and be subject to the same liabilities thereon as an individual or holder would be. It is contended that, as appellant cannot engage in the improvement of real estate not necessary for its own use, it had no power to acquire this stock subject to assessment for the improvement of real estate other than that used by it. In acquiring this stock, as it is conceded it had a right to do, appellant did not engage in the business of improving real estate. What we have said disposes of all the questions argued, and leads to the conclusion that the judgment of the district court should be AFFIRMED.

CHARLES BENESH, *et al.*, v. THE MILL OWNERS MUTUAL FIRE INSURANCE COMPANY OF IOWA, Appellant.

Insurance Company: VENUE OF SUIT AGAINST. An incidental prayer for reformation of an insurance policy in a petition to recover the indemnity therein provided, does not take the case out of McClain's Code, section 3789, providing that an insurance com-

1   pany may be sued in the county in which it keeps its principal place of business, or in the county where the contract of insurance was made, or in which the loss occurred, even if the section is limited to actions which are primarily upon the contract of

insurance and would not apply to an action brought solely to reform the policy.

Assignment of Policy: NECESSARY PARTIES TO SUIT UPON. After the loss of certain partnership property by fire one of the partners died, and the other assigned his interest in the insurance policy to one of the plaintiffs. A third party, to whom any loss was payable, under the policy, as security on obligations of the 8 owners of the insured property, released his claims on satisfaction of such obligations. The administrator of the deceased partner and the assignee of the other thereupon sued to recover for such loss, and to reform the policy as to the description of the property insured. *Held*, that plaintiffs were the real parties in interest, and had the right to sue on such policy, without joining such assignors.

REORGANIZATION: *Liability.* In a suit upon an insurance policy it appeared that it was issued by a company bearing the same name as defendant, which subsequently re-incorporated in order to remedy certain defects in its original articles, retaining the 2 same officers and the assets of the original company; that the holders of such policy were treated as members, and paid dues and assessments to such reorganized company as to its predecessor; and that it was determined by resolution that the old policies should be continued in force until new ones were issued at the election of the policy holders. *Held*, that defendant was responsible to the same extent as if it had issued such policy.

Appeal from Tama District Court.—Hon. G. W. Burnham, Judge.

SATURDAY, OCTOBER 23, 1897.

SUIT in equity to reform a policy of insurance, and to recover the indemnity therein provided. The defendant moved to transfer the cause to Polk county, which motion was denied. It demurred to the petition because of a defect of parties, and its demurrer was overruled. It then answered, denying the execution of the policy and its corporate existence at the time the policy was issued. The court entered a decree reforming the policy, and gave plaintiffs judgment for the amount claimed. Defendant appeals.—*Affirmed.*

Berryhill & Henry for appellant.

Struble & Stiger for appellees.

DEEMER, J.—McClain's Code, section 3789, is as follows: "Insurance companies may be sued in any county in which is kept their principal place of business, in which was made the contract of insurance, or in which the loss insured against occurred."

1 Appellant argues that this section does not apply to suits to reform policies of insurance; that it has reference to actions which are primarily upon the contract of insurance. If it be conceded that this be a proper construction, yet it does not follow that plaintiff's motion to transfer should have been sustained. The suit was upon a policy of insurance, and as an incident to this relief the court was asked to declare the terms of the contract. The ultimate relief sought was recovery for the loss insured against, and the suit was properly brought in the county where the loss occurred.

II. The policy was issued to Adam Bruner and John Stransky. Bruner died after the fire occurred, and plaintiff Beckley is the administrator of his estate.

2 After the loss, Stransky assigned to plaintiff Benesh all his interest in the policy. By the terms of the policy, loss, if any, was made payable to John Beal and A. Bruner, as their interest might appear. These parties assigned their interests in the policy to the plaintiffs. None of these assignors were made parties to the suit. Appellant contends that these persons should have been made parties, for that reformation cannot be had in a suit by an assignee of a written contract unless the assignors are made parties. The policy was made payable to Beal to secure the payment of certain obligations he had indorsed for Bruner and Stransky. When he made the assignment, he

acknowledged complete satisfaction of his liability on
these obligations, and released the insured of all his
claims to any part of the money due on the policy.
Surely, he was not a necessary party to the suit.
Stransky, who was one of the insured, assigned all his
right, title, and interest in the policy to Benesh, and
transferred to him all claims and demands of every kind
and nature existing in his favor by reason of the policy
of insurance, and authorized Benesh to demand, and in
his own name sue for, the amount due. The reformation asked for was in the description of the property.
The policy located the building upon the west half of
the northwest quarter of section 14, whereas, in truth
and in fact, it was situate upon the west half of the
northwest quarter of section 23. These plaintiffs were
the real parties in interest, and had the right to sue
upon the policy. We can see no reason for making
Stransky a party, as he had sold all his claim and
demand of every kind or nature existing in his favor
under the policy of insurance. It is a general rule that
the assignment of a debt carries with it every remedy
and security for such debt available by the assignor as
an incident thereto. See cases cited in 2 Am. & Eng.
Enc. Law (2d ed.) p. 1084. The case of *Durham v.
Bischof*, 47 Ind. 211, relied upon by appellant, is not in
point. There an attempt was made to defeat liability on
a contract in an action brought by the beneficiaries
thereof, without making the real persons in interest
parties to the litigation. It is not a case relating to
rights of assignors, as the one at bar.

III.   The evidence clearly shows a mistake in the
description of the premises, which mistake was mutual,
and should be corrected, unless it appears, as contended
by appellant, that it did not issue the policy, and is not
bound by it. The defendant is now doing business
under and pursuant to articles of incorporation adopted

and recorded in January, 1889, after the policy in suit was issued. It appears, however, that at the time the policy was issued a corporation bearing the same name as the defendant was doing business in this state, having its principal place of business at Des Moines. On account of an adverse decision, see *Day v. Insurance Co.*, 75 Iowa, 694, it concluded to re-incorporate. The records show that at the January, 1889, meeting of the policy holders, a resolution to re-incorporate was unanimously carried, and the articles under which the corporation is now acting were adopted. The officers remained the same, at least until the following March; the membership remained practically the same, and no one was dropped except at his request. The insured, under the policy in suit, were treated as members, and paid dues and assessments to the re-organized company as to the old. The premium notes and assets of the old company were transferred to the new, and by resolution it was determined that the old policies should be continued in force until new ones were issued, and that, if the policy holders, after notice of the change, did not elect to take new policies, the old should continue. We have no doubt that the companies remained substantially the same, and that what was done was simply a re-incorporation to meet some of the defects in the original articles and amendments thereto. In any event, the defendant, under its own showing, is responsible to the same extent as if it had issued the policy in suit.

Other questions, with reference to the condition of the record, need not be considered. The trial court was right in reforming the policy and giving plaintiffs judgment.—AFFIRMED.

ESTHER RIDLER, Appellant, v. J. W. RIDLER, Administrator of the Estate of GEORGE RIDLER, Deceased.

Contract: PARENT AND CHILD: *Services.* An express promise of
    compensation is not essential to the existence of a valid claim by
    a daughter against the estate of her father for services rendered
    to him while living in the same family, but it is sufficient if the
5 services were rendered with the expectation on her part of receiv-
    ing compensation, and on the part of the father of making com-
    pensation therefor.

MEASURE OF RECOVERY. An instruction, that in determining the com-
    pensation to be allowed the daughter of intestate for services
    rendered to him, the jury should consider the circumstances of the
4 claimant, as well as those of the family of the intestate, and
    award such sum as will be just to the estate and to the claimant,
    and a fair response to the evidence,—is erroneous, as it includes
    improper elements to be considered in arriving at a proper meas-
    ure of compensation.

Evidence: VOLUNTEER STATEMENTS. In a proceeding by a daughter
    to establish a claim for work and labor against her father's estate,
    the statement, "But, then, Esther (claimant) didn't work at home
1 just as a hired girl," volunteered by a witness for the adminis-
    trator, during her examination in chief, was simply a conclusion
    of such witness, and therefore inadmissible.

SAME. Where such witness, in answer to a question on cross-exam-
    ination respecting the manner in which she would treat a girl
1 who was working for her, replied, "Why, Esther was not con-
    sidered a hired girl at my father's house; she was considered
    as one of the children,"—such answer was incompetent, and not
    responsive.

SAME. The answer of a witness for the administrator in proceedings
    by a daughter of the intestate to establish a claim for services
    in reply to a question as to the worth of such services in the
2 neighborhood, that she did not know because people in that
    neighborhood took care of their parents with the assistance of
    the neighbors, except in the evidence of that trial, and that she
    never heard of a charge being made in such a sense, is irrespon-
    sive, and highly prejudicial, and should be stricken out on motion.

PERSONAL TRANSACTIONS WITH DECEDENT. The testimony of a wit-
    ness for the administrator as to the kind of services claimant ren-
    dered the intestate and his wife, makes the testimony of the

claimant as to the character of such services competent under the
3 proviso of Code 1873, section 3639, that the prohibition of the testimony of an interested party to transactions with a deceased
person shall not extend to any transaction or communication as
to which the administrator shall be examined on his own behalf.

*Appeal from Dubuque District Court.—Hon. J. L.
Husted, Judge.*

MONDAY, OCTOBER 25, 1897.

PROCEEDINGS to establish a claim for work and labor
against the estate of George Ridler, deceased. The
administrator denied the claim, and further pleaded
the statute of limitations, and also pleaded that claimant is a daughter of the deceased, and that, during the
time the labor and work was performed, she lived with
the deceased as a member of his family, and performed
the services as such. Trial to a jury; verdict and judgment for the administrator; and claimant appeals.—
Reversed.

R. W. Stewart for appellant.

Longueville & McCarthy for appellee.

DEEMER, J.—This is the second time the case has
been before us. The first opinion will be found in 93
Iowa, 347. Upon a re-trial, claimant introduced the
same evidence and proved the same state of facts as are
recited in that opinion. The pleadings are the same
with this exception: that appellant filed an amendment
to her claim, in which she stated that it was orally
agreed between herself and father that she should
receive compensation for her services, which should be
paid out of his estate after his death. In the former
opinion we held that the case should have gone to the
jury on the evidence adduced. At the trial from which
this appeal is taken, the case was submitted to a jury,

with the result above indicated. A number of errors
are assigned, which we will now consider.

Mrs. Mathias Thompson, a half-sister of appellant,
was a witness for the administrator. During the course
of her examination in chief, she volunteered this statement: "But, then, Esther didn't work at home
1   just as a hired girl." Claimant moved to strike it
out, as a conclusion, incompetent, immaterial,
and improper. The motion was overruled, and exception taken. This question was propounded to her on
cross-examination: "Q. I suppose you didn't allow a
girl that was working for you to go out of an evening,
or have company come to the house to see her? That
would not be consistent with your ideas of a hired girl's
duty, would it?" To which she answered: "A. Why,
Esther was not considered a hired girl at my father's
house; she was considered as one of the children."
Appellant moved to strike this answer, as not
responsive, a conclusion, incompetent, irrelevant, and
immaterial. This motion was also overruled. These
rulings were manifestly incorrect. The voluntary
statement was simply a conclusion of the witness, *Peck
v. McKean*, 45 Iowa, 18; and the answer to the question
was incompetent and not responsive.

A witness for the administrator was asked this
question: "Q. Do you know what the services of taking
care of them during that time would be worth in that
neighborhood?" To which he responded: "A. I
2   don't know, because I never heard of any one
being hired just specially for that. The most of
them out there, the neighbors turn in, and help, and
their own family takes care of them, and I don't know
as we ever heard of a charge being made, only in the evi
dence here yesterday." Appellant moved to strike the
answer, because not responsive, incompetent, irrelevant, and immaterial. That it was not responsive is

clear, and it is just as apparent that the answer was incompetent and highly prejudicial.

The administrator testified as to the physical needs and condition of his parents, and as to the kind of service that appellant rendered. He also testified with reference to the need of attention at night. Claimant was the called in rebuttal, and questioned as to services she had performed, and the manner of such services. Objections to these questions were sustained, on the ground that the witness was incompetent, under section 3639 of the Code of 1873. This section contains this exception: "But this prohibition shall not extend to any transaction or communication as to which such * * * administrator * * * shall be examined on his own behalf." It seems to us that the claimant's evidence should have been admitted, under the exception contained in the statute. *Bailey v. Keyes*, 52 Iowa, 90.

II. The court instructed the jury that it was necessary for claimant to establish an express promise that she should be compensated for her services. We have held that there must be proof of an express promise, or of such facts and circumstances as satisfy the jury that the services, if any, were rendered in the expectation by one of receiving, and by the other of making, compensation therefor. *McGarvy v. Roods*, 73 Iowa, 363; *Cowan v. Musgrave*, 73 Iowa, 384; *Scully v. Scully*, 28 Iowa, 548. The doctrine of implied contract with relation to such cases as illustrated in the foregoing opinions was not submitted. On the contrary, the court erroneously instructed that an express contract must be proven before there can be a recovery.

III. In the instruction with reference to the compensation to be allowed, the court said to the jury that

they should consider the circumstances of the claimant,
      as well as the circumstances of the family (of
5   deceased), and award such sum as would be just
      to the estate and to the claimant, and a fair
response to the evidence. Manifestly, these are not
proper elements to be considered in arriving at a proper
measure of compensation.

For errors pointed out, the judgment of the district
court is REVERSED.

In the Matter of the Estate of Joseph Z. Moore,
Deceased, Nora L. Carroll, Executrix, Appellant.

Ella R. Moore v. Nora L. Carroll, Appellant.

John W. Foster v. Nora L. Carroll, Appellant.

Appeal: ISSUE BELOW. An action against an executrix for an
accounting was referred for that purpose, and it appeared that
the executrix charged herself in her accounts with the rents of
lands. The referee charged her the same in his report, and no
1   exception was taken thereto and passed on by the district court.
Held, the supreme court, on appeal by the executrix, could not
pass on the question whether she was properly charged with such
rents

Review: *Evidence.* Whether an executrix was properly removed,
2   cannot be determined on appeal, unless all the evidence is in the
record.

Same. Whether a judgment that a widow elected to take under the
8   will was proper, cannot be determined on appeal, unless all the
evidence is in the record.

Appeals from Guthrie District Court.—Hon. A. W.
Wilkinson and Hon. J. H. Henderson, Judges.

Monday, October 25, 1897.

APPEALS were taken by Nora L. Carroll from an
order made in an accounting of herself as executrix of
the estate of Joseph Z. Moore, deceased, from an order

removing her as such, and a decree declaring that she had elected to take under the will.—*Affirmed.*

Bishop Bowen & Fleming for appellant.

Powell & Paschal and *J. W. Foster* for appellee.

LADD, J.—Three separate cases are brought here on this appeal. It appears that Joseph Z. Moore died December 18, 1889, leaving a will, which was admitted to probate February 12, 1890, and, as therein
1   directed, his wife, Nora L. Moore, now Nora L. Carroll, was appointed executrix, without bond. The estate consisted of a large amount of land and personal property. The will provided, in substance, that the chattels should be sold by the executrix, that out of the proceeds thereof she be paid one thousand, two hundred dollars, due her, and, after the payment of the debts of the deceased, the balance, together with the proceeds of the sale of the land, which was directed to be sold, be divided into three parts, one to be paid to the executrix, and the remaining two parts to be loaned on real estate security, and the interest thereon be paid to the four children annually, and, when the youngest attain majority, be divided equally among them. It will be noticed that the money derived from the sale of the property, and not the property, was distributed to the widow and heirs. The executrix converted the personal property into money, collected the rents of the land without selling it, and filed several reports. Ella R. Moore, one of the children, filed a petition in equity, November 15, 1894, demanding an accounting. This was transferred to the probate calendar, and an accounting ordered, being referred for that purpose. To the report of the referee several exceptions were filed, and the account finally settled by the court. The executrix was charged with the rents of the land, and was

only allowed family expenses for one year, and these rulings are the only ones complained of in that proceeding. The questions cannot be passed upon by this court. The executrix charged herself with the rents in her report. The referee did likewise in his report, and no exception was taken thereto and passed upon by the district court. On what theory an executrix could be relieved from accounting for the income of property directed by the will to be converted into a trust fund for the benefit of the heirs, during the time necessary for making the sale, or while wrongfully withheld from sale, may be difficult to understand, and, as the question was not raised in the lower court, need not be considered here. Nor was the authority to disallow large sums improperly charged the estate for family expenses in the report of the referee, ever brought in question in the district court. The exceptions filed do not refer in any way to the disallowance of such items by the referee. That the district court must be given an opportunity to pass upon all questions before their consideration here, is not doubted. *Danforth v. Carter*, 1 Iowa, 552; *Patterson v. Stiles*, 6 Iowa, 54; *State v. Cuddy*, 40 Iowa, 419; *Machine Co. v. Richardson*, 89 Iowa, 225; *Porter v. Goble*, 88 Iowa, 565; *Byers v. Johnson*, 89 Iowa, 278.

II. Upon the application of Ella R. Moore, the executrix was removed, and John W. Foster appointed administrator with the will annexed, in her stead, and of this she complains. But it is conceded the evidence is not all before this court, and without it we cannot determine whether the district court properly exercised its discretion.

III. Foster applied to the court for a construction of the will, and to determine whether the widow had accepted thereunder. The court held that she had elected to take under the will. Whether she had done so can only be determined from the consideration of all the evidence, and, as said before, this is not before us.

While the questions raised do not seem difficult of solution, owing to the condition of the record we cannot consider them, and the orders and decree of the district court will stand AFFIRMED.

ANDREW K. MURRY v. MAX WEBBER, Appellant.

Agency: PLEADING CONSTRUED. In an action for the conversion of goods that had been stored in a building under an agreement with the former lessee, it appeared that G, who was in defendant's employ, and in charge of the building, would not allow the goods to be removed without payment of storage fees that he

1 demanded, and that the goods were soon afterwards destroyed by fire. The answer alleged that "defendant, by his agent, demanded that plaintiff should pay the reasonable value of the storage of said goods" before their removal. *Held*, that defendant admitted the agency of G.

Evidence: AFFIDAVITS: *New trial.* An affidavit made in support of

2 a motion for a new trial is not admissible on the new trial where the affiant is called as a witness.

Appeal from Scott District Court.—HON. P. B. WOLFE, Judge.

MONDAY, OCTOBER 25, 1897.

ACTION to recover the value of a lot of boots and shoes, of which plaintiff was the owner, and which he alleges the defendant wrongfully converted to his own use. Defendant answered, denying that he wrongfully converted said property to his own use. Verdict and judgment were rendered in favor of the plaintiff for one thousand, nine hundred dollars. Defendant appeals.— *Affirmed.*

Davison & Lane and *Pam & Kennedy* for appellant.

E. Sharon and *J. D. Shearer* for appellee.

GIVEN, J.—I. Beiderbecke & Miller were the owners of a building containing two storerooms known as
Nos. 111 and 113 West Second street, in the city of Davenport, Iowa. The part known as "No. 111" was three
stories high. The owners leased said building No. 111
to the plaintiff for five years from April 1, 1890, and
the part of the building known as "No. 113" to one Vogelhuth. In December, 1890, plaintiff and Vogelhuth
agreed that the latter would take plaintiff's lease off
his hands, and by consent of the owners, plaintiff's lease
was canceled, and a lease made to Vogelhuth. Thereupon plaintiff packed his stock of boots and shoes theretofore kept in storeroom No. 111, and stored them in the
third story of said No. 111, with the consent of Vogelhuth. There is a dispute as to the terms upon which
plaintiff was permitted to so store said goods. February 4, 1891, the lease to Vogelhuth was canceled, and a
lease executed by the owners to the defendant for the
entire building, Nos. 111 and 113, and was dated back
so as to cover the same five years. Defendant went into
possession under the lease, plaintiff's goods still being
in the third story, and the key to the room in plaintiff's
possession. On March 31, 1891, plaintiff proceeded to
remove his goods from said building, and, after he had
removed a small part thereof, he was prevented by one
Goldsteine from removing the balance. The defendant
was then in Chicago, and Goldsteine was a clerk in his
store kept in said building. Goldsteine told plaintiff he
could take no more shoes out of that place until he paid
thirty dollars, to which plaintiff replied: "I have
nothing to do with you at all. I am renting from Beiderbecke & Miller,"—and that he was going to take his
goods out; whereupon Goldsteine said that he should
not, and locked the door. The goods that were not
removed remained in said third story room, and on the
seventh day of April, 1891, were partially destroyed by

fire. Plaintiff does not question that, in the absence of a contract to the contrary, defendant had a lien on the goods for storage, and might rightfully prevent their removal until the storage was paid or tendered. He claims, however, that he had a contract with Vogelhuth by which he sold to Vogelhuth certain furniture and fixtures at the agreed price of twenty-three dollars and fifty cents, and that it was agreed that the storage should be four dollars per month, and that twelve dollars of said price be credited on the charge for storage, and that, therefore, the defendant had no right to detain the goods.

II. At the close of the evidence for the plaintiff, "defendant asked the court under the evidence to instruct the jury to return a verdict for the defendant," which motion was overruled. It is insisted that the evidence does not show an agreement with Vogelhuth for a definite time, nor that the storage was paid to March 31, 1891, and therefore the motion should have been sustained. While the evidence was somewhat confused it was not only sufficient to warrant the court in submitting the case to the jury, but sufficient to warrant the jury in finding as claimed by the plaintiff. It is also contended that this motion should have been sustained because there was no evidence of conversion of the goods by the defendant, for that there was no evidence that Goldsteine was agent for the defendant or custodian of said third floor. It is said in the answer, when 1 plaintiff commenced to remove the goods, "that defendant by his agent, demanded that plaintiff should pay the reasonable value of the storage of said goods, or for the occupancy of the part of the third floor where said goods were kept; but plaintiff refused to pay any sum whatever for such storage or occupancy, and denied the right of defendant to receive any payment whatever therefor." It is undisputed that Goldsteine, who was in the employ of the defendant in said store, was the person who demanded payment of storage, and who refused to allow plaintiff to take the goods. His agency is recognized in the answer, and the defense is rested upon the right of Goldsteine, as such agent, to refuse to allow the goods to be taken until the storage was paid. There was no error in overruling the defendant's motion for a verdict.

III. Defendant offered in evidence an affidavit made by F. H. Miller in support of a motion for a new trial made on the former trial of this case, and on plaintiff's objection the affidavit was excluded. There was no error in this ruling, as Mr. Miller was present on this trial, and was called and examined by the defendant touching the subject-matter of the affidavit. There was surely no ground for admitting the affidavit.

2

IV. The court instructed to the effect that, if the jury found that plaintiff had a contract for storage with Vogelhuth, as claimed, it should find that the storage had been paid by the plaintiff for the three months. Defendant insists that this was error, that the contract for storage was not for a definite time, and that storage was to be paid for out of the twenty-three dollars and fifty cents at the rate of four dollars per month for whatever time plaintiff's goods remained in storage, and that, therefore, it was not a payment of storage for three months in advance. We think the evidence justifies the instructions. Several other complaints against the instructions are merely mentioned, but we do not discover any error in any of the particulars complained of. Our conclusion is that the judgment of the district court should be AFFIRMED.

D. W. PAINE v. THE INCORPORATED TOWN OF LETTS-
VILLE, IOWA, Appellant.

Highways: DAMAGES: *Municipal corporations.* A municipal corporation is liable for the damages to a building constructed with
1 reference to the natural surface of the lot and street, from a
change of grade of the street, in the absence of an ordinance
fixing any grade.

Appeal: OBJECTION BELOW. The objection that the court did not
give the jury any rule for estimating damages cannot be raised on
2 appeal, where no instruction in regard to that matter was asked
in the trial court and no complaint of the omission was made in
the motion for a new trial.

Appeal from Louisa District Court.—HON. BEN McCOY,
Judge.

MONDAY, OCTOBER 25, 1897.

ACTION at law to recover for damages alleged to
have been caused to a town lot by an unauthorized
change of the grade of a street. There was a trial by
jury, and a verdict and judgment for the plaintiff. The
defendant appeals.—*Affirmed.*

Gray & Tucker for appellant.

C. A. Carpenter for appellee.

ROBINSON, J.—The defendant is an incorporated
town of this state, and the plaintiff is the owner of a lot
and store building which front on one of its streets.
There is no ordinance fixing any grade in the
1   town. In the latter part of the year 1894, the
defendant caused changes to be made in the
street in front of the property of the plaintiff. He claims
that the building on his lot, including brick foundation

walls, was constructed with reference to the natural
surface of the lot and street; that the defendant unlawfully excavated the street in front of his premises to a
depth of three feet below the natural grade, to his
injury in the sum of seven hundred dollars, and for that
sum he asks judgment. The answer of the defendant
contains a general denial, and alleges that the work performed, and the changes, if any, made, in the street,
were under the instructions and directions of the plaintiff, and for that reason he is estopped to claim damages in consequence of what was done. The verdict and
judgment were for the sum of two hundred dollars.

I. The appellant insists that the evidence does
not sustain the verdict, but shows that the earth
removed was not a part of the original soil, and had
been deposited in front of the plaintiff's premises from
excavations made in the vicinity, and perhaps from
other sources, and that the natural grade has not been
lowered. It is not necessary to set out the evidence in
regard to a change of grade, but it is sufficient to say
that witnesses for the plaintiff testified positively that
the street had been excavated in front of the plaintiff's
building to a considerable depth below the original
grade, while witnesses for the defendant testified as
positively that the excavation had not extended
below the natural surface of the ground. In fact, the
greater number of witnesses who testified in regard to
the original grade and the alleged change sustain the
defendant's claim. But there was a fair conflict in the
evidence with respect to that issue, which was properly
submitted to the jury, and we cannot say that its finding
is not supported by the evidence. Moreover, the sufficiency of the evidence to sustain the verdict is not
questioned by the assignments of error.

II. It is said that, before the work complained
of was done, the plaintiff agreed that the changes proposed might be made. It is doubtful if the evidence

would have sustained a finding that an estoppel had
been established. The plaintiff denied some of the
statements charged to have been made by him, and we
think the finding of the jury as to the alleged estoppel
should be regarded as final. It is proper to state that
this question also is not presented by the assignments of
error.

III. The last objection urged against the legality
of the proceedings of the district court is that it did not
give to the jury any rule for estimating damages. It
is true that the jury was not instructed in regard
to the measure of the plaintiff's recovery, but the
case was tried on the theory that, if he was
entitled to recover anything, it would be the difference
between the value of his property immediately before
and immediately after the alleged change of grade.
The defendant did not ask an instruction in regard to
that matter, did not except to any portion of the charge
given, and did not make the omission to charge in
regard to the measure of damages a ground of the
motion for a new trial. Therefore it appears that the
objection now urged is made for the first time in this
court. We think it is made too late. *Kidd v. Pill &
Medicine Co.*, 91 Iowa, 268; *Duncombe v. Powers*, 75
Iowa, 188; *State v. Helvin*, 65 Iowa, 291; *Smith v.
Railway Co.*, 60 Iowa, 514.

IV. The liability of the defendant in case the
averments of the petition are sustained by the evidence
is not questioned. See *Trustees of the Diocese of Iowa
v. City of Anamosa*, 76 Iowa, 539. What we have said
disposes of all questions presented in the arguments.
As there was no error in the proceedings of the district
court of which the defendant can justly complain, the
judgment is AFFIRMED.

T. F. GREENLEE AND J. F. ATKINSON v. THE HOME INSURANCE COMPANY, Appellant.

Amendments: STRIKING OFF. Where a cause in which defendan
had filed an answer consisting of a mere denial was ordered to be
2 tried on depositions, and plaintiff had taken his evidence within
the time prescribed, an amendment to the answer, filed on the day
4 of trial, and setting up facts known to defendant when the original answer was filed, was properly stricken off, plaintiff being
unprepared to try the issues tendered therein, and no excuse being
shown for failure to file it before the testimony was taken.

SAME. The allowance or disallowance of amendments to pleadings
under Code 1873, section 2689, providing that the court may, on
3 motion of either party, at any time, in the furtherance of justice,
and on such terms as may be proper, permit a party to amend any
pleadings or proceedings, is largely discretionary with the trial
court.

Appeal: CERTIFICATION OF EVIDENCE. On appeal in an equitable
action wherein an issue of fact was joined, questions involving
1 the evidence cannot be reviewed, where the trial judge, instead of
certifying that the transcript contains all the evidence "offered"
on the trial, as required by Code 1873, section 2742, merely certifies
that it contains all the evidence "introduced."

*Appeal from Benton District Court.—*HON. G. W. BURN-
HAM, Judge.

MONDAY, OCTOBER 25, 1897.

ACTION in equity to reform a policy of insurance,
and to recover for a loss by fire of the insured property.
Decree for plaintiffs. Defendant appeals.— *Affirmed.*

McVey & McVey for appellant.

J. J. Mosnat for appellees.

KINNE, C. J.—I. This is an action in equity, in
which it is sought to reform a policy of insurance upon

a certain building and fixtures, and for a judgment
thereon, the insured property having been destroyed
by fire. Reformation was sought to show that the
plaintiff Atkinson's interest was that of a mechanic's
lien holder, instead of a mortgage, as stated in the
policy; also, to correct the description of the real estate
upon which the property insured was in fact situated;
also, to correct a statement in the policy to the effect
that eleven thousand dollars other insurance was permitted. The original answer was a denial. September
6, 1895, the defendant filed an amendment to its
answer, setting up certain provisions of the policy,
relating to misrepresentations of the insured and their
effect; touching the ownership of the property; also providing that the policy should be void, unless otherwise
provided by agreement indorsed thereon, if, with the
knowledge of the insured, foreclosure proceedings be
commenced or notice given of the sale of any of the
property covered by the policy, by virtue of any mortgage or trust deed, or if any change other than death of
the insured takes place in the interest, title, or possession of insured (except change of occupants without
increase of hazard), whether by legal process or
judgment, or by voluntary act of the insured, or otherwise. Other provisions of the policy were pleaded.
The answer then pleaded facts which it is claimed were
in violation of the provisions of the policy, and which
avoided the same. A motion was made to strike this
answer, which was sustained. Thereupon the defendant filed a motion for leave to re-file said amendment,
which motion was overruled. A decree was entered
as prayed, in favor of plaintiffs.

II. The first question arising upon this record is
the sufficiency of the certificate of the trial judge to the

evidence. The certificate recites that "the within and
foregoing transcript is a correct, true, and com-
1   plete transcript of all the testimony introduced,
both oral and documentary, in the foregoing
and within-entitled cause, together with the objections
interposed by counsel and the rulings of the court
therein, exceptions taken, as taken down in shorthand,"
etc. Code 1873, section 2742, requires that the certificate be to "all the evidence offered on the trial" in
equitable actions wherein an issue of fact is joined.
The certificate in this case does not embrace the evidence "offered," but only that actually "introduced."
It has always been held by this court that certificates
in form like the one in the case at bar do not comply
with the statute, and we cannot try this case *de novo*,
because it does not appear that we have all of the evidence, which was offered upon the trial below, before us.
Taylor v. Kier, 54 Iowa, 645; *Tuttle v. Story County*, 56
Iowa, 316; *Reed v. Larrison*, 77 Iowa, 400; *Marble
Works v. Linesenmeyer*, 80 Iowa, 253; *Baldwin v.
Ryder*, 85 Iowa, 251; *Bank v. Ash*, 85 Iowa, 74.

III.   Errors are assigned, and we may consider any
question thus raised which may be determined without
a resort to the evidence. There is but a single question
raised which can be determined without con-
2   sidering the evidence. The court, on motion,
struck the amendment to defendant's answer.
Defendant filed objections to this motion, which were
overruled. It also asked leave to re-file the amendment
after it was stricken, and this was refused. Exceptions
were taken to all of these rulings. We do not think that
the court erred in these rulings. The original answer,
which was merely a denial, was filed April 1, 1895.
The amendment was filed September 6, 1895. The
motion to strike out was based in part upon the grounds
that the amendment was filed just as the case was

reached for hearing, and long after all the testimony on
the part of the plaintiffs had been taken, and no reason
was given why the amendment was not sooner filed.
The plaintiffs had no knowledge of defendant's intention to file it. The facts pleaded existed, and were well
known to defendant, when it filed its original answer,
and no reason is given why they were not then pleaded.
If the amendment is permitted to stand, plaintiffs
would be compelled to take further testimony. No evidence of the facts pleaded is admissible, for the reason
that at the last term of this court an order was made
that this cause should be tried on written depositions,
and a time was fixed by the court within which the
depositions of each party should be taken. The showing in resistance and in support of the motion for leave
to re-file was, in effect, that the facts pleaded were
known to plaintiffs; that no additional testimony would
be needed, and, if it was, defendant consented that it
might be produced without notice; that the facts were
not pleaded at the prior term through inadvertence
and oversight; that without the amendment defendant
cannot safely go to trial; that the defendant would,
upon the hearing of the notice to re-file, take the testimony of the plaintiff Greenlee and his attorney. In
support of the motion to re-file, said testimony was
taken. There was nothing in this testimony benefiting
the defendant, and we give it no further consideration.
Our statute provides that "the court may, on motion of
either party at any time, in furtherance of justice, and
on such terms as may be proper, permit such party to
amend any pleadings or proceedings." Code 1873, section 2689. It may be admitted that the general rule is
to allow amendments, and to deny the right is the exception. So, too, we have held that the statute is to receive
a liberal construction. Subject to these general
3   rules, the allowing of amendments is largely in
the discretion of the trial court. It is the rule
also that an amendment should not be allowed, or, if

filed, may be stricken, where it appears that it will
delay the trial of the case, and it might have been
sooner filed. *Newell v. Bank*, 51 Iowa, 178; *Bays v.
Herring*, 51 Iowa, 286; *Nelson v. Hays*, 75 Iowa, 671;
Chlein v. Kabat, 72 Iowa, 291. The only reason given
for not filing this amendment at the prior term is that

4
of inadvertence and oversight. It it to be
remembered that the original answer was a
simple denial, and it was filed April 1, 1895. At
that same term of the court, and on May 2, 1895, the
order was made for the trial of the case upon written
evidence in the form of depositions. That order provided that plaintiffs should take their depositions in
chief by June 20, 1895. The defendant was to take its
evidence by July 20, 1895, and the plaintiffs to take evidence in rebuttal by August 15, 1895. The plaintiffs
took their testimony within the time provided. Defendant knew when this order was made that the evidence
would soon be taken. It knew that it had nothing but
a denial on file. It knew of the defenses it afterwards
pleaded in the amendment; and no reason or excuse is
given why defendant did not plead these matters after
it filed its original answer, and before the time fixed
by the court for taking the testimony. The court was
not bound to seek for an excuse for the failure of the
defendant to file its amendment sooner, no excuse whatever being offered as to why it was not filed at some
time after it filed its original answer, and before the
testimony was taken. The court might well presume
there was none, and, if such was the case, there was no
abuse of discretion in the action taken by the court.

The amendment was filed the day of the trial, and
against the objection of plaintiffs. The amendment,
if allowed, would have worked prejudice to plaintiffs.
It appears that they had not prepared for trial of any
such issues as these therein tendered. They had no

reason to expect that new and material issues would be raised for the first time upon the trial. The failing to file the amendment sooner appears to have been a case of inexcusable neglect, and, while the law relating to the filing of amendments is liberal, it cannot be extended to cover such a case. There was no error in the rulings. As we have said, all of the other questions raised require us to resort to the evidence; and, as we do not have all of the evidence before us, we cannot determine them.—AFFIRMED.

CLARK M. PEEBLES AND JULIA A. WHITE, Appellants,
v. RICHARD BUNTING AND THE McCORMICK
HARVESTING MACHINE COMPANY.

Homesteads: WIDOW. Where a widow lived on her husband's farm
for six months after his death, then left it, and went to another
1 place, where she resided about nine years, then returned to the
farm, where she lived for seven years, when she again left, and
4 resided in another place for three or four years, and made an
arrangement with her children whereby she received the rent for
the whole of the farm, she cannot claim a homestead right in the
farm.

SAME. A widow can elect to take homestead rights in the land in
lieu of dower under Code 1873, sections 2007, 2008, only, when the
2 premises, or some part of them, were occupied by the husband as
a homestead prior to his death, so as to make it his homestead at
the time of his death.

PRESUMPTIONS. In the absence of evidence showing the election of
the widow to take a homestead in lieu of dower, the presumption
3 is that she took her primary right, which under the provisions of
Code 1873, section 2440, is a one-third interest in all of her husband's real estate.

JUDGMENT LIEN. When a widow does not elect to take her homestead right in her husband's land, in lieu of dower, and judg-
5 ments are obtained against her, they attach immediately to her
one-third interest in his real estate.

Judgments: PARTIES: *Issues.* In an action brought by the children
of a judgment debtor to quiet their title to premises sold under
an execution issued on the judgment, on the ground that the
debtor held homestead rights in the property sold, the court may,

7   upon a finding that the debtor held an undivided one-third inter-
    est in the land, which was subject to the judgment, enter a decree
    against such debtor, although she was in default as to the plain-
    tiff's petition and was not served with notice of the defendant's
    cross-bill, to which she was made a party.

Appeal: OBJECTION BELOW   Where a case was tried below as if the
6   answer applied to an amended and substituted petition, it will
    be so treated on appeal.   ~

Appeal from Calhoun District Court.—HON. Z. A
CHURCH, Judge.

TUESDAY, OCTOBER 26, 1897.

SUIT in equity to quiet the title to certain lands
theretofore owned by Albert Peebles in his lifetime.
The defendants are judgment creditors of Mary E.
Morton (*nee* Peebles), and, as such, claim a lien upon
the lands. The trial court dismissed the plaintiff's petition, and they appeal.—*Affirmed.*

M. R. & J. B. McCrary for appellants

M. E. Hutchison for appellees.

DEEMER, J.—Albert Peebles died, intestate, on the
fourth day of October, 1875, seized of the land in
dispute. He left, surviving him, Mary E. Peebles, now
Morton (his widow), and Clark M. Peebles, and Julia A.
     Peebles, now White, his children. After the
1   death of Peebles, his widow resided upon a part
     of the land in controversy for the term of about
six months, when she removed to Lake City, at which
latter place she resided until January, 1884, when she
returned to the land theretofore owned by her husband,
where she remained until February, 1891, at which time
she again removed to Lake City, and remained there
until the commencement of this suit. Appellee Bunting
obtained judgment against Mary E. Morton (*nee*

Peebles), February 23, 1892, and appellee McCormick Harvesting Machine Company obtained judgment against her on February 14, 1894. These judgments were based upon debts contracted by Mrs. Morton in the year 1883. The land was sold under the McCormick judgment in December, 1894. Appellants, who are the children of Albert Peebles, deceased, bring this suit to quiet their title to the lands, claiming that they are the absolute owners thereof, subject to a homestead right in Mary E. Morton, and that appellees' judgments are not liens upon the land. Appellees contend that Mary E. Morton became the owner of an undivided one-third of the land at the death of her husband, and that their judgments are liens upon her said interest. The sole question in the case is whether or not Mary E. Morton (*nee* Peebles) elected to take a homestead interest in the land in controversy. If she did, then appellants are entitled to the relief asked. If not, they must fail.

The statutes relating to this issue are as follows, under the head of "Homestead," Code 1873:

"Sec. 2007. Upon the death of either husband or wife the survivor may continue to possess and occupy the whole homestead until it is otherwise disposed of according to law.

"Sec. 2008. The setting aside of the distributive share of the husband or wife in the real estate of the deceased, shall be such a disposal of the homestead as is contemplated in the preceding section. But the survivor may elect to retain the homestead for life in lieu of such share in the real estate of the deceased. * * *"

Under the head of "Descent and Distribution:"

"Sec. 2440. One-third in value of all the legal or equitable estates in real property possessed by the husband at any time during the marriage * * * shall be set apart as her (the wife's) property in fee simple if she survive him. * * *

"Sec. 2441. The distributive share of the widow shall be so set off as to include the ordinary dwelling house given by law to the homestead, or so much thereof as will be equal to the share allotted to her by the last section, unless she prefers a different arrangement. * * *

"Sec. 2443. The share thus allotted to her may be set off by the mutual consent of all the parties interested when such consent can be obtained. * * *

"Sec. 2444. The application for such admeasurement by referees may be made at any time after twenty days and within ten years after the death of the husband. * * *"

These statutes have provoked a great deal of litigation, and the court has not always agreed upon their construction. The cases are collated and the differences of opinion are shown in *Stephens v. Hay*, 98 Iowa, 37. We need not at this time express our individual views further than to say that, if appellants' contention as to the facts be correct, according to the opinion of the majority the rule announced in the *Stephens-Hay Case* should be adhered to, and the decree of the court affirmed. The writer and Mr. Chief Justice Kinne still adhere to the dissent as expressed in that case. Aside from this, however, we are all of opinion that plaintiffs are not entitled to a decree. In

2   order to recover, they must show that some part of the land in controversy was the homestead of Albert Peebles at the time of his death. Sections 2007 and 2008 of the Code of 1873 contemplate the existence of homestead interests at the death of the husband. It is the homestead then existing which the wife may continue to use and occupy after the death of her husband, and which she may elect to take in lieu of her distributive share.

There is no evidence that any part of the land in dispute was occupied by Albert Peebles as a homestead. There is a showing that Mrs. Morton lived upon the land for six months after her husband's death, and some testimony to the effect that she claimed it as a homestead. But this evidence is of no avail without further proof that it was the homestead of the deceased, which she continued to occupy and elected to take. As there is no evidence of the homestead character of the land, and no showing that she took any other property as a homestead in lieu of dower, the presumption is that she took her primary right, which has been held to be a one-third interest in all of her husband's real estate, under the provisions of section 2440 of the Code. She took this immediately upon the death of her husband, and it was thereafter subject to the debts of the wife. The judgments obtained by appellees became liens upon this interest as soon as they were rendered, and the McCormick Harvesting Machine Company was justified in selling this interest under their judgment.

II. Mention has already been made of the fact that appellants are not entitled to recover, in the opinion of the majority, even if their contention as to the facts be conceded. We do not, however, fully agree with them as to the facts. While Mrs. Morton lived on the farm for six months after the death of her first husband, yet she then left it, and took up her residence in Lake City, at which latter place she lived until January 1, 1884, when she returned to the farm, where she lived until February, 1891, when she again removed to Lake City. True, she says in an indirect way that she always intended to return to the farm, and to hold it as a homestead; yet it also appears that, by arrangement with her children, she was receiving the rent for the whole of the land, and was holding it, as she says, "for my support, for the rent of it, and then leave it for my children, Clark and Julia A. Peebles." If the children sold the farm, they were to make provision for her support. Instead of claiming the land as a homestead, we are satisfied that Mrs. Morton was relying upon the rent for her support, and did not in fact intend to use and occupy the premises under any homestead rights. Confirmation of this is found in the fact that in the year 1891 she mortgaged an undivided one-third interest to Bunting, and in April, 1894, she quit-claimed all her interest in the land to the appellants. The predominant idea in the mind of Mrs. Morton was to secure support out of the rent of the land, rather than to make it a place of

5   abode. Under such a state of facts, it is quite clear that she did not elect to take a homestead right in lieu of her distributive share; and, in the absence of such an election, her primary right to an undivided one-third of the land obtains. This one-third is subject to appellees' judgments, and the trial court correctly denied appellants the relief claimed. This case is ruled by *Hornbeck v. Brown*, 91 Iowa, 316. There is no claim that the land is exempt under the provision of section 2441 of the Code. Hence the authorities cited with reference thereto are not in point.

III. Appellants' counsel contend that appellees did not answer their amended and substituted petition, and that there was no issue presented for trial. This objection seems to be raised for the first time

6   in this court. The case was tried in the court below as if the original answers of appellees applied to the amended and substituted petition, and it will be so treated here. Appellants also say that Mary E. Morton was made a party to defendants' cross-bill, but was not served with notice, and that any decree against her is erroneous. Mrs. Morton was a party

defendant to the main action, and was properly served
with notice. She did not appear and default was
entered against her. Appellees pleaded that this
default was allowed in fraud of their rights, and, while
they say that they make her a party, yet they do not
do so. No decree was rendered against her upon
7   their cross-petition. The trial court found that,
as between the parties litigant, Mrs. Morton
owned an undivided one-third interest in the land,
which was subject to the judgments held by the appellees, and dismissing the appellants' petition. This it
had the right to do, under the issues tendered, although
Mrs. Morton was in default as to appellants petition,
and was not served with notice of appellees' claim. The
decree of the district court is right, and it is AFFIRMED.

ANDREW SCHUSTER v. T. H. GAMBLE, Appellant.

Partition: SETTLEMENT. Where a county contracted with two persons to drain a lake, one of them, in consideration thereof, to be
given a deed of a part of the lake bed, and the other the balance;
but, by reason of a dispute between such persons as to the proportion in which they should bear the cost of a certain drain, the
county, instead of deeding to them such parts severally, executed
a deed to the two conveying all the land, the deed reciting that
the land had been drained by them pursuant to their contract
with the county, the land should be partitioned between them as
provided by their contract with the county, and not on the basis
that, by the deed, each received an undivided half, they having
made no agreement between themselves to accept said deeds as a
settlement of their controversy.

Appeal from Webster District Court.—HON. B. P. BIRD-
SALL, Judge.

TUESDAY, OCTOBER 26, 1897.

ACTION for partition of real estate. The plaintiff
claimed an undivided one-half thereof, and the district

court so found, and entered decree as prayed. Defendant appeals.—*Reversed.*

Wright & Nugent for appellant.

Botsford, Healy & Healy for appellee.

LADD, J.—A slough or lake bed, known as "Bass
Lake," had been meandered in the original survey, and
was situated in the east quarter of section 4, the northwest quarter of section 3, the southwest quarter of section 3, and in the northwest quarter of section 10, in
township 90 north, of range 29 west of fifth P. M.
Webster county assumed to own this lake bed, and
in 1885 its board of supervisors adopted this resolution:
'*Resolved*, that a committee of this board be appointed
to enter into a contract with said Gamble & Schuster to
drain said lake or slough in a complete and satisfactory
manner, and that when the said lake is drained to the
satisfaction of this board, as full compensation for the
labor and expense of said drainage, this board cause to
be delivered a quitclaim deed to said Gamble & Schuster
for the part of the lake lying north of the half section
lying on section 3 and 4, 90—29, and that a part of said
lake bed situated on the southwest quarter of section
3, and the northwest of section 10—90—29, Webster
county, Iowa, and not otherwise. The part lying north
of one-half section line of 3 and 4 to be deeded to T. H.
Gamble, and the balance to Andrew Schuster." In
pursuance of the provisions of this resolution, Gamble
dug the ditches necessary to drain that portion of the
lake bed north of the half section line through sections
3 and 4, and next to his land, and the plaintiff dug a
ditch draining that portion of the lake bed lying in the
southwest quarter of section 3 next to land owned by
him. In order to complete the drainage it was necessary
to extend the ditch from the lower end of Bass Lake

through a part of section 10, and in section 9 to Bass Creek, a distance of about seventy rods. A dispute arose concerning the proportion of the cost of digging this ditch each should pay; the plaintiff insisting that the expense ought to be in proportion to the amount of land each would receive, and the defendant that each ought to pay one-half thereof. This was dug by the plaintiff at an expense of twenty-five cents per rod, and the defendant refused to pay any part thereof, because, as he claimed, the plaintiff had failed to connect the east ditch on the northeast quarter of section 3 with the main ditch in the southwest quarter of section 3, as had been agreed, and as was necessary in order to carry off the water. Owing to this controversy, the county did not convey the land to the parties for several years, but in 1889 executed a quitclaim deed running to Gamble and Schuster, conveying all the land in the lake bed, and containing this clause: "Said lake bed or slough having been drained by said Gamble and Schuster in pursuance of contract entered into by and between said parties and the board of supervisors of Webster county, Iowa, as authorized by resolution of said board, adopted at the January session, 1885, of said board." In reply it is alleged that this deed was made by the county in pursuance of a settlement entered into by and between the plaintiff and defendant that such quitclaim deed should be executed, and each receive an undivided half interest in the land drained; and the only question for our determination is whether there was such a settlement, and, if so, whether the deed was made in pursuance thereof.

The plaintiff does not claim in his testimony that he entered into such an agreement with the defendant. On the contrary, he says that, after receiving the deed, he withheld it from record over two years, that he and the defendant might settle between themselves, and that they could not do so. After receiving the deed,

he told Gamble that, upon the payment of expense
belonging to him, he would let him have the land. He
does not say that Gamble was before the board of supervisors at the session the deed was executed, but testifies
that at the previous session Gamble had said: "We
would settle among ourselves." Gamble testifies that
he was not before the board during the session at which
the deed was executed, and refused to accept it, because
not drawn in accordance with the resolution, but told
the auditor he might mail it to him, and he would see if
he could settle with Schuster. He asked Schuster's
attorneys to have Schuster try to get the county to give
a quitclaim deed, so that they might divide the land.
The testimony of neither party indicates a settlement,
or that the deed was issued in pursuance of a settlement between them. Surely, if there had been a settlement, the very parties alleged to have made it ought
to know something of the transaction. After the execution of the deed, Gamble continued to occupy all the
land drained, north of the half section line running
through sections 3 and 4, and Schuster that below,
according to the resolution. There was no occasion
for Gamble to ask for a division of the land, as he was
already in possession of that to which he was entitled.
Appellee insists that the testimony of Ainsworth and
Wolfinger establishes the settlement alleged. The
former was a member of the board of supervisors, and
says that a deed was recommended "and for some
reason or other it was not agreed to." There is nothing
in the testimony of Wolfinger concerning any settlement between the parties. While some circumstances
tend slightly to show that the deed might have been
executed in adjustment of differences, the weight of
evidence establishes to our satisfaction that the county,
believing that the land had been properly drained, executed the joint deed, instead of separate deeds, as pro-

vided in the resolution, in order to avoid participation in the controversy between these parties, and that
the deed was taken in that form to enable them to settle
between themselves. Gamble had ditched six hundred
and seven and one-fourth rods on the land claimed by
him, while Schuster had ditched one hundred and
seventy-two and one-half rods on the land below the
half section line. After doing this amount of work, it is
unreasonable to suppose that Gamble would yield a
quarter of his land in settlement of the dispute, involving but a small item for ditching. The quitclaim deed
clearly recognizes the resolution, and that the lake bed
has been drained as therein required, and in accordance
therewith the land must be partitioned. The defendant
agreed to pay one-half of the ditch from the lake bed
to Bass Creek, amounting to eight dollars and seventy-
five cents, and he should also pay one-half of the reasonable value of the labor in digging out and keeping it in
repair up to the time the deed was executed by the
county, which amounted to forty-five dollars, making
fifty-three dollars and seventy-five cents in all. The
land will be partitioned so as to give the defendant all
the lake bed in the northeast quarter of section 4 and
the northwest quarter of section 3, and the defendant
all that lying in southwest quarter of section 3 and
northwest quarter of section 10. Judgment will be
entered against the defendant in the sum of fifty-three
dollars and seventy-five cents, with interest at the rate
of six per cent. per annum from January 1, 1889, and
made a lien on his land. Each party will pay one-half
of the costs in this and the district court. The decree
of the district court is REVERSED.

ALLEN COOK, Appellant, v. J. E. FOGARTY.

Collision with Bicycle: NEGLIGENCE: *Evidence.* The failure of a driver approaching a bicycler to turn to the right, is *prima facie* negligence on his part, under Code 1873, section 1000, requiring
3 persons meeting each other on the public highway to give one-half
4 of the same by turning to the right, and rendering all persons failing to observe such requirement liable for damages resulting therefrom.

SAME. In an action for injuries from a collision on a public road at
3 night, between plaintiff, while riding a bicycle, and a buggy
4 driven by defendant in an opposite direction, it appeared that a man on a wheel could be seen readily only a short distance, and that plaintiff had no light or bell. Plaintiff testified that he was dressed in light-colored clothes Defendant testified that he ought to have seen a man so dressed thirty yards or more, but did not see or hear him until the collision occurred, and that he was watching the road ahead. Defendant's companion also stated that he was watching, but did not see plaintiff until the accident. Plaintiff saw defendant and his horse one hundred and fifty yards distant, and began to slacken his speed. He testified that he helloed to defendant when he was fifty feet distant, and again a moment later Defendant did not heed the warning. Plaintiff turned to the right side of the road, and, a moment before he was struck, threw himself from his wheel, but not in time to avoid the collision. *Held,* that the jury was authorized to find that defendant had overcome the presumption of his negligence arising from his failure to turn to the right, and give plaintiff half of the road, as required by Code 1873, section 1000.

CONTRIBUTORY NEGLIGENCE. One who rides a bicycle without a
5 light or other signal of warning, in a public thoroughfare, where he is liable to meet moving vehicles or pedestrians, at a time when objects cannot be discerned readily except at a short distance, is guilty of contributory negligence precluding recovery for injuries received in a collision with a horse and wagon being driven in an opposite direction.

Instruction: HARMLESS ERROR. Plaintiff was not prejudiced by
6 refusal to permit him to testify that he expected defendants to turn out of the road when they met, where he testified that he did not know that defendants would turn out, and the court charged that it was defendant's duty to give plaintiff a share of the road if the approach of the latter was seen or should have been known; especially as plaintiff's testimony showed that, for some moments

before the accident, he must have known that he was not seen and that defendant would not turn out for him.

SAME   Plaintiff had no cause for complaint because the court charged
7   that the failure to carry a light or to ring a bell is not conclusive proof that the plaintiff was guilty of contributory negligence, but that those facts should be considered in reaching a conclusion.

SAME.   Where the court charged that plaintiff and defendant pos-
8   sessed equal rights to the highway when they met, and that whether either was negligent should be determined by all the facts of the case, and did not charge that defendant was not under obligation to carry a light, the rights and obligations of plaintiff were fairly presented, and it was not error to refuse to charge that "plaintiff was not obliged to carry a lamp or bell any more than was defendant."

Jury Panel: SUMMONS.   When a case was called for trial, ten men were drawn from the regular panel, and, no others being present,
2   plaintiff asked that the jury be completed by calling talesmen, but the court continued the cause until the next day, when the jury was completed from the regular panel.   *Held*, that there was no violation of law, or abuse of discretion, in what was done.

CONSTITUTIONAL LAW.   Acts Twenty-fifth General Assembly, chap-
1   70, section 4, providing that in preparing the lists and ballots containing the names of persons who are to constitute the jury list, "the name of each alternate juror on the list from cities and towns where the courts are held shall be deposited in a box to be known as the talesmen box and not the first box," is held not shown to be unconstitutional.

Appeal from Greene District Court.—HON. Z. A. CHURCH, Judge.

TUESDAY, OCTOBER 26, 1897

ACTION at law to recover for damages to the person, clothing, and bicycle of the plaintiff, alleged to have been caused by negligence of the defendant. There was a trial by jury, a verdict for the defendant, and judgment in his favor for costs.   The plaintiff appeals. —*Affirmed.*

J. A. Gallaher for appellant.

No argument for appellee.

ROBINSON, J.—In the evening of August 20, 1895, the plaintiff was riding a bicycle from Grand Junction westward towards Jefferson, on a public highway, and when midway between the two towns met the defendant, who was in a buggy drawn by one horse, and was driving from Jefferson to Grand Junction. At the moment of meeting, a collision occurred between the plaintiff and the horse of the defendant and a shaft of his buggy, which caused the damages for which the plaintiff seeks to recover. The plaintiff claims that he called to the defendant as they were about to meet, and finally dismounted from his wheel, and stood with it by the roadside; but that, in consequence of the negligent and careless driving of defendant, his horse jumped to the side of the road, and into the wheel, destroying it, and causing a buggy shaft to strike the plaintiff in the breast, thereby knocking him down, and bruising him and tearing his clothes. The defendant admits the collision, but denies all negligence on his part, and alleges that he exercised due care; that the accident occurred in the night time, when it was so dark that a man approaching on a bicycle without a light or signal of any kind could not be readily seen; and that the defendant did not see or know of the plaintiff's approach until the collison occurred. The defendant further avers that the plaintiff traveled without a signal light, and was negligent in not carrying a light or in some manner warning the defendant of his approach, or in not turning out of the highway to avoid the horse and buggy.

I. The appellant contends that chapter 70 of the Acts of the Twenty-fifth General Assembly, under which the jury was drawn, is unconstitutional, because

1   it is provided in section 4 thereof that in preparing the lists and ballots containing the names of persons who are to constitute the jury list "the name of each alternate juror on the list from cities and

towns where the courts are held shall be deposited in
a box to be known as the talesman box and not in the
first box." It is said this provison violates both the
constitution of the United States and of this state, but
the part violated is not pointed out. In the absence of
a more satisfactory argument on this point, we deem it
sufficient to say that the appellant has failed to satisfy
us that the act in question is unconstitutional.

2   The appellant also complains of the manner in
which the jury was drawn, as in violation of the
act specified. When this case was called for trial, ten
men were drawn from the regular panel, and, no others
being present, the plaintiff asked that the jury be completed by calling talesmen, but the court refused the
request, and continued the cause until the next day,
when the jury was completed from the regular panel.
We do not think any violation of law or abuse of discretion in what was done is shown.

II.   The evidence authorized the jury to find the
facts to be substantially as follows: At the time of the
accident it was so dark that a man on a wheel could not
have been seen readily further than a short dis-
3   tance. The defendant states that he ought to
have seen a man dressed in light-colored clothing
a distance of thirty yards or more, and the plaintiff
states that he wore such clothing at the time of the accident. But he was not seen by the defendant until the col
lision had occurred. The plaintiff saw the defendant and
his horse, which was gray or white in color, one hundred and fifty yards before meeting them, and began to
slacken his speed. He says he hallooed to the defendant and a companion who was riding with him when
they were fifty feet distant, and again a moment later.
The defendant did not heed nor hear the warning, but
continued to drive his horse in the traveled road,
although the sides were level, and he could have turned

out easily. The plaintiff turned to the north side of the
road, and a moment before he was struck threw himself
from his wheel, but not in time to avoid the collision.
Section 1000 of the Code of 1873 is as follows: "Persons
meeting each other on the public highways shall give
one-half of the same by turning to the right. All persons failing to observe the provisions of this section
shall be liable to pay all damages resulting therefrom.
* * *" The plaintiff was entitled to use the
4   public highway with his wheel, and was entitled
to one-half of it when he met persons going in an
opposite direction. He turned to the right as he
approached the defendant, as the law provides, and the
fact that the latter did not is *prima facie* evidence of
negligence on his part. *Riepe v. Elting*, 89 Iowa, 83.
The appellant contends that the presumption authorized by law has not been overcome, and that the testimony of the defendant shows conclusively that, if he
had been giving proper attention to his horse and the
road, the accident would not have occurred. But we
think the jury was authorized to find that the presumption of negligence on the part of the defendant was overcome. The fact that it would have been possible for
him to discover the approach of the plaintiff in time to
turn to the right does not show that he was negligent in
not doing so. The defendant states that at the time of
the accident he was watching his horse and the road in
advance for the purpose of seeing any one who might be
on the road, but that he was not expecting to meet any
one, and did not see or hear the plaintiff until the accident occurred. The defendant's companion also states
that he was watching the road in advance of the horse,
but did not see the plaintiff until the moment of the
accident. In view of this evidence the jury was justified in finding that the defendant used due care to ascertain the approach of persons on the highway. Until he

knew, or with reasonable care could have known, that
the plaintiff was approaching, it was not his duty to
turn out for him, and he was not negligent in keeping
in the traveled way.

III.   The plaintiff would not necessarily have been
entitled to recover had the defendant failed to discover
him in time to avoid the accident, through inattention to
his duties as driver.   Contributory negligence on
5   the part of the plaintiff would prevent a recovery.   He contends that there was no evidence
whatever that he was guilty of such negligence; but, if
the testimony for the defendant was entitled to credit,
we think the plaintiff must have been negligent. He says
he saw the defendant when he was distant one hundred
and fifty yards.   The defendant was driving at a rate
of five or six miles an hour, and the plaintiff was going
as fast, and probably faster.   If that rate of speed had
been continued, they would have met in about thirty
seconds from the time the plaintiff saw the defendant.
The plaintiff says he slackened his speed, and, if he did
so, the collision may not have occurred until nearly a
minute after the plaintiff was first made aware of
the defendant's approach.   The plaintiff must have
known that he was making little, if any noise;
that he did not carry a light or other means
of attracting attention at a distance; and that his
approach might not be discovered.   True, the law
of this state did not make it his duty to carry a light,
to sound a bell, or to give other signal of his
movements, and the same was true of the defendant.
But a horse and buggy traveling five miles an hour are
apt to make some noise, and, with the occupants of the
buggy, are more readily seen, even in the night time,
than is a single pedestrian or bicycle rider.   These are
matters of common knowledge; and a person who rides
a bicycle without a light or signal of warning, in a public thoroughfare, where he is liable to meet moving

vehicles or pedestrians, at a time when objects can be
discerned readily at a distance of but a few feet, is
guilty of negligence. That appears to be what the
plaintiff did. He does not claim to have called to the
defendant until within fifty feet of him, or but two or
three seconds at most before the collision occurred, and
probably too late for the defendant to avoid it if he had
heard the warning. The plaintiff had no reason to
think that he was seen. In fact, he states that the
occupants of the buggy did not seem to hear him. We
do not think the jury could well have found that the
plaintiff was not negligent.

IV. The appellant complains of the refusal of the
court to permit him to testify that he expected the
defendant to turn out of the road when they met. We
do not think prejudice could have resulted from
6   that ruling. The court charged the jury that it
was the duty of the defendant to give the plaintiff
a share of the road if the approach of the latter was
seen, or should have been known; and the plaintiff
states that he did not know that the defendant would
not turn out. Moreover, we think the testimony of the
plaintiff shows that for some moments before the accident occurred he must have known that he was not
seen and that the defendant would not turn out for him.

V. The eighteenth paragraph of the charge is as
follows: "In the matter of carrying a light or the failure to carry a light, the matter of ringing a bell or not
ringing a bell, you are instructed that the failure
7   to carry a light or failure to ring a bell is not
conclusive proof that plaintiff was guilty of contributory negligence; but these facts, like the other
evidence in the case, should be taken into consideration
by you in reaching your conclusion regarding the circumstances and surroundings of the accident." The
appellant complains of this as instructing the jury,
in effect, that the plaintiff would be guilty of negligence

in not carrying a light or ringing a bell, and would be
excusable for failure to do so only under unusual circumstances. It was evidently designed to meet the
claim made by the defendant in his answer and in the
evidence, and no doubt in argument, that the plaintiff
should not recover because of his negligence in not
carrying a light or sounding a bell, and to that extent
the paragraph was in the interest of the plaintiff. A
light and a bell are well-known means by which wheelmen give notice of their presence. We think that the
plaintiff was negligent in not giving a signal of his
approach, and that he has no just ground for complaining of the part of the charge quoted.

VI. The appellant complains of the refusal of the
court to charge the jury that "plaintiff was not obliged
to carry a lamp or bell, any more than was the defendant." The court did not charge the jury that the
8   defendant was not under obligation to carry a
light, but said that the plaintiff and the defendant possessed equal rights to the highway when they
met, and that whether either was negligent should be
determined by all the facts of the case. We think the
rights and obligations of the plaintiff were fairly presented to the jury, and that there was no occasion to
give the instruction under consideration, which was
refused.

VII. Many other questions are referred to by the
appellant, and a few are discussed in argument. What
we have said disposes of the most important of them.
We need not say more in regard to them than that
we do not find any sufficient reason for disturbing the
judgment of the district court. A motion was submitted with the case to strike an additional abstract
from the files, and to tax the cost thereof to the appellee.
We do not find that the motion is well founded, and it is
overruled. The judgment of the district court is
AFFIRMED.

F. D. McNeely, Appellant, v. G. D. Ford, *et al.*

Usury! PRINCIPAL AND AGENT: *Ratification.* Notes given a wife for money borrowed are usurious, where her husband acted as her agent in loaning the money, and it was understood by them that he should invest it on such terms, as to interest and otherwise, as he saw fit, and he added to the amount of the notes, in excess of the sum actually loaned, certain amounts as his commissions, which, with the rate of interest stipulated in the notes, made the interest exceed the lawful rate, and all such charges were ratified by her by demanding a recovery for the full amount. Citing *Greenfield v. Monaghan,* 85 Iowa, 211, and *Richards v. Purdy,* 90 Iowa, 502.

*Appeal from Marshall District Court.—*Hon. S. M. Weaver, Judge.

Tuesday, October 26, 1897.

Action to recover judgment for the full amount of a promissory note executed by defendant to plaintiff for seven hundred and seventy dollars, with eight per cent. interest, dated March 28, 1893, and due March 28, 1894; also, for a decree foreclosing a mortgage on real estate given to secure said note. Defendant answered, admitting the execution of said note and mortgage, and alleging as defense that said note is usurious, which allegation the plaintiff denies in his reply. Judgment was rendered in favor of the plaintiff for a part of the amount claimed, namely, for four hundred and seventy-eight dollars and eighty-three cents, and decree foreclosing the mortgage for that amount. Judgment was rendered against the plaintiff for the costs. Judgment was also rendered against the defendant for two hundred and eighty-five dollars and twenty-one cents, to be paid to the school fund. Plaintiff appeals.—*Affirmed.*

J M. Whitaker for appellant.

Henry Stone for appellee.

GIVEN, J.—I. We first inquire whether the promissory note sued upon is usurious. The facts out of which its execution grew are these: Plaintiff is the wife of G. W. McNeely, who has been engaged in the loan business. At the time of their marriage, in 1885, the plaintiff had three or four hundred dollars, which had been given to her by her father, and which she placed in the hands of her husband to be loaned. Mr. McNeely placed in her name a sufficient amount of notes owned by him to increase the amount in his hands for her to one thousand dollars. This money was left in his hands to be invested for the plaintiff. On March 21, 1890, the defendant applied to Mr. McNeely for an immediate loan of money, to enable him to redeem his property from an execution sale, the period of redemption of which expired that day. Defendant on that day executed his promissory note, payable to the plaintiff, for six hundred and forty-two dollars, payable March 21, 1891, with ten per cent. interest, for which he received from Mr. McNeely six hundred dollars. Defendant testifies that the forty-two dollars were added as illegal interest. Mr. McNeely testifies that forty dollars of it were added as his commission, to which defendant had agreed. Certain payments were made and credited upon this note. On March 21, 1891, defendant executed his other promissory note for the sum of one hundred and seven dollars and seventy-five cents, payable to the plaintiff, January 1, 1892, with eight per cent. interest, for which he received ninety-seven dollars and fifty cents in money from Mr. McNeely. Defendant testifies that the ten dollars and twenty-five cents were retained as illegal interest, while Mr. McNeely testified that they were for the expense of making and recording the chattel mortgage given to secure the note, and that it was put in the note at defendant's request. On March 25, 1892, the defendant executed his other promissory note to plaintiff for fifteen dollars, payable in sixty days, with eight per cent. interest. Defendant testifies that this was given for additional illegal interest on the first note. Mr. McNeely testifies that it was to pay the costs of extending the six hundred and forty-two dollar note. On April 1, 1892, defendant executed to plaintiff another promissory note for one hundred and eight dollars, payable November 1, 1892, with ten per cent. interest. Defendant testifies that he only received ninety-seven dollars and fifty cents on this note, which is not disputed nor explained by Mr. McNeely, but he says that it was a clerical error that makes the note draw ten per cent. interest, and that it should have been only eight per cent. On March 28, 1893, the note sued upon was given for the balance appearing to be due upon these several notes, according to the face thereof, less credits appearing thereon. Defendant testifies that Mr. McNeely and Mr. Forrey figured the amount due upon these notes to be seven hundred and fifty dollars, and that twenty dollars were added as usury, making the note seven hundred and seventy dollars. Mr. McNeely testifies that the twenty dollars were added on account of his day's travel and expenses in going to St. Anthony to see the defendant, and for the settlement and for the recording and execution of the mortgages. We will not discuss this evidence further than to say that it leaves no doubt that in these transactions Mr. McNeely acted solely as the agent of the plaintiff, and was not entitled to any commission from the defendant for effecting a loan, and that the several amounts added to the promissory notes over and above the amount received by defendant were usurious.

II. Plaintiff cites and relies upon *Greenfield v. Monaghan*, 85 Iowa, 211, and *Richards v. Purdy*, 90 Iowa, 502. In both those cases the excess over the amount actually loaned was retained by the agent solely for his own benefit, without the knowledge of the party whose money was loaned; and there was no evidence that his act in so doing was authorized or ratified by the person whose money he was loaning. In the *Greenfield Case* it is said: "We find no direct evidence that the plaintiff authorized or knew that Griswold was exacting a commission from Monaghan; and it is the well-settled rule in this state that, when a charge is made by the agent for his own benefit in excess of the authorized rate of interest, the transaction is not tainted with usury if the principal did not authorize the charge,"—citing cases. It is further said: "Proof that the agent for the person lending the money retained a portion of it for his own use, which, if for the benefit of the principal, would make the loan usurious, is not proof of usury, because the transaction may be entirely legal; and for that reason the law will presume that it was so. Therefore, in order to sustain the plea of usury, it is necessary for the borrower to show, not only that the agent has retained, from the sum loaned, money sufficient to make the amount the borrower is required to pay, if for the benefit of the principal, greater than that sanctioned by law, but also that the act of the agent in retaining money was authorized or ratified by the principal. In this case the defendants failed to show that Griswold had authority to retain the commission, that the plaintiff knew that it had been retained, or that he derived any benefit from it." This case was followed in the *Case of Richards*. In that case the agent making the loan was also agent for the borrower. In this case Mr. McNeely acted solely as the agent of his wife, and, though she testifies that she never authorized him to receive more than legal interest, we are satisfied that it was intended and understood between them that he should invest her money upon such terms, as to interest and otherwise, as he might see fit. He testifies: "She gave it to me to make investments, and I invested it as best I could. I never consulted her in making these loans; never had to when I put out any money for her. Of course, she did not ask any questions." He also says that she trusted to his judgment and experience to invest the money. She testifies that he was her agent for loaning the money, and that "I would ratify whatever he would do." The six or seven hundred dollars contributed by Mr. McNeely to make the one thousand dollars were never in the possession nor control of the plaintiff. In view of the relation of the plaintiff and her agent and of the other facts, we are satisfied that the plaintiff expected him to loan the money upon whatever terms, as to interest and otherwise, he might see fit. We are in no doubt that they intended that she should have the full benefit of all that might be realized from loaning this money. If it may not be said that he had authority from the plaintiff to take usurious interest, it is certainly clear that what he did take was not for his own, but for her, benefit. The excess over the amounts actually loaned were in each instance included in notes payable to the plaintiff, and in this action she is asking to recover these amounts. Mr. McNeely fails to show in his testimony that his accounts with his wife were so kept as that these excesses were for his benefit, and not for hers. The rule quoted above is grounded on the facts, not only that the excess or usury was taken without the authority or ratification of the person for whom the loan was made, but that it was taken for the benefit of the agent, and not for the benefit of the principal. In this case we think it entirely clear that it was taken for the benefit of the principal, this plaintiff, and that she accepts and ratifies the act by now demanding recovery therefor. The judgment of the district is AFFIRMED.

THE H. E. SPENCER COMPANY, Appellant, v. P. F. PAPACH, Defendant, LYDIA E. VERNER, Garnishee.

Mortgages: CREDITORS: *Recording.* One who sells goods to a mortgagor during ten days between the execution and recording of the 1 mortgage, will not be given priority over the mortgagee, where 2 the latter used reasonable dispatch, under the circumstances, in recording the mortgage, and did not withhold it from record to save the credit of the mortgagor, nor induce any one to extend credit to him.

FORECLOSURE EXPENSES. A mortgagee is not entitled, as against a 3 creditor of the mortgagor, to expenses incurred in selling the 5 mortgaged goods at retail, where the mortgage simply authorizes her to sell the goods at "public auction."

Pleading: ESTOPPEL. The claim that a creditor of a mortgagor is . 4 estopped to complain of the expense incurred by the mortgagee in selling the mortgaged goods at retail, is not available under a pleading setting forth, that such creditor is estopped to claim that the mortgage was illegal and to deny the validity of the sale to the mortgagee and her title derived from the mortgage and the sale thereunder.

*Appeal from Appanoose District Court.—*HON. F. W. EICHELBERGER, Judge.

SATURDAY, APRIL 10, 1897.

PLAINTIFF, a judgment creditor of the defendant P. F. Papach, served notice of garnishment upon Lydia E. Verner, as a supposed debtor of said defendant. The garnishee answered, and issues were joined upon her answer. The case was transferred to, and tried as in, equity, and judgment and decree rendered in favor of the garnishee. Plaintiff appeals.—*Reversed.*

Mabry & Payne for appellant.

T. B. Perry for appellee.

Given, J.—I. The following is a sufficient statement of the facts to show the points in controversy on
this appeal: On and for some time prior to July 14,
1893, the defendant was engaged in the business of
a retail merchant at the town of Mystic, in Appanoose
county. On July 14 he was indebted to the plaintiff in
a considerable sum for goods, and to his mother-in-law,
Mrs. Mary A. Kirkman, and to the garnishee, his sister-
in-law, for borrowed money. On July 14, defend-
1   ant executed to Mrs. Kirkman and to Mrs.
Verner, each, a chattel mortgage on his stock of
merchandise, book accounts, and notes, to secure the
amounts due them, respectively, which mortgages were
filed for record July 24, 1893. On July 25 he executed
two other mortgages on the same property,—one to
William Bradley, and one to T. W. Barhydt,—to secure
amounts due to them, respectively, which mortgages
were filed for record July 25, 1893. The three mortgages last mentioned were assigned to Mrs. Verner,
and on July 29, 1893, by virtue thereof and of the mortgage to herself, she took possession of the stock of
goods, book accounts, and notes, and proceeded to collect the accounts and notes, and to dispose of the goods
at retail until September 26, 1893, when the entire
property was sold in bulk under said mortgages, and
purchased by the garnishee for "four thousand, seven
hundred dollars." On July 24, 1893, the defendant was
indebted to plaintiff in the sum of one thousand, seven
hundred and fifty-seven dollars and four cents for goods
purchased, three hundred and thirty-five dollars and
eighty-six cents of which had been purchased by defendant between July 14 and 24, 1893.

II.   It is not questioned on this appeal that the
defendant was indebted to said several mortgagees in
the sums named in the mortgages; nor is the validity of
the mortgages to William Bradley and T. W. Barhydt
disputed, nor that they were assigned to the
2   garnishee.   Appellant contends that the evidence shows affirmatively that the mortgages to
Mrs. Kirkman and to the garnishee were withheld from
record in pursuance of an understanding. that they
should be so withheld. We will not set out or discuss
the evidence on this subject. It is sufficient to say that
a careful reading of it satisfies us not only that there is
no such understanding proven, but that said mortgagees caused their mortgages to be filed for record as
soon as could be conveniently done in view of their
place of residence, and that there was no intention
upon the part of either of them to withhold the mortgages from record for any fraudulent purpose.   There
can be no doubt but that the plaintiff extended the
credit it did to the defendant between July 14 and 24
in ignorance of the existence of these mortgages, and we
think it may be fairly presumed that that credit would
not have been extended, had the plaintiff known of
their existence.   Appellant's contention is that under
these facts the mortgages are void, as to it, to the
amount of the sales made to defendant between those
dates.   It is said in argument: "What is the difference
in the result to plaintiff whether these relatives simply
withheld their mortgages from record purposely, of
their own accord, to save his credit, or whether they
made an agreement so to do? The design in either case
was the same.   The result to plaintiff in either case
was the same."   What the effect would be if these mortgagees withheld their mortgages from record purposely, of their own accord, to save the defendant's
credit, we need not determine, as we think no such

purpose is shown. We are satisfied that these mortgagees used reasonable dispatch, under the circumstances, in causing their mortgages to be filed for
record, and that neither of them withheld them for the
purpose of saving the credit of the defendant, or of
inducing the plaintiff or any other person to extend
credit to him. Appellant cites a number of authorities
to show that, as to the indebtedness created after July
14, it is an existing creditor, as well as to the indebtedness created prior thereto. The correctness of this
claim may be conceded, but it does not strengthen the
position of appellant, as against these mortgagees,
merely because it was an existing creditor.

III. During the time that the garnishee was
engaged in selling goods at retail, she employed the
defendant and two others to assist in the business from
July 29 to September 26, 1893. The court allowed her
two hundred and sixty dollars on account of amounts
paid to these persons, and for her own services.
3   Each of the mortgages contains the usual pro-
       vision authorizing the mortgagee to take pos-
session, "and to sell the same at public auction" after
giving at least ten days' notice by posting up written
notices. Appellant's contention is that the garnishee
had no authority to carry on the business at retail, and
should not be allowed for expenses incurred in so doing,
and that plaintiff should have judgment against her
       for two hundred and sixty dollars so expended.
4   Appellees contend in argument that, under the
       facts proven, appellant is estopped from now
complaining of the expense incurred in selling the goods
at retail. It is a well established principle that matter in
estoppel must be specially pleaded, or it cannot be considered. See *Independent District of Burlington v.
National Bank,* 68 Iowa, 343; *Folsom v. Fast Freight
Line,* 54 Iowa, 490; *Phillips v. Van Schaick,* 37 Iowa,

229; *Ransom v. Stanberry*, 22 Iowa, 334; *Eikenberry v. Edwards*, 67 Iowa, 14; *Glenn v. Jeffrey*, 75 Iowa, 20; *Eggleston v. Mason*, 84 Iowa, 631. Appellant, in its reply to the amended answer of the garnishee, alleged that said expenses incurred in selling goods at retail, and for an attorney's fee, were not legitimate items of charge in favor of the garnishee. The only estoppel pleaded by garnishee is as follows: "The garnishee claims that, by reason of the acts and conduct of the plaintiff as above described, it is estopped from claiming that said mortgages are illegal, and from denying the validity of the sale to the garnishee, and her title derived from said mortgages and sale thereunder." There being no estoppel pleaded to appellant's claim as to these expenses, the claim of estoppel made in argument cannot be considered. The district court disallowed any credit to the garnishee on account of attorney's fees, but allowed her two hundred and sixty dollars on account of her own services and of clerk hire while engaged in selling goods at retail. Her authority was derived solely from the mortgage. That gave no right to incur expense nor to render services otherwise than in keeping and selling goods as therein provided, namely, at public auction. These items of expense not being a proper credit to the garnishee, it follows that she has that amount in her hands, to which the plaintiff is entitled. The district court found that the garnishee had nine dollars in her hands in excess of the amount due to her, and directed that amount to be applied to the costs, and rendered judgment against the plaintiff for "the costs of this suit except nine dollars." Plaintiff moved to re-tax the costs, upon the ground that, being entitled to the nine dollars, it was the successful party. It is our conclusion that the plaintiff is entitled to recover two hundred and sixty-nine dollars, with six per cent. interest

from the twenty-sixth day of September, 1893, together
with the costs of this suit.   We need not determine
whether the court erred in overruling the plaintiff's
motion to re-tax the costs.   The case will be remanded
for judgment in harmony with this opinion.—REVERSED.

SUPPLEMENTAL OPINION ON REHEARING.

WEDNESDAY, OCTOBER 27, 1897.

PETITION for re-hearing.—*Modified.*

PER CURIAM.—Upon reviewing this case on petition
of the appellant for a re-hearing, we reach the conclusion, upon a reconsideration of the evidence, that the
garnishee should be charged with fifty dollars retained
on account of her own labor, instead of one hundred
dollars, as held in the former opinion.   The former opinion is therefore modified accordingly, and the petition
for re-hearing is OVERRULED.

THE FIRST NATIONAL BANK OF KANSAS CITY, MISSOURI,
Appellant, v. THE MOUNT PLEASANT MILLING
COMPANY, et al.

Bill of Lading: TRANSFER OF TITLE: *Attachment.*   A bank which discounts a draft with bill of lading attached, drawn against a shipment, and credits the amount thereof to the drawer, acquires an
interest in the property shipped, paramount to that of a subsequent attaching creditor of the drawer and shipper, though it
advanced him no money before the attachment was effected;
although this is not the rule in the sale of negotiable paper, and
though a bill of lading is quasi negotiable, and is by a statute made
negotiable by indorsement and delivery, like bills of exchange.
Citing *Oddie v. Bank,* 45 N. Y. 740; *Cragie v. Hadley,* 99 N. Y. 131;
Bank v. Burkhardt, 100 U. S. 636; *Bank v. Gregg,* 28 N. E Rep.
(Ill. Sup.) 839; *Neill v. Produce Company,* 28 S. E. Rep. (W. Va.)
702; *Bank v. Crocker,* 111 Mass. 163.

Appeal from Henry District Court.—Hon. T. M. Fee,
Judge.

Wednesday, October 27, 1897.

Action at law for the conversion of two cars of
wheat. The defendants claimed the property under a
writ of attachment issued in an action wherein the
Milling Company was plaintiff and the Moffatt & Lee
Commission Company was defendant, and alleged that
plaintiff was not the owner thereof, but that it belonged
to the Commission Company. The trial court directed
a verdict for the defendants, and plaintiff appeals.—
Reversed.

Power, Huston & Power and *W. I. Babb* for appellant.

McCoid & Finley and *Blake & Blake* for appellees.

Deemer, J.—The appellant will be designated as
the "Bank," the appellee as the "Milling Company,"
and the Moffatt & Lee Commission Company as the
"Commission Company." January 3, 1895, the Commission Company, having contracted to sell and deliver
two cars of No. 2 wheat to the Derby Roller Mills, of
Burlington, Iowa, drew its draft on the Roller Mills for
the net proceeds, in favor of plaintiff; delivered the bill
of lading for the wheat, indorsed in blank, with weigh-
master's certificates attached, to the plaintiff; and at
the same time received credit on the books of the Bank
for the amount of the draft, less one dollar and twenty
cents discount or exchange. The bank at once entered
the draft upon its books, charged the same to its cor-
respondent at Burlington, Iowa, and sent it forward,
with the attached papers, for payment. The wheat was
shipped immediately, and while enroute, and at Mt.

Pleasant, Iowa, in the custody of the carrier, was seized by the sheriff on a writ of attachment in favor of the Milling Company and against the Commission Company. The Derby Roller Mills learned of the seizure of the wheat, and refused to pay for the same. The draft was protested and returned to the Bank. The Bank thereupon demanded the wheat from the sheriff, but he refused to surrender. This action was then commenced.

As a general rule, a bill of lading represents the goods while in the possession of the carrier for transportation, and its assignment operates as a transfer of the title, and a symbolical delivery of property. *Garden Grove Bank v. Humeston & S. R'y Co.*, 67 Iowa, 526; *Weyand v. Railway Co.*, 75 Iowa, 573; *Ayres, Weatherwax & Reed Co. v. Dorsey Produce Co.*, 101 Iowa, 141.

The statutes of Missouri (Rev. St. 1879, sections 558, 559), where the transfer was made, also provide that:

"558. All bills of lading, transportation receipts and contracts of affreightment issued or given by any person, boat, railroad or transportation or transfer company, for goods, wares, merchandise, grain, flour or other produce, shall be and are hereby made negotiable by written indorsement thereon, and delivery in the same manner as bills of exchange or promissory notes, and no printed or written conditions, clauses or provisions shall in any way limit the negotiability or effect of any negotiation thereof, nor in any manner impair the rights and duties of the parties thereto, or persons interested therein; and every such condition, clause or provision purporting to limit or affect the rights, duties or liabilities created or declared in this chapter, shall be void and of no force or effect.

"How Transferred—Lien Created—Exception.

"559. All bills of lading and transportation receipts of every kind, given by any carrier, boat, vessel, railroad, transportation or transfer company, may be transferred by indorsement in writing thereon, and the delivery thereof so indorsed; and any and all persons to whom the same may be so transferred shall be deemed and held to be the owner of such goods, wares, merchandise, grain, flour, or other produce or commodity, so far as to give validity to any pledge, lien or transfer given, made or created thereby, on the faith thereof, and no property so stored or deposited, as specified in such bills of lading or receipts, shall be delivered, except on the surrender and cancellation of such receipts and bills of lading."

Appellee contends, however, that the Bank did not purchase the bill of lading; that it has no lien upon it or upon the property, except to the extent of advances made; and that as it did not advance anything on the strength of the bill of lading, but merely gave the Commission Company credit upon its account,—which at the time showed a balance in its favor,—it cannot recover. This contention is based upon a rule applicable to the transfer of negotiable paper, to the effect that a mere discount and credit do not of themselves amount to a *bona fide* purchase for value. The rule is announced and applied in the following, among other, cases: *Dresser v. Construction Co.*, 93 U. S. 92; *Mann v. Bank*, 30 Kan. 412 (1 Pac. Rep. 579); *Fox v. Bank*, 30 Kan. 444 (1 Pac. Rep. 789). The trouble with this position, as applied to the facts of this case, lies in the assumption that a bill of lading is to be treated in all respects as a negotiable instrument, and subject to the same rules, as to its transfer and negotiation. The authorities speak of such an instrument as "quasi negotiable," and the statutes of Missouri say that it is negotiable by written indorsement and delivery, in the same manner as bills of exchange. What is meant by this, as we understand it, is to give to such documents negotiability and assignability by indorsement and

delivery, so that the indorsee may sue thereon in his
own name. It does not necessarily follow that, because
a statute has made bills of lading negotiable, all the
consequences of an indorsement and delivery of bills
and notes before maturity ensue, or are intended to
result, from such negotiation. Bills of lading represent
property, and, when indorsed or assigned, operate as
a symbolical delivery to the indorsee or assignee of the
property covered thereby. Such a transfer is quite
different from the negotiation of a bill of exchange or.
a promissory note, which circulates in the commercial
world as an evidence of money. *Shaw v. Railroad Co.*,
101 U. S. 557, 25 Lawy. Ed. 892; *National Bank of Commerce v. Chicago, B. & N. R. Co.*, 44 Minn. 224 (46 N. W.
Rep. 560). Thus it has been held that the indorsement
and delivery of a bill of lading pass the property, when
it is intended to so operate, in the same manner as a
direct delivery of the goods would do if so intended.
Mechanics & T. Bank v. Farmers & M. National Bank,
60 N. Y. 47; *Gardener v. Howland*, 2 Pick. 599;
Brower v. Peabody, 13 N. Y. 121; *Forbes v. Railroad Co.*, 133 Mass. 154; *Lickbarrow v. Mason*, 1 Smith,
Lead. Cas. 848, and note. So, where the shipper
attaches a bill of lading to a draft for the price, and
indorses the same to one who discounts the draft, the
goods are thereby pledged for the payment of the draft,
and a special property therein passes to the transferee.
Conrad v. Insurance Co., 1 Pet. 445; *Bank v. Crocker*
111 Mass. 163; *Holmes v. Bank*, 87 Pa. St. 525; *Bank v
Wright*, 48 N. Y. 1; *Hathaway v. Haynes*, 124 Mass
311; *Dows v. Bank*, 91 U. S. 618; *Emery v. Bank*, 25
Ohio St. 360; *Bank v. Kelly*, 57 N. Y. 34. And the possession of a bill of lading, whether indorsed or not, is
prima facie evidence of title, as against any person not
showing a better title. *Railroad Co. v. Phillips*, 60 Ill.
190; *Pratt v. Parkman*, 24 Pick. 42; *City Bank v. Rome,
W. & O. R. Co.*, 44 N. Y. 136.

The question here presented is not whether the indorsee takes the bill of lading free from equities or defenses in the hands of the original holder, but whether he has a better title to the grain than an attaching creditor of the indorser. If A should purchase a horse from B, and secure the delivery thereof upon a promise to pay for the same at some future time, he certainly has better title than C, who attaches the horse as the property of B after the delivery to A. So when the plaintiff in this case cashed the draft, and took the assignment of the bill of lading from the Commission Company, it secured a better title than the Milling Company, which attached the grain while in transit; and the fact that, when the grain was attached, it had not been called upon to make any direct advances to the Commission Company, is not, in itself, of controlling importance. *Bank v. Dearborn*, 115 Mass. 219. Having given the credit to the Commission Company before the grain was attached, and having secured title to the grain through the indorsement of the bill of lading, it obtained title to the draft and to the bill of lading, and had the right to follow the grain, which had been symbolically delivered as collateral to the draft which it had discounted. *Oddie v. Bank*, 45 N. Y. 740; *Cragie v. Hadley*, 99 N. Y. 131 (1 N. E. Rep. 537); *Bank v. Burkhardt*, 100 U. S. 686; *Bank v. Gregg*, 138 Ill. 596 (28 N. E. Rep. 839). If the bank had simply undertaken the collection of the purchase price as agent of the Commission Company, then the title to the grain remained in the latter company, and it was subject to attachment until delivered to and paid for by the Roller Mills. But if the Bank purchased the draft, and accepted the bills of lading as collateral security, or if it purchased the grain outright, and accepted the bills of lading as evidence of this purchase, or if, in consideration of the indorsement and delivery of the bills of lading, it made or agreed to make certain definite future advances, it acquired a title to the grain which could not be defeated by a subsequent attachment. *Neill v. Produce Co.*, 41 W. Va. 37 (23 S. E. Rep. 702). As said in the case of *Bank v. Crocker*, 111 Mass. 163: "Whether it [the transfer] should be regarded as a sale, a pledge, or a mortgage, there was a sufficient delivery to give to the plaintiff a special property, which they could enforce by suit against any wrongdoer."

In directing a verdict and judgment for the Milling Company the court erred. Each party moved for a verdict at the conclusion of the evidence, and it is contended by appellee that, in so doing, appellant waived the right of submission to the jury, and that the order and judgment of the court have the same force and effect as the finding of a jury upon all questions of fact involved in the case. This seems to be the rule established by the weight of authority. 6 Encyclopedia Pleadings and Practice, page 703, and cases cited. Expressing no opinion at this time upon the question of law thus presented, it is sufficient to say that we do not think there was sufficient evidence to justify the court in directing a verdict for the defendant. If a jury had found for the defendants upon the evidence adduced, the court should have set aside the verdict as without support. The judgment of the district court is REVERSED.

ELI DYER v. THE DES MOINES INSURANCE COMPANY, Appellant.

Insurance: NOTICE AND PROOF OF LOSS. The assured under a policy on a building and goods, which were burned, sent the company, after it had notice of the loss, a list of figures, accompanied by
1   his unsigned affidavit, which he intended for, and which its officers must have understood was intended as proof of loss. They must
2   have also understood that the figures first appearing represented the amount of dimension lumber in the burned building and the

other parts of the statement the other property lost by the fire *Held*, that such proofs, except as to how the loss occurred, and the omission to sign the affidavit, substantially complied with the policy and Acts 1880, chapter 211, section 8, requiring notice of loss, accompanied by an affidavit stating the facts as to how the loss occurred, so far as they are within assured's knowledge, and the extent of the loss.

WAIVER. An insurance company waives the failure of the insured to specify in his proofs of loss how the fire originated, and to verify
2 the same by affidavit, by returning the same with a general state-
3 ment that they contain none of the elements necessary to comply
4 with the policy or statute as to proofs of loss, without subsequently, and within a reasonable time, pointing out such specific objections.

*Appeal from Monroe District Court.—*HON. M. A. ROBERTS, Judge.

WEDNESDAY, OCTOBER 27, 1897.

THE plaintiff shows as his cause of action in substance as follows: That, on October 15, 1894, the defendant, a duly-incorporated insurance company, issued to him its policy of insurance against loss or damage by fire upon the lower story of a certain two-story building not exceeding seven hundred dollars, and on certain furniture and goods therein not exceeding two hundred dollars, for the period of one year; that on the eleventh of January, 1895, said property was totally destroyed by fire, without fault on his part, and that he thereafter gave the defendant written notice of said loss, and within sixty days from the date of said loss he gave the defendant proof thereof; that the defendant fails and refuses to pay said loss, or any part thereof. He alleges that a mistake was made in writing said policy in describing the property insured as being all of said building instead of the lower or first story thereof, which alone belonged to him, and of which fact he fully informed the defendant's agent at the time the application was taken. He prays that said mistake may be corrected, and for judgment on the policy, as corrected, for eight hundred and thirty-nine dollars and thirty-two cents, with interest. The defendant answered, admitting that it issued the policy on the building and goods, written as alleged; denies that any mistake was made in writing the policy, as alleged; and avers that it was written as stated by the assured. Defendant alleges that in his application plaintiff answered that his title was by warranty deed, and did not disclose the fact that he had no title to the upper story of said building; and that because thereof the policy is, by its terms, void. Defendant further

1   alleges that plaintiff did not give notice and proofs of said loss within the thirty days, nor in the manner, required by the policy; and that there has been no waiver of any of the conditions of said policy by the defendant. "The defendant admits that, on the eighth day of March, 1895, it received through the mails a paper upon which was written a list of figures; but said paper did not contain a statement of the origin of the fire, or how the loss occurred, and was not signed by the assured, nor sworn to, nor did it contain an itemized statement of the actual cash value of the property claimed to have been lost by the fire, nor did it possess the essentials plainly pointed out in the policy and in the statutes necessary to make it a proof of loss." On the day following the defendant returned said paper to plaintiff through the mail, with a letter as follows: "Des Moines, Iowa, March 9, 1895. Eli Dyer, Esq., Foster, Iowa—Dear Sir: We received from you yesterday a list of some figures, but, as it contains none of the elements necessary to comply with the policy and statute as to proofs of loss, we return the same herewith, and respectfully refer you to the policy and statute governing such cases. Yours, very truly, J. S. Clark, Sec'y." Defendant states that, notwithstanding assured

was notified of the deficiency of the paper, he did not
thereafter furnish proofs of loss as required by the policy. Defendant asked to be dismissed, with costs.
Plaintiff, in reply, denies the right of the defendant to
insist upon any of the defenses set up in its answer, for
the following reasons: That when defendant's agent
was taking the application he was informed that there
was a mortgage on said premises, amounting to sixty-
five dollars, which was duly recorded; that the plaintiff
claimed to be the owner of the undivided one-half of
the ground on which the building stood; that his claim
of title was based upon a deed, not present, but which
was on record, which he asked said agent to examine,
and that he did not state that he held title by warranty
deed; that the application was signed in blank, said
agent agreeing to fill the blanks when he examined the
record as to plaintiff's title; wherefore plaintiff asked to
have said statement reformed so as to conform to the
facts. Replying to the matters set forth as to proofs of
loss, plaintiff says that by said letter defendant failed
to point out any specific objections to said proofs of loss,
"for which failure it has waived the right, and is now
estopped from making any of the objections it now
urges to the insufficiency of said proofs of loss." Plaintiff alleges that, on the eleventh day of March, 1895, he
transmitted to defendant further proofs of loss, which
were returned to him on the day following, with an
accompanying letter that will be hereafter noticed.
Plaintiff states that in this letter the defendant wholly
failed to specify any one of the objections now urged
against the sufficiency of said proofs of loss. The case
was transferred to and tried as in equity, and a decree
rendered finding that the mistakes alleged do exist by
mutual mistake of the parties, and decreeing that the
policy be corrected accordingly. Judgment was entered
in favor of the plaintiff for seven hundred dollars, with

interest from June 7, 1895. Defendant appeals.—
Affirmed.

McVey & Cheshire for appellant.

T. B. Perry and *N. E. Kendall* for appellee.

Given, J.—I. Appellant does not complain of that
part of the decree granting a reformation of the policy,
nor could it well do so, for the uncontradicted evidence
fully sustains the decree in that particular.
2   Appellant's contention is that the court erred in
rendering judgment against it, "for the reason
that no proofs of loss as required by the policy and the
statute were ever made or delivered to the defendant
company." Appellee contends that "defendant failed
to point out any specific objections to said proofs of loss,
or any of the objections now urged on this trial; for
which failure it has waived the right, and is now
estopped from making any of the objections it now
urges of the sufficiency of said proofs of loss." Much is
said in argument, and many authorities are cited, as to
how and by whom waiver might be made under this
policy, and especially as to whether an adjusting agent
might waive proofs of loss. There is neither allegation
nor evidence of an express waiver of proofs of loss nor
of an express waiver of the insufficiency of the proofs
made. The question is whether, under the facts, appellant is estopped from questioning the sufficiency of the
proofs made, and it is only in this connection that we
are called upon to consider the subject of waiver.
3   The statute requires notice of loss, accompanied
by an affidavit stating the facts as to how the
loss occurred, so far as they are within the knowledge of
the assured, and the extent of the loss. Acts Eighteenth
General Assembly, chapter 211, section 3. This policy
requires that the assured shall render an account of the

loss, signed and sworn to, stating how the fire originated. The proofs received by appellant March 8, and
returned March 9, 1895, consisted of a list of figures in
the form usually employed in giving the dimensions of
framing lumber; thus: "4 2x8 No. Ft. 18," giving the
aggregate value as seventy-three dollars and twenty-
one cents. Following this is a number of items giving
the amount of various kinds of building material, and
the value of each item or group of items. Then appears
the following:

"Foster, Iowa, 3-7, 1895. I, Eli Dyer, duly sworn,
depose and say that I lost the following amount, as
itemized, in a fire January 11, 1895, and which was
insured in policy No. 108,863, given by Des Moines
Insurance Co., of Des Moines, Iowa."

After this there are set out the items of furniture
and goods, such as those covered by the policy, with the
value of each item, and a total of $813.32. The docu-
ment closes as follows:

"I, Eli Dyer, being duly sworn, depose and say that
the above is a true and correct statement of account
against the Des Moines Ins. Co. Eli Dyer.

"Before me, this seventh day of March, 1895, personally appeared Eli Dyer, who is personally known to
me as respectable and entitled to credit, and on oath
swears that the above statement is correct, as he verily
believes. R. Williams, Justice of the Peace."

The certificate and signature of the justice renders
it evident that the statement was verified by Eli Dyer,
and it is probable that his signature was omitted by
oversight; yet the paper cannot be regarded as an affidavit. *Crenshaw v. Taylor*, 70 Iowa, 386. Having previous notice of the loss from Mr. Dyer, appellant's officers must surely have understood from this writing that
it was intended as proof of Dyer's loss; that the figures
first appearing represented the amount of dimension

lumber in the burned building, and the other parts of
the statement the other material and property lost to
Dyer by the fire. The figures as to values could not
have been understood as representing anything else
than the value of the property destroyed. Thus viewed,
these proofs comply substantially with every requirement of the statute and the policy, except as to how the
loss occurred, and in the omission to sign the affidavit.
It appears in evidence, without objection, that, after
receiving notice of the loss, and before these proofs
were made, appellant sent its adjusting agent to the
scene of the loss for the purpose of investigating this
and other losses that occurred by the same fire; that
said agent saw that the loss of appellee's building was
total, and was then informed that the fire originated in
a building some distance from appellee's building, and
was communicated to it through intervening buildings
that were destroyed at the same time. There is no evidence that anything was said to or by the adjusting
agent about proofs of loss. We have seen by
4   appellant's letter of March 9 that these proofs
were returned to appellee with the statement
that "it contains none of the elements necessary to comply with the policy or statute as to proofs of loss."
Appellee was referred to the policy and statute, without any intimation as to the grounds upon which appellant objected to the sufficiency of his proofs. On March
11, 1895, appellee forwarded further proofs of loss, the
receipt of which was acknowledged March 16; but as
these additional proofs are not set out in the record,
and not relied upon, they will not be further noticed.
The only objections that could fairly have been made to
the proofs received March 8 are that they were not furnished within the thirty days, as required by the policy,
and do not state how the fire originated, and were not
verified by affidavit. We have seen that no objection

was made on the score of time in the answer, and no
such objection is insisted upon in argument. We have
also seen that no objection was made to the proofs
received March 8 on the ground that they were not
signed or that they did not state the origin of the
fire, and that no particular objection was specified as
to those proofs. It is probable that appellee omitted
to state the origin of the fire because of the information
previously given to appellant's adjuster; but, be that as
it may, it is clear that appellant knew, through its
adjusting agent, how appellee claimed the fire had originated. In Wood, Insurance, p. 968, it is said: "It
seems to be settled beyond dispute that, where there
are defects in the proofs of loss, whether formal or substantial, or, indeed, in any respect which could have
been supplied if specific or other objections had been
made thereto by the underwriters, a failure on their
part to object to the proofs upon that ground, or to
point out the specific defect, or to call for the information omitted, within a reasonable time, is considered a
waiver, however defective, informal or insufficient
such proofs may be." In *Young v. Insurance Co.*, 45
Iowa, 378, it is said: "Good faith required that, if proofs
were not satisfactory, notice should be given the
assured to that effect within, at least, a reasonable
time. Objections of this kind are technical, and without substantial merit; and the insurer should make
such known with promptitude, to the end that they
may be perfected, if possible." In *Green v. Insurance
Co.*, 84 Iowa, 135, wherein the *Case of Young* is cited
approvingly, this court said as follows: "The plaintiff
was authorized to rest upon the presumption that the
defendant would act in good faith, and give him such
notice if the letter was not regarded as sufficient proof
of loss. The defendant was bound to know that the
plaintiff would so regard its failure to make objection to

the insufficiency or want of proof. It must, therefore, under the familiar rules upon this subject recognized by this court, be regarded as having waived all objection to the insufficiency or want of proof of loss." Appellant insists that, as the facts of those cases were different from this, the principle does not apply. It is but an application of the familiar doctrine of estoppel. Good faith required in this case, as well as in those, that, upon the receipt of the proofs of loss, if appellant was not satisfied therewith, it should have specified its objections thereto, to the end that they might have been perfected, if possible. Appellant having failed to specify the objections now urged to the proofs of loss at a time when they might have been remedied, it should not now be heard to urge these objections.

It is further urged by appellant that the recovery is too large, and that the judgment should not have been for more than five hundred dollars. We think the evidence as to the value of the property destroyed fully sustains the judgment. Our conclusion is that the decree of the district court should be AFFIRMED.

---

*

J. F. WILHELMI v. THE DES MOINES INSURANCE COMPANY, Appellant.

Limitation of Actions: BY CONTRACT: *Insurance.* A provision in a
8 fire policy that no suit thereon shall be sustainable, unless commenced within six months after the fire, is valid.

SAME: *Successive suit.* Code 1878, section 2537, providing that if
1 plaintiff fails in an action, for any cause except negligence in its
2 prosecution, and a new suit be brought within six months thereafter, the new suit shall, for the purposes herein contemplated,
   "be deemed a continuation of the first," applies only to statutory
   limitations, and not to those created by contract.

SAME. An action on a policy providing that no suit on it should lie
   unless commenced within six months after the fire, was defeated
4 because it was commenced within ninety days after notice of
   loss, contrary to Acts Eighteenth General Assembly, chapter 211,

section 8. *Held*, that plaintiff was not entitled to maintain the second action, not commenced within six months after the fire, because defendant did not set up the defense of prematurity in the first action until the six months limitation had expired. The insurer owed the insured no duty to disclose such defense.

SAME. Nor was he entitled to maintain the second action because the first suit was not in fact premature, because of the existence of 5 facts which he failed to show in his first action.

Appeal from Polk District Court.—HON. W. F. CONRAD, Judge.

WEDNESDAY, OCTOBER 27, 1897.

ACTION at law upon a policy of insurance, to recover for a loss caused by fire. A demurrer to the petition was overruled, and the defendant refusing to plead further, judgment was rendered in favor of the plaintiff for the amount of the policy, with accrued interest and costs. The defendant appeals. — *Reversed.*

McVey & Cheshire and *McVey & McVey* for appellant.

Gatch, Connor & Weaver for appellee.

ROBINSON, J.—The petition states that on the fifth day of March, 1889, the defendant delivered to the plaintiff the policy in suit; that it insured him against loss or damage by fire, in the sum of one thousand, eight hundred dollars, on a stock of merchandise which is described; that on the twenty-second day of September, 1889, and while the policy was in force, the property insured was, without fault on the part of the plaintiff, destroyed by fire; that on the same day the plaintiff went personally to the secretary of the defendant, at his office in Des Moines, reported the loss to him, and asked him to send an agent to examine and report upon the loss; that thereupon the secretary directed an

agent of the defendant to go with the plaintiff and
inspect the loss, which was done; that the agent, after
inspecting the loss, reported to the secretary that it
was total; that on the same date the secretary waived
written notice of proof of loss, and questioned the plaintiff fully in regard to the origin of the fire and all things
connected with the loss, and the value of the goods, and
made memoranda from the answers given by the plaintiff; that the secretary then requested the plaintiff to
procure, so far as possible, his bills, copies of account,
and other papers relating to his stock and loss, and
make a sworn statement as to the amount and extent of
the loss and the value of the stock destroyed, all of
which the plaintiff did on the twenty-fourth; that at
that time the statement was reduced to writing by the
secretary, and at his request was verified by the plaintiff; that the plaintiff then asked the secretary if he
required any further proof or notice, and was informed
by the secretary that nothing further was required;
that, by reason of what was said and done as stated,
the defendant waived any further notice or proof of
loss; and that the secretary waived written notice of
proof of loss by refusing to pay the amount of the policy
for the alleged reason that the plaintiff was not the
sole owner of the property insured.   The peti-
1   tion further alleges that on the twenty-sixth day
of December, 1889, the plaintiff commenced an
action at law in the district court of Polk county to
recover the claim for which he sues in this action, and
on the twenty-seventh day of September, 1890, recovered judgment therein for the amount of the policy, but
that on appeal the judgment thus obtained was
reversed by this court on the fourteenth day of October,
1892, for the reason that the action was commenced
within ninety days after notice of loss had been given,
contrary to section 3 of chapter 211 of the Acts of the

Eighteenth General Assembly; that upon the filing of
a *procedendo* in the district court on the eighth day of
December, 1892, the original suit was dismissed without prejudice. The petition also states that the plaintiff was advised by counsel, and believed, that by reason
of what he had done, and what the secretary of the
defendant had said and done, there was a waiver of
other notice or proof of loss than that which had been
given, and in consequence filed his petition in the original action more than ninety days after the alleged
waiver was made; that on the sixteenth day of May,
1890, the defendant filed an answer which set out
several defenses, but did not claim that the action was
prematurely brought, and never, within the knowledge
of the plaintiff, made such a claim until the twentieth
day of September, 1890, on which date the cause was
called for trial; that at that time the defendant filed an
amendment to its answer, which averred that the
action was prematurely brought. The petition alleges
further that the plaintiff prosecuted the action with
due diligence, and that within six months after the
failure thereof, for the reason stated, this action was
commenced in continuation of the former action. The
policy, a part of which is made a part of the petition,
provides that none of the terms and conditions of the
policy can be waived, excepting in writing, by the
secretary of the defendant, and that no action on the ·
policy shall be sustainable in any court of law or equity
unless commenced within six months next ensuing
after the fire. This action was commenced on the
twenty-first day of December, 1892. The grounds of the
demurrer are, in substance, that the issues tendered by
the petition were adjudicated in the former action, and
that this action was commenced more than six months
after the loss occurred, contrary to the provisions of the
policy; that the facts pleaded show that this is not a

continuation of the original action, and do not show
any excuse for the delay in bringing this action, and
that the plaintiff failed in the original action by reason
of negligence on his part; and that he voluntarily dismissed that action, and a new one cannot be brought
after the expiration of the time fixed by the policy. This
is the second submission of this cause for our determination, a re-hearing having been granted after the filing
of the opinion on the first submission.

I.   Section 2537 of the Code of 1873 provides that,
"If after the commencement of an action, the plaintiff
fail therein for any cause except negligence in its prosecution, and a new suit be brought within six
2   months thereafter, the second suit shall, for the
purposes herein contemplated, be deemed a continuation of the first." It was held by this court in the
original action that it was prematurely brought. See
Wilhelmi v. Insurance Co., 86 Iowa, 326.   To avoid the
effect of that decision, and relying upon the section of
the Code we have quoted, the plaintiff dismissed the
original action, and commenced this one, as already
stated. The plaintiff contends that the facts admitted by
the demurrer show that the original action was not prematurely brought; hence, that he was not negligent in
bringing it; and that, under the statute quoted, this
must be regarded as a continuation of the former suit.
It is claimed by the defendant and denied by the plaintiff that the effect of the decision of this court on the
appeal in the original action was to adjudicate finally
that it was commenced prematurely.   We do not find it
necessary to determine that question.   If it be conceded
that the claim of the plaintiff that as the judgment of
the district court was reversed, and the cause was then
dismissed without further proceedings, there was no
final adjudication, is well founded, it does not follow
that this action can be maintained.   The questions

which are controlling in this case were considered and determined in *Harrison v. Insurance Co.*, 102

3   Iowa, 112. It was there held that provisions in policies of insurance limiting the time within which actions thereon may be commenced, similar to the one involved in this case, are valid, and that the section of the Code we have quoted applies to statutory limitations, and not to those created by contract. Therefore this action cannot be regarded as a continuation of the one first brought, and it was commenced after the expiration of the time limited by the policy for the commencement of an action.

It is said that the defendant did not, in the original action, plead that it was prematurely brought, until after the time for bringing an action on the policy, as

fixed by its terms, had expired. The thought

4   expressed is that the defendant was guilty of bad faith in thus delaying to plead that defense, for the reason that, had it been urged sooner, the action could have been dismissed, and a new one commenced within the time allowed by the policy. We do not know of any duty upon the part of the defendant to protect the interest of the plaintiff by pointing out the defects in his proceedings before the case was reached for trial. The amendment to the answer which alleged that the action was prematurely brought appears to have been filed by permission of the court, and, so far as is shown, without objection by the plaintiff.

It is said the plaintiff was not negligent in prosecuting the original action, because he relied upon and followed the advice of competent attorneys in what he

did, and he was sustained in it by the district

5   court. If it be true that he was not negligent in commencing the action prematurely, and prosecuting it as long as he did, that fact does not afford ground for relief in this action. The petition upon which

he now relies shows that the first action was not prematurely brought, for the reason that the secretary,
who was authorized to waive requirements of the policy,
did so, with respect to formal notice and proof of loss.
See *Ruthven v. Insurance Co.*, 102 Iowa, 550. And the
first action was not commenced until after the expiration of ninety days from the time of that waiver. If the
averments of the petition in this case are true,—and
the demurrer admits that they are,—the facts could
have been shown in the former action; and if it be true,
as claimed by the appellant, that there was no final
adjudication by this court as to whether the action was
prematurely brought, the fact could have been inquired
into and determined after the cause was remanded to
the district court. If the plaintiff's theory of the law be
true, he has failed to show any sufficient reason for
discontinuing his first action, and must be held to have
been negligent in not showing in that action the waiver
which he now pleads. It is immaterial whether there
was an adjudication of negligence on the part of the
plaintiff in the first action, or whether he is now shown
to have been guilty of negligence in prosecuting it. The
effect is the same, and there is no equitable ground for
holding that section 2537 of the Code of 1873 applies in
this case. We conclude that the limitation of the right
of action contained in the policy in suit is valid and
binding, and that the plaintiff's right of action is not
saved by the statute cited. It follows that the demurrer
should have been sustained, and the judgment of the
district court is REVERSED.

JANE ANN DUNN v. THE PORTSMOUTH SAVINGS BANK,
Appellant.

Trusts: EVIDENCE. A finding by the court that decedent did not
    hold real property in trust for a woman with whom he was living
1   as his wife will not be disturbed on appeal, where the latter, as

his administratrix, treated the property as belonging to his estate, and the claim of trust was not made until a claim was made by the decedent's legal wife, and the circumstances strongly indicate that the claim of a trust was an afterthought to defeat the legal widow's claim.

Estoppel: CLAIM OF DOWER   The legal widow of deceased is not estopped to claim her dower as against one claiming under a woman with whom deceased at the time of his death was living 2 as his wife, by the mere fact that after learning of his pretended marriage with the latter, she took no steps to enforce her rights during his life.

Appeal from Pottawattamie District Court.—HON. N. W. MACY, Judge.

WEDNESDAY, OCTOBER 27, 1897.

IN 1841 the plaintiff was married to Stephen Dunn, who died in December, 1887, seized of the legal title to certain lots in Council Bluffs, Iowa, and she brings this suit, averring that, as widow, she owns the undivided one-third of said lots, and asks that her title therein be quieted against the defendant bank, which she avers claims some interest therein. It is made to appear that there were born to plaintiff and Stephen Dunn several children, of whom John, Stephen and Almira survive; that plaintiff and Stephen Dunn were married in Mon-·treal, Canada, and afterwards lived in Cincinnati, Ohio, where, somewhere between 1850 and 1856, Stephen Dunn took his children, and abandoned plaintiff; that he reached Council Bluffs some time after, and was married to a Mrs. Carson (known in the record as Mary Carson Dunn) in June, 1857, with whom he lived as his wife to his death in 1887. It appears that after his death Mary Carson Dunn was administratrix, and the estate was settled, and the real estate, by agreement, was divided between her and the heirs at law, being the children and a grandchild of Stephen Dunn. In such division the lots in question were deeded to Mary

Carson Dunn. She conveyed her title to one Paul E. Seabrook, who executed a mortgage thereon, which became the property of the defendant bank, and, by a foreclosure and sale, the bank now claims to be the owner of the lots. The issues present the question, *first*, is plaintiff the widow of Stephen Dunn? If she is, then, *second*, did Stephen Dunn hold the title to the lots in question in trust for Mary Carson Dunn? The district court gave a decree for plaintiff, from which the defendant appealed.—*Affirmed*.

John W. Lytle and *J. J. Stewart* for appellant.

C. G. Saunders for appellee.

Granger, J.—I. We do not think that appellant seriously contends that plaintiff is not the widow of Stephen Dunn, deceased, and entitled to a distributive share in his real estate. The only escape from such a conclusion is that they had been divorced, and no such claim is made in argument. In fact, the contrary quite clearly appears. It affirmatively appears that plaintiff never obtained a divorce, and has no knowledge of her husband doing so. Besides, it appears that Dunn, when he married Mary Carson, made no pretense of a divorce, but represented that he understood his wife to be dead, that she had died since he left her.

II. The claim that Dunn held the title to the lots in trust for Mary Carson Dunn is made to depend on the facts that when she married Dunn she was keeping a boarding house at Council Bluffs, and had for

1   some time been doing so, and was the owner of considerable property, and that when she quit that business she went onto a farm, and conducted it and other business successfully, and that the real estate in question, and other real estate, was bought with her money, and that, while the title was taken in the name

of Dunn, it was in trust for her. She represents in her
testimony that Dunn was a cutter and tailor by trade,
and not a farmer, but worthless for such a business;
that he was drunk considerable of the time, and spent
more than he earned for drink. Her testimony shows
him to have been a worthless man, and especially so for
any business purpose. Other evidence shows him to
have been a man of at least fair business capacity and
habits. After his death, Mary Carson Dunn returned
an inventory into court, showing him to have been the
owner of six lots, including those in question, and one
hundred and sixty acres of land, all valued at two thousand, six hundred and thirty-one dollars, and a personal estate, other than money in bank, of one thousand,
two hundred and thirty-five dollars. It also appears
that he had a credit balance in bank of five hundred
and eleven dollars and seventy-four cents. The estate,
thus inventoried, was settled as his in all respects by
Mary Carson Dunn, she taking what the law gave her as
widow, and his heirs taking the balance. The record
shows a bank account with Stephen Dunn from April,
1885, to his death, with an almost constant credit balance in his favor. She claims that she was the owner of,
practically, all this property, and that his right was
simply that of a trustee for her. One cannot well escape
the conclusion that the fact of Dunn being a trustee for
Mary Carson Dunn was first thought of to escape the
claims of plaintiff. In no other connection is there a
word or deed in harmony with such a purpose. There
is also strong reason to think that the idea of the utter
worthlessness of Dunn originated when such an escape
became desirable. While he lived, he was trusted by
her as a man possessing business merit, and who was
trustworthy. It is further insisted that the plaintiff is estopped by her acts to claim an interest
in the property. This claim is based on the facts
that she, for many years, knew that her husband was

2

married to Mary Carson Dunn; that she knew that Mary was caring for her children; that Stephen was without means; and that Mary supposed him to be a single man. It is also said that plaintiff caused it to be advertised in a paper that she was dead. Most of the claimed facts have no support in the evidence. It is true that plaintiff, after the marriage of Stephen and Mary, came to look for Stephen, and found him at St. Joe, and was told of the marriage, and that she left him after some conversation, saying that she hoped he would do well. There was little else for her to do. She had been abandoned years before, causelessly, so far as the record shows, and for years knew nothing of her husband or children; the latter having grown to man and womanhood. The claim of her having caused her death to be published is without support; in fact, the claim of estoppel has no substantial support in the record. The decree is clearly right, and it is AFFIRMED.

GEORGE W. DIETZ v. THE CAPITAL CITY BRICK AND PIPE COMPANY, Appellant.

Appeal: TRIAL DE NOVO. *Transcript.* A trial *de novo* may be had upon evidence which is, in part, oral and taken in shorthand by the reporter, and, in part, documentary and written evidence, though said reporter does not sign any transcript of his shorthand report, or certify his shorthand notes, provided the trial judge certifies all the evidence under Code of 1873, section 2742.

Appeal from Polk District Court.—HON. W. A. SPURRIER, Judge.

WEDNESDAY, OCTOBER 27, 1897.

NOTE —The judge's certificate at bar was as follows: "The foregoing is a correct, full and complete transcript of all the evidence, including documentary evidence and testimony of witnesses, produced and sworn upon the trial and whose evidence was taken down in writing at the trial, and which was produced, offered, or introduced upon the trial of said cause, and the foregoing constitutes a complete record of the evidence of said cause and is now hereby made a part of the record of the said cause." —REPORTER.

PLAINTIFF, a judgment creditor of the Central Brick
& Tile Company, brings this action in equity, alleging
that said Central Company has sold and transferred all
of its assets and property to the defendant; that the
purchase price thereof has not been paid; that by the
terms of the agreement of sale there was to be paid out
of the purchase price the debts of the Central Company in cash, and the balance to be paid in stock of the
defendant company, issued ratably to the stockholders
of the Central Company; that by fraudulent collusion
between the defendant and the stockholders of the Central Company all of the said purchase price, exceeding
in amount the debts due plaintiff, is about to be paid
by the issuance of stock, and that plaintiff will lose his
debt, inasmuch as some of the stockholders in the Central Company are insolvent.   The plaintiff claims an
equitable lien on the fund in the defendant's hands, and
a decree for payment of the amount due him.   The
defendant admits the purchase of the property from
the Central Company; that it was to be paid for by
seven hundred dollars cash and the balance to be paid
by the issuance of stock in the defendant company to
the Central Company's stockholders ratably; that such
cash payment was made, and that the rights to stock
in the defendant company have all been purchased and
are now held by one McGorrisk; denies that the defendant now has any property of the Central Company;
denies all fraud and collusion.   There was a trial to the
court, and on January 12, 1895, a decree was entered in
favor of the plaintiff and against the defendant for one
thousand, eight hundred and sixty-two dollars, and
attorney's fees and costs.   Defendant appeals.—
Reversed.

Bishop, Bowen & Fleming for appellant.

J. W. Lindsay, A. M. Miller, and *B. I. Salinger* for appellee.

KINNE, C. J.—I. Appellee insists that the evidence in this cause has never been made of the record, or in any way been properly preserved, so as to entitle this cause to be heard *de novo* in this court. It is said that no translation or transcript of the shorthand notes of the evidence taken in the case, and duly certified by said reporter, has ever been filed, and therefore we have no evidence before us. The situation, as shown by the transcript, is this: This cause was tried on oral evidence, taken in shorthand by the official reporter; also in part upon documentary evidence and written evidence. June 13, 1894, the trial judge made a proper certificate to the shorthand notes, but said reporter's notes do not appear to have been certified by him, nor does he certify to what is claimed to be a transcript or extension of said notes into longhand. The notes appear to have been filed in time. What is claimed to be a transcript or translation of said notes into longhand, though not certified to by the reporter, was filed within the time required. The trial judge, within the time required, makes a proper certificate to all of the evidence. The case then presents this question: Can an equity case, triable *de novo* in this court, be so tried when the official shorthand reporter's notes have never been certified by him, and when he has never certified to the translation of said notes? Appellant's contention is that the certificate of the judge is all that is required. The statutes bearing upon the question are as follows: "But in equitable actions, wherein issue of fact is joined, all the evidence offered in the trial shall be taken down in writing or the court may order the evidence, or any part thereof, to be taken in the form of depositions, or either party may, at pleasure, take his testimony, or any part thereof, by deposition. All the evidence so taken shall be certified by the judge at any time within the time allowed for the appeal of said cause, and be made a part of the record, and go on appeal to the supreme court, which shall try the case anew." Code 1873, section 2742. In section 3777 of the Code of 1873, relating to shorthand reporters, it is provided that "the original notes of any testimony taken in any case shall be filed in the office of the clerk of the court, and become a part of the record in said case, * * * and said original notes, or the transcript thereof, or any part thereof, may be referred to in any bill of exceptions, and when duly transcribed and certified, shall be inserted therein on appeal. * * *" Under section 2742 of the Code of 1873 it has been held that the shorthand notes do not constitute written evidence. *Godfrey v. McKean*, 54 Iowa, 127. And we have said that, if such shorthand notes are afterwards transcribed by the shorthand reporter into longhand, and certified to by him, and filed, such transcript will be deemed written evidence; and we adhere to this holding. *Ross v. Loomis*, 64 Iowa, 432. In *Richards v. Lounesbury*, 65 Iowa, 587, the judge alone certified the shorthand notes. Neither court, judge, nor reporter certified to the translation of the notes, and it was held that the cause could not be tried *de novo* in this court. In that case it is said: "Surely, the reporter, who probably alone can correctly read the notes, ought to certify to the translation; and the certificate of the judge, who cannot read them, ought not to be regarded as alone sufficient. * * * It is plain that the certificate of the judge, who cannot read the notes, cannot give them the character of written evidence in the case. Evidence taken in shorthand can only become the written evidence when translated, and the translation is certified to by the reporter." In *Merrill v. Bowe*, 69 Iowa, 654, the judge alone certified to the shorthand notes, which were filed in time. After the lapse of more than six months, the reporter certified to his translation of the notes, which was filed over eleven months after the entry of the decree. It was held that the evidence had not been properly certified in time. It will be observed that the facts in the case at bar are different. In this case the reporter never certified to his notes, or to the translation of them; and under the holding of the cases cited the mere certificate of the judge to the notes would not be sufficient, as the notes do not become written evidence until translated, and the translation is certified by the reporter. Now, the statute provides for certification to evidence in equitable actions by the judge, and says when it is so certified it shall, on appeal, go to this court, which shall try the case anew. It seems to us, in such cases, the law makes the trial judge the party who must finally determine what the evidence is in a case tried before him, and that whether the notes and the translation of them be certified by the reporter is quite immaterial, except as such certified notes or translation may aid the judge in determining as to what the evidence offered was. Suppose an equitable cause is tried, as it may be, without the aid of a reporter, manifestly, in such a case, the judge alone certifies to the evidence. Suppose an equitable cause is tried on oral evidence taken by a shorthand reporter, and he transcribes his notes into longhand, and certifies to both the notes and the translation, and a controversy should arise as to whether certain of the evidence thus taken had been correctly taken and translated, who would determine the controversy? Say that in such a case, by a proper proceeding by motion, it was sought to correct the notes and the translation, who would be empowered to say whether or not the correction sought

was proper, and should be made? Clearly, in such a
case, the trial judge, who heard the evidence, must
determine what it in fact was. While it is desirable
that the reporter should certify to his notes, as well as
to the translation of them, to the end that the same may
be given whatever force and effect such certificate may
add thereto, and to the end that the judge who tried the
case may be thus officially assured that the notes or
translation presented to him for his certificate are genuine and correct, still no certificate of a shorthand
reporter to the notes, or to the translation, or to both
notes and translation, can relieve the judge who tried
the case from the duty of finally deciding what the evidence offered on the trial was, and certifying it as such.
He may refresh his recollection from the notes, if he
can read them, or from the translation of them, in
determining what the evidence offered was; but he is
not obliged to certify that the notes, or a transcript of
them, as presented to him, in fact correctly set forth the
evidence actually offered upon the trial. Being vested
by the statute with the authority to certify the evidence, he may use the notes, if he can, and the translation of them, and any other means he may have of
determining what evidence was offered upon the trial.
Without desiring to pass upon questions not before us,
it is proper to say that, in case the trial judge is in
doubt as to the correctness of the shorthand notes, or
as to the translation of them, or in case he is satisfied
said notes, or the translation of them, or both, are not
correct, he should, before certifying to either, notify
counsel, so that the record in that respect may be corrected by proper proceedings, if found necessary, before
his certificate is made. Some language used in *Merrill
v. Bowe* and *Richards v. Lounsberry*, *supra*, may seem
to be in conflict with what we have said, and with our
holding in the case at bar. Some of us think, when the

facts of these cases are considered, there is no conflict
between the rules therein stated and what we have said
in this case.   Others of us think that there are statements in said cases which are not reconcilable with
what we have said in the case at bar.   We are united,
however, in holding that, as the evidence in this case
was certified by the judge, and filed in time, it is properly before us; and the motion to strike is overruled.

II.   The appellee has not argued the case upon the
merits, but relied upon the claim that the evidence was
not made of record.   We have held that the evidence is
properly before us.   We shall not enter into a discussion of the evidence.   After carefully considering all of
it, we are satisfied that the decree below should be
reversed.   The evidence shows that before this defendant, or those acting for it, purchased the property of
the Central Company, they insisted that the claim
involved in this action should be settled.   The claim
was then the property of Dietz & Dietz, a firm of which
this plaintiff was a member.   Plaintiff authorized the
other member of the firm to make a settlement of the
claim, and to take stock in the new company for it; and
this he did, and thus satisfied in full the obligation.
The property of the old company was all turned over
to the new company.   The new company never became
in any way liable for this debt.   The claim itself, as we
have said, was, with plaintiff's consent, adjusted and
settled, and he has neither a legal nor moral right to
recover.   The decree below is REVERSED.

103 54
106
108
121
103
134
●134
134
134

STATE OF IOWA, Upon the Relation of JOHN Y. STONE, Attorney General, Plaintiff, v. THE UNION STOCK YARDS STATE BANK AND HOWARD G. PIERCE, Defendants, E. C. TOMPKINS, Receiver, Appellee, MARY C. COOK, Intervener, Appellant.

Banks: INSOLVENCY: *Assessment of stockholder.* The court may
1 make a valid assessment on the stockholder of an insolvent bank
in an *ex parte* proceeding, where the purpose of such assessment
is simply to ascertain the probable condition of the bank, with
the right of stockholders to have their liability judicially deter-
6 mined whenever an attempt is made to enforce the assessment,
under Acts Eighteenth General Assembly, chapter 208, section 1,
making stockholders in banking corporations individually liable,
in addition to the amount of stock held by them, to an amount
equal to their respective shares.

ON REHEARING.

ADJUDICATION. A matter considered and determined in making an
1 order of assessment in proceedings for the appointment of a
receiver of an insolvent corporation is conclusively settled, except
6 so far as it may be changed by vacation or modification of the
receivership proceedings, and will not be reconsidered in an
action to enforce payment of the assessment.

SAME: *Receivers* Under Acts Eighteenth General Assembly, chapter
5 201, section 1, providing that all stockholders shall, in addition to
the amount of stock held by them, be individually liable to an
amount equal to their shares of stock for all liabilities accruing
while they remained such stockholders, and that if any bank
becomes insolvent and its assets are found insufficient to pay its
debts and liabilities, the stockholder may be compelled to pay such
deficiency in proportion to the amount of stock owned by each,
not to exceed the extent of such additional liability, the full stat-
2 utory liability of a stockholder in an insolvent bank may be collected before the assets of the bank are exhausted, subject to an
3 interest in the fund for his proportion of an unexpended balance,
although the amounts collected cannot be distributed until after
the exhaustion of the assets.

SAME. In a suit by the state, under Code 1873, section 1572, to wind
2 up an insolvent bank, the liability of the stockholders under Acts
3 Eighteenth General Assembly, chapter 208, is not directly to the

5 creditors, but constitutes a fund for the debts of the bank, which
the receiver is authorized to collect and distribute.

CONSTITUTIONAL LAW. The provision of constitution, article 8, section 5, that no act authorizing or creating corporations or associations with banking powers, nor amendments thereto, shall take
4 effect until they have been submitted to the people, refers to banks
of issue only, and does not apply to Acts Eighteenth General
Assembly, chapter 208, fixing the liability of stockholders of banking associations and corporations, but not authorizing banks of
issue.

Appeal from Woodbury District Court.—HON. G. W.
WAKEFIELD, Judge.

SATURDAY, APRIL 10, 1897.

THE defendant bank became insolvent, and the
present suit was instituted, under the provision of the
law, Code, section 1572, to wind up the bank and distribute the assets among the creditors. To that end, a
receiver was duly appointed, who took possession of the
property of the bank, and proceeded in the discharge
of his duties. The receiver was appointed June 26,
1893, and in October, 1894, he made a report of his
doings, and of the condition of the bank estate, showing an estimated deficit of ninety-nine thousand and
fifty-nine dollars and twenty-two cents. From the
report it appeared that, of the two hundred and fifty
thousand dollars of outstanding stock of the bank,
fifty thousand dollars was uncollectable. The receiver
asked an order for an assessment, based on such estimates, of seventy-five per cent. against the stockholders
of the bank, under the provisions of chapter 208, Acts
Eighteenth General Assembly. No creditor or stockholder was made a party to the proceeding in which the
order was asked. The order was granted making the
assessment, with authority to the receiver to proceed to
use all legal means to collect the same, by suit or otherwise. Intervener herein is a stockholder, and upon

notice from the receiver of the asessment, and a demand
for payment, she presented her petition of intervention,
in which she claims that the court had not jurisdiction
to make the assessment; that the assessment was
erroneous, because premature, and not supported by
adequate and proper proceedings; and that the act creating the liability was unconstitutional and void. She
asked, as relief, that the order of assessment be set
aside, and that the receiver be directed to take no
further steps or proceedings thereunder. The court
sustained a demurrer to the petition, and the appeal is,
by the intervener, from such ruling.—*Affirmed.*

Kean & Sherman for appellant.

Swan, Lawrence & Swan, J. S. Lothrop, and *Black
& Goodwin* for appellee.

GRANGER, J.—I. The question is first presented
whether the court, in an *ex parte* proceeding, can make
a valid assessment on the stockholders. Much depends
on the effect to be given to the assessment when
1   made. If it is to have a conclusive effect,—that
is, if it is to have the effect of an adjudication so
as to preclude an inquiry thereafter into its correctness
in any essential particular,—we think it cannot be
done. But, if such an assessment is only intended for,
and to have the effect of, an ascertainment by the court
of probable conditions, with the right of a stockholder to
take issue and have his liability judicially determined
whenever there is an attempt to enforce the assessment, then we think such an assessment can properly
be made. This is no more than to say that the court
may, from the record, aided by other information,
determine *prima facie* the extent of the fund necessary
to discharge the liability of the stockholders under the

act, and, upon such a determination, authorize the collection of the same, when, in a suit to enforce such payment, the stockholders may contest his liability
unaffected by such determination. We regard the
assessment in this case no more than such a determination, and with no other legal effect than as we have
stated. Of this determination or assessment appellant
was notified. She thus had the opportunity to investigate and know of her liability, and make payment without cost, if she thought herself liable, or, if not, to contest her liability without prejudice from the assessment made. Such a procedure seems to be in accord
with good business judgment, and without a disadvantage in the preservation of legal rights. In a quite
recent case in Washington, to be hereafter cited, speaking of such liabilities under the laws of the different
states, in considering a method of procedure under a
law similar to ours, it is said that some statutes "provide the mode of enforcing the right; others leave it for
the judiciary to work out the method,"—and the case
adopts a method designed to give effect to the spirit of
the law in that state, as no method of procedure is prescribed. The same is true of our law. It is also to be
said that preliminary assessments, varying in form and
method, are of general observance, where liabilities of
such a nature are to be enforced. Our statute
2   creating the liability is section 1, chapter 208,
Acts Eighteenth General Assembly, as follows:
"That all stockholders or shareholders in associations
or corporations organized under said chapter one aforesaid, for the purpose of transacting a banking business,
buying or selling exchange, receiving deposits of
money, or discounting notes, shall be individually and
severally liable to the creditors of such association or
corporation of which they are stockholders or shareholders, over and above the amount of stock by them

held therein, to an amount equal to their respective shares so held for all its liabilities accruing while they remained such stockholders; and should any such association or corporation become insolvent, and its assets be found insufficient to pay its debts and liabilities, its stockholders may be compelled to pay such deficiency in proportion to the amount of stock owned by each, not to exceed the extent of the additional liability hereby created." The case of *Le Mars Ins. Co. v. Hildreth*, 55 Iowa, 248, may seem not to be in harmony with our conclusion in this case. An assessment was held in that case to be an adjudication, and void, where the stockholder was not made a party. An examination of that case shows a purpose in making the assessment, because of a form of notice, and the character of the assessment made, to fix the liability of the stockholder by the assessment. The action was to recover on the assessment as fixing the liability of the stockholder. It is therein stated that "the plaintiff claims in his petition that the defendant is bound by the assessment made against him." With our construction of the order of assessment in this case, that case is clearly distinguishable, for, in an action to recover, the assessment will serve only as a guide to the amount of recovery.

II. There is also a claim that, before the stockholders can be made liable under the act in question, the assets of the bank must be exhausted; that is, as we understand, all the assets in the hands of the receiver must be applied, and the liability 3 is for the deficiency. We have no doubt that the deficiency measures the extent of the liability of stockholders under the act; but we do not concur in the claim that the assets must first be applied, so that the receiver has no part of them on hand. It is likely true that, pending

the collection, conversion, and application of the assets,
the precise deficiency cannot be known, and if the
thought is that the only right of the creditors of the
bank is to have the exact liability of each stockholder
first determined, and that amount, and that only, collected, we cannot concur in it. Section 2 of the act is
important in this connection. It is as follows: "Should
the whole amount for which the stockholders are made
individually responsible as provided by section 1 of
this act be found in any case to be inadequate to the
payment of all the debts of any such association or corporation, after the application of its assets to the payment of such debts, then the amount due from such
stockholders on account of their individual liability
created by this act, as such, shall be distributed equally
among all the creditors of such corporation in proportion to the amount due to each." It will be seen that
the law contemplates the collection and distribution
of a fund, the distribution to be after the application
of the assets, if we follow the letter of the law. But the
liability for the payment, to create the fund, is not
made to depend on the application of the assets, but on
the fact of the insolvency of the bank. The first section
of the act fixes the conditions as to liability for payment, and the second section fixes the conditions under
which the payment, when made, shall be applied. It
will be noticed, and it is important, that the first section simply deals with the facts that create and limit
the liability of the stockholders. The second section
deals only with the facts to govern the application of
the money when collected. Now, our thought is, conceding for the present the right of a receiver, in such
a case, to collect and distribute the fund, that the liability of the stockholder for payment does not depend
on conditions that accurately fix the extent of his liability, but on the facts of the insolvency of the bank and a

liability of the stockholder, because such when the debts accrued. With the facts established to fix a liability to the fund, we think it is, primarily, for the full amount contemplated by the act, subject to such an interest in the fund, when created, as will entitle him to his proportion of any balance unexpended upon final settlement. If the conditions are such that the court or receiver shall attempt to collect less than the full amount, of course it is nothing of which the stockholder can complain, and we are not saying that more should be collected or demanded than the conditions seem to justify. But it can be readily seen that accuracy, as to amount, is impracticable, if not impossible, because the expenses of collection and distribution cannot be known beforehand, and, if the assets of the bank were previously exhausted, there would be no other fund from which to pay such expenses. We think, in such cases, the time for collection, and amount to be collected, can best be left to the sound discretion of the court; for we deal now only with cases where the bank estate is in process of liquidation, by a proceeding in court, by direction of the auditor of state. It is a case in which the state has in charge the settlement of the bank affairs. See Code, sections 1571, 1572.

III. It is claimed that chapter 208, Acts Eighteenth General Assembly, being the act under which the liability of stockholders is created, is unconstitutional because not submitted to a vote of the people, under the provisions of article 8, section 5, of the constitution of the state, as follows: "No act of the general assembly authorizing or creating corporations or associations with banking powers, nor amendments thereto, shall take effect, or in any manner be in force, until the same shall have been submitted, separately, to the people, at a general or special election, as provided by law, to be held not less than

three months after the passage of the act, and shall
have been approved by a majority of all the electors
voting for and against it at such election." This article
of the constitution received construction in *Allen
v. Clayton*, 63 Iowa, 11, and it was there held that
section 5, with other sections, had reference only to
banks of issue. Chapter 208 is amendatory of the
general incorporation act, being chapter 1, title 9,
Code. Neither the act amended, nor the amendment,
creates or authorizes a corporation or association
with banking powers as intended by the constitutional
provision. The acts do not authorize banks of issue.

IV. Another claim against the validity of the
assessment is that the liability of stockholders under
the act is not an asset of the bank, so that it is a matter
within the power or authority of a receiver, and
5   hence that the liability of the stockholder is
directly to the creditors of the bank after the
bank assets are exhausted. In this respect reliance is
placed on many authorities which hold that such liabilities, or the money received therefrom, are not assets of
the bank, and that a receiver has no authority to collect
or apply them. That may be stated as the general rule.
The rule, however, is not without its exceptions, caused
sometimes by statutory enactments, and at others by
judicial construction. The general rule, as stated, has
usually been announced in cases of voluntary assignments or receiverships, at the instance of creditors,
with no statutory limitation or direction as to the application of the money when collected. Mr. Thompson, in
his Commentaries on the Law of Corporations (volume
3, section 3561), having stated the general rule, says the
rule has been changed by statute. The text is supported
by a citation to *Story v. Furman*, 25 N. Y. 214. That
case deals quite elaborately with the right of a receiver
to collect and distribute money due from stockholders

under such an act. It is said in the case that "this stockholders' liability constituted a fund for the payment of all the corporate debts after its assets were exhausted, and, if it was insufficient to pay all the debts, it must be distributed among the creditors upon equitable principles," etc. That is the law of this state. In that case, after a full discussion of the facts and law to justify a recovery by the receiver, it is said: "Independently of these views, which relate chiefly to the arguments addressed to us on the hearing, I should be prepared to reverse the judgment of the court below, and affirm the judgment of the referee, upon another distinct ground. I do not see why the order appointing the plaintiff receiver did not vest him with ample authority to enforce the stockholders' liability under the statute. Such liability is clearly a fund in equity for the payment of the debts of the corporation. The receiver was appointed in a suit instituted by creditors, and in behalf of all the creditors of the corporation. He was expressly authorized, by the order of the supreme court, to commence an action against each and all of the stockholders of said corporation who are solvent, for the recovery of such a contributory sum from each solvent stockholder, not exceeding the whole amount of stock owned by them, as will be necessary to satisfy any deficiency that might exist in the payment of the debts of the said corporation." It is further said in the opinion: "I do not see why this order was not entirely within the authority and jurisdiction of the supreme court as a court of equity as an original equity power at common law. The appointment of a receiver was the only appropriate mode to reach and collect this equitable fund, the personal statute liability of the stockholders, for distribution among the creditors." This extended quotation is justified because of the importance of the rule announced. It will be seen that, after

the conclusion that a fund is to be collected for distribution among creditors, it announces a broad common law
rule, that is an exception to the general rule, that a
court of equity possesses an inherent common law jurisdiction to appoint a receiver with authority to collect
and distribute the fund. This case is frequently cited
in the books, and is nowhere criticised. In High on
Receivers (section 317a), the exception to the general
rule is noticed, and it is there said: "But under a
statute making all persons composing the corporation
liable to the extent of their respective shares of stock,
for all debts due at the time of the dissolution of the
corporation, a receiver, appointed in an action brought
in behalf of all the creditors to wind up the corporation,
may enforce the liability against the shareholders."
This text is also supported by a reference to *Story v.
Furman, supra*. In the authorities cited as sustaining
the right of a receiver to collect and distribute this fund,
it is stated that the rule obtains where all the stockholders are liable for all the debts of the corporation.
Our law provides that stockholders shall only be liable
for debts accruing while they remained stockholders,
and it is thought by some that this provision operates
against the authority of the receiver. While this language is included, with the other language, in announc-
ing the rule, it nowhere appears that it is regarded as
a controlling fact, or one essential to the application of
the rule. Without exception, we think, where the law
contemplates a fund for distribution, it must be done by
a receiver, assignee, trustee, or some such officer of the
court. If it be in an equitable proceeding by a creditor,
wherein all persons interested are made parties, the
fund must be collected and distributed under the direction of the court, and this must be done, of course, by
some person selected for that purpose. It is difficult to
understand why the court, with the receiver as its agent,

may not as equitably deal with the situation to arise
from this provision of our statute as it could in the same
kind of an action, at the instance of a creditor, with
some person appointed to make a distribution. In both
cases the entire matter is under the control and direction of the court. This provision of the statute does not,
of course, operate to defeat the provision as to *pro rata*
distribution, and, wherever that is to be done by the
court, it is one of equitable cognizance. It may be said
that, so far as we have observed, our statute is unlike
any under which the general rule, above stated, has
been announced. It is also to be said that chapter 208,
giving rise to this liability of stockholders, is made, by
its terms, a part of the general incorporation law under
which the defendant bank was organized. That law
contains the provisions under which the state, on the
relation of the attorney general, is to commence such
suits to wind up such corporations, and all its provisions are to be construed together. It would seem
like a strange and uncalled for state of affairs for the
suit, at the instance of the state, to proceed until the
assets of the bank were exhausted, and then subject the
creditors to delays, and the annoyance of another like
suit, at their own instance, to collect and distribute this
fund. See, for a case in point and quite fully considered, *Wilson v. Book*, 13 Wash. 676 (43 Pac. Rep. 939).
See, also, *Watterson v. Masterson*, 15 Wash. 511 (46 Pac.
Rep. 1041). We reach the conclusion that the assessment is not invalid because of a want of authority for a
receiver, in case of a valid assessment, to collect and
distribute the fund under orders of the court. From
these considerations it follows that the judgment of the
district court must be AFFIRMED.

SUPPLEMENTAL OPINION ON REHEARING.

THURSDAY, OCTOBER 28, 1897.

Overruled.

GRANGER, J.—In an application for a re-hearing, it is
urged that the opinion, wherein it states the effect of the
order of assessment when a suit is brought to enforce
payment, is not in harmony with the rule stated
6   in *Schoonover v. Hinckley,* 48 Iowa, 82, and *Stewart v. Lay,* 45 Iowa, 604. In view of the language
used, the claim is not without support. We understand
the rule to be, as to the appointment of a receiver and
the making of such an assessment, that all matters
that necessarily inhere in the orders by which such
results are attained,—that is, matters to be considered
and determined in making the orders,—are adjudicated
and conclusively settled, except in so far as they be
changed by vacation or modification in the receivership proceeding upon application of parties interested,
whether stockholders or others. It is definitely settled
in *Stewart v. Lay, supra,* that none of these matters
can be set up in an action brought by the receiver under
direction of the court. It is urged to us that one of the
district courts of the state has held,—following the
opinion in this case,—that in an action on such an
assessment the amount of recovery cannot be contro-
verted. Such a holding is correct. It was one of the
matters considered and determined in making the order
of assessment, and, if erroneous, the error must be
cured in the same proceeding. With the opinion thus
modified, we are content with its conclusion, and the
petition for a re-hearing is OVERRULED.

E. MANNING V. D. W. FERGUSON, Appellant.
103 561
114
4114

Execution Sale: RIGHTS OF PURCHASER. A purchaser at execution
5 sale takes subject to the rights of the parties as they shall be
adjudicated in the action then pending, and by virtue of which
the property is sold.

Subrogation: DEFAULT. By reason of a defendant's guaranty of the
1 note, he was entitled, even before payment of the note, to have
4 provision made for his subrogation to the rights of the mortgagors,
6 entitling him to relief, and the decree in favor of the judgment
creditor should be set aside for want of notice to him and wrongful entry of default.

DEEMER, J., dissenting.

Default: APPLICATION TO OPEN. An application to set aside a
4 default and a decree wrongfully entered, is not governed by Code
7 1873, sections 2837, 2838, providing for applications for new trial.

Appeal. Where appellee denies that an agreed statement of facts has
2 been made a part of the record on appeal, and there is no response
to the denial, except in argument, the statement will be stricken
out from the abstract.

DEFAULT: *Estoppel to appeal.* Defendant was the payee and guar-
1 antor of a note, secured by mortgage, given for the price of the
land mortgaged. A bill was filed by the assignee of the note
and mortgage Defendant was defaulted and judgment was
8 rendered against him and the mortgagors for the amount of the
note, and the mortgage was foreclosed. A counter-claim was filed
4 by a judgment creditor claiming a lien prior to the mortgage,
which was allowed. Defendant was made a party to but was not
served with notice of the filing of said counter-claim, and default
was entered against him. *Held,* that though the owner of the
mortgage did not appeal from the order allowing the said claim
as a prior lien, defendant, as guarantor of the note, was not
thereby estopped from appealing from the refusal of the court to
set aside so much of the decree as affected his rights.

Appeal from Van Buren District Court.—HON. T. M.
FEE, Judge.

THURSDAY, OCTOBER 28, 1897.

·ACTION in equity to recover the amount due on a promissory note and for the foreclosure of a mortgage given to secure its payment. Marion Poling and Luella Poling, who were the makers of the note, the payee and guarantor, Ferguson, and Nichols, Shepard & Co., were made parties defendant. Judgment by default was rendered against the Polings and Ferguson for the amount due on the note, and the mortgage was foreclosed as to them, and the cause was continued as to Nichols, Shepard & Co. At a subsequent term the plaintiff dismissed his action as against that company, and a decree was rendered in its favor. Ferguson afterwards appeared, and asked to have his default and the decree rendered in the cause set aside. The court granted but a part of the relief he demanded, and from its refusal to grant more, he appeals.—*Reversed.*

Mitchell & Sloan for appellant.

Wherry & Walker for appellee.

ROBINSON, J.—The note upon which the plaintiff obtained judgment was dated December 31, 1891. The mortgage was upon one hundred and twenty acres of

1   land in Van Buren county, and was recorded on the twenty-second day of January, 1892. Its date is not shown. The answer of Nichols, Shepard & Co. is in the nature of a counter-claim, and states that on the twenty-fifth day of November, 1885, the company recovered in the circuit court of Van Buren county against the defendant Marion Poling a judgment of which a large amount was unpaid; that Marion Poling purchased the land, and received a conveyance therefor on the thirty-first day of December, 1891; and that from that date the judgment became and was a lien on the land, and that the mortgage became a lien

upon the land as against the judgment creditors only
from and after its filing for record. Nichols, Shepard
& Co. asks that its judgment be declared to be a lien
upon the mortgaged premises prior and senior to the
lien of the mortgage, and that the equity of redemption
of the plaintiff and all of the defendants, in the mortgaged premises, be foreclosed and forever barred. To
that answer the plaintiff filed a reply, in which he
admitted the rendition of the judgment, but denied that
it was superior to the lien of the mortgage, and alleged
that the mortgage was given for purchase price of the
mortgaged premises. The decree rendered in favor of
Nichols, Shepard & Co., adjudged the Polings and Ferguson to be in default, and that the judgment in its
favor was a lien upon the mortgaged premises senior
to the lien of the mortgage. The equity of redemption
of the Polings was foreclosed. The motion of Ferguson
to set aside the default and decree was based upon his
affidavit, which showed that he was one of the defendants in the action; that he had no notice or knowledge
of the counter-claim of Nichols, Shepard & Co., and that
he first learned of the default against him and the
decree in favor of the company on the day the affidavit
was made. The affidavit further states that Ferguson
sold the land in question to the Polings, and that the
mortgage was for the purchase price of the land; that
the judgment in favor of the company was obtained
long prior to the sale of the land and the execution of
the mortgage, and is not, in law or in equity, senior to
the mortgage, and that such an issue did not necessarily arise in the foreclosure proceedings; that Ferguson sold the mortgage to the plaintiff, and that in the
proceedings to foreclose it Ferguson was made a
defendant because of the fact that he was indorser of
the note. Upon considering the motion of Ferguson

the district court found that, no notice of the counter-
claim having been served upon him, the motion should
be sustained so far as the decree purported to be
against him, and the decree was accordingly modified
by striking therefrom that part which purported to
enter a default or decree against him. The motion, so
far as it applied to the decree against Manning, was
overruled, and of that part of the order the appellant
complains.

I. The abstract contains what purports to be an
agreed statement of facts, signed by the attorneys for
the plaintiff and for Nichols, Shepard & Co. The
appellee, in an additional abstract, denies that
2   it was ever made a part of the record. To that
denial there is no response except in argument,
and it must therefore be taken as true, and a motion to
strike it from the abstract has been sustained.

II. The application of Ferguson did not show any
ground for setting aside the default and judgment
which Manning obtained, and the judgment in his favor
must be regarded as final and conclusive as against
Ferguson. It is contended that the decree in
3   favor of Nichols, Shepard & Co. as against Manning is also final, and that, as he has not
appealed therefrom, Ferguson cannot. It is also
claimed that the attempt of the latter to have the decree
against Manning set aside must be regarded as an
attempt to intervene, and that it was too late. The
appeal of Ferguson is not from the decree against Manning, but must be regarded as from the refusal of the
court to set aside so much of it as affected his claim to
the mortgaged property. The fact that Manning dismissed his petition before the decree was rendered did
not affect the right of the defendant company to insist
upon a hearing on its counter-claim; and, since Manning did not appeal from the decree rendered on that

hearing, that decree is final as to him. But the counter-
claim asked affirmative relief as against the appellant,
and he was entitled to notice of, and an opportunity to
be heard as to that claim.   The district court could,
therefore, upon a proper application, rightly set aside
the default in favor of the company, ánd so much of
the decree as affected the rights of the appellant;
but the court refused to set aside so much of it as
was against the property involved in the action.
Ferguson was not a mere intervener, but had been
made a party to the counter-claim by reason of the
demand for relief against him which had been made,
and an application by him to set aside the decree so far
as it affected his interests was proper. By reason of his
application he submitted himself to the jurisdiction of
the court as to the counter-claim, and is bound by the
decree rendered thereon so long as it is in force. Therefore he has the right to have the ruling of the district
court which denied him the relief he asked reviewed by
means of an appeal.

III. We are next required to determine whether
the appellant showed such an interest in the mortgaged
property as to entitle him to have the decree as to that
set aside or modified. The effect of the action

4   of the district court was to set aside the default
and decree so far as they affected the appellant
personally, and to refuse to set them aside so far as
they affected the mortgaged property. To entitle the
appellant to have the default set aside it was necessary
for him to file an affidavit of merits which should contain a statement of facts from which the court could
determine whether he had a meritorious defense to the
counter-claim. Code 1873, section 2871; *King v. Stewart*, 48 Iowa, 334. We have set out so much of the affi-
avit which the appellant filed in support of his application as can be claimed to show the interest which he

asserts in the property in question. In its additional
abstract, Nichols, Shepard & Co. shows that, in July,
1894, which was more than nine months before the
decree in question was rendered, the mortgaged premises were sold to the appellant under a special execution which issued on the judgment in favor of the plaintiff and against the Polings for about the sum required
to satisfy the judgment. The indorsement of the appellant on the note which the mortgage in question
secured was in words as follows: "For value received,
I guarantee the payment of the within note at maturity.
[Signed] D. W. Ferguson." The record submitted to
us does not contain the evidence upon which the cause
on the counter-claim was tried, and it must be presumed
that it was shown that the judgment of Nichols, Shepard & Co. was a lien upon the land in question senior
to that created by the mortgage. The alleged stipulation of facts which has been stricken from the abstract
did not show that the mortgage was given to secure the
purchase price. But for the purpose of appellant's
application it must be assumed by us that the statements of his affidavit, so far as they recite alleged facts,
and not conclusions of law, are true. The question,
then, arises whether the fact that the note was given
to secure the purchase price of the land, and that it was
indorsed as stated, and, with the mortgage, was sold
to the plaintiff, gave to the appellant an interest in the
land which he is entitled to have protected in this
action. We do not think he can claim anything
5   in this case from his mere purchase of the land
at execution sale, for the reason that he purchased subject to the rights of the parties as they should
be adjudicated in the action which was then pending to
determine whose lien upon the land was the senior one.
Rider v. Kelso, 53 Iowa, 369. Nor do we understand

him to make any claim of that kind, although it is discussed by the appellant; but he bases his objection to
the ruling of the district court upon the interest which
he claims was created by his indorsement of the note.

He insists that by reason of that indorsement he
6   had a vested right, contingent upon his payment
of the note, to be subrogated to the rights of the
plaintiff as against the land, and that a court of equity
would take cognizance of that contingent right, and
make provisions for its enforcement. As between themselves, Ferguson was surety for the makers of the note.
It represented their debt, the payment of which he had
guaranteed; and it is well settled that in such cases, if
the surety pay the debt, he is entitled to the benefit of
all securities which the principal debtor has placed in
the hands of his creditors to secure the debt. *Rand v.
Barrett*, 66 Iowa, 736; *City of Keokuk v. Love*, 31 Iowa,
123; 3 Pomory, Equity Jurisprudence, section 1419, and
note; 24 Am. & Eng. Enc. Law, 187; 2 Brandt, Suretyship and Guaranty, section 298. In *City of Keokuk v.
Love, supra*, the right of sureties to have provision for
subrogation made before they had paid the debt of their
principal was considered, and held to exist. In that
case the sureties had not paid the debt when the judgment was rendered, and the trial court did not provide
for subrogation. The sureties afterwards paid the debt,
and it was urged against them on appeal that the right
of subrogation did not exist when the judgment was rendered, and that a new case could not be made on appeal.
This court said of those claims: "All this is answered
by the single proposition that the power of a court of
equity is not limited to settling the rights of parties
upon what has been done in the past, but it reaches
forth, and declares their duties and rights for the future;
and in the exercise of this latter power it should have
decreed that when the sureties paid the debt of their

principal they should be subrogated to the rights of the creditor." What was thus said is applicable in this action, and is decisive of the controlling question involved in this appeal.

IV. The appellee contends that the application of the appellant is governed by sections 2837 and 2838 of the Code of 1873, and that it is not sufficient to meet their requirements. But those sections refer to 7 applications for a new trial, and do not apply in this case. The appellant had not had the benefit of a trial before the decree in question was rendered, and his application was not for a new trial, but to set aside a default wrongly entered, and a decree wrongly rendered, in order that a trial might be had.

V. We conclude that the application of the appellant was made in due time, and that he showed a meritorious defense to the claim of Nichols, Shepard & Co., and a contingent right to subrogation which entitled him to relief. It was a proper action in which to settle the claims of the various persons who were interested in the subject-matter of the litigation. The appellant was a party to the action, and affirmative relief had been asked against him by Nichols, Shepard & Co., and granted. It was his right to be heard in his own behalf before judgment was rendered against him; and, as the company had not notified him of its adverse claim, it was his right, if his affidavit be true, to have the default set aside, and to be heard on the merits of his claims. The district court, therefore, erred in not fully setting aside the default of the appellant, and requiring him to plead forthwith, and issuably. Code 1873, section 2871. Its ruling, so far as it is involved in this appeal, is REVERSED.

DEEMER, J. (dissenting.)—The opinion holds that the decree, as between Nichols, Shepard & Co. and Man-

ning, is conclusive, and yet finds that Ferguson, by
reason of his being a guarantor of the Poling note, is
entitled to subrogation, and to rights superior to that of
the creditor, Manning. Concede that in a proper case
subrogation may be enforced in equity before payment
of the debt, yet the right of the guarantor is to be substituted in the shoes of the creditor. Subrogation is
the substitution of some other person in the place of
and to the rights of a creditor. If Ferguson has any
right, it is to be placed in the same position, and
given the same rights, as Manning has, when he (Ferguson) pays the judgment. It is universally held that the
party subrogated can obtain no greater rights than
were possessed by the one in whose place he is substituted. *Knapp v. Sturges*, 36 Vt. 721; Sheldon, Subrogation, section 6; Harris, Subrogation, section 489; 24
Am. & Eng. Enc. Law, page 192. The opinion says that
the decree is final as to Manning, and also finds that
there was a showing upon the trial that Nichols, Shepard & Co.'s judgment was superior to Manning's mortgage. The effect of the conclusion reached by the
majority is to give to Ferguson, in virtue of his right of
subrogation, greater rights than his creditor has
against Nichols, Shepard & Co. It must be remembered
that Ferguson was in default as to Manning's petition,
and that he made no claim of a right to subrogation in
that case. The decree on the Nichols, Shepard & Co.
petition was set aside as to Ferguson. This is all he
was entitled to, and, in my judgment, the case should be
AFFIRMED.

S. K. MYERS, Appellant, v. KITTIE TOWNSEND.

Sales: RESCISSION—REPLEVIN. Plaintiff in replevin, who relies in
    his petition upon the breach of a contract for conditional sale of
    the property, cannot recover where the defendant establishes a

right to rescind the contract for fraudulent misrepresentations, that rescission and return were offered and demanded and that plaintiff has never acquiesced in such rescission.

Appeal from Webster District Court.—Hon. B. P. Birdsall, Judge.

Thursday, October 28, 1897.

Action at law to recover the possession of a piano in the defendant's possession under a written contract, by the terms of which defendant agreed to pay therefor in installments. By the terms of the contract the title, ownership, and possession remained in plaintiff, and he was authorized to take possession of it at any time, even before the maturity of the contract. He alleged that but ten dollars had been paid on the instrument, that he had demanded possession, and that defendant had refused to surrender it. Defendant pleaded that the contract under which she purchased was partly in writing and partly in parol; that the instrument was warranted; that fraud was practiced upon her in its sale; that she offered to rescind the contract, by tendering back the instrument she received, and demanding the ten dollars she had paid, and the return of an old piano which she had given the plaintiff as part payment on the new one, which he refused to do. In reply the plaintiff denied the alleged fraud, and further pleaded that when defendant offered to rescind he had sold the piano, and could not return it. Trial to a jury, verdict and judgment for defendant, and plaintiff appeals.— *Affirmed.*

Blake & Mitchell for appellant.

Yeoman & Kenyon for appellee.

Deemer, J.—The court instructed the jury, in effect, that if defendant was induced to enter into the contract by means of false and fraudulent representations of the plaintiff, which she relied upon; and
1   if such representations were known by plaintiff to be false when made, and they were made for the purpose of deceiving the defendant, and were such as a person of ordinary intelligence and prudence would ordinarily act upon; and if the defendant, not knowing of their falsity, was induced thereby to execute the contract and part with her property, and she was damaged thereby; and if she, in reasonable time after the discovery of the fraud, offered to return said piano to plaintiff upon his returning to her the old piano, and plaintiff was in a condition so to do, but refused to do so, —then they should find for her. This instruction is complained of. We think that it was correct, as applied to the issues tendered. The plaintiff in such an action must recover solely upon the strength of his own title, and not upon the weakness of that of his adversary; and he must, in his petition, state the nature and extent of his interest in the property sought to be recovered. Having stated the nature and extent of his interest, and the grounds of his recovery, he must prove it, in order to be entitled to the verdict. Proof of some other state of facts entitling him to possession is not sufficient. *Kern v. Wilson*, 73 Iowa, 490. As plaintiff was seeking to recover under the terms of a written contract, the defendant could have defeated his recovery by pleading and proving any state of facts which would have avoided the contract. This, defendant attempted to do by pleading fraud in the inception of the contract, and the jury found that her claim was established. If established, the contract was avoided, and plaintiff could not recover thereon. It is said, however, that the facts pleaded in answer do not negative the plaintiff's right

of possession. These facts show an attempt at rescission
on the ground of fraud and breach of warranty. It
appears that defendant gave an old piano, valued at one
hundred and twenty-five dollars, and ten dollars in
cash, in part payment for the new instrument; that, as
soon as she discovered the fraud and breach of warranty, she demanded the return of her old piano and the
money paid, and offered to return the instrument she
received; and that plaintiff refused to comply with her
demands. If these demands had been complied with,
plaintiff would, under proper allegations, have been
entitled to the return of the instrument sold. Plaintiff
did not consent to the rescission. On the contrary, he is
now insisting upon the terms of his contract,—a contract which the jury found was fraudulent and void.
Upon what theory, then, may he recover? He had no
right to rescind the contract; for he is the party who
was guilty of the fraud, and consequently can found no
rights thereon. Had there been a mutual agreement
for rescission, and plaintiff had made the necessary
allegations in his petition, it is likely he could recover.
Downey v. Riggs, 102 Iowa, 88. But that is not this
case. Here plaintiff is seeking to assert his rights under
the contract, and he is not entitled to the instrument,
on account of rescission by the defendant for fraud,
unless he acquiesced therein, and pleaded facts entitling
him to recover by virtue of a mutual rescission of the
contract. Any other rule would permit the seller to
take advantage of his own wrong, and would give him,
not only possession of the. property sold, but confer
upon him the fruits of his fraudulent bargain, as well.
Surely this is not the law. It must be remembered that
defendant is not pleading a counter-claim. She meets
the plaintiff's claim under the contract by pleading and
proving that it is void for fraud. Having done this, she
meets the plaintiff's demand, and defeats his right to

recover. When it is conceded, as it must be, that plaintiff had no right of rescission, and that he must recover either upon the contract, or upon a mutual rescission which gives him the right to the possession of the instrument, the case is determined. Counsel argue at length the questions as to the character of the contract, the right to rescind, the necessity of a return of the property in order to effectuate a rescission, and many other question which we do not regard as controlling. True, the court instructed as to what it was necessary for defendant to do in order to rescind the contract on her part, and this instruction appears to be correct. It seems to be well settled that an offer to return the property is sufficient, where the contract is induced by fraud. *Hendrickson v. Hendrickson,* 51 Iowa, 68; 2 Parsons, Contracts, 780; Beach, Modern Contracts, section 792. Defendant did everything on her part essential to a rescission. Plaintiff did not assent to it, however, and is now insisting upon a recovery, under the terms of the contract, of the instrument sold; and at the same time is insisting upon retaining the money and piano received in exchange. This, as we have seen, he cannot do, and the court was right in so instructing the jury.—AFFIRMED.

H. W. HAWLEY v. THE CITY OF FORT DODGE, *et al.,* Appellants.

Sidewalk Construction: ORDINANCES. Where an ordinance authorizes the city council to order the construction of a sidewalk, by resolution which shall be served on the adjoining lot owners, and provides that in case the owner fails to construct the walk within the time fixed, the work shall be done on contract at his expense, service of the resolution is a condition precedent to the right to have the walk constructed at the expense of the lot owner.

Appeal from Webster District Court.—HON. B. P. BIRD-
SALL, Judge.

THURSDAY, OCTOBER 28, 1897.

ACTION to enjoin the collection of an assessment for
the cost of constructing a temporary sidewalk in front
of lots owned by plaintiff in the defendant city. Decree
for plaintiff, and the defendants appealed.—*Affirmed.*

Blake & Mitchell for appellants.

Frank Farrell for appellee.

GRANGER, J.—The Defendants, other than the city,
are the treasurer of the city and the treasurer of the
county. In 1873 the city council of Fort Dodge adopted
an ordinance of which the following is a part: "The city
council may, by resolution passed by two-thirds of the
whole number of councilmen composing such council,
order the laying of a temporary plank sidewalk at a cost
not to exceed forty cents per lineal foot, and may
require the same to be kept in repair. Such temporary
sidewalk shall be laid upon the natural surface as near
as practicable without regard to grade, until the street
wherein they are laid shall have been permanently
improved, and the cost of such temporary sidewalk shall
be assessed against the property in front of which the
same shall be laid, and the resolution therefor shall
describe the kind and character of said walk, and the
material of which the same shall be constructed, and
the time within, and the street and place along which
the same shall be constructed." In 1877 the city council amended the ordinance of 1873, and the following is
a part of the amendment: "Section 1. Be it ordained
by the city council of the city of Fort Dodge, that whenever such construction, improvement or repair is

ordered as provided in section first, second and fifth of
the above named ordinance, such resolution shall be
served by the city marshal upon resident lot owners,
and agents of non-resident owners, and if there be
none, then by publication for two consecutive weeks, on
non-residents, in some newspaper printed in said city,
and in case the owner of the property along the said
street or highway, where such construction, improvement or repair is ordered, shall fail to make the same
within the time fixed in such resolution, then the same
shall be constructed as provided by said resolution, and
the officer, contractor or person under whose supervision such construction, improvement or repair shall have
been made, shall return to the city council a detailed
statement of the cost thereof, opposite each lot, or part
of lot, parcel of land along which the said construction,
improvement or repair shall have been made, with the
name of the owner or owners thereof, when known to
him, and thereupon the city council shall, by resolution,
declare an assessment against such lot, part of lot, or
parcel of land, and the owner or owners thereof, if
known, of the costs of such construction, improvement
or repair, together with all the costs and expenses connected therewith." In March, 1892, the following resolution was adopted for the construction of the sidewalk in question: "Be it resolved by the city council of
the city of Fort Dodge, that there is hereby ordered
temporary sidewalks from west end of Farley street
bridge along blocks 33 and 37, Duncombe's subdivision
of West Fort Dodge, Iowa; thence running along the
south side of the street on the north side of block 10,
and on the west side of block 10 of West Fort Dodge,
Iowa."

It will be seen that the ordinances of the city under
which the council proceeded specify the notice to be
given to lot owners where it is sought to make the cost

of sidewalks a burden on the lots. There is something of a showing of the service of a notice by the marshal of the city, but it is too slight to be entitled to credence. His testimony amounts to no more than saying: "I guess I did serve the notice, but I have no knowledge on the subject." The service of the resolution in one of the ways provided in the ordinance was a condition precedent to a right to have the walk constructed on contract at the expense of the owner of the lots. The city was as much required to observe the ordinance as the lot owner. The ordinance contemplates the right of the lot owner to construct the walk himself, after notice. The lot owners, whether resident or non-resident, must take notice of the ordinances as they may operate for or against them; and the city must, to justify the imposition of such burdens by virtue of such ordinances, do the things necessary to give them effect. The giving of the notice in the way and of the kind specified in the ordinances is precisely what the city had engaged to do by its enactment, of which all persons were required to take notice. This case is not within the rule of *Gatch v. City of Des Moines*, 63 Iowa, 718; *Ford v. Town of North Des Moines*, 80 Iowa, 636; or *Trustees of Griswold College v. City of Davenport*, 65 Iowa, 633, and like cases. They treat of an absolute right to notice before the assessment can be made effective. In this case there is a failure to give a prescribed notice. It is not necessary to consider other questions. The judgment is AFFIRMED.

MARY S. FOOTE, Appellant, v. THE BURLINGTON GAS-LIGHT COMPANY.

Damages: SUPPLEMENTAL PETITION. In an action to recover dam-
1   ages for injury to property, resulting from the maintenance of a nuisance, a claim for additional damages accruing since the commencement of the action, from a continuance of the same nuisance, may be set up by supplemental petition.

Pleadings: SUPPLEMENTAL PETITION. Facts occurring after the com-
2   mencement of an action which merely strengthen, develop, or

reinforce the original cause of action or enlarge the extent of or change the relief sought thereby, may properly be introduced by supplemental petition, although they would support an independent action.

CONTINUANCE.   The filing of an amendment or a supplemental peti-
3 tion does not alone entitle defendant to a continuance, but he must show some good reason why he cannot safely proceed with the trial.

Appeal from Des Moines District Court.—HON. HENRY BANK, JR., Judge.

THURSDAY, OCTOBER 28, 1897.

ACTION for damages occasioned by filling the air with gas, smoke, soot, and obnoxious odors from defendant's gas and electric plants, and carried to the premises of plaintiff, injuring her property, and interfering with the enjoyment of her homestead. There was a trial to the court, and judgment for the plaintiff. From an order granting a new trial, she appeals.— *Reversed.*

C. L. Poor and *W. C. McArthur* for appellant.

Smyth & Lewald and *Blake & Blake* for appellee.

LADD, J.—This action was begun August 31, 1892, and the substituted answer filed September 21, 1895. The original petition alleges that from January 6, 1892, the plaintiff's property was injured, and its enjoyment interfered with, by the gas, smoke, soot, and obnoxious odors emitted from defendant's gas and electric plants, and claims damages in the sum of eight hundred dollars. The substituted answer sets up three defenses: (1) The statute of limitations; (2) that the operation of the plants was authorized by the laws of the state and the ordinances of the city; (3) a general denial. The case was set down for trial November 20, 1895, and on that day the plaintiff filed a supplemental petition alleging the wrongs complained of had been continued since the beginning of the action, and asking one thousand, two hundred dollars additional damages. The defendant thereupon moved to strike the supplemental petition because not pertaining to the original petition, setting up a new cause of action, and filed too late. This motion was overruled, and the defendant asked for a contin- uance on the ground that "the supplemental petition claims for time subsequent to the filing of the original petition up to the present time, about three years and one-half, and for one thousand, two hundred dollars additional damages; this being, as defendant's counsel deem it, entirely new matter, and a claim for recovery of new money, and different from the recovery on the original petition, and one which they have not investi- gated or conferred with their clients or their witnesses concerning." To this the plaintiff objected because "there is no allegation that defendant cannot be ready to fully present the facts in defense to the supplemental petition, as well as to the original petition. * * * The president and general manager are in court, and can be consulted, if counsel desire. The defense for the time covered by the original petition must be the same as for the time covered by the supplemental petition." The court overruled the motion, remarking that, "in the absence of an averment, in a motion for continuance, that the counsel are not prepared to go to trial, and that they cannot properly present the case without a postponement, the court would not be warranted in con tinuing the cause." The same defense was made as to the original petition, and the parties proceeded to trial. December 13, 1895, the court entered judgment against the defendant for nine hundred dollars. Motion for new trial was filed January 11, 1896, time for so doing having been extended to that date, and was afterwards sustained on the ground that the court erred in over- ruling the motions to strike and for continuance. In a written opinion filed, the presiding judge, who, by the way, did not sit at the trial, expressly states that he

does not pass on the other grounds of the motion for
new trial, and for this reason they will not be considered here.

I.   Why not permit damages since the beginning
of an action to be claimed in a supplemental petition,
when of the same nature, and occasioned by the same
cause?   The nuisance was a continuing one.
1   Had no supplemental petition been filed, another
action could have been maintained for the damages therein alleged.   But, if the original action had
been dismissed, the plaintiff might well have claimed,
in a new petition, damages for the entire period, and
no one would contend two causes of action were stated.
It follows, then, that the original and supplemental
petitions, when read together, state but one cause of
action, and the relief sought is only enlarged.
2   The true criterion for determining the propriety
of a supplemental petition does not lie in ascertaining whether it states a cause of action which might
be independently maintained.   If it may be read with
the original petition, and both considered as one pleading, and if its scope is limited to strengthening, developing, or re-enforcing the original cause of action, or of
enlarging the extent of or changing the relief sought,
then it meets the very purpose of such a pleading.
Leach v. Association, 102 Iowa, 125.   The new cause of
action which the law will not permit to be thus pleaded
is one not related to that stated in the original petition,
and which, under the rules of pleading, must be set up
in a separate count or division.   It is the policy of the
law to grant relief as far as possible, for all wrongs complained of growing out of the same transaction, and
thus put an end to litigation.   *Childs v. Railroad Co.*,
117 Mo. Sup. 414 (23 S. W. Rep. 373); *Richwine v. Pres-
byterian Church*, 135 Ind. 80 (34 N. E. Rep. 737); Boone,
Code Pleadings, section 40.   It was held in *Childs v. Rail-*

road Co., supra, that a continuance of the same griev-
ance after the commencement of the suit might be
pleaded by way of supplemental petition. See *Buckley
v. Buckley,* 12 Nev. 423; Phillips, Code Pleadings, sections 317, 318. No good reason has been suggested for
not disposing of this entire controversy between these
parties in one action, and we think the ruling of the
district court in permitting the supplemental petition
was correct.

II. It will be observed that the right to a continuance as claimed is based on the mere filing of the supplemental petition. Surprise is not alleged, nor is it
said that counsel were not then prepared to properly
present their defense to the court. The filing of
3   an amendment or of a supplemental petition will
not alone authorize a continuance. For all the
court may have known, the parties might have been
fully prepared to proceed with the trial, and, if so,
there was no occasion for delay. If the defendant had
desired a continuance, some good reason for granting it
ought to have been suggested. *Barnes v. Insurance Co.,*
75 Iowa, 11; *State v. Tieman,* 39 Iowa, 474; *York v.
Clemens,* 41 Iowa, 95. No continuance should be
granted except for the absence of evidence, unless the
court is satisfied that substantial justice will thereby be
more nearly obtained. Code 1873, section 2749. Such a
showing was not made, and no prejudice appears to
have resulted from the ruling. It follows that the district court erred in granting a new trial, and its order
must be REVERSED.

CAROLINE NOTEBOOM v. FRED WATKINS AND THE FIRST
    NATIONAL BANK OF HAWARDEN, Appellant.

Evidence. In an action for the proceeds of a note which was claimed
1 by plaintiff, and which her husband had delivered to defendant,

either for collection, or as collateral to a debt of his own, where the answer was a general denial, it was not error to permit plaintiff to show the manner in which she acquired the money that she loaned her husband as a consideration for the note.

CROSS-EXAMINATION.   In an action for the proceeds of a note, plain-
2 tiff was asked on cross-examination whether she had made certain answers in a petition previously given, and defendant sought to produce the answers in the petition as part of the cross-examination. *Held*, properly rejected

HARMLESS ERROR.   Error cannot be predicated on the exclusion of
2 evidence which was afterwards admitted

Witnesses: IMPEACHMENT   It is not competent to ask a witness on
3 cross-examination if he was not the defendant in a criminal case tried the day previous, as preliminary to the further question whether he had not been convicted of a felony, as the latter question may be asked without any preliminary inquiry.

Instruction: CONSTRUED.   In an action for the proceeds of a note which was claimed by plaintiff, and which her husband, J, had
4 delivered to defendant, either for collection, or as collateral for a debt of his own, the jury were instructed that if certain facts were found they should find for plaintiff, even though they should believe that J had agreed to deliver the note to the defendant, "but if you do not so find, then you will find for defendant," and that if they found that J had agreed to deliver the note as security for his debt, and defendant, in the presence and hearing of plaintiff, demanded that he deliver it in accordance with his agreement, and thereafter, on the same day, without objection by plaintiff, J delivered the note as security, they should find for defendant. *Held*, not objectionable as requiring defendant to prove an estoppel, even though plaintiff failed to establish her case.

Bills and Notes: BONA FIDE PURCHASER.   One who takes a note wholly as collateral security for an antecedent indebtedness, with
5 no extension of time, is not a holder for value.

Appeal from Sioux District Court.—HON. GEORGE W. WAKEFIELD, Judge.

THURSDAY, OCTOBER 28, 1897.

PLAINTIFF states as her cause of action that defendant Watkins is the cashier of the defendant bank; that during the spring of 1895 plaintiff was the absolute owner of a certain promissory note described, signed by

Cornelius and Annie Noteboom, which was secured by mortgage upon real estate described; that during said spring the defendants received from her said note for collection; that defendants have collected the same, and converted said note and the proceeds thereof to their own use, and fail and refuse to return the said note or the proceeds thereof to plaintiff,—wherefor she asks judgment for six hundred dollars, with interest, and for costs. Defendants answered, admitting that the First National Bank is a corporation, and that defendant Watkins is the cashier thereof, and denying every other allegation of plaintiff's petition. The case was tried to a jury, and a verdict and judgment rendered in favor of the plaintiff. Defendants appealed.—*Affirmed.*

Palmer & Van Dyke, Hobson & Olmstead, and *Milchrist & Robinson* for appellants.

Hutchinson & Reininger and *Allen & Cullen* for appellee.

GIVEN, J.—I. The following facts appear without conflict: Plaintiff is the wife of John Noteboom, with whom she joined in the conveyance of the land described in the petition, to their son, Cornelius Noteboom, in consideration of which Cornelius Noteboom and his wife, Annie, executed to John Noteboom their three promissory notes, each for five hundred dollars, due in one, two and three years, and secured by mortgage on said real estate. John Noteboom transferred the two notes last falling due, to the defendant bank as collateral security for an existing indebtedness from himself to the bank. This action is as to the note first falling due. There is no question but that John Noteboom did deliver this note, indorsed by him in blank, to the defendants, in the spring of 1895. The contentions are these: The plaintiff claims that, immediately after the

execution of said note, John Noteboom indorsed and
delivered it to her on account of an existing indebtedness from him to her; that it was represented to her and
to her husband by defendant Watkins that Cornelius
Noteboom desired to make a new loan upon the land,
and to take up all three of said notes, and that it would
be necessary for the bank to have this note to consummate the matter, and upon payment by Cornelius
she would receive her money; that, relying thereon, she
afterwards sent the note to the defendants, by her husband, for that purpose. The defendants contend that
all three of the notes were promised to the bank by John
Noteboom as collateral security for his indebtedness to
the bank, and that in the spring of 1895, the defendants
insisting thereon, the note in question was delivered to
them by John Noteboom as such security, he receiving
at that time from the bank on account thereof an additional sum of forty dollars in money. The jury found
specially that at the time this note was delivered to the
defendants the plaintiff was the owner hereof; also,
that the defendant Watkins did not know of the claim
of plaintiff that she was the owner of said note, before
the same was delivered to the bank.

II. Appellants' first seven assignments of error
relate to the rulings of the court upon the admission of
evidence. We have examined each of these assignments with care, and do not find that there was any
prejudicial error in the rulings of the court. It
1   is complained that the plaintiff was permitted
to show the manner in which she acquired the
money that she loaned to her husband, on account of
which she claims this note. It is said that there is no
issue as to the consideration which she gave for the
note. Under plaintiff's allegation of ownership of the
note, and defendants' general denial, this evidence was

competent to show the ownership, and was certainly
without prejudice to defendants. Upon cross-
2   examination of the plaintiff, she was asked as to
whether she had not made certain answers in a
petition previously given, and appellants complain that
they were not permitted to introduce the answers in
the petition as a part of the cross-examination. It was
not a part of the cross-examination, and, if it had been,
there was no prejudice, inasmuch as the answers were
afterwards introduced by the defendants. Plain-
3   tiff's husband was asked on cross-examination
whether he was defendant in a criminal case
tried the day previous. It is insisted that this was competent, as preliminary to the further question whether
he had not been convicted of a felony. This latter question the appellants had a right to ask without any preliminary inquiry. Other questions made on the rulings
on evidence do not seem to us to merit special mention.

III. Appellants' next complaint is of the second
instruction. This complaint is, in part, at least,
grounded upon an error in improperly punctuating and
capitalizing the instruction in the abstract, as is shown
by appellee's amendment to the abstract. The
4   first part of the instruction directed the jury
that, if it found certain facts enumerated to be
established, it should find for the plaintiff, "even though
you should also believe that John Noteboom had
agreed to deliver the same to defendant. But if you
do not so find, then you will find for the defendants."
Following this, they were directed, in effect, that if they
found that John Noteboom had agreed with the defendants to deliver the note as security for his indebtedness;
that in the spring of 1895 Watkins demanded of John,
in the presence and hearing of the plaintiff, that he
deliver the note as security, in accordance with his
agreement; and that thereafter, upon the same day,

without objection by the plaintiff, John delivered the note as security,—they should find for the defendants. Counsel insist that under this instruction defendants were required to prove an estoppel against the plaintiff before the verdict could be rendered in their favor, even if the plaintiff wholly failed to establish her case. But this is not a fair construction. The effect of the instruction was to tell the jury that, if the plaintiff failed to establish her case, it should find for the defendants, and even if she did establish her case, and the note was demanded in her presence, and delivered, without objection on her part, in pursuance of the agreement of John, and as security for his debts, the jury should find for the defendants. We fail to discern any error in this instruction.

IV. Appellants' further contention is that the court erred in overruling their motion for judgment on the special findings. The special findings are that the plaintiff owned the note, and that the defendants received it without knowledge of her ownership. In the case of *Bank v. Barber,* 56 Iowa, 560, it is said: "The question in the case at bar is as to whether the intervener's title can be defeated by reason of the wrongful indorsement and delivery made by Elliott to the plaintiff. It certainly cannot unless the plaintiff is a holder for value. Now, the mere fact that the plaintiff took the notes as collateral security would not show that it is a holder for value. It would not be such if they were taken wholly as collateral security for an antecedent indebtedness, and no extension was given." Appellants contend that they were good-faith purchasers of this note, for value, and that, although they purchased after maturity, having done so without knowledge of

plaintiff's ownership, they took the note free from any
claims thereto by her. It will be seen by the
5   foregoing authority that if they took the note
wholly as collateral security for an antecedent
indebtedness, and with no extension of time, they are
not holders for value. Whether they were purchasers
of the note is one of the issues, and upon that issue the
evidence is in marked conflict. Plaintiff and her husband testify quite positively that it was taken for plaintiff to collect; and Mr. Watkins testifies with equal posi-
tiveness that it was taken as collateral security for the
indebtedness of John Noteboom, including forty dollars
then loaned to him. Under the evidence and instructions the jury were warranted in finding for the plaintiff on this issue, and it is apparent from the general
verdict that they did so find. The findings that plaintiff
owns the note, and that defendants received it without
knowledge of her ownership, do not, alone, entitle
appellants to a judgment. It must further appear that
they took it as purchasers, and on this issue, as already
said, the jury found against appellants. There was no
error in overruling appellants' motion for judgment on
the special findings, nor in any of the respects complained of.—AFFIRMED.

THE BROWN SHOE COMPANY, Appellant, v. FRANK HUNT.

586|
490|

Innkeeper's Lien. The lien given by Acts Eighteenth General
Assembly, chapter 18¹, section 2, to hotel keepers, on all property
1   "belonging to or under control of their guests, which may be in
such hotel," and so forth, attaches to sample goods carried by a
traveling salesman. though the hotel keeper knew, when he
received the salesman as a guest, that the goods belonged to his
employer.

CONSTITUTIONAL LAW. Said act is not unconstitutional as depriving
2   the owner of his property without due process of law. since it
makes no provision as to how the lien shall be enforced, but
simply provides for the lien and for possession under it.

Appeal from Woodbury District Court.—HON. JOHN F.
OLIVER, Judge.

THURSDAY, OCTOBER 28, 1897.

Lynn & Foley for appellant.

S. J. Quincy and *Wright & Hubbard* for appellee.

KINNE C. J.—I. This cause was determined upon
the following agreed statement of facts: "This is an
action in replevin, in which the Brown Shoe Company,
a corporation organized under the laws of the state of
Missouri, is plaintiff, and Frank Hunt, of Sioux City,
Iowa, is defendant. That immediately prior to and
within the last two years before the commencement of
this action, the defendant was the agent and general
manager of and for Lola M. Hunt, the proprietor of the
New Oxford Hotel, in Sioux City, Iowa. That said hotel
was kept for the general accommodation of the general
traveling public. That one M. K. Sheehan applied for
and was furnished meals, lodgings, extras, and accommodations usually furnished the general public at inns
and hotels as a guest of said hotel, which said accommodations were furnished by defendant. That said accommodations so furnished were of the value of $68.60, all
of which remains due and unpaid. That, at the time
the accommodations for which defendant claims a lien
were furnished to the said M. K. Sheehan, the said
Sheehan was the authorized traveling agent and
salesman of the plaintiff and engaged in the
prosecution of its business; and that the goods
described in plaintiff's petition, and taken under the
writ of replevin herein, were the samples of stock and
the cases containing the same furnished by the plaintiff to the said M. K. Sheehan, for his use in the prosecution of the plaintiff's business. That the amount

charged against the said M. K. Sheehan, and for which
defendant claims a lien upon the goods in controversy,
is the fair and reasonable price of the accommodations
furnished by the defendant to the said M. K. Sheehan.
That, at the time the said M. K. Sheehan became a guest
of said hotel, the property and goods described in the
petition were in his actual possession and under his
control in said hotel, and remained in his possession
and under his control in said hotel up to the time when
said M. K. Sheehan departed therefrom, and said goods
and chattels remained at said hotel until the same were
taken under the writ of replevin issued in this action.
That the defendant took possession of said goods and
chattels described in the petition, and held possession
thereof as security for the accommodations furnished
to said M. K. Sheehan at said hotel as a guest thereof,
and does not claim to have any other or further interest
in said goods and chattels, except that defendant claims
he is entitled to a lien thereon for the value of the
accommodations so furnished to the said M. K. Sheehan, under the statutes of this state. That the said goods
and chattles were such at all times the property of
plaintiff, and were at the time the said defendant took
possession thereof. That plaintiff's ownership of said
goods was well known to the defendant while said M.
K. Sheehan was a guest at said hotel, and at the time he
took possession of the same. That the plaintiff, before
the commencement of this action, demanded the possession of said goods and chattels. That the value of
said property is as stated in the petition. That the
goods and chattels described in plaintiff's petition were
taken under the writ of replevin in this action, and
delivered to the plaintiff, and have ever since remained
in the possession of the plaintiff. That, in case the
plaintiff recovers in this action, it is entitled to the
possession of said property, and judgment against the

defendant for costs. That, in case defendant prevails
in this action, he is entitled to a judgment against the
plaintiff, and upon the replevin bond filed in this action
and the securities thereon, to the amount of $68.60, and
costs of this action." The cause was tried to the court
and a judgment entered in favor of the defendant, and
against the plaintiff, for sixty-eight dollars and sixty
cents, and for costs, from which plaintiff appeals.

II.   Our statute provides: "All hotel, inn or eating-house keepers, shall have a lien upon and may take
and retain possession of all baggage and other property
belonging to or under the control of their guests,
1   which may be in such hotel, inn or eating-house,
for the value of their accommodations and keep,
and for all money paid for or advanced to, and for such
extras and other things as shall be furnished such
guest, and such property so retained shall not be
exempt from attachment or execution to the amount of
the proper and reasonable charges of such hotel, inn or
eating-house keeper against such guest, and the cost
of enforcing the lien thereon." Acts Eighteenth General Assembly, chapter 181, section 2. It appears from
the statement of facts that defendant knew that the
goods upon which he claims a lien did not belong to his
guest, but were the property of the plaintiff. It is
therefore contended that his inn keeper's lien did not
attach to them. Counsel cite several cases in support
of such contention. They were cases where the lien
claimed was the common law lien, and not one created
by the statute. This applies also to the claim that the
goods were not of such a character as to be considered
as for the convenience or comfort of the guest, but
rather such as enabled the guest to carry on a trade or
business. The common law doctrine that the inn keeper
could have no lien as against the property of third
parties, he knowing their ownership when he received

the guest and the property, has been changed by our statute. Under our statute, the inn keeper may "take and retain possession of all baggage and other property belonging to or under the control of their guests, which may be in such hotel or inn." Clearly, the legislature intended by the words used to give a lien, not only upon the property in fact belonging to the guest, and which was in the hotel or inn, but likewise a lien upon property placed therein which was under the guest's control. The guest in this instance was a traveling man, selling goods by sample, and the lien is claimed upon these sample goods and the receptacles in which they were contained. These goods were used in the prosecution of his business as a salesman. The nature and character of his occupation were such that plaintiff must be held to know he would be compelled to stop at hotels or inns, and that, in the proper prosecution of his avocation, he would need his sample goods in such hotels or inns. The statute clearly covers such goods as they were, under the control of the guest.

III. The statute is not unconstitutional. It does not deprive the owner of his property without due process of law. It simply provides for a lien and 2   a possession, and makes no provision as to how the lien shall be enforced. The judgment below is AFFIRMED.

A. W. HEISS, Appellant, v. THE CHICAGO, ROCK ISLAND & PACIFIC RAILWAY COMPANY.

Railroads: LICENSE: *Trespassers.* A depot platform had at the north end steps for the use of the public, and at the south an apron from the ground, for the same purpose. There was a well-1   defined footpath going from the public street across the track to the platform   It would not have been proper to have the grounds fenced, nor could the path have well been obstructed. *Held,* that the railroad company gave no license or invitation to anyone to approach the track by the path, and cross the track to the east side of the platform, so as to render it liable to a person injured in so doing, without negligence on its part.

Negligent speed: *Ordinances.* In the absence of any ordinance, 2 no particular rate of speed on depot grounds would, alone, be proof of negligence.

Appeal from Greene District Court.—Hon. Charles D. Goldsmith, Judge.

Friday, October 29, 1897.

The plaintiff, while at Minburn, attending to business as a traveling salesman, heard the whistle of a train on which he expected to return to Perry, and hastened towards the depot. The street passed so that the crossing at the railroad was twenty-one feet north of the depot platform, to which there were steps. He followed this street until near a corncrib about sixty four feet east of the crossing, when he took a footpat diagonally southwest, towards the waiting room, at the south end of the depot, where he had left his satchel. When five or six feet from the track, he left the path, and went directly across to the platform, which was between two and three feet above the ties, and in some way, unexplained, stumbled and fell, striking his head on the platform, and became unconscious. The train, which he had noticed approaching, ran over one leg, and rendered amputation necessary. This action is brought for damages resulting. Trial to jury, judgment on verdict directed for defendant, and plaintiff appeals.—*Affirmed.*

Cardell & Nichols for appellant.

Cummins & Wright for appellee.

Ladd, J.—The controlling question argued is whether the plaintiff was a trespasser, or on the track

with the license and invitation of the defendant. If a
mere trespasser, the defendant owed him no
1   active duty, and would be liable only in event of
his discovery in time to avoid the injury. If
there with a license and invitation of the defendant,
then its employes were bound to keep a lookout for
him; and if, by the exercise of ordinary care, he might
have been discovered in his perilous situation in time
to have avoided the injury, the defendant is liable.
Murphy v. Railway Co., 38 Iowa, 542; *Clampit v. Railway Co.*, 84 Iowa, 71. The street north of the depot platform passes very near to it,—one witness placing the
distance at ten feet and another twenty-one feet from
t⁰ᵒ crossing,—and at this end of the platform are steps
for the use of the public in going to and from the depot.
At the south end there is an apron from the ground to
the platform, for the same purpose. Instead of making
use of these, the plaintiff abandoned the street, and
took a footpath near a corncrib to a point opposite the
platform, thirty-eight feet south of the north end, and
there left the path, and attempted to cross the rails and
mount the platform. The path was not very distinct
until near the corncrib, but clearly defined from there
until it reached the track, where it disappeared or
widened out, the ground being trodden six or eight feet
wide. The path had been used more or less in going
"cross lots" to the depot for several years. The platform at that place was between two and three feet
above the ties, and was left open under. It is possible
that the mere use of a path across a railroad track may,
under some circumstances, imply a license for such use,
but in this case every circumstance negatives such an
inference. The defendant had furnished safe and convenient approaches to the platform. These were for
the use of the public, and an invitation to thus approach
the depot. Their existence in the immediate vicinity

rebuts any inference that might be drawn from the mere use of the path. The approach to the depot could not well have been made more difficult than it was by way of the footpath. No obstruction could well be made use of, nor could the grounds properly be fenced. That people persisted in the use of such an approach, when others, safe and convenient, in the immediate vicinity, were provided, will not be construed to imply an invitation for its use. The facts are essentially different from those in *Clampit v. Railway Co., supra.* There the ties across the ditch, the stairway, and the beaten path clearly indicated an intention to appropriate a crossing by footpath; and from the fact that there was no other near by, and no obstruction to its use by the defendant, where these might have been placed, consent was implied. Such consent is indicated by no act or omission on the part of the defendant in this case. It could not obstruct mounting the platform at a point where passengers passed to and from the train, and it was not required to employ servants to warn people from doing so, when safe and convenient approaches were plainly visible near by.

II. In the absence of any ordinance to the contrary, no particular rate of speed on depot grounds would, alone, be proof of negligence. *Cohoon v. Railway Co.*, 90 Iowa, 169. The evidence fails to show that plaintiff was discovered by those in charge of the train, in time to avoid the injury, and he cannot recover.—AFFIRMED.

2

THOMAS HAGAN v. C. H. S. POWERS, Appellant.

Evidence: PERSONAL TRANSACTIONS WITH DECEDENT. Where a husband buys land, and has it deeded to his wife without her knowl-
2   edge, there is no personal transaction between him and her, within Code 1873, section 3639, providing that no party can be examined

as to any personal transaction or communication between him
and a person at the time of such examination deceased, etc.

SAME. In an action by a surviving husband against his deceased
wife's father to quiet in plaintiff title to land purchased by him,
8　and deeded to his wife, plaintiff, under Code 1873, section 3639,
was not competent to testify that the wife promised to take care
of it for him.

Resulting Trusts. The provisions of Code 1873, section 1935, with
8　reference to the creation of a trust in real property, do not apply
to a trust raised by operation of law, and not by reason of any
declaration or creation of the parties.

PRESUMPTIONS: *Husband and wife.* In 1873 plaintiff purchased unimproved land near the farm on which he resided, and had it deeded
1　to his wife without her knowledge, with the intention thereby to
create a trust. When informed of what he had done, she acquiesced therein; and the title remained in her until her death, in
2　1894. In the meantime the husband improved, controlled, and
used the land as his own. *Held*, that the presumption that the
land was an advancement to the wife was overcome by evidence
of his control and improvement, and her repeated admissions that
the land was his, and that she held the title in trust for her husband, and his own evidence as to his intention.

Appeal from Union District Court.—HON. W. H. TED-
FORD, Judge.

FRIDAY, OCTOBER 29, 1897.

PLAINTIFF states as his cause of action that in
December, 1873, he purchased from Joseph Shaw a certain quarter section of land in Adair county, with his
own property and funds, and caused the same to be
conveyed to his then wife, Mary E. Hagan, by reason of
which she thereafter held the title as trustee for plaintiff; that she received said trust, and agreed to safely
hold said land for plaintiff's benefit; that at the purchase the land was unimproved; that plaintiff improved
it, and has ever since controlled it; that Mrs. Hagan
died, inestate, without issue, October 10, 1894, leaving
the defendant as her only surviving parent; that defendant claims an undivided one-half of said land by inher-

itance through said Mary E. Hagan, but that, in truth
and in fact, said Mary E. Hagan did not own said land
at the time of her death, but held it as trustee, as aforesaid. Plaintiff prays that he may be decreed to be the
owner in fee simple in said premises, and that he be
quieted in his title as against the claims of the defendant. The defendant answered, admitting that the title
was in Mary E. Hagan, but denying that the plaintiff
paid for the land with his own money or property, and
denying that Mrs. Hagan held the same in trust for the
plaintiff, or ever recognized such trust; admits the death
of Mrs. Hagan, and that he is her only surviving parent.
He avers that Mary E. Hagan had owned and controlled
said land since December, 1873, and that her possession
and claim of ownership were adverse to the claim of the
plaintiff, and that the claim of the plaintiff is barred.
He prays for a decree awarding him the ownership of an
undivided one-half interest in said land. The action
was brought in Adair county, where the land is situated,
but, by stipulation of parties, was transfered to and
heard in the district court of Union county, by which a
decree was entered in favor of the plaintiff as prayed,
from which the defendant appealed.—*Affirmed.*

D. W. Higbee for appellant.

Maxwell & Winter for appellee.

GIVEN, J. --1. A consideration of the question
involved renders it necessary that we first determine the
facts. There is no dispute that the plaintiff purchased
the land in controversy in 1873, it being then
1   unimproved; that he caused the title to be conveyed to his wife, who continued to hold the same
until her death, October 10, 1894, when she died, intestate, and without issue, leaving the defendant her only
surviving parent. During these years the plaintiff and

his wife resided upon an adjacent farm in Union county,
and the plaintiff improved, controlled, and used the land
in question, as his own.   Plaintiff, being somewhat
addicted to the use of strong drink, and not always
prudent in the management of his financial affairs,
caused the deed for this land to be made to his wife,
without her knowledge, intending that she should hold
it in trust for him; and thereafter, when informed of the
fact, Mrs. Hagan acquiesced in it, and repeatedly and
uniformly throughout said years acknowledged that the
land was the property of her husband. Appellant states
his contention as follows: "The matters necessary to
be proven in order to create the resulting trust claimed
by appellee (neither fraud nor mistake being claimed)
are: (1) Payment by appellee with his own money; (2)
intention on the part of appellee at time of conveyance
to create a trust; (3) conveyance to deceased; (4) knowledge on the part of deceased of appellee's intention to
create a trust, and assent or failure to dissent after that
knowledge."   The claim of the plaintiff that he paid for
said land with his own money is denied, and the defendant contends that after the contract of purchase from
Shaw, and prior to the execution of the deed or payment
of the purchase price, appellant promised appellee that,
in consideration of a promise on the part of the appellee
that he would place the title in the name of Mrs. Hagan,
appellant would furnish him help in various ways, to the
amount of the cost of the land, and that appellant did
so furnish such help by contributing horses and other
property at various times.   Upon this issue of fact, we
think, the appellant has failed to support his contention.
It is true, he did furnish to the plaintiff and his wife
horses and other property at various times, but it was
mostly before this land was contracted for, and without
reference thereto.   It fairly appears that in every
instance that money or property was received from

appellant it is accounted for as having been a gift without condition, or as being settled for otherwise than on account of the purchase of this land. That appellee paid for the land, and caused the conveyance to be made to deceased, with the intention to thereby create a trust, and that, after knowledge of these facts, deceased assented thereto, we think, is abundantly proven.

II. It is contended on behalf of the defendant that much of the evidence from which these facts are found is incompetent, because it relates to communications between husband and wife, and communications and transactions with the deceased Mrs. Hagan. In *Dysart v. Furrow*, 90 Iowa, 59, it is said: "If the transaction or communication was personal, it must be known alike to both, and therefore either may deny. * * * Personal transactions and communications, as contemplated by the statute, are communications between the parties of which both must have had personal knowledge." This rule is approved in the later cases of *Cole v. Marsh*, 92 Iowa, 379, and *Martin v. Shannon*, 92 Iowa, 375.

2   The purchase, payment, and conveyance of the land were exclusively transactions between the plaintiff and the vendor, Mr. Shaw. It was not until after the transaction was completed by the making of the conveyance that Mrs. Hagan learned that the conveyance was to her, and assented thereto, as shown by a number of witnesses other than appellee.

3   The only evidence appearing in the record that comes within the objection is the statement of the plaintiff, as follows: "I then told her I had deeded to her, to take care of it for me, and she said, 'I can do it.'" This statement is clearly incompetent, and must therefore be disregarded.

III. We now inquire whether, under the facts as we find them, the law raises a resulting, or, as it is

sometimes called, a presumptive, trust in favor of appellee. In *Cotton v. Wood*, 25 Iowa, 44, the familiar rule
is thus announced: "Where, upon the purchase of
property, the consideration is paid by one, and the legal
title conveyed to another, a resulting trust is thereby
raised, and the person named in the deed will hold the
property as trustee of the party paying the consideration." In Perry on Trusts (section 124) it is said: "The
general foundation of this kind of trusts is the natural
equity that arises when parties do certain things. Thus,
if one pays the purchase money of an estate, and takes
the title deed in the name of another, in the absence
of all evidence of intention the law presumes a trust
from the natural equity that he who pays the money
for property ought to enjoy the beneficial interest."
The parties to this transaction being husband and wife,
another rule requires consideration. In *Cotton v. Wood*,
it is further said: "But if the person to whom the conveyance is made be one for whom the party paying the
consideration is under obligation, natural or moral, to
provide, the transaction will be regarded *prima facie* as
an advancement, and the burden will rest on the one
who seeks to establish the trust for the benefit of the
payee of the consideration to overcome the presumption
in favor of the legal title by sufficient evidence." In
the absence of the obligation to provide, it could not be
questioned that the law would raise a trust in favor of
appellee, from the facts established. We think
4   appellee has fully overcome the presumption of
advancement, by his own evidence as to his intention, by evidence of repeated admissions of Mrs. Hagan
that the land was his, and his continued occupation and
improvement of it. This being a trust raised by opera-
ation of law, and not by reason of any declara-
5   tion or creation of the parties, section 1935 of the
Code of 1873 does not apply. The facts in this
case are in many respects the same as those alleged in

Cotton v. Wood, supra, and the rulings in that case support our conclusion in this. We think the decree of the district court is correct.—AFFIRMED.

GEORGE W. BAXTER, Administrator, v. THE CITY OF CEDAR RAPIDS, Appellant.

Municipal Corporations: SIDEWALKS: *Jury question.* In an action against a city for injuries resulting from a fall caused by the end of a plank of a street crossing next the sidewalk projecting above the sidewalk, witnesses for plaintiff testified that the plank was
2 so decayed and worn that it would not hold nails, and that it was warped so that the end next the walk was sprung, and when not under pressure, its upper surface was three or three and a half
4 inches above the level of the walk   Other witnesses for plaintiff stated that the difference in level was less, some placing it at an inch. Defendant's witnesses stated that the end of the plank was securely nailed, and that it was only one or one and one-half inches higher than the other planks. *Held*, that it was for the jury to determine the condition of such plank, and its height above the walk.

SAME. It cannot be said as a matter of law, that an obstruction two
9 inches high in a sidewalk or street crossing is not such a defect as will render the city liable for injuries caused by it.

NOTICE OF DEFECT. Where such defect in the crossing had existed for
3 ten days or two weeks, and it was in a thickly inhabited part of
5 the city, and much used, defendant was chargeable with notice of its condition in time to repair it before the accident.

CONTRIBUTORY NEGLIGENCE: *Jury question.* Plaintiff had lived in the city only five days at the time of the accident   It was almost
2 dark and the street lamps had not been lighted. She had passed over the crossing seven or eight weeks before, but it was not shown that the defect then existed, or that she knew of it at the time of the accident. She testified that at the time of the accident it was quite dark, and, as she went from the pavement upon the crosswalk, her foot caught in the middle plank, and it threw her; that "I was walking fast as I usually do. I am a very spry walker. The middle plank of the three on the crosswalk caught my foot. It was done so quick I could hardly tell. * * * I was walking as I usually walk,—lifting my feet well from the ground. I did not notice anything that night in reference to the sidewalk." *Held*, that the evidence did not show that she was negligent in not discovering the condition of the walk.

Evidence: PRIVILEGED COMMUNICATION. In an action against a city
for injuries caused by a defective sidewalk, evidence of plaintiff's
6 physicians regarding her condition, and the information obtained
while treating her, when called as witnesses for defendant, is within
the prohibition of Code 1873, section 3643, providing that no
physician shall be allowed to disclose any confidential communication properly intrusted to him in his professional capacity, and
necessary and proper to enable him to discharge the functions of
his office according to the usual course of practice.

SAME. The court properly excluded a question by defendant, asking
8 one of such physicians to state "any conversation, if any you had,
with plaintiff, in which she asked you whether or not the injury
in the hip could not arise from the fact that she had to do the
most of her standing on her right hip, and because she was compelled to use a crutch, and not use her left limb?" Since the evidence called for, was within the statute, and said evidence was
immaterial.

WAIVER The fact that plaintiff produces one of several physicians
7 as his witness does not warrant defendant in claiming that the
statutory privilege has been waived as to the testimony of the
other physicians whom he offers as witnesses for the defense.

INSTRUCTION. Though an instruction that a person, in passing along
a street, is required to use more caution when it is dark than in
10 the day time may properly be given, it merely states a fact which
is a matter of common observation, and which the jury must consider under other proper instruction, and hence a refusal to so
instruct is not prejudicial to defendant.

Misconduct of Jurors. In an action against a city for injuries
caused by a defective sidewalk, several members of a jury urged
12 that a large verdict be returned to teach defendant a lesson, for
the reason that, if any one became involved in trouble, when
within its limits, defendant would punish him. *Held,* not to
show passion, prejudice, or misconduct, and that the matters in
question so inhered in the verdict that they may not be shown by
affidavit.

New Trial. In a personal injury case a new trial was asked by
defendant because of newly discovered evidence that plaintiff's
health was impaired before the accident. An affiant stated that
he knew plaintiff at a certain town for fifteen years, and until she
13 moved to defendant city; that he knew she was continually complaining of ill health while she lived there; "that it was generally
reputed that she had ill health, and I know the same myself," and
she claimed the climate there did not agree with her, "but the
climate where she did live after leaving here did agree with her "
Held, too indefinite to require the granting of a new trial.

SAME. A new trial will not be granted because of newly-discovered
14 evidence that is inherently conflicting.

REDUCING VERDICT. It is questionable whether a case where the
    court overrules a motion for new trial and *then* gives plaintiff an
 1 "opportunity" to take judgment for less than the verdict, comes
    within the practice under which courts make the overruling of a
11 motion for new trial depend upon the acceptance of a reduced
    verdict. However that may be, it is proper to attach such condi-
    tion to overruling such motion and a reduction so ordered is not
    a finding by the court that the verdict was excessive or the result
    of passion and prejudice

APPEAL Where affidavits in support of a motion for new trial are
14 contradicted by counter-affidavits, a denial of a new trial will not
    be disturbed on appeal.

Appeal from Linn District Court.—HON. WILLIAM G.
THOMPSON, Judge.

FRIDAY, OCTOBER 29, 1897.

ACTION at law to recover for personal injuries
which are alleged to have been caused by negligence on
the part of the defendant. There was a trial by jury,
and a verdict and judgment for the plaintiff. The
defendant appeals from that judgment. After its
appeal was perfected, it filed a petition for a new trial.
A demurrer to that petition was filed and sustained,
and, the defendant refusing to plead further, the petition was dismissed, and costs were taxed to the defendant. From that order, the defendant, also, appeals.—
Affirmed.

Warren Harman and *J. J. Powell* for appellant.

Rickel & Crocker for appellee.

ROBINSON, J.—In the evening of September 3,
1894, Mrs. C. A. Baxter, the plaintiff's intestate, while
walking in a street of the defendant, fell, and, it is
claimed, received severe and painful injuries, which

caused her death about the first day of July, 1895. The plaintiff alleges that the fall and injuries of the decedent were caused by a defective street crossing, for which the defendant is liable. The defendant denies all negligence on its part, and alleges that the injuries sustained by the decedent, for which a recovery is sought, were caused by negligence on her part. The verdict of the jury was for the sum of five thousand, seven hundred and fifty dollars. A motion for a new trial was filed by the defendant, and proceedings were had thereon as shown by the following record: "The court overruled defendant's motion for new trial, to which ruling the defendant duly excepted. The court then gave the plaintiff the opportunity of accepting three thousand dollars judgment and costs, instead of amount of verdict. Plaintiff accepts the three thousand dollars judgment and costs of suit. Defendant excepts. Thereupon the court entered judgment for three thousand dollars in favor of plaintiff. Defendant excepts." This action was commenced by Mrs. Baxter to recover for the injuries she claimed to have sustained. In an amendment to her petition she alleged the assignment to her by her husband, George W. Baxter, of all claims which had accrued to him in consequence of the injuries she had sustained. After her death, Baxter, as administrator of her estate, was substituted as plaintiff, and the cause was prosecuted in his name until after judgment was render and an appeal therefrom taken. After the petition for a new trial was filed, the death of Baxter was suggested, and E. H. Crocker, as administrator, was substituted as plaintiff.

I. On the twenty-ninth day of August, 1894, the decedent and her husband moved from Spirit Lake to

Cedar Rapids. At the time of the accident in question
the plaintiff was walking rapidly to her
2   home. At the corner of Fifth street and
Sixth avenue, she turned from the sidewalk
to step onto the street crossing. Her right foot
was caught by a plank of the crossing, which was
raised above the surface of the sidewalk; and she
was thrown with much force to the crossing, and
severely injured. The sidewalk at that point was of
stone, and the part of the crossing next to it was made
of three planks, two inches thick, nailed together to
crosspieces, and abutted against the walk. The upper
surfaces of two of the planks were about level with the
top of the sidewalk, but the end of the middle plank,
which was the one which caused the decedent to fall,
was somewhat above that level. There is much dispute
as to the condition of that plank, and its height above
the walk. Witnesses for the plaintiff contend that it
was so decayed and worn that it would not hold nails;
that it was warped in such a manner that the end next
the walk was sprung, and, when not under pressure, its
upper surface was three or three and a half inches
above the level of the walk. Other witnesses for the
plaintiff state that the difference in level was less, —
some placing it at one inch. Witnesses for the defendant state that the end of the plank was sound and
securely nailed and that it was only an inch or an
inch and a half higher than the other planks. In
view of this conflict in the testimony, it was the province
of the jury to determine the condition of the plank, and
its height above the walk. There was testimony
3   which tended to show that the defect in the
crossing of which the plaintiff complains had
existed for ten days or two weeks, and that the crossing was in a thickly inhabited part of the city, and
much used. The plaintiff had, during a visit to Cedar

Rapids, passed over the crossing seven or eight weeks
before; but it is not shown that the alleged defect then
existed, nor that she knew of it at the time of the accident. When that occurred, it was almost dark, but the
street lamps had not been lighted. Her testimony was
taken and used on the trial. She stated that:
4   "It was quite dark, and when I came to the
      corner I turned; and, as I came from the pave-
ment onto the crosswalk, my foot caught on the middle
plank and threw me on my left knee. I was walking
fast at the time, as I usually do. I am a very spry
walker. The middle plank of the three on the crosswalk caught my foot. It was done so quick I could
hardly tell. * * * I was walking as I usually
walked,—lifting my feet well from the ground. I
didn't notice anything that night in reference to the
sidewalk." We do not think the evidence shows that
the decedent was negligent in not discovering the con
dition of the walk. *Owen v. City of Ft. Dodge*, 98 Iowa,
      281. And it appears from the length of time the
5   defect in the crossing had existed, and its loca-
      tion, that the defendant is chargeable with
knowledge of it in time to have put the crossing in.
good condition before the accident occurred.

II. Several different physicians treated the
decedent after the accident, and one of them testified
as a witness for the plaintiff. The defendant placed
several of the others on the witness stand, and asked
them questions in regard to the condition of the
      decedent, and the information they obtained
6   while treating her. The court, on the objection
      of the plaintiff, refused to receive their testi-
mony, on the ground that the information sought to be
obtained from them was privileged. The ruling was
based on section 3643 of the Code of 1873, which contains the following: "No * * * physician shall

be allowed, in giving testimony, to disclose any confidential communication properly intrusted to him in his
professional capacity, and necessary and proper to
enable him to discharge the functions of his office
according to the usual course of practice. * * *
Such prohibition shall not apply to cases where the
party in whose favor the same are made waives the
rights conferred." The information sought to be
elicited from the physicians was within the prohibition of that section. *Prader v. Association*, 95 Iowa,
149. But the defendant contends that the plain-
7   tiff waived the prohibition by placing one of the
physicians on the stand as a witness in her
behalf. Nothing in the statute justifies such a claim,
and we are of the opinion that the ruling of the court
was right. We think the court was also right in refusing to permit one of the physicians of the
8   decedent, called by the defendant, to answer a
question which it asked, as follows: "Will you
state any conversation, if you had any, with Mrs.
Baxter, in which she asked you whether or not that
injury in the hip could not arise from the fact that
she had to do most of her standing on her right hip, and
because she was compelled to use a crutch, and not use
her left limb?" Whether the decedent ever asked the
question indicated was wholly immaterial, and, if the
facts were as assumed in the interrogatory, they were
privileged, and within the prohibition of the statute.

III. The defendant asked the court to instruct
the jury that, if "the crosswalk was only raised about
two inches above the sidewalk to which it was an
approach, then the crosswalk was reasonably safe and
convenient for the public. A simple rise of two inches
from a sidewalk to a crosswalk would not be such an
obstruction that you could find that it was not in a
reasonably safe condition, and in that case you will

find for the defendant." The court refused the instruction, and of that ruling the defendant complains.

9   It seems that there is authority for the claim
that the loose end of the plank in a walk which
rises two inches above the other portions of the walk
is not a defect for which the municipality in which it
exists is liable. *Weisse v. City of Detroit,* 105 Mich.
482 (63 N. W. Rep. 423). See, also, *Yotter v. City of
Detroit,* 107 Mich. 4 (64 N. W. Rep. 743). It may be that
the conclusions reached in those cases were authorized
by the facts upon which they were based, but we do not
think it can be said, as a matter of law, that an obstruction in a sidewalk or street crossing two inches high
cannot be such a defect that the city or town in which
it exists may be liable for injuries which it causes. It
is manifest that such an obstruction may easily cause
most serious accidents to persons using the walk, even
though they be free from negligence. Indeed, at times
they may be much more dangerous than larger obstructions, because less readily discoverable. Whether an
obstruction or other defect in a walk is of a character
to make the municipality which permits it to exist
responsible for it, does not necessarily depend upon
the size of the defect, but upon the effects which may
reasonably be apprehended from it upon persons who
use the walk in a proper manner. These will vary with
the circumstances of different cases, and whether the
municipality is liable for a defect in its streets or walks
will, as a rule, be a question of fact, to be determined
by the jury under the instruction of the court, and not
a mere question of law, to be determined by the court
alone. The evidence in this case authorized the jury to
find that the defect in question was of a serious character, even though the plank which tripped the
decedent was not more than two inches higher than
the sidewalk, and the instruction under consideration
was properly refused.

IV. The appellant complains because the court refused to give an instruction which it asked, to the effect that a person, in passing along a public street, is required to use more caution and be more watchful when it is dark than in the daytime. The instruc-

10   tion might properly have been given, but it merely stated a fact which is a matter of common observation, and which the jury must have considered under the charge given. Hence we do not think the defendant could have been prejudiced by the refusal of the court to give the instruction asked.

V. The appellant insists that the court erred in not granting a new trial because the damages allowed by the jury were excessive, and showed passion and prejudice. It is said that the action taken by

11   the court which caused the plaintiff to accept judgment for much less than the amount fixed by the verdict shows that it found that the jury was influenced by passion and prejudice to fix an excessive amount in its verdict. The record shows that the action of the court in regard to a new trial was unusual. It overruled the motion for a new trial, apparently without condition, and then gave the plaintiff "the opportunity" to take a judgment for three thousand dollars and costs, and the plaintiff took advantage of the opportunity to remit a part of his recovery. That does not show that the court found that the verdict was for an excessive amount, and we cannot say that it was. But conceding that the effect and purpose of what was done were to overrule the motion for a new trial on condition that the plaintiff would accept judgment for the amount for which it was rendered, and, if he would not, that the motion would be sustained, that does not show that the district court found that the jury was influenced by passion and prejudice in reaching its verdict. It merely shows that in the opinion of the court the evidence did not authorize a verdict for so

large an amount as that fixed by the jury. Juries may, and frequently do, err in estimating the amount of a recovery, when there is no ground for claiming that they were influenced by prejudice or passion. Authorities are cited to sustain the claim that, when a trial court finds that a verdict for damages is not sustained by the evidence, it should grant a new trial, and cannot rightly fix a smaller amount, which the successful party may accept, or submit to a new trial. We are aware that there are authorities of high standing which support the rule for which the appellant contends. But the well established rule in this state is for a trial court, which is of the opinion that a verdict for an excessive amount has been returned, to give the successful party the option to accept judgment for the amount which the court believes to be just, or to submit to a new trial. *Duffy v. City of Dubuque*, 63 Iowa, 176, and cases cited therein; *Van Winter v. Henry County*, 61 Iowa, 691, and cases therein cited. The case of *Darland v. Wade*, 48 Iowa, 548, upon which the appellant relies is not in point. The facts and the opinion in that case distinguish it from cases like this. What was done in this case to avoid a new trial on the ground of an excessive recovery, appears to have been authorized by the settled practice in this state.

VI. The motion for a new trial was supported by the affidavits of jurors which stated, in effect, that several members of the jury urged that a large verdict be returned against the defendant, to teach it a lesson and punish it, for the reason that, if any one became involved in trouble when within its limits, the defendant would punish him. It is urged that those affidavits show passion and prejudice and misconduct on the part of the jury. They were contradicted by counter-affidavits, but, if they had not been, they would not have shown ground for setting aside the verdict, because they merely tended to show arguments

12

or reasons which were urged to increase the amount of the recovery. Matters of that kind so far inhere in the verdict that they cannot be given any weight for the purpose of setting it aside. *Wright v. Telegraph Co.*, 20 Iowa, 196; *Griffin v. Harriman*, 74 Iowa, 438; *Wilkins v. Bent*, 66 Iowa, 531; *Fox v. Wunderlich*, 64 Iowa, 192; *Brown v. Cole*, 45 Iowa, 603; *Bingham v. Foster*, 37 Iowa, 340; *Garretty v. Brazell*, 34 Iowa, 104; *Cowles v. Railroad Co.*, 32 Iowa, 517; *Hall v. Robison*, 25 Iowa, 92.

VII.   The last claim of the appellant which needs to be considered at any length is that the court erred in refusing to grant a new trial on the ground of newly-discovered evidence.   That ground was set out in both the motion and the petition for a new trial. It was included in the motion by an amendment filed seventeen days after the verdict was returned, and fourteen days after the original motion was filed, and was supported by affidavits. Some of those relate to a mistake alleged to have been made by a witness for the city which is of so little consequence that it will not be further considered. So far as the affidavits can be regarded as material, they relate to the claims made on the trial, and testimony offered to support it, to the effect that Mrs. Baxter's general health was good before the accident. The affidavits tend to show
13   that an attorney for the defendant went to the former home of Mrs. Baxter, in Spirit Lake, in July next preceding the trial, which commenced in the latter part of October, 1895; that the purpose of his visit was to ascertain something as to the condition of Mrs. Baxter's health during the many years she resided there; that he spent two or three days in the town, and talked with a large number of people who had been her neighbors, and with men who had business dealings with her family, and with all persons, so far as he could ascertain, who would be likely to know

anything of her health, but that he found that a strong
sympathy for the Baxter family, and a strong prejudice
against the defendant, prevailed, and he could not
learn anything to the advantage of the defendant. The
affidavits also tended to show that the attorney talked
before the trial with all the persons in Cedar Rapids
who, so far as he was able to learn, could give him
any information in regard to the health of Mrs. Baxter,
but without success; that, after the trial, he had
obtained the affidavit of A. M. Johnson, a resident of
Spirit Lake, and that much testimony could now be
procured to show that Mrs. Baxter's health was poor
for years prior to her death. The affidavit of Johnson
was also attached to the motion, and showed that he
knew Mrs. Baxter at Spirit Lake about fifteen years,
and until she moved to Cedar Rapids; that he knew that
she was continually complaining of ill health while she
lived there; "that it was generally reputed that she had
ill health, and I know the same myself, and she claimed
the climate at Spirit Lake, Iowa, did not agree with
her, but the climate where she did live after leaving
here did agree with her." We are of the opinion that
this affidavit was not sufficiently definite and certain
to require that a new trial be granted. Whether the
statement, "and I know the same myself," refers to
what Mrs. Baxter's health was reputed to be, or to the
affiant's knowledge of what it was in fact, is not clear,
and the affidavit does not show that her health was
impaired before the accident. On the contrary, if the
closing statement is of any value, it tends to show that
the cause of her alleged ill health was removed when
she went to Cedar Rapids. We think the motion for a
new trial was properly overruled. The statements in
regard to newly discovered evidence contained in the
petition for a new trial are more important. The petition was filed about four months after the trial was
ended, and shows that after the motion for a new trial

was overruled and judgment was rendered, an attorney
for the defendant again went to Spirit Lake, and talked
with a number of persons, and discovered much evidence which can be obtained, and which will contradict
testimony given for the plaintiff, and show that for
years before the accident, while Mrs. Baxter resided
at Spirit Lake, she complained of a stomach trouble, of
a heart trouble, of dropsy and swollen limbs, of bloat-
ing, of difficulty in breathing, of being unable to sleep
when lying down, and that she was improved in health
by going away from home. The petition shows that
some of the newly discovered evidence will be given by
persons who reside in Cedar Rapids, and of whom some
were witnesses on the trial; that some of those persons
will show that Mrs. Baxter stated after the accident
that she had suffered much while residing at Spirit
Lake from stomach trouble; that others will tetstify
that she was quite strong and well after the accident,
doing a large part of the work and all of the cooking
for a family of ten or twelve persons, including board-
ers; and that the physicians who attended her after
the accident will prove that her sickness and death
were not in any manner caused by the injuries she
received in falling on the street crossing. Some
14   of this testimony would doubtless have been
material and competent on the trial of the cause,
but that of the physicians would have been incompetent, for reasons already shown, or it should have been
offered on the trial. No sufficient reason for not examining more fully the witnesses who actually testified is
shown, and we are satisfied that if the averments of the
petition are true, and if the defendant had been as dili-
gent before as since the trial, it would have discovered
the competent and material evidence for which it now
asks a new trial. Moreover, it is to some extent conflicting. To show that Mrs. Baxter was vigorous and

apparently well after the accident would tend to show
that her health was not permanently impaired when
she was at Spirit Lake. None of the newly discovered
evidence tends to show that the defendant was not
liable for the injuries which resulted from the accident.
Upon a consideration of the entire record, we conclude
that the court was right in sustaining the demurrer to
the petition for a new trial because of a lack of diligence to procure the newly-discovered evidence for use
on the trial, and for the further reason that it does not
impress us as being of sufficient importance to justify a
new trial. The evidence is ample to sustain the judgment, and there was no error in the proceedings which
was prejudicial to the defendant. The judgment of the
district court, and its order sustaining the demurrer to
the petition for a new trial, and taxing costs thereon
to the defendant, are AFFIRMED.

ED. BENEDICT, Appellant, v. W. D. BIRD AND J. H.
ENGLE.

Statute of Frauds: ADMISSION IN PLEADINGS. The admission by
defendants in their original answer, introduced in evidence, of an
8 oral contract to convey land, materially different from that pleaded
by plaintiff, does not bring the case within Code 1873, section
3666, providing that the prohibition by section 3664, subdivision
4, of parol evidence to establish a contract creating interest in
real estate shall not prevent the enforcement of such a contract,
if it is not denied in the pleadings, nor oral testimony of the
adverse party from being evidence.

PART PAYMENT. The "part payment" which takes a case out of the
1 statute of frauds is not constituted by an arrangement that the
agent of the seller shall pay him part of the purchase price for
which the buyer agrees to reimburse said agent, which he never
did, though the seller actually received such payment. It is the
same as though the seller had made partial payment to himself.

POSSESSION. Evidence that, after an oral contract for the sale of
land, the vendee went to the premises with his son, to whom he
2 rented the place, picked up some lumber, and drove a few nails,

and that the vendor, when told by the vendee that he had rented
the premises, said it was all right, and that neither the vendee
nor his son was ever afterwards on the place, was insufficient to
show that such a vendee had "taken and held possession * * *
under and by virtue of the contract," within Code 1873, section
3665, which, excepts the contract from the statute of frauds.

SAME. To bring an oral contract to convey land within Code 1873, section 3665, providing that the prohibition by section 3664, subdivision
2 4, in such case of parol evidence to establish a contract creating an
interest in land shall not apply where the vendee with the actual
or implied consent of the vendor has taken and holds possession
of the land "under and by virtue of the contract" it is indispensible that the possession shall have been taken and held under and
by virtue of the contract.

WAIVER BY FAILURE TO OBJECT TO EVIDENCE. Defendant in an
action for breach of an oral contract to convey land does not
6 waive his plea of the statute of frauds by failing to object to the
parol evidence when offered, where the plaintiff pleads facts
which if established would show the contract to be valid because
embraced within some of the exceptions stated in the statute; as
plaintiff's order of proof was discretionary with him, defendant
could not tell until it was closed whether plaintiff would not
prove himself within some of said exceptions.

SALES—COMPLETION. An oral contract for the sale of land provided
that the deed should be placed in a bank, and delivered when title
was approved and payment made The person employed by the
4 vendee, after examining the deed and abstract, returned them to
the bank, with his opinion that there was some defect in the title,
whereupon the vendor took back the papers. *Held*, that the contract of sale was not completed.

INCONSISTENT CLAIMS: *Statute of frauds.* One who grounds his
5 action upon damages sustained because the seller failed to complete his sale according to contract cannot urge therein that deed
was fully delivered and that, hence, an oral bargain to sell land is
taken out of the statute of frauds.

Appeal from Ida District Court.—HON. Z. A. CHURCH,
Judge.

FRIDAY, OCTOBER 29, 1897.

ACTION at law to recover damages for a breach of
· an oral contract to convey land. Verdict directed for
the defendants. Plaintiff appeals.—*Affirmed.*

Warren & Johnston for appellant.

B. I. Salinger and *J. C. Walter* for appellees.

KINNE, C. J.—I.   Plaintiff claims: That on October 8, 1895, the defendants sold and agreed to convey to plaintiff eighty acres of land, at the agreed price of thirty-two dollars and fifty cents per acre, the deed and abstract showing title to be delivered at once, and price to be paid on said delivery.   That Engle, who was in fact the agent of Bird, his co-defendant, said he would pay Bird, who held the legal title to the land, twenty dollars on the purchase price, and that thereafter both of the defendants told plaintiff it had been paid.   That plaintiff took possession of the land, and leased it, and notified Bird that he had done so, and that the latter assented thereto.   That it was agreed that the deed should be delivered to Baxter, Reed & Co., for plaintiff, and he would arrange with them to pay over the money when Mr. Bradshaw approved the title. That plaintiff placed money with said firm, with instructions to pay it to the defendants when the deed and abstract had been delivered and Bradshaw had approved the title.   That the deed and abstract were delivered to Baxter, Reed & Co., and by them handed to Bradshaw.   Thereafter, Bradshaw returned them to the bank, with his opinion to the effect that there were some defects in the title.   That defendants went to the bank, and procured the deed and abstract, and conveyed the land to another party for an increased price.   In a substituted answer, the defendants denied making the contract, and denied, in substance, all the allegations of the petition, and pleaded that the contract relied upon was void under the statute of frauds.   At the close of the evidence for the plaintiff, the defendants moved for a verdict in their

favor upon several grounds, some of which will hereafter be considered. The motion was sustained, and a
verdict returned accordingly, upon which a judgment
was entered.

II. Our statute provides that, except when otherwise expressly provided, no evidence of certain contracts is competent unless in writing, and signed by the
party charged, or by his lawfully authorized agent.
Code 1873, section 3663. Among the contracts mentioned are those for the creation or transfer of any
interest in lands, except leases for a term not exceeding
one year. Code 1873, section 3664, subdivision 4. By
Code 1873 (section 3665) it is provided that the provision last referred to shall not apply when the purchase money, or any portion thereof, has been received
by the vendor, or when the vendee, with the actual or
implied consent of the vendor, has taken and held possession thereof under and by virtue of the contract. It
is also provided that the regulations referred to relate
merely to the proof of contracts, and do not prevent the
enforcement of those which are not denied in the pleadings (Code 1873, section 3666); and nothing in the foregoing provision shall prevent the party himself, against
whom the unwritten contract is sought to be enforced,
from being called as a witness by the opposite party,
nor his oral testimony from being evidence (Code 1873,
section 3667). It is contended that the fact of a
1   part payment on the land is established, and
       hence the statute does not apply. The exception
of the statute relating to a payment of the purchase
price applies only to cases where "the purchase money,
or any portion thereof, has been received by the vendor." The claim is that Engle, who was acting as agent
for his co-defendant, Bird, paid the latter twenty dollars
on the land for plaintiff. The petition charges that
Engle acted as Bird's agent. It would be a case, then,

of the seller making a part payment to himself. This
is not a case where one may properly act as the agent
of both parties. The interest of the principals being
adverse, Engle could not be the agent of both parties.
Therefore, if he had paid the twenty dollars to his principal, it would not avail the plaintiff as a part payment,
under the provisions of the statute. Engle being Bird's
agent, his act was in law the act of his principal. The
evidence shows without conflict that plaintiff never
paid any part of the purchase price of this land to either
of the defendants.

III. A further contention is that plaintiff took
possession under the contract, and hence has brought
himself within the exceptions provided in the statute.
To take a case out from the rule of the statute,
2   the possession must be taken and held under the
      contract, and with the actual or implied consent
of the vendor. Code 1873, section 3665. The evidence
shows: That plaintiff went over the place, and examined the house and cellar. Took his son with him, and
rented the place to him. Picked up some lumber around
the barn, and drove a few nails that were loose about
the barn. That he told Bird he had rented the place,
and he said it was all right. That neither he nor his
son ever slept in the house, or occupied it, and neither
of them were ever on the place afterwards. This sale
of the property and the examination of the house
occurred in October, 1894, and this suit was begun in
March, 1895. Even if it be conceded that all the acts
recited were done, still there is no evidence that such
acts had reference to, or were done under and by virtue
of, the contract of sale. The cases relied upon by appellant were not in their facts like that at bar. In *McCoy
v. Hughes*, 1 G. Greene, 373, the party had entered upon
the land and made improvements with the consent of
the seller, and had tendered the purchase money. In

Thayer v. Reeder, 45 Iowa, 273, the deed was delivered, purchase money paid, and possession taken. In *Sweeney v. O'Hora,* 43 Iowa, 38, there was a clear taking of possession established. Other cases are cited which are not applicable. It is indispensable that it appear that the possession is taken and held under and by virtue of the contract. If the acts mentioned would amount to a taking of possession, still it is not shown that they were done under the contract. We do not think that the plaintiff has shown that he has "taken and held possession" under the contract, as contemplated by the statute.

IV. It is contended that the defendants in their original answer, which was introduced in evidence, admitted the contract pleaded by the plaintiff. While said answer admits the execution of a deed to the 8   plaintiff, it does not admit the contract as claimed by the plaintiff. The facts touching the contract, which are pleaded in the original answer, are in material respects different from those pleaded by plaintiff. It cannot therefore be said that the contract, as pleaded in the petition, is admitted by the defendants. There is nothing in the answer which removes the case from the operation of the statute. Browne, Statutes, Frauds, section 501.

V. Upon the facts in this record, we do not think that the sale was ever completed. A fair view of the evidence shows that the deed was not delivered so as to pass the title. It is clear that the deed was 4   placed in the hands of Baxter, Reed & Co., to be held by them until the abstract was approved and the title found to be all right. When title was approved, and the money paid, it was to be delivered. As Bradshaw did not approve the title, and no part of the purchase price was paid, there was no delivery to the purchaser. Again, it appears that no absolute

delivery was intended by the parties at the time the
deed was placed in the hands of Baxter, Reed & Co.
Furthermore, the contract, as claimed by the plaintiff,
was silent as to what should be done in case the title
was found to be imperfect. This action is for
5   damages for a failure to complete a contract of
sale, and must be grounded upon the fact that
the deed was never in fact delivered. If it was so
delivered, then the grantor would not be liable, in an
action like this, for failure to comply with his promise,
and the plaintiff could not be damaged by a breach of
the contract to convey, which breach never existed.

VI. It is insisted that, as the defendants permitted the contract to be proven by oral testimony
without objection, they cannot thereafter invoke the
aid of the statute. *Crossen v. White*, 19 Iowa, 111
6   did not involve the question we have here, where
it is claimed that the facts take the case out of
the statute, and bring it within the exception. In *Holt
v. Brown*, 63 Iowa, 322, the statute was not pleaded,
and no objection made at any time, or in any manner,
to the evidence. Neither case deals with the question
we have in this record. The question is, when the contract is alleged by the defendant to be within the statute
of frauds, and the plaintiff pleads facts which, if established, would show the contract to be valid, because
embraced within some of the exceptions stated in the
statute, does the defendant waive his right to insist
upon the provisions of the statute if he fails to object to
the evidence when offered? It was discretionary with
the plaintiff as to the order in which he would introduce
his evidence. He could introduce proof of his contract
first, and thereafter proof to take the contract out of
the statute. Nor could the defendant have successfully
objected to the proof of the contract until it appeared
that the plaintiff had failed to establish the exceptions

he had pleaded. *Campbell v. Ormsby*, 65 Iowa, 521. As we have considered the case upon its merits, no ruling upon the motions submitted is necessary. We have considered all the questions made in the record, and discover no error.—AFFIRMED.

THE FORREST MILLING COMPANY, HARRIS & COLE BROTH-ERS, NORMAN H. HARRIS, RUTHEDGE HARRIS, J. J. COLE, J. W. COLE, and W. R. COLE, Appellees, v. THE CEDAR FALLS MILL COMPANY, THE CEDAR FALLS PAPER MANUFACTURING COMPANY, and G. N. MINER, Appellants, and H. H. CLAY, H. OLBRICH, W. R. GRAHAM, J. T. KNAPP, Trustee, C. C. KNAPP, J. T. KNAPP, and MARY G. OVERMAN, JESSIE F. COLLINS AND LIZZIE ROGERS, Heirs of D. C. OVER-MAN, Deceased, Appellees.

Water Power: HEAD: *Deeds*. A conveyance of a mill lot and the right to one hundred inches of water, which describes the lot by
1 metes and bounds, does not, by fixing its river boundary at low
18 water mark, limit the "head" of water, so as to prevent the
4 grantee increasing it by excavating the tail race below the then
5 low water mark.

SAME. Each of the parties to whom the owner of a water power conveys parts thereof, describing it in each case as so many
6 inches of water, without any limitation as to the "head," but with
7 conditions making the grantees liable for their proportionate
8 share of the expense necessary to repair or improve the race, dam and other structures creating the water power, is entitled to as nearly the same head as the conditions will permit of.

Same. The various owners of water rights in connection with a mill
3 dam and race have the right to the same head of water, or as
4 nearly the same as the topography of the ground, the fall of the
7 main race, and other conditions admit of, in the absence of con-trary provisions in the deeds conveying such rights, where they have been accustomed to excavate about the tail races leading from their mills, as they see fit, without any objection from other owners.

SAME. The rule that the grant of a mill or of a privilege of a mill
9 carries with it not only the land on which it stands, but the land

10 and water actually and commonly used therewith and necessary
to its enjoyment, does not apply to a conveyance of a specifically
described lot, though there be a mill upon it.

SAME: *Tenants in common.* Where four persons own a water power
9 in common, the land on which it was developed, and adjoining
10 land divided into lots, and three of the persons, at their own
11 expense, erect a mill on one of the lots, and conduct water thereto
from the head race, and the fourth likewise constructs a mill on
another lot, and conducts water thereto, the deed of the latter to
the former of an undivided one-fourth of several lots, including
that on which was their mill, or the deed of the former to the latter
of an undivided three-fourths of other lots, including that on
which was his mill, conveys none of the water rights of the
grantors, either as an easement or otherwise.

NOTICE: *Partition.* The use of water rights, as appurtenant to
16 land, by grantees of the land in possession thereof, does not of
itself operate as notice that there has been a parol partition of
17 the water rights which had previously been held in common by
the grantors in such deeds and other persons, where such use is
referable, as well, to their rights as tenants in common.

Same. The record of a deed to land on which a mill operated by
16 water is located does not charge a subsequent purchaser of water
17 rights in the race from which the water for the mill is obtained,
with notice of any interest of the grantee, in such water rights.

WATERS: *Deeds.* A conveyance by one of four tenants in common
of land, to the other co-tenants, of an undivided fourth interest
in a certain part of the land which is used for milling purposes,
does not carry with it, as a necessary incident to the beneficial
16 enjoyment of the land conveyed, a similar interest in water rights
owned by the same persons in common, as the grantees would
have the right to use the water because of their interest therein
as co-tenants.

Co-tenancy. A conveyance of an undivided fourth interest in a lot
2 and mill, together with all the rights and privileges appurtenant
thereto, does not convey any interest in the water power used for
such mill, owned in common by the grantors in such deed and
another person, which will be valid as against subsequent grantees
of such water power under deed by all the persons owning an
interest therein.

Same. A tenant in common of lands on which his co-tenants have
9 built a mill with their own means, and at their own expense have
turned the water on their wheels from a mill race owned in common by the same parties, does not, by conveying his undivided
interest in such land to his co-tenants, so enhance the value of
the land sold, by any artificial arrangement of his property, as to
cause the right to use the water to pass by the deed.

Same. A conveyance by part only of the tenants in common of a
13 water power, of an aliquot part thereof, is invalid as against
subsequent purchasers from all the co-tenants.

Same. Less than all the tenants in common cannot create an
13 easement in the common property and convey it to another.

ESTOPPEL. One whose remote grantors of a lot conveyed therewith
only part of the water which had been made appurtenant thereto,
and conveyed the remainder to another, is, like such grantor,
14 estopped to assert invalidity of the latter conveyance, on the
ground that water which has been made appurtenant to land
cannot be severed and sold separate from it.

Same. Where all the parties owning a water power formed a volun-
8 tary association for the purpose of repairing and keeping up the
power, the payment by certain members of assessments levied
15 against them, based on their ownership of certain water, will
estop other members to assert the invalidity of the conveyances
of water to them.

*Appeal from Black Hawk District Court.—*HON. C. F.
COUCH, Judge.

FRIDAY, OCTOBER 29, 1897.

THIS is a contest over the rights and interests of
the respective parties in and to a water power located
upon and along the Cedar river, at the city of Cedar
Falls. From a decree fixing and declaring the rights
of the several parties and enjoining the defendants from
making certain excavations in the main race, and
declaring that plaintiffs had the right to excavate and
deepen the tail races from their mills, so that they
might have a "head" equal to the greatest on the aforesaid water power, the defendants, the Cedar Falls Mill
Company, the Cedar Falls Paper Manufacturing Company, and G. N. Miner appeal.—*Affirmed.*

Mullen & Pickett for appellant Cedar Falls Mill
Co.

J. J. Tolerton for appellant Cedar Falls Paper
Manufacturing Co.

Hemenway & Grundy and *J. D. Nichols* for appellant G. N. Miner.

Boies, Husted & Boies for appellees W. R. Graham and others.

DEEMER, J.—The facts are complicated, and the issues so involved that we find it very difficult.to make a clear and comprehensive statement of the case. It appears that prior to the year 1848 one Sturgis was the owner of the land now known as the "Old Mill Square," at the city of Cedar Falls. This tract comprises about thirty-eight acres of land, and included the water power which is now the subject of controversy. In April of that year, he conveyed an undivided three-fourths of this land to J. M. Overman, D. C. Overman, and Edwin Brown; and on the same day, but by a different instrument, he conveyed the remaining one-fourth to James Newell, who, in turn, in July of the same year, conveyed the said one-fourth to William F. Overman. Before selling the land, Sturgis had commenced building a dam across the Cedar river. This dam was completed by Brown and the Overmans, and they also constructed a head race from a point some distance above the dam, along and across the land owned by them, for the purpose of conveying water to the mills thereafter to be erected. In 1854 William F. Overman conveyed his interest in the land and water power to Henry H. Meredith; and from that time, until the execution of the conveyances hereinafter referred to, the two Overmans, Brown, and Meredith owned the entire tract of land and water power thereto appurtenant, as tenants in common. In 1856, and after the head race had been constructed as far as the tract known as "Lot 21," the Overmans and Meredith, at their individual expense, erected a flouring mill upon said lot

21, and put in four water wheels, of an aggregate capacity of one thousand, two hundred inches of water, to furnish power, and used and appropriated that amount of water from the main race. In 1857 and 1858, Brown, at his expense, erected a mill upon what is now known as "Lot 24." This mill was also connected with the head race, and was supplied with four wheels, using an aggregate of one thousand, two hundred inches of water.

The parties to this controversy claim title by various mesne conveyances from these original owners. The Forrest Milling Company claims title and a right to draw three hundred inches of water from the race, under the following grants: In 1864 the Overmans, Meredith, and Brown executed and delivered to Charles Elliott and Micajah Collins a deed, by metes and bounds, to what is known as "Lot 28," in Mill Square addition, together with three hundred inches of water to be used in driving machinery upon the premises. This interest the Forest Milling Company acquired through certain mesne conveyances. The plaintiffs the Forrest Milling Company and Harris & Cole Bros. also claim title to what is now known as "Lot 32," in Mill Square addition, together with the right to draw one thousand inches of water from the mill race, through certain mesne conveyances from the Cedar Falls Starch · Company, that obtained title through a conveyance to it by the Overmans, Meredith, and Brown on August 31, 1866. The defendant J. F. Knapp claims the right to one hundred inches of water from the main race, to be taken opposite lot 24, as successor in interest to Sophronia M. Wilcox and Henry Budge, who obtained their title as follows: In 1865 the co-tenants above described executed to said Wilcox and Budge a deed to a right to use one hundred inches of water from the mill race, and Wilcox and Budge sold their interest and

right to this defendant. Clay & Olbrich, defendants,
and G. N. Miner, claim an interest in said water power
as successors in interest to Henry C. Overman, who
acquired it as follows: In June, 1866, D. C. Overman
executed and delivered to H. C. Overman a deed for lot
20 in Mill Square addition, and on the same day the
co-tenants above mentioned sold to H. C. Overman the
right to draw two hundred inches of water from the mill
race on the east bank, and directly in front of lot 20.
These deeds were not recorded, however, until November 9, 1866. H. C. Overman conveyed the right to one
hundred inches of this water to G. N. Miner, and
the other one hundred he conveyed to Clay &
Olbrich. Miner also claims that he is the owner of and
entitled to draw from the race one thousand, four hundred inches of water, as appurtenant to lot 21 of Mill
Square addition, under the following conveyances: (1)
A deed in July of the year 1858, from Brown to the
Overmans and Meredith, covering an undivided one-
fourth interest in and to lots 2, 3, 4, 5, 7, 8, 9, 11, 21, 22,
and 23 in Mill Square addition. The Overmans and
Meredith, at the same time, and evidently as a part of
the same transaction, deeded to Brown an undivided
three-fourths interest in lots 1, 6, 10, 14, 15, and 24, in
the same addition. A second deed, in April of the year
1861, from the Overmans and Meredith, conveyed an
undivided one-fourth of the premises known as "Lot
21," with all rights, privileges, and appurtenances
thereto belonging, to Elizabeth Wright; she, in turn,
conveying the same to Miner. He also claims a right to
the other three-fourths interest as successor to the
rights of the Overmans and Meredith under a foreclosure sale of their interest under a mortgage executed
after the conveyance to appellees' grantors. Miner also
claims that he is entitled to three hundred inches of
water as the partial successor in interest to the rights

of J. M. Overman, D. C. Overman, and Ellen C. Meredith, under the following conveyances: In April of the year 1863, the Overmans and Meredith conveyed the undivided one-half of lot 26, with the right to one thousand, six hundred inches of water from the race, to Shepard Wilson. But one thousand inches of this water was used by the mill on lot 26, and Wilson and another (one Van Saun, who had become interested with him), and who together owned all of said lot, conveyed six hundred inches of this water to L. N. and D. H. Fabrick, as an appurtenance to lot 27. D. H. Fabrick conveyed his interest in lot 27 to L. N. Fabrick, and L. N. Fabrick conveyed three hundred inches of the water, without any land, to Alexander Graham. L. N. Fabrick then conveyed lot 27 to Rhodes & Dayton, through whom the Cedar Falls Mill Company holds title. Thereafter, and in 1879, Fabrick executed a deed to Miner, purporting to convey to him the right to draw three hundred inches of water from the mill race. The Cedar Falls Paper Manufacturing Company claims title to and the right to draw one thousand two hundred inches of water from the race, through foreclosure of a mortgage executed by Edwin Brown, who obtained title, as is claimed, under the deed from his co-tenants, of date July 18, 1858. The mortgage so foreclosed was executed on the sixth day of October, 1866, after appellees' grantors had obtained title. The Cedar Falls Mill Company claims title to one thousand, six hundred inches of the water as successor to the interest of Shepard Wilson, who obtained his title through a deed of conveyance from the Overmans and Meredith, dated April 18, 1863, covering the undivided one-half of lot 26 in Mill Square addition, and the right to use the undivided one-half of one thousand six hundred inches of water. In October, 1867, Brown conveyed to the Overmans and Meredith his one-fourth interest in and to lots 26 and 27, and a

right to draw one.thousand, six hundred inches of
water, as appurtenant to lot 26; and thereafter the
Overmans and Meredith conveyed the remaining half
of lot 26, with the water rights appurtenant to lot 26,
to Wilson, who thereafter conveyed the same, as we
have stated, to the Cedar Falls Mill Company. The
Cedar Falls Mill Company also claims title and the
right to three hundred inches of water, obtained
by the conveyance from Rhodes & Dayton, heretofore
referred to.

In April of the year 1853, and before Meredith
acquired any interest in the lands, the Overmans and
Brown made and caused to be recorded a plat of the
town of Cedar Falls, which plat included in its
2   boundaries a portion of the lands in controversy,
and caused to be surveyed and set apart as a
water site the tract of land comprising thirty-eight
acres heretofore referred to. The Cedar river flows in
a southeasterly direction through this tract, and furnishes the power which is the subject of controversy.
In 1858 the Overmans, Meredith, and Brown caused to
be surveyed and platted into lots (numbering from 1 to
24, inclusive) certain lands adjoining the town of Cedar
Falls and the thirty-eight acre tract hitherto mentioned, and caused the same to be denominated "Mill
Square Addition" to the town of Cedar Falls. None of
the original thirty-eight acres were divided into lots,
nor were they included within the boundaries of this
addition. In October of the year 1867, Brown executed
and delivered to the Overmans and Meredith a deed to
an undivided one-fourth of the right to draw water from
the main race to be used upon lot 21 in the Mill Square
addition, and his undivided one-fourth interest in and
to lots 26 and 27, with the right to draw from the mill
race one thousand, six hundred inches of water. And,
on the same day, the Overmans and Meredith executed
and delivered to Brown a deed conveying to him an

undivided three-fourths interest in the right to draw one thousand, two hundred inclies of water to be used upon lot 24 in Mill Square addition. These deeds were a part and parcel of the same transaction, and the only consideration therefor was the mutual conveyances and promises between parties. They all contained this condition: "Subject, however, to the payment of such part of the expenses for necessary repairs and improvements to the race, dam, and other structures creating the water power in Cedar Falls, aforesaid, as the amount of water herein conveyed bears to the amount of water used on said race, or as may be hereafter used at the time such expenses are incurred; and subject to the further right of the parties owning water rights to draw off the water from said race for necessary repairs and for improvements to said water power. And provided, further, that if, at any time hereafter, there shall not be sufficient water in said race to propel all the machinery driven by the same, that then the grantees herein shall only draw their just proportion of the same." Since the commencement of this action, the Forrest Milling Company has acquired the undivided one-half of the residue of the property known as the "Old Mill Square," and the defendant G. N. Miner is the owner of the other undivided half. In the year 3 1875 an association composed of the various owners of the water power was formed, under the name of the Cedar Falls Water Power Company, for the purpose of maintaining the dam and the race, and of assessing the expenses thereof against the various owners of the power. These assessments, made from time to time, were paid by the various owners, as follows: The Cedar Falls Mill Company paid upon one thousand inches of water; the Cedar Falls Paper Manufacturing Company paid upon one thousand inches; Miner paid, during a part of the time at least, upon two thousand inches; Harris & Cole Bros. paid upon five hundred inches; and the Forrest Milling Company upon five hundred inches. Harris & Cole Bros. and the Forrest Milling Company refused to pay one of these assessments, and withdrew from the association. Thereafter the other members of the association proceeded to improve the race, by making excavations below the mills of these parties who withdrew from the association. To this, plaintiffs objected, and commenced this suit to prevent work on the race below their mills.

The defendants insist upon their rights to improve the property in the manner contemplated, averring that such work was for the mutual benefit of all the owners.

In answers and cross-petitions, defendants 4 assert their respective rights to the water power, and further say that plaintiffs were excavating the head race in such manner as to impede the flow of water, and also charge that plaintiffs have extended their tail race below low water mark, thus giving them a greater head than that to which they are entitled under their deeds. Each of the parties plaintiff and defendant claim a prior and superior right to that of all others, in the water power. The supply of water is frequently insufficient to operate all the mills upon the race, or to furnish to the owners the number of inches called for in their deeds. As this suit was originally brought to restrain defendants from excavating in the race below plaintiffs' head gates, and as the defendants in their cross-petition ask an injunction to restrain the plaintiffs from excavating their tail race below low water mark, and from using more than one thousand inches of water from the main race, we will consider the rights of the parties in these respects before determining their respective rights and priorities under the various conveyances to which we have referred.

The trial court found that each of the several parties was entitled to draw the amounts of water

which shculd be allotted, from the same common head,
and that, to obtain it, any or all of the parties might
excavate and extend their tail race into the bed of the
river and the thirty-eight acres of land aforesaid, so far
as might be necessary for the purpose. It also found
that the proper method of improving the main race is to
place the bottom thereof substantially upon a level, and
the provisional injunction theretofore granted was so
modified as to permit the improvement of the race below
the head gates of the plaintiff's mill by the removal
of substances therein, commencing at the highest points
and projections, and continuing such removals with a
view to placing the bottom of said race as nearly upon
a level as possible. The lower court found, as
5   we think correctly, that the conveyance from the
tenants in common of the Old Mill Square, and
the water power connected therewith, to the starch
company, of lot 32, and the right to draw at all times
one thousand inches therefrom, which right is now
owned by the plaintiffs, described the lot by metes and
bounds, and fixed the river boundary at low water
mark; that, at the time the property was improved, the
tail race was excavated about one foot below low water
mark as it then existed, and, since the acquisition of the
property by the plaintiffs, the said tail race has been
excavated and extended considerably further below
low water mark; that none of the deeds or other written
instruments fixed the amount of head to which any of
the owners are entitled; and that the present head at
plaintiff's mill is seven and one-half feet, at the Cedar
Falls Mill Company's mill eight and one-half feet, at
Miner's mill ten and one-half feet, and at the Paper
Manufacturing Company's mill something in excess of
any of these figures; that, since the dam was constructed, it has been raised about one foot, at the common expense of the owners of the power; that the highest point in the main race is above the plaintiffs' head

gates, and that below such head gates the surface of the
bottom of the race is irregular and uneven, detracting
from the value of the power furnished by said race, by
reason of the water having to pass over such obstructions, and the accumulation of ice in the winter season,
and the action thereof; that the better and more
effective power is produced by making the bottom of
the race as nearly level as possible, and with but a slight
incline therein.

From these facts it clearly appears, we think, that
the court was right in its decree directing how the main
race should be improved. As to the excavations made
by plaintiffs in their tail race, it is sufficient to
6   say that there is nothing in any of the conveyances limiting the "head" to which they are
entitled, unless it be in the description of lot 32, which
fixes the river boundary of the lot at low water mark.
We do not think this has anything to do with the head
to which they are entitled. By going upon the land
not covered by their deeds, they may be committing a
trespass, but defendants do not complain of this. They
say that plaintiffs have no right to excavate the tail
races from their mills, so that the head of water used
by them may be increased, and that they are limited by
the deed to which we have called attention.
7   Until this litigation arose, the various owners
excavated about the tail races leading from their
mills as they saw fit, and without any objection from
any of the others; and, in the absence of limitation not
found in these deeds, we think each of the parties had
the right to the same head of water, or to as nearly the
same as the topography of the ground, the fall of the
main race, and other conditions would permit of. This
position is strengthened by the fact that nearly all the
deeds to which we have referred contain conditions
making the grantees liable for their proportionate

share of the expense necessary to repair or improve
the race, dam, and other structures. Of course, no one
can so excavate as to deprive others of their just proportion of the power. The excavation proposed will not
have this effect, and we are satisfied that the decree is
correct in these respects. Mention has already been
made of a fact to which attention should be given in
connection with the matters now under consideration,—that the Forrest Milling Company and defendant
Miner are the owners of what remains of the water
power and original Mill Square not covered by the conveyances to which we have referred.

The most serious contention in the case, and the
one involving the most doubt, relates to the rights and
interests of the various parties in and to the water
power in question. The conveyances under
8   which defendants and appellants claim are all
prior in point of time to those under which the
plaintiffs claim, and defendants are entitled to priority,
provided these deeds conveyed a right to any part of the
water, and were executed by the necessary parties. The
conveyance which is at the foundation of Miner's claim
is the deed from Brown to the Overmans and Meredith,
of date July 19, 1858. It conveyed, among other things,
"the undivided one-fourth of lot 21, Mill Square, town
of Cedar Falls." Nothing is said about water rights.
At that time, however, the main race had been extended
from the southerly boundary of Mill Square, and the
four joint owners of the same had, at their own expense,
conveyed the water from the main race to the mill
erected by the Overmans and Mered.th upon lot 21,
which adjoined the thirty-eight-acre tract on the south.
At the time this deed, as well as the others bearing the
same date to which we have referred, were made, a large
part of the land owned by these co-tenants was undivided; and, unless this deed from Brown to his co-tenants operated as a partition of the water power or a

transfer of a part thereof to the grantees therein named, then there was no valid sale or conveyance of water rights until the deeds of October 19, 1867, which were subsequent to the dates of the original conveyances under which the plaintiffs claim. The deed itself does not purport to convey any water rights. It is said, however, that they passed, to the extent the water was then in use, by implication, as an easement in or appurtenance to the land. To this question we will first give our attention.

The mill erected on this lot was built by the Overmans and Meredith at their own expense, just as the mill upon lot 24 was built by Brown from his own funds. The water, it is true, had been carried 9 from the main race, which was upon the thirty-eight-acre tract, to these lots, and was being used by the builders of these mills, as we have stated. In equity, the mill belonged to the tenants who erected it; for it is an elementary rule that, when one co-tenant erects permanent improvements upon the common property, he is, as between himself and the co-tenants, the separate and individual owner thereof, and they will be allotted to him upon partition. Freeman, Co-Tenancy, sections 262, 505. This rule was also enforced in this case by agreement of the parties, in virtue of which they improved separate and distinct tracts of land. As no water rights were expressly conferred, they did not pass unless by implication. In some cases it has been held that a grant of a mill or of a privilege of a mill carries with it not only the land upon which it stands, but the land and water actually and commonly used therewith, and necessary to its enjoyment, on the theory that such a general description carries with it all things which have been used with the principal thing, and which in fact constitutes or is reputed to be a parcel of it. Gould, Waters, section 307; *Taylor*

v. Bradley, 18 N. Y. 109; *Ogden v. Jennings,* 62 N. Y.
526. This rule does not apply to the case at bar, for
the reason that the description is specific in its terms,
and refers to a lot which had certain well defined
boundaries; and the water right did not pass as a part
of the thing granted, unless as a necessary incident to
the beneficial enjoyment of the thing granted. *Parsons
v. Johnson,* 68 N. Y. 62. Easements of necessity sometimes pass by implication where no mention of them is
made in the conveyance. The foundation of such a
right is a necessity, and not convenience. Gould,
Waters, section 362; *Ward v. Robertson,* 77 Iowa, 161.
It has already been noted that the original conveyances
of the land were between tenants in common, not only
of the premises, but of the water power as well, and
there was no reason for implying the grant of an easement in the water power. When Brown conveyed to
the Overmans and Meredith, they then owned three-
fourths of the water power in controversy, and had in
their own right plenty of water with which to run the
mill. Nothing passed by implication from necessity.
Ogden v. Jennings, 62 N. Y. 526; *Ward v. Robertson, supra.*

Appellants claim that the power passed as an
appurtenant to the mill. It is no doubt true that, as a
general rule, an existing easement appurtenant to an
estate will pass by a grant in general terms.
10   But an easement which is extinct or which has no
legal existence, though used *de facto,* does not pass
as an appurtenance. 3 Hillard, Real Property, p. 514,
section 40. It is also elementary that no one can create
an easement against himself in his own land. For this
reason, it has been held that a tenant in common who
owns other property in severalty cannot so use the last
as to acquire for the benefit of the individual estate an
easement in the property held in common. *Crippen v.
Morss,* 49 N. Y. 63; *Great Falls Co. v. Worster,* 15 N. H.

412. The land conveyed by Brown to his co-tenants, in favor of which the claimed easement would exist, was owned by the Overmans, Meredith, and Brown in fee, prior to the conveyance; and the land upon which the water power was developed was owned by the same parties. No easement existed at the time of the conveyance, for at that time there was unity of title and ownership in both the so-called dominant and servient estates. Washburn, Easements, pp. 684, 685. It has sometimes been held that when an owner of the whole tenement has, by some artificial arrangement of the material parts of his estate, added to the advantage and enhanced the value of one portion of it, he cannot, after selling that portion with the advantage openly and visibly attached, voluntarily break the arrangement, and thus destroy or materially diminish the value of the portion sold. *Simmons v. Cloonan*, 47 N. Y. 240; *Lampman v. Milks*, 21 N. Y. 505; *Insurance Co. v. Patterson*, 103 Ind. 582 (2 N. E. Rep. 188); *Kelly v. Dunning*, 43 N. J. Eq. 62 (10 Atl. Rep. 276); *Lammott v. Ewers*, 106 Ind. 310 (6 N. E. Rep. 636). This rule does not

11   apply to the case at bar, for the reason that the Overmans and Meredith built the mill upon lot 21 from their own means, and at their own expense turned the water from the main race upon their wheels, as they had a right to do, for they owned an undivided three-fourths of the water power. Brown, the grantor in the deed under which appellants claim, had nothing to do with this artificial arrangement, except to consent to it; and it certainly should not be held that he, as grantor in the deed, made such an artificial arrangement of his property as that the right to use the water passed by the deed under the rule last above referred to. Again, this doctrine, to some extent at least, is based upon the rule of necessity; and we have already seen that there is no room for implying a grant from necessity. One other thought seems to be conclusive of the

proposition that no right to the water passed by the deed from Brown to the Overmans and Meredith, of date July 19, 1858. The mill itself, which was erected upon lot 21, belonged exclusively to the Overmans and Meredith at the time the conveyance was made. It was built upon common property, but at the separate cost of the grantees in the deed. In the absence of a promise, either express or implied, Brown could not be made liable for any part of the cost of the mill; and, as he was not the owner of any part of the improvement, no interest in it passed by the deed under consideration.

It quite clearly appears that the deeds of date July 19, 1858, between the tenants in common of this property, operated as a voluntary partition of the lands described therein, and of nothing else, and that each retained his joint interest in and to the water power until the making of the conveyances to appellees' grantors, and of the partition deeds of water rights, of date October 19, 1867, heretofore referred to, unless it be found that there was a parol partition of the water rights at an earlier day, as claimed by some of the appellants, to which claim we will hereafter give attention. We have seen that the deed from Brown to the Overmans and Meredith did not convey any water rights, and we have further discovered that, aside from the claim of parol partition, there was no division of any part of the water power, or of any rights therein until the deed of date October 19, 1867. In the meantime, however, the plaintiffs and W. R. Graham's grantors obtained conveyances, from all the tenants in common of the water power, of certain rights and interests therein, which they claim to be prior and superior to any rights of the other parties under these partition deeds. These partition deeds, of date October 19, 1867, granted the right to draw from the mill race a certain specified number of inches of water, "to be a

12

right and privilege appurtenant to the land described
in the deeds." This is the first attempt of the parties to
make an express written partition of the water rights,
and is entitled to great weight in construing the deeds
made in the year 1858, between these same parties.
The deed from the Overmans and Meredith to Elizabeth
O. Wright, under which appellant Miner claims, was of
an undivided one-fourth of lot 21, together with all the
rights and privileges appurtenant or in any manner
thereto belonging, and the mill and appurtenances
thereto belonging. It does not purport to convey more
than an undivided one-fourth of the lot and appurtenances thereto. These "appurtenances" now claimed
by appellants, to be availing, must have existed at the
time of the conveyance, and must have been owned by
the grantors in the deed. That they did own the lot
and the mill situated thereon must be conceded. But
they did not own all of the water power. Brown had
an interest in it at that time, and a conveyance by three
of the four co-tenants of an aliquot part of the water
power was of no validity against subsequent granters
of all the proprietors, unless such interest in the water
power had theretofore been made appurtenant to the
lot. We have already seen that it was not so partitioned by any deed between these co-tenants. The
voice of authority is nearly uniform to the effect that,
"while a tenant in common may make a valid sale of
any undivided fraction of his undivided interest which
he sees fit, he cannot be allowed to sell his interest of
any portion thereof in a part of the premises by metes
and bounds, because this would interfere with his
co-tenants' right of partition." *Farr v. Reilly*, 58 Iowa,
399, and cases cited. Likewise, it has been held "that
less than all the tenants in common cannot create an
easement in the common property, nor convey such
easement to another." *Rush v. Railroad Co.*, 57 Iowa,

201; *Marshall v. Trumbull*, 28 Conn. 183; *Adams v. Iron Co.*, 7 Cush, 361; Freeman, Co-tenancy; section 185; *Pfeiffer v. Regents*, 74 Cal. 156 (15 Pac. Rep. 622). This thought disposes of the claims made by Miner as successor in interest to three of the four tenants in common, and of the Cedar Falls Mill Company, under conveyances by the parties to Shepard Wilson.

Miner's claim to certain interest in the water power superior to that of appellees, as a partial successor to the interest of Henry C. Overman, under deed of date June 26, 1866, is not sustained, for the 13 reason that this deed was not delivered or recorded until after appellees' grantors obtained title. The claim of the Cedar Falls Paper Manufacturing Company rests upon a conveyance made in the year 1858, by the Overmans and Meredith, to Brown, of an undivided three-fourths of lot 24; and the same rules of law are applicable to it as to the claim made by Miner of rights under the conveyance by Brown to the Overmans and Meredith, and need not be further noticed. And the same may be said with reference to the claim of this defendant to one thousand inches of water as appurtenant to lot 32.

Plaintiffs claim title to five hundred inches of water, known as the "Graham water." Three hundred of this they acquired by certain mesne conveyances from L. N. Fabrick (he being the then owner of 14 lot 27, with six hundred inches of water), which he acquired from Shepard Wilson and one Van Saun. The Cedar Falls Mill Company claims title to this water under a subsequent deed from the same L. N. Fabrick. The other two hundred inches plaintiffs obtained through certain mesne conveyances from Alexander Graham, who obtained his title from G. N. Miner, to lot 24, with one thousand two hundred inches of water appurtenant thereto, one thousand of which

he conveyed to one Neff, and the remaining two hundred he conveyed to William Graham, plaintiffs'
grantor. The Cedar Falls Paper Manufacturing Company claims title to this two hundred inches under a
conveyance from Neff of lot 24. These five hundred
inches of water were attempted to be separated from
the estates to which they were appurtenant, and conveyed by deeds covering nothing but water rights.
Appellants contend that such a conveyance is not valid
in this state, because water which has been made appurtenant to land cannot be severed and sold separate from
the land. We need not decide this difficult and interesting question, for the reason that we find appellants
are estopped from denying the validity of these conveyances, which were prior in point of time, to those
under which they claim. Defendants' remote grantors,
who made the original severance of the water, would
be estopped from denying the validity of their conveyances; and, as defendants stand in their shoes, they
cannot be heard to say that the conveyances are invalid.
Weare v. Williams, 85 Iowa, 253, and authorities cited.

15   Moreover, it appears that all the parties formed
a voluntary association for the purpose of repairing and keeping up the power, and plaintiffs paid
assessments levied against them by this association, of
which defendants were members, based upon their
ownership of the water in dispute. Such fact operates
as an estoppel upon the defendants, and they cannot
now be heard to say that the conveyances were invalid.

We have now disposed of every claim in the case
save that of parol partition, which the defendants and
appellants, or some of them, say was made in the year
1858. The exact claim is that the original

16   owners, by their acts and agreements, made a
parol partition of a part of the real estate, water
and water rights owned by them in common. That

they did make a voluntary partition of a part of the
real estate must be conceded. But the more important,
and indeed the only, question in this connection, is, did
they partition the water or water rights owned by
them at or about the time the conveyances were made
in the year 1858? There are authorities which hold that
parol partition may be made of property owned in
common, and that, when such partition is followed by
actual possession in severalty, each tenant will thereafter hold the part assigned to him in the severalty, in
fee. *Wood v. Fleet*, 36 N. Y. 506; Freeman, Co-tenancy,
section 393. Where this rule prevails, it no doubt
applies to a water power and to water rights. *Cooper
v. Water Power Co.*, 42 Iowa, 398; *Kennedy v. Scovil*,
12 Conn. 317; *Hanson v. Willard*, 12 Me. 142; *Brown
v. Cooper*, 98 Iowa, 444. If it be conceded that such
rule obtains in this state,—a point not now decided,—
it follows that the question is one of fact, and the burden is upon the defendants who tender such issue to
prove it. Two of the original co-tenants were witnesses
upon the trial, and each of them denied any partition of
the water power or water rights until the execution of
the deeds, in the year 1867. There are some facts pointing to such a voluntary division of the water, but in the
face of the denials of these witnesses we are not justified in finding that such an arrangement was entered
into. The written documents which have been offered
in evidence belie the claim made, and give support to
the plaintiffs' contention that no partition was made
until the year 1867, after they had acquired their rights
by conveyances from all the tenants in common. The
possession and use made of the water by the co-tenants
was no more referable to ownership in severalty
than to the right of each to have the use of
the common property belonging to all the parties. But,
aside from this, we are constrained to believe that

plaintiffs are innocent purchasers of the property, without notice of any such parol partition as is claimed. When they became the owners of the land and water rights, the conveyances which we have noticed were all of record. From these conveyances they were justified in believing that the conveyances to the starch manufacturing company, Wilcox & Budge, and to Elliott & Collins were the first which attempted to grant any water rights. True, there were conveyances antedating these referring to water rights, but none of them were made by all the owners of the property. The only partition of record was that made in the year 1867, after plaintiffs' grantors obtained the title under which appellees now claim. The deeds of 1858 did not on their face purport to convey any water rights or privileges. True, Brown or his grantees, and the Overmans and Meredith and their grantees, were in the use of the water power and the rights; but there was nothing of record to indicate that either the mills or even the water power were in existence in the year 1858. The first reference of record to the mills is in the deed to Elizabeth Wright, of date April 1, 1861; but this, as we have seen, was made by but three of the four tenants in common, and was invalid as against subsequent purchasers from all of the co-tenants. Aside from this, had they known that Brown and the Overmans and Meredith were making use of the water to propel the machinery of their respective mills, still they might well infer that it was in virtue of their rights as tenants in common, and the deeds of partition made in the year 1867 would be confirmatory evidence of this fact.

When plaintiffs purchased their property, they acquired what appeared from the face of the records

to be a superior interest in the water power to that of
any of the appellants in this suit. It is true that
17   Elliott & Collins and Budge & Wilcox and their
grantees have rights superior to those acquired
by the appellees Harris & Cole Bros.; but they were
fully protected by the decree rendered by the trial
court. Appellees were charged by the record with
notice of rights created by the instruments as recorded,
and not with notice arising from unrecorded instruments, or from facts surrounding the instruments
which were not of record. *Miller v. Ware*, 31 Iowa, 524;
Disque v. Wright, 49 Iowa, 538. And while it is true
that some of appellants were in possession of lands,
and were using water rights as appurtenant thereto,
at the time the plaintiffs purchased, yet such use did
not of itself indicate that there had been a parol partition of the property between the original tenants in
common before the conveyances were made to plaintiffs' grantors. *May v. Sturdivant*, 75 Iowa, 116; *Bon-
nell v. Allerton*, 51 Iowa, 166. Again, the possession by
appellant Miner of a part of the water power at the time
plaintiffs, or some of them, purchased their interest in
the power, might properly be referred to the title orig-
inating by the deeds of partition executed in the year
1867. See authorities above cited, and Webb, Record
Titles, section 232, where it is said: "Where a person
occupies premises, and the record shows a conveyance
under which he would be entitled to the possession, in
such case his possession will be referred to the record
title, and a subsequent purchaser will not be charged
by it with notice of any other undisclosed title or equity
which the occupant may have. The possession is a
matter tending to excite inquiry, but the fact that the
occupant has placed upon the public records written
evidence of his right, with the terms of which his possession is consistent, arrests inquiry at that point, and

reasonably informs the purchaser that he may rest upon
the knowledge thus obtained."

The trial court found that the Forrest Milling Company, as successor to the interests of Elliott & Collins,
is entitled to draw three hundred inches of water from
the race, provided that, if at any time there is
18   an insufficient supply to propel all the machinery
which was on the race in 1864, it shall only draw
such proportionate part of the three hundred inches as
the whole at such time supplied by the dam and race
shall bear to the whole number required to run all the
machinery which was on the race at that date; that
Knapp, as sucessor to Wilcox & Budge, was entitled
to draw one hundred inches, subject to the prior right
of the Forrest Milling Company, and subject to diminution when there was failure of supply; that the Forrest
Milling Company and Harris & Cole Bros., as successors
to the Cedar Falls Starch Company, are entitled to
draw one thousand inches, subject to the prior rights
of the parties above mentioned; that, subject to these
rights, appellants Miner and Clay & Olbrich, as successors in interest of Henry C. Overman, are entitled
to draw two hundred inches of water; and that after
the parties named have been supplied with the number
of inches of water to which they are, respectively,
entitled, as aforesaid, the residue is to be divided as
follows: One thousand inches to Cedar Falls Mill Company, one thousand inches to Cedar Falls Paper Manufacturing Company, one thousand seven hundred inches
to G. N. Miner, and five hundred inches to Forrest Milling Company and Harris & Cole Bros.; that none of the
owners of said residue are entitled to any priority over
the others; and that, in case of insufficient supply, then
the parties are entitled, after the owners of the prior
rights are supplied, to appropriate the residue as follows: The Cedar Falls Mill Company ten-forty-seconds

thereof, the Cedar Falls Paper Manufacturing. Company ten-forty-seconds thereof, G. N. Miner seventeen-forty-seconds thereof, the Forrest Milling Company and Harris & Cole Bros. five-forty-seconds thereof; and, in case of excess in the supply, then the Forrest Milling Company and G. N. Miner are entitled to an equal share of such excess. Our extended examination of the record leads us to the conclusion that this disposition of the case is approximately correct. We have not considered all questions argued, for the reason that to do so would unduly extend an opinion which, at best, is entirely too long. Our effort has been to decide what appear to be the controlling points, and our conclusion is that the decree should be AFFIRMED.

SOPHIA M. RICE, Guardian, v. THE GRAND LODGE OF THE ANCIENT ORDER OF UNITED WORKMAN OF IOWA, Appellant.

Insurance: SUSPENSION. A mutual benefit society does not waive the requirement of a certificate of health as a condition of the reinstatement of a member who has defaulted in the payment of
2 assessments, by receiving and crediting to him the amount of the assessments from him, and retaining the money for a reasonable time, where it sent him a marked copy of the order calling his attention to the necessity of reinstatement.

SAME. A member of a benefit society, whose laws provided that failure of any member to pay an assessment by the twenty-eighth day of the month should operate as a suspension, subject to rein-
2 statement on compliance with certain requirements, mailed an
5 assessment on the twenty-fifth of the month, and died on the
6 twenty-ninth, several days before the money reached the society, which refused to accept it. Held, that deceased was legally suspended at the time of his death.

WAIVER. The fact that a benefit society, whose laws provided that
4 non-payment of an assessment by a particular date should operate
5 as a forfeiture of a member's rights, subject to reinstatement on payment of arrearages within four months thereafter, had frequently received assessments from a member after they became

due, did not waive a subsequent suspension for non-payment of an assessment when due.

Same. That a member of a mutual benefit society had at times, as 3 a matter of convenience to him, been allowed to pay his assessments before maturity, does not tend to show a license for, or even acquiescence in, non-payment of other assessments as they became due.

Appeal. Legal propositions determined on appeal stand as the law of 1 the case on a subsequent appeal.

Appeal from Black Hawk District Court.—Hon. A. S. Blair, Judge.

Friday, October 29, 1897.

This cause was before in this court, and reported in 92 Iowa, at page 417. The facts are there fully stated, and need not be re-stated here. On the former trial the district court sustained a motion by plaintiff for a verdict in her favor, and on the hearing in this court the action of the district court was reversed on the ground that the evidence did not authorize such action, and the cause was remanded for further proceedings. At the next trial in the district court, when the evidence was concluded the defendant moved for a verdict in its favor for several reasons, which the court denied, and submitted the cause to the jury, that returned a verdict for the plaintiff, and from a judgment thereon the defendant appealed.—*Reversed.*

J. D. & C. Nichols for appellant.

Hunt & Morrill and *O. C. Miller* for appellee.

Granger, J.—Some legal propositions were settled on the former appeal, and they must stand as the 1   law of this case. *Windsor v. Cobb,* 74 Iowa, 709; *Heffner v. Brownell,* 75 Iowa, 341.

It is not, and could not well be, contended that, if Rice was legally suspended at the time of his death, there could be a recovery by plaintiff. Looking to the case on the other appeal, it will be seen that the financier of the subordinate lodge was required to send to each member a copy of the assessment not later than the eighth day of each month, and that any member failing to pay the assessmnet against him by the twenty-eighth day of the same month forfeited all rights under his certificate. The effect of this non-payment was a suspension, by operation of the law of the order. By the same law it is provided that, if all assessments shall be paid at any time within four months, the mere fact of payment shall operate to reinstate the person suspended. If not thus reinstated within the four months, a reinstatement thereafter must be by such payments, a certificate of health, and a vote of the local lodge. Rice had been suspended for more than the four months when he sent the twenty dollars which paid all arrearages to the date of such payment, but he furnished no certificate of health, and no vote of the local lodge had been taken. This twenty dollars was to cover seventeen assessments in the year 1891, and three quarterly dues. The twenty dollars was mailed at Niehart, Mont., August 24, 1891, and received at Guttenberg, Iowa, by the local lodge, September 2, 1891, and placed to the credit of Rice on the books. The secretary acknowledged the receipt of the money, and inclosed in the envelope a copy of the laws of the order, so marked as to call attention to the requirement that a health certificate shoul l be furnished before reinstatement. On the eighth of September, 1891, the secretary of the local lodge mailed to Rice, at Niehart, Mont., notice of another assessment, which was received about the fifteenth of the month; and on the twenty-fifth of the month Rice sent by mail, five dollars, which was received by the lodge October 3, 1891. By the law of the order, the payment must be made by the twenty-eighth of the month, or suspension follows. On the former appeal it was held, under the same state of facts, that there was no payment until after the twenty-eighth day of the month, and hence from the twenty-eighth Rice stood suspended, because of such non-payment, unless certain facts relied on would defeat such a result. He died on

3

the twenty-ninth. Among the reasons urged in support of a waiver by the order is the manner in which Rice had been permitted to pay his assessments. It does appear that he had at times paid his assessments before due; that is, he would make payments before notice of assessments. It does not appear that he was to do so. It was a matter of choice with him, and we know of no rule or reason by which it can be said that such a payment tends to show a license for, or even acquiescence in, non-payments of assessments as they should become due. It appears to have been done as a matter of convenience to. or choice by Rice, and not in any way at the instance of the order. It also appears that he many times

4

paid after the twenty-eighth of the month. That was his absolute right. The lodge was bound to accept such payments, and they had the effect of a reinstatement. To have denied them would have been violating the contract, and the result would have been. probably, a reinstatement without payment. There is absolutely nothing in such an act to show a purpose to permit or sanction an irregular course of dealings. To illustrate the argument, it is said that in 1890 assessments 8 and 9 were paid three months after due, "and no question was raised, so long as defendant got the money." What question could be raised? Notices were given of the assessments regularly, so far as known,

and it was for Rice to pay or not, as he might elect.
Whether paid before or after the twenty-eighth of the
month, the lodge must accept it, within the four
months, and the law fixed his status. We are not told
in argument what the lodge should have done in such
a case to avoid a waiver, and it is difficult to anticipate
any duty, except to receive and give credit for the
money.

It is said that "every act and relation between
Rice and defendant for a course of years, even up to
Rice's death, showed a disregard of strict compliance."
Taking the dealings prior to the receipt of the
5   twenty dollars, September 2, 1891, we do not
find a single act on the part of the lodge, not in
harmony with the prescribed course of dealings, from
which it could be reasonably understood that the lodge
intended to sanction a course of dealings on the part of
Rice not prescribed by his contract, which included
the law of the order. As to receiving and giving credit
for the twenty dollars September, 1891, we find nothing to indicate just the course to be pursued by the
lodge. It was one step, and the first, required for reinstatement. The doing of that could only be considered
as tending to show an intent to treat Rice as reinstated,
but any such purpose is disproved by sending the
marked copy of the laws, to call his attention to what
was necessary for reinstatement. It is not known that
Rice ever saw the marked portion of it, but the purpose
of the lodge is as conclusively shown, and Rice is presumed to have known his duty under his contract. The
time was short between the receipt of the money and
his death, and the lodge might well anticipate that he
intended to complete his reinstatement. Till the health
certificate came, the lodge could not accept him by a
vote. We said on the other appeal, to meet an argument by defendant, that, "if the financier and treasurer

as _____ received payments of assessments, of the local lodge were held and applied to the purposes of the order, it does not appear to us that the defendant is in any position to claim that these acts were without authority." That rule obtains in the case. There is nothing, except the giving of the credit, to indicate that it was applied to the purposes of the order. There was not a lapse of time, or other facts to indicate that Rice did not intend to complete his reinstatement, so that a presumption might arise that the order intended to keep the money and treat him as reinstated. It is to be said that, pending a sufficient time for Rice to complete his reinstatement, the financier should have made a record of the receipt of the money, so that in his absence the fact of the payment could be known. It is not easy to see why a credit was not a proper course to pursue; the money to be afterwards charged back, if returned for any reason. If, for any reason, it could be held that there was a reinstatement from suspension because of defaults in the payments of the seventeen assessments, it still remains that there was a default in the payment of the eighteenth assessment, because we before held, under the same facts, that the payment was not made in time, and that the financier was not required to, and did not, receive it. What we
6   have said shows our conclusion that there was no course of dealing to avoid a suspension if the assessment was not paid by the twenty-eighth of the month. His death was after the twenty-eighth, and before payment, so that he died suspended for that particular default, if not for previous ones. There is really not a dispute as to facts determinative of the case. It is thought that *Mayer v. Insurance Co.*, 38 Iowa, 304, authorizes a payment after the death of the assured, though it was due before. That is true wherever, by the terms of the contract, or a course of dealings, there is no suspension or forfeiture from which there must

be a reinstatement. In this case we have said that there are no facts to show a waiver of the obligation to pay by the twenty-eighth of the month. The payments after that date were made because the laws gave that right. We think the court should have directed a verdict for the defendant.—Reversed.

Kinne, C. J., took no part.

L. W. Thomas, Appellant, v. The Chicago, Milwaukee & St. Paul Railway.

103   64
114   1

1
1
103
122
e122
122
103
f126
103
f132
103
134
103
e138
138

Railroads: trespassers. A railroad company owes no duty to a
4 trespasser upon the track until its employes actually see him in a place of danger.

License. A license to use a railroad track may be inferred from
2 facts and circumstances short of an actual invitation or consent on the part of the company.

Rule applied. For many years the bridge and track of the railroad company at and near the place of an accident had been in almost constant use as a footpath, so that a path had become well worn.
1 Persons living in the neighborhood of the bridge and track, and also the villagers, used the path in going to and from the depot, village and school. The bridge passed over a highway, and access to the bridge was had by means of a ladder. It did not
8 appear who erected the ladder. There was no evidence that the company had ever given license to use the bridge or track as a footpath, or that it had ever attempted to prevent such use. The company's employes knew of the ladder. It was in plain view of all train operatives, and defendant's superintendent had been in a position where he might have seen it. *Held*, that a finding that the bridge and track were used as a footpath, with the consent of the company, was warranted. *Burg v. Railway*, 90 Iowa, 106, *distinguished*.

Duty of employes. Employes operating a train are bound to keep a lookout for persons on the track with the license or invitation
5 of the company, express or implied, and to exercise ordinary care to discover the presence of and avoid injuring such persons.

Same. Employes operating a train are charged with the duty of exercising care, diligence and watchfulness to discover whether
5 persons are on the track at a point where the company has

impliedly assented to the use of the track as a footpath, and the
rule applicable to trespassers does not apply to one upon the
track by virtue of such license.

Appeal from Marshall District Court.—HON. B. P. BIRD-
SALL, Judge.

SATURDAY, OCTOBER 30, 1897.

ACTION to recover damages for injuries sustained
by Earl B. Thomas, a minor son of the plaintiff, through
the alleged negligence of the defendant company. Jury
trial. Verdict directed for the defendant by the court,
and judgment accordingly. Plaintiff appeals.—
Reversed.

J. L. Carney for appellant.

Charles B. Keeler and *T. Binford* for appellee.

KINNE, C. J.—I. This is the second appeal in this ,
case. The opinion on the former appeal will be found
in 93 Iowa, 248. After the reversal upon the former
appeal, certain amendments were made to the petition.
the substance of which are incorporated in the statement of the case. Just before noon, on May 15, 1890,
Earl B. Thomas, a minor son of the plaintiff, aged three
years and nine months, was, with another child younger
than himself, upon an open uncovered bridge, which
was located upon the defendant's line of railway, about
one thousand nine hundred feet west of the station of
Rhodes, in Marshall county, Iowa, and, while there,
was run over by a train going west, and his right foot
was so crushed as to require its amputation. The petition charges that, without fault on the part of his parents, the child went upon the track and bridge, and
was in plain sight from the station, and at all points
upon the road between the station and the place of the

accident; that the defendant's employes, knowing that
the children were on the track, started a train from
the water tank at the station, a distance of about ninety
rods from the bridge, westward (the engine being in
front, but with the pilot attached to the cars), and negligently and carelessly ran the train over the plaintiff's
child; that all of the persons upon the engine knew
that the child was upon the track and bridge, but did
not look along the track over which they were going, or
exercise any care or caution whatever in the operation
of said train or to discover whether or not the track
was clear; that it was a wild train, not running on
schedule time, and was running with the engine back-
ward; that the train was not manned with a sufficient
number of brakemen, and the engine was without steam
or air brakes. It is also charged that the engineer and
other employes on the train saw the said child in time
to have stopped the train and prevented the accident;
that they negligently allowed the engine and cars to
approach and reach said bridge without signal of bell
or whistle, and without any effort to stop said train,
and ran over the foot and leg of said child; that the
roadway and track of defendant's line of railroad
extending from the overhead bridge, just west of the
bridge where the injury occurred, to the station of
Rhodes, was daily and almost hourly frequented by
men, women and children, traveling upon foot, east and
west upon said line of railway; that, for the purpose of
convenience in access to said railway track from the
overhead bridge in connection with the highway, there
had been constructed a ladder by the defendant's
employes, or with their knowledge and consent, so that
persons could have ready access from the highway to
the railway track, and also from the railway track to
the highway; that with the knowledge and consent of
the defendant, and for more than ten years prior to the
accident, people residing in the vicinity of the bridge

and in the town of Rhodes had constantly used the
track of the defendant's railway for the purpose of
traveling to and from the depot, school, and village of
Rhodes, and had used said ladder for the purpose of
reaching the track of the defendant; that the public
generally had leave and license to use said railway
track as a footway, and the child Earl was not a trespasser thereon; that defendant's employes were negligent in not exercising watchfulness and care in reference to the train while it was passing over such part of
the track where pedestrians had license to walk, and
such negligence caused said accident. To the answer
the defendant interposed a general denial, except that
it admitted its corporate capacity, and that the accident
was caused by one of its trains. When plaintiff's evidence was in, the defendant moved the court for a
verdict in its favor, because there was no evidence war-
ranting a verdict for plaintiff; that there was no
evidence sufficient to sustain a finding of negligence on
part of the defendant company or its employes which
was the cause of the accident; that the evidence did not
warrant a finding that the defendant owed to the child
any legal duty of watchfulness and care before his position was known, and it is not shown that there was any
want of care after his position was known; that no
license or right upon the part of the child to be upon
the track and bridge had been shown, but he was a
trespasser; that the evidence failed to show any invitation or consent by the defendant to use its track and
bridge as a footway; that the evidence failed to show
that the engineer or other trainmen actually saw the
child upon the bridge before the accident, or, if they
did see him, that they had failed to use all the means
and appliances at their command to stop the train and
avert the accident. This motion was sustained.

II. An important question in this case is as to
whether the child Earl was upon the track and bridge

of the defendant company by leave or license of the
defendant. The former trial was had upon the theory
that the child had no right upon the track; that he was
a trespasser; and that there was nothing in the situation or surroundings requiring the trainmen to be on
the lookout for persons on the track. If the child
1   was a licensee, instead of a trespasser, another
rule of law may obtain. The evidence which it
is claimed shows a license to use the track and bridge
as a footway by pedestrians may be briefly stated as
follows: For many years prior to the accident, the
bridge and track of the defendant company, from the
place of the accident to the station of Rhodes, had been
in almost constant use by people living in the vicinity
of this bridge as a footway in going to and from the
depot, school and village. Children of from four or five
years old and upward used it as a means of going to and
from school. The bridge passed over a private highway, and access to the bridge and track were had by the
use of a ladder reaching from this highway to the head
block of the bridge above. It does not appear as to
who erected this ladder. The bridge was fourteen feet
above the highway. There were paths leading from the
track to this ladder. These paths were well worn. This
track and ladder were also used by persons living in
the village who had occasion to visit those living in the
vicinity of this bridge. The distance to the village was
much less by way of the track than by the highways.
There was no evidence to show that the defendant company ever gave leave or license to use this bridge and
the track as a footpath, nor does it appear that the
defendant company ever made any attempt to prevent
such use. The ladder could be seen from the track. The
road master of the defendant company and other of its
employes had seen this ladder. The superintendent of
the company was present at one time while the bridge

was being raised, and the ladder was then attached to
the bridge. There is nothing to show that the use of
this ladder was ever interfered with by the defendant
company. From all of the evidence, it is clear that the
footpath and ladder were seen by some of the defendant's employes, and that they were so situated as to be
seen by any employe of the defendant company engaged
in the operation of its trains.

We held in *Murphy v. Railway Co.*, 38 Iowa, 542,
that an instruction in the following language was
proper: "If you find from the evidence that the
deceased had for a considerable time prior to the accident been accustomed to walk over and upon the track
of the railroad company, at and near the place where
the accident occurred, by the acquiescence of the company, then the deceased was not a trespasser upon the
track, and such permission may be implied if deceased
was long in the habit of so walking over the track, with
the knowledge of the company or its employes in charge
of that part of the road, without objection on their part;
and it is for you to determine from all the facts in evidence before you whether or not the deceased had such
implied permission." It was said in that case that facts
which would be sufficient to constitute ordinary diligence as against a trespasser might not establish such
diligence as against a person there by permission. In
Masser v. Railway Co., 68 Iowa, 604, it is said: "The
evidence tended to show that the track at that point
was traveled to some extent by footmen, and that there
had been such an amount of travel as to make a path."
It was held the facts did not show a license. The court,
however, said: "If the travel had been at a point where
the defendant's employes were stationed, and it were
shown that the footmen occupied the track without
their dissent, it may be that the company's assent
should be implied." In *Burg v. Railway Co.*, 90 Iowa,
106, it was held that an allegation in a petition that

"for more than ten years defendant's roadbed and right
of way, from a point west of where the accident happened to the city of Des Moines, has been used by the
public as a thoroughfare to and from said city of Des
Moines, which fact was well known to the defendant
and its employes," did not state facts from which the
law would infer a license. In that case it was said: "We
are not saying that there might not be such a use of the
track as that the assent of the company might be understood and implied therefrom, but no such state of facts
is pleaded." In *Richards v. Railway Co.*, 81 Iowa, 430,
it was held that the facts did not show a license or
invitation to people to walk along the defendant's
tracks, and that the fact that it did not forbid their
doing so could not be given the force of an invitation.
The court said: "It may be there was evidence of such
habitual use of the tracks by the public, which use was
known to the employes of defendant, and not disproved, that the jury would have been authorized to
find that plaintiff had an implied license to use the
right of way as he did. But, if that be true, defendant
was under no obligation to protect plaintiff from harm
by taking steps to prevent it, unless it had so
acted as to mislead him. It was the duty of defendant
not to injure him wantonly or wilfully, but if it had
done no act to mislead, and had no reason to anticipate
the danger to which plaintiff exposed himself, it owed
him no active duty." In *Clampit v. Railway Co.*, 84
Iowa, 71, it was held that, one using a railway track
for crossing at a place daily used for a considerable
time by a number of persons, some of whom had constructed a stairway by the track for the use of pedestrians, and when a crossing over a ditch had been made
by some one unknown, and the defendant had done
nothing to prevent persons from crossing said track,
and the use of such place as a crossing was known to

the employes of the defendant, it would be presumed to
assent to such use, and that it was a license, and the
plaintiff, in using it, was not a trespasser. On the former trial of this case we said: "It may also be
2   remarked in this connection that a license to use
the track of a railroad company may be inferred
from frequent use, in connection with other circumstances from which an implied invitation may be
inferred."

From the foregoing cases it appears that this court
has often recognized the doctrine that a license to use a
railway track may be inferred from facts and circumstances short of an actual invitation or consent on the
part of the railway company. The question,
3   then, before us, is: Are the facts and circumstances disclosed in this record such as to warrant a jury in finding an implied invitation or license
to use the track by footmen? It may be admitted that
the facts in this case touching the circumstances surrounding the use of the track are in some respects not
the same as in *Clampit's Case;* yet they are in all essential respects save one much alike. In the case at bar
the use of the track was not merely for crossing purposes. In that case the court said: "The stairway and
the ties across the ditch, as well as the path made by
footmen, prominently advertised the place as a crossing
used by pedestrians. No engineer or fireman passing
along the tracks at that place, with his eyes open, in
the exercise of reasonable watchfulness and care, could
have failed to see these indications of a footpath, and to
understand therefrom that it was used by pedestrians.
if he possessed ordinary intelligence." This language
applies as well to the facts in the case at bar. Here
was an almost constant use of this track. Here were
well-defined footpaths, and a ladder in use for years.
for the purpose of reaching the track. The track
repairers knew the ladder was there. The road master

had actual knowledge of it. The superintendent had
once, at least, been where, if he used his eyes, he must
have seen it. It was in plain view of all of the train
operatives. It does not appear that the ladder was ever
used for any purpose except as a means of getting onto
the track; and, with the fact undisputed of the use of
the ladder, paths, and track for years without objection from the defendant or any of its employes, all
these and other facts would warrant a finding by a jury
that the use of the track was by the consent of the
defendant, and therefore the child Earl was not a trespasser.

III.   If the rule of law as to care to be exercised
by the employes of the company operating its train is
the same towards one who is a mere licensee by virtue
of an implied invitation from the defendant as it is in
case of a trespasser upon the track, it was not necessary
to submit this case to the jury for the purpose of determining which of these relations this child occupied
towards the defendant company.   As is said in
4   the opinion on the former appeal in this case, if
the child was a trespasser, then the company
owed him no duty until its employes actually saw him
on the track in a place of danger; that they were not
bound to keep a lookout for trespassers, and were not
negligent in failing to discover trespassers upon its
track.   *Masser v. Railway Co., supra; Burg v. Railway
Co., supra; Morris v. Railway Co.,* 45 Iowa, 29; *Richards
v. Railway Co., supra; Thomas v. Railway Co.,* 93 Iowa,
248.   Appellant contends that this should not be the
rule even as to trespassers.   Such has been the uniform
holding in this state, and, unless there are cogent reasons for departing from it, it should not be changed.
We discover no sufficient reason for changing this rule,
which has always been consistently adhered to by this
court.   The important question now is, does this rule
apply with like force and effect to one who may be

found to be a licensee by invitation of the company, implied from all the surrounding circumstances? The general current of authority undoubtedly is that the same rule ordinarily applies in both cases. 3 Elliott, Railroads, sections 1154, 1249-1251, and cases cited; Beach, Contributory Negligence, section 212, and cases cited. Indeed, it is held that one using a railway track as a place of crossing or a footpath, with the silent acquiescence of the company, or with the knowledge or passive permission of the company, is, at most, a bare licensee, who takes his license with all of its concomitant risks and perils; and, as a general rule, the company owes him no greater duty than that which is due to a mere trespasser. 3 Elliott, Railroads, section 1154, and cases cited. Such is undoubtedly the general trend of the authorities in this country. In our own state, in *Richard's Case*, this doctrine seems to be recognized and applied as to one walking along the track; while in *Clampit's Case* (the last expression of this court upon this subject) it is expressly held that one crossing the track of a railroad company under circumstances as to uses of the track much like those of the case at bar "was entitled to all the rights and protection of one rightfully upon it with the license of the defendant. He may recover for injuries resulting from the defendant's want of care, if not contributing thereto by his own negligence." Owing to the age of the child Earl, there can be no question of contributory negligence in this case. If the rule laid down in *Clampit's Case* is to be adhered to as to one crossing the track, we see no escape from the conclusion that this case should have been submitted to the jury under proper instructions of the court, for them to determine whether the child was a trespasser or licensee, and, if a licensee, whether the employes of the defendant exercised that care to discover his presence upon the track, where, from the

license given, they had a right to expect persons might
be. We believe the rule announced in *Clampit's Case* a
just one, as applied to the facts in that case. It amounts
to saying that, when the company had impliedly
assented to the use of its track by persons as a footpath, its employes operating trains are charged with
the duty of exercising care, diligence, and watchfulness
to discover if persons are on the track at these places
where they have recognized their right to be. We are
not holding that at every place, and continuously along
the line of a railway, the employes operating trains
must be on the watch for trespassers. What we do hold
is that as to persons rightfully on the track by the
license and consent of the company, whether such consent be expressed in words or arise by implication, a
duty rests upon the company and its employes to be on
the watch for such persons at the places they may be
expected to be, in view of the license and consent given.

5   So, in this case, if the boy Earl was a licensee,
and not a trespasser, and at a place where the
company had impliedly assented to the use of its
track as a footpath, it was the duty of those operating
the train to exercise watchfulness and care to ascertain
if persons were on said track at said place. If the jury
should find that Earl was a licensee, then they must
determine, in view of all of the evidence, whether the
employes of the company properly discharged that duty,
and, if they did not, whether the failure so to do
resulted in causing the injury.

IV. Without referring specifically to the several
complaints as to the rulings upon the introduction of
evidence, it may properly be said that most of the rulings against the plaintiff impress us as technical, and
some of them as incorrect. We do not say more, as it
is not likely that on a re-trial the same questions and
rulings will appear. We have, in view of another trial,

refrained, so far as possible, from discussing the weight
of the evidence. The appellee's objection to tne record
is not well taken, and appellant's motion to strike the
additional abstract is overruled. For the reasons given,
the judgment below is REVERSED.

J. A. FUNK v. THE IOWA BUSINESS MEN'S MUTUAL FIRE
ASSOCIATION, Garnishee, Appellant.

Insurance: AMOUNT ALLOWED: *Construction of policy.* The time
when total insurance must not exceed three-fourths the value of
the property is not the time of loss, but the time when insurance
is taken, notwithstanding a provision of policy and application
"Total Insurance Permitted. Limited to three-fourths the cash
value of property insured at the time of loss, and to be concurrent herewith," the only other reference in the policy to the
amount allowed being that the policy shall be void if, without
permission there be "other insurance, whether valid or not, in
excess of the amount permitted herein;" and direction being
given in the application "Do not insure for more than three-
fourths of what it would cost to replace it;" and the amount of
stock on hand, and the value of the average stock, and the concurrent insurance being there given, with the statement that
assured understood and agreed that the total insurance on the
property should not exceed three-fourths its cash value.

*Appeal from Polk District Court.—*HON. W. A. SPUR-
RIER, Judge.

SATURDAY, OCTOBER 30, 1897.

PROCEEDINGS by garnishment. There was a trial
by jury, and a verdict and judgment in favor of the
plaintiff. The garnishee appeals.—*Affirmed.*

Berryhill & Henry for appellant.

Geo. R. Sanderson for appellee.

ROBINSON, J.—The plaintiff is a judgment creditor
of L. H. Mudge. In October, 1894, the appellant issued

to Mudge a policy of insurance which purported to
insure him against loss or damage by fire or lightning
on a stock of merchandise and trade fixtures and furniture specified, to the amount of one thousand dollars.
During the life of the policy the property insured was
destroyed by fire, and the appellant was then garnished
as a supposed debtor of Mudge by reason of the policy
and loss. The only questions presented by this appeal
which we find it necessary to determine relate to the
validity of the policy, the appellant contending that it
became void by reason of over-insurance contrary to its
provisions. The contract of insurance consists of an
application and a policy. The application contains the
following:

"Notice to Applicants. The answers to questions
in this application are your statement, and the sole
basis on which we take the risk, and misrepresentations or false statements will void the policy. Please
read your application after blanks are filled, to make
sure that questions are answered correctly. The estimate of the value of the property must be made by you.
Do not insure for more than three-fourths of what it
would cost to replace it, allowing for all depreciation
by age or use.

"Total Insurance Permitted. Limited to three-
fourths the cash value of property insured at the time
of loss, and to be concurrent herewith.

"I offer the following statement and agreement as
the basis for insurance on the above-described property:
What is the net amount of stock on hand? Answer.
Three thousand and twenty-nine dollars. What is your
average amount of stock? Answer. Three thousand
dollars. What other insurance have you on stock?
Answer. One thousand, two hundred and fifty dollars.
Do you understand and agree that the total insurance
on this property shall not exceed three-fourths its cash
value, exclusive of land? Answer. Yes.

"I have read the above application, and hereby
warrant the answers to all the questions therein to be
true."

The policy contained the following:

"Iowa Business Men's Fire Association. (Mutual).
In consideration of the stipulations herein named,
* * * and on the faith of the representations and
agreements made in the application for the insurance,
* * * does insure L. H. Mudge from noon of the
fourth day of October, 1894, until canceled by act of the
insured or by this association, against all direct loss or
damage by fire or lightning, except as is hereinafter
provided, to an amount not exceeding one thousand
dollars. * * * Total insurance permitted limited
to three-fourths the cash value at the time of loss, and
to be concurrent herewith. It is hereby understood
and agreed by the assured that neglect to comply with
the conditions of the contract signed in this application * * * shall forever bar him from making any
claim against this association. * * * This policy
shall be void in each of the following instances, unless
permission by the secretary be indorsed hereon or
attached hereto: * * * Other insurance, whether
valid or not, in excess of the amount permitted herein.
* * *"

The jury found the value of the insured property
destroyed to be two thousand, six hundred and twenty-
two dollars and seventy cents, and it is admitted that
the insurance upon it, including that in controversy,
amounted to two thousand, two hundred and fifty dollars, or to more than three-fourths the value of the
property insured, at the time it was destroyed. Was
there, in that respect, such a violation of the conditions
of the policy as made it void? A careful examination
of the policy and application shows that the only reference to the amount of insurance, as compared with the

value of the property insured, which relates in terms to a time subsequent to the issuing of the policy, is contained in the following statement found in both instruments: "Total insurance permitted limited to three-fourths the cash value at the time of loss, and to be concurrent herewith." If that stood alone, there would be ground for claiming that the "total insurance" referred to might be in addition to, because it was to be concurrent with, that given by the policy in suit. If the provision be taken literally, the policy would be valid, to the time of the loss, in any event, and void, according to the theory of the defendant, at the moment of the loss, if the insurance at that time exceeded the limit prescribed. In other words, in such a case it would be valid for the purpose of collecting assessments, but void as a protection against loss to the insured. Of course, the real intent of the parties must be gathered from all parts of the contract construed together. Commencing with the application, we find that it requires the estimate of value to be made by the assured, and that it cautions him not to insure for more than three-fourths of what it would cost to replace the property insured. That part of the application refers clearly to the time of taking insurance, and not to what may occur after it is taken. The next clause we have already considered in connection with the same one in the policy. Then follow the questions and answers which were "the basis for insurance." They show the net amount of stock on hand, and the value of the average stock, and the concurrent insurance. It may be said that the next paragraph, which states, in substance, that the assured understood and agreed that the total insurance on the property should not exceed three-fourths of its cash value, exclusive of land, refers to time subsequent to the date of the application, but not necessarily so. The question was, no

doubt, printed in blank applications, and so framed as to apply to cases where concurrent insurance had not been, but might be, taken to the limit named. The reference to land contained in the question tends to show that it was intended for general use, as the application in this case did not ask for insurance on any building. The only portions of the policy which refer to the amount of insurance permitted are the ambiguous paragraph already considered, and the one which makes the policy void, if, without permission of the secretary, duly indorsed, "other insurance, whether valid or not, in excess of the amount permitted herein" is taken. That may refer to the amount of insurance as compared with the value of the property at the time a loss occurs, but it would refer as well to insurance at the time it was taken; and, if that was what the parties to the contract intended, nothing in the policy makes it void in case the total insurance on the property in question at the time it was destroyed exceeded three-fourths of its value. Although that interpretation is not free from difficulty, yet, when all the provisions of the contract are considered, it seems to be the most reasonable one to adopt, and it will effect justice. It is the one which the assured would be most apt to conclude was the one intended. The form for the application and the policy were prepared by the defendant. After having framed the contract in ambiguous terms, it should not be given the benefit of the interpretation most favorable to itself. That the assured lost property covered by his policies, of a value greater than the amount of his insurance, and that the loss was honest are not questioned, and there is no good reason why the garnishee should not pay its contract obligation. There does not appear to be any ground for disturbing the judgment of the district court, and it is
AFFIRMED.

MILTON D. BRYCE, as Trustee for MILO H. LOUNSBURY,
v. THE CHICAGO, MILWAUKEE & ST. PAUL
RAILWAY COMPANY, Appellant.

10
12
103
129

Railroads: NEGLIGENCE: *Jury question.* A railroad track curved
1 somewhat on a bridge, so that at one corner the ends of bolts in
a truss at the side of a bridge would be only fifteen inches from
a car. It was the duty of brakemen on freight trains to loosen
hand brakes while near and passing over the bridge, and plaintiff,
while going down a ladder on a car, in discharge of such duty,
was struck by said bolts. *Held*, that he may recover damages

EVIDENCE. Evidence that no accident had happened for nine years is
2 not admissible to show that the railroad company was not negligent in constructing the bridge.

RISK OF EMPLOYMENT: *Contributory negligence.* An experienced
3 brakeman on a moving train crossed a bridge twice a day for
fourteen months, and usually on the top of box cars, which were
twice as high as trusses built along the side of the bridge The
track curved all the way over the bridge, rendering it difficult for
him to estimate the distance from the car to the trusses, at any
one point. *Held*, it cannot be said, as matter of law, that he
should have known it was dangerous to be on a car ladder at the
northeast corner of the bridge, where the ends of bolts projecting
from the truss were only fifteen inches from the car.

Same. A brakeman, whose attention was taken up in the discharge
4 of his duties, was struck by bolts projecting from a truss built on
the side of a bridge, when he was on the ladder of a freight car.
Held, it cannot be said, as matter of law, that he was negligent in
not looking out for dangers which resulted from improper construction of the bridge, and of which he had no knowledge.

Same. A servant assumes the risk not only of dangers which he
8 appreciates, but of dangers which, by the exercise of ordinary
diligence, he ought to know and appreciate.

Appeal from Cedar District Court.—HON. WILLIAM P.
WOLF, Judge.

SATURDAY, OCTOBER 30, 1897.

license given, they had a right to expect persons might be. We believe the rule announced in *Clampit's Case* a just one, as applied to the facts in that case. It amounts to saying that, when the company had impliedly assented to the use of its track by persons as a footpath, its employes operating trains are charged with the duty of exercising care, diligence, and watchfulness to discover if persons are on the track at these places where they have recognized their right to be. We are not holding that at every place, and continuously along the line of a railway, the employes operating trains must be on the watch for trespassers. What we do hold is that as to persons rightfully on the track by the license and consent of the company, whether such consent be expressed in words or arise by implication, a duty rests upon the company and its employes to be on the watch for such persons at the places they may be expected to be, in view of the license and consent given.

So, in this case, if the boy Earl was a licensee, 5   and not a trespasser, and at a place where the company had impliedly assented to the use of its track as a footpath, it was the duty of those operating the train to exercise watchfulness and care to ascertain if persons were on said track at said place. If the jury should find that Earl was a licensee, then they must determine, in view of all of the evidence, whether the employes of the company properly discharged that duty, and, if they did not, whether the failure so to do resulted in causing the injury.

IV. Without referring specifically to the several complaints as to the rulings upon the introduction of evidence, it may properly be said that most of the rulings against the plaintiff impress us as technical, and some of them as incorrect. We do not say more, as it is not likely that on a re-trial the same questions and rulings will appear. We have, in view of another trial.

ACTION for damages brought by plaintiff, as trustee
for Milo H. Lounsbury, for injuries received while in
the employment of defendant. Trial to jury. Verdict
and judgment for the plaintiff, and defendant appeals.
—*Affirmed.*

Burton Hanson, Chas. B. Keeler, and *T. B. Hanley*
for appellant.

Preston, Wheeler & Moffit, F. L. Anderson, and
Wright & Wright for appellee.

LADD, J.—The bridge was a Hawe truss, constructed nine years ago over a stream and highway
about one thousand, five hundred feet east of defendant's station at Anamosa, on its line of road running
from Marion to Farley, and was fourteen feet wide,
and a few inches more than thirty-four feet in'
1   length. The track over the bridge was curved
         so that the north rail was five or seven inches
nearer the truss at the northeast corner than the south
rail to the end opposite, and a few inches lower,—the
track curving to the north,—causing the cars to
"shuck" over and lean to the north in passing over the
bridge. The trusses on either side were about one-half
the height of a box car, with timbers held together by
long iron bolts, with nuts on the inside. These bolts
extended through the timbers about two inches beyond
the nuts at the northeast corner of the bridge, and came
within fifteen inches of a common stock car standing
on the track. This distance would vary with the width
of the car, the way it was loaded, and the speed of the
train. The bridge was in a valley, with up grades in
both directions; that to the east being a quarter of a
mile east of the bridge and up a considerable hill, while
that to the west commenced at the bridge, and was not
heavy. From each extremity of the bridge the

track curved to the north. In approaching the bridge
from the east, it was usual to set the brakes at the
summit of the elevation or hill, and loosen them at the
foot of the grade towards the bridge. The train on
which Lounsbury was employed at the time of the accident consisted of fifteen or eighteen freight cars and a
combined baggage and passenger car, without air
brakes, and approaching Anamosa from the east. The
hand brakes had been set at the top of the grade, as
usual; and, as the train reached the bottom, Lounsbury,
who was on the cars, near the center, began releasing
the brakes as he moved forward.   There were two
refrigerator cars immediately behind the tender;
then a flat car, used for coal, and boxed in, except about
two feet on the end towards the engine, with sides and
end about two and one-half feet high; and back of this
a stock car. The train was moving at the rate of eight
to ten miles per hour. After releasing the brake at the
east end of the stock car, Lounsbury attempted to go
down the iron ladder on the north side of the west end
thereof, to the flat car,—the only way then possible,—
in order to release its brake and report on the engine
in event another car was to be taken at Anamosa.
When he had swung over the edge of the car, and had
descended about four rounds of the ladder, he was
caught by the end of one of the iron bolts referred to,
and permanently injured.   The court, in substance,
told the jury that the defendant had the right to lay its
track upon such a curve as it might deem best, and to
elevate the outside rail, and that it was not required
to conform the bridge to the curve, or to lay the track
so its center would be in the center of the bridge. See
Patton v. Railway Co., 73 Iowa, 310; *Tuttle r. Railway
Co.*, 122 U. S. 194 (7 Sup. Ct. Rep. 1166). The one question submitted was "whether the defendant was negligent in placing the truss of the bridge in question as

thereon, or if such misrepresentations were made
merely as a matter of opinion, and not as an assertion
of fact, then no damages can be based on this branch
of the defense." Plaintiff contends that under the facts
the defendant had no right to rely upon this representation, and that, having opportunity to know the fact,
the law will give him no relief; citing 5 Am. & Eng. Enc.
Law, 340; *Longshore v. Jack*, 30 Iowa, 298; and other
cases. It is a familiar rule that: "It is the duty of
every person, in transacting business, to use ordinary
care and prudence. If false representations are made
regarding matters of fact, and the means of knowledge
are equally open to both parties, and then one party,
instead of informing himself, sees fit to put himself in
the hands of the other, whose intention is to mislead
him, the law will give him no remedy for his injury."
In *Gee v. Moss*, 68 Iowa, 318, it is held that the question
as to whether the injured party acted with due care and
prudence in relying upon the representation of the
other is a question for the jury, and not for the court;
and that is the very question submitted to the jury
under this instruction.

III.   Defendant alleges that, as inducement to him
to sign said lease and notes, the plaintiff agreed to put
in a well and pump on said land, suitable for use at the
house and for watering stock, and that without said
         promise he would not have executed said lease:
2   that the plaintiff wholly failed to make a well or
         provide a pump, whereby defendant was left
without water on the farm, and was compelled to go
one-half a mile for water for use in the family and for
his stock, to his damage one hundred and fifty dollars.
The court instructed the jury that, if it found these
allegations to be true, the defendant would be entitled
to recover the difference in the rental value of the farm
with and without such supply of water during the term.

Appellant's contention is that: "There was no basis in the evidence for this instruction. No evidence was offered showing the difference in the rental value." The only evidence was that of the defendant, that plaintiff's agent promised to furnish a well, that he did not do so, and that defendant had to go to the neighbors', part of the time a half mile, and at other times a mile, distant, for water. He was asked, "What was it worth?" to which he answered, "One hundred and fifty dollars." There is no evidence to support the instruction, and, while it states the measure of damages correctly, we think it should not have been given, on this evidence. To get water as defendant says he did is not shown to have necessarily resulted from plaintiff's failure to make a well. Defendant could not adopt an unnecessarily expensive mode of securing a supply of water, and make that the measure of his recovery. There is no evidence that the mode adopted was a reasonable one, and the evidence indicates that a supply could have been procured at less expense by making a well.

IV. The court gave this further instruction: "(6) I now call your attention to the defendant's counter-claim based upon the alleged wrongful seizure of his property under the writ of attachment issued in this cause. If you find by a preponderance of the evidence that the consideration for the note in suit was not for rent alone, but was in part for the purchase price of a horse sold to the defendant by the agent, Little, then the plaintiff was not entitled to have a writ of attachment issued to secure the payment of such note, and, if you so find, then the seizure of so much of the plaintiff's property as was taken under the writ issued in this cause was wrongful; and in such case he would be entitled to recover on this counter-claim the value, if anything, of the use of said attached property from the date of said seizure to the present time, together with the depreciation, if any, in the reasonable market value of said property from the date of said seizure to the present time, as well as the fair market value of the hay and corn, if any, which has been used, or fed out to the stock. Plaintiff says: "It is conceded that the twenty dollars were included in the rent. This, however, would not deprive the plaintiff of his right to a landlord's attachment. Neither would the suing out of the attachment be wrongful." He cites *Merrit v. Fisher*, 19 Iowa, 354. In that case there were several distinct causes of action, one of which was exc'isively for rent. In *Smith v. Dayton*, 94 Iowa, 102, the landlord had taken the note of the tenant for rent due and for other items, and a mortgage to secure the same. It was held, "He has so blended his accounts with reference to the rents for the years 1890 and 1891 with other items, and has so acted with reference to the securities taken, that we think he has waived any lien he might have had for the rent reserved in the lease for these years." The instruction complained of is in harmony with this decision.

V. The court further instructed to the effect that, under the clause of the lease quoted above, if the jury found that the plaintiff relied upon the contract lien thereby created, and seized property thereunder, it would operate as a waiver on his part of any right to insist upon or enforce a landlord's lien under the statute, and that if he thereafter caused an attachment to issue, and to be levied upon other property of the defendant, such writ and seizure would be wrongful, and that, if they so found, the defendant would be entitled to damages for the use of the attached property, and the depreciation of the value thereof. In *Rollins v. Proctor*, 56 Iowa, 326, it is held that a landlord's lien for rent is not waived by taking personal

security, unless such was the intention of the parties.
In *Bank v. Honnold*, 85 Iowa, 353, the lease con-
4   tained a clause as to exempt property, similar to
that quoted above.   It was held to be, in effect,
a mortgage, and that it must be recorded, to bind third
persons.   In *Smith v. Dayton, supra*, the lease provided
for a lien on exempt property, as in this case, and it was
held that this did not waive the statutory lien.   The
defendant had a right to mortgage his exempt property
to secure the rent, and this he did by said clause in the
lease, and manifestly it was not the intention of the
parties that the statutory lien was thereby waived.
Plaintiff having the right to pursue both his contract
and statutory lien, the seizure of the property under
neither was wrongful.   For the errors pointed out, the
judgment of the district court is REVERSED.

S. H. SHOEMAKER v. J. S. ROBERTS AND SARAH ROBERTS,
Appellants.

Newspaper Subscription: IMPLIED CONTRACT: *Evidence.*   Cause of
action is not stated by complaint for subscription price of a
1   newspaper, alleging that plaintiff became owner of the subscription list which contained the name of defendant, and that the
paper was mailed to him at A; it not being alleged that A was his
2   place of residence or that he accepted or received the paper, or
that it was sent to the address appearing on the list, or that his
name was on the list by his authority.

SAME.   To establish an implied contract on the part of a person to
whom a newspaper was regularly addressed and mailed, it must
affirmatively appear that he received it, or that such a state of
facts exists as will raise a presumption that it was received by
him, and no such presumption arises in the absence of proof that
the address to which the paper was sent was his proper address.

Plea and Proof: RESIDENCE.   Even if the fact that the original
notice in an action was served on defendant at a certain town
8   could be used in aid of the petition, it affords no evidence that
defendant's residence was at such town; the statute with reference to service of notice recognizing no smaller governmental
sub-divisions than counties. (Sections 2602, 2604, Code of 1873'.

Appeal from Hardin District Court.—Hon. D. R. HIND-
MAN, Judge.

SATURDAY, OCTOBER 30, 1897.

ACTION at law to recover the subscription price of
a certain newspaper alleged to have been sent to J. S.
Roberts. The trial court overruled a demurrer to the
plaintiff's petition, and defendants appeal.—*Reversed.*

J. S. Roberts, J. H. Scales, and *W. F. Beck* for
appellants.

No appearance for appellee.

DEEMER, J.—The case involves less than one hundred dollars, and comes to us on the following certificate
from the trial judge: "I, D. R. Hindman, presiding
judge in the above entitled cause, do hereby cer-
1   tify that said cause involves the determination
of the following questions of law, upon which it
is desirable to have the opinion of the supreme court:
(1) Does the fact that the plaintiff, who became the
owner of the Hampton *Chronicle*, a weekly family newspaper, published at Hampton, Iowa, who was also the
owner of the subscription list of said paper, among
which was the name of the defendant J. S. Roberts, and
mailed regularly each week a copy of said paper, with
the postage paid, to him, at Ackley, Iowa, from the time
plaintiff became the owner, by purchase, of said newspaper and subscription list, viz.: August 10, 1890, up to
September 6, 1894, create a liability on the part of said
J. S. Roberts to pay the subscription price of said paper
during the time it was so mailed to him, from said
August 10, 1890, to September 6, 1894? (2) Where the
plaintiff alleges that he is the owner, by purchase, in

the year 1890, of the Hampton *Chronicle*, a weekly family newspaper, with the subscription list of regular subscribers, among which is the name of defendant, and, as such owner, mailed a copy of said paper each week, with the postage paid, at Hampton, Iowa, addressed to J. S. Roberts, defendant in the action, at Ackley, Iowa, which allegations are admitted by demurrer filed by defendant, do such allegations, including the fact that service of the original notice in the case was made on defendant at Ackley, Iowa, show a liability on the part of the defendant Roberts for subscription to said newspaper?" While the certificate is somewhat involved, we take it that the real inquiry is whether or not the defendant J. S. Roberts is liable, in the absence of an allegation that Ackley was his place of residence, or that he received the paper and had the benefit thereof.

That one who receives a newspaper without objection, and has the benefit thereof, is liable upon an implied contract to pay for the same, is conceded. But,

2 to establish such liability, it must be shown affirmatively that defendant received the paper, or such a state of facts must be recited as that the presumption arises that it was received by the person to whom it was addressed. No such presumption arises in the absence of proof that the address to which the paper is sent is the address of him from whom recovery is sought. Liability in such case is based upon the doctrine that when one accepts and receives the beneficial results of another's labor or services, which he has no reason to suppose were gratuitous, and which he could or not accept at his option, the law will imply a previous request and a promise to pay. Without proof of the acceptance of benefits, no such implication will obtain. In the case at bar there is no allegation that Ackley was the defendant's place of residence, no statement that he accepted or received the paper, no claim that the

paper was sent to the same address as appeared upon
the subscription list, and no showing that his name was
upon the list by his authority. The fact that the
3   original notice was served upon the defendant at
Ackley is of no moment. If such fact could be
considered in aid of the pleading, it affords no evidence
that Ackley was defendant's place of residence. The
statutes with reference to service of notice recognize no
smaller governmental subdivisions than counties. Code
1873, sections 2602, 2604. The questions presented
should each be answered in the negative. The judgment is therefore REVERSED.

JOHN B. CRANDALL, Appellant, v. THE DES MOINES,
NORTHERN & WESTERN RAILROAD COMPANY
AND THOMAS MILLER, Sheriff.

Railroad: CONDEMNATION OF ADDITIONAL DEPOT GROUNDS: *Conditions precedent.* Code 1873, section 1241, provides that a railway
corporation may take and hold "so much real estate as may be
necessary for the location, construction and convenient use of the
railway. The land so taken otherwise than by the consent of the
owners, shall not exceed one hundred feet in width, except for
wood and water stations, unless where greater width is necessary
for excavation, embankment or depositing waste earth." Acts
Twentieth General Assembly, chapter 190, section 1, provides that
any completed and operating railway company "shall have power
to condemn lands for necessary additional depot grounds in the
same manner as is provided by law for the condemnation of the
right of way," but also provides that before such condemnation
the company shall apply to the railroad commissioners who shall
notify the land owners, and certify to the district court of the
county the amount and description of additional lands necessary
for the company *Held,* that where a railroad completed and in
operation, desires land one hundred feet in width for additional
depot grounds the action of the commissioners must precede the
effort to condemn, without regard to whether the land already
occupied by the company was obtained by purchase or condemnation

Appeal from Calhoun District Court.—HON. S. M. ELWOOD, Judge.

SATURDAY, OCTOBER 30, 1897.

THE defendant company owns a line of road from Des Moines to Fonda, passing through Calhoun county. When the road was built, the company building it purchased at one of the stations a strip of land two hundred feet in width, and located thereon its depot and side tracks. This proceeding is to condemn an additional one hundred feet in width. Proceedings were had to that end, so that a jury to make the appraisement was appointed; and, before the appraisement was made, a preliminary injunction was obtained in this suit and proceedings stayed. The district court dismissed the petition, and dissolved the injunction, from which order the plaintiff appealed.—*Reversed.*

Stevenson & Lavender for appellant.

Cummins, Hewitt & Wright for appellee.

GRANGER, J.—The following is a part of the law for the condemnation of private property for works of internal improvement, being section 1241 of the Code of 1873: "Any railway corporation organized in this state, or chartered by or organized under the laws of the United States, or any state of territory, may take and hold, under the provisions of this chapter, so much real estate as may be necessary for the location, construction and convenient use of its railway, and may also, take, remove and use for the construction and repair of said railway and its appurtenances, any earth, gravel, stone, timber, or other materials, on or from the land so taken; the land so taken otherwise than by

the consent of the owners, shall not exceed one hundred feet in width, except for wood and water stations,
unless where greater width is necessary for excavation,
embankment, or depositing waste earth." It is conceded in argument that the additional strip of land is
not for wood or water stations, or for excavation or
embankment or deposit of waste earth. The only other
purpose for which it could be taken by the company
in such a proceeding would be "for the location, construction, and convenient use of its railways," and such
is the purpose for which the company claims the right.
Without question, the additional land is desired for
additional depot ground, at a station called "Lohr-
ville;" and there is no dispute but that the additional
land is needed for such purposes. The following is
section 1, chapter 190, Acts Twentieth General
Assembly: "Any railway corporation owning or
operating a completed railway in the state of Iowa,
shall have power to condemn lands for necessary additional depot grounds in the same manner as is provided
by law for the condemnation of the right of way; provided, that before any proceedings shall be instituted
to condemn such additional grounds the railway company shall apply to the railway commissioners, who
shall give notice to the land owner and examine into
the matter and report by certificate to the clerk of the
district court in the county in which the land is situated, the amount and description of the additional
lands necessary for the reasonable transaction of the
business, present and prospective, of such railway company. Whereupon said railway company shall have
power to condemn the lands so certified by the commissioners." The contentions arise over the construction
of the sections of the law quoted, it being that of appellant that, as the land is not needed for wood or water
stations, nor for excavations, embankment, or deposit
of earth, the company is only entitled to one hundred

feet in width of right of way, whether it is obtained by
purchase or by condemnation, except for additional
depot grounds, when it must, as a condition precedent
to proceedings to condemn for such purpose secure the
action and report of the railway commissioners.
Appellee's contention is that the purchase by the company of lands for a right of way or for depot grounds is
no limitation on its right to condemn the one hundred
feet prescribed by the statute; that, as to the action of
the commissioners, the law has no application, except
when it is sought to condemn grounds additional to
the one hundred feet that has been condemned.
Several cases are cited by appellant which are determined upon facts that do not give them force or authority in this case. The case relied upon by appellee is
that of *Stark v. Railroad Co.*, 43 Iowa, 501. It is said
by appellant that the case is not in point, because the
record, as seen by a reference to the abstract, shows
that the application in that case was to condemn the
land for wood and water stations. We have examined
the record, and the use for which the land was sought
was for the "convenient use of said railroad, and for
wood and water stations." The opinion, in terms,
makes no reference to wood and water stations; and
how much weight was given that particular fact in
reaching the conclusion does not appear. There is
reason to think the conclusion was reached independent
of such considerations, because of such want of reference and the general thought of the opinion. The law
contemplates that a company constructing its line of
railroad may have, for a just compensation, a right of
way one hundred feet in width. The theory of the law
is, as to its acquisition, that it shall be, first, by an
agreement with the owner for the grant and the compensation to be paid. If the grant is refused, the law
makes it; and, if there is a failure to agree upon compensation, the law provides a way for its adjustment.

If we have appellee's position correctly, it is that in
cases where the landowner grants the right of way by
a deed therefor, so that it is called a "purchase," such
a grant is no limitation on the company to afterwards
take one hundred feet more by condemnation for the
convenient use of the road; but, if the landowner so
refuses, that an assessment is made by a jury, and the
right of way is thus taken, then the limit of the law
applies, and no more can be taken by condemnation for
such use. We speak now of the right of way generally,
without reference to depot grounds, where more than
the one hundred feet are needed.

It seems to us that appellee's contention embraces
questions not necessarily involved in this case. The
section providing for a right of way for the construction of a road and the one providing for additional
depot grounds should be construed together. The
general law as to rights of way for railroads, and
the manner of obtaining them, has reference mainly to
the location and construction of the road, so as to put
it in operation when it is, in legal contemplation, a
"completed railway." Before the proceeding in question, to condemn, the defendant company was operating
a completed railway in Iowa, and at the point in question it had its depot and side tracks. Had the land, at
this particular point, been obtained by condemnation
proceedings, there would be no question but that
before the proceedings to condemn for additional
depot grounds, there must have been the action of the
railway commissioners as a condition precedent. The
entire subject is on of legislative control, and the Act
of the Twentieth General Assembly providing for such
action by the railway commissioners makes no limitations on their right to act, except that it must be a
"railway corporation owning and operating a completed railway in the state of Iowa." There is nothing

in the act to indicate a legislative purpose to distinguish between cases in which the right of way, at the point in question, was obtained by a purchase of the land, or by condemnation. It is as much a completed railway in one case as in the other, and, in express terms, the law is made applicable to a completed railway in operation. With the most liberal construction placed on section 1241 of the Code of 1873, permitting the company to take and hold so much real estate as may be necessary for its location, construction, and convenient use, it still remains that the Act of the Twentieth General Assembly ingrafts on it the modification that if the road is completed and in operation, and the land is for additional depot grounds, the action of the commissioners must precede the effort to condemn. In dismissing the petition and dissolving the injunction the court erred.—REVERSED.

EMMA KLAES v. CONSTANCE KLAES AND R. F. JESS, Appellants.

Alimony Decree: SETTING ASIDE. A decree for alimony obtained
1 by a husband in a suit for divorce, in which his wife did not
2 appear. upon false testimony that the land awarded as alimony
was purchased with the husband's money, though the title was in
the wife, will be set aside in a suit brought for that purpose

HUSBAND AND WIFE: *Liability for attorneys' fees.* The defendant in
1 a divorce action is liable for a personal judgment for the services
5 of the attorney of plaintiff in securing the divorce, where she
procures an award of alimony made to plaintiff and a mortgage
from plaintiff to his attorney in payment of the latter's contingent interest in the alimony decreed, to be set aside because the
award was obtained through plaintiff's false testimony.

BONA FIDE PURCHASER A client contracted to pay his attorney one-
half the alimony which might be recovered in a divorce suit
1 brought by the client A divorce having been secured, and certain land, title to which was in the wife, having been awarded as
3 alimony, the client gave his attorney a mortgage on the property

to secure said contract and certain advances made by the attorney. The decree for alimony was thereafter set aside for fraud. *Held*, that the attorney was not a *bona fide* mortgagee, beyond the amount of his advances, the rest of the consideration having failed by reason of the fact that the decree awarding alimony was set aside.

Appeal from Dubuque District Court.—Hon. J. L. Husted, Judge.

Saturday, October 30, 1897.

Suit in equity to set aside a decree for alimony rendered in an action for divorce, wherein Constance Klaes was plaintiff and the plaintiff herein was defendant; also, to set aside a mortgage given by Constance
1   Klaes to R. F. Jess on the twenty-sixth day of January, 1895, covering certain property which was awarded the mortgagor as alimony in the divorce suit. Jess contested appellee's right to have the decree set aside, and further pleaded that he took his mortgage in good faith. He also pleaded that appellee and her husband had entered into a conspiracy to defraud him by bringing this suit, and further pleaded an estoppel. The trial court set aside the decree awarding alimony, canceled the mortgage upon the property, but gave Jess judgment against the plaintiff for the sum of one hundred fifty dollars. Plaintiff and Jess both appeal. As Jess first perfected his appeal, he will be called the appellant.—*Affirmed.*

R. F. Jess pro se, appellant.

Lyon & Lenehan for appellee.

Deemer, J.—On the twenty-fifth day of January, 1895, Constance Klaes obtained a divorce in the district court of Dubuque county, from his wife Emma Klaes, on the ground of adultery. The court also awarded him, as permanent alimony, certain lots in the city of Dubuque, which, he claimed in his petition, and supported by his oath upon the trial, were purchased with his own money, although the legal title stood in the name of his wife. On the next day Constance Klaes mortgaged the said lots to the appellant to secure a note for the sum of one thousand five hundred dollars. This note was given to represent one-half the value of the property secured in the divorce proceedings, under an agreement by the terms of which Jess, who was the attorney for plaintiff in those proceedings, should have one-half of what was recovered as alimony. Notice of the divorce suit was served by publication, the appellee at that time being in California. Soon after appellee learned of the decree, she returned to Iowa, and commenced this proceeding to set aside the decree in so far as it awarded the husband alimony, and to cancel the mortgage upon the lots. The petition recites that the decree, in so far as it relates to alimony, was based upon fraud and perjury committed by Constance Klaes in obtaining the order. She claims that the lots were purchased with her own money, and that her husband furnished no part of the consideration therefor; that her husband was a drunkard and a spendthrift, and that he contributed nothing to the purchase of the property in controversy, or to any other property which she at that time claimed to own; and that the mortgage to Jess was fraudulent and void, and without any consideration other than a reasonable attorney's fee, which appellee avers should not exceed the sum of fifty dollars. Constance Klaes appeared, and filed written consent to setting aside the order for alimony. Appellant denied the allegations of appellee's petition, and further stated that he was a good-faith purchaser of the lots, for value, to the extent of his mortgage interest. He also alleged that appellee and her husband are now conspiring to cheat and wrong appellant out of his note and mortgage. Appellant also pleaded an estoppel based upon the fact that, after his suit was commenced. Constance Klaes executed and delivered a quit-claim deed of the property to his wife, the appellee herein. Defendant Klaes, in his petition for divorce, alleged that the lots in question were purchased with his own money, except to the extent of about one hundred and fifty dollars; that the said lots were the homestead of the family, and that the title was allowed to remain in his wife because of his belief in her honesty and fidelity; that appellee was worth from eight to nine thousand dollars when she left Dubuque; and that he (Constance) had always devoted his earnings to the support of his wife. The prayer of the petition was that he be divorced, and awarded the lots in controversy as his permanent alimony. The evidence given by Klaes in his own behalf was in support of these allegations, and at the conclusion of the trial the court granted his prayer for relief.

The evidence introduced upon the trial of this action shows that the testimony given by plaintiff in the divorce proceeding was false and untrue; that he

2   neither purchased the property, nor paid anything for the improvement thereof; that he did nothing towards the support of the family, and was, in sooth, a drunkard and spendthrift This showing calls for the setting aside of the decree, in so far as it relates to the alimony, unless appellant Jess is entitled to protection under his mortgage. *Whitcomb v. Whitcomb*, 46 Iowa, 437; *Rush v. Rush*, 46 Iowa, 648; *Whetstone v. Whetstone*, 31 Iowa, 276. Appellant claims that he is an innocent purchaser of the property,

3   and that his rights under the mortgage should not be disturbed. We are abundantly satisfied that he had an arrangement with Constance Klaes by which he was to receive as compensation for

his services, one-half of the alimony recovered; and it further appears that the mortgage which appellee attacks was made to secure the fulfillment of this contract. At the time the mortgage was executed, Jess gave Constance Klaes a contract, by the terms of which he was to surrender the note and mortgage upon a conveyance to him, by warranty deed, of an undivided one-half interest in the lots. The lots were valued at two thousand, five hundred dollars, but the note was for one thousand, five hundred; two hundred and fifty dollars more than Jess' claim. This excess was to be advanced to Klaes to pay certain claims against him him. Pursuant to this agreement, Jess paid him seventy-two dollars and seventy-five cents. Now, as we have said, this note and mortgage were given to secure the contract by which Klaes agreed to give Jess one-half the alimony recovered, and to secure advances, and for no other purpose. It is likely true that, to the extent of the advances made, Jess is a *bona fide* holder. But he is not such holder as to the remainder, for the reason that the consideration has failed. While the lots were at one time awarded to Klaes as permanent alimony, yet the decree has been corrected, and Klaes has in fact recovered nothing. The original order and decree were subject to timely attack, and a mortgage executed as this one was is not exempt from the results of such an attack. It was given to represent the alimony recovered. If, in the end, no alimony was recovered, then the mortgage was without consideration. It is not a case where one purchases property decreed to another as alimony, without notice of any defects in the decree, paying a valuable consideration therefor, but rather a contract made on the strength of the recovery of a certain amount as alimony, which recovery is afterwards set aside and held for naught.

In such latter case the mortgage is without consideration, and is subject to all legal defenses existing against
it.   There is no merit in appellant's claim of
4   estoppel.   Appellee is not relying upon the quitclaim deed from her husband, and, if she were,
there is an express declaration in the deed that appellant's mortgage is void.   Nor do we find sufficient evidence of fraud and collusion between Constance Klaes
and his wife to justify us in refusing the relief she prays.
Appellant says in argument that he does not claim the
one thousand, five hundred dollars called for by the
mortgage, but that he is entitled to one thousand, two
hundred and fifty dollars, and interest on the note; to
one hundred dollars claimed to have been advanced to
one Hoeffling; and to seventy-two dollars and seventy-
five cents paid to Klaes.   We may observe, in passing,
that there is no evidence that Jess advanced any money
to Hoeffling.   We have disposed of his claim to the one
thousand, two hundred and fifty dollars by showing
that the consideration for it has failed, and we take up
the claim for money advanced in the next division of
this opinion.

II.   Emma Klaes appeals from the order of the
court allowing Jess a judgment for one hundred
fifty dollars and costs against her.   Seventy-two
dollars and seventy-five cents of this amount was
properly allowed because of advancements made by
       Jess upon the strength of the mortgage.   The
5   remainder was, no doubt, allowed as attorney's
       fees in securing the divorce.   The evidence fully
justified this allowance, and the court, under the circumstances disclosed, did not err in taxing it to the
plaintiff.   The mortgage might have been held a valid
lien, to the extent of these allowances, but the court
did not see fit to so order; and, as no complaint is
grounded upon this omission, there is no occasion to

consider the question further. The evidence shows
that appellant's services were well worth the amount
allowed. The decree of the district court is AFFIRMED.

J. W. NEASHAM, Appellant, v. ANNA I. McNAIR.

FAMILY EXPENSES: *Husband and wife.* A diamond shirt stud procured for personal use, and actually used and worn by a husband,
is a family expense within the meaning of Code, section 2214,
charging family expenses upon the property of both husband and
wife, or either of them.

ROBINSON, J., dissenting.

Appeal from Wapello District Court.—HON. F. W.
EICHELBERGER, Judge.

SATURDAY, OCTOBER 30, 1897.

THE petition alleges that the defendants are husband and wife, a family of large fortune, high social
rank, and luxurious habits; that O. E. McNair purchased an article of jewelry for his personal use and
adornment, and used the same for such purpose; that
he afterward executed a note therefor, no part of which
has been paid. It was admitted that the article referred
to is a diamond shirt stud. Anna I. McNair demurred
on the ground that such stud is not an expense for the
payment of which she is liable. The plaintff elected to
stand on the ruling by which the demurrer was sustained, and appeals from the judgment dismissing the
petition.—*Reversed.*

Work & Lewis for appellant.

W. S. Coen for appellee.

LADD, J.—Is a diamond shirt stud, worn by the
husband for personal use and adornment, an expense

of the family, for which the wife may be liable? Section 2214 of the Code of 1873 provides that "the expense of the family and the education of the children are chargeable upon the property of both husband and wife, or either of them, and in relation thereto they may be sued jointly or separately." At common law the husband was liable for any expense incurred in the clothing and maintenance of the wife and children, suitable to his situation in life. The term "necessaries" was not confined to food and clothing, but was construed to include articles of utility and ornament ordinarily enjoyed by families of persons of estate and station similar to that of the husband. The wife, however, was not chargeable for necessaries, and there was no remedy for articles purchased by her and used in the family, when not included in that term. The statute obviates determining the vexatious question of what are necessaries, and affords an adequate remedy against both husband and wife. *Smedley v. Felt*, 41 Iowa, 588; *Schrader v. Hoover*, 80 Iowa, 243; *Blachley v. Laba*, 63 Iowa, 22; *Devendorf v. Emerson*, 66 Iowa, 698. The expense, however, is limited to that of the family, and must have been incurred for something used therein, or kept for use of or beneficial thereto, and may include articles which enhance domestic comfort and increase social enjoyment. *Fitzgerald v. McCarty*, 55 Iowa, 702; *Smedley v. Felt, supra*. In the latter case a piano was adjudged a family expense. "Family" is defined as a collective body of persons who live in one home, under one head or manager. *Menefee v. Chesley*, 98 Iowa, 55, and authorities cited. That husband and wife, when living together, as they are presumed to do, are both members of the family, and included in this definition, will not be questioned. Necessaries for which the husband was liable will certainly now be conceded to be a part of the family expense. Clothing

seems to have been treated as such. *Finn v. Rose*, 12
Iowa, 565; *Devendorf v. Emerson, supra; Smedley v.
Felt, supra.* It is said that this is beneficial to each
member only, and not to the entire household. The
clothing of every member is a source of comfort and
enjoyment to all. It is as essential as the food placed
on the table. Indeed, the services of a physician to one
member of the family have been deemed a family
expense; and so a watch and chain used by the wife and
daughter only. *Schrader v. Hoover, supra; Marquardt
v. Flaugher*, 60 Iowa, 148. Wearing apparel is not confined in its meaning to clothing, but includes the idea of
ornamentation as well. A watch and chain have been
adjudged such. *Brown v. Edmonds*, 8 S. D. 271 (66 N.
W. Rep. 310); *McClung v. Stewart.* — Or. — (8 Pac. Rep.
447); *Bumpus v. Maynard*, 38 Barb. 626. Contra, see
Smith v. Rogers, 16 Ga. 480; *Rothschild v. Boelter*, 18
Minn. 331; *Gooch v. Gooch*, 33 Me. 535; *Sawyer v. Sawyer*, 28 Vt. 252. See 29 Am. & Eng. Enc. Law, 38. In
Sawyer v. Sawyer, supra, a breastpin is held to be a
part of the wearing apparel of a deceased husband,
which, under the Vermont statute, goes to the widow.
But the supreme court of New Hampshire adjudged a
breastpin "not to be wearing apparel necessary for the
debtor and his family." *Towns v. Pratt*, 66 Am. Dec.
726. The question of value and necessity is somewhat
controlling in some of the cases referred to. By "wearing apparel" is usually meant clothing and garments
protecting the persons from exposure, and not articles
of ornament merely. Originally it included, not only
the vesture, but all the ornaments and decorations
worn with it. That jewelry, when of no purpose other
than that of ornament, as a ring, will not be so classified, may be conceded. But if it serves the double
purpose of being an article of use, in fastening the garments, or otherwise, and also of adornment to the person, there appears no good reason for not adjudging it

a part of the wearing apparel; else much that is pleas-
ing in dress must be excluded from the meaning of the
word, as generally accepted. The ornamentation of a
lady's wardrobe is of little utility, yet it is always
included in the term. If an article of jewelry is used
with and as a part of the clothing, it may well be
deemed a portion of the wearing apparel. It may thus
serve as necessary and useful a purpose as the garments themselves. Articles of jewelry were often
adjudged necessaries for which the husband was liable
at common law. *Raynes v. Bennett,* 114 Mass. 424;
Porter v. Briggs, 38 Iowa, 166. These are quite as commonly worn by many people as the clothing that covers
them. The make of a shirt or the taste of the wearer
may be such as to require some kind of a button or stud.
If the inexpensive pearl were used, no one would question the propriety of making it a family charge. But it
might be as much out of place in the shirt front of a
person of fashion or fortune as a diamond in that of
one who earns his bread by the sweat of his face. If
the cost, the utility, or the necessity is to be the criterion, then the line must be drawn on many articles of
furniture, clothing, and food. What shall be the deli-
cacies of the table, the adornments of the person, and
the character of the furnishings, must be left to the
better judgment and discretion of each family, which
is presumed to, and ordinarily does, act as a unit in
such matters. Many families would have no use for
terrapin, silks and satins, or Smyrna rugs, or costly
jewelry, and in such cases neither husband nor wife
would be liable for indebtedness incurred by the other
therefor. But, if these are purchased for and used in
the family, it is not perceived on what ground they
may not be deemed a family charge. Under our statute,
there is no occasion for inquiry as to the cost or necessity. Nor is there better reason to investigate the character or value of a button or stud worn, in determining

whether it is a family expense, than that of a costly
dress, an artistically trimmed bonnet, or a silk hat. The
article may be unnecessary, or such as the family ought
to have dispensed with, or of no actual utility; still, if
purchased for and used in the family, the liability of
the wife cannot be avoided. *Dodd v. St. John,* 22 Or.
250 (29 Pac. Rep. 618). If the diamond stud was worn
by the defendant's husband, as is alleged, for personal
use, as well as adornment, it is an expense such as is
contemplated by the statute. Nor does such a holding
involve necessary hardship. It is said in the petition
that the McNairs are a family of large fortune, high
social rank, and luxurious habits. If this be true, the
jewelry may well be deemed appropriate to their situation in life, and a source of no inconsiderable outlay in
maintaining the family according to their station, and
in harmony with their associations. The price of a
diamond shirt stud will not in all cases be a family
expense, but where procured for personal use, and
actually used and worn by the husband, it becomes
such. The same rule must be applied to the diamond
and the pearl, to the rich and the poor.—REVERSED.

ROBINSON, J. (dissenting).—I do not agree to what
is said in support of the conclusion of the majority.

STATE OF IOWA v. ELIAS DOTY, Appellant.

SALE OF OBSCENE PHOTOGRAPHS: *Criminal law.* A photographer
who took the pictures of two women who exposed themselves
when naked before the camera; and of one of them alone, when
nude, and delivered the pictures to them, receiving pay therefor, is guilty of selling obscene, lewd, indecent or lascivious
photographs, within the meaning of Acts Twenty-first General
Assembly, chapter 177, section 1.

Appeal from Linn District Court.—HON. WILLIAM G.
THOMPSON, Judge.

WEDNESDAY, DECEMBER 15, 1897.

THE defendant was convicted of the crime of keeping for sale and selling obscene pictures, and was
adjudged to pay a fine of fifty dollars and costs. From
that judgment he appeals.—*Affirmed.*

Elias Doty for appellant.

Milton Remley, attorney general, for the state.

ROBINSON, J.—The admitted facts in regard to the
transaction in question are as follows: The defendant
carried on in Cedar Rapids a picture gallery called the
"Riverside Studio." While thus engaged, two women
applied to him to take pictures of themselves, and he
complied with their request, and made several tin type
pictures of them. One of the pictures was taken of
both women, and another of one of them, when nude.
The pictures were completed by the defendant, and
delivered to the women, who paid him twenty-five cents
for each picture. It is clear, and not denied, that the
pictures taken of the women when nude were obscene.
The defendant was convicted under section 1 of chapter
177 of the Acts of the Twenty-first General Assembly,
which contains the following: "Whoever sells, or offers
for sale or gives away * * * any obscene, lewd,
indecent, or lascivious books, pamphlets, paper drawing, lithograph, engraving, picture, photograph, model,
cast, or any instrument or article of indecent or
immoral use, * * * on conviction thereof, shall
be punished by a fine of not more than one thousand
dollars, nor less than fifty dollars, or by imprisonment
in the county jail not more than one year, or both such

fine and imprisonment at the discretion of the court."
It is the theory of the appellant that he did not keep
for sale, nor sell, nor give away, the pictures, within the
meaning of the statute; that what he did was merely to
make the pictures, the indecent portions of which were
furnished by the women represented. The theory does
not find support in the facts of the case, nor is it reasonable. The women desired and bargained for the
obscene pictures, and that they contributed to the pictures by exposing themselves, when naked, before the
camera, did not affect the character of the transaction.
The products of that exposure and of the materials and
skill used by the defendant were the obscene pictures.
If it be true that the women had some rights in the
pictures before they were delivered, as a right to prevent their use or delivery to other persons,—a question
we do not decide,—the fact did not give the women any
right to possess the pictures before the purchase price
had been paid. Until that time the pictures belonged
to the defendant, and his liability for the sale was not
affected by the fact that his ownership may have been
qualified by some rights possessed by the women. When
he delivered the pictures to them, and received in return
twenty-five cents for each picture, he sold them within
the meaning of the statute, and the fact that he made
them was an aggravation of, rather than a defense to,
the crime of which he was convicted. No excuse for
what he did is shown or attempted. When the women
applied for the pictures, they told him they had a bet
with a man, whom they named, to the effect that they
dared to have pictures taken of themselves when nude.
No question as to the development of art, or the dissem-
ination of useful knowledge for lawful purposes, is
involved in the case, and we have no occasion to determine whether the acts of the defendant would have
been sanctioned by law under any circumstances. That

his act in selling the obscene pictures he had made,
under the facts admitted in this case, was a violation of
law, is clear. The views we have expressed dispose of
all the questions presented for our consideration. We
do not find that the district court erred in refusing
instructions to the jury asked by the defendant, nor in
the charge given, and its judgment is AFFIRMED.

STATE OF IOWA V. FRANK JACKSON, Appellant.

Manslaughter: EVIDENCE It appeared that after defendant and W
had an altercation with deceased, and the latter became separated
from them, they went into the street to meet him. There was
1 evidence, though it was contradicted, that W urged that he and
defendant get out of deceased's way; that defendant opposed that
course; and that, when they met deceased in the street, deceased
was knocked down and stunned by defendant, and was pounded
on the head by W, without any effort by defendant to interfere.
Death was caused by the blow struck by W. *Held*, that the evidence supported a verdict of manslaughter.

Included Offenses: INSTRUCTIONS. Where an indictment charges
murder in the first degree, and there is evidence showing the elements of that crime, it is not error to instruct as to murder in the
5 first and second degrees, though a verdict of murder in either
degree might be set aside as not sustained by the evidence; since
it is only when the evidence, "without conflict," does not prove
the essential elements of the higher offense, that it is error to
submit an issue as to it.

Corroboration: INSTRUCTION. An instruction given to the jury in a
murder trial, that a conviction could not be had on the uncorrob-
4 orated testimony of an accomplice, is not erroneous in not specifying in what particular the evidence of such accomplice must be
corroborated

Evidence: ADMISSIONS Where there was evidence of verbal admissions, it was not error to fail to instruct that verbal admissions
3 should be received with great caution, where the statements were
made deliberately and understandingly, in a conversation in
which defendant's purpose was to state the particular facts of his
connection with the affray.

Impeachment: INSTRUCTION There was some evidence, by way of
contradictions, affecting the credibility of W, who was a witness

for the state and defendant's accomplice; and there was impeaching evidence directed to the general character of the defendant, who was a witness for himself, and of L, who was a witness for the state The court charged that, if the general character of
2   either of the two witnesses was bad, the jury should consider that fact only in weighing his evidence; and, that, if the jury found that the character of defendant was bad, that fact could rightfully be considered only in determining the weight to be given his evidence *Held*, that the charge was not open to the objection that the singling out of such two witnesses unduly emphasized the fact of the impairment of defendant's credibility, leaving the inference that, if W was found to be corroborated in any particular, his credibility was unaffected.

Appeal from Pottawattamie District Court.—HON. WALTER I. SMITH, Judge.

WEDNESDAY, DECEMBER 15, 1897.

INDICTMENT for murder of the first degree. Verd'ct of guilty, and a judgment thereon, from which the defendant appealed.—*Affirmed.*

Sims & Bainbridge and *D. B. Bailey* for appellant.

Milton Remley, attorney general, and *Jesse A. Miller* for the state.

GRANGER, J.—I. The defendant, Jackson, was indicted, jointly with one Richard Wallace, for the murder of Richard Baker, a colored man, commonly known as Texas Baker, on the night of November 4, or early morning of November 5, 1895, at Council Bluffs, Iowa.
　　Some facts are without dispute. One John
1　　Webs'er, the defendant, and Baker, with many
　　others, were in front of the Metropolitan saloon, on Broadway street, in said city, when an altercation arose between Webster and Baker because Webster had taken a cigar from Baker's mouth. Baker left the crowd, and crossed the street, and soon returned; and, as he had crossed the motor track that ran along the

street, he was met by Jackson, who either knocked or pushed him down, so that he lay on his back, with his head between the rails of the motor track, and, while in this position, he was struck by Webster with a club, in the face and on the head two or three times, from which wound Baker died the following morning. Some facts, about which there is a dispute, are these, as claimed by the state: During the altercation over the cigar, Baker put his hand on his hip, as if to take from his pocket a weapon, upon which Webster said, "Look out, boys! He is going to shoot," and started for the saloon door, when Jackson took him by the arm, and said, "Hold on! I'll see you through with it." Baker was then returning from across the street, where he had picked up a couple of bricks, and Jackson and Webster left the sidewalk, and met Baker just as he had crossed the motor track. When within a few feet of Baker, Jackson said to Webster, "Let him come; I will stop him," or "Let him come; I will fix him." That Jackson stepped in front of Webster, and knocked Baker down with his fists. That Baker fell "like a log," his head striking the pavement first, after which he did not speak or move. That Jackson then rushed to his head, and kicked him on the head or face. That then Webster came up, and struck the blows with the club, while Jackson stood within four or five feet of him. That, after Webster had struck the blows, Jackson grabbed hold of him, and said, "Come on; let's get out of here." That they left together, and, when a short distance away, Jackson said, "I am going back, to clear myself with the people." That he soon joined Webster again on a bridge, about a block from the scene, and they went on together, and Jackson tried to have Webster throw the club into the creek. That it was afterwards thrown into an alley, and there found, covered with hair and blood. That, as they proceeded to their homes, Jackson put his finger to Webster's face, and said, "I never hit a prettier lick in my

life." Appellant's version of the disputed facts is that
they did not occur as stated; that Webster made no
such remark about shooting, and that Jackson did not
take him by the arm and say, "Hold on! I'll see you
through;" that he did not advance towards Baker with
Webster, but alone, and only pushed Baker down when
he drew the brick to strike and threatened to kill him;
that he did not kick Baker, but that the kicking was
done by one Roper; that, when he saw Webster striking
Baker with the club, he rushed between Baker and
Webster, and told Webster to stop, that he was killing
him; and that he (Jackson) caught the third blow on his
own leg, to save Baker. The other facts as claimed by
appellant are also denied.

II.   There is a strenuous contention that the verdict of manslaughter had not support in the evidence.
We do not think it is contended that the death resulted
from the blow struck by Jackson, but rather from the
blows given by Webster with the club. The testimony
of the physician who examined Baker before and after
death is to the effect that death resulted from hemor-
rhage. The testimony would clearly sustain a finding that Baker was stunned, and temporarily helpless,
from the blow given by Jackson, not, however, saying
but that the testimony in that respect is in conflict.
The argument deals with the matter of intent or motive
on the part of Jackson to do the act. Neither motive
nor intent is necessarily an element of the crime of
manslaughter. It is true that, under the facts of this
case, the fatal blows being given by Webster, there
must have been the intention to do an unlawful act,
and that the act resulted in the homicide. The intent
to do the unlawful act has a clear support in the evidence if some of the facts urged by the state are established. If it is true that when Webster and Baker

engaged in the quarrel of words, and Webster, appre-
hending that Baker was going to shoot, sought safety
by retreating from him,—which was clearly the proper
course to pursue,—Jackson intercepted him with the
remark, "Hold on! I'll see you through," and then
went into an affray with Baker and Webster, the intent
to do the unlawful act is clearly manifest. That they
did go into the affray is not a disputed fact, and we
think a finding that they went into it under such circumstances has support in the evidence, n twithstand-
ing the conflict. It is true that the movements were not
seen alike by all the witnesses, and this variance in
the testimony is urged as discrediting the evidence to
the effect that Webster and Jackson acted understandingly in their movements, and in what they did. Particular stress is placed on the fact that some of the
witnesses for the state say that, when Webster came
to Baker, he came from the west, instead of from beside
Jackson, or near him, where some of the witnesses
placed him. On the question of intent the variance is
not material. That Webster was close by when Jackson struck the blow, intending to aid in an affray, is not
to be doubted; nor is it to be seriously doubted that
Jackson designed to assist Webster in an encounter
against Baker if he (Baker) should attack him. These
facts, aided by the other, which the jury could have
found, that Webster and Jackson invited the affray by
going into it, rather than by avoiding it, quite conclusively fixed Jackson's relation to the affair as a partici-
pant with Webster in a purpose to do an unlawful act,
which resulted in the death of Baker. That such a
state of facts would justify a verdict against Jackson,
see *State v. Mushrush*, 97 Iowa, 444; *State v. Munch-
rath*, 78 Iowa, 268; *State v. McCahill*, 72 Iowa, 111;
State v. Malow, 44 Iowa, 104; *State v. Shelledy*, 8 Iowa,
477. There is something of an attempt, in argument,

to clothe the act of Jackson, in going out to meet Baker, with a chivalrous rather than a criminal motive; that he generously exposed himself to danger in the interest of Webster or others in the crowd of people assembled there. Nothing is clearer to a disinterested reader of the record than that such was not his motive. It is in evidence, but disputed, that, when Webster and Baker were having words about the cigar, Jackson said, "Why don't you stop quarreling and go to fighting?" and also that, as he and Webster advanced towards Baker on the street, Jackson said to Webster, "Let him come; I will stop him." It is true that the latter words might well be used by one about to act solely for the protection of others in a lawful manner, but the record here shows, rather, a disposition to bravado, and a desire to be foremost in the affray. We conclude that, under the state of the evidence, we have no right to disturb the finding of the jury.

III. The defendant was a witness in his own behalf, and one Lawson was a witness for the state. Impeaching evidence directed to the general moral character of each was admitted. The court, in an instruction, referred to such impeaching evidence, and directed that, if the jury found the general moral character of either to be bad, it should take that fact into consideration in determining the weight due to his testimony, and that the evidence could not be considered for any other purpose. The court then said: "And, if you find that the general moral character of this defendant is bad, that fact can rightfully be considered by you only in determining the weight to be given his evidence, and it should not receive any weight aside from that in passing upon his guilt or innocence." It is urged that, inasmuch as there was no dispute over the introduction of the testimony, the instruction could only be considered by the

jury as a command to look with some distrust upon the
testimony of the defendant. There was some evidence,
by way of contradictions, affecting the credibility of
Webster as a witness; and it is thought that the singling out of the two witnesses by the court
"unduly emphasized the fact of the impairment of the
credibility of the defendant, leaving the inference for
the jury that, if John Webster was found to be corroborated in the testimony that he had given, in any particular, his credibility as a witness was unaffected." It
seems to us that the language of the instruction refutes
the criticism. The instruction attempted to deal with
the effect of impeaching evidence as affecting general
moral character, and, in doing so, it made no distinction, but was general as to all witnesses of that class.
There seemed to be a manifest purpose in the instruction to guard the rights of the defendant from prejudice
by strictly limiting the effect of the impeaching testimony, and not permitting the fact of impeachment, if
found, to weigh against the defendant otherwise than
as affecting his testimony. Of that, appellant should
not complain.

IV. One Lawson was a witness for the state, and
gave testimony as to admissions made to him by Jackson while both were confined in jail. The testimony
was as to what occurred at the time Baker was
3   killed, and in some important particulars it contradicts Jackson's testimony given on the trial.
Appellant refers to *Allen v. Kirk*, 81 Iowa, 658, and
other cases, in which a rule has been stated to the effect
that, as a general rule, verbal admissions of a party
should be received with great caution, as that kind of
evidence is subject to imperfections and mistakes; and
it is urged that it was error for the court not to caution
the jury in regard to the testimony of Lawson. The
same authority that announces the above rule also holds

that such admissions of a party to a suit, when made understandingly and deliberately, often afford satisfactory evidence. The reason for the general rule is that such admissions often come from loose and random conversation, without a purpose to express what the hearers may understand. Conceding Lawson's statements to be true, the statements by Jackson seem to have been made deliberately and understandingly, in a conversation in which his purpose was to state the particular facts of his connection with the affray. Under such circumstances, we do not think a failure to caution the jury in the respect suggested involved error.

V. In an instruction, the court gave the statutory rule that a conviction could not be had on the testimony of an accomplice without corroboration, and that the corroboration was not sufficient if it merely showed the commission of the offense or the circumstances thereof. Webster was the accomplice, and a witness, and it is said that the court should have gone further, and enlightened the jury as to the particular feature of the case in which Webster should have been corroborated. The corroboration, under the statute, must have been such as would tend to connect the defendant with the commission of the offense charged, and the jury was so told. The instruction placed upon the jury the statutory limitation that the corroboration could not come from facts that merely showed the commission of the offense or the circumstances thereof, and then left it to the jury to say whether or not there was corroboration in the other evidence. We think such an instruction conforms to the requirements of the law. That other evidence did so tend is not open to question. It may further be said that the instruction, at the time of the trial, seemed to be so satisfactory that no modification of it was asked,

VI. The indictment was for murder of the first
degree, and the court submitted the case to the jury
upon instructions as to the crime charged and all
degrees of crime included therein; and it is now
5   urged that it was error to instruct upon the
crime of murder of either degree, b꞉cause the
evidence is so clearly insufficient to sustain a verdict
for murder that a court could not permit such a verdict
to stand. It is conceded in argument that there has
been an acquittal of the crime of murder, because of
the verdict of manslaughter. In *State v. Kyne*, 86
Iowa, 616, we held that under an indictment for rape,—
and there was a conviction only of an assault with an
attempt to commit rape,—it was error to put the
defendant on trial for the higher degree of the crime
when the evidence showed, without conflict, that all
the essential elements of the crime had not been proven.
It is thought that rule should apply to this case, but
we think not, for the reason that it does not appear
without conflict in this case that defendant was not
guilt, of the higher crimes. We have not held that in
a case where we might set aside a verdict for a higher
crime, as not sustained by the evidence, it would be
error for the trial court to submit to the jury the issue
as to such crime; but wh n, without conflict, the essential elements of a crime are not proven, it is error to
submit such an issue. We are far from believing that
there is no evidence in this case tending to show the
elements of even murder of the first degree. There is
evidence tending to show an understanding with Webster to go into the affray; that Jackson knocked Baker
down, and rendered him helpless; that he stood by and
saw Webster give the fatal blows, after he had felled
the victim, without a word of dissent or protest, until
he thought Baker was dead, when he said to Webster,

"Go on now; you have killed him," and suggested mak·
ing their escape. These are facts tending to show delib·
eration, premeditation, and malice. Even though other
evidence might so outweigh this as to require a court
to set aside a verdict for an offense higher than man·
slaughter, it was not error for the court to submit to
the jury the issues presented by the indictment and
plea as to murder. The judgment will stand AFFIRMED.

STATE OF IOWA V. JOE SPIERS, Appellant.

Instructions: INTOXICATING LIQUORS. Where defendants were
proved to have received a car load of a beverage that was billed
as mineral water, but was contained in ordinary beer kegs, and
witnesses testified that they drank of it, and that it was beer, and
the defendants offered no testimony, and the court charged the
8 jury that the burden was upon the state to show beyond a reasonable doubt that the defendants sold intoxicating liquors, the failure of the court to specifically instruct the jury that the defendants' claim was that the beverage was mineral water, and not
intoxicating, was not error.

Evidence: CONDITIONAL ADMISSION. In a prosecution for liquor
selling, a witness was permitted to testify concerning sending an
agent to defendants' place, upon the condition that the state
2 should prove that whatever was obtained by the agent was obtained
at defendants' place. When the state failed to show the required
facts, the testimony, in regard to the agent, was stricken out.
Held, no error.

Trials: QUESTIONING WITNESS BY JUDGE. Where, in a criminal
prosecution, the state's witnesses show a disposition to evade giv-
1 ing direct answers, and to equivocate, and the questions of the
state's attorney are not well calculated to develop material facts
it is not error for the trial court to question the witnesses and
compel answers.

Appeal from Sioux District Court.—HON. JOHN F.
OLIVER, Judge.

WEDNESDAY, DECEMBER 15, 1897,

THE defendant Spiers was convicted of the crime of nuisance, alleged to have been committed by maintaining a building and keeping therein for sale and selling therein intoxicating liquors, in violation of law, and appeals from that judgment, which required that he pay a fine and costs.—*Affirmed.*

Geo. W. Argo for appellant.

Milton Remley, attorney general, and *Jesse A. Miller* for the state.

ROBINSON, J.—I. The appellant and one Carl Kroll were indicted and tried jo'ntly f r the crime of nuisance, but Kroll was acquitted. The appellant complains that he was not given a fair and impartial trial, for the alleged reason that the trial judge asked numerous questions of witnesses, made objectionable remarks, and took such an active part in the trial in behalf of the

1   state as to prejudice the appellant. The record shows that the trial judge interrogated different witnesses, and that the questions he asked were frequently more direct and better answered than were those asked by the county attorney. But an additional abstract, filed in behalf of the state, and not denied, shows that many of the claims of error made by the appellant are based upon a misapprehension of the record. Several of the witnesses for the state showed a disposition to evade giving direct answers, and to equivocate; and the questions of the county attorney were not in all cases well calculated to develop material facts, and the questions and rulings of the court were of a character to prevent evasions, and compel the witnesses to disclose the truth. A trial court should not, as a rule, interfere with the examination of witnesses when the examination is being fairly conducted, unless

to rule upon objections and motions. But the trial court is not required to remain silent when unwilling witnesses persist in such a course as will conceal the truth, and make the trial a travesty of justice. We do not find that the district court exceeded the power which rightfully belonged to it, in assisting in the examination of witnesses, and in compelling answers.

II. It is claimed that the court erred in permitting objectionable questions asked Mrs. Farrand to be answered. The state sought to prove by her that she had sent an agent to the place where the defend-
2   ants were doing what was claimed to be an illegal business, and that he procured something there for her. What was thus procured, if anything, is not shown, and the court permitted questions of which complaint is made to be asked and answered only on condition that the state should prove that whatever the agent delivered to the witness was obtained at the place kept by the defendants; and, when it became apparent that the required fact would not be shown, the evidence in regard to the sending of the agent to the place specified was stricken out. No evidence which could have prejudiced the defendant was given by the witness, and nearly all of what she said was withdrawn from the jury. There was nothing in her examination of which the appellant can justly complain.

III. The appellant complains that the court did not submit to the jury his theory of the case, which was that the beverage sold at the time and place in question was mineral water only, and not intoxicating.
3   The beverage was kept and sold on the fourth day of July, A. D. 1896, in a temporary structure erected for the day. A car load of what was billed as mineral water, but which was contained in ordinary beer kegs, was delivered to the defendant on the preceding day. Witnesses who drank of the beverage testified

that it was beer, although some of them stated that it
was of a poor quality, and it was shown that the appellant was responsible for the sales. No evidence was
offered by the defendants. The court charged the jury
that the burden was on the state to prove beyond a
reasonable doubt the maintaining of the building, and
the keeping therein for sale of intoxicating liquors by
the defendants; and that, if the jury had a reasonable
doubt as to the guilt of either or both of the defendants,
then it should find such defendant or defendants, as the
case might be, not guilty. It was not claimed that the
defendants had any legal right to sell any intoxicating
liquor at the time and in the place in question. Proof
that they sold beer was *prima facie* evidence that they
sold an intoxicating liquor, and the burden was on them
to show, if they could, that it was not intoxicating.
State v. Cloughly, 73 Iowa, 626. We do not think it was
necessary, under the circumstances stated, for the court
to instruct the jury specifically that the defendants
claimed that the beverage sold was mineral water, and
that it was not intoxicating. So far as those claims
were made by the defendants and supported by evidence, they were as apparent to the jury as to the court,
and under the plea of not guilty entered by the defendants, and the charge of the court, could not have
escaped due consideration by the jury. We conclude
that the evidence is ample to sustain the verdict, and
that no error prejudicial to the appellant was committed during the trial. The judgment of the district
court is AFFIRMED.

STATE OF IOWA v. C. S. PICKETT, Appellant.

Challenge to Juror: COMPETENCY: *Waiver.* Under Code 1873, sections 4405, 4407, 4408, providing, among other things, that a want

of any of the qualifications prescribed by statute to render a person a competent juror, shall be ground for a challenge for cause, and that a juror challenged, and other witnesses, may be examined, to prove or disprove the challenge, the right to challenge for cause is discretionary, and may be waived; and, where a juror in a criminal case could not read or write the English language, defendant, by failing to examine said juror, will be taken to have waived the objection, notwithstanding that Laws Twenty-sixth General Assembly, chapter 61, section 1, provide, as a qualification for a competent juror, that he must be able to read and write the English language. *State v. Groome*, 10 Iowa, 308, *overruled.*

Appeal from Jefferson District Court.—HON. F. W. EICHELBERGER, Judge.

WEDNESDAY, DECEMBER 15, 1897.

AT the February term, 1897, of said court, the defendant was indicted, tried, and convicted of the crime of adultery, and his motion for a new trial overruled, and judgment of imprisonment in the penitentiary for the period of nine months entered against him, from which he appeals.—*Affirmed.*

A. W. Jaques for appellant.

Milton Remley, attorney general, and *Jesse A. Miller* for the state.

GIVEN, J.—One ground of appellant's motion for a new trial is that one of the jurors who sat on the trial cannot read or write the English language, and that appellant did not know that fact until after the trial. It is shown that one of the jurors, a native of Sweden, who had resided in this country for nineteen years, and become a citizen thereof, and an elector of this state, could not read or write the English language. Such being the fact, appellant contends that the court erred in overruling his motion for a new trial. Section 1, chapter 61, Laws Twenty-sixth General Assembly, is as follows: "All qualified electors of the state, of good moral character, sound judgment and in full possession of the senses of hearing and seeing, and who can speak, write and read the English language, are competent jurors in their respective counties." See section 332 of the Code. Section 4405 of the Code of 1873 (section 5360, present Code) provides, among other grounds of challenge for cause: "A want of any of the qualifications prescribed by statute to render a person a competent juror." Sections 4407, 4408, Code 1873 (sections 5361, 5362, present Code), provide that the juror challenged, and other witnesses, may be examined, to prove or disprove the challenge. It does not appear that any challenge was made to said juror, or that he, or any other witness, was examined as to his competency. Appellant contends that the fact of the juror's incompetency, and that appellant did not know that fact until after the trial, was a sufficient ground for granting a new trial; and he cites and relies upon *State v. Groome*, 10 Iowa, 308. In that case the defendant moved in arrest of judgment, and for a new trial, for the reason that one of the jurors who tried the case was not an elector of the state; and such was found to be the fact. The court says: "It is claimed by the state that the defendant cannot take advantage of this objection to the juror by a motion for new trial, that he passed his time by not challenging the juror before the trial, for cause. We think it is the duty of the state to place twelve legal jurors in the box, and that it is not the duty of the defendant to inquire whether the jurors are qualified or not. It is presumed that the officer whose duty it is to select the jurors will select those who are competent and legal. The law tenders to defendant a jury for the trial of his cause, and by accepting the jury he waives any objection thereto for bias or prejudice, of any character whatever, in the minds of any of the

jurors; but, if either of the jurors was disqualified to act
as such, the defendant does not waive his right to objection for this cause, but has a right to a new trial. If
the defendant knew at the time the jury was sworn that
any of them were not qualified to act as jurors, he would
have waived his right to object thereto. It must appear
that defendant had knowledge of this fact before it can
be inferred that he waived his objection. Without this
knowledge, a waiver cannot be inferred;" citing *Cowles
v. Buckman*, 6 Iowa, 162. In the cited case, only eleven
jurors were called, and both parties, not observing or
knowing that fact, accepted the jury. It was held that
the parties were entitled to a full jury, that there was
no waiver, and that appellant was entitled to a new
trial. In *Faville v. Shehan*, 68 Iowa, 242, this court held
that when, in a civil action, in the absence of conceal-
ment or fraud on the part of his adversary, a party
accepts a juror without examination as to his qualifications, he waives objections on account of want of qualifications discovered afterwards. It is said: "A different rule, applicable to criminal cases, was recognized in
State v. Groome, supra. We are not disposed to extend
the doctrine of that decision in civil cases;" citing a
number of cases. In *State v. Kaufman*, 51 Iowa, 578,
one of the jurors, becoming ill, was, with consent of the
defendant, discharged; and, with defendant's further
consent, the trial was concluded before the eleven
jurors. It was held that a defendant in a criminal case
may waive a statute enacted for his benefit, and therefore could consent to a trial with eleven jurors. It will
be observed that in these cases this court has recognized
the right of an accused to waive objections to jurors on
the ground of incompetency, or to the panel on the
ground of number. In *Groome's Case* the defendant
was held not to have waived the objection to the juror,
because it did not appear that he had knowledge of the

juror's incompetency until after the trial. The contention before us is not as to the right of an accused to
waive an objection to an incompetent juror, but whether
he should be held to have waived it by not challenging
for that cause, and examining the juror, or other witnesses, to sustain the challenge. Counsel for the state
concede that, if the doctrine announced in *State v.
Groome* is to stand, this case must be reversed. They
insist, however,—upon a very full citation and review
of the authorities on both sides of the question,—that
the rule in *Groome's Case* is so against reason and the
current of decisions that it should be overruled. Their
citations are so complete that we will not refer to other
cases. The following cases do tend quite directly to
support the conclusion in *Groome's Case*, namely:
Guykowski v. People, 1 Scam. (Ill.) 476; *Schumaker v.
State*, 5 Wis. 324; *Hill v. People*, 16 Mich. 351; *Rice v. State*,
16 Ind. 298; and *State v. Babcock*, 1 Conn. 401. These
cases are modified, if not overruled, in the following
later decisions by the same courts: *Chase v. People*, 40
Ill. 352; *Davison v. People*, 90 Ill. 221; *State v. Vogel*,
22 Wis. 471; *People v. Scott*, 56 Mich. 154; *Croy v. State*,
32 Ind. 384; *Kingen v. State*, 46 Ind. 132; *Gillooley v.
State*, 58 Ind. 182, and *State v. Tuller*, 34 Conn. 280. The
following cases fully sustain the claim that the rule
generally observed is that a failure to challenge a juror
for cause, as to his competency, and to examine him, or
other witnesses, in support of the challenge, is a waiver
of the right of challenge, though the fact of incompetency is not known to the party until after trial: *Rex
v. Sutton*, 8 Barn. & C. 417; *Rex v. Despard*, 2 Man. & R.
406; *Wharton's Case*, 1 Yel. 24; *State v. Powers*, 10 Or.
145; *U. S. v. Baker*, 3 Ben. 68; *Hickey v. State*, 12 Neb.
490; *Meeks v. State*, 57 Ga. 329; *Costly v. State*, 19 Ga.
614, at page 628; *Gillespie v. State*, 8 Yerg. (Tenn.) 507; .
McClure v. State, 1 Yerg. (Tenn.) 208; *State v. Davis*, 80 N.

C. 412; *State v. Fisher,* 2 Nott. & McC. (S. C.) 261; *State v. Quarrel,* 2 Bay. (S. C.) 150; *George v. State,* 39 Miss. 570, at page 590; *Jones v. People,* 2 Colo. 351; *Beck v. State,* 20 Ohio St. 228; *State v. Hinkle,* 27 Kan. 308; *People v. Coffman,* 24 Cal. 230. These cases are grounded upon the fact that the right to challenge for cause, and to examine the juror, or others, in support thereof, is discretionary, and may be waived, and that, when the party fails to avail himself of this right, he must be taken to have waived all objection on the ground of incompetency. A failure to challenge and examine for cause virtually says: "I am content with that jury, so far as cause is concerned; and, if any juror be incompetent for any reason, I waive my right to challenge for that cause." It is not questioned but that a failure to challenge and examine as to any other of the fifteen grounds of challenge for cause provided in said section 4405 of the Code of 1873 would be a waiver as to said causes. We fail to discover why the same rule should not apply to all those causes, and in all cases, civil and criminal. *Groome's Case,* and those supporting it, are grounded upon the thought that it is the duty of the state to put none but competent jurors in the box, and the accused may presume, in the absence of knowledge to the contrary, that those called are competent. This is certainly at variance with the spirit and purpose of our statute as to the mode of selecting and impaneling juries. The right given to challenge for any of the causes named, and to examine the juror, or other witnesses, in support of the challenge, precludes the conclusion that the law assumes to present none but competent jurors, or that a party has a right to so assume. The right to examine for such cause would be an idle provision, if such were the law. The state makes no guaranty as to the competency of jurors, but says to litigants, "Examine for yourselves." In *Groome's Case* it is held that, by accepting the jury without inquiring as to bias or prejudice, the defendant waived any objection on those grounds. We think that, by the same reasoning, he should be held to have waived the objection for incompetency. No sufficient reason is given for the distinction that is made in some of the cases, between civil and criminal cases, and between capital and other criminal cases. The same statutes govern as to the selection of jurors for all cases, civil and criminal. True, different provisions are made for impaneling juries, but none that impose upon the state the duty of presenting none but competent jurors. There is no reason why every party to an action, civil or criminal, should not be held to exercise the right given him to examine as to the qualifications of jurors called to act in his case, and, if he waives that right, to be concluded thereby, unless actual prejudice is otherwise shown. See, also, *State v. Belvel*, 89 Iowa, 405. Our conclusion is that the rule announced in *State v. Groome, supra,* on this question, is not sustained by the better reasoning, and is not in harmony with the general current of decisions, and that it should be overruled. This disposes of the only question presented in the partial record before us, and it follows from what we have said that the judgment of the district court should be AFFIRMED.

STATE OF IOWA v. ANDREW KOUHNS, Appellant.

Incest: EVIDENCE   Defendant was charged with incest with his
daughter, who testified that he took her by the arm, and threatened to whip her if she did not submit; and she cried; that he
1 threw her on the ground, and had intercourse; and she became
pregnant, and was delivered of a child; that she never had inter-
4 course with any other person, that she told defendant of her
pregnancy, and he denied the paternity of the child. *Held,* that
there was evidence sufficient to support a verdict of guilty.

RAPE: *Corroboration.* The woman with whom a man has incestuous intercourse by means of threats and force is not such an accom-
2 plice that he cannot be convicted upon her uncorroborated evi-
dence, as provided by Code 1873, section 4559.

SAME. That an incestuous intercourse was had under such circum
3 stances that the act would amount to rape will not bring it
within Code 1873, section 4560, providing that a conviction for
rape shall not be had upon the uncorroborated evidence of the
. prosecutrix.

Misconduct of Counsel. In a prosecution for incest with a daughter,
the court struck out an answer by witness to the effect that
the defendant had had sexual intercourse with another daughter,
whereupon the county attorney stated that he understood that to
5 show sexual intercourse of the defendant with any other daughter
was corroborative of the fact that he had sexual intercourse with
the complaining witness. *Held,* that in the absence of any showing that the county attorney did not make the statement in good
faith, an omission by the court to instruct the jury to disregard
the statement, as requested by the defendant, is not reversible
error.

Jurors: SELECTION. Code 1873, section 241 (Laws 1886, page 44), provides that not more than one grand juror shall be drawn from a
township; and the law also provides that the clerk shall give the
6 sheriff his precept within three days after the grand jury is
drawn. The record shows that the sheriff received the notices on
November 30, and made his return December 6. *Held,* that a
juror who changed the township of his residence on November
20, but was summoned as a resident of the town from which he
removed, – there being another juror summoned from the town to
which he removed, – was an illegal juror.

Waiver. Where it does not appear from the record that a defendant
did not know of an irregularity in the drawing of the grand jury
which indicted him, until after he pleaded to the indictment, he
will be held to have waived the irregularity by his plea of not
guilty.

*Appeal from Boone District Court.--*HON. B. P. BIRD-
SALL, Judge.

WEDNESDAY, DECEMBER 15, 1897.

THE defendant was indicted for the crime of incest,
and was convicted, and sentenced to the state penitentiary for the term of five years. He appeals.—*Affirmed.*

Dyer & Stevens for appellant.

Milton Remley, attorney general, and *Jesse A. Miller* for the state.

Kinne, C. J.—I. The defendant was charged with having committed the crime of incest with his daughter Mattie Kouhns. The daughter testified that defendant took her by the arm, and said that he would whip her if she did not do what he wanted her to do; that she cried; that she said nothing; that he took her and threw her on the ground, and had intercourse with her; that she afterwards became pregnant, and was delivered of a child; that she never had intercourse with any other person; that she told defendant that she was pregnant, and he denied the paternity of the child. The defendant denies having had connection with his daughter Mattie,
—in fact, denies all of the statements. It is con-
1   tended that the verdict is supported only by the
uncorroborated evidence of the complaining wit-
ness, and the argument is that in this case there can be no conviction unless her testimony is corroborated. Sec-tion 4560 of the Code of 1873 provides that "the defend-ant in a prosecution for rape, or for enticing or taking away an unmarried female of previously chaste charac-ter for the purposes of prostitution, or aiding or assist-ing therein, or for seducing and debauching any unmar-ried woman of previously chaste character, cannot be convicted upon the testimony of the person injured, unless she be corroborated by other evidence tending to connect the defendant with the commission of the offense." Section 4559 provides: "A conviction cannot be had upon the testimony of an accomplice, unless he be corroborated by such other evidence as shall tend to connect the defendant with the commission of the offense; and the corroboration is not sufficient if it

merely shows the commission of the offense or the circumstances thereof." The crime of incest is not mentioned in section 4560 as one wherein a conviction is
dependent upon corroboration. Counsel argue that the
evidence required to convict should be the same in case
the crime charged is incest as in the cases expressly
mentioned in the statute. If that should be conceded,
it would furnish no ground for this court's ingrafting
something upon the statute which is not provided for
therein. The legislature has not seen fit to require
corroboration of the complaining witness as a pre-·
requisite to conviction of the crime of incest, and therefore such corroboration is not necessary. In the case
referred to by counsel the question of the necessity of
corroboration in such a case was not raised. It was
therein insisted that the evidence of the prosecutrix
was not corroborated, and this court held that it was,
without determining the necessity for corroboration
when the crime charged was incest. Under the
2   section of the Code of 1873 last quoted, it is contended that the complaining witness was an
accomplice, and hence no conviction could be had in the
absence of corroboration. But we have held that the
woman with whom one has incestuous intercourse is not
necessarily an accomplice. *State v. Chambers*, 87 Iowa,
1; *State v. Hurd*, 101 Iowa, 391. If it should be conceded that, if the intercourse was voluntary on part of
the prosecutrix, she would be an accomplice, still we
have no such case before us. The prosecutrix in the
case at bar was some fifteen or sixteen years of age, and
it appears from her evidence that the defendant accomplished the act by threats and force. There could therefore have been no acquiescence on her part, and under
such circumstances it cannot be said that she is an

accomplice. *State v. Chambers* and *State v. Hurd,*
3   *supra.* Nor is it material that under the facts
     the acts would also constitute rape. A convic·
tion may be had of the crime of incest although
the facts show that the acts would also constitute rape.
State v. Hurd, supra. It appears, therefore, that in such
a case no corroboration is necessary. There is evidence,
—though, perhaps, not very conclusive,—which corrob-
orates the prosecutrix. Under our view of the law, the
jury might find the defendant guilty, in the absence of
all corroborating evidence, if they believed from the evidence that his guilt was established beyond a reason-
     able doubt. Without entering into a further dis-
4   cussion of the evidence, it is sufficient for us to
     say that, after a careful examination of the entire
record, we are constrained to hold that the evidence was
ample to support the verdict.

II. The county attorney, in the course of the examination of witnesses, said, in the presence and hearing
of the jury, "I understand that to show sexual inter-
     course of the defendant with any other daughter
5   is corroborative of the fact that he had sexual
     intercourse with the complaining witness in this
case, and that he had sexual intercourse with the complaining witness another time is corroborative evidence." Now, this statement was made just following
a ruling by the court striking out an answer by a witness to the effect that defendant had had sexual intercourse with one of his daughters other than the prosecutrix. We have often held that it is not error for a
county attorney to state to the jury what he thinks has
been shown by the evidence. *State v. Beasley,* 84 Iowa,
83; *State v. Cater,* 100 Iowa, 501. So we have held that
an erroneous statement as to the law, made by the
county attorney in an argument to the jury, is not

reversible error. *State v. Toombs*, 79 Iowa, 741. And we have said that it is not reversible error for a county attorney in good faith to offer evidence that is incompetent. *State v. Gadbois*, 89 Iowa, 25; *State v. Beal*, 94 Iowa, 39. Now, following the adverse ruling of the court, the statement was made by the county attorney. It was objected to by the defendant's counsel, and at the same time they asked that the jury be instructed to disregard it. Defendant contends that the statement constituted prejudicial error, in the absence of an instruction to the jury to disregard it. So far as the record shows, the county attorney was acting in good faith in making the statement, and even though it may not have been, in all respects, a correct statement of the law, if made by him in good faith, believing it to be such, we cannot say that it constituted reversible error. If every statement of a county attorney to a court, in the presence of a jury, which may be erroneous as to the law, is to be held prejudicial error, regardless of the circumstances or of the evidence, it is apparent that few verdicts in criminal cases could be sustained. The evidence introduced in the further progress of the trial was such that it affirmatively appears that the statement under consideration could not have prejudiced the defendant's case.

III.   It is said that the grand jury was not legally selected. The exact complaint is that two of the grand jurors finding the indictment were residents of the same township. The county contains seventeen civil townships. Code 1873, section 241, after providing for drawing jurors, says, "Provided that in drawing such grand jury not more than one person shall be drawn as a grand juror from any civil township, excepting where the grand jury is by law required to be drawn from a district containing fewer civil townships

than the number of grand jurors required to be summoned." Laws 1886, p. 44. The record shows that one Piper, a member of the grand jury which returned the indictment in this case, was, when the poll list was returned to the county auditor, May 25, 1895, a resident of Marcy township, in said county, and so remained until November 20, 1895. At that date he removed to Yell township, in the same county, where he resided at the time the indictment was found. This list was one from which the grand jurors were selected for the January, 1896, term of court. It appears from the evidence of the clerk of the district court that the notices to be sent to grand jurors were given by the clerk to the sheriff on November 30, 1895, and that the sheriff made his return on them December 6, 1895; so that Piper must have been a resident of Yell township when he was summoned by the sheriff as a grand juror. As the law provides that the clerk shall give the sheriff his precept within three days after the grand jurors are drawn, commanding him to summon them, it must be presumed, we think, in view of the statements of the clerk, and notwithstanding Piper's statement in his letter as to the date he was notified, that when drawn, as well as when summoned, he was a resident of Yell township; and it is without dispute that at the drawing one Clark, who was also a resident of Yell township, was drawn as a grand juror. It does not appear from this
7   record that defendant did not know of the irregularity complained of before he pleaded to the indictment. In view of the holding of a majority of the court in *State v Belvel*, 89 Iowa, 405, it must be held that the defendant waived the irregularity, as he might have raised the question by attacking the indictment. *State v. Belvel, supra; State v. Reid*, 20 Iowa, 413. We

do not, therefore, consider what the effect of such an irregularity would be, if the question had been made at the proper time. On the whole record, it appears that the defendant had a fair trial, and that there was no prejudicial error.—AFFIRMED.

SUPPLEMENT.

[This case did not reach me in time to be published in its chronological order.—REPORTER]. ·

J. P. BLOOD v. THE HAWKEYE INSURANCE COMPANY, Appellant.

Insurance: ACTIONS ON POLICIES: *When premature.* Acts Eighteenth General Assembly, chapter 211, section 3, provide that, to maintain an action on an insurance policy, the assured need only prove the loss and notice in writing to the company within sixty days, accompanied by an affidavit as to how the loss occurred and its extent, but that no ac ion shall be begun within ninety days after giving such notice. *Held,* that the requirement of the statute as to the time within which an action may be brought cannot be waived, and an action in less than ninety days after notice of loss not accompanied by an affidavit, or after a waiver of such notice and affidavit, was premature. Following *Wilhelmi v. Insurance Co.,* 86 Iowa, 326. ·

Appeal from Woodbury District Court.—HON. GEORGE W. WAKEFIELD, Judge.

MONDAY, FEBRUARY 1, 1897.

ACTION on a policy of fire insurance. Judgment for plaintiff, and the defendants appealed.—*Reversed.*

J. B. Johnson for appellant.

Marks & Mould and *J. P. Blood & Co.* for appellee.

GRANGER, J.—The cause was submitted to the court without a jury. At the close of the evidence the defendant moved the court for judgment in its favor, for the reason, among others, that the action was prematurely brought, because it was less than ninety days after the "affidavit and proofs of loss" required by the statute were served on defendant. The petition shows that the loss occurred on the twenty-second day of September, 1894, and that proofs of loss were prepared and agreed upon October 20, 1894. The action was commenced December 27, 1894. A part of section 3, chapter 211, Acts Eighteenth General Assembly, is as follows: "In order to maintain his action on the policy it shall only be necessary for the assured to prove the loss of building insured, and that he has given the company or association notice in writing of such loss, accompanied by an affidavit stating the facts as to how the loss occurred, so far as they are within his knowledge, and the extent of the loss, which notice shall be given within sixty days from the time the loss occurred: provided, further, that no action shall be begun within ninety days after notice of such has been given." On the twenty-fourth of September a letter was written to the company, which the company answered, stating that the matter would have its attention. This letter is construed by appellee as a notice. It was not accompanied by any affidavit, as required by the act above quoted. This letter, or notice, somewhat elaborately stated the facts, and it may be conceded that it did so as fully as would be required in an affidavit under the statute.

It is claimed by appellee that because of its letter to the company notifying it of the loss, and the answer by the company, and because plaintiff gave to the company, at its request, about October 20, 1894, an affidavit stating the facts as to how the loss occurred, and because of a compliance by plaintiff with the terms of the policy as to adjustments, notice and proofs of loss, and his observance of other requirements of the policy, defendant waived the provisions of the law above quoted as to the time in which such actions may be brought. It is held in *Von Genechtin v. Insurance Co.*, 75 Iowa, 544, that the notice required by the statute includes the affidavit. See, also, *Wilhelmi v. Insurance Co.*, 86 Iowa, 326. Under the express language of the last-cited case the notice in this case, without the affidavit, is not the notice required by the statute. As to the waiver of the provisions of the statute it is said, in the same case: "Whatever may be the rule as to the power of the company to waive formal notice and proof of loss, as required by the statute, the question of their right to waive the provisions of the statute, prohibiting the commencement of an action prior to the expiration of 90 days after notice and proofs of loss are given, must be regarded as settled."

Appellee contends, and the contention is supported by the facts in this case, that the affidavit to accompany the notice, and the proofs of loss, as contemplated by the policy, are not the same. The requirements of the statute as to the affidavit are not as comprehensive as those of the policy as to the proofs of loss. The statute, as to the affidavit simply requires that it shall show the facts as to how the loss occurred, so far as the assured knows, and the extent of the loss, while, by the terms of the policy, the proofs of loss must contain specific items of information not essential to a compliance with the statute as to the affidavit. We leave it as an open question whether proofs of loss, other than such as are required by the affidavit, under the statute, can be required by the terms of a policy. There is some confusion in the cases, arising from the use of the terms "affidavit" and "proofs of loss," by not at all times having in view the distinctions between the requirements of the law and of policies, and speaking of the affidavit as proof of loss, which, in a sense, it is, but distinguishable from proofs of loss as generally required by policies.

It is appellee's thought that the requirement in the policy as to the proofs of loss being complied with by him, with other facts as to notice, agreeing to the amount of the loss, etc., operates to waive the requirements of the law as to the time in which the suit may be brought. The *Wilhelmi Case, supra,* is decisive of the question as to time, and the ninety days must run. If the notice, accompanied by the affidavit, is given, the time commences to run from that date. If the company may waive the notice and affidavit, which questions we do not decide, then some other fact must fix the commencement of the ninety days, and such question is in no way argued by counsel. If we assume it to be from the date of the waiver, which would seem to be the reasonable one, we think there is no evidence in the case from which the fact of a waiver can be found. The facts pleaded as a waiver occurred from September 25 to October 20, 1894, and the petition was filed December 24, 1894; so that, in no event could there have been the period of ninety days before the commencement of the action. We do not know that appellee could question this proposition. His argument is directed, in something of a general way, to a waiver of a "strict compliance with the law," and we understand the claim to be that the ninety days' period may be waived. As we have said, that question is settled by the *Wilhelmi Case.*

The action is prematurely brought, and there should be a judgment for defendant.—REVERSED.

APPENDIX

Notes of Cases Not Otherwise Reported.

ALLAN SMITH, Appellant, v. FANNIE A. V. KNIGHT, Administratrix, Etc., et al.

APPEAL. Refusal to allow a credit claimed by plaintiff cannot be considered on appeal, where the evidence is not properly in the record.

SAME. A statement in appellee's abstract, denying that the evidence set forth in appellant's abstract was properly preserved or filed of record, and that appellant's abstract and appellee's amendment together contain all the evidence, will be taken as true where appellant does not reaffirm his original abstract.

Appeal from Boone District Court.—HON. B. P. BIRDSALL, Judge.

WEDNESDAY, OCTOBER 13, 1897.

THIS is a branch of the case of *Smith v. Knight,* which was determined in this court on May 18, 1893, wherein the judgment of the lower court was affirmed. 88 Iowa, 257. After the affirmance, an execution issued upon the judgment, and certain property of the appellant was levied upon thereunder. Appellant then brought this action by supplementary proceedings in the original case, asking to be entitled to certain credits upon the execution, and praying for an injunction restraining the sheriff from proceeding until such claimed credits were determined. An injunction issued as prayed. In the original action it was ordered that the defendants deed an undivided one-half of lot 11, in block 67, in Boone, Iowa, to the plaintiff, Allan Smith, and plaintiff was ordered to pay to defendants a sum there'n stated; and in default of a conveyance of the undivided one-ha'f of said lot to Smith the amount he was to pay the defendants was to be reduced to the extent of the value of the one-half of said lot. Plaintiff in this proceeding seeks to have the value of the undivided one-half of said lot 11 credited on the execution against him. This relief the lower court refused, and plaintiff appeals.— *Affirmed.*

(733)

James G. Day and *E. L. Penfield* for appellant.

Dyer & Stevens and *R. F. Jordan* for appellees.

KINNE, C. J.—I. Appellees have filed a paper in which they deny that the evidence set forth in appellant's abstract was properly preserved or filed of record in this case, and deny that there is any evidence relating to the value of the undivided one-half of lot 11, in block 67, Boone, Iowa, before this court, and deny that the appellant's abstract and appellees' amendment together contain all of the evidence. Appellant has not re-affirmed his original abstract, and therefore we must treat the statements in appellees' abstract as being true. Not having all of the evidence before us, this case cannot be tried *de novo*.

II. Appellant has filed an assignment of errors, and we may therefore consider any question the determination of which is not dependent upon an examination of the evidence. Appellant claims a credit on the execution against him to the extent of the value of an undivided one-half of lot 11. If it be conceded that in this proceeding he would be entitled to such credit, still, before it could be given, the value of such interest must be shown. As we have already said, we have no evidence before us, and hence cannot say that the court below erred in not allowing such credit on the execution. Whatever may be the merits of this case, we see no way, under the law, in view of the record, of granting relief.— AFFIRMED.

E. H. GIBBS v. THE CITY OF OSKALOOSA, Appellant.

APPEAL. A certificate by the reporter that the abstract is a true rendering into longhand of his shorthand notes and that it contains all the testimony offered or introduced, is no part of the record, unauthorized, and of no effect.

Appeal from Mahaska District Court.—HON. D. RYAN, Judge.

WEDNESDAY, OCTOBER 13, 1897.

APPEAL from a decree canceling certain receipts purporting to satisfy a judgment in the Poweshiek county district court.—*Affirmed.*

J. C. Williams for appellant.

J. F. & W. R. Lacey for appellee.

DEEMER, J.—The abstract contains a certificate of the reporter to the effect that it is a true rendering into longhand of his shorthand notes, and that it contains all the testimony offered or introduced, together with motions and objections of counsel, and rulings of the court thereon. The reporter has nothing to do with the preparation of the abstract, and his certificate thereto is of no more effect than if made by any other stranger to the proceedings. Moreover, appellee has expressly denied that the evidence was ever certified, except by the reporter, and no response is made to this denial.

There are no assignments of error. For these reasons, we cannot try or consider the case, and the decree is AFFIRMED.

HEALY BROTHERS, *et al*, V. GEORGE V. JORDAN, Appellant

DISTRAINT OF ANIMALS: *Notice* Under Code 1873, section 1454, providing that, in case of distraint of trespassing cattle and failure of the owner to satisfy the damages, the land owner shall notify the township trustees to assess the damages, "such notice to be either verbal or in writing," and "the owner of stock, or person entitled to the possession thereof, when known, shall also be notified of the time and place of the meeting of the trustees to assess said damages," a verbal notice of such meeting to the owner of the cattle or person entitled to the possession thereof is sufficient.

Appeal from Crawford District Court.—HON. C. D. GOLDSMITH, Judge.

THURSDAY, OCTOBER 15, 1897.

DEFENDANT distrained plaintiffs' hogs doing damage in his field. He notified plaintiffs, and one of them came, but they failed to agree upon the damages, and defendant notified the township trustees to assess the damages. This action is replevin for the possession of the hogs. The defense is a right of possession because of the distraint. The court directed a verdict for the plaintiffs, and the defendant appealed.—*Reversed.*

Shaw & Kuehnle for appellant.

P. E. C. Lally for appellees.

GRANGER, J.—The following is a part of section 1454 of the Code of 1873: "Within twenty-four hours after the stock has been distrained,

Sunday not being included, the party so injured, or his agent, shall notify the owner of said stock, when known, and if said owner sha l fail to satisfy the owner of or occupant cultivating said land, he shall within twenty-four hours thereafter, notify the township trustees to be and appear upon the premises to view and assess the damages; such notices to be either verbal or in writing. * * * The owner of the stock, or person entitled to the possession thereof, when known, shall also be notified of the time and place of the meeting of the trustees to assess said damage." It is not questioned but that, if the distraint proceedings were legal, the defendant would be entitled to the possession of the hogs. The objection to such proceedings was that no notice was given plaintiffs of the time and place of the ass ssment by the trustees. Defendant offered to prove a verbal notice of that kind, which the court refused to permit; and the only quest on for us is, is a verbal notice in such case sufficient? We think it is. It seems to us the language of the section practically settles it. In the first part of the section it is provided that the notice to the owner of the stock and to the trustees may be either verbal or in writing. That, it is true, is a notice of the distraint, but is the important notice, for it is the first one, and gives notice of the taking of the stock, and other proceedings are to follow, by way of settlement or assessment. Surely, if a verbal notice is good in the first place, such a notice after a failure to settle the damage ought to be good as to the time and place for the assessment. There seems to be nothing to elaborate. We think a verbal notice was sufficient. The judgment is REVERSED.

THE CITIZENS STATE BANK v. ANNA WESTON, et ol., Appellants.

FRAUDULENT CONVEYANCE: *Evidence.* A father and his daughter made a contract, when she was about twenty-five years old, whereby she agreed to stay at home and care for her parents, and he agreed to clothe and support her and pay her one hundred and fifty dollars a year; said sum to be paid when she required it. After she had worked pursuant to such contract for some thirteen years, during which time she had been paid nothing, a bank brought suit against the father, and obtained judgment   Pending the suit she demanded that she be paid for her services. He had no money, and it was agreed between them that he should convey to her certain land in full satisfaction of her claim. *Held,* that the conveyance made by him and accepted by her pursuant to the latter agreement was not fraudulent as to the bank

Appeal from Pottawattamie District Court.—Hon. W. I. Smith Judge.

Tuesday, October 19, 1897.

Action in equity to set aside a conveyance of certain land. Decree for plaintiff, and defendants appeal.—*Reversed.*

Flickinger Bros. for appellants.

Mayne & Hazelton for appellee.

Kinne, C. J.—Owing to the contention of counsel as to the condition of the record, we have carefully read the transcript in this case; and from it and from the pleadings we find the following, among other, facts established: Plaintiff bank secured a judgment against the defendant James Weston, who is the father of the defendant Anna Weston. About the time the judgment was rendered, the said James Weston conveyed the premises in controversy to the defendant Anna Weston, his daughter. This action is brought to set aside said deed, and to establish the lien of the plaintiff's judgment against the said land. Anna Weston, the daughter, when about twenty-five years of age, entered into an agreement with her father whereby she agreed to stay at home and work and care for her parents, in consideration of which the father agreed to support and clothe her and pay her at the rate of one hundred and fifty dollars per year; said sum to be paid when she required it. Under this arrangement, Anna stayed at home, did the housework, and cared for her parents for some thirteen years prior to the execution of the deed to her. She had never been paid anything under the agreement until the property was conveyed to her, which she accepted in full for all her services theretofore rendered. The mother was during all of this time in poor health, and required constant care. While plaintiff's suit was pending against her father, Anna demanded that she should be paid for her services. The father then had no money, and it was agreed between them that he should convey this land to her in full satisfaction of her claim. We th nk the evidence establishes the contract of employment, and the performance of the labor by Anna thereunder, and that the deed was accepted by her for the purpose of settlement of the sum due her. It may be conceded that in some respects the evidence of the father is not satisfactory, but, taking all of the evidence, it is reasonably clear that the plaintiff has failed to establish its claim that the conveyance was made for the purpose of defrauding it. As the father was in fact indebted to the daughter, he had a legal right to convey this land in satisfaction of her claim, even though the effect of it was to hinder, delay, or prevent the plaintiff from collecting its claim. We have no doubt of the justness of the daughter's claim, and we think the evidence shows that the transaction was legitimate. The law is so well settled, relating to such conveyances, that we need not here cite the authorities. The evidence is not sufficient to sustain plaintiff's claim, and a decree should have been entered for the defendant Anna.—REVERSED.

IN THE MATTER OF THE ESTATE OF W. P. GARDNER, Deceased.

HOMESTEADS: *Debt of decedent.* A homestead is not subject to the debts of the deceased owner, unless they were incurred prior to the acquisition of the homestead.

Appeal from Carroll District Court.—HON. Z A CHURCH, Judge.

FRIDAY, OCTOBER 22, 1897.

THIS is an application by the administrator of the estate of W. r. Gardner, deceased, to sell certain real estate belonging to the deceased in order to pay debts. The widow of deceased claimed certain of the real estate as exempt to her as a homestead. One of the creditors, to-wit, J. W. Gardner, opposed this claim on the ground that his debt antedated the acquisition of the homestead. The trial court found that the property was a homestead, and denied the application to sell. The creditor appeals.—*Affirmed.*

Geo. W. Paine for appellant.

B. I. Salinger for appellee.

DEEMER, J.—That the property was and is a homestead is conceded. It was acquired in the year 1882, and is not subject to the debts of the deceased unless these debts were contracted prior to the acquisition thereof. The claim of J. W. Gardner is based upon two promissory notes in the sum of three hundred dollars each, which are dated April 15, 1883, and April 15, 1887, respectively. He contends, however, that these notes were given in renewal of a debt contracted in the fall of 1873. To establish this contention he introduced the evidence of a former wife and of a grandson of the deceased. It is not important that we set out this evidence. It is sufficient to say that we do not think it establishes the appellant's contention. Certainly it does not so clearly establish it that we are justified in holding that the order of the trial court lacks support in the evidence. The notes are not sufficiently connected with any previous loan of money as to justify us in saying they are renewals. The judgment and order of the district court are AFFIRMED.

H. J LEDWARD & COMPANY V. GEORGE W. KUDER, Appellant.

MOTION TO STRIKE: *Sufficiency.* After a witness had been examined and cross-examined touching all the matters in controversy, and had given much competent testimony, defendant moved "to strike out the testimony in relation to this transaction, for the reason that same is not competent." *Held,* that the motion was too indefinite, as not advising the court what particular transaction was referred to.

Appeal from Louisa District Court.—HON. BEN McCOY, Judge.

FRIDAY, OCTOBER 22, 1897.

Gray & Tucker for appellant.

C. A. C, penter for appellee.

KINNE, C. J.—I. This action is brought to recover a balance claimed to be due the plaintiff from the defendant on account of certain corn which defendant shipped the plaintiff, and which plaintiff stored and sold on commission for the defendant. The defendant, in substance, denies the allegations of the petition, and denies any indebtedness to the plaintiff. A jury was waived, and the cause tried to the court. Judgment was entered for plaintiff, and the defendant appeals.

II. While several assignments of error are made, but two are argued. After the witness J. H. Ledward had been examined and cross-examined at considerable length touching all of the matters in controversy, the defendant's counsel moved the court "to strike out the testimony in relation to this transaction, for the reason that the same is incompetent." The court took the motion under advisement, and, when deciding the case, overruled it. The correctness of this ruling is challenged by appellant. We think the ruling was proper. The court was not advised by the form of the motion, and in view of the extended examination of the witness which preceded the motion, as to what particular transaction was sought to be stricken. If it was the object of the mover to strike out all of the testimony of the witness, the motion was properly overruled, as much of his evidence was competent. If it was the thought of counsel to strike out certain parts of the evidence, as to which the witness showed he had no personal knowledge, then the motion should have pointed out with some certainty the portions of the evidence desired to be stricken. This the motion did not do.

III. It is said that the plaintiff's claim is not established by any evidence. This case was tried to the court, and its finding and judgment stand as the verdict of a jury, and we cannot disturb it if the evidence supports the judgment. That there was sufficient evidence to support the finding and judgment we have no doubt.— AFFIRMED.

ELIZA TOMLINSON, *et al*, v. JOSEPH TOMLINSON, Appellant.

CANCELLATION OF DEED: *Evidence*. A decree setting aside a deed is sustained by evidence that the grantor and grantee were brothers; that the grantor was seventy years old, and mentally and physically weak; that he was financially embarrassed, had been sued for slander, reposed special confidence in the grantee, who was several years his junior, and of good business capacity, and acted on the grantee's advice, without consideration for the deed,—the grantee himself admitting that when he took the deed he knew that the grantor was mentally incapable of protecting his own interests.

Appeal from Jones District Court.—HON. WILLIAM G. THOMPSON, Judge.

TUESDAY, OCTOBER 26, 1897.

ACTION in equity to set aside and cancel a deed of certain lands which was made to the defendant, and for a decree quieting the title in the plaintiffs. Decree for plaintiffs. Defendant appeals.— *Affirmed.*

Robert G. Cousins for appellant.

L. A. Ellis and *F. O. Ellison* for appellees.

KINNE, C. J.—The grounds alleged for the relief demanded are: (1) Fraud and undue influence on the part of defendant in obtaining the deed to the land in question, and (2) a fraudulent alteration of the deed, after its execution and delivery, in a material part, rendering it inoperative as a conveyance. The answer is a general denial, and averments that the defendant is the absolute owner of the land. As usual in such cases, the evidence is, as to some material matters, conflicting, but a careful consideration of all of the competent evidence satisfies us that the following, among other, facts are established: Eliza Tomlinson is the widow of Jesse Tomlinson, who died December 17, 1894. The other defendants are the children of said Jesse and Eliza Tomlinson. Jesse Tomlinson, in his lifetime, was the owner of two hundred and forty acres of land in Jones county, Iowa. That the defendant was a brother of Jesse Tomlinson. Jesse Tomlinson and his wife were both over seventy years of age. Jesse Tomlinson was mentally and physically infirm. He placed great confidence in and reliance on the defendant, who was several years younger than himself. That he was indebted in the sum of about five thousand dollars, and was sued for slander. That he was a man easily irritated, and his obligations and this slander suit annoyed and worried him. Some ten years prior to his death, he had fallen from a horse, and for several years before he died he had failed much in mind and health. He had grown peculiar; would take the farm tools, and hide them; left considerable sums of money in rubbish, in old buildings, and in barns; left promissory notes in old tin cans; preached to himself in the fields in a loud voice; was afraid his son would squander his money. The defendant, taking advantage of the weak mental condition of said Jesse, and with the pretense on his part of aiding Jesse to pay his debts, and of assisting him in the management of his affairs, obtained a conveyance from Jesse and his wife of all their land under the promise that their title to the same should not be affected; that he would not place the deed of record; that when Jesse's debts were paid he wou'd re-convey the land to him. Relying upon the representations of the defendant, and by reason of his influence over Jesse and his wife, he secured said conveyance, placed the same of record, and, as a part of his scheme to defraud his brother, he pretended to lease said land to Jesse, and entered into a written contract of lease with him. Eighty acres of said land was sold, and with the proceeds of it, and of certain personal property, the defendant paid off all of Jesse's debts. The one hundred and sixty acres of land which was left has always been in the possession of Jesse or his wife and heirs. Said land embraced the homestead of Jesse Tomlinson and his wife, and said homestead had never been set apart. There was not a dollar's consideration for the conveyance of the land by Jesse Tomlinson and his wife to the defendant, and, after the eighty acres had been sold, and Jesse had turned over the crops raised, or their proceeds, to the defendant, to aid in paying his debts, and after the debts were all paid, there still remained one hundred and sixty acres of land, worth about ten thousand dollars, which is the land the defendant seeks to hold as against plaintiffs. Finding that his title to the land, acquired without any consideration, was of doubtful validity, the defendant, without the knowledge or consent of Eliza Tomlinson, went with Jesse before a notary, and had a provision inserted in the deed to the effect that the deed was subject to all mortgages and liens against the property. Jesse Tomlinson's situation was this: He had a farm worth about fourteen thousand dollars, and owed five thousand dollars. The defendant, without having invested a dollar of his own money, insists on a right to hold title to the one hundred and sixty acres, worth ten thousand dollars. The defendant had often expressed his opinion to the effect that his brother, Jesse, had not been fit to do business, that he had about lost his mind, that he was not responsible, and was not capable of doing business. To others he said that his brother, Jesse, had not been capable of doing business for seven or eight years. He also told the parties, prior to the time the deed was made, that he was going to try and persuade Jesse to put this property in his (defendant's) hands, to keep his son and others from squandering it, and that Jesse was not capable of attending to his own business. It thus appears, according to the defendant's own statements, he knew, when he took the conveyance, and when he had the same altered by inserting the provisions heretofore referred to, that the brother he was dealing with was mentally incapable of protecting his own interests, and that he now seeks to take advantage of a conveyance, which, in view of all of the evidence, it is fair to say he induced his brother to execute to him without any consideration whatsoever. We think it clearly appears that this conveyance was induced by the acts of the defendant and his promises, that he never paid anything for the land, that he has perpetrated a fraud, and that he ought not to be permitted to profit by it. He took advantage of the condition and confidence of his brother to secure the title to this land, and he should be compelled to restore that which he took to those to whom it rightfully belongs. The motion to reinstate the case is sustained. The motion to strike

the amendment to the abstract need not be considered, in view of
the disposition made of the case. The decree below was correct, and
it is AFFIRMED..

E. H. BARNES V. J. B. HOGATE, *et al.*, Appellants.

CONTRACT BY AGENT. Where the owner of land employs another to
cultivate the same, specifying the manner of payment for the
work to be done, and providing that the owner is to be at no
other expense for labor done on said land, if the owner afterwards directs the employe to do additional work, and to get some
one to help him, the owner is liable for the reasonable value of
labor done by a third person, hired by the party employed, to cultivate the land.

Appeal from Pottawattamie District Court. — HON. W. R. GREEN,
Judge.

TUESDAY, OCTOBER 26, 1897.

THE defendant J. B. Hogate leased a farm to one Brubaker by
written lease for the season of 1894. In August of that year, Hogate
being in Spain, and learning that the corn crop in this country had
failed, wrote his tenant a letter to have the corn cut and shocked.
The tenant employed the plaintiff to cut and shock the corn at an
agreed price of four cents per shock, and he cut and shocked one
thousand, two hundred and forty-three shocks, and this action is to
recover from Hogate therefor. The district court gave judgment for
plaintiff, and the defendants appealed.—*Affirmed.*

A. W. Askwith for appellants.

A. B. Johns for appellee.

GRANGER, J.—The amount in controversy is less than one hundred dollars, and hence our jurisdiction is fixed by the question
presented by the district court. It is as follows: "When the owner
of land employs another to cultivate the same, by written contract
specifying the manner of payment for the work to be done, the
horses and tools to be furnished by the owner, and providing the
owner is to be at no other expense for tools or labor done on said
land, if the owner afterwards writes to the employe, directing him
to do additional work in the way of cutting corn, not provided for
by the contract, and to get some one to help him, is the owner liable

for the reasonable value of labor done by a third party, hired by the
party employed to cultivate the land, in pursuance of said directions,
notwithstanding he does not have the corn cut in the manner
directed, but in a more expensive way? If the foregoing question is
answered in the affirmative, then this case should be affirmed; but,
if in the negative, then this case should be reversed." We are
limited by the question, and we do not go outside for the facts. We
think a question is argued by appellants with facts different from
those stated in the question. The question seems to us to be hardly
an open one. It is argued to us as if Hogate had merely requested
Brubaker to do what his lease required him to do, and to get some
one to help him. We are to determine if Hogate would be liable if
he directed Brubaker to "do additional work in the way of cutting
corn, not provided for by the contract, and to get some one to help
"him." The proposition is not debatable By the direction, he makes
Brubaker his agent to employ some one to do what he (Hogate)
wants done. It is not a matter that the lease or contract controls.
The argument takes no note of the latter statement in the question
as to the departure from the directions, and we need not cons'der it.
Our answer to the question submitted by the court is in the affirmative, and the judgment is AFFIRMED.

CHARLES A. LLOYD, et al , v. W. A. SPURRIER, et al.

CERTIORARI: *Premature.* A writ of *certiorari* from the supreme
    court to the district court and the judges of such court, to review
    the proceedings in a certain case in such court, is prematurely
    issued where a motion is pending to set aside the order and judg-
    ment and order complained of.

KINNE, C. J., taking no part.

TUESDAY, OCTOBER 26, 1897.

CERTIORARI proceedings against the district court and judges of
the ninth judicial district.—*Dismissed.*

A. W. O. Weeks for plaintiffs.

O. O. Cole for defendants.

PER CURIAM.—Upon the petition of plaintiffs a writ of *certiorari*
issued from this court, directed to the district court and judges of the
Ninth judicial district, commanding them to certify the records and

proceedings in a case before them wherein James Bellangee, chairman of the state central committee of the people's party of Iowa, was plaintiff, and George L. Dobson, *et al.*, constituting the election board of the state of Iowa, were defendants. Due return was made, and the case was submitted upon such return and certain oral evidence offered by the petitioners. From an examination of the return, we discover that a motion to set aside the order and judgment of the district court in the case hitherto referred to is still pending in that court, and is undisposed of. The presumption is that all errors, if any there be, will be corrected by that court, and that there will be no occasion to review its proceedings by writ of *certiorari*. Until that motion is disposed of, there is no reason for invoking the writ. As an attempt has been made in the district court to correct the errors complained of, the writ was prematurely issued, and it is DISMISSED.

KINNE, C. J., taking no part.

H. G. FISHER, Appellant, v. THE CARROLL COUNTY FAIR AND DRIVING PARK ASSOCIATION, *et al.*

SPECIFIC PERFORMANCE. In ejectment, defendant asked specific performance of a contract for the exchange of land owned by defendant for the land in dispute, of which defendant has possession when plaintiff purchased it. The contract did not fix any time for exchanging deeds, but the same year it was made, and four years before suit was brought, plaintiff asked for a deed. Defendant did not then or at any time refuse to carry out the contract, but only stated reasons for delay; those given being that it was unable to execute the deed, owing to a mortgage on the land. Plaintiff made no tender of a deed, nothing had been lost by delay, and the parties were in the same situation as when the contract was made. Defendant tendered performance. *Held*, that plaintiff should be required to perform the contract.

Appeal from Carroll District Court.—HON. S. M. ELWOOD, Judge.

WEDNESDAY, OCTOBER 27, 1897.

THE defendant association acquired in 1887 the south half, north half, southwest quarter of section 30, township 84, range 34. It erected its hall and amphitheater along the south side of the north half, north half, of the same quarter, then owned by O. A. Kentner. On April 1, 1889, Kentner sold this land to the plaintiff, the contract providing that "for above consideration the said H. G. Fisher agrees to transfer to the Carroll Driving Park Association a strip of land now occupied by them, being a part of the above described land, and received from the Carroll Driving Park Association in exchange, and free from incumbrance, a like amount of land off the east end of the south half of the north half of the southwest quarter of section 30, township 84, range 34, Carroll county, Iowa." The defendant retained possession of the strip of land referred to, though deeds were not exchanged; and in August, 1893, petition in ejectment was filed. The defendants answer by demanding specific performance of the contract. Issue was joined, and the cause tried as an equitab'e action. Decree was entered for defendants, and plaintiff appeals.—*Affirmed.*

M. W. Beach for appellant.

F. M. Powers and *Geo. W. Paine* for appellees.

LADD, J.—The defendant is owner of the south half, north half, southwest quarter, of section 30, township 84, range 34, and the plaintiff the owner of the north half of the north half of the same quarter. The defendant had constructed its hall and amphitheater on a portion of the north half, and was in possession of between three and four acres thereof, when the plaintiff purchased it, in 1889, of Kentner, a part of the consideration being that he would convey the land so occupied to the defendant in exchange for a deed to a like parcel at the east end of the south half by the defendant. Some time during that year the plaintiff asked Hinrichs, then secretary of defendant, to execute a deed; but this the association was unable to do, owing to a mortgage on its land. The plaintiff insists that he then declared the "trade off," but this is denied by Hinrichs and others. The circumstances and the subsequent course of the plaintiff clearly indicate that he did not consider his obligation under the contract te minated, or the information derived from Hinrichs a refusal to carry out its terms. The defendant continued in possession of the strip of land without objection until 1893, and the plaintiff was in possession cf six or eight acres at the east end of the south half, but whether under the contract or an oral lease is in dispute. As the rental value appears to have been two dollars and fifty cents to five dollars per acre, it would seem that, in paying only six dollars for the use of six or eight acres, that referred to in the contract must have been excluded. This conclusion is strengthened by the fact that defendant's possession was without objection. There is some dispute about the way the land should be surveyed. The fence along the north side of that occupied by the defendant was crooked. It was blown down in 1893, and another constructed after a careful survey. The plaintiff had suggested that this line be straightened, and that the part that defendant received extend back to that it was to convey, so as to leave but one corner; and in pursuance of this suggestion or understanding the east end of the new fence was placed at substantially the same point occupied by the east end of the old fence, and it was then run due west, reaching the west line several feet north of that end of the old fence. This included some land lying north of that formerly occupied by the defendant, owing to a jog to the south in the old fence. While the plaintiff had not suggested the manner of straightening the fence, the only feasible way was by beginning at one end of the old fence, and running it in a straight line parallel with the boundary line of the land, and this was done. After the work of straightening this line had begun, the plaintiff protested, and then instituted this suit. The contract fixes no date for the exchange of deeds. The defendant never refused to carry out the contract, but only stated reasons for delay. It was entitled to a reasonable time to clear its land of the mortgage and make the deed. The plaintiff made no tender. He was bound to perform his part of the contract before insisting on its forfeiture, and he was not excused from so doing because the defendant was not ready at the time referred to. The parties are in the same situation as when the contract was made, and the exchange can be as well made now as then. Nothing has been lost by the delay. The defendant has tendered performance upon its part, and the plaintiff will be required to convey the land as agreed. There is a controversy as to whether the plaintiff was to convey according to the line of the old fence or the new, and whether the strip ran back to that to be conveyed to him. Before this litigation, the evidence shows, his wish was that the line be straightened, and conveyances made in accordance with the surveys as made and the fences as constructed by the defendant. The adjustment according to the line of the new survey and the new fence is clearly to the interest of both parties, and the objections thereto are only captious. While on many of the questions the evidence is in sharp conflict, it warrants the conclusion reached by the district court, and its decree is AFFIRMED.

STATE OF IOWA v. NOAH J. THOMAS, Appellant.

EVIDENCE: *Seduction.* A conviction for the crime of seduction will not be sustained, where, although the defendant paid his attention to the prosecutrix for a time, yet the letters which passed between them contained no reference to an engagement or any improper act, and the associates of the prosecuting witness and her conduct with other men indicate that she was not a chaste woman. See opinion for other facts.

Appeal from Franklin District Court.—HON. B. P. BIRDSALL, Judge.

WEDNESDAY, DECEMBER 15, 1897.

DEFENDANT was indicted for the crime of seduction, was convicted, and appeals.—*Reversed.*

Taylor & Evans for appellant.

Milton Remley, attorney general, and *Jesse A. Miller* for the state

KINNE, C. J.—I. Counsel for appellant contends that the evidence does not sustain the verdict. There are certain facts in the case which are either admitted or established beyond any reasonable doubt, viz.: That Grace Porter, the prosecuting witness, went to the house of Mr. and Mrs. Hemm to do housework June 12, 1895, and continued to work there up to and after she claims to have been seduced; that the defendant began working for the same Mr. Hemm about July 11, 1895, and so continued until January 8, 1896, when he went on a visit to his parents, in Wisconsin. He returned from Wisconsin the March following, and resumed his work at Hemm's. Several other men were working for Hemm at the same time, and all of them, including the defendant, slept upstairs. The prosecutrix also slept upstairs, and in a room through which all of these men had to pass in going to their room. About the fifteenth to twentieth of September, 1895, defendant and prosecutrix went from the Hemm place to Belmond and Meservey together, and returned early on the following morning. Prior to this she had ridden with the defendant to Alexander, and also to the place where one Butterwick worked, about two miles east of Alexander. At another time she rode with him to a point about eighty rods west of Alexander, where they met Butterwick, and she left defendant, and got in Butterwick's buggy. He once gave her a pair of shoes, let her have money to go to Hampton, and at another time gave her a dollar. He sat up with her often, was seen to embrace and kiss her, and, after the Belmond trip, except as to the matter of carnal knowledge of each other, they seem to have conducted themselves as lovers usually do. It appears also that from some time in September until in January, 1896, the prosecutrix had no regular company except the defendant. It is established beyond a doubt that the prosecutrix had carnal connection with some one in the fall of 1895, and that on December 29, 1895, she had a miscarriage. She claims that her seduction was accomplished by the defendant on November 6, 1895, under a promise of marriage and protestations of love and affection on his part, and that thereafter they had carnal intercourse five times, at intervals of a week or over apart. The medical evidence showed that pregnancy had existed for not less than two nor more than three months, and, if this time be computed from the date of the miscarriage (December 29, 1895), conception must have taken place as early as October 30, 1895. She says that the night the defendant accomplished her seduction he was in her room an hour. The men who slept in the room with the defendant never knew of his visiting her room after he had retired for the night. She claims he came to her bed from his room some time after he had gone to bed with the other men in their room. She testified that she missed her monthly sickness November 29, 1895, but said nothing about it. A month later she claims to have had a miscarriage, and, though seeing the defendant daily, she did not disclose to him her condition, according to her own evidence, until January, 1896, about the time he went to Wisconsin. She testifies that, on January 1, 1896, defendant asked her if there was anything wrong, and she told him "how she felt, and told him, if such was the case, it was all laid at his door." In other words, she was then, according to her own evidence, intimating to him that she thought she was in the family way, when she now claims to have had a miscarriage two days before. During the absence of the defendant in Wisconsin, several letters passed between them, and she admits that "there was nothing said in any letter by either of us about any improper act. Our engagement was not mentioned in the letters."

The defendant admits paying his attentions to the prosecuting witness for a time, denies any engagement or promise of marriage or profession of love, and denies that there were ever any carnal relations between them. He says she never said anything to him about being in the family way, or about having a miscarriage, and he knew nothing of it until she testified to it in court. Some of the facts above recited are, in our judgment, hardly reconcilable with the claim of the prosecutrix that defendant seduced her or had carnal connection with her. After all the protestations of love and promises which she says he made in order to induce her to submit to his wishes, it is strange she could, according to her own admissions, conceal from him for weeks the fact that she was with child. Stranger yet that when he, as she claims, sought from her information as to her condition, she, although knowing that she had already had a miscarriage, said nothing about it until days afterwards. Counsel for the state seem to think that it was natural that the letters which were exchanged between them should be silent as to their marriage engagement or their acts of illicit intercourse. She was, when she says this seduction took place, a woman twenty-one years of age. It would have been the natural,—the usual,—thing between lovers who were engaged to speak of it in their correspondence. It does not require much knowledge of human nature to acquaint one with the fact that engaged lovers, who are separated for a time, and who carry on a correspondence, are prone to often refer to the time when their hopes are to be consummated by the marriage, and in various proper ways to refer to the fact of the existing engagement. It is to our minds an exceedingly strong circumstance tending to show that no engagement ever existed, and many of the recited facts make the defendant's guilt a matter of serious doubt.

We are at a loss to determine how the jury could have found, as they must, under the instruction, that this prosecutrix was of previous chaste character. It appears without conflict that in the summer of 1895 she was intimate with one Miss Kruse, who was, according to the undisputed evidence, a woman of bad reputation. According to her letter of date June 12, 1895, to one Mr. Butterwick, she was staying with this woman. In that letter, after asking Butterwick to get Grant, and come and see them, between 9 and 10 o'clock at night, she says it is "pleasure we are fishing for, and that we will gain, for I am going to make up for lost time," and signs herself "Lady Grace." In company with Miss Kruse, the prosecutrix went one Sunday to the town of Alexander. There they were joined by this same Butterwick and one Palmer. Prosecutrix testified that they all went to church; that after church she went back to get her handkerchief, and then they went for a drive, Butterwick and she being in one buggy, and Palmer and Miss Kruse in another; that they drove until two o'clock in the morning, or after. They then came back to the hotel, and could not get in, and they then drove in various directions until daylight. Palmer testifies that church was out about nine o'clock, and after that they all walked around town for a while, and then Butterwick and prosecutrix went into the church, and he does not know whether they came out of the church then or not. He and Miss Kruse left them there, and saw no more of them until 3 o'clock in the morning, when they met on the street; that there was no all-night ride, and no ride at all prior to 3 o'clock in the morning. Palmer testifies also that he had a conversation with prosecutrix after the preliminary examination of the defendant about this case, and she told him what she had sworn to, and wanted him to testify to the same thing. The prosecutrix did not deny this attempt to induce Palmer to tell the same story she had told. Now, if Palmer told the truth, the prosecutrix did not, in her evidence, as to the night she put in with Butterwick; and if she did not, and, in addition to having testified falsely, was endeavoring to induce Palmer to do the same, to bolster up her testimony, we think it must be conceded that her testimony as to other matters may well be looked upon with suspicion, in view of the contradictions and the improbability of its being true. If she did not solicit Palmer to swear as he says, she would be quick to deny it, and to take the stand in her own behalf. Butterwick was in court, and, if her story was true as to how he and she spent the night, it would have been the most natural thing to do to have herself denied Palmer's testimony, and sustained her own by Butterwick. No effort was made so to do. During her early acquaintance with the defendant, and prior thereto, she wrote several letters to this man Butterwick. Many expressions in these letters, unexplained, and in connection with other facts and circumstances, indicate that the prosecutrix was not a chaste woman. Some of the letters were explained by her as a witness on the stand. Others, which were of more doubtful character, she did not attempt to explain. It is admitted that one Piatt, who lodged in the same house with the prosecutrix, and during the time she claims the engagement between her and the defendant existed, did, late at night, and after the prosecutrix was in bed, visit her, and sit on the edge of the bed, and talk to her for some time.

In view of the facts disclosed by this entire record, some of which we have set forth, we are forced to the conviction that the evidence of the prosecutrix is in material matters untrue, as it is certainly contradictory. Other material facts which she testifies to are, as we have endeavored to show, unusual, unnatural, improbab'e, and, in view of all of the other established facts in the case and her claims as to the seduction and marriage engagement, ought not to be accepted as true. While it is the duty of courts and juries to protect woman against the wiles of the seducer, and to punish the guilty, a man ought not to be sent to the penitentiary for the crime of seduction upon evidence so unsatisfactory as to his guilt as that in the record before us. When the evidence is all analyzed and given its proper force, it cannot be said that it could satisfy any fairminded man of the defendant's guilt beyond a reasonable doubt. Indeed, to our minds, properly viewed, the defendant's guilt does not appear by a preponderance of the evidence.

II. Several errors are assigned upon rulings of the court upon the introduction of evidence, the giving of instructions, the misconduct of the jury and of the county attorney. In view of the conclusion reached, we need not consider the questions just stated. We hold that the evidence is not sufficient to warrant the conviction of the defendant, and the court should have sustained the motion for a new trial.—REVERSED.

INDEX

ABANDONMENT—See Homesteads, [1]; Levy, [1].

ACCOMPLICE—See Crim. Law, [2], [3].

ACCRETIONS.

1. Accretions between the meander line and a navigable river belong to the riparian proprietor.—Bennett v. Natl. Starch Mfg. Co., 207.

2. Defined—In a suit commenced in 1893 and tried in 1895, between the respective owners of adjoining lots, numbered ten to fifteen, bounded on the south by the Des Moines river at a point where it flows east, the question was whether certain ground south of the original river bank, forming the boundary of lot ten was accretion. When the section of which such lots are a part was surveyed by the United States, the river near such lots was separated by an island, into two parts, and the place in controversy was covered by the north one of the two channels. Subsequently a large part of the island was cut away, and the north channel partially filled, discharges from sewers above contributing to such result; and for several years prior to 1895 water had not covered the tract in question, except in times of high water. In October, 1895, a rise of nine feet would have been required to cause water coming down the river to flow over it, though a considerable portion would have been covered by back water, from a smaller rise. The deposits in the old north channel are of sand and refuse from sewers. The soil thus formed does not produce grass, and is not suitable for agricultural purposes; cottonwood trees, willows, weeds, and sand burrs growing on it. The two banks are distinct, and in most places several feet higher than the place in question; and the river would overflow all of that, before it could overflow either bank. For several years before the trial such tract had not been overflowed, and it had on it cottonwood trees and willows of three or four years' growth; but the river had been unusually low for several years. *Held*, that the ground in question was not an accretion.—*Idem*.

Small figures refer to subdivisions of Index. The others to page of report.

ACTIONS.

Joinder of Causes—An action for forcible entry and detainer of real property cannot be consolidated with an action relating to the same land to set aside a tax deed and permit redemption from a sale for taxes, under Code 1873, section 2784, providing that two or more actions pending in the same court which might have been joined may be consolidated; as one is a law action, and the other an equitable one, and therefore may not be prosecuted by the same kind of proceedings, which, under Code 1873, section 2630, is a condition of joining causes of action.—Hodowal v. Yearous, 32.

ADJUDICATION.

A matter considered and determined in making an order of assessment, in proceedings for the appointment, of a receiver of an insolvent corporation, is conclusively settled, except so far as it may be changed by vacation or modification of the receivership proceedings, and will not be reconsidered in an action to enforce payment of the assessment.—State v. Union Stock Yards State Bank, 549.

ADMISSIONS—See CRIM. LAW, [5]; EVID. [48].
ADULTERY—See CRIM. LAW, [1].
ADVERSE POSSESSION—See REAL PROPERTY, [1], [2].
AFFIDAVITS—See EVID. [1]; JURISDICTION, [1]; PRACT. SUP. CT. [9], [19], [25].
AGENCY—See INS. [4], [7], [9]; PRIN. AND AGENT.

ALIMONY.

1. Decree—SETTING ASIDE—A decree for alimony obtained by a husband in a suit for divorce, in which his wife did not appear, upon false testimony that the land awarded as alimony was purchased with the husband's money, though the title was in the wife, will be set aside in a suit brought for that purpose.—Klaes v. Klaes, 680.

2. Husband and Wife—LIABILITY FOR ATTORNEYS' FEES—The defendant in a divorce action is liable for a personal judgment for the services of the attorney of plaintiff in securing the divorce, where she procures an award of alimony made to plaintiff and a mortgage from plaintiff to his attorney in payment of the latter's contingent interest in the alimony decreed, to be set aside because the award was obtained through plaintiff's false testimony.—Idem.

3. Bona Fide Purchaser—A client contracted to pay his attorney one-half the alimony which might be recovered in a divorce suit brought by the client. A divorce having been secured,

Small figures refer to subdivisions of Index. The others to page of report.

and certain land, title to which was in the wife, having been
awarded as alimony, the client gave his attorney a mortgage
on the property. *Held*, he was not such *bona fide* purchaser as
that his mortgage might not be cancelled.—*Idem.*

AMENDMENTS—See PRACTICE, ², ³.

ANIMALS.

1. **Dogs**—*Liability of Owner for Injury By*—Under Code, section
   1485, making the owner of a dog liable to a person injured, for
   all damages done by it, except when such person is doing an
   unlawful act, negligence of the person injured does not exempt
   the owner from liability, unless the negligence amounts to an
   unlawful act.—Shultz v. Griffith, 150.

2. **RULE APPLIED**—Plaintiff left his horse and buggy in defendant's livery stable, and at about 8 P. M. went into the barn
   yard to see that his buggy was put under shelter; and to get
   some articles therefrom. While at the buggy, he was bitten
   by defendant's dog. *Held*, that though the property was in
   care of defendant, plaintiff was not a trespasser in going to it
   when and for the purpose he did, without permission, and it is
   immaterial whether defendant's employes knew of his presence.—*Idem.*

3. **EVIDENCE OF OWNERSHIP**—A person having a dog in his possession, and harboring it on his premises, as owners of dogs usually do, will be deemed the owner of the dog, in an action under
   Code, section 1485, for injuries done by it.—*Idem.*

4. **Distraint**—*Notice*—Under Code 1873, section 1454, providing that,
   in case of distraint of trespassing cattle and failure of the
   owner to satisfy the damages, the land owner shall notify the
   township trustees to assess the damages, "such notice to be
   either verbal or in writing," and "the owner of stock, or person
   entitled to the possession thereof, when known, shall also be
   notified of the time and place of the meeting of the trustees to
   assess said damages," a verbal notice of such meeting to the
   owner of the cattle, or person entitled to the possession thereof
   is sufficient.—Healy Bros. v. Geo. V. Jordan, 785.

APPEAL—See PRACT. SUP. CT.

1. **Appeal From Justice**—AMENDMENT—An answer in an action
   commenced in a justice's court to recover the possession of
   leased property from a tenant, may be amended in the district
   court after an appeal from the justice's court, by setting up
   facts showing a payment of the rent, under Code 1873, section
   3591, permitting amendments in the district court in cases
   appealed from the justice's court, where they do not set up any

new demand or counter-claim; and such an amendment may
be filed at any time before trial in district court begins.—Boos
v. Dulin, 331.

2. Affirmance of Justice's Judgment—OPENING UP—The district court should not open a judgment affirming a judgment of a justice of the peace entered on the motion
of appellee, because of failure of the appellant to docket
the case by noon of the second day of the term to which
the same was returnable as required by Iowa district court
rule 4, of the rules of practice in the Iowa district courts,
upon an affidavit of appellant which affirmatively shows neglect to have the case docketed after taking the appeal, or which
merely shows that the matter was left with the appellant's
attorney, who, for some reason, did not attend to it.—Hodowal
v. Yearous, 82.

ARBITRATION—See INSURANCE, [10], [11], [19].

ASSESSORS' BOOKS—See EVIDENCE, [2], [47].

ASSIGNEES.

An assignee for creditors is not entitled to judgment against a
receiver of a bank for the purchase price of property conveyed
by the assignor to the bank for the purpose of making good
an impairment of its capital stock, under an agreement that
he should be paid out of the undivided profits of the land, where
there are no special profits, notwithstanding that a release by
the assignor, of the agreement for payment, is set aside at the
instance of the assignee, as fraudulent.—Brown v. Bradford,
378.

ASSIGNMENT—See INSURANCE, [13], [14], [15], [16].

ASSUMPTION—See DEEDS, [1], [2], [3].

ATTACHMENT—See BILL OF LADING; LEVY, [1].

1. JOINT OBLIGORS—That the surety on a note is financially
responsible, does not affect the right of the holder to an attachment in a suit against the maker, if any of the grounds of
attachment specified by the Code exist as against him; and it
is prejudicial error to admit testimony showing the existence
of such a surety.—Richardson v. Probst, 241.

2. Levy—PROPERTY HELD ON CONDITIONAL SALE—*Notice to Officer*—A levy of an attachment on all the goods, wares, merchandise, furniture and fixtures "belonging to" defendant, and
contained in a certain building, covers an article sold to
defendant on condition that the title is not to pass from the
seller until the purchase price is paid in full, where the contract of sale is not recorded, and neither the officer making the

stockholders, and that if any bank becomes insolvent and its assets are found insufficient to pay its debts and liabilities, the stockholders may be compelled to pay such deficiency in proportion to the amount of stock owned by each, not to exceed the extent of such additional liability.—*Idem.*

CORROBORATION—See CRIM. LAW, [1], [3], [4].

COSTS—See MTGS. [2]; PRACT. SUP. CT. [18].

Estates—The personal representatives of a decedent cannot avoid liability for costs under Code 1873, section 2933, providing that costs shall be recovered by the successful party, upon the ground that the defense to the petition of the successful party was made in good faith and on reasonable grounds —In re Proctor's Estate, 232.

COUNTIES.

Bridges—LIABILITY OF COUNTY—A county chargeable with knowledge of defects in the railing on an approach to a county bridge, is liable for injuries of which the defective railing was the proximate cause.—Faulk v. Iowa County, 442.

COURTS—See ATTY'S FEES, [1]; MUNICIPAL CORP. [4], [5].

COVENANTS.

1. **Release of Mortgage**—A covenant in a mortgage for the partial release of one or more acres from its operation, on the payment at any one time of eight hundred dollars for each acre so released, runs with the land, and inures to the benefit of the grantee of the mortgagor, though the words "heirs and assigns" are not used in the covenant —Gammel v. Goode, 301.

2. SAME—The right to a partial release, by the payment of a stipulated sum "at any one time," is available after default in payment, and the commencement of a foreclosure suit.— *Idem.*

3. PARTIAL RELEASE—A mortgage on platted land stipulated for a partial release of one or more acres on the payment of a specified sum per acre, or of lots "on the same basis" *Held,* that, in determining the proportionate amount to be paid on the release of one of the lots, the streets and alleys in the acre should be taken into consideration, and payment need not be made for the land included in such streets and alley.—*Idem.*

CREDITORS—See MORTGAGES, [1]; PLEADINGS, [4].

CRIMINAL LAW—See CONST. LAW, [5]; EVID. [4]; EXCEPTION, [1], [2]; GRAND JURY; PRACT. [7].

---

and directed his mother-in-law to give to his child, and a bond found in the house of his father-in-law, and not taken from a locked drawer, are admissible as a standard of comparison for the purpose of determining the genuineness of his signature to an alleged confession, notwithstanding an objection that they were taken surreptitiously and that he is thus compelled to give evidence against himself.—*Idem.*

8. DECLARATIONS OF ACCOMPLICE—*Conspiracy*—Declarations of a thief, made before the theft, that he had made arrangements to sell property of plaintiff to defendant, and declarations after the theft that he had sold the property to defendant, are not a part of the *res gestæ* and are not admissible against defendant, if made in his absence, unless a conspiracy between him and the thief is shown.—Hackett & Freeman v. Graves, 296.

9. CONFESSION—Where one makes a confession of murder in the belief that he thus proves his capacity to commit crime and to become an accomplice in future crimes, the confession is voluntary.—State of Iowa v. Van Tassel, 6

10. IDENTIFICATION—*Sufficiency*—The evidence fully identified and accounted for certain organs from the time they were taken from deceased's body until they reached H, a toxicologist in Chicago, except for an hour or so, when they were left sealed in the office of the doctor that removed them from deceased's body, and while they were in transit by express to Chicago. Said doctor, during such hour or so, left them in a commode in his office, the door of which was locked, while he was gone, and no one was in the room. The city marshal assisted the doctor in packing the jars containing the organs, and as soon as they were packed, the marshal took the box and delivered it to the express agent, who held it in his possession, and had it under his immediate supervision, until it was shipped to Chicago, where H received the box in the apparent condition in which it was when shipped, and analyzed the contents of the jars. *Held*, that there was sufficient identification of deceased's organs to justify the admission of H's evidence of his analysis thereof, and its results, and this, though there was some conflict as to the number of jars sent and received.—*Idem.*

11. Fraudulent Banking—A bank which is still receiving deposits, although most of its business has been transferred to another bank, is within Acts Eighteenth General Assembly, chapter 153, making it a felony for any officer of a bank to knowingly receive any deposits when the bank is to his knowledge insolvent.—State of Iowa v. Boomer, 106.

CRIM. LAW Continued

Accomplice—See *post*, [6].

Admissions—See *post*, [5].

1. Adultery—*Evidence*—The woman in a cemetery, i... half an hour, is not adultery; especiall... both parties d... parties who ... Iowa v. W ...

2. Corrob... in a ... ur ...

...e after a stated time, with ...gainst fraudulent banking.— ...nother action tending to show by ...t he was sole owner of a bank are ...a a prosecution for knowingly receiv... in such bank, while it was insolvent.— ...ce—On a trial for fraudulent banking, where ...fendant's bank are in his possession and he ...quired to produce them, witnesses that have ...oyed by defendant and have become familiar ...e books in the course of their employment, may ...ss to their contents.—*Idem.*

...*Evidence*—Such witnesses, being familiar with the ...king business, the bank books, and the value of the ...perty then owned by defendant could state their opinions ...ss to defendant's solvency when the deposit in question was ...ceived —*Idem.*

...PUNISHMENT—Under Acts Eighteenth General Assembly, chapter 153, section 2, making it a felony for an insolvent bank to receive a deposit, a judgment of conviction requiring defendant to be imprisoned in the penitentiary, at hard labor, for the term of five years, is not reversible for being excessive punishment.—*Idem.*

17. Grand Jury—WAIVER—Where it does not appear from the record that a defendant did not know of an irregularity in the drawing of the grand jury which indicted him, until after he pleaded to the indictment, he will be held to have waived the irregularity by his plea of not guilty.—State v. Kouhns, 720.

Harmless Error—See *post*, [29].

Identification—See *ante*, [10].

Impeachment—See *ante*, [6]; *post*, [31].

18. Incest—See *ante*, [4]—*Evidence*—Defendant was charged with incest with his daughter, who testified that he took her by the arm, and threatened to whip her if she did not submit; and she cried; that he threw her on the ground, and had intercourse; and she became pregnant, and was delivered of a child; that she never had intercourse with any other person, that she told defendant of her pregnancy, and he denied the paternity of the child   *Held*, that there was evidence sufficient to support a verdict of guilty.—State v. Kouhns, 730.

19. Included Offenses—*Instructions*—Where an indictment charges murder in the first degree, and there is evidence showing the

Small figures refer to subdivisions of Index. The others to page of report.

VOL. 103 Ia—49

Small figures refer to subdivisions of Index. The others to page of report.

CRIM. LAW Continued

and directed his mother-in-law to give to his child, and a
bond found in the house of his father-in-law, and not taken
from a locked drawer, are admissible as a standard of comparison for the purpose of determining the genuineness of
his signature to an alleged confession, notwithstanding an
objection that they were taken surreptitiously and that he is
thus compelled to give evidence against himself.—*Idem.*

8. DECLARATIONS OF ACCOMPLICE—*Conspiracy*—Declarations of a
thief, made before the theft, that he had made arrangements
to sell property of plaintiff to defendant, and declarations
after the theft that he had sold the property to defendant, are
not a part of the *res gestœ* and are not admissible against
defendant, if made in his absence, unless a conspiracy between
him and the thief is shown.—Hackett & Freeman v. Graves,
296.

9. CONFESSION—Where one makes a confession of murder in the
belief that he thus proves his capacity to commit crime and to
become an accomplice in future crimes, the confession is voluntary.—State of Iowa v. Van Tassel, 6

10. IDENTIFICATION—*Sufficiency*—The evidence fully identified and
accounted for certain organs from the time they were taken
from deceased's body until they reached H, a toxicologist in
Chicago, except for an hour or so, when they were left sealed
in the office of the doctor that removed them from deceased's
body, and while they were in transit by express to Chicago.
Said doctor, during such hour or so, left them in a commode in
his office, the door of which was locked, while he was gone, and
no one was in the room. The city marshal assisted the doctor
in packing the jars containing the organs, and as soon as they
were packed, the marshal took the box and delivered it to the
express agent, who held it in his possession, and had it under
his immediate supervision, until it was shipped to Chicago,
where H received the box in the apparent condition in which
it was when shipped, and analyzed the contents of the jars.
Held, that there was sufficient identification of deceased's
organs to justify the admission of H's evidence of his analysis
thereof, and its results, and this, though there was some conflict as to the number of jars sent and received.—*Idem.*

11. **Fraudulent Banking**—A bank which is still receiving deposits,
although most of its business has been transferred to another
bank, is within Acts Eighteenth General Assembly, chapter
153, making it a felony for any officer of a bank to knowingly
receive any deposits when the bank is to his knowledge
insolvent.—State of Iowa v. Boomer, 106.

experts had been permitted to give their opinions, based in part on the result of such analysis, and their opinions were proper to be considered; that the opinions were based on the assumption that the facts recited in the hypothetical questions were true; that whether or not the conditions so stated were true was for the jury to determine; that they should give careful consideration to all the evidence bearing on all the facts involved in the hypothetical questions, and to the opinions of witnesses founded thereon, and that it was for them to decide whether the death was caused by poisoning *Held*, that the objection that the quoted part of the instructions assumed the existence of certain facts with reference to such analysis was not well taken when all the instructions were considered together. —State of Iowa v. Van Tassel, 6.

25. *Same*— On an issue whether defendant's wife was murdered or committed suicide, the court directed the jury to carefully consider her health, mental traits, and condition prior to her · death, and that such evidence should not be permitted to obscure the "well-proven facts," nor lead them to indulge in fanciful suppositions *Held*, that the instruction was not open to the objection that it clearly intimated that all the state's evidence consisted of well-proven facts, when considered in connection with instructions relating to reasonable doubt and to what the state must prove in order to convict.— *Idem.*

26. *Reasonable Doubt*—An instruction that to authorize a conviction, the minds of the jury must be brought to an abiding conviction beyond a reasonable doubt of the defendant's guilt after a full consideration of the whole case, is not erroneous because it fails to use the wo ds "to a moral certainly," as, "abiding conviction beyond a reasonable doubt," is equivalent to that.— *Idem.*

27. DEGREES —Where the evidence conclusively shows that deceased's death was caused by poison, and there is no evidence that it was negligently administered, so that defendant is either guilty of murder in the first degree or not guilty, it is not error to submit to the jury the first degree, only.— *Idem*

28. DEGREE OF LARCENY— *Reasonable Doubt* — An instruction giving substantially the provision of Code 1873, section 4129, that where there is a reasonable doubt of the degree of defendant's offense, he shall only be convicted of the lower degree, is not required on trial for larceny of hogs, where the uncontradicted evidence shows that defendant, if guilty at all, was guilty of grand larceny.—State of Iowa v. Burton, 28.

judgments, is sufficient to authorize the examination of such clerk and identification by him of papers in a case to which defendant has been a party, tending to show that he was the owner of the bank.—State of Iowa v. Boomer, 106.

87. **Obscene Photographs**—A photographer who took the pictures of two women who exposed themselves when naked before the camera; and of one of them alone, when nude, and delivered the pictures to them, receiving pay therefor, is guilty of selling obscene, lewd, indecent or lascivious photographs, within the meaning of Acts Twenty-first General Assembly, chapter 177, section 1.—State of Iowa v. Doty, 698.

Poisoning—See *ante,* [21], [22], [24], [25], [27], [29], [35].

Rape—See *ante,* [3], [4].

Reasonable Doubt—See *ante,* [15], [30].

88. **Seduction**—*Evidence*—A conviction for the crime of seduction will not be sustained, where, although the defendant paid his attention to the prosecutrix for a time, yet the letters which passed between them contained no reference to an engagement or any improper act, and the associates of the prosecuting witness and her conduct with other men indicate that she was not a chaste woman. See opinion for other facts.—State of Iowa v. Thomas, 748.

89. *Same*—Evidence as to the relation between the prosecutrix in seduction and one other than defendant, after the alleged seduction, which does not tend to explain their relation before that time is inadmissible in behalf of defendant.— State of Iowa v. Abegglan, 51.

Sentence—See *ante,* [16].

Voluntary Testimony—See *ante,* [6], [7], [9].

Waiver—See *ante,* [17].

DAMAGES—See ANIMALS, [1], [2]; INSTRUCTIONS, [2]; MUNICIPAL CORP. [1]; PLEADINGS, [2], [3]; PLEA AND PROOF, [3].

1. **Measure**—The expense to which a tenant was put in procuring water from neighboring farms is not the measure of damages for the landlord's failure to put in a well according to agreement, where water could have been procured at less expense by making a well.—Ladiner v. Balsley, 674.

2. *Same*—Evidence that a lessee was obliged to go to his neighbors, a half mile, or more, distant, for water, and his testimony that it was for a specified amount, is insufficient to support an instruction correctly stating the measure of damages for the breach of the lessor's promise to dig a well to be the difference in rental value.—*Idem.*

Small figures refer to subdivisions of Index. The others to page of report.

EQUITY JURISDICTION.

Plaintiff, who had been twice convicted and fined for violating an ordinance requiring grain to be weighed on the city scales, and had appealed, brought suit, during pendency of the appeals, to restrain the city from enforcing the ordinance, and from further prosecuting plaintiff or any of his customers thereunder, on the ground that the ordinance was void; alleging that plaintiff's corncribs were one-half mile from the city scales, that all the eligible locations near the scales were occupied by other dealers, that sellers of corn refused to sell to plaintiff unless the corn could be weighed near his cribs, and that the granting of the relief demanded would avoid a multiplicity of suits. *Held,* that plaintiff could avoid a multiplicity of suits by obeying the ordinance, and that, though he must suffer some loss of business pending his appeals, or pay enough to secure the corn he desires, the loss would not be so great as to warrant the interference of equity.—Ewing v. City of Webster City, 226.

ESTATES—See Costs; Pract. ¹¹; Sales, ¹.

1. **Descent and Distribution—Husband and Wife**—The heirs of a widow may have her distributive share of the estate of her deceased husband set off to them in personalty where she made no such election to take under her husband's will as to divest her of such share, as, upon her husband's death, it vested in her immediately, subject to her right of election to take under the will — In re Proctor's Estate, 232.

2. **Dower**—The heirs of a widow whose dower was not assigned during her lifetime may have it set off to them, in the absence of an election on her part to take under her husband's will in lieu of dower.—*Idem.*

3. **Election**—A widow is not necessarily put to her election between dower which in Iowa is an estate in fee simple, and a devise in her husband's will, of a life estate in all his real property, as such a devise is not inconsistent with the right of dower.—*Idem.*

4. **Same**—A widow will not be held to have elected to take under her husband's will in lieu of dower, by her asking for the probate of the will which nominates her as executor, and accepting her appointment as such and selling real property which under the will she had power to dispose of if necessary for her support, and keeping possession of the personal estate which the will bequeathed to her for life, where all her acts are referable to her position as an executor, and there is

Small figures refer to subdivisions of Index. The others to page of report

purchase price for which the buyer agrees to reimburse said agent, which he never did, though the seller actually received such payment. It is the same as though the seller had made partial payment to himself.—*Idem*.

44. *Possession*—Evidence that, after an oral contract for the sale of land, the vendee went to the premises with his son, to whom he rented the place, picked up some lumber and drove a few nails, and that the vendor, when told by the vendee that he had rented the premises, said it was all right, and that neither the vendee nor his son was ever afterwards on the place, was insufficient to show that such a vendee had "taken and held possession * * * under and by virtue of the contract," within Code 1873, section 3665, which in such case excepts the contract from the statute of frauds.— *Idem*.

45. *Same*—To bring an oral contract to convey land within Code 1873, section 3665, providing that the prohibition by section 3664, sub-division 4, of parol evidence to establish a contract creating an interest in land, shall not apply where the vendee with the actual or implied consent of the vendor has taken and holds possession of the land "under and by virtue of the contract" it is indispensible that the possession shall have been taken and held under and by virtue of the contract.—*Idem*.

46. WAIVER BY FAILURE TO OBJECT TO EVIDENCE—Defendant in an action for breach of an oral contract to convey land does not waive his plea of the statute of frauds by failing to object to the parol evidence when offered, where the plaintiff pleads facts which if established would show the contract to be valid because embraced within some of the exceptions stated in the statute; as plaintiff's order of proof was discretionary with him, defendant could not tell until it was closed whether plaintiff would not prove himself within some of said exceptions.—*Idem*.

47. ¶Tax Books—Tax books are inadmissible in evidence to show that a specified person paid the taxes, where the testimony of the witness who produced the books shows that they furnish no guide as to who, in fact, paid the taxes.—Allbright v. Hannah, 98.

Title—See *ante*, ³⁶.

48. Volunteer Statements—In a proceeding by a daughter to establish a claim for work and labor against her father's estate, the statement, "But, then, Esther (claimant) didn't work at home just as a hired girl," volunteered by a witness for the administrator, during her examination in chief, was simply a conclusion of such witness, and therefore inadmissible.—Riddler v. Riddler, 470.

49. SAME—Where such witness, in answer to a question on cross-examination respecting the manner in which she would treat a girl who was working for her, replied, "Why, Esther was not considered a hired girl at my father's house; she was considered as one of the children," such answer was incompetent and not responsive.—*Idem.*

50. SAME—The answer of a witness for the administrator in proceedings by a daughter of the intestate to establish a claim for services, in reply to a question as to the worth of such services in the neighborhood, that she did not know because people in that neighborhood took care of their parents with the assistance of the neighbors, and that she never heard of a charge being made in such a sense, except in the evidence of that trial, is irresponsive, and highly prejudicial, and should be stricken out, on motion.—*Idem.*

Waiver—See *ante,* ²⁵, ⁴⁶.
Warranty—See *ante,* ⁶, ⁷.
Witness—See *ante,* ⁹.

51. Writings—See *ante,* ¹⁴—Where a paper that has written on it the name of a particular person, is not itself admitted in evidence, it cannot properly be used as the basis of a comparison of handwriting, for the purpose of showing whether a certain signature is such person's.—State of Iowa v. Van Tassel, 6.

EXCEPTIONS.

1. CRIMINAL LAW—A statement of the court, made in its decision overruling a motion for a new trial, may be excepted to, because of Code 1873, section 4480, reserving the right to except to a decision or action of the court, whether made "before or after the trial of the indictment or on such trial."—State of Iowa v. Taylor, 22.

2. SAME—*Bill of Exceptions*—The statement of the trial court in overruling a motion for a new trial, indicating doubts as to defendant's guilt, is a matter of exception, and affects a "material or substantial right" of defendant within Code 1873, section 4480; and a bill of exceptions containing such statement may, if time to settle the bill has been extended beyond the term, be settled by the signature of bystanders, where the judge refuses to sign the bill. under section 4480, providing that if the judge refuses to sign the bill it may be signed by two or more attorneys or officers of the court or disinterested bystanders. *St. John v. Wallace*, 25 Iowa, 21, *distinguished —Idem.*

EXECUTION.

1. **Abandonment**—The issuance of a void execution does not operate as an abandonment of a prior execution.—Dunham v. Bentley, 186.

2. **Return**—The return of an execution does not, under Code, 1873, section 3052, affect garnishment proceedings commenced after the issuance of the execution.—*Idem.*

8. **Revivor**—An execution issued in the name of a deceased plaintiff is absolutely void where there is no indorsement thereon of the name of his representatives, as required by Code 1873, section 3130.—*Idem.*

EXECUTION SALE.

Rights of Purchaser—A purchaser at execution sale takes subject to the rights of the parties as they shall be adjudicated in the action then pending, and by virtue of which the property is sold.—Manning v. Ferguson, 561.

EXECUTORS—See PRACT. SUP. CT. 20, 24.

EXEMPTIONS—See LEVY, 1, 3, 4.

EXPERTS—See CRIM. LAW, 16; EVID. 14.

FALSE REPRESENTATIONS—See FRAUD, 2, 3, 4, 5, 6, 7, 8, 9.

FAMILY NECESSARIES—See HUSB. AND WIFE, 2.

FELLOW SERVANTS—See RAILWAYS, 21.

FORCIBLE ENTRY—See ACTIONS.

FORECLOSURE—See MORTGAGES, 2; REDEMPTION, 1.

FORFEITURE—See COVENANTS, 2.

FORMER ADJUDICATION—See ADJUDICATION.

FRAUD—See ATTORNEYS FEES, 2; ESTOPPEL, 2; EVID. 6, 7, 25; MORTGAGES, 2.

1. **Cancellation of Deed**—*Evidence*—A decree setting aside a deed is sustained by evidence that the grantor and grantee were brothers; that the grantor was seventy years old, and mentally and physically weak; that he was financially embarrassed, had been sued for slander, reposed special confidence in the grantee, who was several years his junior, and of good business capacity, and acted on the grantee's advice, without consideration for the deed,—the grantee himself admitting that when he took the deed he knew that the grantor was mentally incapable of protecting his own interests.--Tomlinson v. Tomlinson, 740.

2. **False Representations**—DEED IN BLANK--*Deceit*—Defendant made a deed. At the request of the grantee he erased the

Small figures refer to subdivisions of Index. The others to page of report.

VOL. 103 Ia— 50

money paid for stock, is an expression of an opinion, and the fact that the corporation became insolvent and ceased to do business six months later, does not invalidate a note given in payment for stock.—Swan v. Mathre, 261.

9. SAME—In an action on a note given in payment for stock, bought by a purchaser before maturity, the defense was that the note was void for want of consideration, and for fraud in its inception, and that plaintiff had knowledge of its invalidity when he purchased it. *Held,* evidence as to the insolvency of the corporation, as to plaintiff's knowledge of the insolvency, as to the sum plaintiff had paid for his own stock in the corporation, and as to why he did not sue the indorser of the note, is irrelevant, and inadmissible.—*Idem.*

FRAUDULENT BANKING—See CRIM. LAW, [11], [12], [13], [14], [15], [16], [22], [24].

FRAUDULENT CONVEYANCE—See BANKS, [2]; HUSBAND AND WIFE, [1].

1. Action to Set Aside—JOINDER—Several judgment creditors may join in an action to set aside a fraudulent conveyance.—Gamet & Ogden v. Simmons, 163.

2. Badges—That a transaction which was in fact a mortgage was put in the form of a conveyance absolute on its face, while a badge of fraud as to creditors of the mortgagor, is not conclusive as to fraud.—Brown v. Bradford, 378.

3. DEED AS MORTGAGE—A conveyance absolute on its face is not fraudulent in law because of a secret trust rendering it a mortgage, where no fraud was intended, and none of the grantor's creditors were in fact misled.—*Idem.*

4. Consideration—A transfer of land to one's stepdaughter, based on a promise which is not binding on the promisor, is voluntary and fraudulent as to creditors, where he has no other property left with which to pay debts.—Gamet & Ogden v. Simmons, 163.

5. *Rule Applied*—The promise by a stepfather, to deed land to his stepdaughter, as soon as she was married, if before that time she will travel with and take care of him, is not binding upon him where she is a minor, and he is standing in *loco parentis.*—*Idem.*

6. Evidence—DISCONNECTED TRANSFERS—A note given by a husband to his wife for a good and sufficient consideration, is not void as to the husband's creditors because another note was given by him to her without consideration, in an entirely distinct transaction.—Muir v. Miller, 127.

7. HUSBAND AND WIFE—The defendant, being indebted to his wife for various loans made to him, evidenced by his two

intent of the grantor to hinder or delay his creditors, the conveyance is fraudulent.—Gamet & Ogden v. Simmons, 163.

14. **Recording**—A conveyance absolute on its face is not fraudulent in law because of a secret trust, where such trust does not enter into the consideration for the deed. The mere non-recording of deeds does not render them fraudulent in law as to creditors, where no fraud was intended, and no one was misled.—Brown v. Bradford, 878.

GAMBLING CONTRACT.

1. **Evidence**—Defendant telegraphed plaintiff: "Buy five thousand Sept. oats below thirty-one. Draw on me for margins," and by a subsequent telegram directed plaintiff to "sell September, and buy May " Defendant failed to put up margins and the May oats were sold at a loss. Plaintiff paid the loss, and sued to recover the same, but failed to disclose from whom he purchased, or to produce any memorandum of the transactions; while defendant denied that the purchases were actually made, and testified that in ordering such purchases he did not intend any delivery of the grain to him. *Held*, that a verdict for defendant was warranted.—Counselman & Co. v. Reichart, 430.

2. SAME—To render a contract in grain futures void as a mere speculation on the chances of rise and fall of the market, with no intention to deliver the grain, both parties thereto must have contemplated that no delivery would be made; and the contract between commission merchants and a customer is not void on that ground, although the customer intended, only, to speculate on margins without a delivery of the grain, if the commission merchants intended an actual delivery.—*Idem*.

3. PRESUMPTIONS—The jury are warranted in drawing an inference unfavorable to the existence of the intention on the part of a commission merchant in purchasing "futures" grain for a customer, that there should be an actual delivery, from his failure to produce the paper and documents showing a purchase by him on the market, in response to the demand of the other party.—*Idem*.

4. INTENT—A party to a contract in grain futures may attack it on the ground that it is a mere gambling contract and may testify as to his intention with reference to the delivery of the grain when he made the purchase.—*Idem*.

GRAND JURY— See CRIM. LAW, [17], [20].

Change in Statute—A grand jury drawn prior to July 1, 1895, for that year, pursuant to the laws then in force, is competent to return an indictment subsequent thereto, though acts April 26, 1894, which took effect July 1, 1895, changed the law concerning the drawing of grand juries.—State of Iowa v. Wiltsey, 54.

GUARANTY—See DEFAULT, [1]; EVID. [18].

HARMLESS ERROR—See EVID. [16], [16], [17], [18], [19]; INSTRUCTIONS, [5], [6], [7], [8]; PRACT. [18].

HEIRS—See ESTATES, [1], [2]; PRACT. [11].

HIGHWAYS—See MUNICIPAL CORP. [1]; RAILROADS, [10], [12].

HOMESTEADS—See CONTRACTS, [2]; FRAUD. CONV. [6].

1. **Abandonment**—A wife will be deemed to have abandoned her homestead in land held by her husband, under a contract of purchase reserving the title to the vendor, where her husband, with her knowledge and apparent acquiescence, surrendered the contract to the vendor, who in pursuance of the husband's request, conveyed the land to a purchaser from him, and she afterwards remained on the land with him under a lease from the grantee, apparently recognizing a title unincumbered by the homestead, in the latter.—Bradshaw v. Remmick, 90 Iowa, 409, *followed.*—Anderson v. Cosman, 266.

2. **Leased Lands**—A homestead right under the Iowa statute may exist in lands leased, or held under a contract of purchase, the legal title remaining in the vendor.—*Idem.*

8. **Debt of Decedent**—A homestead is not subject to the debts of the deceased owner, unless they were incurred prior to the acquisition of the homestead.—In re Gardner's Estate, 738.

4. **Judgments**—PARTIES—*Issues*—In an action brought by the children of a judgment debtor to quiet their title to premises sold under an execution issued on the judgment, on the ground that the debtor held homestead rights in the property sold, the court may, upon a finding that the debtor held an undivided one-third interest in the land, which was subject to the judgment, enter a decree against such debtor, although she was in default as to the plaintiff's petition and was not served with notice of the defendant's cross-bill, to which she was made a party.—Peebles v. Bunting, 489.

5. **Widow**—Where a widow lived on her husband's farm for six months after his death, then left it, and went to another place where she resided about nine years, then returned to the farm,

where she lived for seven years, when she again left, and resided in another place for three or four years, and made an arrangement with her children whereby she received the rent for the whole of the farm, she cannot claim a homestead right in the farm.—*Idem.*

6. SAME—A widow can elect to take homestead rights in the land in lieu of dower under Code 1873, sections 2007, 2008, only, when the premises, or some part of them, were occupied by the husband as a homestead prior to his death so as to make it his homestead at the time of his death.—*Idem.*

7. *Presumptions*—In the absence of evidence showing the election of the widow to take a homestead in lieu of dower, the presumption is that she took her primary right, which under the provisions of Code 1873, section 2440, is a one-third interest in all of her husband's real estate.—*Idem.*

8. JUDGMENT LIEN—When a widow does not elect to take her homestead right in her husband's land, in lieu of dower, and judgments are obtained against her, they attach immediately to her one-third interest in his real estate.—*Idem.*

HUSBAND AND WIFE—See ALIMONY, ²; ESTATES, ¹; FRAUD. CONV. ⁶, ⁷, ⁹, ¹²; HOMESTEADS, ¹; INS. ¹⁶; PRIN. AND AGENT, ⁴; TRUSTS, ².

1. Conversion—CREDITORS—While money given by a wife to her husband, without promise of repayment, will not enable her to base a claim against his creditors, this rule has no application to cases where her rights against the husband might be enforced by suit under section 2204, Code 1873, and hence a settlement in which the wife takes an assignment of a note on account of her property which her husband has *converted*, is valid against his creditors.—Dunham v. Bentley, 136.

2. Family Expenses—A diamond shirt stud procured for personal use, and actually used and worn by a husband, is a family expense within the meaning of Code, section 2214, charging family expenses upon the property of both husband and wife, or either of them.—Neasham v. McNair, 695.

IMPEACHMENT—See CRIM. LAW, ³¹; EVID. ²⁰, ²¹, ²²; VERDICT, ¹.

INCEST—See CRIM. LAW, ⁴, ¹⁸.

INCLUDED OFFENSES—See CRIM. LAW, ¹⁹, ²⁷, ²⁸.

INCUMBRANCES—See INS. ²⁵, ³⁰.

INDICTMENT—See CRIM. LAW, ¹², ²¹, ²², ²³; GRAND JURY.

INDORSER—See NEGOT. INST. ³, ⁴, ⁵, ⁶; PRACT. SUP. CT. ⁷.

INJUNCTIONS.

1. Penal Ordinances—Proceedings to enforce a penal ordinance enacted by authority of the legislature are criminal, within

the rule that the validity of a criminal statute will not be tested, nor its enforcement enjoined by a court of equity, unless the party seeking such relief will otherwise sustain irreparable injury for which he has no plain, speedy, and adequate remedy at law.—Ewing v. City of Webster City, 226.

2. **Water**—The discharge of sewage from a manufactory into a running stream will not be enjoined on the complaint of a lower riparian owner that it emits disagreeable odors, where the causes of offense for which the defendant was responsible were almost wholly removed before the action was commenced, and the use which it is making of the river is a proper one, in view of the business which it carries on and the conditions which exist in the locality.—Bennett v. National Starch Mfg. Co., 207.

INNKEEPER'S LIEN.

1. The lien given by Acts Eighteenth General Assembly, chapter 181, section 2, to hotel keepers, on all property "belonging to or under control of their guests, which may be in such hotel," and so forth, attaches to sample goods carried by a traveling salesman, though the hotel keeper knew, when he received the salesman as a guest, that the goods belonged to his employer. —Brown Shoe Co. v. Hunt, 586.

2. **Constitutional Law** — Said act is not unconstitutional as depriving the owner of his property without due process of law, since it makes no provision as to how the lien shall be enforced, but simply provides for the lien and for possession under it.—*Idem*.

INSANITY—See EVID. ²⁴.

INSOLVENCY—See ADJUDICATION; CORPORATIONS, ¹, ⁹, ¹³, ¹⁴.

INSTRUCTIONS—See CRIM. LAW, ², ⁵, ¹⁹, ²⁴, ²⁶, ⁹, ¹⁷, ²⁸, ²⁹, ³⁰, ⁵¹, ²²; MALICIOUS PROS. ⁷; NEGLIGENCE, ⁹.

1. Where the court charged that plaintiff and defendant possessed equal rights to the highway when they met, and that whether either was negligent should be determined by all the facts of the case, and did not charge that defendant was not under obligation to carry a light, the rights and obligations of plaintiff were fairly presented, and it was not error to refuse to charge that "plaintiff was not obliged to carry a lamp or bell any more than was defendant."—Cook v. Fogarty, 500.

2. **Applicability** — Testimony by a mother as to the value of her time, and as to the amount of time given by her to her

knew, when the application was made, that the insured was actually arranging for other insurance and had definitely fixed its amount, which by the agent's mistake was understated in the application, and such right is not dependent upon the authority of the agent to contract with reference to insurance, as the company is estopped to avail itself of the agent's mistake.—*Idem.*

85. PLEADING—*Prayer*—A prayer in a petition in an action in equity on a policy of insurance, that the policy be so reformed as to permit concurrent insurance of a specified amount and for such other and further relief as plaintiff may be or show himself entitled to, is broad enough to include relief from a provision of the policy rendering it void if the insured "now" has or shall "hereafter" procure any other insurance unless consent in writing is indorsed hereon.—*Idem.*

86. VENUE OF SUIT AGAINST—An incidental prayer for reformation of an insurance policy in a petition to recover the indemnity therein provided, does not take the case out of McClain's Code, section 3789, providing that an insurance company may be sued in the county in which it keeps its principal place of business, or in the county where the contract of insurance was made, or in which the loss occurred, even if the section is limited to actions which are primarily upon the contract of insurance and would not apply to an action brought solely to reform the policy.—Benesh v. Mill Owners Mut. F. Ins. Co., 465.

87. Reorganization—LIABILITY—In a suit upon an insurance policy it appeared that it was issued by a company bearing the same name as defendant, which subsequently re-incorporated in order to remedy certain defects in its original articles, retaining the same officers and the assets of the original company; that the holders of such policy were treated as members, and paid dues and assessments to such reorganized company as to its predecessor; and that it was determined by resolution that the old policies should be continued in force until new ones were issued at the election of the policy holders. *Held,* that defendant was responsible to the same extent as if it had issued such policy.—*Idem.*

88. Special Interrogatories—In an action on a life policy, a refusal to submit a special finding, "Do you find that the deceased committed suicide?" was proper, where the defense was suicide, as such finding was directly involved in the general verdict.—Ingbram v. National Union, 395.

Small figures refer to subdivisions of Index. The others to page of report.

VOL. 103 Ia—51

45. *Same*—The fact that a benefit society, whose laws provided that non payment of an assessment by a particular date should operate as a forfeiture of a member's rights, subject to reinstatement on payment of arrearages within four months thereafter, had frequently received assessments from a member after they became due, did not waive a subsequent suspension for non-payment of an assessment when due.—Rice v. Grand Lodge A. O. U. W., 644.

46. *Same*—That a member of a mutual benefit society had at times, as a matter of convenience to him, been allowed to pay his assessments before maturity, does not tend to show a license for, or even acquiescence in, non-payment of other assessments as they became due.—*Idem.*

INTERROGATORIES—See PRACT. [13], [14], [15], [16].

INTOXICATING LIQUORS.—See CRIM. LAW, [33].

1. **Abatement of Nuisance**—A decree ordering that a building be closed, and that the owner shall pay the costs and attorney fees incurred in proceedings to enjoin the continuance of a liquor nuisance in such building, is unauthorized where the sale of intoxicating liquors was made by a trespasser without the owner's knowledge or consent, and the sale of the liquor and the occupancy of the trespasser had ceased before the petition was filed.—Merryfield v. Smith, 167.

2. **Contracts**—PUBLIC POLICY—*Sureties*—At a time when selling liquor in original packages was legal, a non-resident appointed an agent to so sell. He sold by the glass in violation of his contract of appointment, and, the liquors of his principal being thereupon seized, he became the surety of the principal on a replevin bond in an action to reclaim the liquors. He was ultimately compelled to make payment on account of said bond. *Held*, he is not estopped to recover such payment.—Green v. Schoenhofen Brew. Co., 252.

8. **Mulct Law**—CONSENT OF VOTERS—Section 17, chapter 62, Acts of the Twenty-fifth General Assembly, provides, among other things, that the payment of a specified tax, and filing with the county auditor of a written consent to the sale of liquor, signed by a majority of the voters of a city, shall, upon the "following conditions," be a bar to proceedings under the statute prohibiting such sale. One of the succeeding conditions is the filing with the auditor of a copy of a resolution of consent of the city council. *Held*, that the action of the city council in passing such a resolution is not a determination of the sufficiency of the statement of consent signed by the voters, which will protect it from collateral attack in a suit to enjoin a liquor nuisance.—State of Iowa v. Pressman, 449.

4.   Evidence—In an action involving the sufficiency of such statement of consent, the best evidence of who were legal
   · voters of the city at the last election is the poll books and registration lists of that election, although they are not records in such sense, as that they may not be attacked for fraud.—*Idem.*

INTOXICATION—See CRIM. LAW, ³⁰, ³⁴.

JOINDER—See FRAUD. CONV. ¹.

JOINDER OF CAUSES—See ACTIONS.

JOINT OBLIGORS—See ATTACH. ¹.

JUDGMENTS—See MECHANICS LIENS, ²; PRACT. ⁹.

1.   Lien—When a widow does not elect to take her homestead right in her husband's land, in lieu of dower, and judgments are obtained against her, they attach immediately to her one-third interest in his real estate.—Peebles v. Bunting, 489.

2.   Parties--ISSUES—In an action brought by the children of a judgment debtor to quiet their title to premises sold under an execution issued on the judgment, on the ground that the debtor held homestead rights in the property sold, the court may, upon a finding that the debtor held an undivided one-third interest in the land, which was subject to the judgment, enter a decree against such debtor, although she was in default as to the plaintiff's petition, and was not served with notice of the defendant's cross-bill, to which she was made a party.—*Idem.*

3.   Vacation—MOTION AND PETITION—Under Code 1873, section 3154, authorizing the vacation or modification of a judgment for irregularity or for fraud practiced by the successful party in obtaining it, a claim of irregularity in obtaining the judgment cannot be considered, unless made by motion on the second day of the next succeeding term, as provided by the Code, though a petition to vacate for want of jurisdiction or for fraud of the successful party may be considered if filed within one year after such judgment was rendered.—Priestman v. Priestman, 320.

JUDGMENT BY CONFESSION--See PRINCIPAL AND AGENT,¹.

1.   Statement—A statement of the facts under the statutes for confession of judgment upon a certificate of deposit against a bank and guarantors is sufficiently specific where it sets forth a copy of the certificate which purports to be issued to the payee for a deposit made by him of a specified amount on a specified date and to be payable to him in current funds on

---

Small figures refer to subdivisions of Index. The others to page of report.

return of the certificate four months after date, and a guaranty and waiver of protest signed by two of the defendants and a transfer from the payee to the plaintiff, and states that there is "now" justly due the plaintiff on the certificate a specified sum.—Briggs v. Yetzer, 342.

2. VERIFICATION—A statement for confession of judgment signed by defendants, followed by the jurat of a notary public, in the usual form, stating that it was subscribed and sworn to, without stating by whom, is verified by defendants as required by Code 1873, section 2896.—*Idem*.

JURISDICTION.

1. Notice by Publication—Under Code 1873, section 2618, providing that "service may be made by publication when an affidavit is filed that personal service cannot be made on the defendant within the state, where the action is for a divorce, if the defendant is a non-resident of the state, or his residence is unknown" and section 2620, that, "when the foregoing provisions has been complied with, the defendant, so notified, shall be required to appear as though personally served within the county in which the petition is filed on the day of the last publication,"—there was no service where such affidavit was not filed until after three publications of the notice; as the filing of such affidavit is a condition precedent to such publication.—Priestman v. Priestman, 320.

2. IDEM SONANS—Where service, in an action for divorce against a non-resident, is by publication, and defendant makes default, and does not appear, the court cannot assume that the name "Keesel" in the published summons should be understood as "Keisel," defendant's real name, on the principle of *idem sonans;* and a decree based on such a service is void, and is subject to collateral attack.—Hubner v. Reickhoff, 368.

8. *Collateral Attack*—An adjudication that such prerequisite had been complied with, is subject to attack in a proceeding to vacate such judgment.—Priestman v. Priestman, 320.

JURORS.

1. Challenge—COMPETENCY—*Waiver*—Under Code 1873, sections 4405, 4407, 4408, providing, among other things, that a want of any of the qualifications prescribed by statute to render a person a competent juror, shall be ground for a challenge for cause, and that a juror challenged, and other witnesses, may be examined, to prove or disprove the challenge, the right to challenge for cause is discretionary, and may be waived; and, where a juror in a criminal case could not read or write the English language, defendant, by failing to examine said juror, will be taken to have waived the objection, notwithstanding that Laws Twenty-sixth General Assembly, chapter 61, section 1, provides, as a qualification for a competent juror, that he must be able to read and write the English language.—*State v. Groome*, 10 Iowa, 806, *overruled*.—State of Iowa v. Pickett, 715.

2. SELECTION—Code 1873, section 241 (Laws 1886, page 44), provides that not more than one grand juror shall be drawn from a township; and the law also provides that the clerk shall give the sheriff his receipt within three days after the grand jury is drawn. The record shows that the sheriff received the notices on November 30, and made his return December 6. *Held*, that a juror who changed the township of his residence on November 20, but was summoned as a resident of the town from which he removed,—there being another juror summoned from the town to which he removed,—was an illegal juror.—State of Iowa v. Kouhns, 720.

JURY PANEL.

1. Summons—When a case was called for trial, ten men were drawn from the regular panel, and, no others being present, plaintiff asked that the jury be completed by calling talesmen, but the court continued the cause until the next day, when the jury was completed from the regular panel. *Held*, that there was no violation of law, or abuse of discretion, in what was done.—Cook v. Fogarty, 500.

2. *Constitutional Law*—Acts Twenty-fifth General Assembly, chapter 70, section 4, providing that in preparing the lists and ballots containing the names of persons who are to constitute the jury list, "the name of each alternate juror on the list from cities and towns where the courts are held shall be deposited in a box to be known as the talesmen box and not the first box," is held not shown to be unconstitutional. —*Idem*.

JURY QUESTION—See CRIM. LAW, 20, 34; FRAUD. 4; INSTRUCTIONS, 10; MUNICIPAL CORP. 5, 10, 11; NEGLIGENCE, 6, 7, 8; RAILROADS, 2, 4, 22, 24, 26.

JUSTICE OF THE PEACE—See APPEAL, 2.

LANDLORD AND TENANT—See DAMAGES, 1, 2; PLEADING, 4; PRACT. SUP. CT. 19.

1. Lien—BLENDING OF ITEMS—Where a landlord accepts two notes amounting to two hundred and thirty dollars, and twenty dollars of the consideration therefor is not for rent, he

has no right to a landlord's attachment.—Ladner v. Balsley, 674.

2. WAIVER—A lien of a landlord for rent under the Iowa statute is not waived by the reservation in the lease of a lien on all the personal property of the lessee on the premises, whether exempt from execution and attachment or not, and the seizure of the exempt property thereunder.—*Idem.*

LARCENY—See CRIM. LAW, [28].

LAW OF CASE—See CRIM. LAW, [34].

LEASE—See EVID. [5]; HOMESTEADS, [2]; INS. [20].

LEVY.

1. Abandonment—The abandonment of personal property by the receiver of a corporation by failing to inventory and appraise it, and to include it in the sale of the property of the corporation, does not constitute an abandonment of a levy legally made by him as marshal prior to his appointment as receiver, in an attachment issued at the instance of a creditor who subsequently became a purchaser at the receiver's sale.—Nat'l Cash Reg. Co. v. Broeksmit, 271.

2. Exempt Property—As the judgment debtor need not give such notice when he claims such property as exempt, no notice need be given by one who purchases from him after the levy, since he takes it with all the rights of the seller.—Whitney v. Gammon, 363.

8. NOTICE TO SHERIFF—After exempt property had been seized on execution, the judgment debtor sold it to plaintiff. To induce the sheriff to sell the property, the judgment creditor executed bond to indemnify the sheriff and any claimant. Code 1873, section 3055, provides that if, on levy of execution, the officer receives notice that the property is claimed by a third person, he may release the levy, unless bond is given, but that he shall be protected from liability until he receives such notice. *Held*, that plaintiff's right to sue on the bond was unaffected by failure to give the sheriff notice of his claim; the object of the notice being merely to enable the officer to protect himself by demanding indemnity which, here, he had taken without such notice.—*Idem.*

4. PUBLIC POLICY—A bond given to indemnify a sheriff against damages from the seizure and sale of personal property under an execution, and to secure to any claimant of the property any damages he may sustain by reason of such seizure and sale, is not void, although it turns out that the property was exempt and not subject to levy, where there was a controversy between the parties at the time the bond was given, as to the character of the property.--*Idem*.

LIBEL.

To publish of one that he has for several years owed for medical services; that his attention has been repeatedly called thereto to no purpose; that finally, being sued therefor, he, having no other defense, has cowardly slunk behind that of the statute of limitations; and that such a course is not in accordance with the writer's idea of strict integrity,—is not actionable, within Code 1873, section 4097, defining libel as malicious defamation of a person by writing tending to expose him to public hatred, contempt or ridicule, or to deprive him of the benefits of public confidence and social intercourse.— Hollenbeck v. Hall, 214.

LICENSE—See RAILROADS, [14], [15], [16], [17], [18].

LIENS—See HOMESTEADS, [8]; INNKEEPER'S LIEN, [1]; LANDLORD AND TENANT, [1], [2].

LIMITATION OF ACTIONS.

1. **Commencement of Suit**—*Action to Redeem*—Code 1873, section 2582, which is found in the general chapter on the limitation of actions, and provides that delivery of the original notice to the sheriff of the proper county, to be served immediately, "is a commencement of the action," is applicable to an action to redeem from a tax sale and to quiet title, though there is a special limitation for such action not found in the general chapter of limitations.—Smith v. Callanan, 218.

2. **Contract**—*Insurance*—A provision in a fire policy that no suit thereon shall be sustainable, unless commenced within six months after the fire, is valid.—Wilhelmi v. Des Moines Ins. Co., 532.

3. **Indemnity Bond**—While an action against the sheriff for wrongful levy must be brought within three years, an action seeking to recover damages on account of such levy may be brought against those who made a bond to indemnify the sheriff for making it, within ten years after the execution of such bond. —Whitney v. Gammon, 863.

4. **Open Account**—Settling the amount due upon an open running account and giving a note for such amount interrupts the continuity of the account for the purposes of the rule that the statute of limitations does not commence to run against an open running account until the last item is furnished.—Hoag & Griffith v. Hay, 291.

5. *Same*—The doctrine that the statute of limitation does not commence to run against an open running account until the last item is furnished does not apply to a cause of action for lumber, furnished under separate contracts.—*Idem*.

6. Policy of Insurance—A policy of insurance provided that no action thereon should be maintained unless commenced within six months after the fire. *Held*, that the limitation did not begin to run until sixty days after notice of proof of loss were furnished the company, which was the time of payment fixed by the policy.—Read & Traversy v. State Ins. Co., 807.

7. Successive Suit—Code 1873, section 2537, providing that if plaintiff fails in an action, for any cause except negligence in its prosecution, and a new suit be brought within six months thereafter, the new suit shall, for the purposes herein contemplated, "be deemed a continuation of the first," applies only to statutory limitations, and not to those created by contract.—Wilhelmi v. Des Moines Ins. Co., 532.

8. SAME—An action on a policy providing that no suit on it should lie unless commenced within six months after the fire, was defeated because it was commenced within ninety days after notice of loss, contrary to Acts Eighteenth General Assembly, chapter 211, section 3. *Held*, that plaintiff was not entitled to maintain the second action, not commenced within six months after the fire, because defendant did not set up the defense of prematurity in the first action until the six months limitation had expired. The insurer owed the insured no duty to disclose such defense.—*Idem*.

9. *Same*—Nor was he entitled to maintain the second action because the first suit was not in fact premature, because of the existence of facts which he failed to show in his first action.—*Idem*.

MALICIOUS PROSECUTION.

1. Evidence—Evidence showing that the prosecution on which an action for malicious prosecution is based has been ended is admissible, where the answer denies that it has been ended.—Noble v. White, 852.

2. ADVICE OF COUNSEL—An attorney who has testified as to the advice he gave defendant as to the bringing of prosecution cannot be asked, on cross-examination, what his advice would have been on a state of facts which was not disclosed to him by defendant.—*Idem*.

MALICIOUS PROSECUTION Continued

8. RELEVANCY—Evidence that it was a damage to a place to have
sod plowed up is inadmissible in an action by a tenant against
his landlord for malicious prosecution based on charges made
by the latter against the former for wilful trespass in plowing land, where the plaintiff's guilt or innocence of the criminal charges depended upon whether or not he had authority
under the lease to plow the grass land.—*Idem.*

4. SAME—The testimony of defendant in an action for malicious
prosecution based on charges of wilful trespasses upon his
land, that some of the best men said that the plaintiff was
damaging his property to the amount of five hundred dollars, is inadmissible even if defendant has a right to show
what rumors as to the destruction of his property had come
to his knowledge, before filing the information.—*Idem.*

5. *Reputation of Plaintiff*—Evidence as to the reputation of
plaintiff in an action for malicious prosecution for being
quarrelsome and a bully is inadmissible, where the plaintiff's guilt or innocence of the criminal charges made
against him depends upon whether or not he had authority
under a lease from the latter to plow the latter's grass
land.—*Idem.*

6. Malice—Bringing a criminal prosecution for wilful trespass on
land, knowing that the only remedy is a civil action for the
possession of the land, shows malice, even if the person instituting the prosecution is entitled to the possession of the land.
—*Idem.*

7. Instructions—An instruction in an action for malicious prosecution, that the fact that the grand jury ignored the information,
and that the defendant was acquitted before a justice of the
peace, is no evidence of want of probable cause, but the testimony on that point is only admitted to show that the prosecution has ended, is as favorable to defendant as a requested
instruction, that the ignoring of the indictment by the grand
jury cannot be considered in evidence to show absence of probable cause or as showing malice on his part.—*Idem.*

MANSLAUGHTER—See CRIM. LAW, [22], [24].
MASTER AND SERVANT—See RAILROADS, [5], [6], [22].
MAYORS—See MUNICIPAL CORP. [1], [3], [4].

MECHANIC'S LIEN.

1. Contract for Owner—A son who is farming his father's land,
and with his father using the proceeds as he sees fit, had no

---

interest in the land; and no lien attaches to the land for lumber furnished for improvements thereon under a contract with the son in his own name, and for the purchase price of which he executed his individual notes.—Hoag & Griffith v. Hay, 291.

2. JUDGMENT AGAINST MAKER OF CONTRACT—One who contracted for material used in the construction of a building on another's property is not liable to a personal judgment in a suit in which it is sought unsuccessfully to charge the property with a mechanic's lien, where the plaintiffs have not surrendered, and do not offer to surrender, the notes made by him, which cover the claim.—*Idem.*

MISCONDUCT—See NEW TRIAL, ²; PRACT. SUP. CT. ⁶, ⁷, ⁹, ¹².

MORTGAGES—See PLEAD. ⁴; REDEMPTION, ¹.

1. Creditors—RECORDING—One who sells goods to a mortgagor during ten days between the execution and recording of the mortgage, will not be given priority over the mortgagee, where the latter used reasonable dispatch, under the circumstances, in recording the mortgage, and did not withhold it from record to save the credit of the mortgagor, nor induce any one to extend credit to him.—Spencer Co. v. Papach, 518.

2. Foreclosure Expenses—A mortgagee is not entitled, as against a creditor of the mortgagor, to expenses incurred in selling the mortgaged goods at retail, where the mortgage simply authorizes her to sell the goods at "public auction."—*Idem.*

3. Fraudulent Payment, What is Not—The failure to file a chattel mortgage does not render a mortgagee liable for the proceeds realized on a sale of the mortgaged property by the mortgagor with his permission, and received by him under arrangement with the latter, to creditors whose claims accrued after the mortgage and before the sale, but who acquired no lien on the mortgaged property.—Hammill Co. v. Van Loon, 249.

MOTION TO STRIKE—See PRACT. ⁸.

MULCT LAW—See INTOX. LIQ ³, ⁴.

MUNICIPAL CORPORATIONS—See CONST. LAW, ¹, ³, ⁴; NEGLIGENCE, ⁵.

1. Highways—DAMAGES—A municipal corporation is liable for the damages to a building constructed with reference to the natural surface of the lot and street, from a change of grade of the street, in the absence of an ordinance fixing any grade.—Paine v. Incorp Town of Lettsville, 481.

made upon the plans and specifications furnished by the city, and the detailed plans furnished by the bidders were merely to advise the authorities of the bidder's interpretation of the plans and specifications and their method of execution.—*Idem.*

9. **Sidewalk Construction**—*Ordinances*—Where an ordinance authorizes the city council to order the construction of a sidewalk, by resolution which shall be served on the adjoining lot owners, and provides that in case the owner fails to construct the walk within the time fixed, the work shall be done on contract at his expense, service of the resolution is a condition precedent to the right to have the walk constructed at the expense of the lot owner.—Hawley v. City of Fort Dodge, 578.

10. JURY QUESTION—In an action against a city for injuries resulting from a fall caused by the end of a plank of a street crossing next the sidewalk projecting above the sidewalk, witness for plaintiff testified that the plank was so decayed and worn that it would not hold nails, and that it was warped so that the end next the walk was sprung, and when not under pressure, its upper surface was three or three and a half inches above the level of the walk. Other witnesses for plaintiff stated that the difference in level was less, some placing it at an inch. Defendant's witnesses stated that the end of the plank was securely nailed, and that it was only one or one and one-half inches higher than the other planks. *Held*, that it was for the jury to determine the condition of such plank, and its height above the walk.—Baxter v. City of Cedar Rapids, 599.

11. *Same*—It cannot be said as a matter of law, that an obstruction two inches high in a sidewalk or street crossing is not such a defect as will render the city liable for injuries caused by it.—*Idem.* .

12. NOTICE OF DEFECT—Where such defect in the crossing had existed for ten days or two weeks, and it was in a thickly inhabited part of the city, and much used, defendant was chargeable with notice of its condition in time to repair it before the accident.—*Idem.*

MURDER—See CRIM. LAW, [6], [7], [9], [10], [21], [22], [24], [25], [26], [27], [29], [35].

NEGLIGENCE—See ANIMALS, [1], [2]; INSTRUCTIONS, [9]; INS. [33]; RAILROADS, [19], [20], [21], [22], [23], [24], [25], [26].

1. **Bridges** —The frightening of a horse, and its consequent backing of a vehicle off a bridge approach, are not such unusual occurrences as to excuse reasonable precautions by the bridge authorities to provide against the accident.—Faulk v. Iowa County, 442.

NEGLIGENCE Continued

2. **Collision with Bicycle**—*Evidence*—The failure of a driver
approaching a bicycle to turn to the right, is *prima facie*
negligence on his part, under Code 1873, section 1000, requiring
persons meeting each other on the public highway to give
one-half of the same by turning to the right, and rendering all
persons failing to observe such requirement liable for damages resulting therefrom.—Cook v. Fogarty, 500.

3. *Same*—In an action for injuries from a collision on a public
road at night, between plaintiff while riding a bicycle, and
a buggy driven by defendant in an opposite direction, it
appeared that a man on a wheel could be seen readily only a
short distance, and that plaintiff had no light or bell. Plaintiff testified that he was dressed in light-colored clothes.
Defendant testified that he ought to have seen a man so
dressed thirty yards or more, but did not see or hear him
until the collision occurred, and that he was watching the
road ahead. Defendant's companion also stated that he was
watching, but did not see plaintiff until the accident.
Plaintiff saw defendant and his horse one hundred and fifty
yards distant, and began to slacken his speed. He testified
that he helloed to defendant when he was fifty feet distant,
and again a moment later. Defendant did not heed the
warning. Plaintiff turned to the right side of the road, and,
a moment before he was struck, threw himself from his
wheel, but not in time to avoid the collision. *Held*, that the
jury was authorized to find that defendant had overcome the
presumption of his negligence arising from his failure to
turn to the right and give plaintiff half of the road, as
required by Code 1873, section 1000.—*Idem*.

4. **Contributory Negligence**—*Bridges*—A driver whose horse
took fright and backed off a bridge approach was not chargeable with contributory negligence because he was driving
without a whip, where it appeared that none was ordinarily
used or required, and that he had no reason to anticipate the
act of the horses.—Faulk v. Iowa County, 442.

5. *Bicycles*—One who rides a bicycle without a light or other
signal of warning, in a public thoroughfare, where he is
liable to meet moving vehicles or pedestrians, at a time
when objects cannot be discerned readily except at a short distance, is guilty of contributory negligence precluding recovery for injuries received in a collision with a horse and
wagon being driven in an opposite direction.—Cook v.
Fogarty, 500.

6. **JURY QUESTION**—*Bridges*—Plaintiff, her husband and her child
were driving over a bridge, and when on the graded approach

_____
Small figures refer to subdivisions of Index. The others to page of report.

NEGOTIABLE INSTRUMENTS.

1. Bona Fide Purchaser—One who takes a note wholly as collateral security for an antecedent indebtedness, with no extension of time, is not a holder for value.—Noteboom v. Watkins, 580.

2. Demand and Notice—Presentment and demand on one of two makers of a note is not sufficient to hold the indorser.—Closz & Mickelson v. Miracle, 198.

3. SAME—There can be no such demand of payment as to charge an indorser of a note, by mailing a letter to the maker.—*Idem.*

4. SAME.—The necessity of a demand payment upon a maker of a note after maturity, as a condition of holding an indorser, is not obviated by making a demand upon him before maturity, and the statement of another maker that he could not make the payment.—*Idem.*

5. WAIVER—To prove a waiver of demand and notice by an indorser, it must be shown that he made a waiver with knowledge of the facts that discharged him from liability. —*Idem.*

6. *Proof*—A waiver of demand and notice of non-payment cannot be proved in an action against the indorser of a promissory note, under a petition alleging demand and notice. —*Idem.*

7. Indorsement of Draft—*Title to Proceeds*—Defendant indorsed a sight draft to a bank, with which he had an account, and the same was placed to his credit. Said bank forwarded it to the drawee bank, where it was protested, and on its return, it was given back to defendant, and charged to him. Defendant then sent it the second time to the drawee, to whom the drawer then paid it. *Held,* that defendant was the owner of the funds in the hands of the drawee, in such sense, that he might recover damages of the drawer because he attached said fund without sufficient reason to believe that the drawee was indebted to him.—Pickering v. Cameron, 186.

NEWSPAPER SUBSCRIPTION—See CONT. ⁶, ⁷.

NEW TRIAL—See EVID. ¹; EXCEPTIONS, ¹; PRACT. SUP. CT. ²⁶.

1. Where a motion for a new trial urges that a motion for verdict should have been sustained in spite of a conflict in the evidence, that conflict must be resolved against the moving party. If, then, there is not sufficient evidence to sustain a verdict the motion for new trial should be sustained, and otherwise, overruled.—Inghram v. National Union, 395.

---

2. Misconduct of Jurors—In an action against a city for injuries caused by a defective sidewalk, several members of a jury urged that a large verdict be returned to teach defendant a lesson, for the reason that, if any one became involved in trouble, when within its limits, defendant would punish him. *Held*, not to show passion, prejudice, or misconduct, and that the matters in question so inhered in the verdict that they may not be shown by affidavit.—Baxter v. City of Cedar Rapids, 599.

3. Newly Discovered Evidence—In a personal injury case a new trial was asked by defendant because of newly discovered evidence that plaintiff's health was impaired before the accident. And affiant stated that he knew plaintiff at a certain town for fifteen years, and until she moved to defendant city; that he knew she was continually complaining of ill health while she lived there; "that it was generally reputed that she had ill health, and I know the same myself," and she claimed the climate there did not agree with her, "but the climate where she did live after leaving here did agree with her." *Held*, too indefinite to require the granting of a new trial.— *Idem.*

4. *Same—*A new trial will not be granted because of newly discovered evidence that is inherently conflicting.—*Idem.*

5. *Same—*A new trial for newly discovered evidence which is merely cumulative is properly refused.—Allbright v. Hannah, 98.

NOTICE—See ANIMALS, ⁴; ATTACH. ²; CRIM. LAW, ³⁰; CORPORATIONS, ⁴, ⁵, ⁶, ¹²; COUNTIES; FRAUD. CONV. ¹⁰; INS. ⁸, ³¹; LEVY, ², ⁸; MUNICIPAL CORP. ¹²; NEG INSTR ⁵, ⁶; PRACT. SUP. CT ⁷; TAXATION. ²; WATER POWER, ¹⁰, ¹⁴.

NOTICE BY PUBLICATION—See JURISDICTION, ¹, ².

NUISANCE—See INJUNCTION; INTOX. LIQ. ¹; JURISDICTION, ²

NUNC PRO TUNC ORDER—See PRACT. SUP. CT. ¹⁶.

OBJECTIONS—See EVID. ⁴⁶; PRACT. SUP. CT. ¹², ¹³, ¹⁴, ¹⁵.

OFFICER OF CORPORATION—See INS. ²³, ³⁴.

ORDINANCES—See EQUITY JURISDICTION; INJUNCTION; ¹; MUNICIPAL CORP. ⁹; RAILROADS, ¹¹, ³⁶.

PARENT AND CHILD—See CONT. ³, ⁴, ⁵; EVID. ⁴⁸, ⁴⁹, ⁵⁰; FRAUD. ⁴; FRAUD. CONVEYANCE, ⁴, ⁵, ¹⁰; SALES, ².

1. Services—An express promise of compensation is not essential to the existence of a valid claim by a daughter against the estate of her father for services rendered to him while living in

Small figures refer to subdivisions of Index. The others to page of report.

the same family, but it is sufficient if the services were rendered with the expectation on her part of receiving compensation, and on the part of the father of making compensation therefor.—Riddler v. Riddler, 470.

2.   MEASURE OF RECOVERY—An instruction,—that in determining the compensation to be allowed the daughter of intestate for services rendered to him, the jury should consider the circumstances of the claimant, as well as those of the family of the intestate, and award such sum as will be just to the estate and to the claimant, and a fair response to the evidence,—is erroneous, as it includes improper elements to be considered in arriving at a proper measure of compensation. —*Idem.*

PARTITION—See WATER POWER, [14].

Settlement—Where a county contracted with two persons to drain a lake, one of them, in consideration thereof, to be given a deed of a part of the lake bed, and the other the balance, but, by reason of a dispute between such persons as to the proportion in which they should bear the cost of a certain drain, the county, instead of deeding to them such parts severally, executed a deed to the two conveying all the land, the deed reciting that the land had been drained by them pursuant to their contract with the county, the land should be partitioned between them as provided by their contract with the county, and not on the basis that, by the deed, each received an undivided half, they having made no agreement between themselves to accept said deeds as a settlement of their controversy. —Schuster v. Gamble, 495.

PERSONAL TRANSACTIONS—See EVID. [29], [30], [51], [33].

PHOTOGRAPHS—See CRIM. LAW, [37].

PLATS.

1.   Dedication by—VACATION—*Acceptance*—Where the owners of land which had been dedicated as a street in the plat of an addition to a city had disposed of none of the abutting lots, and such dedication had not been accepted by the city, they had the right to vacate such street, under Code 1873, section 564, authorizing such vacation of any part of a plat, provided it does not affect the rights and privileges of other proprietors in such plats.—Brown v. Tabor, 1.

2.   SAME—*Deeds*—Under Code, 1873, section 559, providing that descriptions of lots according to the number and designation thereof on the plat shall be deemed sufficient for the purposes of conveyances thereof, and section 561, declaring the

acknowledgment and recording of such plat equivalent to a deed in fee simple of lands therein set apart for streets and other public uses, a deed describing the lands thereby conveyed as lots, by numbers as designated in the plat, included only the several parcels so specified therein; as such reference to the lots by numbers, in the deed, had the effect identical with describing them by metes and bounds as delineated on the plat, and therefore included no portion of a vacated street on which they abutted but to which no reference was made in the deed.—*Idem.*

8.   TITLE TO STREETS ADJOINING—Where a "street" as platted was vacated, under Code 1873, section 564, a proportionate part thereof did not become a part of each of the abutting lots; by virtue of section 565, authorizing the proprietors of vacated *lots* to inclose a proportionate part of the adjoining street, and section 567, providing for the re-platting of such lots; as such sections relate only to the owners of "lots" which have been vacated.—*Idem.*

PLEA AND PROOF—See CONT. [7]; MALIC. PROS. [1]; NEG. INST. [4].

1.   **Evidence**—In an action for the proceeds of a note which was claimed by plaintiff, and which her husband had delivered to defendant, either for collection, or as collateral to a debt of his own, where the answer was a general denial, it was not error to permit plaintiff to show the manner in which she acquired the money that she loaned her husband as a consideration for the note.—Noteboom v. Watkins, 580.

2.   **Failure of Proof**—Where plaintiff sued for a breach of a written contract for the sale of land, and the evidence showed merely a contract made by defendant's agent, and signed by plaintiff alone, there was a total failure of proof, within Code 1873, section 2688, providing that when the allegation to which the proof is directed "is unproved in its general meaning" it shall not be deemed a variance, but a failure of proof.—Saatoff v. Scott, 201.

3.   **Variance**—Damages for breach of an oral contract to convey land cannot be recovered under a petition on a written contract, in the absence of an amendment thereof to conform to the evidence.—*Idem.*

4.   RESCISSION—*Replevin*—Plaintiff in replevin, who relies in his petition upon the breach of a contract for conditional sale of the property, cannot recover where the defendant establishes a right to rescind the contract for fraudulent misrepresentations, that rescission and return were offered and

demanded and that plaintiff has never acquiesced in such
rescission.—Myers v. Townsend, 569.

PLEADING—Appeal, [1]; Instruction, [11]; Plea and Proof, [2]; Practice, [4].

1. **Agency**—*Pleading Construed*—In an action for the conversion
of goods that had been stored in a building under an agreement with the former lessee, it appeared that G, who was in
defendant's employ, and in charge of the building, would not
allow the goods to be removed without payment of storage
fees that he demanded, and that the goods were soon afterwards
destroyed by fire. The answer alleged that "defendant, by his
agent, demanded that plaintiff should pay the reasonable value
of the storage of said goods" before their removal. *Held*, that
defendant admitted the agency of G.—Murry v. Webber, 477.

2. **Damages**—*Future Suffering*—Future pain and anguish cannot
be considered in assessing damages under a pleading which
alleges pain and injury in the past tense only, where the petition does not allege that there has been a failure to make
recovery, and where the evidence is confined to showing disablement up to time of trial.—Shultz v. Griffith, 150.

3. **Damages**—Supplemental Petition—In an action to recover
damages for injury to property, resulting from the maintenance of a nuisance, a claim for additional damages accruing
since the commencement of the action, from a continuance
of the same nuisance, may be set up by supplemental petition.—Foote v. Burlington Gaslight Co., 576.

4. **Estoppel**—The claim that a creditor of a mortgagor is estopped
to complain of the expense incurred by the mortgagee in selling the mortgaged goods at retail, is not available under a
pleading setting forth, that such creditor is estopped to claim
that the mortgage was illegal and to deny the validity of the
sale to the mortgagee and her title derived from the mortgage
and the sale thereunder.—Spencer Co. v. Papach, 513.

5. **Prayer**—*Insurance*—A prayer in a petition in an action in
equity on a policy of insurance, that the policy be so reformed
as to permit concurrent insurance of a specified amount and
for such other and further relief as plaintiff may be or show
himself entitled to, is broad enough to include relief from a
provision of the policy rendering it void if the insured "now"
has or shall "hereafter" procure any other insurance unless
consent in writing is indorsed hereon.—Fitchner v. Fidelity
Mut. Fire Ass'n, 276.

---

6. Verification—An amendment of the answer in an action to recover the possession of real property from a tenant, alleging a reduction of the rent because of a mistake as to the acreage, upon which no affirmative relief is asked, does not introduce a new and distinct cause of action or counter-claim, within Code 1873, section 2680, authorizing courts to permit unverified amendments to pleadings unless a new and distinct cause of action or counter-claim is thereby introduced.—Boos v. Dulin, 331.

POSSESSION—See REAL PROP. *.

PRACTICE—See ALIMONY, ¹; ACTIONS; CORPORATION, ¹³, ¹⁴; CRIM· LAW, ¹⁷; DEFAULT, ¹; ESTATES, ²; EVID. ¹⁷; EXCEPTIONS, ¹, ²; FRAUD. CONV. ¹; JURORS, ²; JURY PANEL, ¹; NEW TRIAL, ².

1. Actions on Policies—*When Premature*—Acts Eighteenth General Assembly, chapter 211, section 8, provides that, to maintain an action on an insurance policy, the assured need only prove the loss and notice in writing to the company within sixty days, accompanied by an affidavit as to how the loss occurred and its extent, but that no action shall be begun within ninety days after giving such notice. *Held*, that the requirement of the statute as to the time within which an action may be brought cannot be waived, and an action in less than ninety days after notice of loss not accompanied by an affidavit, or after a waiver of such notice and affidavit, was premature. *Following Wilhelmi v. Insurance Co.*, 86 Iowa, 326.— Blood v. Hawkeye Ins. Co., 728.

2. Amendments—*Striking Off*—Where a cause in which defendant had filed an answer consisting of a mere denial was ordered to be tried on depositions, and plaintiff had taken his evidence within the time prescribed, an amendment to the answer, filed on the day of trial, and setting up facts known to defendant when the original answer was filed, was properly stricken off, plaintiff being unprepared to try the issues tendered therein, and no excuse being shown for failure to file it before the testimony was taken.—Greenlee v. Home Ins. Co., 484.

3. SAME—The allowance or disallowance of amendments to pleadings under Code 1873, section 2689, providing that the court may, on motion of either party, at any time, in the furtherance of justice, and on such terms as may be proper, permit a party to amend any pleadings or proceedings, is largely discretionary with the trial court.—*Idem*.

4. Certiorari—*Premature*—A writ of *certiorari* from the supreme court to the district court and the judges of such court, to

---

Small figures refer to subdivisions of Index. The others to page of report.

PRAC. Continued

10. ASSIGNMENT OF POLICY—After the loss of certain partnership property by fire one of the partners died, and the other assigned his interest in the insurance policy to one of the plaintiffs. A third party, to whom any loss was payable, under the policy, as security on obligations of the owners of the insured property, released his claims on satisfaction of such obligations. The administrator of the deceased partner and the assignee of the other thereupon sued to recover for such loss, and to reform the policy as to the description of the property insured. *Held*, that the plaintiffs were the real parties in interest, and had the right to sue on such policy, without joining such assignors.—Benesh v. Mill Owners Mut. F. Ins. Co., 465.

11. Probate—The heirs of a widow may maintain a petition against representatives of the deceased husband to have the widow's dower assigned to them, and her distributive share admeasured and set apart to them, although they were not legatees or devisees under the husband's will.—In re Proctor's Estate, 232.

12. Reserving Ruling—*Prejudice*—The taking under advisement a motion to strike out testimony is without error where the ruling finally sustaining the motion is accompanied by an instruction to the jury not to regard the testimony.—Faulk v. Iowa County, 442.

13. Special Interrogatory—To require the submission of an interrogatory to the jury under Code 1873, section 2807, the fact to be found must be one inhering in, and necessary to determine in arriving at, the general verdict, and the method or elements considered in reaching the ultimate facts cannot be called for by special interrogatories —Read & Traversy v. State Ins. Co., 307.

14. RULE APPLIED—Under Code 1873, section 2807, providing that a special verdict shall find only the ultimate facts as established by the evidence, special interrogatories, in an action on an insurance policy, calling for the damages to goods in different parts of the store, and the value of those totally destroyed, are properly refused, as calling for the method or elements considered in reaching the facts.—*Idem*.

15. SAME—*Accidental Death*—A refusal to submit a special finding, "Do you find the deceased was killed by any other person?" was properly refused, as not presenting a controlling issue, for defendant would be liable if the death was by accident, no matter who caused it.—Inghram v. National Union, 395.

PRACTICE SUPREME COURT.

---

5. **Appealable Orders**—An order setting aside a default is not appealable, because it is not one which affects a substantial right and, in effect, prevents a judgment from which an appeal might be taken and such appeal will be dismissed on the court's own motion.—Odell v. Coquolette, 485.

Argument—See *post*, [17].

6. **Bill of Exceptions**—*Misconduct of Counsel*—It does not follow from the fact that affidavits showing remarks by attorneys in their arguments to the jury were made a part of the record on appeal by bill of exceptions, that they are competent to prove a disputed fact.—Faulk v. Iowa County, 442.

7. TIME OF SIGNING—The trial judge has no power, in the absence of an agreement of consent, to sign a bill of exceptions after the final adjournment of the term; and if consent is given, the bill must be filed within the time agreed upon, or it will not be considered, under Code 1873, section 2831.—Hershey, Brown & Co v. Nyenhuis, 195.

8. ESTOPPEL—Appellee is not estopped to deny that the bill of exceptions was filed in due time, by correcting in i's amended abstract alleged errors and inaccuracies in the appellant's abstract, where the appellee denies the statement that the evidence was immediately after the trial certified by the trial judge and made a part of the record, and states the facts showing that the bill was not allowed by the judge during the term of court, or within the time after adjournment allowed therefor.—*Idem*.

9. RECORD BY AFFIDAVIT—*Misconduct*—An affidavit alleging misconduct of counsel in making improper statements in their arguments to the jury is not competent evidence of such misconduct, on appeal, but the alleged improper statements should be set out in the bill of exceptions.—State of Iowa v. Burton, 28.

Certification—See *ante*, [4]; *post*, [23].

Costs—See *post*, [18], [19].

Estoppel—See *ante*, [8]; *post*, [10].

10. **Estoppel to Appeal**—DEFAULT—Defendant was the payee and guarantor of a note, secured by mortgage, given for the price of the land mortgaged. A bill was filed by the assignee of the note and mortgage. Defendant was defaulted and judgment was rendered against him and the mortgagors for the amount of the note, and the mortgage was foreclosed. A counterclaim was filed by a judgment creditor claiming a lien prior to the mortgage, which was allowed. Defendant was made a party to but was not served with notice of the filing of said

17. ARGUMENT—Where an appellee presents no brief or argument, the supreme court will consider only such questions as are essential to determine the appeal.—Richardson v. Probst, 241.

18. COSTS—The supreme court will not disturb the taxation of costs where the record does not show what the costs were, and no abuse of the court's discretion is shown.—Ottumwa Screen Co. v Stodghill, 437.

19. FORCIBLE ENTRY—*Abandonment by Tenant*—The supreme court will not undertake to set out and discuss alleged errors which, at most, are merely technical, and do not affect any substantial right of the parties, where the only practical effect its decision can have is to determine who is liable for the costs.—Boos v. Dulin, 331.

20. EVIDENCE—Whether an executrix was properly removed, cannot be determined on appeal, unless all the evidence is in the record.—In re Moore's Estate, 474.

21. *Same*—Whether a judgment that a widow elected to take under the will was proper, cannot be determined on appeal, unless all the evidence is in the record.—*Idem*.

22. *Same*—Refusal to allow a credit claimed by plaintiff cannot be considered on appeal, where the evidence is not properly in the record.—Smith v. Knight, 733.

23. *Certification of Evidence*—On appeal in an equitable action wherein an issue of fact was joined, questions involving the evidence cannot be reviewed where the trial judge, instead of certifying that the transcript contains all the evidence "offered" on the trial, as required by Code 1873, section 2742, merely certifies that it contains all the evidence "introduced " —Greenlee v. Home Ins. Co., 484.

24. ISSUE BELOW—An action against an executrix for an accounting was referred for that purpose, and it appeared that the executrix charged herself in her accounts with the rents of lands. The referee charged her the same in his report, and no exception was taken thereto and passed on by the district court. *Held*, the supreme court, on appeal by the executrix, could not pass on the question whether she was properly charged with such rents.—In re Moore's Estate, 474.

25. NEW TRIAL—Where affidavits in support of a motion for new trial are contradicted by counter-affidavits, a denial of a new trial will not be disturbed on appeal.—Baxter v. City of Cedar Rapids, 599.

Transcript—See *ante*, ¹⁶; *post*, ²⁶.

26. VERDICT—Under Code, section 2837, subdivision 6, providing that when a verdict is not sustained by sufficient evidence, or is contrary to law, a new trial can be granted, a verdict will not be disturbed on the ground that it is not sustained by the evidence, unless it is so manifestly against the weight of evidence as to show that it was the result of passion or prejudice.—Inghram v. National Union, 395.

27. *Rule Applied*—In an action on a life policy the defense was suicide. Deceased was county clerk. A witness testified that on Sunday morning about nine o'clock he went into the clerk's office, and heard two shots, and on opening the vault door found the gas burning, and deceased's body at the foot of the stairs in the vault, and a revolver, with two empty chambers, lying near. There were two wounds on the body of deceased, one of which was sufficient to cause death. *Held*, that a verdict that deceased did not commit suicide was not supported by the evidence.—*Idem*.

28. **Trial De Novo**—*Transcript*—A trial *de novo* may be had upon evidence which is, in part, oral and taken in shorthand by the reporter, and, in part, documentary and written evidence, though said reporter does not sign any transcript of his shorthand report, provided the trial judge certifies all the evidence under Code of 1873, section 2742.—Dietz v. Capital City Brick and P. Co., 542

Waiver—See *ante*, ²⁶, ²⁷.

PREMATURE SUIT—See PRACT. ⁴.
PRESENTMENT—See PRACT. SUP. CT. ⁷.
PRESUMPTIONS—See HOMESTEADS, ⁷; REAL PROP. ²; TRUSTS, ².

PRINCIPAL AND AGENT—See INS. ⁴, ⁷, ⁸; NEG. INSTR. ¹⁸; PLEADINGS, ¹.

1. **Contract by Agent**—Where the owner of land employs another to cultivate the same, specifying the manner of payment for the work to be done, and providing that the owner is to be at no other expense for labor done on said land, if the owner afterwards directs the employe to do additional work, and to get some one to help him, the owner is liable for the reasonable value of labor done by a third person, hired by the party employed, to cultivate the land.—Barnes v. Hogate, 743.

2. **Duty of Agent**—An agent to collect a certificate of deposit is bound to exercise the degree of diligence and foresight an ordinarily prudent man would under like circumstances, and has implied authority to procure a confession of judgment thereon.—Briggs v. Yetzer, 342.

Small figures refer to subdivisions of Index. The others to page of report.

RAIL.

PRIVILEGED COMMUNICATION—See EVID. [32], [34], [36].
PUBLIC IMPROVEMENTS—See MUNICIPAL CORP. [6], [7], [8].
PUBLIC POLICY—See INTOX. LIQ [2]; LEVY. [4].
PURCHASER--See EXECUTION SALE; HUSBAND AND WIFE. [2].
QUIETING TITLE—See EVID. [36].

RAILROADS.

Assumption of Risk—See *post*, [4], [5], [6].

Attachment--See *post*, [6].

1. **Condemnation of Additional Depot Grounds**—See *post*,
   [27], [28]—*Conditions Precedent*—Code 1873, section 1241, provides
   that a railway corporation may take and hold "so much real
   estate as may be necessary for the location, construction, and
   convenient use of the railway. The land so taken otherwise
   than by the consent of the owners, shall not exceed one hundred feet in width, except for wood and water stations, unless
   where greater width is necessary for excavation, embankment
   or depositing waste earth." Acts Twentieth General Assembly,
   chapter 190, section 1, provides that any completed and operating railway company, "shall have power to condemn lands for
   necessary additional depot grounds in the same manner as is
   provided by law for the condemnation of the right of way,"
   but also provides that before such condemnation the company
   shall apply to the railroad commissioners, who shall notify the
   land owners, and certify to the district court of the county the
   amount and description of additional lands necessary for the
   company. *Held*, that where a railroad completed and in operation, desires land one hundred feet in width for additional
   depot grounds, the action of the commissioners must precede
   the effort to condemn, without regard to whether the land
   already occupied by the company was obtained by purchase or
   condemnation.—Crandall v. D. M., N. & W. R. R. Co., 684.

2. **Contributory Negligence**—JURY QUESTION—A boy fourteen
   years old is not, as matter of law, guilty of contributory negligence in permitting his attention to be diverted to a moving
   train as he was crossing a railroad track running laterally
   through a city street, precluding recovery for injuries from
   being struck by moving cars while his foot was held between
   the main and the guard rail of the track, although he could
   have easily avoided catching his foot if he had noticed the condition of the track—where he was unaware of such condition.—
   Goodrich v. B., C. R. & N. R'y Co., 412.

RAIL. Continued

8. *Same*—Contributory negligence of a boy in catching his foot between the main and guard rail of a switch track does not preclude his recovery for injuries from being run over by moving cars if the cars could have been stopped before reaching him, by the use of due diligence on the part of the employes, after seeing his dangerous condition —*Idem.*

4. SAME—A brakeman, whose attention was taken up in the discharge of his duties, was struck by bolts projecting from a truss built on the side of a bridge, when he was on the ladder of a freight car. *Held,* it cannot be said, as matter of law, that he was negligent in not looking out for dangers which resulted from improper construction of the bridge, and of which he had no knowledge.—Bryce v. C., M. & St. P. R'y Co., 665.

5. RISK OF EMPLOYMENT—An experienced brakeman on a moving train crossed a bridge twice a day for fourteen months, and usually on the top of box cars, which were twice as high as trusses built along the side of the bridge. The track curved all the way over the bridge, rendering it difficult for him to ·estimate the distance from the car to the trusses, at any one point. *Held,* it cannot be said, as matter of law, that he should have known it was dangerous to be on a car ladder at the northeast corner of the bridge, where the ends of bolts projecting from the truss were only fifteen inches from the car — *Idem.*

6. *Same*—A servant assumes the risk not only of dangers which he appreciates, but of dangers which, by the exercise of ordinary diligence, he ought to know and appreciate.— *Idem.*

7. **Conversion**—*Tender*—A shipper who, after a wrongful delivery of the goods by the carrier to a third person, agrees to wait for a delivery of the goods until the return of the station agent, may treat the goods as converted and maintain an action for their value, where the carrier fails for seven days after the return of the agent to recover and deliver the goods, and a tender made thereafter, and after notice to the carrier of the shipper's election to treat the goods as converted, is too late.—Hamilton v. C , M. & St. P. R'y Co., 325.

8. ATTACHMENT—*What May be Seized*—Where a common carrier fails and refuses to deliver to the consignee property shipped over its line, the consignee has a right to elect to claim damages for the value of the property, and to waive all title to it; and, after the carrier has been notified of such election, the property belongs to it, and is not subject to attachment in its hands as being the property of the consignee.—*Idem.*

Small figures refer to subdivisions of Index. The others to page of report.

VOL. 103 Ia—53

brakemen on freight trains to loosen hand brakes while near
and passing over the bridge, and plaintiff, while going down a
ladder on a car, in discharge of such duty, was struck by said
bolts. *Held*, that he may recover damages.—Bryce v. C., M. &
St. P. R'y Co., 665.

26. SPEED—*Ordinances*—In the absence of any ordinance, no
particular rate of speed on depot grounds would, alone, be
proof of negligence.—Heiss v. C., R. I. & P. R'y Co., 590.

Ordinances—See *ante*, [11], [26].

27. Right of Way—The interest in a railroad right of way is the
same whether granted or condemned.—Smith v. Hall, 95.

28. SAME—The nature and quality of the interest taken and conferred in a railroad right of way is fixed by the legislature,
and whether it shall be only an easement or a full fee title is
purely for its determination. It is therefore competent for the
legislature to say to whom the land shall revert when abandoned by the company.—*Idem.*

29. REVERSION—A conveyance of all the remaining portions of a
tract of land from which a railroad right of way had been
taken, passes to the grantee whatever right to the reversion
the grantor then had.—*Idem.*

Risk of Employment—See *ante*, [4], [5], [6].
Stock—See *post*, [31].

30. Trespassers—A railroad company owes no duty to a trespasser
upon the track until its employes actually see him in a place of
danger.—Thomas v. C., M. & St. P. R'y Co., 651.

31. TRESPASSING STOCK—An engineer has the right to presume that
the track is clear of stock at a point where the company has
inclosed the right of way, and he owes no duty to the owner
in relation to trespassing horses until their presence is discovered, and then only the duty of using ordinary care to avoid
injuring them.—Mears v. C. & N. W. R'y Co., 208.

Trespass—See *ante*, [14], [18].

RAILROAD COMMISSION—See RAILROADS, [1].
RAPE—See CRIM. LAW, [3], [4]; EVID. [19].
RATIFICATION—See PRIN. AND AGENT, [3], [4]; SALES, [2].

REAL PROPERTY—See ACCRETIONS, [1], [2]; CONTRACTS, [3], [5]; COVENANTS, [1]; EVID. [26]; PLATS, [1], [2,3]; RAILROAD, [28], [29].

1. Adverse Possession—Adverse possession of a part of the
land will be considered, for the purpose of title by adverse
possession, under the Iowa statute, to extend to the whole subdivision to which the occupant holds color of title or makes
claim of right.—Libbey v. Young, 258.

2. PRESUMPTIONS—The presumption that possession of land extends to the entire congressional sub-division called for by the occupant's conveyance or claim of right, does not obtain where, with his knowledge, and that of his grantors, another person has been in possession of part of the sub-division, under color of title or claim of right, for more than ten years.—*Idem.*

3. Possession—Possession of land is a matter tending to excite inquiry, but the fact that the occupant has placed written evidence of his rights upon the public records, with the terms of which his possession is consistent, arrests inquiry at that point, and reasonably informs the purchaser that he may rest upon the knowledge thus obtained.—Forest Mill Co. v. Mill Co., 641.

4. Riparian Rights -- BOUNDARIES — The title to land derived under conveyances made while the Des Moines river was regarded as navigable, describing the premises conveyed as bounded by the bank of such river, only extends to the edge of the bank, notwithstanding that the river is not now regarded as navigable.—Bennett v. Nat'l Starch Mfg. Co., 207.

5. SAME-·The line which separates the bed of a navigable stream from the land owned by the riparian proprietor is not the line reached by unusual floods, but that which is shown by the character and condition of the soil and vegetation to be the limit which high water ordinarily reaches.—*Idem.*

6. SAME—The owners of land bordered by a navigable stream own only to ordinary high water mark,—that is, to the edge of the bank,—and the whole bed of the river belongs to the public.—*Idem.*

REASONABLE DOUBT—See CRIM. LAW, [26], [28], [30].

REBUTTAL—See EVID. [37], [39].

RECEIVERS—See BANKS, [3]; CORPORATIONS, [13], [14]; LEVY, [1].

RECORDING—See FRAUD. CONV. [14], MORTGAGES, [1]; WATER POWER, [10].

REDEMPTION—See TAXATION, [1].

1. Foreclosure—The statutes give the mortgagor twelve months in which to redeem from sale under foreclosure. During the first six and the last three months, this right is exclusive in him. During the other three months his lien creditors may redeem from the sale and from each other. A sale was had under first mortgage and plaintiff bought the certificate. Within a few days later he bought a second mortgage. He foreclosed it, without objection by the mortgagor, and purchased at the sale. The mortgagor never offered to redeem

REDEMPTION Continued

from either sale, but within a few days before the year of redemption from the first sale expired, he made deed to a stranger, who then paid in sufficient to redeem from the first mortgage sale, and thereupon insists that all rights under the second sale were lost. *Held,*

a. The general rules of statutory redemption under which a mortgagor may redeem from sale under first mortgage without paying the second mortgagee who has not redeemed, have no application to cases where, during the period in which lien creditors may redeem, the same person holds the certificate of sale resulting from the foreclosure of both the first and second mortgages.

b. Under such circumstances, equity will consider that done which ought to have been done, and no rights will be lost because a party who owned all rights under a first and second mortgage and all liens, failed to pay the clerk enough money to redeem from the first sale, which money he would have been entitled to withdraw from the clerk as soon as it was paid in.

c. Under these circumstances, the purchase of the second certificate would operate as a redemption if it were bought within six and nine months after the first sale, and though the right of redemption was exclusively in the mortgagor for the first six months, and such purchase within the first six months was, therefore, technically, not a redemption, it will operate as one where the certificate was held during both said periods, without an attempt at redemption by the mortgagor.

d. Consequently, a grantee of such mortgagor could not make an effective redemption from the sale under the first mortgage without paying enough to satisfy both sales.—Stephens v. Mitchell, 65.

2. ENTRY OF CREDIT—The only effect of the failure of the assignee of a certificate of the sale under execution to enter on the sale book the amount he is willing to credit on his claim, under the provisions of Code, section 3115, is to require him to credit the debtor with the full amount of his claims on the land.—*Idem.*

SALES

SALES—See CONTRACTS, ³, ⁴, ⁵; EVID. ⁶, ⁷, ²⁵; HOMESTEADS, ⁶.

1. **Completion**—An oral contract for the sale of land provided that
   the deed should be placed in a bank, and delivered when title
   was approved and payment made. The person employed by
   the vendee, after examining the deed and abstract, returned
   them to the bank, with his opinion that there was some defect
   in the title, whereupon the vendor took back the papers. *Held*,
   that the contract of sale was not completed.—Benedict v.
   Bird, 612.

2. **Contingent Interest**—RATIFICATION—Though an assignment
   of a son's prospective interest in a father's estate is invalid,
   yet it may become operative by a ratification after the father's
   death.—Dunham v. Bentley, 186.

3. **Delivery**—Plaintiff sold to defendant not less than sixteen hundred nor more than twenty-three hundred bushels of corn at
   so much a bushel, and received fifty dollars of the purchase
   money. The corn was in two cribs, one containing sixteen
   hundred bushels intact, and the other, which had been opened,
   about seven hundred bushels. Plaintiff reserved the right to
   retain two hundred or three hundred bushels, if he needed
   them, and a third party was entitled to fifty bushels. Before
   any corn had been separated from the mass the entire lot was
   burned. *Held*, that, as to sixteen hundred bushels, at least,
   the title had passed to defendant.—Welch v. Spies, 389.

4. EVIDENCE—Evidence that the seller of personal property notified the wife of the person having the possession thereof that
   he had sold the same, is admissible on the question as to
   whether the title had passed before the destruction of the
   property, as tending to show what he did to complete delivery.—*Idem.*

5. *Same*—The fact that part of the corn was to be shelled and
   delivered by plaintiff at a place designated by the defendant,
   did not prevent the title from passing.—*Idem.*

6. *Same*—The intent of the parties is of controlling importance
   in determining whether or not the title to personal property,
   the subject of the contract of sale, has passed to the purchaser, and the fact that it remains to weigh or measure the
   property sold is not conclusive as to such intent.—*Idem.*

Small figures refer to subdivisions of Index. The others to page of report.

7. **Vendor's Liens**—A deed absolute on its face was made to a bank by an officer thereof to cover an impairment of the capital stock, with a collateral agreement for payment of the price out of future profits of the bank. This agreement was released upon the promise of the bank examiner that the management of the bank would not be interfered with. Through the bank examiner, a receiver was subsequently appointed for the bank. *Held*, that, as the payment was to be made from a particular fund the grantor could not have a lien established on the land for the price.—Brown v. Bradford, 878.

SEDUCTION—See CRIM. LAW, [38], [39].
SETTLEMENT—See PARTITION.
SHERIFFS—See LIMITATION OF ACT. [8].
SIDEWALKS—See MUNICIPAL CORP. [9], [10], [11], [12].

SPECIFIC PERFORMANCE.

In ejectment, defendant asked specific performance of a contract for the exchange of land owned by defendant for the land in dispute, of which defendant has possession when plaintiff purchased it. The contract did not fix any time for exchanging deeds, but the same year it was made, and four years before suit was brought, plaintiff asked for a deed. Defendant did not then or at any time refuse to carry out the contract, but only stated reasons for delay; those given being that it was unable to execute the deed, owing to a mortgage on the land. Plaintiff made no tender of a deed, nothing had been lost by delay, and the parties were in the same situation as when the contract was made. Defendant tendered performance. *Held*, that plaintiff should be required to perform the contract. —Fisher v. Carroll County F. and Driv. P. Ass'n, 746.

STATUTE OF FRAUDS—See CONTRACTS, [4], [5]; EVID. [41], [42], [43], [44], [45], [46]; PRACT. [6].
STOCKHOLDERS—See CORPORATIONS, [1], [9], [13], [14].
STOCK REDUCTION—See CORPORATIONS, [11].
STOCK TRANSFER—See CORPORATIONS, [3], [6], [7], [8], [10], [13].
SUBROGATION—See DEFAULT, [3].
SUPPLEMENTAL PETITION—See PLEADINGS, [3]; PRACTICE, [5].
SURETIES—See ATTACHMENT, [1].

TAXATION—See ACTIONS; CONST. LAW, [2], [3], [4].

1. **Tax Book**—*Sale*—Code 1873, section 845, provides for the placing upon the tax books, opposite each parcel of land, the year or years for which taxes remain due and unpaid, and that sales for taxes not so entered are invalid. The treasurer's tax book, in the

column "1878," showed the figures "75," written with lead pencil, and crossed over, as if to mark them out. In column "1879," appeared "74" in the same condition. In the column ."1880," appeared the letters "ad," unexplained. *Held*, not a compliance with the statute.—Smith v. Callanan, 213.

2.   REDEMPTION NOTICE—Code 1873, section 894, provides that, after the expiration of two years and nine months from the date of sale of land for taxes, notice may be served on the person in possession of the land, and also on the person in whose name the same is taxed, stating that the right of redemption will expire, and a deed for said land be made unless redemption is made within ninety days from service of said notice. *Held*, that the notice should be given to the person in whose name the property is taxed, at the time the notice is in fact given, and not necessarily to the person to whom it is taxed at the end of the two years and nine months from the date of sale.—*Idem*.

TENANTS IN COMMON—See WATER POWER, 4, 5, 6, 7, 8, 9.
TENDER—See PRIN. AND AGT. 6; RAILWAY, 7.
TRANSACTION WITH DECEDENTS—See EVID. 32.
TRANSCRIPTS—See PRACT. SUP. CT. 22.
TRESPASS—See RAILWAY, 1, 14, 17, 18, 20.
TRUSTEES—See INS. 15.

TRUSTS.

1.   EVIDENCE—A finding by the court that decedent did not hold real property in trust for a woman with whom he was living as his wife will not be disturbed on appeal, where the latter, as his administratrix, treated the property as belonging to his estate, and the claim of trust was not made until a claim was made by the decedent's legal wife, and the circumstances strongly indicate that the claim of a trust was an afterthought to defeat the legal widow's claim.—Dunn v. Portsmouth Savings Bank, 588.

2.   PRESUMPTIONS—*Husband and Wife*—In 1878 plaintiff purchased unimproved land near the farm on which he resided, and had it deeded to his wife without her knowledge, with the intention thereby to create a trust. When informed of what he had done, she acquiesced therein; and the title remained in her until her death, in 1894. In the meantime, the husband improved, controlled, and used the land as his own. *Held*, that the presumption that the land was an advancement to the wife was overcome by evidence of his control and improvement, and her repeated admissions that the land was his, and his own evidence as to his intention, and that she held the title in trust for her husband.—Hagan v. Powers, 593.

8. Resulting Trusts—The provisions of Code 1878, section 1985, with reference to the creation of a trust in real property, do not apply to a trust raised by operation of law, and not by reason of any declaration or creation of the parties.—*Idem.*

USURY—See PRINCIPAL AND AGT. [5].

VACATION—See ALIMONY, [1]; JUDGMENTS, [2]; PLATS, [1], [2], [6].

VENDOR'S LIEN—See BANKS, [3].

VENUE—See INS. [36].

VERDICT—See NEW TRIAL, [1], [2]; PRACT. [18]; PRACT. SUP. CT. [36].

Impeachment of—Statements made by jurors to others of the panel, after retiring to consider of their verdict, which are calculated to arouse sympathy for defendant, and to reduce the verdict against him, cannot be assigned as error by him, *first*, because they inhere in the verdict, and *secondly*, because they were not prejudicial to *defendant.*—Noble v. White, 852.

VERIFICATION—See JUDGMENTS BY CONFESSION, [1]; PLEADINGS, [6].

VICIOUS ANIMALS—See ANIMALS, [1], [2], [3].

WAIVER—See CRIM. LAW, [17]; EVID. [25], [46]; INS. [1], [42], [44], [45], [46]; JURORS, [1]; LANDLORD AND TENANT, [2]; NEG. INSTR. [5], [6]; PRACT. SUP. CT. [12].

WARRANTY—See EVID. [6].

WATER POWER.

1. Head—*Deeds*—A conveyance of a mill lot and the right to one hundred inches of water, which describes the lot by metes and bounds, does not, by fixing its river boundary at low water mark, limit the "head" of water, so as to prevent the grantee increasing it by excavating the tail race below the then low water mark.—Forest Mill Co. v. Cedar F. Mill Co., 619.

2. SAME—The various owners of water rights in connection with a mill dam and race have a right to the same head of water, or as nearly the same as the topography of the ground, the fall of the main race, and other conditions admit of, in the absence of contrary provisions in the deeds conveying such rights, where they have been accustomed to excavate about the tail races leading from their mills, as they see fit, without any objection from other owners.—*Idem.*

3. SAME—Each of the parties to whom the owner of a water power conveys parts thereof, describing it in each case as so many inches of water, without any limitation as to the "head," but with conditions making the grantees liable for their proportionate share of the expense necessary to repair or improve the race, dam and other structures creating the water power, is entitled to as nearly the same head as the conditions will permit of.—*Idem.*

AUTHORITIES CITED

IN THE OPINIONS REPORTED IN THIS VOLUME.

P

S

T

W

CASES CITED

IN OPINIONS REPORTED IN THIS VOLUME.

E

F

U

V

W

STATUTES ·CITED, CONSTRUED, ETC.,

IN THE OPINIONS REPORTED IN THIS VOLUME.

Lightning Source UK Ltd.
Milton Keynes UK
UKHW020806191218
334261UK00009B/412/P